THE DICTIONARY OF
MYTHOLOGY

THE DICTIONARY OF MYTHOLOGY

AN A-Z OF THEMES, LEGENDS AND HEROES

J. A. COLEMAN

ARCTURUS

ARCTURUS

This edition published in 2019 by Arcturus Publishing Limited
26/27 Bickels Yard, 151–153 Bermondsey Street,
London SE1 3HA

Copyright © Arcturus Holdings Limited

ISBN: 978-1-83857-027-9
AD004418UK

Printed in China

CONTENTS

INTRODUCTION

W ho made the world, the sun, the moon and the stars? Where did
people come from, and where do they go when they die? Where does
the sun go at night, or during an eclipse, or in the wintertime? What causes
thunder, and why are there earthquakes and floods? These are questions that
people have asked themselves from time immemorial, and myths are the
stories that have been told in answer to these questions.

Of course, different peoples and cultures in different parts of the world
have come up with different answers to questions such as these and therefore
have developed different mythologies, but as will be seen from a reading of
the myths included in this book, many of the answers proposed by widely

The Greek goddess of the moon, Selene, in a flying chariot drawn by two white horses.

separated and totally unrelated peoples and cultures can be remarkably similar. That is one of the fascinating features of mythology.

This *Dictionary of Mythology* is an abridgement of J. A. Coleman's monumental work, *The Dictionary of Mythology: An A–Z of Themes, Legends and Heroes*. As Coleman himself explained in his introduction to that book, he took a very broad view of what could or should be included in a mythology dictionary. To paraphrase his remarks slightly, we may say that while scholars divide stories of the imagination into such categories as, for example, myths, legends, fairy-tales and folklore, one could very well argue that, given that the stories may relate to postulated beings such as gods and demons, to completely imaginary characters such as Ali Baba, to real historical characters such as Charlemagne, and to characters such as King Arthur who exist in a place somewhere between history and fiction, it is hard to see how one could slot them all neatly into separate classes. Furthermore, the boundary between 'myth' and 'religion' is far from clear, if indeed such a boundary could be set at all; what is an interesting myth to one person may be a matter of deep religious faith to another. Coleman, therefore, adopted what he referred to as a 'relaxed' view of what constitutes mythology, and this abridgement of his book adopts a similarly broad position.

Abridging a book inevitably involves choices: what to keep, what to cut down, and what to drop completely. The original *Dictionary of Mythology* provides its readers with a very wide coverage indeed of the mythologies of the world, from the well known to the little known. Such breadth of coverage is also reflected in this version. But to ensure that what remained after the abridgement was not simply an unstructured mass of unrelated entries, the decision was made to focus, to some extent, on certain recurring themes in world mythology and on stories relating to certain characters and events. So here the reader will find, for example, many stories about the creation of the world, the first people, and the great Flood that destroyed the world, along with stories about the Trojan War, the Argonauts, and King Arthur and the Knights of the Round Table, and characters from the *Arabian Nights* tales.

Gods and goddesses, monsters, demons, tricksters and culture-heroes are all to be found in these pages. And preference was given to longer entries that told a story, as opposed to short entries which simply said 'X: A god of Y' (though there are a few of these that were considered to be of sufficient interest to be included, short though they are).

Among these pages readers will find not only gods and goddesses of love, war and death, of the seas, the forests and the mountains, of the winds and the weather, but also of beer-making and intoxication, of pigs, tattoos and turnips, even a goddess of sewers; a gecko-god, a shark-god, a squid-god, and many others. Those who are familiar with J. R. R. Tolkien's *The Lord of the Rings* will recognize names such as Balin, Dvalin and Gandalfr. Those who have enjoyed the adventures of *Asterix the Gaul* will find information here about the god Toutatis (Teutates) by whom many of the Gauls swear. And readers with an interest in geography may be surprised to learn how Sicily, Sri Lanka, Iceland and the Orkney Islands came to be formed.

Much of mythology is not directly about humans, but nevertheless 'all human life is there'. It is people who asked the questions, and people who came up with answers. And that is what makes the study of mythology so stimulating, so thought-provoking and so important (but also great fun!).

George Davidson
Edinburgh

The Beguiling of Merlin by Edward Burne-Jones depicts a scene from Arthurian legend, when Nimue, the Lady of the Lake, ensnares the wizard in a hawthorn bush.

A *Central American*
A Mayan deity of uncertain identity, referred to as God A (*see* **alphabetical gods**); perhaps the god of death, Ah Puch. This deity is depicted with an exposed spine and skull-like features, wearing a snail on his head and a pair of cross-bones.

A-mi-t'o-fo *Chinese*
= *Japanese* Amida
The Chinese Buddhist name for *Amitabha*.

A-mong *Burmese*
A progenitor of the Karen. A-mong and Lan Yein descended from heaven bearing a drum given to them by Sek-ya, the god of supernatural weapons, and founded the tribe. The drum was one of Sek-ya's magic weapons, which, when sounded, drove off the enemy.

A-shih-to *see* **Asita**

Aalu *Egyptian*
also Aaru
The paradise of Osiris, far to the west. To reach this land, the soul had to pass through many gates (15 or 21), each guarded by demons.

aart *Egyptian*
A symbol of Ra. When washed in a sacred lake, it became the crocodile-god, Sebek.

A'as *Mesopotamian*
A Hurrian god of wisdom, the keeper of the tablets of destiny.

ab *Egyptian*
The symbolic heart, as distinguished from the corporeal heart hati, judged at death.

Ababinili *North American*
also Sitting Above
The supreme god of the Chickasaw tribe; a sun god and a god of fire, regarded as the creator of all living things.

Abaddon *Hebrew*
The devil; the king of scorpions; the angel ruling over the damned. This name is sometimes used for hell itself rather than its ruler.

Abaia *Pacific Islands*
A magic fish. Abaia became angry when a woman fished in the lake where he lived, and he caused a deluge.

Abakan Khan *Siberian*
A rain god, the khan of the Abakan River.

Abassi *African*
Creator-god and sky god of the Efik. He reluctantly allowed his two children to descend to earth but imposed conditions that they neither mated nor engaged in agriculture, returning to heaven for their meals. Inevitably, the pair mated and soon the earth was fully populated. Abassi endowed these people with the gift of argument and instituted death so that, ever since, people have quarrelled and killed each other.

Abassylar *Siberian*
A demon which is said to devour the souls of the dead.

abatawa *African*
also abativa
A fairy. These beings are envisaged

as being so small that they can walk under grass. They are said to sleep in anthills and to shoot poisoned arrows at their enemies.

abawinae   *North American*
In the lore of the Tubatulabal tribe of California, a ghost. This entity is the soul of a dead person which appears in the form of a human being.

Abdallah the Fisherman   *Arabian*
A character in the *Arabian Nights' Entertainments*. He visited Abdallah the Merman under the sea and killed a sea-monster merely by shouting at it.

Abderus   *Greek*
An armour-bearer for the hero Hercules. He helped Hercules on his eighth Labour but was eaten by the mares of Diomedes.

Aberewa   *African*
A primordial woman in the lore of the Akan. When she pounded maize in her mortar, the pestle bumped the sky, annoying the god Nyame who soon moved further away. Aberewa collected many mortars and piled them one on top of another, trying to reach Nyame. The pile was too short and when she persuaded a child to remove a mortar from the bottom of the pile so that she could put it on top, the whole edifice collapsed. (*See also* **Abuk**.)

Abhirati   *Buddhist*
The Eastern paradise.

Abigor   *European*
A demon said to foretell the future; one of the 72 Spirits of Solomon. He is depicted as a soldier on horseback, armed with a lance.

abiku   *African*
In Dahomey, the spirit born with each child. The abiku tries to take the child to its forest home. To prevent this, some parents put

the child in chains while others disfigure the child's face so that the spirit will reject it or fail to recognise it. These spirits are said not to like bells, so some parents fix bells to a child harbouring an abiku or rub pepper into cuts in the child's skin, hoping the pain will drive the spirit away. In some accounts these demons eat children.

Ablach   *Irish*
An Irish name for *Avalon*. (*See also* **Emain Ablach**.)

Abokas   *Pacific Islands*
The home of the dead in the lore of the New Hebrides.

Abou Hassan   *Persian*
A rich merchant in the *Arabian Nights' Entertainments* story, *The Sleeper Awakened*. He was mysteriously transported to the bed of the caliph and was then treated as if he were the caliph.

Abuda   *Buddhist*
In Japan, the eight cold hells. (*See also* **To-Kwatsu**.)

Abuk   *African*
A primeval woman of the Dinka. She and her husband Garang originally lived in a small pot on one grain of corn per day but they grew bigger when the pot was opened. She annoyed the god Deng when she struck the sky with her pestle as she was grinding corn and he made the work harder than ever. (*See also* **Aberewa**.)

Abyla *see* **Calpe**

Acacitli   *Central American*
A leader of the Aztecs when they left their homeland, Aztlan.

Acala   *Buddhist*
A tutelary god, lord of the three worlds. He is responsible for guarding the north-east quarter of the world. He is depicted with

four faces and eight arms, one foot on the goddess Parvati's bosom, the other on the god Maheshvara's head.

Acastus   *Greek*
King of Iolcus, he was one of the Argonauts and took part in the hunt for the Calydonian boar. After the return of the *Argo* to Iolcus, the sorceress Medea induced the daughters of Pelias, the father of Iolcus, to kill him (Pelias). For this crime, Acastus, the new king, banished Medea and Jason (the leader of the Argonauts). His wife, Hippolyta, accused Peleus, who had come to his court to be purified, of rape. Acastas abandoned his guest, unarmed, on Mount Pelion, hoping that wild animals would kill him. Peleus was saved by the centaur Chiron and attacked Iolcus with a band of former Argonauts, killing Hippolyta and, some say, Acastus.

Acca Larentia   *Roman*
An Etruscan mother-goddess, said by some to be the mother of the Lares (household gods) and the hero Hercules. In some accounts, she was a prostitute who was won by Hercules in a game of dice, in some accounts she became wealthy and later married a man called Tarutius. Others say she was the wife of a shepherd, Faustulus, and adopted Romulus and Remus.

Accolan of Gaul   *British*
A treacherous knight, lover of Morgan le Fay.
    When King Arthur executed one of Morgan's lovers, she stole the sword Excalibur and gave it to Accolan, another lover.
    Accolan was hunting with Arthur and Urien, Morgan's

husband, when a ship on a lake came into the shore. They boarded it and were bewitched by Morgan. Urien was transported back to his home but Arthur, duped by Morgan, fought Accolan who was expected to kill the king. Morgan then planned to kill Urien, marry Accolan and rule as queen at his side. Instead, although he sustained severe wounds, Arthur, with the help of the magic of the Lady of the Lake, recovered Excalibur and killed Accolan.

Acephali   *Greek*

A headless race said to live in Libya. Some say that these beings had their face on their chests.

Ach-chazu   *Mesopotamian*
also Ahhazu

A monster causing death and disease.

Achates   *Greek*

Armourer and faithful friend of Aeneas, the Trojan hero. He is said to have killed Protesilaus, the first Greek to land when the Greeks invaded Troy. He accompanied Aeneas on his wanderings after the fall of Troy.

Acheflour   *British*

In some accounts, a sister of King Arthur and mother of Percival, a knight of King Arthur's court. She reared Percival, after the death of his father (there are a number of different suggestions as to who this was), in the solitude of the Waste Forest, hoping to keep him from knightly pursuits. When she believed that Percival had been killed, the thought drove her mad. Percival found her living in the woods and took her home.

Acheron   *Greek*

One of the rivers of Hades; son of the goddess Demeter. Acheron was condemned to the

underworld by Zeus for helping the Titans in their struggle against the gods and was turned into a river. This was the river of woe over which Charon ferried the souls of the dead.

The word sometimes refers to the underworld itself.

Achilles   *Greek*

A Greek hero; son of King Peleus of Phthia and Thetis, a sea-nymph. At his birth, his mother dipped him in the river Styx to make him invulnerable, holding him by one ankle. This part of his body did not go into the water and consequently remained unprotected. Another version says that Thetis held the child by his ankle over a fire but Peleus snatched him from her in time to save him from being completely consumed.

Like many famous Greeks he was a pupil of the wise centaur Chiron and of Phoenix. Thetis sent him to the court of King Lycomedes of Scyros where, dressed as a girl, he hoped to escape service with the army at Troy. Odysseus, in the guise of a pedlar, saw through the disguise when Achilles chose weapons, rather than trinkets, from the wares on offer, and persuaded the younger man to join the expedition to rescue Helen from the Trojans.

He fought at Troy, leading his band of Myrmidons but fell out with King Agamemnon over a girl, Briseis, awarded to him as a prize, and refused to fight any more. When the Greeks were on the verge of defeat, Achilles' best friend, Patroclus, put on Achilles' armour and led a renewed attack but was killed in single combat

with Hector (a Trojan prince) who took the armour. Spurred into action by the death of his friend, Achilles donned new armour made for him by the god Hephaestus and led the Greeks in a fresh assault on the Trojan forces. He met and killed Hector and defiled his body by dragging it round the city walls behind his chariot and when the Ethiopian prince, Memnon, intervened with his army on the side of the Trojans, Achilles met him also in single combat and killed him, driving the defenders right back to the gates of the city. He also killed Penthesilea, the Amazon queen who was fighting on the side of the Trojans, and when a Greek soldier, Thersites, mocked him for mourning her death, he killed him too. In the fighting near the gate, Achilles was struck by an arrow fired from the walls by Paris (Hector's brother) which, striking his ankle, the only vulnerable part of his body, killed him.

Another account says that the Trojan princess, Polyxena, given to Achilles as a prize, persuaded him to divulge the secret of his vulnerability and she passed on the knowledge to her brother, Paris, who stabbed Achilles in the heel at his wedding to Polyxena.

It is said that he married either Helen (of Troy) or the sorceress Medea in Hades.

Actaeon   *Greek*

A hunter who was changed into a stag by the goddess Artemis, who caught him watching her as she bathed.

In other versions of the story, he approached the goddess when he was wearing the skin of a stag or she threw a goat-skin over him. He was torn to pieces by his own hounds.

Yet other versions say that he suffered this fate for boasting that he was a greater hunter than Artemis herself or because he was a competitor of Zeus for the love of Semele, a princess of Thebes.

Actl   *Central American*
A god of tattooing.

Actor   *Greek*
One of the Argonauts. Various genealogies are suggested for this Greek hero. Perhaps a son of the sea god Poseidon.

Adad   *Mesopotamian*
A Babylonian storm god, a form of the god Marduk. In some early accounts, Adad was created from Chaos. After usurping the power of his father, Prince Sea, he challenged Mot, the god of death, who invited him to the underworld. There he ate the food of the dead and died. He was rescued by the goddess Anat who dragged Mot out of the underworld and chopped him up, so restoring Adad to life.

He is depicted as wearing a horned head-dress and a robe decorated with stars, etc. He may also be shown holding thunderbolts.

Adad-Ea   *Mesopotamian*
= *Greek* Charon
The ferryman in the Babylonian underworld.

Adaheli   *South American*
The sun personified. Some Carib peoples say that, in the beginning, Adaheli descended from the sky and mated with the cayman to produce the first tribes.

Adaro   *Pacific Islands*
A spirit of the sea. These beings are envisaged as half man, half fish, riding on waterspouts and rainbows.

In the Solomon Islands they are said to shoot people with flying fish.

In some versions, the soul has two parts – the aunga (good) which dies and the adaro (bad) which remains as a ghost.

Addanc   *Welsh*
In Arthurian legend, a dwarf or monster living in a lake. He killed the sons of the King of Suffering each day (though they were restored to life again every evening when bathed by their wives). He lived in a cave and hid behind a pillar, killing all who entered with his poisoned spear. Peredur, a Knight of the Round Table, protected by a magic stone given to him in some accounts by the Empress of Constantinople, saw where he was hidden, killed him and cut off his head.

In an alternative story, he was the cause of the Flood and was killed when he was dragged from his underwater lair by the oxen of the god Hu Gardarn after being lulled to sleep on the bosom of a maiden.

Adeyn y Corph   *Welsh*
A fabulous bird said to foretell death.

Adham-Algal   *Mesopotamian*
Purgatory, where the wicked undergo torture.

Adiri   *East Indies*
The Papuan land of the dead; also the name of the ruler of the dead. Originally the cheerless home of Adiri, ruler of the dead, and his daughter, Dirivo. When Dirivo married Sido, the first man to die, Adiri became a more cheerful place (*see more on this at* **Sido**).

Adityas   *Hindu*
A group of early gods, variously given as a triad (Aryaman, Mitra and Varuna) or a group of six (with Anisa, Bhaga, and Daksha) or eight. In later years the number was increased to twelve (guardians of the months of the year) by adding Dhatri, Indra, Ravi, Savitri, Surya, and Yama. Some lists include Aditya, Marttanda, Varuna, Vishnu and Vivasvat.

Adlet   *Inuit*
The Dog People in the lore of the Inuit. These beings are said to be the descendants of a red dog and an Inuit woman. Five of her ten offspring were dogs who became the ancestors of the white races; the other five were monsters who gave birth to even greater monsters, the Adlet.

Adliparmiut   *Inuit*
The lower level of Adlivun (*see below*). Those permitted to penetrate to this level enjoy the privilege of being allowed to carry on hunting but must endure great extremes of weather in so doing.

Adlivun   *Inuit*
Home of the wicked dead. This underworld is ruled by Sedna and her father Anguta. Murderers are kept forever in this grim place but others can progress to the lower level, Adliparmiut. Those who stay in Adlivun, the tupilag, sometimes return as spirits carrying illness and disease.

Admete   *Greek*
Daughter of King Eurystheus of Argos. As his ninth Labour, Hercules was required to get the girdle of Hippolyta, the queen of the Amazons, as a gift for Admete.

Admetus   *Greek*
King of Pherae, he was one of the Argonauts and took part in the

hunt for the Calydonian Boar.

When the god Apollo killed the Cyclops, the god Zeus ordered him to serve as a slave to Admetus for one year.

With the help of Apollo, Admetus won the hand of Alcestis, daughter of King Pelias of Iolcus, by driving a chariot drawn by a boar and a lion. He forgot to make a sacrifice to Artemis when he got married and the goddess filled his bed with snakes. Artemis promised that he would escape death if one of his family offered to die in his place. Alcestis poisoned herself to save him but was rescued from Tartarus either by Hercules who wrestled with Thanatos ('Death') or by the mercy of Persephone, queen of the underworld.

Adno-artina   *Australian*

An ancestral lizard; he fought and killed the ancestral dog Marindi during the Dreamtime.

Adonis   *Greek*

= *Babylonian* Tammuz; *Etruscan* Atunis; *Phrygian* Attis

God of re-birth, vegetation, etc; son of Myrrha by her own father, King Cinyras.

The king's wife upset the goddess Aphrodite by saying that Myrrha was more beautiful than the goddess, who thereupon caused Myrrha to fall in love with her father who slept with her when he was drunk. The result of this union was Adonis who was saved from Cinyras's sword by Aphrodite, who put Adonis in a box and handed him over to Persephone (queen of the underworld) to be reared. Some say that Myrrha was changed into a myrtle tree and that the baby was delivered from the trunk of

the tree when it was split open by the tusk of a charging boar.

When Aphrodite wanted him back, Persephone refused to hand him over and Zeus had to intervene to settle the argument. He had the Muse Calliope adjudicate and she decreed that Adonis should spend half of each year with the two women who loved him or, in some versions, four months with each of the women and the rest of the year by himself.

Some stories say that he was married to Aphrodite and they had two children.

Adonis was killed by Ares, the god of war, in the form of a boar when he was out hunting with Aphrodite, and the crimson flower of the anemone grew where his blood stained the earth. Alternatively, his blood became red roses and Aphrodite's tears became anemones.

After his death, Aphrodite successfully pleaded with Zeus to allow Adonis to spend half the year with her and half in the underworld.

He is sometimes depicted carrying a lyre.

Adonis flower   *Greek*

The rose, the anemone or the pheasant's-eye. It was said that the rose was originally a white flower which became stained with the blood of Aphrodite who was scratched by a thorn when she went to help the dying Adonis.

The anemone was said to have sprung either from the blood of Adonis or from the tears of Aphrodite.

The pheasant's-eye, like the anemone, was said to have sprung from Adonis's blood.

Adroa   *African*

The creator-god and sky god of the Lugbara, a people of Uganda and the Democratic Republic of the Congo.

Adroanzi   *African*

The children of Adroa. They have the habit of following humans and killing those who look back at them. Other accounts describe them as having the form of water-snakes which drown and eat humans.

Adventures of the Sons of Mugmedon, the   *Irish*

The story of the exploits of Niall, a high-king of Ireland, and his step-brothers.

This story tells of Niall's encounter with a witch, the Loathly Lady. Niall and his four step-brothers were out hunting and needed water for cooking their supper. Fergus went to a nearby well and found it guarded by an extremely ugly woman who demanded a kiss as the price of the water. Fergus and all the others except Niall refused the offer. Niall not only kissed her but slept with her and she turned back into the beautiful woman she really was – Flaitheas, the embodiment of Irish sovereignty. She decreed that Niall and his descendants should be the kings of Ireland forever.

Adventurous Bed   *British*

also Perilous Bed

A bed in Castle Carbonek. In some accounts, Galahad slept here and was wounded by a fiery lance, while others say that this was where Lancelot spent an uncomfortable night. (*See also* **Lit Merveile**.)

Aegeus   *Greek*

King of Athens; father of Theseus.

His father had been driven from the throne of Athens but, with the help of his brothers, Aegeus regained the kingdom. He seduced – or, some say, married – Aethra of Troezen and went off to Athens (where he expelled the king Lycus), leaving his sword and sandals hidden behind a huge rock to be reclaimed by any son of their union. That son was Theseus and, in some stories, it was the sea god Poseidon who fathered the child, which was accepted by Aegeus as his own. He recognised Theseus as his son just in time to prevent the sorceress Medea from poisoning him at a banquet.

On his return from Crete after killing the Minotaur, Theseus forgot to hoist the white sail that would signal success and his father, seeing a black sail and thinking him dead, died when he fell from the Acropolis.

Aegir   *Norse*
= *Anglo-Saxon* Eager

God of the deep seas. He was one of an early trinity of gods with his brothers Kari and Loki, and he wrecked ships and dragged them down to the ocean depths.

aegis   *Greek*
The breastplate or shield of Zeus, carried by the goddess Athena. It was originally said to be a breastplate made by the god Hephaestus and was later depicted as a goatskin with the mask of the Gorgon Medusa in the centre.

Aeneas   *Greek*
A Trojan hero. He was said to have been raised by the nymphs of Mount Ida and, in some accounts, was regarded as an ancestor of King Arthur.

At the siege of Troy he was wounded by Diomedes but Apollo carried him off to safety at Pergamos where his wounds were treated by the goddess Artemis. When the city fell, his mother, the goddess Aphrodite, ensured his safety and he was able to escape with his father Anchises and his young son Ascanius but not his wife Creusa, who became separated from the others and died.

Another version says that he betrayed Troy to the Greeks and was rewarded by being given safe-conduct when the city fell, another that he was captured by Neoptolemus, the son of Achilles.

After many adventures (*see Aeneid*) he settled in Italy and married Lavinia, daughter of the king of the Latins, so founding the Roman race. In some accounts, he had a daughter, Rhome, who murdered Latinus and bore Romulus and Remus.

On his death, in a later battle with the Rutulians (a tribe living to the south-east of Rome), he became one of the gods with the title Indiges.

Aeneas Silvius   *Roman*
King of Alba Longa (an ancient city south-east of Rome); a descendant of Aeneas.

Aeneid   *Roman*
Virgil's account (in twelve volumes) of the adventures of Aeneas after the fall of Troy.

The story is as follows:

Aeneas sailed from Troy looking for a new place to settle and dreamed that he should go to Hesperia (the land to the west, Italy) and find a home on the west coast.

His ship was driven off course by the Harpies (female monsters) and when they next made land in Epirus they found that the rulers were Helenus the Trojan seer and Andromache, formerly the wife of the Trojan prince Hector who had been killed at Troy. Helenus advised him to look for a white sow with thirty piglets. Other accounts say that Aeneas was given this advice, some time after he arrived in Italy, by the god of the River Tiber.

Their next stop was in Sicily where only the warning given them by a starving sailor Achaemenides, who had been left behind when Odysseus and his crew escaped from the cave of the Cyclops Polyphemus, saved Aeneas and his crew from the clutches of the Cyclopes who still inhabited that part of the island. Anchises, his old father, died soon afterwards.

A storm contrived by the gods blew the ship to the north coast of Africa where they were feted by Dido, queen of Carthage, who fell in love with Aeneas. He knew that his destiny lay in Italy and eventually forced himself and his crew to give up their life of luxury and set sail once more, heading north. Dido was distraught at the loss and killed herself.

Arriving in Italy, Aeneas was advised by the Sibyl of Cumae to arm himself with a golden bough and seek advice from his father in the underworld who was able to tell him of the problems that lay ahead.

The inhabitants of the area where they finally landed were the Latins under King Latinus and the Rutulians under King Turnus. When Ascanius, the son of Aeneas, inadvertently killed a highly acclaimed pet stag, the Latins were greatly angered. Latinus had been told that his daughter, Lavinia, would marry a stranger from another country and he accepted Aeneas in that role but Turnus married Lavinia and was only too ready to help the Latins against the Trojans when they went to war.

Aeneas, on the advice of the river god of the Tiber, consulted Evander, king of an impoverished state, who told him to seek help from the Etruscans who had been oppressed by the tyrant Mezentius who was now fighting with the Rutulians against the Trojans. They readily provided an army which, after much fighting, defeated the Latins and Rutulians. Aeneas was wounded by an arrow and, when the physician Iapis could not heal him, the goddess Aphrodite intervened with a magic herb and he was soon back in action. Evander's son Pallas was killed in the battle by Turnus. The warrior-queen Camilla also died. Aeneas himself killed Turnus in single combat and also Mezentius and his son Lausus. On one occasion, the goddess Cybele intervened to prevent Turnus from setting fire to the Trojan ships, which turned into swans and swam away.

The white sow and her litter, referred to in the prophecy of Helenus, were found on the site of what was later to be the city of Alba Longa, south-east of Rome.

Aeolus *Greek*
God of the winds. He lived on the floating island of Aeolia with his wife Eos (goddess of the dawn).

aeon
An age of the universe. In some accounts, there have been 365 such ages, though others say only 30.

aes sidhe *Irish*
People of the hills; fairies. This name applied to the Danaans after their defeat by the Milesians.

Aesir *Norse*
also Elder Gods
The twelve early sky deities of the Norse pantheon. They were originally at war with the later gods, the Vanir, but made peace with them and exchanged hostages. Some versions say that they came later than the Vanir.

At one time or another, the following (among others) have been regarded as belonging to the Aesir: Balder, Bragi, Forseti, Frey, Frigga, Heimdall, Hermod, Hoder, Hoenir, Iduna, Loki, Mimir, Odin, Thor, Tyr and Uller.

Afrikete *African*
A sea goddess of the Fon. She was regarded as a trickster and a gossip.

afrit[1] *Arabian*
An evil demon, a type of jinnee. These beings sometimes take human form and may even marry mortals. They are said to live in the ground from whence they may appear as clouds of smoke. They can appear in different sizes, varying from giant size to miniature beings small enough to enter a bottle, but they are said to be enormously strong, capable of lifting and flying off with a complete city, flying at lightning speed on their bat-like wings.

afrit[2] *Egyptian*
A spirit which was manifest in the whirlwind and could be called up by Set.

afterbirth
In some cultures, the placenta is regarded as having mystic powers, ruling the life of the person concerned or acting as guardian or twin; should it be eaten by an animal, the child will grow up with the characteristics of that beast.

African
The Baganda are among those who regard the afterbirth as the twin of the child. They put the afterbirth in a pot which is then buried under a tree. Here it becomes a spirit which enters the tree. If the tree is damaged or if someone outside the tribe should eat the fruit of that tree, the spirit leaves, whereupon the twin is forced to follow and will die.

In the case of a king, the so-called twin is housed in a specially built small temple where it is guarded by an official known as the kimbugwe. Part of his duties is to expose the placenta to the light of the moon once in each month and, after anointing it with melted butter, return it to its resting place.

Australian
Some of the Aboriginal tribes believe that part of the soul, known as the choi-i, is to be found in the placenta, which is buried in a spot marked by a small mound of twigs. This enables the fertility spirit, Anjea, to locate the afterbirth which she can use, they say, to make another baby.

Chinese
The Chinese had a practice of making medicines from the afterbirth.

East Indies
(1) In Java the afterbirth is cast adrift in a small boat decorated

with fruit, flowers, etc to be eaten by the crocodiles who, it is said, are themselves the products of afterbirths or are ancestors of the tribes.

(2) In Sumatra, some tribes say that the afterbirth holds a tutelary spirit which will guide the person concerned during his or her lifetime.

Others say that one such guardian exists in the afterbirth while a second exists in the embryo.

Some bury the afterbirth under the house, others keep it after preserving it in salt.

Finno-Ugric

In countries occupied by various branches of the Finno-Ugric peoples, the placenta was hung on the branch of a tree in the forest and sacrifices offered to it in recognition of its role in nourishing the child.

Hebrew

An ancient custom involved burning the placenta and mixing the ashes with flowers or milk as an antidote to disease or a charm to protect the user from witchcraft.

New Zealand

The Maoris plant a tree when a baby is born and bury the placenta under it so that both the child and the tree will develop together.

North American

(1) The Hupa place the afterbirth in a tree which has been split open to receive it and then bind the split; if the tree thrives, so will the child – and vice versa.

(2) The Kwakiutl treat the afterbirth differently according to the sex of the child. That of a boy is put out to be eaten by the ravens in the

belief that this will endow the child with the power to read the future; that of a girl is buried on the shore to ensure that she will become expert at digging up clams, a useful accomplishment in the coastal area of British Columbia.

(3) Other tribes, including the Cherokee, Creek and Pawnee, say that a real living twin can emerge from the afterbirth.

Siberian

The Yukaghi people tie the afterbirth inside a reindeer skin together with miniature hunting weapons for a boy and sewing implements for a girl so that they will acquire the skills appropriate to their sex.

South American

The Aymara bury the afterbirth alongside tools for a boy and cooking utensils for a girl. In some cases the afterbirth is burned so that the ashes can be used to make medicines.

Agamemnon   *Greek*

King of Mycenae (or Argos); husband of Clytemnestra; father of Chrysothemis, Electra, Iphigenia and Orestes by Clytemnestra, and of twins by Cassandra.

As an infant, he was saved with his brother Menelaus when his father Atreus was killed by his [Atreus's] nephew Aegisthus, and fled to Sparta. Later, helped by Tyndareus, the king of Sparta, he regained his father's throne.

He killed Tantalus, king of Pisa, and married his widow Clytemnestra.

When the Greek forces were assembled ready to invade Troy to recover the beautiful Helen, adverse winds kept them

shore-bound. To propitiate the gods, Agamemnon sacrificed his daughter Iphigenia, so ensuring favourable winds for the voyage.

In the fighting at Troy he was given the girl Chryseis as a prize and refused to release her when her father came to plead for her. The father was a priest of Apollo and the god intervened in the dispute, bringing much sickness to the Greek forces. To avoid further trouble, Agamemnon released the girl but, in compensation, demanded the girl Briseis who had been given to Achilles, whereupon Achilles swore vengeance and refused to fight any more.

When Troy fell, Agamemnon returned to Mycenae with Cassandra who had borne him twin boys to find that his wife, Clytemnestra, had taken Aegisthus as a lover while he was away. These two plotted Agamemnon's death and killed him with Cassandra and her two children.

Agares   *European*

A demon, duke of hell, one of the 72 Spirits of Solomon. He is said to have taught languages and is depicted as a human riding a crocodile.

Agas Xenas Xena   *North American*

In the lore of the Chinook, the deity of the evening star.

Agassou   *African*

A panther-god of the Fon.

Agbon   *African*

The palm tree. In the lore of the Yoruba, this was the first living thing to be created by the god Olorun.

Age   *African*

A desert god of the Fon, god of animals.

Agent of Earth *see* **Ti-kuan**

Agent of Heaven *see* **T'ien-kuan**

Agent of Water *see* **Shui-kuan**

Agiel *Hebrew*

One of the seven Intelligences, ruler of the planet Saturn.

Aglaia *Greek*

One of the three Graces – splendour; daughter of Zeus and the goddess Eurynome; wife of the god Hephaestus, some say.

Aglookik *Inuit*

The spirit of the hunt. He is said to live beneath the ice and to direct the hunter in his search for game.

Agnar *Norse*

Son of King Hrauding; foster-son of the goddess Frigga.

He and his brother Geirrod were cast ashore on an island and were given shelter by the god Odin who was living there disguised as an old man. When they finally returned home, Geirrod abandoned his brother to the sea in their small boat.

Later, Geirrod succeeded to the throne and, when Odin visited his court in disguise to test his hospitality, he had the god tied to a stake between two fires. During the eight days of this ordeal, Odin received no food or drink except a draught of ale brought to him by Agnar. When Odin revealed himself as a god, Geirrod tripped over and impaled himself on his sword and Agnar was elevated to the throne by the grateful Odin.

Agni *Hindu*

The god of fire. He is depicted as having two or three heads, seven tongues and four hands (or seven arms) and sometimes with a goat's head, carrying a flaming spear.

In some accounts, he was born of the lotus, or was kindled from wood by the sage Brighu. Some say that he ate his parents (the two pieces of wood) when he was born. He is said to appear when two pieces of wood are rubbed together.

He is one of the eight Dikpalas, the guardian of the south-eastern quarter of the world with his elephant, Pundarika, and rides either a goat or in a chariot drawn by parrots or red horses.

His voracious appetite led him, on one occasion when he was exhausted, to consume the Khandava forest. Some versions have it that his huge appetite was not something that he was born with but was inflicted on him by a curse by Brighu when Agni told a demon that Brighu was the one who had stolen the demon's wife, Puloma. Some regard the reference to his huge appetite as a metaphor for Agni's fire-raising propensities.

In some accounts he is revered as Trita (lightning) and Surya (sun); the three forms are referred to as Tryambaka.

Agramant *European*

In the legends of Charlemagne, a king of Africa. His father had been killed in battle with Charlemagne and he planned an invasion of France to exact revenge. The king of the Garamantes, on his death-bed, advised that the venture would succeed only with the help of the knight, Rogero, and he could be freed from the clutches of his foster-father, the magician Atlantes, only with the magic ring of the enchantress Angelica which rendered the wearer invisible.

During his battles in France, he heard that his capital, Biserta, was besieged by Abyssinians led by Astolpho and withdrew his forces. On the return voyage, he met Gradasso, king of Sericune, who had left France earlier to return to his own country, and who offered to help Agramant. The two of them, along with Sobrino, a Saracen, challenged three paladins of Charlemagne – Florismart, Oliver and Roland – to fight to settle their differences. Agramant was killed in this fight.

Agras *Finnish*

A god of twins; also a turnip god.

Agrasandhari *Hindu*

A book of judgement: the register of an individual's deeds. This book, which records all one's life on earth, is kept by Chitragupta, the registrar of the dead, in the realm of Yama, ruler of one of the courts of the underworld.

Agravain *British*

A Knight of the Round Table. He and his brother Mordred set out to prove that Lancelot and Guinevere were having an affair and, when King Arthur was away from Camelot, they caught the lovers in bed together. In the ensuing fight, Lancelot wounded Mordred and killed not only Agravain but all the other knights who had helped.

Other sources say that he was killed by Lancelot when he rescued Guinevere from the stake (*see more at* **Guinevere**).

Agunua *Pacific Islands*

A serpent creator-god of the Solomon Islands; chief of the figona (spirits).

He created a woman and they mated to produce a daughter. When the woman grew old she disappeared, returning after she had changed her skin. Her daughter then rejected her, so she resumed her old skin. As a result, humans can no longer renew their youth by sloughing their skins and growing a new one, as snakes do.

Ah Bolom Tzacab *Central American*
A Mayan fertility god. Some identify him as the deity God K.

Ah Ciliz   *Central American*
The Mayan god of eclipses. He was thought to swallow the sun when it disappeared during an eclipse.

Ah Cuxtal   *Central American*
The Mayan god of birth.

Ah Kin   *Central American*
A Mayan sun god. He was carried back every night through the underworld by Sucunyum, the god of the underworld, ready to start his journey through the sky the following day. He was regarded as the source of cures for illness.

He is depicted as having a third eye, square in shape, and teeth filed into the shape of the letter T.

Ah Kumix Uinicob   *Central American*
Mayan water gods. These small deities assume the duties of their larger counterparts, Ah Patnar Uinicob, when there is less work to do in the dry part of the year.

Ah Patnar Uinicob   *Central American*
Mayan water gods. These deities are depicted as giants pouring water from jars to nourish the earth. They cause rain by beating the clouds with axes made of stone. In the dry season, their duties are taken over by their small counterparts, Ah Kumix Uinicob.

Ah Puch   *Central American*
= *Aztec* Mictlantecuhtli
The Mayan god of death; chief demon. He is depicted as a

decaying corpse or as a skeleton wearing bells.

Ahalya   *Hindu*
The first woman; wife of the sage Gotama. She was seduced by the god Indra, and Gotama cursed Indra with the loss of his testes. Ahalya was forced to lie in ashes for centuries, living only on air, until she was rescued by Rama, the seventh incarnation of the god Vishnu.

Ahat   *Egyptian*
A cosmic cow which acted as nurse to the sun god.

Ahau Kin   *South American*
also Lord of the Sun Face
A Mayan sun god. After sunset, he became lord of the underworld, the Jaguar god.

Ahayuta achi   *North American*
also War Brothers, War Twins
Twin war gods of the Zuni; sons of the Sun by the goddess Dripping Water.

In some versions these twins are regarded as mischievous boys forever disobeying their grandmother, Spider Woman, and getting into scrapes from which they always emerge triumphant.

As culture heroes, they are credited with building mountains, digging canyons and introducing irrigation.

Ahhazu *see* **Ach-chazu**

Ahmed   *Arabian*
A prince in the *Arabian Nights' Entertainments*. He owned a tent which could house a whole army but which could be folded so as to fit into a pocket. He also owned an apple which could cure illness.

Ahnfrau   *German*
The spirit of a noblewoman which warns her descendants of approaching death.

Ahriman   *Persian*
also Angra Mainya
The Zoroastrian evil principle, the god of darkness. In some accounts he and Ahura Mazda are the twin sons of Zurvan 'Infinite Time'. He was envisaged as a black toad and was constantly in opposition to Ahura Mazda, creating ashes where Ahura Mazda had made fire, poison where Ahura Mazda had created a cure, and so on.

He is said to have sunk a shaft to the centre of the earth and there created a hell.

This deity killed the primeval ox and introduced disease and all the other ills of mankind and, in some stories, sent a flood. He will be defeated at the final battle and confined eternally to hell.

Ahsonnutli   *North American*
also Turquoise Man
Supreme god of the Navaho; consort of the Turquoise Woman (*see* **Estanatlehi**).

He is regarded as a hermaphrodite deity who placed men at the four corners of the earth to support the heavens.
(*See also* **Turquoise Man**.)

Ahti   *Finnish*
also Ahto
An ancient god of the waters. This primordial ocean preceded creation but mated with Ilmatar, goddess of the air, when she fell from the heavens, to produce countless creatures.

Ahura Mazda   *Persian*
also Auramazda, Ohrmazd, Spenta Mainya, Wise Lord
God of light and creator-god; the Zoroastrian good principle; father of Haoma, Mithra, Zoroaster and others. In some accounts he and Ahriman are the twin sons of Zurvan, 'Infinite Time'.

He created a bull which, when it escaped from its cave, was found and killed by Mithra, the blood-spots forming living beings where they touched the earth. He sent his son Atar to chain the dragon Azhi Dahaka to a mountain to stop his persecution of mankind.

He is depicted as a venerable, bearded figure, usually inside a circle, holding a ring and with one hand held up in blessing. Sometimes he is shown enveloped in flames and wearing a mantle of the sky.

Ahurani   *Persian*

A Zoroastrian water goddess, goddess of fertility, health and prosperity.

Aichleach   *Irish*

One of the five sons of the warrior Uigreann who killed Finn mac Cool after he killed their father.

In one version, he killed Finn when the Fianna (*see* **Fianna**) staged a rebellion. In another account, all five sons threw their spears simultaneously so that they could all share in Finn's death.

Aidne   *Irish*

A Milesian (*see* **Milesians**), said to have created fire by rubbing his hands together.

Aikiren   *North American*

also Duck Hawk

A guardian spirit of the Karok tribe of north-west California.; He is said to live on top of Sugarloaf Mountain.

When he found two maidens weeping at the loss of their lovers, he reunited them for a year, at the end of which the girls had to return to their tribe but not before they had been given the secret of reviving the dead by rubbing salmon flesh on their lips.

Ailleann   *Irish*

A woman of the Otherworld. She was said to have appeared from time to time as a deer. Some say that she married King Arthur when she took him and his men to the Otherworld.

Aillen   *Irish*

A creature from the Otherworld. Every year he emerged from his cave and, putting the garrison to sleep with his music, burned down the king's palace at Tara with his fiery breath. The warrior Finn mac Cool killed him and cut off his head. In some accounts, it is Amergin (a son of Milesius), not Finn, who is the hero of the story.

Aim   *European*

A demon, one of the 72 Spirits of Solomon. He is depicted with three heads – one of a man, one of a cat and one of a snake – and riding a snake.

Aimon Kondi   *South American*

A creator-god of the Arawak Indians. He is said to have set the world on fire and followed that with a flood.

Ain Shams   *Egyptian*

A well. It was said that the sun was born in, and renewed itself by bathing in, this well.

Aine   *Irish*

A sun goddess, goddess of love and fertility.

In some stories she is equated with Morrigan, the goddess of war; in others she is the moon goddess of Munster who was raped by Ailill Olom whom, some say, she killed. Some say that she was killed by Ailill who drove a spear through her chest when she pulled his ears off.

Some accounts equate her with Ana, the beneficent version of the goddess Dana, while in

some stories she is a fairy queen in Limerick. She was sometimes seen in the form of a mermaid, bathing in a lake, while in other versions she became a banshee living in a palace inside a hill where she wove sunbeams into cloth of gold.

In some accounts, she fell, in love with the sea god Manannan and her brother gave her to him in exchange for Manannan's wife, Uchdealb.

Ainge   *Irish*

Daughter of the Dagda, god of life and death. It is said that the forests of Ireland were created from a bundle of twigs which she had collected and which were stolen by Gaible, son of Nuada the leader of the Danaans, who scattered them on the wind.

Airavata   *Hindu*

also Airabata, Airavana

The white elephant of the god Indra. This animal was the eleventh thing to be created at the Churning of the Ocean.

Some say that it was created from shavings from the sun by Vishvakarma, the god of artisans, others that it was created by the god Brahma. This animal is sometimes depicted with several heads and four tusks.

airbedruad   *Irish*

An impenetrable magic hedge. It was said that druids could conjure up such a hedge round opposing armies.

aitvaras   *Baltic*

= *Estonian* ai; *Finnish* ajata

A Lithuanian house-spirit. This spirit was variously described as a cockerel or as a flying dragon with the head of a snake and a fiery tail.

Such a bird can be obtained

by giving one's soul to the Devil in exchange or it can be reared from an egg laid by a seven-year-old cockerel. Fed on omelettes, the bird can increase its owner's wealth by stealing food and money.

Aizen-myoo *Japanese*
A Shinto (later Buddhist) god, the personification of love. He is depicted seated, with two, four or six arms and sometimes two heads. He often wears a lion's mask on his head and carries a five-pointed thunderbolt.

Ajagava *Hindu*
The bow of the god Shiva.

Ajax[1] *Greek*
also Ajax the Greater
A warrior-hero, king of Salamis.

During the Trojan War, he attacked Teuthrania (in Mysia), killed the king, Teuthras, and seized his daughter, Tecmessa. He also killed Glaucus in battle.

When Achilles was killed at Troy the chieftains had to decide whether Ajax or Odysseus should have the wonderful arms made for Achilles by the god Hephaestus. When the choice fell on Odysseus, Ajax decided to kill both Agamemnon and Menelaus since they had, he thought, swayed the decision against him but Athena intervened to strike him with temporary madness, causing him to kill the Greek flocks, thinking they were soldiers. When he came to his senses and realised what he had done, he killed himself with his own sword, one given to him by Hector, prince of Troy, when they fought an inconclusive duel. It was said that the hyacinth sprang up where his blood stained the ground (*see also* **Hyacinthus**).

In other versions, Odysseus killed Ajax, or the Trojan prince Paris killed him with an arrow, or the Trojans captured him and buried him alive.

Ajax[2] *Greek*
also Ajax the Less
A Greek warrior. At the fall of Troy he raped Cassandra (a Trojan princess and prophetess) who had taken refuge in the temple of Athena. For this sacrilege the gods caused a storm to disperse the homeward-bound Greek fleet and he was drowned.

Others say he was killed by a thunderbolt hurled by the sea god Poseidon when he boasted that he would escape the sea despite the gods.

Aje *African*
A Yoruba goddess of wealth. She is said to appear in the form of a hen.

Aji-Shiki-Taka-Hiko-Ne *Japanese*
A Shinto rain god or thunder god. As a child, he made so much noise that he was placed in a boat which sails for ever round the islands of Japan.

Ajysyt *Siberian*
The mother-goddess of the Yakuts. She brings the soul from heaven at the birth of a baby and records each one in the Golden Book of Fate.

Akaf *African*
A king of Kordofan in Sudan.

The custom was that each king was killed at a time decreed by the priests who read the stars. Akaf proposed to take the story-teller, Far-li-mas, and his own sister, Sali, with him when his time came. Sali induced Far-li-mas to recite such marvellous stories that the priests forgot the stars and no date was ever fixed for the king's

death. (*See also* **Arabian Nights' Entertainment.**)

Akakanet *South American*
A vegetation-deity of the Araucanian tribe. This deity, who lives in the Pleiades, is said to provide flowers and fruit for the use of the tribe.

In some accounts, he is the benevolent aspect of an evil spirit, Guecubu, while others say they are brothers.

Akongo *African*
A creator-god of the Ngombe people. He found the people that he had created to be so noisy that he left them and went to live in the sky.

Others say that at first they all lived in the sky, but Akongo sent the humans to earth to be rid of therm.

Ala *African*
Earth goddess and fertility goddess of the Ibo; goddess of the underworld.

Aladdin *Arabian*
The owner of a magic lamp in the *Arabian Nights' Entertainments*. He could conjure up a genie that would obey his orders merely by rubbing the lamp and, with its help, won the hand of a beautiful princess, Badr al-Budur. He later killed the magician who tried to take the lamp from him and, on the death of his father-in-law, became emperor of China.

Alan *British*
also Alain le Gros
In some versions of the Grail story, he was the son of Pellimore and father of Percival and took over as keeper of the Holy Grail after Josephus. In other accounts, he is the Fisher King.

Alasnam *Arabian*
The owner of eight precious statues in the *Arabian Nights'*

Entertainments. He filled a ninth empty pedestal with his wife, the most beautiful woman in the land. He also owned a magic mirror that could tell him whether a maiden was faithful.

Alberich   *German*

In the Nibelungen stories, a king of the dwarfs. In one story, he was the father of Ortnit, king of the Lombards, and gave him a magical suit of armour and the sword Rosen. He helped Ortnit when he laid siege to the fortress of Muntabure.

In the Wagnerian version of the story, he stole the Rhinegold from the Rhine-daughters, and his brother, Mime, made from it the Helmet of Invisibility and the Ring of Power.

In some accounts he was the father of Hagen by Krimhild.

(*See also* **Andvari**.)

Albion   *Greek*

King of the giants; ruler of Britain; son of the sea god Poseidon.

He led an assault on the gods, climbing a pile of stones that reached the sky. Hercules came to the aid of the gods, killing many of the giants. In one story, Albion, who survived, planned to kill Hercules and waited in ambush in the Pyrenees. Hercules came on him from the rear and killed him.

In another version, he and his brothers went to Gaul and fought against Hercules. When they tried to steal some of Geryon's cattle that Hercules had brought back from his tenth Labour, all the giants were killed.

alchera   *Australian*

also alcheringa, Dreamtime, the Dreaming

The period when the ancestors of the Aborigines rose out of the ground to shape the earth and make mankind by singing. When they had finished their work they returned to their sleep under the earth.

Alchera is the term generally in use in central Australia; further north in Arnhem Land the tribes refer to this period as *bamum* and to their ancestors of that period as *Wongar*; to the west and south, the usual name for the Dreamtime is *tjukui*.

Alderley Edge   *British*

A site in Cheshire, England, where King Arthur and his knights are said to be sleeping.

Other suggested sites are at Cadbury, Craig-y-Dinas, Mount Etna, Ogof Lanciau Eryri, Ogo'r Dinas, Richmond Castle and Sewingshields.

Ale of Goibhniu   *Irish*

A drink which conferred immortality on those who drank it.

Alecto   *Greek*

'relentless'

One of the three Furies.

Alfheim   *Norse*

also Liosalfheim, Nibelheim

The home of the good elves. This domain is said to be poised between heaven and earth. It is also regarded as the home of the god Frey. (*See also* **Liosalfheim, Svartalfheim**.)

Algon   *North American*

A Chippewa hunter. He found a fairy-ring on the prairie and watched as twelve star-maidens descended from the sky in a basket and danced round the ring. He tried several times to catch the youngest star-maiden, without success, and finally turned himself into a mouse.

When she tried to kill him, he returned to his normal form and carried her off. They married and had one son. Some years later, she made another wicker-basket and, taking the child with her, ascended to her home in the sky.

When the boy was grown up, he asked to see his father so they came back to earth in the basket. Algon returned to the skies with them, taking parts of all the animals and birds with him. The star-people each took one of the fragments and became the animal or bird whose part they had chosen. Algon, his wife and son, all became falcons.

Ali Baba   *Arabian*

The hero of a story in the *Arabian Nights' Entertainments*. He discovered the password ('sesame' or 'simsim') to the robbers' cave and stole their treasure. His slave, Morgiana, killed the robbers, when they hid in large jars, by pouring boiling oil over them and later killed their leader. As reward, Ali gave her her freedom and allowed her to marry his son or nephew.

Aliduke   *British*

A Knight of the Round Table. He was one of the many knights captured and imprisoned by the giant Turkin (or Tarquin), who hated all Arthur's knights, until rescued by Lancelot.

All-father

A name given to supreme gods such as Odin and Zeus: the pre-existing, uncreated ruler of all things.

In North American tribal lore, the sky.

All-seer *see* **Odin**

All-spirit *see* **Maheo**

All-wise   *Norse*

also Alvis(s)

A dwarf. All-wise had been promised the hand of the goddess Freya but, when he arrived to claim her, the god Odin, who had been away from Asgard when the promise was made, saved Freya from this union. He said that he needed to test the dwarf's claim to great knowledge and kept him up all night answering questions about the gods and creation. He kept the questions going until the sun came up and its rays turned the dwarf into stone.

A similar story is told involving the god Thor and his daughter Thrud.

alligator

(1) In Bolivia, the Guarani envisage an underworld ferryman, akin to the Greek Charon, in the form of an alligator.

(2) In Central America, some tribes revere a deity depicted with the body of a man and the head of an alligator.

(3) Some Indonesian tribes tell how the trickster mousedeer induced the alligator to line up his family nose to tail and used them as a bridge to cross a swamp.

(4) A Japanese story has a monkey in place of the mousedeer of the Indonesian story.

(5) One North American story tells how Rabbit lured the alligator into a field and then set fire to the grass; this accounts for the beast's scaly skin. The story of walking on the backs of alligators to cross a swamp appears again in the southern states and, in this case, the last alligator in the line bit off Rabbit's tail.

The alligator's dented nose is said to be the result of a blow when he was playing a ball-game with the birds.

(6) In the Pacific Islands, the teeth of the alligator are worn as a charm to protect the wearer from illness and witches.

Allocer   *European*

A demon, a duke of hell; one of the 72 Spirits of Solomon.

alphabetical gods   *Central American*

Unidentified gods of the Maya. The Spaniards destroyed many of the records of the Maya, making identification of some deities difficult or impossible. These have been given labels, A to I and K to P.

Altjira   *Australian*

also Altjirra

Creator-god and sky god of the Aborigines. He was one of the ancestral deities of the Dreamtime but, when the others returned to their underground sleep, he ascended into the highest heaven. He is depicted as having the feet of an emu.

Alulim   *Mesopotamian*

A Sumerian deity, the first man. He is said to have descended from heaven and ruled on earth for 28,000 (or 67,200) years.

Aluluei   *Pacific Islands*

A god of navigation. When his brothers killed him, his father brought him back to life. The stars are regarded as his many thousand eyes.

Alvis(s) *see* **All-wise**

Alvor   *Norse*

A race of small people, the hog-folk: a form of elves. These people are said to dance in the fields at night.

Ama-Tsu-Kami   *Japanese*

Gods of heaven, as opposed to the Kuni-Tsu-Kami.

Ama-Tsu-Mara   *Japanese*

The Shinto smith-god. He made the mirror which was used to persuade Amaterasu to come out of her cave. The mould for the mirror was made by Ishi-Kore-Dome.

He is depicted as having only one eye.

Amaimon   *European*

A medieval devil, ruler of the eastern part of hell. One of the cardinal demons, one of the 72 Spirits of Solomon.

Amaka   *Siberian*

One of the two aspects of the supreme being of the Evenk people. In this aspect, the creator looks after the interests of human beings; in his other aspect, as Ekseri, he is the guardian of animals and forests.

Amaterasu   *Japanese*

A Shinto sun goddess; daughter of the god Izanagi and goddess Izanami. She was said to have been produced from the eye (right or left according to which story is read) of Izanagi when he washed his face.

When she was born, her parents sent her up the Ladder of Heaven to take her place as the sun goddess.

The god Susanowa challenged her to a contest in attempt to take over her kingdom of heaven. She chewed up his sword and spat out three female deities and he swallowed her five-strand necklace and spat out five male deities. He then claimed her realm and so upset Amaterasu that she shut herself in the cave Ama-no-iwato and darkness descended on the earth until the Eighty Myriad Gods persuaded her to emerge when they invented the mirror, Kagami, for her and had Uzume (the goddess of dancing and merrymaking) dance to make them all laugh.

Her sacred bird is the Yatagarasu (sun-crow).

Amazons *Greek*

Warrior-maidens, daughters of the god Ares and the goddess Artemis, some say.

In some accounts their mother was the goddess Aphrodite or Otrere, queen of the Amazons. They came from Asia Minor or Scythia and made a practice of breaking the arms and legs of all male infants to keep them subservient. They cut off one breast to make it easier to use a bow or spear. There were three tribes, each with its own city and ruled by one of three queens.

Some say that they killed and ate any who landed on their shores.

They were defeated in battle by Theseus leading the Athenians.

In Arthurian lore, they appear as a subject race under King Lucius. In one story they were engaged in battle by Gawain and the Crop-eared Dog is said to have killed their queen.

In Arabian lore, each had one male, one female breast or one breast in the centre. Some say men and women lived on opposite sides of the river in West Africa and met only in the dry season when the river could be forded. Others say the women lived without men, conceiving by bathing in a certain pool, perhaps inhabited by a jinnee who mated with them.

ambrosia *Greek*

The food of the gods conferring everlasting youth; oil used for anointing and healing.

Ambuscias *European*

A demon, duke of hell; one of the 72 Spirits of Solomon.

Ame-no-iha-kina *Japanese*

The throne of God.

Ame-no-Toko-Tachi-no-kami *Japanese*

A primordial female deity; the female principle.

Ame-no-Uzume-no-mikato *see* **Uzume**

Ame-no-wo-ha-bari *Japanese*

The magic sword of the god Izanagi. Izanagi used this weapon to decapitate his son, the fire god Kazu-Tsuchi.

Amen *Egyptian*

also Amon, Ammon;

= *Greek* Zeus; *Roman* Jupiter

Supreme creator-god, god of fertility and life, god of Thebes; one of the three Lords of Destiny (with Khnum and Ptah). Some say that he was born from the voice of the god Thoth.

As a god of the primitive waters he represented, together with the goddess Amaunet, the unknowableness of the waters.

In one account, he engendered Athor and Kneph who were the parents of the god Osiris and the goddess Isis.

His bird is the goose and he is depicted variously as a man with a human head or that of a frog, a ram or a serpent, or as an ape or a lion, and sometimes wearing a cap with two tall feathers.

Amenhotep *Egyptian*

The god of healing. He was originally a mortal pharaoh, later deified.

Ament *Egyptian*

A serpent-headed or cat-headed mother-goddess; wife of Amen.

Originally she was a Libyan goddess. In Thebes, she is Mut.

Amenti *see* **Sons of Horus**

Amfortas *British*

also Grail Keeper, Grail King, Pelles, Fisher King, Sinner King

In the Wagnerian version of the Grail story, he took over the guardianship of the Holy Grail when his father Frimutel became too weak. Relying on the power of the Sacred Spear, he set out to destroy Klingsor, the evil magician who had built a garden of delight to seduce those knights seeking admission to the Temple of the Grail, but he himself was seduced into losing the spear to Klingsor who wounded him in the side with it. Nothing would heal this wound but the touch of this spear and he suffered great pain for many years until Parsifal regained the spear and cured him.

An alternative version says that, forgetting his vows of purity, he looked lustfully on a maiden, whereupon the Holy Spear wounded him of its own accord. Other accounts say that he sustained a wound in a jousting match.

He appears as Peredur's uncle in the Castle of Wonders and shows him the Grail and the Holy Lance.

Amida *Buddhist*

also Amida Butsu, Amitayas, Buddha of Infinite Light;

= *Chinese* A-mi-t'o-fo; *Hindu* Shiva; *Indian* Amitabha

The Japanese version of Amitabha. He is the supreme Buddha of the Shin sect, revered in Pure Land Buddhism, and taught that one could attain Nirvana by faith as an alternative to meditation

Amina *Arabian*

A ghoul in the *Arabian Nights' Entertainments*. She treated her three sisters very badly and led them about on leads like dogs.

Amitabha   *Buddhist*

= *Chinese* A-mi-t'o-fo; *Hindu* Shiva; *Japanese* Amida

An Indian bodhisattva, 'god of infinite light'; the first (or fourth) of the five Dhyanibuddhas.

He generated the god of mercy Avalokiteshvara from a beam of light issuing from his right eye.

He was the ruler of the Western Pure Land, Sukhavati, and revered in Pure Land Buddhism, in which he is equated with the Japanese Shakyamuni.

(*See also* ***Amitayas***.)

Amitayas   *Buddhist*

The Buddha of infinite light; a name of the Buddha as 'eternal Buddha'.

In some accounts, this deity is the same as Amitabha.

Amma   *African*

Supreme god of the Dogon people of Mali.

The primordial egg he created had two yolks: from one came the evil god Ogo and his sister Yasigi, the other produced the twins known as the Nummo.

He created the sun and the moon by baking a clay pot with bands of copper for the sun and brass for the moon and he made white people from moonlight and black people from the light of the sun.

Some say that he mated with the earth goddess to produce Ogo the jackal, the first of the animals.

In some accounts, Amma was the primordial egg from which sprang the Nummo who created the earth and everything in it.

Amon¹   *Greek*

also Ammon

The Greek and Roman version of the Egyptian god Amen.

Amon²   *European*

A demonised version of the god Amon, one of the 72 Spirits of Solomon.

In some versions, this being is regarded as a serpent-tailed wolf while earlier versions may show the head of an owl.

Amon-Ra   *Egyptian*

An assimilation of Amon with the sun god Ra; god of Thebes. He is depicted as having the head of a snake.

Amor *see* **Cupid**

Amori   *Pacific Islands*

A female kangaroo, in the lore of New Guinea. It is said that she produced a human son, Sisinjori, after swallowing the sperm which she found on the spot where the first human couple mated.

Amotken   *North American*

The creator-god of the Salish Indians. He created five goddesses from hairs from his own head and arranged for them to rule in succession. The present age is ruled by the goddess of evil.

He is envisaged as a wise old man, living alone.

Amphitrite   *Greek*

A sea goddess, one of the Nereids; wife of Poseidon.

She fled from Poseidon's advances but Delphinus, king of the dolphins, wooed her on the sea god's behalf and she agreed to marry him

Jealous of her husband's interest in the lovely Scylla, she changed her into an ugly monster by putting herbs into the water where she bathed.

She is depicted as crowned with seaweed in a pearl-shell chariot drawn by sea-horses and dolphins.

amrita   *Hindu*

The drink of the gods; the water of life. The drink which conferred immortality was originally made by the gods and demons who coiled the world serpent, Vasuki, round Mount Mandara and spun it, so 'churning the ocean'. Amrita was the first of the fourteen things to emerge from the waters.

amrita-khumba   *Hindu*

The phial which contained the original amrita which appeared at the 'churning of the ocean'.

Amy   *European*

A demon in hell, one of the 72 Spirits of Solomon. This being can appear as a beautiful woman and is said to be a teacher of astrology.

An¹   *Egyptian*

A name for Osiris as a sun god.

An²   *Mesopotamian*

= *Babylonian* Anu

Sumerian creator-god, god of heaven. He was killed and flayed by the god Marduk.

He is usually depicted as a bull.

Ana   *Irish*

A goddess of war. She was one of a trinity of names (Ana, Badb and Macha) known as the Fate Trinity and regarded as an aspect of the war goddess Morrigan or Nemain.

Anahita   *Persian*

A water goddess, fertility goddess and goddess of the dawn; one of the Yazatas.

She purified the original primitive waters. Her female temple slaves acted as religious prostitutes.

In some accounts, she was regarded as a war goddess who drove a chariot drawn by four white horses.

She is depicted as a tall handsome woman in a cloak

embroidered with gold thread and ornamented with otter skins.

She is identified with the planet Venus.

Anansi   *African*
also Aunt Nancy, Mr Spider; = *Ashanti* Kwaku Ananse; *Hausa* Gizo; *West Indian* Annency, Nansi, Ti Malice

A trickster-god of the Yoruba. He was originally a creator-god but was changed into a spider when a king kicked him for killing his huge ram which had eaten Anansi's crops. Others say that he was defeated in a shape-changing contest by the chameleon and came down to earth on a rope. He now appears both as a spider and a man.

He begged a single cob of corn from God, promising to provide him with a hundred slaves. By pretending the cob had been stolen, he tricked a chief into giving him a basketful of cobs to keep him quiet. He swapped the cobs for a hen, the hen for some sheep and the sheep for a corpse. Pretending that this was a son of God who had been killed by the sons of a chief, he persuaded the chief to give him a hundred young men whom he presented to God as slaves.

To prove that he was as clever as God himself, he captured the sun, the moon and darkness in a bag. When he produced the sun from the bag, some people were blinded.

On one occasion he got stuck to the Gum Girl, on another an antelope carried him to safety from a bush-fire. To repay this kindness, he wove a web around the antelope's baby, so hiding it from hunters.

When he asked the sky gods to sell him some stories, he was told that the price would be a fairy, a hornet, a leopard and a python. The gods were so impressed when Anansi produced all these items that they gave him all their stories which they called *Anansesem*.

In one story, he owned a pot which was always full of food and when his children broke the pot he punished them with a whip. The inquisitive children examined the whip which then started to beat them and would not stop.

On another occasion, he boasted that he could ride a tiger but the king asked the tiger who said that this was a lie and tried to get Anansi to retract in the king's presence. By pretending to be ill, the spider induced the tiger to carry him on his back – and, of course, he needed a bridle, a saddle and a whip. When the king saw the spider riding the tiger, he welcomed him to the royal palace.

Ananta   *Hindu*
also World Serpent; = *Buddhist* Muchalinda

A serpent with 1000 (or seven) heads; king of the Nagas (snakes).

He is the ruler of Patala and lives in a palace, Mani-Mandapa. The world is said to rest on his heads. The world is destroyed at the end of each kalpa by the fiery breath of Ananta and Vishnu sleeps on the coils of the serpent, floating on the primordial waters, in the intervals between cosmic cycles.

He or Vasuki (another Naga) was used as a rope, coiled round Mount Mandara and pulled by the gods and demons to cause the Churning of the Ocean.

Either Ananta or Vasuki, tried to poison the amrita that emerged at the Churning of the Ocean but the god Shiva sucked up all the snake's venom and held it in his throat to save the lives of the other gods.

Anat   *Canaanite*
also Queen of Heaven; = *Babylonian* Ishtar; *Phrygian* Cybele; *Sumerian* Inanna

A goddess of the heavens, fertility, mountains, springs and war; sister and wife of Baal or Anu.

She offered the prince Aqhat immortality for his marvellous bow and when he rejected the offer she had him killed by a soldier, Yatpan. As a result, darkness ruled the earth and plants and animals started to die. With the help of the god El, Anat rescued Aqhat from the underworld and restored the bow to its rightful owner, whereupon things returned to normal.

When her son (or in some accounts, her husband) Baal died, she went to the underworld to plead for his release. Mot, the god of death, refused, so she killed him and ground him under a millstone.

She is often depicted with a lance and a shield.

(*See also* **Ashtoreth, Astarte**.)

Anaulikutsai'x   *North American*
A river goddess of the Bella Coola or Nuxalk Indians of British Columbia. She lives in the cave Nuskesiu'tsta and controls the movement of salmon.

Ancient Old Man *see* **Kmukamtch**

Ancient Spider *see* **Areop-Enap**

ancile   *Roman*
plural ancilia

The shield of the god Mars. When the Romans prayed to the god Mars to relieve them of a plague, he not only obliged but dropped a shield from heaven which, it was said, would always protect the city. The king, Numa Pompilius, had eleven copies made and then hung all twelve in the temple of Mars to frustrate anyone wanting to steal the original. The shields were guarded by priests known as the Salii.

Andras   *European*
A demon, a marquis of hell, one of the 72 Spirits of Solomon. He is depicted as bird-headed angel with wings, riding a black wolf and holding a sword.

Andrealphus   *European*
A demon, a marquis of hell, one of the 72 Spirits of Solomon. He is depicted as a peacock and has the power to teach mathematics and to change humans into birds.

Andromache   *Greek*
The wife of Hector, prince of Troy; mother of Astyanax by Hector. At the fall of Troy she was captured by the Greeks and given as a prize to Pyrrhus, the son of Achilles, who abandoned her after fathering three sons on her. She later married Helenus, the Trojan prophet, and bore him a son.

Andromalius   *European*
A demon, one of the 72 Spirits of Solomon. He appears as man holding a snake and has the power to expose thieves and recover what they have stolen.

Andromeda   *Greek*
When her mother Cassiopeia boasted that her daughter was more beautiful than any of the Nereids, Andromeda was chained to a rock in the sea as a sacrifice to the sea-monster sent by the

sea god Poseidon. She was rescued by Perseus, who married her, and, at her death, was placed in the heavens by the goddess Athena.

Andvari   *Norse*
= *German* Alberich
King of the dwarfs. He was a dwarf who lived in a gem-studded palace underground and owned, in addition to a fabulous hoard of treasure, a magic ring, a magic belt that could increase his strength and a wonderful sword.

In different countries he had different names. As Alberich he was said to own the red cap, Tarnkappe, which allowed him to appear in daylight without being turned to stone.

On a visit to earth with the gods Odin and Hoenir, Loki, the god of mischief, had killed Otter, son of Hreidmar, a king of the dwarfs, and demanded that Andvari should hand over his treasures to satisfy Hreidmar's demand for compensation in gold and to secure the release of Odin and Hoenir who had been imprisoned with Loki for the murder. Andvari handed over the gold and the Helmet of Invisibility but when Loki also snatched his magic ring, Andvaranaut, he put a curse on the treasure.

In some accounts Andvari is equated with Oberon, king of the fairies. Some describe him as a fish or fish-shaped.
(*See also* **Alberich**.)

Angra Mainya *see* **Ahriman**

Angus Og   *Irish*
God of love and beauty; son of the Irish leader, the Dagda.

He was raised by Midir, a god of the underworld, and, when he reached manhood, he lived in the palace of Bruigh after displacing

his nominal father, Elcmar or, some say, the Dagda as king of the Danaans. He carried off Etain, wife of Midir.

It was said that four swans always hovered round his head and he owned a huge horse, and a dun cow given to him by the god Manannan.

He helped one of the Fianna, Dermot, in battle by making each enemy soldier appear in the likeness of Dermot so that they were all killed by their fellow-soldiers. When Dermot was killed by a boar, Angus kept his body in his palace and, by breathing life into the corpse, could talk to Dermot whenever he wanted.

Another story says that he pined for the love of a girl until his parents discovered that she was Caer Ibormeith, daughter of the king of Connaught who lived as a swan on a lake with 150 other swans. He was able to identify her and she went to live with him in his palace. In some versions, Angus changed himself into a swan.

Anguta   *Inuit*
Creator of earth, sea and sky; father of the sea goddess Sedna.

This deity is said to live in Adlivun.

When Sedna fell or was thrown into the sea and clung to the side of his boat, he chopped off her fingers so that she sank to the bottom. He also had some fingers missing and had only one eye.

animals
Many animals (and birds) appear in mythologies worldwide, often as supports for the world.
(1) The Chinese say that the world is supported on the back of

a tortoise. Animals ruling the months and double-hours are the rat, ox, tiger, hare, dragon, serpent, horse, goat, monkey, cock, dog and boar.

(2) The European version of the animals which support the sun gives ram, bull, (twins), crab, lion, (virgin), (scales), scorpion, centaur, (waterman), fish (or ship).
In Greece the list was cat, dog, snake, crab, ass, lion, goat, ox, hawk, monkey, ibis and crocodile.

(3) In Hindu lore, the god Vishnu appears as the turtle, Kurma, in his second incarnation while the turtle Chukwa supports on its back the elephant, Mahapadma, which in turn supports the earth.

(4) The Japanese say that a tortoise supports the Cosmic Mountain on its back.

(5) The supporters of the sun in Mongol lore are given as mouse, cow, tiger, hare, dragon, snake, horse, sheep, monkey, cock, dog and sow.

(6) In North America, many tribes say that the world is supported on a tortoise – or on four such animals.
(*See also* **sacred animals**.)

Ankalamman   *Hindu*
A guardian goddess of the Tamil; an aspect of the goddess Kali.

ankh   *Egyptian*
A symbol of life worn by the gods and royal personages; one of the three symbols (*tet* and *was* were the others) carried by the god Ptah.

Annency   *West Indian*
also Nansi, Ti Malice
The name given to Anansi in the West Indies. In many tales, he tricks the character known as (Uncle) Bouki.

Annowre   *British*
A sorceress. She once trapped King

Arthur and, when he rejected her advances, would have killed him but for a timely intervention by Lancelot, who killed the witch.

Antigone[1]   *Greek*
When her blinded father, Oedipus, was an outcast wandering the earth, it was Antigone who guided him.

After the battle at Thebes where her brothers Eteocles and Polyneices were killed, Creon, who had taken over Thebes, ordered that the body of Polyneices should not be buried. Antigone herself buried him under cover of a sandstorm but was condemned for disobeying the edict of Creon, who ordered his son Haemon to bury her alive in her brother's grave. Instead, he married her secretly and she bore him a son. In later years, Creon recognised this boy and ordered that he be killed. He refused to change his mind and Haemon killed both himself and Antigone.

In some stories she was buried alive or sealed in a cave where she hanged herself.

Antigone[2]   *Greek*
Wife of Peleus, king of Phthia. When Peleus came to her father's court in Phthia to be purified of the murder of his half-brother Phocus, she married him. He accidentally killed Antigone's father, and went to Iolcus to be purified by King Acastus. He went off on the Argonauts' expedition and then returned to Iolcus. The king's wife sent Antigone a message that Peleus was about to marry Sterope, her daughter, and Antigone hanged herself.

Anu   *Mesopotamian*
= *Sumerian* An

The supreme Hurrian god. He usurped the throne of Alalu, the king of heaven, but was emasculated by his [Anu's] son Kumarbi who took over his father's throne.

Anubis   *Egyptian*
= *Greek* Hermes
The dog-headed or jackal-headed god of embalming and the dead. He weighed the hearts of the dead in the Hall of Judgement.

Nephthys, a goddess of the dead, had no children by the storm god Set so she seduced the god Osiris into fathering Anubis. To keep the child safe from Set, she hid him in reeds where he was found and reared by Isis.

He is depicted as a black dog or a jackal lying down or as a jackal-headed human.

Ao Ch'in   *Chinese*
also Kuang-li
The Dragon King of the South.

Ao Jun   *Chinese*
also Kuang-jun
The Dragon King of the West.

Ao Kuang   *Chinese*
also Kuang-te, Lung Wang ('dragon king')
The Dragon King of the East, the chief of the four Dragon Kings.

He acted as a water god, responsible for rain, and appeared in the form of all kinds of animals and birds.

Ao Shun   *Chinese*
also Kuang-she
The Dragon King of the North.

Aoife   *Irish*
The second wife of the sea god Lir. She married Lir on the death of his first wife, her sister, Aobh, and turned her four step-children into swans condemned to spend three periods each of 300 years on a lake, the passage between Ireland and Scotland and the Atlantic.

Lir turned them back to human form but they had become old and wrinkled. For her wickedness, Aoife was turned into a demon by Bodb Dearg, a king of Munster.

Apauk-kyit-hok   *Burmese*
A man who was the cause of death. In the days when man was immortal, he had already lived nine lifetimes and had been rejuvenated. Then, one day, he hid himself and the others in the tribe thought he was dead and conducted a funeral ceremony. When the sun god discovered the old man's deception, he was angry and thereafter allowed man to die.

Apaya   *Buddhist*
The four lower worlds. These are given as the animal world, the demon world, the world of ghosts and hell.

ape
This animal is featured in a number of mythologies.
(1) In Egypt, the ape is an aspect of Thoth, the god of wisdom, writing, science and the law.
(2) European tradition has the ape in the role of Satan.
(3) Hindu symbolism regards the ape as a raincloud.
(4) In the Philippines, the ape is a trickster-hero who always seems to escape punishment for his escapades.

Aphrodite   *Greek*
= *Babylonian* Ishtar; *Canaanite* Anat; *Phoenician* Astarte; *Phrygian* Cybele; *Roman* Venus; *Sumerian* Inanna
Goddess of beauty and love, one of the Olympians; patroness of prostitutes; wife of the god Hephaestus. There are conflicting versions of her birth. In one, she

was the daughter of the god Zeus and the nymph Dione, in another she was born from the foam where the phallus of the god Uranus was thrown into the sea by his son Cronus, who cut it off. Other stories thought she developed inside a cockle shell or regard her as one of the Fates.

It was she who gave the golden apples to Melanion enabling him to win the foot-race against Atalanta.

She saved the Argonaut Butes from the sea when he was seduced by the song of the Sirens and jumped overboard from the *Argo*, and made him her lover. She seems to have had many other lovers and a number of children including:

Aeneas by Anchises
Eros by Ares, Hermes or Zeus
Hermaphroditus by Hermes
Priapus by Dionysus, Hermes,
Pan or Zeus
and in one such affair she was caught in bed with Ares, the war god, by Hephaestus who trapped them both in a fine-meshed net of metal for all to see. She had an affair with Achises, a Trojan herdsman, and protected their son Aeneas during the battle of Troy. She also fell in love with Adonis, the god of vegetation and rebirth, and her tears when he was killed by a wild boar turned into anemones.

At the wedding-feast of Peleus and Thetis, she was a contender, with Athena and Hera, for the golden apple tossed into the assembly by Eris, the goddess of discord. She won by bribing the Trojan prince Paris, who was asked to be the judge, by promising him access to Helen, the most

beautiful woman in the world. As a result, she supported the Trojans against the Greeks during the Trojan War.

In some versions she appears as an androgynous deity with a beard, a combination of Hermes and Aphrodite (hermaphrodite).

Her birds were the dove, the sparrow and the swan, her tree was the myrtle and her symbol a shell.

Her chariot was drawn by eight unicorns.

Apis   *Egyptian*
A bull-god: the sacred bull; son of the goddess Isis, conceived by lightning or a sunbeam.

At Memphis he was worshipped in the form of a bull, an animal which was said to become the god Osiris or the god Ptah on its death. The bull was sacrificed when it was 25 years old and a new bull was installed. It was required to have the proper markings: a white triangle on the forehead, the shape of an eagle on the back and a lump shaped like a scarab under the tongue.

He is depicted as a black bull with wings bearing the solar disc and the uraeus between the horns.

Appiades   *Roman*
Five goddesses of peace, represented on horseback. They were Concordia, Minerva, Pax (Peace), Venus and Vesta.

Apollo   *Greek*
also Phoebus Apollo
One of the Olympians; mouse-god and god of archery, beauty, doors, embarkation, light, medicine, music, poetry, prophecy, public places, roads, shepherds, truth and wolves; in the Roman pantheon, the god of light and the sun; son of

Zeus by Leto, daughter of the Titan Coeus and his sister; son of the smith-god Hephaestus by Athena, some say; twin brother of Artemis.

He was born on the island of Delos and reared by Themis. While still an infant he killed the serpent Python at Delphi.

He loved the youth Hyacinthus and, grieving at his death, caused by a discus thrown by the god Apollo but deliberately diverted by the West Wind, made the hyacinth flower spring up where the boy's blood stained the earth.

He also loved the Trojan princess Cassandra and gave her the power of prophecy but, when she rejected his love, he decreed that her prophecies should never be believed.

In similar fashion, he granted the Sibyl of Cumae the power of prophecy and as many years of life as she held grains of sand but withheld the gift of youth when she rejected his advances, so that she grew old and shrivelled and asked to die.

Another lover, the young hunter Cyparissus, died of grief when he accidentally killed the god's pet stag and he was changed by Apollo into a cypress tree.

He fell in love with the nymph Daphne who ran away at his approach. Before he could overtake her, her father, the river god Peneus, turned her into a laurel tree which became a tree sacred to Apollo.

He fell in love with Coronis and seduced her. When his bird, the raven, told him that she was having an affair with Ischus, he killed her but rescued his unborn son, Asclepius, who became the

god of healing. He turned the raven, until then a white bird, black.

In some stories he fathered Asclepius on Arsinoe rather than Coronis and in some the black bird involved is a crow.

He had many other affairs. He changed one of his sons, Cycnus, into a swan.

When Zeus slew Asclepius for attempting to raise the dead Hippolytus, Apollo avenged his death by killing the Cyclopes Arges, Brontes and Steropes. For this he was punished by Zeus, who condemned him to serve as a slave. In some versions he served King Laomedon, helping the sea god Poseidon to build the walls of Troy, in others, King Admetus of Thessaly. Some say he served the two kings in separate punishments.

He and his sister Artemis killed all the fourteen children of Niobe for a slight to the goddess.

He engaged in a musical contest with Pan and when Midas adjudged the latter to have won, awarded Midas the ears of an ass. In a similar contest with the satyr Marsyas, Apollo won and flayed the loser alive. His music helped him when he and Poseidon built the walls of Troy since he was able to charm the stones into position merely by playing his lyre.

He turned the Lemnian serpent to stone and when Orion showed signs of having designs on Artemis, Apollo arranged with Mother-Earth to have him harried by a huge scorpion but set him and his lyre in the heavens when he died.

At the siege of Troy, he helped the Trojans against the Greeks

and guided the arrow that killed Achilles.

He is credited with the invention of the lute and the cithara and was given the lyre by the god Hermes.

He is usually depicted with a bow and arrows and accompanied by lions. His chariot was drawn by griffins. His animal was the dolphin and his bird was the crow (or raven).

Apple of Discord   *Greek*
The golden apple tossed by Eris, goddess of discord, into the wedding feast of Peleus and Thetis.

This apple, said to be inscribed 'For the fairest', caused an argument between the goddesses Aphrodite, Athena and Hera, and Paris was appointed to adjudicate. His decision to award the prize to Aphrodite, who promised him Helen, wife of the Greek king Menelaus, as reward, led to the Trojan War.

The apple was one of the Apples of the Hesperides, stolen by Eris.

Apples of Iduna   *Norse*
also Apples of Youth
The apples produced from the magic basket owned by Iduna, goddess of youth. Iduna gave these apples to the gods to maintain their state of eternal youthfulness. Some of them were once stolen by the Frost-giant Thiassi and recovered by Loki.

Apples of Samarkand   *Persian*
Apples which, in the *Arabian Nights' Entertainments*, could cure any illness.

Apples of the Hesperides   *Greek*
The golden apples which grew on the tree given to the goddess Hera at her wedding. This tree was

guarded by the Hesperides, the daughters of Atlas, and its apples were the object of the eleventh labour of Hercules.

The apples themselves were the colour of gold and tasted like honey. Used as missiles, they always struck whatever they were aimed at and returned to the thrower's hand. They also had the power of healing.

Arabian Nights' Entertainments
Arabian

also The Thousand Nights and a Night

The story of Shahriyar who married a new wife every day and executed her next morning. Scheherazade saved her life by telling him fascinating stories, including the seven epic voyages of Sinbad, *Ali Baba and the Forty Thieves, Aladdin's Lamp* and others, for a thousand and one nights until he was over his madness. (*See also* **Akaf.**)

Arachne *Greek*
A Lydian weaver. She challenged Athena at weaving. When her work turned out to be the equal of that of the goddess, Athena beat her severely, whereupon Arachne hanged herself. The remorseful Athena changed her into a spider so that she could continue spinning and weaving.

In some versions she is described as the goddess of weaving.

arak *Cambodia*
A guardian spirit. This spirit, often that of an ancestor, lives in the house or in a nearby tree so that it can watch over the family. If a member of the family should fall ill, the shaman called in to attend the patient can cause the arak to materialise and help with the cure

which involves exorcising the evil spirit which is causing the illness.

Arawn *Welsh*
= *British* Herne
God of the underworld, Annwfn. He was hunting one day when Pwyll, king of Dyfed, drove off his hounds and set his own pack on to the stag Arawn had been pursuing. To make recompense, Pwyll took Arawn's place as king of the underworld for one year while Arawn ruled Dyfed for Pwyll.

King Arthur raided his realm to seize his magic cauldron.
(*See also* **Augusel.**)

Arcas *Greek*
Son of Callisto by Zeus; husband of Erato.

In some accounts, Arcas shot a bear that turned out to be his mother. Callisto and Hera changed both Callisto and Arcas into bears and Zeus had them placed in the heavens as, respectively, the Great Bear and the Little Bear (or, some say, the star Arcturus).

Another account says that his grandfather, Lycaon (Callisto's father), killed Arcas and served his flesh to the god Zeus who restored Arcas and turned Lycaon into a wolf. A similar story is told of Nyctimus, Lycaon's son.

archer god
A god armed with bow and arrows, such as the Greek Eros or the Roman Cupid; and also Apollo.

Areop-Enap *Pacific Islands*
also Ancient Spider
A primeval spider, a creator-deity of Nauru Island.

She was swallowed by a huge clam but, helped by a caterpillar, Rigi, and a shellfish, she opened the clamshell to make the earth. The top of the shell became the

sky, the caterpillar became the sun and the shellfish became the moon. She made men from stones and had them support the sky.

Some say that the caterpillar's sweat formed the oceans but he was drowned in the ocean and placed in the sky as the Milky Way.

Areop-It-Eonin *Pacific Islands*
A young spider. He was born from a boil on the body of the tortoise, Dabage, and is said to have brought the gift of fire to mankind.

Ares *Greek*
= *Roman* Mars
God of war, one of the Olympians; son of Zeus and Hera; brother of Hephaestus.

He was caught in bed with Aphrodite by her husband Hephaestus, the smith-god, who trapped them both in a fine metal net.

When his daughter, Alcippe, was raped and abducted by Halirrhothius (a water god), he pursued them and killed the abductor. He was tried for murder and acquitted.

The young giants, Ephialtes and Otus, once imprisoned him in a bronze jar where he stayed for over a year until released by the god Hermes.

In the Trojan War he was on the side of the Trojans but was wounded by Diomedes, king of Argus. On another occasion, he was wounded in a fight with Hercules. In the form of a boar, he killed the god Adonis.

His animal was the dog, his bird the vulture, and his symbol a spear.

Arethusa *Greek*
A goddess of springs; one of the Nereids.

She was a huntress. When

she was bathing in a river after a chase, the river god Alphaeus tried to seduce her and pursued her when she ran off. To save her, Artemis turned her into a spring that runs under the sea from Greece to Sicily. Alphaeus found her after a long search and they were re-united, their waters flowing together to form one stream.

In one version of the story of Demeter and Core, it was this nymph whose voice, in the burbling of the stream, told Demeter where her lost daughter could be found. She had seen Core in the underworld as she passed through en route to Sicily. (An alternative version is told about another nymph, Cyane.)

Argo   *Greek*

The ship of Jason and the Argonauts. This 50-oared ship (some say 54-oared) was built by Argus for Jason and his men for their quest for thc Golden Fleece. The prow, made from one of the talking oaks from Dodona and provided by the goddess Athena, acted as an oracle on the voyage. After the voyage, the ship was beached at Corinth where, years later, the rotting prow fell on the aged Jason and killed him. The rest of the hull was placed in the heavens by the god Poseidon.

Argonauts   *Greek*

also Minyans

The crew of the ship *Argo* who sailed with Jason to recover the Golden Fleece.

Jason had undertaken to bring back to Iolcus the ghost of Phrixus, a former prince of Boeotia, and the fleece of the golden ram on which Phrixus had fled from Iolcus to escape

death engineered by his step-mother. Assembling a crew from all parts of Greece, Jason set sail for Colchis where the fleece was hanging on a tree guarded by a serpent or dragon that never slept.

At Lemnos, the crew fathered many sons on the women who had earlier killed every man on the island except the king, Thoas.

Later in the voyage they landed on Arcton, Bear Island, where they were entertained by the king. A group of six-armed giants, the Gegeneis, attacked the ship but Hercules, who had been left on guard, killed them all. After leaving the island, the ship was driven back by adverse winds and they landed at night on Arcton where they were mistaken for pirates. The king, Cyzicus, was killed in the ensuing battle.

When they stopped at Mysia, Hylas who was acting as armour-bearer to Hercules, went ashore to find water. When he failed to reappear, Hercules and Polyphemus searched but failed to find him – he had been carried off by water-nymphs to their underwater grotto. The searchers had not returned when *Argo* was ready to sail and they were left behind in Mysia. Hercules then resumed his Labours which he had interrupted to join the expedition.

At Bebrycos the king, Amycus, a boxer who challenged (and beat) all comers, challenged the crew. Polydeuces, an Olympic champion boxer, accepted the challenge and killed Amycus after a tremendous fight.

At Salmydessus, they found the king, Phineus, harried by the female monsters, the Harpies, and

the winged brothers Calais and Zetes drove them off.

Escaping the clashing rocks of the Symplegades they landed at Mariandyne where Idmon was killed by a boar and Tiphys became ill and died. Great Ancaeus took over the role as navigator.

They recruited Autolycus, Deleon and Phlogius at Sinope and were attacked by bronze birds – those of the Stymphalian birds that had escaped in the sixth Labour of Hercules – when Oileus was wounded. Later they picked up four castaways, Argeus, Cytisorus, Melanion and Phrontis, sons of Phrixus and his wife Chalciope.

At Colchis, Jason asked Aetes to hand over the fleece which he agreed to do if Jason could yoke his fiery-breathed bulls, plough the Field of Ares and sow the serpents' teeth remaining from those sown by Cadmus at Thebes. At the behest of Aphrodite, Eros, the god of love, caused the sorceress Medea to fall in love with Jason and she provided him with a lotion that protected him from the scorching breath of the bulls so that he was able to carry out the appointed task. When armed men sprang from the soil, he provoked them to fight amongst themselves until none survived. Aetes reneged on his undertaking and threatened to kill the Argonauts, so Medea led Jason and a few of his men to the place where the fleece was guarded by the immortal dragon which she lulled to sleep while Jason took the fleece. They all ran back to the *Argo*, escaping the ships of the Colchian fleet with just a few wounded and one man, Iphitus, killed.

At the entrance to the Danube the Colchian ships overtook *Argo*. What happened next is the subject of different accounts. In one version, Medea killed her half-brother, Apsyrtus, flinging pieces of his body overboard to delay the pursuers who stopped to collect the pieces for burial. In another, Apsyrtus was in one of the following ships and agreed to a truce with Jason whereby Medea should be put temporarily in charge of a priestess and the king of the Brygians would decide whether she and the fleece should stay with Jason or be returned to Colchis. Medea, however, led Apsyrtus to believe that Jason had abducted her and induced him to come ashore where Jason killed him from ambush. Without their leader the Colchian ships were easily routed and the Argonauts escaped, passing safely between the monster Scylla and the whirlpool Charybdis.

Jason and Medea were purified of the murder of Apsyrtus by Circe the sorceress and then married.

On the final leg of their return journey the *Argo* was forced by a strong wind to the shores of Libya where a huge wave carried the ship miles inland, leaving it high and dry in the desert. They managed to drag the ship to Lake Tritonis but could find no outlet to the sea. Two of the crew died during this period: Canthus was killed by the shepherd Caphaurus when he tried to steal some of his flock and Mopsus died from a snake-bite. In the end, Triton himself dragged the ship overland

to the Mediterranean and they sailed for Crete, where the bronze guardian, Talos, attacked them with rocks. Medea quietened him with a sleeping draught and then pulled out the pin from his ankle, allowing the vital fluid to drain from his single vein, so killing him. An alternative story says that she prayed to Hades who caused Talos to graze his ankle on a rock with the same fatal result.

Arriving back at Iolcus, Jason found that his parents, Aeson and Alcimede, had killed themselves to escape death at the hands of Pelias, who had then killed their infant son, Promachus. To avenge these deaths, Medea deceived the daughters of Pelias into believing that she had divine powers and then ordered them to kill and dismember their father. Alcestis refused but Evadne and Amphinome complied. A torch signal from the roof brought the Argonauts from hiding and they took Iolcus unopposed. Jason handed the throne to Acastus, son of Pelias, who had been one of the Argonauts and he promptly banished Evadne and Amphinome to Arcadia.

Others say that Jason was banished by the Iolcans who were appalled at the killing of Pelias.

From Iolcus, Jason sailed to Orchomenus where he placed the Golden Fleece in the temple of Zeus and then on to Corinth where he finally beached the *Argo*. Here Medea successfully claimed the throne of Corinth which rightfully belonged to her father and, with Jason as her king, ruled for ten years. When he found out that she had poisoned the previous ruler, Corinthus, he

set about getting a divorce so that he could marry Glauce, – in some stories, Creusa – daughter of King Creon of Thebes. Medea stopped that by killing with fire not only Glauce and her father but all the guests except Jason, although some say that he too died in the flames. By putting aside Medea, Jason had broken a promise, made in the name of the gods, never to desert her and he was thereafter an outcast. Late in life, sitting by the remains of *Argo*, he was killed when the prow or, in some accounts, the stern-post, fell on him. In another version, Jason took his own life.

Argus[1]   *Greek*
also Argos
The builder of the *Argo*.

Argus[2]   *Greek*
also Argos
A giant watchman with 100 eyes. In some accounts, he had only three eyes (one in the back of his head) or four, while others say that he had 1000 eyes.

When Zeus turned Io into a heifer, she was handed over to be guarded by Argus.

He was killed by the god Hermes who released Io on the orders of Zeus. His eyes were placed in the peacock's tail by Hera.

Ariadne   *Greek*
A minor goddess of vegetation; daughter of King Minos of Crete.

When she saw Theseus, who had come to Crete as one of seven youths to be sacrificed to the Minotaur, she fell in love with him and gave him the ball of magic twine that enabled him to escape from the Labyrinth after he had killed the Minotaur. She left Crete with him but he left her on Naxos, either deliberately or, in some stories, inadvertently. There she was found by the god Dionysus who married her and fathered her children.

Other versions say that Theseus killed her on Naxos or that she died there in childbirth.

When she died, Dionysus threw the crown she had worn at their wedding into the sky where it became the constellation Corona. She was later restored to Dionysus by Zeus.

Aribadale   *British*

The bearer of the Holy Grail after Repanse, mother of Prester John.

Arimaspi   *Greek*

One-eyed horsemen; Scythians. These inhabitants of the north were said to be permanently at war with the griffins who guarded a stream flowing with gold.

Arjuna   *Hindu*

A warrior-hero of the *Mahabharata*.

He was betrothed to Draupadi but when her father believed that Arjuna was dead, he organised an archery contest between her other suitors for his daughter's hand. The contest, and the hand of Draupadi, was won by a hermit who turned out to be Arjuna, who had merely been in hiding.

In the battle between the Kauravas and the Pandavas (of whom Arjuna was one), the god Shiva acted as Arjuna's charioteer.

In one story, he was accidentally killed by his own son, Babhru-Vahana, but was restored to life with the magic jewel given to Babhru-Vahana by his stepmother Ulupi.

In some stories he is described as an incarnation of the gods

Indra or Vishnu.

Armageddon   *Persian*

= *Norse* Ragnarok

The final battle. In this struggle, Ahura Mazda will defeat Ahriman and the world will thereafter be at peace and all people will once again speak the same language. The Christian version of the story postulates the same triumph of virtue over evil.

arrow

The use of the bow and arrow dates from the early Stone Age period and the arrow itself has great significance in many mythologies:

(1) The Bushmen use arrows as sacrifice to their ancestors who live in the rivers. Other stories include the worldwide tale of the arrows shot one after the other to form a bridge to heaven up which the archer, a culture-hero, ascends.

(2) In Arabia, arrows are used as charms to keep the blood in good order.

(3) The Assyrians associated arrows with the deities Ashur and Ishtar.

(4) In Buddhism, an arrow in five colours is used in demon-worship. In Tibet, this arrow is called dar-dar.

(5) In Greek myths, arrows feature in stories of the hunter deities Apollo and Artemis and the love god Eros as well as in the tale of Chiron, the centaur, who was wounded by one of the poisoned arrows of Hercules. Achilles was killed by an arrow, shot by Paris, which struck his only vulnerable spot – his ankle

A sunbeam is called the Arrow of Apollo and the Arrow of Artemis is a moonbeam.

(6) Hindu myths associate arrows

with both the love god Kama and the war god Karttikeya, Shiva killed the demon Tripura with an arrow, and they tell of a magic arrow (the sabdabhedi arrow) which can seek out and strike the origin of a sound.

(7) In Ireland, an arrow might be carried as an amulet to ward off the arrows fired by the elves, while water drunk after being poured over an arrowhead was said to be effective as a remedy for croup.

(8) Italian stories allege that an amulet in the form of an arrow would ward off the jettatura, the evil eye.

As a weapon, the arrow was an attribute of the Etruscan sun-god Usil or Cautha.

(9) In Japanese myths, the god Susanowa had a bow and arrows and a magic whistling arrow.

(10) North American Indian tribes have many stories involving arrows.

The Cheyenne have a set of four arrows, used in religious cermonies, which, they say, have been in the possession of the tribe from time immemorial. They are used in rites which cleanse any man who has killed one of his own tribe.

A Kwakiutl woman will place an arrow under her bed to ensure that any child she conceives will be male.

The Ojibway, fearing that the sun extinguished during an eclipse may never return, fired burning arrows to re-ignite it.

The Nez Percé have a story in which the trickster god, Coyote, turns himself into an arrow.

The chain-of-arrows story is common to many tribes. One

such story has it that when a man was killed and decapitated by a man from the sky, the dead man's brother shot such a chain and climbed up it to the heavens where he rescued his brother's head. When this was joined to the still bleeding torso, it became the red-headed woodpecker.

(11) In Mexico, arrows are associated with both the gods Mixcoatl and Quetzalcoatl.

(12) In the Pacific, the Philippine god Abog is placated with offerings of arrows while in Melanesia Qat went to heaven via an arrow-chain to retrieve his wife.

(13) In Siberia, the Buriats relate how Ten Geris, a thunder god, used flaming arrows as his weapons when fighting demons while the Koryaks have the story of Eme'mqut who opened the road to the underworld to retrieve his wife by throwing an arrow into the fire. They also tell a slightly different chain-arrow story; in their version, just one arrow is fired but it carves out a road to the heavens.

(14) Some South American tribes, like the Ojibways of North America, fire flaming arrows into the sky to restart the sun after an eclipse.

Another arrow-chain story has the two sons of Tamoi climbing to the heavens where they become the moon and sun.

Arrow Boy   *North American*
A hero of the Cheyenne. Arrow Boy was born after four years in his mother's womb and grew quickly, becoming a medicine man. In an early demonstration of his powers, he allowed others to pull

a noose so tightly round his neck that his head was cut off but the boy merely replaced it. When they lifted the robe that covered him, he was an old man, then a pile of bones, then nothing at all and finally the completely restored boy.

When the chief of his tribe tried to take the bull-calf that Arrow Boy was skinning for a robe, the boy killed him and was then attacked by the tribe who had lost their leader. He escaped by rising into the sky on a plume of smoke and left his people. At his departure, the buffalo disappeared. Later he entered a cavern in a mountain where, for four years, he was instructed in the arts of the medicine men. When his time was up, he returned to his people and the buffalo returned to fill the plains.

Artemis   *Greek*
also Mistress of Animals, Bear Goddess;
= *Roman* Diana
A virgin goddess of childbirth, fertility, hunting, the moon, youth; one of the Olympians; daughter of Zeus by Leto (a daughter of the Titan Coeus and his sister Phoebe); twin sister of Apollo.

As a child she chased and captured four golden-horned stags and harnessed them to her chariot. A fifth animal escaped and featured in later stories as the Ceryneian Hind.

She could be Selene (a moon goddess) in the sky, the goddess Hecate in the underworld and Artemis the huntress on earth where she carried a silver bow made by the Cyclopes.

During the battle of the Giants with the gods, she killed the giant

Gration.

As Selene she fell in love with the shepherd, Endymion, but, as a virgin-goddess, she could not yield to her passion and contented herself with hiding him in a cave on Mount Matmus where she alone could visit him every night and kiss his eternally sleeping lips.

She changed Actaeon to a stag when she caught him watching her as she bathed but another version says that Actaeon was dressed in the skin of a stag when he approached the goddess. In one version, Actaeon was torn to pieces by his own hounds.

She changed Callisto into a bear when the nymph was seduced by Zeus and she avenged the death of Ameinius (who killed himself when he was rejected by Narcissus) by causing Narcissus to fall in love with his own reflection.

At the behest of Leto, she slew the seven daughters of Niobe, and Apollo slew the seven sons, because Niobe had boasted that she was greater than Leto and should be worshipped in her place.

She shot and killed Orion in the mistaken belief that he had raped her priestess, Opis, or from jealousy of Eos, goddess of the dawn, who was also in love with him, or by shooting at a floating target in the sea which she did not realise was Orion's head.

She was said to be able to assume the form of any animal or tree and, on one occasion, took the form of a fish to escape the unwelcome attentions of Alphaeus.

In some accounts, she was the

mother of the Amazons by the war god Ares. Some versions show her with three heads, as a form of Hecate.

Her animal was the deer and her tree the cypress.

Artemis Tauria was Artemis as the goddess to whom were sacrificed all sailors cast ashore in Tauris. She rescued Iphigenia, who was about to be sacrificed by King Agamemnon, and carried her off to Tauris where she became a priestess of Aphrodite and carried out the same rites of sacrificing strangers.

Arthur[1]   *British*

King of Britain; son of Uther Pendragon and Igraine; in some accounts, husband of Guinevere.

The ancestry of both Arthur and Igraine is variously portrayed by early authors but the usual version says that Uther gained access to Igraine, the wife of Gorlois, the Duke of Cornwall, in the form of Gorlois, thanks to the magic of Merlin, and fathered the infant Arthur (and, in some stories, a daughter, Anna) on her. Another version says that the baby was brought in by the sea and found by Merlin and Bleys. Some say Arthur spent his boyhood with Ector, his foster-father and father of Kay (who later became a Knight of the Round Table), not knowing who his real father was; others say that he was reared by the magician, Merlin.

At the assembly to decide on a successor to Uther Pendragon, his feat of pulling the sword from the stone (and, in some versions, an anvil) in which it was set, marked him as the future king of Britain. This sword, which some say was Excalibur, had been set in

place by Merlin and, when it later broke in combat, Merlin promised another and better sword. Arthur became king at the age of fifteen but the barons took advantage of Uther's death and Arthur's youth to carve up the kingdom amongst themselves. When he was older, he tried to subdue the barons but lacked the necessary forces. He sent Ulfius and Brastias to the Continent where they enlisted the help of King Bors of Gaul and King Ban of Benwick (Bayonne) who brought an army of 10,000 to reinforce Arthur's 20,000 men and together they defeated the 50,000 men of the north in the bloody Battle of Bedgrayne. He became a great warrior, reputedly killing 470 (or 960) Saxons at the Battle of Mount Badon. He took his army to help King Leodegrance of Cameliard against King Royns and fell in love with Guinevere, the daughter of Leodegrance. He killed the giant Retho in single combat on Mount Snowdon. Retho had sewn the beards of all those he had killed into his cloak; Arthur used Retho's beard to make his own cloak. In a joust with Pellimore, king of the Isles, Arthur was defeated and his life was saved only by the intervention of Merlin who put Pellimore into a trance. Arthur's sword was broken in this encounter and it was then, in some stories, that Merlin provided Excalibur as a replacement. They rowed into the middle of a lake where a hand, clutching the sword Excalibur, rose out of the water. While Arthur wore the scabbard, he could never lose blood, no matter how badly he was wounded. The sword itself was

said to be capable of remarkable feats.

Having defeated the Saxons, Scots and Picts, he conquered Ireland, Iceland, Norway and Denmark. When the Roman emperor demanded taxes, he led an army into Brittany. Here he killed the giant of Mont St Michel who had carried off Helen, daughter of his friend Hoel, king of Brittany. He then marched on Rome, defeated their army and killed their leader, Lucius. In some accounts he then returned to Britain and was not further troubled by the Romans; in others he conquered Rome itself, killing Frollo (a Roman ruler of Gaul) in single combat, forcing Leo to abdicate and being himself crowned as emperor. He left Kay in charge of Anjou and Bedivere in charge of Normandy. He dug up the buried head of Bran (*see* **Bran**[1]), relying on his own ability to protect the kingdom rather than on the superstitious belief in the power of a long-dead king. He was said also to have dug up the head of Adam near Jerusalem.

He once made a journey to Annwfn, the underworld, to get a magic cauldron.

He was once entrapped by the sorceress, Annowre, and only the timely intervention of Lancelot saved him from death at her hands. In some Spanish accounts, he was imprisoned by the king of Constantinople who released him when Arthur's sister, Urganda, intervened.

Merlin told the king that one born on May Day would cause his death so Arthur ordered that all the children born on that day should be put into a boat and cast adrift. The ship was wrecked in a storm and the only one to survive was Mordred, the boy fathered by Arthur on his own sister, Morgause.

He married Guinevere but she loved Lancelot and was unfaithful to her husband, although they were later reconciled. At his wedding feast, the proceedings were interrupted by a white stag which was chased into the hall by a white bitch and a pack of black hounds. One of his knights seized the bitch and rode away with it. A lady rode in and complained that he had stolen her bitch and a knight then rode in and dragged the woman away. Arthur sent Gawain to find the stag, Torre to find the knight who had taken the bitch and Pellimore to find the lady and the knight who had taken her off.

Once when he was hunting with Urien and Accolan, they saw a ship on a lake come into the shore and they went aboard. They were bewitched by Morgan le Fay, Urien found himself back with his wife, Accolan on the edge of a deep void and Arthur in prison. He was duped into fighting with Accolan who was using the sword Excalibur which had been stolen by Morgan and given to Accolan as part of her plan to destroy Arthur, kill Urien and marry Accolan who would take over the king's throne. After a great fight, Arthur felled Accolan, reclaimed his own sword and forgave his opponent who died of his wounds a few days later.

Shortly after his return to Camelot, a damsel arrived with a jewelled mantle, a gift to Arthur from Morgan. On the advice of Nimue, Arthur required the girl

to try it on. She did so reluctantly and dropped dead, shrivelled to a cinder. While the king was recovering from wounds, Morgan tried once again to steal Excalibur but got away only with the magic scabbard which she threw into a lake. Arthur and a companion, Outlake, pursued her but she and her men escaped when she turned them all into stones until their pursuers had given up the chase.

Arthur helped his cousin Culhwch to meet the 39 conditions laid down by the giant Ysbaddaden before he would allow his daughter, Olwen, to marry Culhwch and, during this quest, Arthur personally killed the Black Witch with his knife Carnwennan.

On one occasion, Melwas, the king of Summer Land, abducted Guinevere but Arthur invaded the country and forced the king to release her.

When Agravain and Mordred told the king of his wife's affair with Lancelot he said that he would believe them only when they could produce proof. Mordred caught the two lovers together in her room and told the king who condemned Guinevere to the stake, ordering Gawain to carry out the execution. Gawain refused but his younger brothers, Gaheris and Gareth, obeyed. They were both killed by Lancelot when he rode in and rescued the queen, carrying her off to Joyous Gard. Arthur raised an army to assault the castle and a fierce battle ended only when the Pope intervened to order that Guinevere be handed back to her husband. Lancelot then returned to his home in Brittany, taking

many of his followers but Arthur's army of 60,000 men invaded France and laid siege to Bayonne where Lancelot had his court. The king would have accepted a truce with Lancelot but Gawain, who hated Lancelot who had killed Gawain's two brothers when rescuing Guinevere, pressed Arthur to continue the war. News that Mordred, who had been left in charge of the country during the king's absence, had usurped the throne caused Arthur to break off the engagement and hurry back to Britain. After several battles in which many thousands were killed on each side, Arthur met Mordred in single combat during the Battle of Camlan and killed him but was himself badly wounded in the fight. Lucan and Bedivere moved him to a nearby chapel but Lucan died from his wounds soon after. The king ordered Bedivere to throw Excalibur into the lake, which he did only after twice disobeying the king's orders. A hand came out of the water to receive the sword and carry it down into the depths. Bedivere then carried Arthur to the edge of the lake and placed him in the boat that was waiting there to receive the king and carry him to Avalon. The king sailed off, attended by Morgan le Fay, the Queen of Northgales, the Queen of the Waste Land and, in some stories, Nimue, the Lady of the Lake. Some say that he still lives, renewing his youth by visiting the Holy Grail; some say he is sleeping on the mountain Yr Wyddfa (Snowdon) or in a cave (various sites are suggested) awaiting recall when Britain is in need of him. A dolmen in

Trebuerden in Brittany is also said to be the king's tomb. Others maintain that he was turned into some bird such as a raven. His soul is said to be housed in a glass castle or, in some stories, embodied in the chough, the puffin or the raven.

In the Welsh version, Arthur was killed by arrows in Snowdonia while pursuing the forces he had defeated at the Battle of Tregalen. His killer was said to be Eda Elyn Mawr.

In Continental lore, Arthur went to Fairyland after his death. When Oberon, king of the fairies, handed the kingdom to Huon, Arthur, who had expected to receive the throne, objected. Oberon threatened to turn him into a werewolf, whereupon Arthur accepted the position. Other stories say that Arthur was in love with Oberon's daughter, Gloriana.

In some accounts, Arthur is equated with Charlemagne. (*See also* **Artos**.)

Arthur
A number of places and objects are by tradition associated with King Arthur:
Arthur's Cave
A cave on the island of Anglesey. The king was said to have hidden some of his treasure, guarded by a monster, in this cave, during his war with Ireland.
Arthur's O'on ('oven')
A small Roman temple near Falkirk, Scotland, said to have been used by King Arthur.
Arthur's Quoit
A cromlech in Wales incorporating a stone or quoit said to have been thrown by King Arthur; similarly,

a cromlech in Anglesey.
Arthur's Stone
(1) A megalith in Wales, said to have appeared when King Arthur, en route to the Battle of Camlan, found a pebble in his boot and threw it out. Some say that the ghostly figure of the king emerges from under this stone when the moon is full.
(2) A boulder in Hertfordshire which some say was the stone from which the young Arthur drew the sword which established his right to the throne. Others say that it marks the site of the grave of a king – some say King Arthur himself.
Arthur's Table
(1) A rock in Wales which bears depressions said to represent the Twenty-Four Knights of King Arthur's court.
(2) A barrow in Wales.
Arthur's Tor
A fortification in Durham, an earthwork which, like Arthur's Cave, is said to contain some of the king's treasure, guarded in this case by the ghosts of some of his knights.

Arthur[2]   *Irish*
Son of Arthur[1], also a king of Britain. He went to Ireland in search of adventure, taking twenty-eight warriors with him. They stole the Irish leader Finn mac Cool's hounds, Bran and Sceolan, and took them to Scotland. A party of Fianna warriors under Goll mac Morna surprised them in camp at night and killed all twenty-eight men and took Arthur prisoner. He became a loyal follower of Finn.
Artos   *British*
also the Bear
A British sky god. He returned

occasionally to earth in human shape to mate with mortal women. In one such visit, he was incarnate as King Arthur.

Asclepius   *Greek*
also Asklepios;
= *Egyptian* Imhotep; *Roman* Aesculapius
A god of healing; one of the Argonauts; son of Apollo, some say.

Apollo had seduced the nymph Coronis but she preferred a mortal lover, so Apollo killed her but saved her unborn child and gave him to the centaur Chiron to be reared. In other accounts, the child was abandoned on Mount Myrtium, found by a shepherd Aristhamas, who called him Aiglaer, and suckled by goats.

He tried to bring Hippolytus (in some versions, Glaucus) back to life in Hades, but Zeus killed him with a thunderbolt. Some say that when Apollo then killed the Cyclopes who made the thunderbolts for Zeus, the god relented and restored Asclepius to life.

Some say that he was able to bring the dead back to life by using blood from the right side of the Medusa slain by Hercules; blood from her left side killed those to whom it was administered.

His animal is the snake and he appears in the heavens as Ophiuchus.

Asgard   *Norse*
= *Greek* Olympia
City of the gods in Godheim; home of the gods, the Aesir heaven; the site of Valhalla.

In some accounts, Asgard comprised twelve separate

regions, each ruled by one of the twelve original gods, the Aesir.

Ash *see* **Ask**

Ash-pate *see* **Assipattle**

Asherah[1]   *Canaanite*

= *Phoenician* Astarte

A Canaanite mother-goddess and sea goddess, mother of the gods; wife of the supreme god El. In some accounts she is Anat as 'Lady of the Sea'.

Some accounts distinguish between Asherah, a Ugaritic mother-goddess who was the mother and wife of Baal, and Asherah, a Canaanite mother-goddess.

Asherah[2]   *Hebrew*

plural Asherim

A wooden image of the goddess Anat.

Ashtaroth[1]   *European*

In the Charlemagne stories, a spirit summoned by the magician Malagigi to bring the paladins Ricciardetto and Rinaldo to the pass at Roncesvalles. He and his servant, Foul-mouth, entered the horses of the two paladins, who were then in Egypt, and flew with their riders to Spain, putting them down in the midst of the Battle of Roncesvalles.

Ashtaroth[2]   *European*

One of the 72 Spirits of Solomon.

Ashtoreth   *Mesopotamian*

= *Babylonian* Ishtar; *Egyptian* Hathor; *Greek* Astarte; *Phoenician* Astarte

A Semitic love goddess. In some accounts she is envisaged as a horned goddess.

Asita   *Buddhist*

= *Chinese* A-shih-to

One of the Eighteen Lohan; in some accounts, regarded as an incarnation of the Buddha Maitreya.

He is depicted with long

eyebrows, sitting on a rock and clasping one knee.

Ask   *Norse*

also Ash, Askr

The first man, made by Odin from an ash-tree. Husband of Embla.

Asklepios *see* **Asclepius**

Asmodeus   *Hebrew*

An evil spirit, the spirit of lust or vengeance; one of the 72 Spirits of Solomon; leader of the shedeem, a tribe of clawed demons.

In some accounts, he was originally a prince of the seraphim who fell from heaven.

He was said to know where to find the shamir, a worm which had the power to split rocks.

This demon takes the form of a being with three heads (bull, man and ram), riding on a dragon, who is said to instruct people in arithmetic and the magic arts.

He was overcome by the archangel Raphael.

In black magic, as one of the Masters of the Revels, he supervises theatres.

Asphodel Fields *see* **Tartarus**

Assipattle   *Scottish*

also Ash-pate

The seventh son of a seventh son; an idle day-dreamer who made good his promise of great deeds.

When the Stoorworm (a venomous water-monster) was ravaging the country, he went out in his little boat to fight it. When the monster swallowed him, Assipattle cut open its liver and pushed in some burning peats which he had brought with him. The beast regurgitated Assipattle, its teeth fell out and became the Orkney Islands and its dead body formed Iceland. For his valour,

Assipattle received the hand of the princess, Gemdelovely.

Astarte   *Phoenician*

also Great Mother, Queen of Heaven; = *Babylonian* Ishtar; *Canaanite* Asherah; *Greek* Aphrodite; *Phrygian* Cybele; *Sumerian* Inanna

A Phoenician fertility goddess, goddess of shepherds; consort and mother of Baal.

She was adopted by the Egyptians as the daughter of the gods Ptah or Ra and became a consort of Set, the god of darkness and storms. In this role, she is depicted naked on horseback.

She is sometimes depicted as a cow or as a woman with a cow's head.

Astolat   *British*

also Shalott

The home of Elaine the White (*see* **Elaine**[3]). This town in Arthurian stories has been identified with Guildford.

Asura   *Hindu*

A demon; a titan. Originally supreme deities, Asuras were later demon spirits opposing the minor gods (the Suras) and living on Mount Sumeru in four towns known as Deep, Golden, Shining and Star Tassel. In some accounts, they live in a magnificent house, Patala.

In some accounts, they were born from the groin of the creator-god Brahma while others say that they were the sons of the sage Kasyapa. Alternatively, the Asuras were early Indian tribes who were overcome by the invading Aryans, regarded in some accounts as giants who fought the gods.

Ataensic   *North American*

also Sky Woman; = *Seneca* Eagentci

A sky goddess and earth goddess;

the first woman in the lore of the Iroquois.

She is said to have fallen from heaven and her body was used by her twin sons Hahgwehdaetgah and Hahgwehdiyu to build the world.

In some accounts, the twins were the children of Ataensic's daughter Breath of Wind and it was her body that they used to build the world.

A different story says that when she was ill, her father dug up a tree. A young man, angry at the loss of the tree, pushed her into the hole from which it has been dug and she fell through to earth. Her fall was broken by the birds which formed a sort of fireman's blanket to save her. Some birds dived into the primeval waters and brought up mud which, plastered on the back of a turtle, formed dry land on which Ataensic could live. She produced a daughter called Breath of Wind who, in time, bore twins known as Djuskaha and Othagwenda.

Ataintjina   *Australian*

A rain-maker god of the Aborigines. He is said to make rain by throwing a young man into the sea where he is swallowed by a huge snake. Two days later the man is disgorged and, carrying some of the snake's scales, ascends into the sky where he hangs head down, his hair forming rain. The scales are thrown to earth as thunder and lightning. Then Ataintjina joins the man in the sky as the rainbow. The rain stops and, after a period of drought, Ataintjina starts the whole cycle again.

Atalanta   *Greek*

Abandoned by her parents Iasius and Clymene when she was born, Atalanta was raised by a she-bear and grew up as a very fleet-footed maiden.

Some say that she sailed with the Argonauts, the only woman in the crew. She joined the hunt for the Calydonian boar and shot and killed the centaurs Hylaeus and Rhoecus when they tried to rape her. She wounded the boar so that the Argonaut Meleager was able to get close and kill it and Meleager insisted that she be given the pelt of the boar, a gesture which brought much trouble on his own head.

She would marry only the man who could beat her in a foot-race, killing all who tried and failed. Melanion eventually beat her by dropping golden apples, given to him by Aphrodite, in her path which delayed her as she stopped to pick them up.

She and her husband were changed into lions or leopards by Zeus for defiling his precinct or, in some versions, by Aphrodite for failing to give thanks to the goddess.

Atamalqualiztli   *Central American*

An Aztec festival in honour of the gods. During the ceremony, held once every eight years, all the people dressed as animals or birds and imitated their ways. At the end of the ceremony, all jumped into a lake filled with snakes and frogs attempting to catch one of the reptiles in their mouths, eating them, if successful, alive.

Atargatis   *Syrian*

A mother-goddess and goddess of vegetation. She was born in the form of an egg, floating in the Euphrates, which was pushed ashore by a fish.

In one story, she fell into the sea and was changed into a fish and her daughter Semiramis was changed into a dove.

As Atargatis Derketo she was a fish-goddess, half woman, half fish.

In some accounts she is equated with Anat.

Ate[1]   *Greek*

Goddess of mischief; daughter of Ares or Zeus. In some accounts, she is Eris, goddess of discord, in others the daughter of Ares and Eris. (*See also* **Eris**.)

Ate[2]   *Mesopotamian*

also Great Mother

A creator goddess.

Athena   *Greek*

also Athene, Pallas (Athena);
= *Egyptian* Isis; *Roman* Minerva

A virgin goddess of agriculture, cities, handicrafts, war and wisdom; one of the Olympians; daughter of Zeus, the giant Pallas, the smith-god Hephaestus or the sea god Poseidon; mother of Apollo by Hephaestus, some say.

Zeus had seduced the nymph Metis and swallowed her and her unborn child. When he later developed a headache, Hephaestus – or in some versions, Prometheus – split his skull open with an axe and out sprang Athena, fully developed and armed.

Another version says that she was the daughter of Poseidon, born in Lake Tritonis in Libya, or of the giant Pallas whom she killed when he tried to rape her.

She became patron of Athens by winning a competition with Poseidon. Whereas he produced only salt-water (or the horse), she invented the more useful olive-tree.

During the battle of the

Giants with the gods she fought alongside the male deities and killed the giants Enceladus and Pallas.

It was she who gave Perseus the bright shield which he used when killing the Medusa.

When Paris awarded the golden apple to Aphrodite at the wedding of Peleus and Thetis, Athena and Hera, the other losing contestant, became her enemies and supported the Greeks against the Trojans during the Trojan War.

She is said to have invented the flute, the bridle and several tools. Her own flute, which was later acquired by the satyr Marsyas, was said to play itself.

When the Theban Teiresias saw her bathing, she struck him blind but gave him inner sight in compensation.

She is depicted wearing a helmet and carrying a shield and spear. Her birds were the cock and the owl (or crane), her tree the olive and her animal the serpent.

Athrwys *British*
A king of Glenvissig (now Gwent). In some accounts, he is equated with King Arthur.

Atl *Central American*
A creator-god of the Aztecs. He represents the fourth of the five ages of the world, each of which lasts for 105,456 years. At the end of this period came the Flood and all humans were turned into fish.

Atlantides *see* **Hesperides**

Atlantis *European*
A supposed lost continent or island. Refugees from Atlantis, which was said to have disappeared beneath the sea when the gods became alarmed at the degenerate behaviour of the island's inhabitants are reputed

to have settled in Spain. Some say it was situated to the west of the entrance to the Mediterranean. Other suggested sites are in South America and the Pacific Ocean.

Some say that this island was originally the realm of the Titan Atlas; others, that it was the original home of Igraine, mother of Arthur, and Merlin.

Atlas *Greek*
A Titan, leader of the Titans in their war with the gods and when they lost he was condemned by Zeus forever to carry the sky (or, in some accounts, the world) on his shoulders.

He helped Hercules in his fourth Labour to get the golden apples from Hera's garden.

He was turned to stone when Perseus displayed the severed head of Medusa when Atlas refused him hospitality on his flight back from his attack on the Gorgons.

Some accounts have Atlas as the ruler of Atlantis.

Atli *Norse*
also Etzel
King of the Huns. Some say that Atli is Attila, the 5th-century leader of the Huns. In the *Nibelungenlied* he is called Etzel.

He coveted the treasures of the Nibelungs and planned to kill them in order to lay his hands on it, so he sent his servant, Knefrud, to invite them to his court. Despite a warning from Atli's wife Gudrun and others, King Gunnar accepted but took the precaution of burying the gold in the bed of the Rhine where it was guarded by the three Rhine-maidens. Atli ambushed the party at his palace and killed all of them except Gunnar and Hogni, Gudrun's

brother, who, having killed Knefrud amongst others, were captured and tortured. Atli had Hogni's heart cut out and shown to Gunnar but he still refused to reveal the hiding place of the gold even when he was thrown into a snake-pit where he was bitten to death.

At the banquet after the battle, Gudrun killed her young sons and served their hearts and blood to Atli and his guests. She then killed her husband either by sword or, in another story, by burning down the palace and all in it, including herself.

Atrahasis *Mesopotamian*
= *Sumerian* Ziusudra; *Syrian* Utnapishtim
A king of Shurupak, the Babylonian Noah. Warned by Enki, he survived the flood sent by the god Enlil in his ship, Preserver of Life, saving also his wife, animals, plants and seeds. He was granted immortality by the sea god Ea or by Enlil.

Some accounts refer to two people of this name – one, the survivor of the Sumerian Flood, the other said to be the father of Utnapishtim, the survivor of the Babylonian version.

Atreus *Greek*
King of Mycenae; son of Pelops and Hippodamia; father of Agamemnon, Menelaus and Pleisthenes.

Atreus was involved in a dispute with his brother Thyestes over the throne of Mycenae. He had stuffed the fleece of a golden-horned lamb made by Pan or Hermes which became acknowledged as a symbol of the right to the throne. He was tricked by Thyestes into killing his own son Pleisthenes. His second wife, Aerope, was infatuated with Thyestes and gave him the lamb. He assumed the throne but soon abdicated when Zeus reversed the motions of the sun as a warning. Atreus took over again as king and banished Thyestes. When he discovered his wife's treachery he invited his brother back to Mycenae and killed and boiled the pieces of Thyestes' sons, serving them to his brother as a meal.

After executing Aerope he married Pelopia, not realising that she was a daughter of Thyestes who had raped her and left her with child. The infant, Aegisthus, was abandoned but rescued by shepherds, suckled by a goat and then recovered by Atreus who thought he was his own son. When Aegisthus was seven years old, Atreus ordered him to kill Thyestes whom he had imprisoned but Thyestes disarmed the boy and, recognising the sword he held, knew that the boy was his own son. Thyestes then reversed the order and this time there was no mistake; the boy killed Atreus and Thyestes was left in control of Mycenae.

Atropos   *Greek*
One of the three Moirae (Fates), the one who cuts the thread of life.

Atse Estsan and Atse Hastin
           North American
In the lore of the Navaho, the first woman and first man, created by the gods from two corn seeds. When the couple taught the rudimentary beings existing at that time how to form communities, the water-monster, Tieholtsodi, caused a flood and drowned these people. The two humans escaped through a hole in the sky made by a hawk and came

into the fifth world. Here they created the present world and, when it was completed, they both vanished. The five pairs of twins which they produced mated with the Kisani to populate the earth.

Attis   *Phrygian*
= *Greek* Adonis; *Sumerian* Tammuz
A Phrygian god of shepherds and vegetation. In some stories he is the son of Cybele, in others her lover. In another version he is the son (or the male half) of the hermaphrodite deity Agdistis whose blood, when he was castrated, produced a tree from which a young girl, Nana, picked the fruit. When she dropped the fruit into her lap she became pregnant, producing Attis. The infant was abandoned and reared by a goat. When he grew up, Cybele (or, in some accounts, Agdistis) fell in love with him and when he deserted her for a nymph, Sagaritis, the goddess drove him mad so that he castrated himself and died but was restored to life and reunited with Cybele. In some accounts, she turned Attis into a pine-tree.

Some say that Attis fathered a child on the goddess Cybele and her father, Meion, king of Phrygia, killed both Attis and the baby. Cybele restored Attis to life. Another version has Agdistis breaking in on the wedding celebrations of Attis and Sagaritis with the result that Attis castrated himself and his bride died from self-inflicted wounds. Some say that the castration was not self-inflicted but resulted from an attack by a wild boar.

He was associated with the planet Jupiter.

Atum   *Egyptian*
King of gods, an early sun god. He was either a son of the water god Nun or a self-created god who brought light to the primeval universe and, as Iusau, a bisexual being, created his son Shu and his daughter Tefnut. Others say that he appeared out of the primordial chaos as a serpent, created by the four frogs and four snakes which existed in the primordial waters. He was later assimilated with the god Ra as Ra-Atum (or Atum-Ra) and is depicted as a black bull, Mnevis, or as a snake.

Auberon *see* **Oberon**

Augeas   *Greek*
King of Elis; in some versions, the son of the sea god Poseidon.

He owned huge herds of sheep and cattle which, being immune to disease, multiplied exceedingly. It was his stables that Hercules cleansed as his fifth Labour. He had agreed to pay Hercules one-tenth of the value of his herds but reneged on his promise and he was killed by Hercules who returned later to exact his revenge.

Augusel   *British*
also Arawn
A king of Scotland.

When King Arthur defeated the Saxons he restored to Augusel the lands which the invaders had taken from him. Augusel fought with Arthur on his expeditions against the Romans on the continent but was later killed by Mordred.

In some accounts, he is regarded as the mortal form of the underworld god, Arawn.

August Female, August Male *see*
     Izanami, Izanagi

aunga   *Pacific Islands*
The islanders say that the soul is

in two parts, the aunga (good) which dies and the adaro (bad) which remains in the form of a ghost.

Aunt Nancy

A name for Anansi in parts of North America, South America and the West Indies.

Aurelius Ambrosius   *British*

= *Welsh* Emrys

A king of Britain. When his brother, King Constans, was killed by the soldiers of Vortigern, prince of Gwent, he and his brother Uther fled to the court of King Boudicius of Brittany to escape from Vortigern but returned later to kill him by burning him in his castle. In another story, they reappeared as the dragons once buried on Mount Erith by the river god and British king Lud and released when Vortigern uncovered the cavern where they were buried. They flew to France, returning in mortal form at the head of an army to recapture the kingdom. They burned down the tower that Vortigern had built on Mount Erith and he was killed. Renwein, Vortigern's wife, avenged his death when she provided her servant Ambion with a phial of poison which he administered, saying it was a cure for the illness from which Aurelius was suffering at the time. Other stories relate that Vortigern's son, Paschent, who had fled to Hibernia, returned with an army provided by the chieftain Gilloman who was angry because Merlin had stolen the stones of the Giants' Ring. While Uther was fighting Paschent, a Saxon soldier, Eopa, tricked his way into the presence of Aurelius, who was ill in bed, and poisoned him.

In some accounts, Aurelius is equated with King Arthur.

Auramazda *see* **Ahura Mazda**

Aurora Borealis

The Northern Lights appear in the folklore of several cultures.

Baltic

(1) In Estonian tales, the lights occur when a celestial war or wedding is taking place and are caused by light reflected from the sumptuous trappings of the sleighs and the horses which draw them.

(2) Finnish lore attributes the lights to the souls of the dead.

(3) Lappish lore attributes the lights to the spirits of those killed in war or murdered.

Greece and Rome

In classical times, the lights were generally regarded as natural phenomena but some said that they portended some fateful event.

Norse

The lights were said to be sunlight reflected from the shields of the Valkyries.

North America

(1) The Inuit say that the lights are the dance of the dead.

(2) In the lore of the Iroquois, the supreme spirit made the maiden Awenhai pregnant but came to believe that she had been seduced by Fire Dragon or Aurora Borealis so he pushed all three of them out through the hole in the sky that appeared when he tore up the Onodja Tree.

(3) The Kwakiutl also say that the lights are the spirits of the dead but add that they can portend death in the family of the deceased.

(4) In the lore of the Makan, the lights are the fires of a small race in the sky cooking their meat.

(4) The Mandan say that the lights occur when medicine men boil their enemies in big pots.

(5) The Tlingit say that the lights are the spirits of the dead playing together in the sky.

Siberia

(1) The Ostyak say the lights are the fires lit by the fish-god, Teman'gryem, to guide travellers.

(2) The Chukchi regard this area of the heavens as the home of those who died a violent death.

Austri   *Norse*

One of the four dwarfs supporting the sky (east). (*See also* **Nordri, Sudri, Westri**.)

Autolycus[1]   *Greek*

also Autolykos

Son of the god Hermes and Chione. A thief who could change the animals he stole into new forms. He stole some cattle from Sisyphus who in revenge seduced his daughter Anticleia.

Autolycus[2]   *Greek*

also Autolykos

A follower of Hercules. He and his brothers Deileon and Phlogius helped Hercules on his ninth Labour and later joined the Argonauts.

Avalokiteshvara   *Buddhist*

= *Chinese* Kuan Yin; *Hindu* Vishnu; *Japanese* Kwannon; *Tibetan* Chen-re-zi

God of mercy; son of Amitabha. He is regarded as a bodhisattva who is reincarnated in each new Dalai Lama.

In the Tibetan scheme of things, he is the supreme national god and can assume any form such as a cloud, a figure with a thousand arms and eleven heads, and various animals. To help his charitable works he was given a thousand hands. He produced a monkey which mated with an ogress to produce a race of hairy beings. These mated with the forest monkeys and when Avalokiteshvara gave them food they lost their hair and tails and became human beings.

He delayed his own release from the cycle of death and rebirth to help others achieve enlightenment. Having brought release to all, he set off to return to paradise but, when he chanced to look back and saw that people had reverted to their former sinful ways, he broke into a million pieces from which arose the version with 11 heads and 1000 arms. The goddess Tara was born from the tears he shed.

He is regarded as a manifestation of Amitabha who generated him from a beam of light issuing from his own eye.

As Padmapani, he created the world and Brahma, Indra, Lakshmi and Sarasvati, from various parts of his own body.

He is represented as a handsome youth holding in his left hand a lotus blossom and was later identified with the Chinese goddess of mercy, Kuan Yin.

In some accounts he is identified with the god Shiva, in others he occupies one of the two thrones in Amitabha's heaven (Mahasthama has the other).

Avalon[1]   *British*
also Island of Apples, Island of Blessed Souls;
= *Irish* Ablach, Emain Ablach; *Welsh* Ynys Avallach
The spirit world; an earthly paradise. This was the home of Morgan le Fay and the site of the forge, operated by fairies, in which Excalibur was made.

On his death, King Arthur was placed on a boat and taken to Avalon where, some say, he was healed of his wounds and survives to this day, awaiting some future call to save Britain.

Another story makes this an island in the far west, concealed from view by a wall of spray, where the giants kept the golden apples that they had stolen from the gods. Some say it was ruled by Morgan le Fay, leader of nine fairy queens.

Avalon[2]   *European*
In legends relating to Charlemagne, the island home of the sorceress Morgan le Fay.

In the story of Ogier the Dane, he was transported to Avalon where he still sleeps. Some accounts say that both Oberon, the king of the fairies, and Ogier held their courts in Avalon.

Avernus   *Roman*
also Lake Avernus
Hell, or the entrance to it.

Awabi *see* **Great Awabi**

Axo-Mama   *South American*
The Peruvian goddess of the potato harvest.

Azure Dragon *see* **Ch'ing Lung**

B

B *Central American*

A Mayan deity of uncertain identity, referred to as God B (*see* **alphabetical gods**); perhaps the rain god, Chac. This deity is depicted with a nose somewhat like that of a tapir. He can walk on water and wields a fiery torch.

Rather than Chac, some say he represents Kukulcan or Quetzalcoatl.

Ba[1] *Egyptian*

A god manifest in the form of a pharaoh.

ba[2] *Egyptian*

The soul, one of the five elements comprising the complete person. The ba is depicted as a bird with a human head which flies between this life and the afterlife.

The representation of the ba in the form of a human-headed bird is known as the ba-bird.

Ba-Toye *African*

A Hausa spirit causing destructive fires.

Baal[1] *Canaanite*

= *Egyptian* Set; *Greek* Cronus; *Phoenician* Melkarth; *Sumerian* Adad, Enlil

A fertility god, god of storms; son of the supreme god El; twin brother of Mot, the god of death; husband and brother of Anat, goddess of fertility.

He fought a battle with the sea god Yam for control of the earth and killed the serpent Lotan. He lived in a huge palace called Sapan which had a hole in the floor through which he watered the earth. When he died, Anat fought and killed Mot, god of the underworld, and ground him under a millstone. Baal was later restored to life and the throne.

He is depicted as a warrior wearing a horned helmet and standing on wave-top.

In some accounts he is equated with Moloch.

Baal[2] *European*

A demon, duke of hell; one of the 72 Spirits of Solomon.

Baal-Dagon *see* **Dagan**[2]

Baalzebub *see* **Beelzebub**

Baatsi *African*

The first man, in the lore of the Efe. To please his wife, he picked the forbidden tahu fruit and God punished them by decreeing that all future generations should die.

Baba-Yaga *Russian*

An ogress or witch; a goddess of death. She had teeth and breasts of stone and was said to steal children, having first turned them to stone merely by looking at them, and then, having returned them to normal, cooked and ate them. She moved around in a mortar by using the pestle as a propelling pole. Her home was a hut which had the legs of a chicken on which, some say, it moved about, and which was enclosed within a fence made of bones.

In the Czech version, these beings had the face of a woman, the body of a sow and the legs of a horse. They lived in caves and put out the eye of any humans they caught.

Babe   *North American*

A huge ox, the companion of Paul Bunyan, hero of a modern American myth.

It was white at birth but turned blue during a particular winter when blue snow fell.

Babe could eat bales of hay, including the baling wire, and was said to be very fond of hot-cakes. He was so heavy that his hoofs sank into solid rock and lakes formed in his hoofprints. He was reputed to have pulled a river (or a road) straight, scooped out Puget Sound by hauling a glacier and pulled dry oil-wells out of the ground.

Babe caused his own death by swallowing a batch of hot-cakes – including the stove. Some say that the Black Hills were piled up over his grave.

Bacab   *Central American*

A rain god; son of the sun god Itzamna and the moon goddess Ix Chel. He was killed at birth and rose three days later into the sky, where he became a rain god.

Bacabs   *Central American*

= *Aztec* Tlalocs

Four giant Mayan deities, sons of the sun god Itzamna and the moon goddess Ix Chel.

These four brothers supported the world, one at each corner, and controlled the winds.

Bacchus   *Roman*

A name for Dionysus in the Roman pantheon.

In one story, Bacchus allowed his lions to attack a maiden simply because he was upset when she failed to offer him the worship to which he thought

he was entitled. He immediately regretted his action and turned the girl into pure crystal. He then poured wine over the crystal which took on the colour of the wine and became what we now know as amethyst.

Bachué   *South American*

A mother-goddess and fertility goddess of the Chibcha Indians. She emerged from Lake Iguague as a snake, produced a baby son, mated with her son to produce the human race and then both resumed their shape as snakes and returned to the lake.

Bad Dog Village   *Buddhist*

A part of hell. Here the good are allowed to pass while the evil ones are torn to pieces by dogs.

Badb   *Irish*

A goddess of war; an aspect of the goddess Morrigan or Nemain.

She was one of a trinity of names (Ana, Badb and Macha) known as the Fate Trinity and regarded as aspects of Morrigan. The list is sometimes Badb, Macha, Nemain. Badb often appeared in the form of a crow or raven.

Badger   *North American*

A hero of the Shoshone Indians. He saved Dove and her children by luring the monster Dzoavits into a hole in the ground and then sealing the entrance with a boulder.

Badger Prey-god   *North American*

One of the six Prey-gods guarding the home of Poshaiyangkyo, the first man. He is responsible for the area to the south.

Badr al-Budur   *Arabian*

also Badoura

In the *Arabian Nights' Entertainments*, a sultan's daughter or a Chinese princess, the wife of Aladdin.

Bagadjimbiri   *Australian*

Creator-gods of the Aborigines.

These two brothers came up out of the earth in the form of dingos, mated a toadstool with a fungus to produce humans, and gave the gift of reproduction to the first people. The brothers grew into giants as high as the sky but were killed in a dispute with the cat-man, Ngariman, and his tribe. The earth goddess, Dilga, drowned the killers with a flood of milk from her breasts, restoring the brothers to life at the same time. When they finally died they turned into water-snakes.

Bagdemagus   *British*

A Knight of the Round Table.

He resented it when Torre, a younger knight, was elected to the Round Table in preference to himself and rode away from Camelot in search of adventure. He found Merlin imprisoned in a rock by Nimue, the Lady of the Lake, but could do nothing to help him.

When his son Meliagaunt abducted Guinevere, he intervened to save her from rape.

He was later made a member of the Round Table and set out from Camelot with the other knights on the Grail Quest. He found a white shield beside an altar in a chapel and took it although it carried a warning that it was intended for the True Prince, an epithet for Galahad. He was challenged by a knight in white armour and found that he could not lift the shield to defend himself. He was unhorsed and badly wounded in the thigh. As a result he had to give up the quest and returned to Camelot with Owain who tended him. He was later killed by Gawain.

Bahloo   *Australian*

A moon god.

Bahloo was originally Mulandi, a happy man who, when he died, was taken up to heaven by Baime and became the moon. He was responsible for making girl babies.

bahr geist   *German*

A spirit; a banshee. (*See also* **bargaist**.)

Bahram Yasht   *Persian*

A fabulous bird of fire. This bird's feathers were used to repel demons and Zoroaster brushed his body with them to make himself invulnerable.

Baime   *Australian*

A sky god of the Aborigines. Some say that the sky is supported on large crystals resting on Baime's shoulders.

Baime is normally asleep. When he woke on one occasion, he turned over and, in doing so, caused the Flood. It is said that when he next awakes, he will destroy the world.

Bajanai   *Siberian*

A Yakut forest spirit. He often leads travellers astray and sometimes appears in the form of an animal.

bajang   *Malay*

An evil spirit which can be evoked when the proper incantations are recited over the spot where a still-born child has been buried. If the bajang mews, another child will die.

Some say that the bajang takes the form of a polecat and can be kept as a sort of family pet, fed on milk and eggs, which can be sent to bring illness and disaster to others.

baka   *West Indies*

In Haitian voodoo lore, a zombie turned into an animal.

bakemono   *Japanese*

Evil spirits with long hair but no feet.

Baku   *Japanese*

also Eater of Dreams

A supernatural being, envisaged as a horse with the face of a lion and the feet of a tiger. In some versions it had a trunk like an elephant. It was said that it could be invoked to eat bad dreams, so averting ill-fortune for the dreamer.

Balam   *European*

A demon, one of the 72 Spirits of Solomon.

This being is said to have one human and two animal heads and can foretell the future.

In some versions, he is depicted as a bull or as a naked man riding a bear and carrying a hawk.

Balam Agab   *Central American*

also Tiger of the Night

In Mayan lore, one of the first four men; brother of Balam Quitze, Iqi Balam and Mahucutah.

He and his brothers were created from maize-flour and broth brewed by the creator-goddess Xmucan. (Other accounts say it was the creator-gods Tepeu and Gucumatz who made them.) Each had his own guardian spirit. The gods created a woman for each of the brothers and they produced children who became the ancestors of the tribes when their parents returned to their original home in paradise.

Balam Bacham   *Malay*

The bridge leading from this world to Belet, the home of the dead.

Balam Quitze   *Central American*

also Tiger with the Sweet Smile

In Mayan lore, one of the first four men; brother of Balam Agab, Iqi Balam and Mahucutah (*see more at* **Balam Agab**).

Balan   *British*

A Knight of the Round Table.

Out of favour with King Arthur, Balan and his brother Balin rode to Castle Terribil, which was besieged by Royns, king of North Wales, hoping to kill Royns and regain the king's favour. They captured Royns and handed him over to the warders at Camelot and subsequently helped the king in his battles with Nero, the brother of Royns.

In a later adventure Balan was appointed by the lady of a castle to defend an island nearby against all-comers. One of these turned out to be his brother Balin and they fought each other to the death, realising only when they raised their visors at the end that they had fulfilled the prophecy that the second sword acquired by Balin would be used to kill his best friend.

Balder   *Norse*

God of day, light, tears; son of the creator-god Odin and the goddess Frigga; brother of Hermod, Hoder and Thor.

Balder was the best-loved of all the gods and when he dreamed of some great danger to himself, his mother extracted an oath from all things that they would never cause him harm. But she had overlooked the humble mistletoe.

Loki, the god of mischief, always out to cause trouble, persuaded the blind Hoder to throw a branch of mistletoe at his brother, so killing him. Nanna, wife of Balder, died of grief and their bodies were placed side-by-side on his funeral pyre. Odin leaned over the dead body of his son and whispered in his ear "Rebirth", reminding Balder that he was to be reborn into a new world after Ragnarok, the great final battle.

Other versions say that Balder was killed by the magic sword, Mistellteinn, when fighting a duel with Hoder for the favours of Nanna.

Hermod rode to Niflheim to ask for the release of Balder and Hela, goddess of the underworld, would have returned him to life if all the world had wept for him but one giantess, Thok, who some say was Loki in disguise, refused to shed a tear for him and he was kept in the underworld. He sent Odin's ring, Draupnir, which had been placed on his funeral pyre, back to Odin with Hermod.

An alternative story makes Balder a harsh character and Hoder the virtuous one.

Bale Fe'e　　　　　　　*Pacific Islands*
An undersea palace, home of Fe'e, the Samoan war god.

Bali　　　　　　　　　　　　*Hindu*
A demon-god, king of Sutala, part of the underworld; one of the Daityas (giants).

He acquired so much power he might have ousted the god Indra. The god Vishnu, as his fifth avatar, the dwarf Vamana, asked the king for three paces of land. He then grew so enormous that he covered the world in two paces, leaving Bali only the underworld, Patala.

Balin[1]　　　　　　　　　　*British*
A Knight of the Round Table; brother of Balan.

Balin had killed a cousin in a fair fight and had been unjustly imprisoned.

He was the only knight at Arthur's court who could draw the sword which was brought by a damsel from Lyle, the Lady of Avalon. It had been her lover's

sword and the Lady of Lyle had put a spell on it. The maiden, Colombe, warned him that he would use it to kill his best friend but he kept it and became the Knight of the Two Swords.

He was then accused by the Lady of the Lake of killing her brother. He recognised her as the witch who had brought about the death of his mother and he cut off her head with the sword. Banished from the court, he sent the witch's head to his relatives and set out to find adventure. He was overtaken by Launceor who was intent on avenging the death of the Lady of the Lake and acquiring the magic sword but Balin killed him in single combat. The damsel, Colombe, then arrived on the scene and killed herself by falling on her lover's sword.

Riding on, he met his brother Balan. They planned to ride to Castle Terribil and kill King Royns of North Wales who was besieging the castle, hoping thereby to regain Arthur's favour. They ambushed Royns and took him as their prisoner to Camelot, handing him over to the warders.

The brothers helped Arthur in his subsequent battles with Nero, brother of Royns, and King Lot of Lothian (in Scotland) and Orkney. When Harleus was killed by the invisible knight Garlon, Balin escorted the dead knight's lady in pursuit of his quest. She was attacked by a group of men when they arrived at a castle but Balin drove them off. They said they needed the blood of a virgin to save the life of the lady of the castle, so the girl gave them some of her blood but it failed to cure the sick woman.

Balin attended a tournament arranged by King Pelham and, when challenged by the king's brother Garlan, cut off his head. Pelham then attacked Balin with a battle-axe and broke his sword. In searching for another weapon, Balin came to a room in which lay the perfectly preserved body of an old man and a strange spear. He seized the spear and killed or wounded Pelham, whereupon the castle was destroyed, killing most of those inside.

Merlin told Balin that the body was that of Joseph of Arimathea and the spear was the one used by the centurion Longinus to pierce Christ's side at the Crucifixion. This spear and the Holy Grail had been brought to Britain by Joseph, an ancestor of Pelham.

His journeying then brought him to a castle where he was lavishly entertained until the lady of the castle said he must joust with the knight who guarded the nearby island. He crossed to the island by boat and fought the knight in red armour who rode out to challenge him. They fought so fiercely and each wounded the other so severely that they both died but, before they expired, Balin discovered that the knight in red armour was his own brother, Balan. The prophecy of the sword had been fulfilled.

Balin[2]　　　　　　　　　　*Hindu*
He was said to have been born from his half-brother Sugriva's hair.

He challenged the demon Ravana to a contest and tied him in the coils of his long hair, parading round the country to show off the captive demon.

He also challenged his half-brother for his throne and used his magic power of reducing any opponent's strength merely by looking at him. Rama, the seventh incarnation of the god Vishnu, was helping Sugriva and he grew stronger as Sugriva grew weaker until he finally burst out of hiding and killed Balin.

Balios *Greek*
A horse given to Peleus by Poseidon or Zeus. This animal, fathered by Zephyrus on Podarge, was later the chariot-horse of Achilles at Troy.

Baliu *Pacific Islands*
A god who controls the human life-span.

Balkis *Arabian*
also Balqis, Bilqis
A queen of Sheba.

The Abyssinians claim that Balkis married King Solomon and they had a son, Menelik, from whom the royal family is descended.

In the Biblical version, Balkis visited Solomon and left when she discovered that his famed wisdom was not as great as advertised.

In Moslem lore, she submitted to Solomon and converted to his religion. She was said to have hidden a dagger in her veil and used it to kill Solomon, so becoming queen of Sheba.

Baloo *Australian*
An Aborigine moon god in New South Wales.

Men were once immortal but when two of them refused to carry Baloo's dogs (or snakes) across a river, he took away man's immortality.

Balor *Irish*
The one-eyed Fomoire god of the underworld; grandfather of Lugh.

He lost one eye from poison administered by the druids when

he saw their secret rituals. His remaining eye had the power to kill by a mere glance. It was said that it required four men to raise his eyelid.

In some accounts, he had one eye in the middle of his forehead. This eye had seven lids and the heat from the eye progressively increased as each lid was raised until, finally, it could set the countryside on fire. Others said it could turn animals or men into stone.

A prophecy said that Balor would be killed by his grandson so he locked his daughter Ethlinn in a tower, Tur Bhalair, so that she could not be touched by any man. Cian gained access to her by disguising himself as a woman and seduced her. The child of this union, Lugh, was thrown into the sea on Balor's orders but was rescued by the sea god Manannan.

He once stole the magic cow, Glas Gabhnach, from Gobhniu who retrieved it by subterfuge. Some say that Balor invaded Ireland to recover the cow and the second Battle of Moytura ensued and here Lugh killed Balor with his spear or with a magic stone, Tathlum, flung from his sling into his grandfather's eye.

Balqis *see* **Balkis**

Bamapana *Australian*
An Aborigine trickster-hero who delights in causing trouble.

Bamboo Princess *Malay*
A princess who lived inside a bamboo cane. She was discovered by a man, Khatib, when he split open a bamboo cane and they both disappeared.

Although they cannot be seen, they both still live and their help

can be invoked and they will do anything they are asked to do.

Bamum *Australian*
The name of the Dreamtime (alchera) used in Arnhem Land.

Ban *British*
King of Benwick (in Brittany); brother of Bors; husband of Elaine; father of Lancelot.

He and his brother brought an army to Britain to help King Arthur in his battles with the rebellious barons.

In one account, he left his castle in the hands of his steward and left for Britain to seek help from King Arthur in his battles with Claudas, King of the Desert Land, taking his wife and the infant Lancelot with him. He died of grief when the steward surrendered the castle without a fight. His brother Bors died of grief on hearing of Ban's death.

bandicoot *Australian*
Aborigines say that the bandicoot was the owner of fire until it was stolen by the hawk or the pigeon.

banshee *Irish*
A wailing spirit foretelling doom; a female fairy. Banshees are rarely seen but are said to look like old women with long white hair.

Barbatos *European*
A demon, one of the 72 Spirits of Solomon. He is depicted as the leader of a band of hunters and can foretell the future.

barbegazi *European*
Mountain spirits of the Alps. They sleep through the summer but emerge in the winter to help climbers.

bargaist *British*
A goblin in dog-like or bear-like form. This spectral beast, which makes a splashing sound as it walks, is said to be unable to cross

water and is regarded as an omen of death in the north of England. (*See also* **bahr geist, gytrash**.)

Barinthus   *British*
A sea god. He was the pilot of the boat which carried King Arthur to Avalon.

Baris   *Mesopotamian*
The place where, according to the Babylonian story, the Ark landed when the Flood subsided.

Barmecide's Feast   *Arabian*
In the *Arabian Nights' Entertainments*, a meal at which the beggar, Schacabac, is offered empty plates instead of the meal promised by Barmecide.

Barong   *Pacific Islands*
A lion-king, a good spirit opposed by the witch Rangda.

basilisk   *European*
A fabulous monster, part cockatrice, part dragon, which could kill with its eyes or its breath.

In some accounts the basilisk is equated with the cockatrice; others refer to it as the king of the serpents. Some say that it was hatched from an egg laid by a cockerel and incubated by a toad.

It is depicted as about a foot long with a white mark or golden cross on its head and with its tail in its mouth.

Bast   *Egyptian*
also Bastet, Bubastis, Pasht, Ubastet, Ubasti;
= *Greek* Artemis
A cat-headed or lion-headed fertility goddess and fire goddess; consort of the god Ra.

In some versions she is the daughter of Ra, in others she is merged with the lion-headed goddess Sakhmet or with Isis.

In some accounts, she is Bubastis, after the city which was

the centre of her influence, in others Bubastis was her son.

In her cat-headed form she was known as Pasht.

Batara Guru   *Malay*
A sky god and creator-god; a name for Indra or Shiva in Java, Malaya, etc.

In Sumatra, he is a creator-god whose daughter, Boru Deak, jumped into the primordial waters. Her father sent a bird with some soil to form the land and then a hero who defeated the underworld serpent, Naga Pahoda. This hero married Boru Deak and they produced the first mortal.

In Sulawesi, he is regarded as the son of Guru ri Seleng who married his cousin, Nyilitimo, and they became the ancestors of the tribes.

Batara Kala   *Pacific Islands*
A creator-god and god of the underworld, in the lore of Bali. He was said to rule jointly with the goddess Setesuyara.

Bathym   *European*
A demon, one of the 72 Spirits of Solomon. He is depicted as a serpent-tailed man riding a horse and he is said to be wise in the lore of herbs.

Bato   *Japanese*
also Bato-Kwannon
A name of Kwannon as 'horse-headed' and guardian of horses. The reference is not to the head of the goddess but to the horse's head set into her tiara.

Battle Maidens *see* **Valkyries**

Battle of Camlan   *British*
The battle between King Arthur and the knight Mordred, who Merlin had prophesied would kill Arthur.

In this battle, said to have been fought at Slaughterbridge on

Bodmin Moor in 580, Arthur killed Mordred, running him through with his spear, but the dying man inflicted a fatal wound on the king with his sword. Only Arthur, Bedivere and Lucan survived the battle (in other accounts, other names are given). The dying king was carried off to Avalon, and Lucan died of his wounds.

Battle of Roncesvalles   *European*
In legends of Charlemagne, a battle (in 778) between the Franks and the Moors.

The rearguard of Charlemagne's army, withdrawing from Spain after an expedition to punish the king, Marsilius, who had earlier invaded France, was ambushed in the pass at Roncesvalles. Roland, in charge of the force, put up a desperate struggle against overwhelming odds, refusing to sound his horn to summon help until the very last moment. The main force under Charlemagne arrived too late to save Roland and his little band but the sun stopped its journey across the heavens to allow the Franks to avenge their comrades, routing the Moors.

In an alternative version, Charlemagne had exacted an annual tribute from Marsilius as his price for withdrawing from Spain and the force under Roland was sent to collect the tribute, only to be ambushed by three armies as they left Spain.

Some 100,000 Moors and 20,000 Franks were killed in the battle which resulted from the treachery of Gano (Count of Mayence and one of Charlemagne's paladins) who, out of jealousy of Roland, betrayed the emperor to Marsilius.

Battle of Tailltinn   *Irish*

In Irish legend, a battle between
the Milesians and the Danaans.
It is said that the three kings and
queens of the Danaans died in
this battle which resulted in the
defeat of the Danaans.

Battle of Tregalen   *British*

A site in Wales said to be the scene
of King Arthur's last battle. In this
Welsh version of the king's death,
he was shot with arrows while
pursuing his defeated enemy.

Battles of Moytura   *Irish*

The battles in which the Danaans
gained supremacy in Ireland,
defeating the Fir Bolg and the
Fomoire.

   The first battle ensued when
the Danaans arrived in Ireland
and defeated the Fir Bolg, the
second when an army of Fomoire
attacked the Danaans and was
defeated.

   Other accounts refer only to
battles between the Danaans and
the Fomoire.

Baucis   *Greek*

Wife of Philemon. She and her
husband were the only ones who
showed hospitality to the gods
Zeus and Hermes when they
travelled as poor wayfarers. While
their inhospitable neighbours
perished in a flood, they were
rewarded by having their hovel
transformed into a magnificient
dwelling which they kept as a
temple to the gods. In old age
they were still together and
the gods changed them into a
lime tree and an oak tree, both
growing from one trunk.

Baxbakualanuchsiwae   *North American*

also Cannibal Mother

In the lore of the tribes of the
north-west, a guardian spirit.

The Aurora Borealis and the
Milky Way were regarded as the
smoke from this deity's camp-fire
in the Arctic. He was regarded as
a cannibal, variously described as
male or female. (*See also* ***Tsonqua***.)

bDud   *Tibetan*

Forest-dwelling demons. These
beings, armed with axes, were
early precursors of the human
race. Next came the Srin.

Bean *see* **Deohako**

bear[1]   *Greek*

The animal of Artemis in Greek
mythology and of Thor in Norse
mythology.

bear[2]   *Japanese*

A mountain god of the Ainu.

Bear[3]   *North American*

In the lore of the Tlingit, he was
killed by Yetl the raven.

Bear[4]   *North American*

A Navaho bear-spirit. He was
involved with Frog, Snake and
Turtle in a plan to capture two
maidens from an underwater
village. The plan went awry; the
two girls were killed and Frog and
Turtle were lucky to escape with
their lives but Bear and Snake
fared better. This pair captured
two girls who were overcome by
the smoke from the kidnappers'
pipes which made Bear and Snake
appear as braves with whom the
girls mated.

Bear[5] *see* **Artos**

Bear[6] *see* **Ya-o-ga**

Bear Goddess *see* **Artemis**

Bear Prey-god   *North American*

One of the six Prey-gods guarding
the home of Poshaiyangkyo, the
first man. He is responsible for the
area to the west.

Beaver[1]   *North American*

A spirit who brought light to the
earth.

   The earth was originally dark

because Snoqalm, the moon god
of the tribes of the north-west,
kept the sun in a box. When the
spider wove a rope that linked
earth and sky, Beaver climbed up
and stole the sun which he placed
in the heavens to light the earth.

Beaver[2]   *North American*

In Algonquian lore, one of the four
animals which survived the Flood.
After the Flood, Beaver, Mink and
Otter all died in an attempt to
find soil from which Manabush
could recreate the world (*see more
at* ***Manabush***) and it was left to
Muskrat to succeed.

Bebo   *Irish*

Queen of the fairies. She and her
husband fell into a bowl of porridge
when they went to Ulster and
were captured by the king, Fergus
mac Leda. She had an affair with
the king who released her and her
husband Iubdan only when Iubdan
gave Fergus his magic shoes.

Bedawang   *Pacific Islands*

A cosmic turtle. This animal,
on which the earth rests, was
engendered by the serpent
Antaboga. On his back are two
snakes and the black stone which
covers the underworld.

Bedd Arthur   *British*

A supposed site of King Arthur's
grave in Dyfed, Wales.

Beddgelert   *Welsh*

also Beth Gelert

A village in Wales, site of the grave
of the hound, Gelert (*see story at*
Gelert).

Bedivere   *British*

A one-handed Knight of the Round
Table; a personal attendant on
King Arthur.

   In the story of Culhwch and
Olwen, he was one of the party of
Arthur's men helping Culhwch in
his quest.

When the king invaded and conquered much of the Continent, he helped the king in his fight with the giant of Mont Saint-Michel and, when Arthur returned to Britain, Bedivere was left in charge of Normandy.

He and Lucan helped the wounded king into the shelter of a chapel after the final battle with Mordred. Lucan soon died from wounds received in the battle and Arthur instructed Bedivere to throw Excalibur into the lake. Bedivere coveted the sword and twice told the king he had done as instructed when, in fact, he had hidden the sword under a tree. He finally obeyed the king's orders and threw the sword into the lake where a hand came out of the water and took the sword beneath the surface. He then carried the king on his back to the edge of the water where a boat waited to carry Arthur to Avalon.

Bedivere wandered for some time and finally came to a hermitage where the Bishop of Canterbury lived and there, in the chapel, saw the tomb of the king. He gave up all his knightly pursuits and lived the rest of his life as a hermit.

In some accounts, he was made Duke of Neustria and was killed in King Arthur's campaign against Rome.

Bedreddin Hassan   *Arabian*

A prince who, in the *Arabian Night's Entertainments*, was captured and became a cook.

bee

Bees feature in many mythologies:
(1) In Christian tradition, the bee represents the risen Christ.

(2) In Egypt , bees are said to be the tears shed by Ra.
(3) European lore says that plants and animals will suffer if bees are used in barter and some go so far as to invite bees to the funeral of their deceased owner.
(4) The Germans regard the bee as a symbol of the sun.
(5) In Greece, the priestess at Delphi took the form of a bee.
(6) The Hindu god Krishna is sometimes envisaged as a bee hovering over Vishnu's head.

Beelzebub[1]   *Canaanite*

also Baalzebub, God of the Dunghill, Lord of the Flies

A Philistine deity, the personification of evil. (*See also* **Beelzebul**.)

Beelzebub[2]   *European*

A demon of pride and false gods. In black magic, he is one of the Grand Dignitaries, chief of the Infernal Empire.

Beelzebul   *Canaanite*

A Philistine god. This name was corrupted to become Beelzebub, said to mean God of the Dunghill and hence, Lord of the Flies.

Beetle[1]   *South American*

A creator-spirit of the Chaco Indians. He first made the world and then used the few grains left over to make the first humans.

Beetle[2] *see* **Ishits**

beetle

An insect featured in many mythologies:
(1) The Egyptians believed that there was no female of the species and that reproduction occurred when a male beetle rolled a ball of ox-dung from east to west and buried it for twenty-eight days. On the twenty-ninth day the beetle pushed the ball of dung into water and a new insect emerged.
(2) The Finns regard beetles as the souls of the dead and they are consulted by young girls wishing to know their marriage prospects.
(3) In Hebrew lore, beetles reproduced themselves while walking backwards towards the west.
(4) In North America, the Hopi carried beetles in battle, saying that they were helpful spirits who could cover their owner's tracks. The Zuni feed a beetle to one struck by lightning as an antidote. They also say that the trickster Coyote buried a beetle in the neutral land he marked off between tribes and anybody who cultivated this land would go blind – like a beetle.

Befana   *European*

also La Strega, La Vecchia

A benevolent spirit in Italy. She was said to be too busy to go with the Magi when they travelled to Bethlehem to see Jesus and later got lost when she tried to find her own way there. Every year she looks in vain for the baby Jesus but leaves presents at each house she visits.

An alternative version says that she was too busy to entertain the Magi who were on their way to Jerusalem but would do so on their return. In the event, they went home by a different route and she missed them. She looks out for them every year on Twelfth Night but never finds them.

Begdu San   *Chinese*

A mountain range. It is said that this range of mountains was formed from the excreta of a giant who, having drunk sea-water and eaten earth because he had devoured everything else, became ill.

Bego Tanutanu   *Pacific Islands*
A Melanesian creator-spirit, the younger of two brothers. The other was lazy and left it to Bego to form the landscape and make all the plants. The Flood was caused when his wife released the sea which she had earlier impounded.

Begochiddy   *North American*
The great god of the Navaho Indians.

Bel-Marduk *see* **Marduk**

Beleth   *European*
A demon king; one of the 72 Spirits of Solomon. He is depicted as riding a pale horse and accompanied by musicians.

Beli   *Norse*
A Frost-giant; god of storms.
When his sister Gerda married the god Frey, Beli tried to kill him. Frey had given his sword to someone else and he used a stag's horn (or his fist) to defend himself and kill Beli.
In some accounts he abducted Freya, hoping to force her to marry one of his three sons, but she refused all of them.

Belial   *European*
A demon of sodomy, arrogance or trickery; a fallen angel; one of the 72 Spirits of Solomon.
The name is also used to refer to the underworld, She'ol, or to the devil.
In black magic, he is regarded as an ambassador to Turkey.

Bell-bird brothers   *Australian*
Culture-heroes of the Aborigines of Central Australia.

Bellengerus le Beuse   *British*
A Knight of the Round Table; earl of Laundes; son of Alisander and Alice le Beale Pellerin.
In some accounts, he killed Andred, a knight at the court of King Mark of Cornwall and was killed by Mark. Some say that he killed Mark as well as Andred.

Bellerophon   *Greek*
A prince of Corinth; son of Glaucus, king of Corinth, or the sea god Poseidon.
His original name was Hipponous and he was called Bellerophon after he killed the Corinthian noble Bellerus in an accident. (Others say it was his own brother, Deliades, who was killed.) He fled to Tiryns where the king, Proetus, purified him of murder; Anteia, the king's wife, accused him of attempting rape when he rejected her advances. Neither Proetus nor his father-in-law, Iobates, to whom Bellerophon was sent, wished to kill a guest so Iobates asked Bellerophon to destroy the monster Chimaera, hoping he would be killed in the attempt.
The prophet Polyidus advised him to capture Pegasus, the winged horse, for the attempt and Athena gave him a golden bridle which made this possible.
Riding on Pegasus over the monster he killed it by shooting his arrows into it or, in another version, forcing lead into its mouth which, melting in its hot breath, choked it to death.
Iobates sent him off to fight the Solymi and then the Amazons and he was again the victor in each case, so Iobates allowed him to marry his daughter, Philonoe.
In some accounts, he avenged himself on Anteia by taking her for a ride on Pegasus and pushing her off when they were flying at a great height.
He foolishly tried to ride up to Olympus but was thrown either because Pegasus was not prepared to attempt the journey or because the god Zeus sent a gadfly to sting Pegasus. In either case, he fell into a thorny bush and was blinded or lamed, ending his days wandering the earth.

Belleus   *British*
A Knight of the Round Table.
He found Lancelot asleep in his bed and mistook him for his lover. Lancelot reacted violently and wounded his unwelcome paramour.
A different version says that Lancelot was sleeping with the wife of Belleus who challenged Lancelot to a duel.

Bellona[1]   *Roman*
An Italic goddess of war; daughter, sister or wife of the war god Mars. She drove the chariot of Mars.

Bellona[2]   *Roman*
A war goddess; sister of the war god Mars.
This deity, originally the Anatolian war goddess Ma, was brought to Rome from the east. Her black-clad priests mutilated themselves and then drank their own blood. Her festival was originally on 3rd June but was later merged with that of the Italic Bellona on 24th March.

Benten   *Japanese*
A sea goddess, goddess of music, speech and wealth; one of seven Shinto deities of good fortune known as the Shichi Fukujin.
In one story, she descended to earth and married a dragon-king, persuading him to give up his wicked habit of eating young children.

Another story tells how she helped the young poet, Baishu, who had found a poem written by a maiden and had fallen in love with her without having met her. He prayed to Benten, who arranged that he should meet the girl as he left the shrine. It later turned out that this girl was, in fact, the soul of the maiden whom he later met and married.

Some of her statues show her with snakes while others show her as having eight arms, six of which are raised with hands holding various objects such as a bow and arrow, the other two being folded in prayer.

She is sometimes depicted playing a kind of flute known as a biwa.

Beowulf   *Norse*
A warrior-prince.

He and his friend Breca swam, fully clothed in mail armour, across the sea from Denmark to Geatland for a dare.

When the monster Grendel made raids on Heorot, the palace of the Danish king Hrodgar, Beowulf volunteereed to try to kill the monster. It ate his companion, Hondscio, and since it was invulnerable to weapons, Beowulf tackled it with his bare hands when he trapped the monster on its next attack. Unable to break Beowulf's grip, Grendel pulled away leaving one its arms behind and later died from the wound. The monster's mother carried off Hrodgar's retainer, Aeschere, and when she emerged to avenge Grendel's death, Beowulf dived into the lake with the sword Hrunting which proved useless against her. He snatched up a huge sword that the monster had

acquired earlier and used it to cut off her head and also that of Grendel.

After this triumph, Beowulf was handsomely rewarded with, amongst other things, the necklace Brisingamen which is normally said to be the necklace of the goddess Freya. In some versions, he became king of Denmark; in others, he returned to Geatland where he acquired land and set up his own kingdom. When his uncle Hygelac, king of Geatland, was killed, Beowulf raised the king's son to be the next ruler but when he too was killed, Beowulf himself took the throne.

In old age he killed a dragon, the Firedrake, which lived beneath a burial-mound guarding a hoard of treasure and which was ravaging the countryside. In killing the dragon, he was mortally wounded but before he died he gave his armour and weapons to the youth Wiglaf, the only one of his retainers to have stood with him in the fight with the dragon.

Bergelmir   *Norse*
A giant, progenitor of the race of Frost Giants. He and his wife were the only ones to survive the rush of blood from the body of the giant Ymir when he was killed by the god Odin and his brothers, and they lived to start a new race of giants.

Berggeist   *German*
A mountain spirit.

Berith   *European*
A demon of alchemy; a duke of hell; one of the 72 Spirits of Solomon. He is depicted astride a red horse and is said to foretell the future.

Beth Gelert *see* **Beddgelert**
Bhima   *Hindu*
A giant warrior-prince, hero of the Hindu epic, the *Mahabharata*; brother of Arjuna.

On a journey to find the magic lotus which restores health and vigour, he met Hanuman, the monkey-god, and from him learned the history of the universe. He killed the yakshas (demons) which guarded the lotus and drank the healing waters of the lake.

In one account, he killed Purochana, an enemy, by setting fire to his house, because he had learned that Purochana planned to burn down the Pandavas' palace (Bhima and Arjuna were two of the five Pandava brothers) and he also killed the demons Hidimba and Vaka and many others.

Two men, Jayadratha and Kitchaka, tried to rape Draupadi (wife of the Pandavas), and Bhima gave them both a beating, making the former work as a slave of the Pandavas. Bhima later saved Draupadi from death at the stake,

In the *Mahabharata* he was poisoned and thrown into the river by his cousin, Duryodhana, one of the Kaurava brothers (their enemies), but the water snakes revived him and gave him tremendous physical strength which he used to great effect in the battle with the Kauravas. One of the Kauravas he killed was Duhsasana and he drank the dead man's blood. In the final episode, Duryodhana, the sole surviving Kaurava, fought Bhima in single combat and was defeated. During the fight, Bhima used an unfair blow which broke his opponent's thigh. Thereafter, he was called Jihma-yodhin, the unfair fighter.

Bhima, and all the Pandavas except Yudhishthira, died on a journey to Mount Meru.

bhumi *Buddhist*

Any member of a group of twelve deities who represent the spiritual stages through which a bodhisattva must pass.

Bifrons *European*

A demon, one of the 72 Spirits of Solomon. This demon takes the form of a monster which can change shape on command. It is said to impart knowledge of magic herbs and of astrology.

Bifrost *Norse*

The rainbow bridge leading from Asgard to Midgard.

This bridge, built of air, fire and water, was guarded by Heimdall, god of the dawn, whose palace, Himinbiorg, was built on top of the bridge. Thor was not allowed to use the bridge – his tread was too heavy for its frail construction. It was broken down by the onrushing forces from Muspelheim at Ragnarok, the final battle.

Big Grandfather *see* **Raven**[1]
Big Raven *see* **Quikinna'qu**
Biggarroo *Australian*

In the lore of the Aborigines, a huge snake, a good being in contrast to the evil Goonnear.

Bilqis *see* **Balkis**
Bil's Way *see* **Irmin's Way**
Bilwis *German*

also Bilmesschneider

An evil spirit said to devastate crops with a sickle attached to his big toe.

Bindinoor *Australian*

When he was wounded, his father Walleyneup, though the supreme

god, could not heal him and he died. As a result, his father decreed that mankind should thereafter lose their immortality.

birds

Birds in various forms feature in many mythologies:

(1) In Australia, the Aborigines regard birds as their original gods.

(2) The Buddhists say that Garuda, half man, half eagle, is the transport of the gods.

(3) Celtic lore regards birds as the souls of the dead.

(4) In the East Indies, the islanders of New Britain say that a bird and a stone, offspring of the sun and moon, became the progenitors of the human race when the bird turned into a woman and the stone into a man.

(5) The Finns, like the Celts, regard birds as the souls of the dead.

(6) In Persia birds were regarded as the transmitters of wisdom.

(7) In the Pacific Islands, birds are referred to in stories where they act as messengers for the gods, appear as deities who lay eggs from which islands emerge and are sent to locate dry land after the flood.

(8) In Siberia the thunder god can be a bird and a raven is sent to assess the size of the expanding world. They also talk of the bucu, a bird said to help the shaman when he travels the world.

(9) The Sumerians said that the dead in the underworld take the form of birds.

(10) A universal story tells of a bird sitting in the tree of life near a pool in which lives a monster (a fish, serpent, dragon or toad) which holds back the waters. This bird often battles

with the monster to release the waters.

Bird's Way *Baltic*

In Lithuanian lore, the name of the Milky Way along which the dead are said to travel to Dausos, the kingdom of the dead.

Bisagit *East Indies*

A smallpox god in Borneo. He gave Kinharingan the soil from which the creator-god made the earth.

Some say that he imposed a condition that he should have half the people made by Kinharingan, an objective he achieves by causing a smallpox epidemic every 40 years.

Bishamon *Japanese*

A Shinto god of war and wealth. One of seven deities of good fortune, the Shichi Fukojin.

He is depicted in full armour with a spear in his hand.

Black Bear[1] *North American*

A sky-spirit of the Slavey tribe of Canada.

When the animals sent a representative of each species to ask why the world was dark and full of snow, Black Bear told them that bags hanging from his lodge contained the cold, the rain and the wind but would not say what the fourth bag held. When Black Bear went out, the animals threw the fourth bag back to earth where it split open and out came the sun, the moon and the stars. The sun lit up the world and its heat soon melted the snow, so the animals returned to earth. En route, many suffered accidents that left them permanently in the form in which we now find them – the bison with the hump, the moose with a flat nose, and so on.

Black Bear[2] *North American*
also Wacabe
A guardian spirit of the Osage.

Black Elves *see* **Nibelungen**

Black One *see* **Kali**

Black Worm of the Barrow *Welsh*
A huge worm or serpent living in
the Mound of Mourning. This
monster held a stone in its tail
which could produce gold for
whoever owned it. The mound
was protected by 300 knights,
each of whom wanted the stone.
When the Black Oppressor tried to
steal the stone, the worm blinded
him in one eye. Peredur, Knight of
the Round Table, killed the worm
and gave the stone to his helper,
Edlym.

Blackbird of Cilgwri *Welsh*
A bird of great knowledge. This
ancient bird was consulted by
Culhwch in his quest for the hand
of Olwen.

Blamor de Ganis *British*
A Knight of the Round Table; a
duke of Limousin; son of Lancelot,
some say.
  He and his brother Bleoberis
accused King Anguish of killing a
relative. Tristram repaid the king's
earlier kindness by taking up his
defence and defeated Blamor in
single combat but spared his life
and they became friends.
  After the death of Arthur, he
joined Lancelot, Bedivere and
other knights in a hermitage.
When Lancelot died, Blamor and
Bleoberis went off to the Holy
Land and fought the Turks.

Blatant Beast *British*
A fiendish beast, offspring of
Cerberus, the dog that guards the
gates of Hades, and the monster
Chimaera, or of another monster,
Echidna.
  This 100-tongued beast was

hunted by Pelleas and captured
by Calidore, who carried it off to
fairyland. It later escaped.

Bleoberis de Ganis *British*
A Knight of the Round Table; a
duke of Poitiers; son of Lancelot,
some say.
  He and his brother Blamor
accused King Anguish of killing a
relative. (*See* ***Blamor de Ganis***.)

Blessed Islands *see* **Fortunate
  Islands**

Blind Old Man *see* **Yokomatis**

Blissful Isle *North American*
In the lore of some Native
American tribes, the land of the
dead.

Blood Clot *North American*
A Ute culture-hero. He was reared
by an old hunter who had found
the blood clot from which the boy
emerged. He grew very quickly
and killed larger and larger
animals as he grew bigger, finally
killing a buffalo. He then left his
foster-father and travelled to
another village where he married
a daughter of the chief.
  One day he borrowed an arrow
from the chief and called up
a huge storm. When the wind
abated, a dead buffalo was
found outside side each tent in
the village. His life in the village
ended when his wife uttered the
forbidden word 'calf' – Blood Clot
then turned into the buffalo he
really was.

Blue Jay *North American*
A culture-hero and trickster-
god, in the lore of the Mohawk
Indians, the bird who scared off
the demon Tawiskaron. He also
separated the Siamese twins born
to Aqas-Xena-Xenas and his wife.
  The Chinook say that Blue
Jay exhumed the body of the
daughter of a chief and took her

to the land of the Supernatural
People where she was restored
to life and married Blue Jay.
When her father demanded Blue
Jay's hair as compensation, he
changed into a bird and flew
off. His wife died a second death
and his sister Ioi was claimed by
the dead. When he found Ioi,
she was surrounded by piles of
bones which then became human
beings again. Blue Jay turned
them back into bones and mixed
them all up so that they all had
mismatched parts when they next
materialised.
  In another story, Ioi gave him
five buckets of water with which
to put out the prairie fires. He was
badly burned and died.
  Another story says that, while
in the land of the Supernatural
People he accepted a challenge to
a diving contest and won by the
trick of coming up several times
to draw breath under a mat of
reeds while his opponent tried to
outlast him on only one lungful.
In another contest, climbing a
pinnacle of ice, he again cheated
and won by using his wings to
fly upwards but, when a whale-
catching contest was arranged,
Blue Jay fell into the sea and was
drowned.

Blue World *North American*
The second of the four worlds
which the Navaho passed through
before emerging into the upper
world. This land was the home
of the Swallow People and the
Navaho reached it as they fled
upwards from the Red World to
escape the flood which was sent
to punish their adultery. Here, too,
they committed the same offence
and were compelled to leave the
Blue World.

bluebottle *East Indies*
In the lore of Java, an insect which may be an ancestor. It is said that bluebottles lead the spirits of the dead to the underworld.

Bne-aleim *see* **Ischin**

boar
This fierce animal of the pig family features in many stories worldwide:
(1) In China the boar is said to carry the sun for part of its journey across the heavens and is regarded as guardian of the north-west quadrant.
(2) Several boars feature in Greek myths, notably the Calydonian boar which was hunted down and slain by a group of heroes and heroines. Another is the Erymanthian boar hunted and captured by Hercules as his fourth Labour.
(3) In Hinduism the boar is a source of cosmic power and appears as Vahara, the third avatar of Vishnu, and as the incarnation of various other deities, including Prajapati who, with his hundred arms, raised the earth. Another version says that the black boar, Enusha, raised the earth on its tusks.
(4) Irish stories include the death of Dermot, slain by the boar which has earlier been charged to kill him.
A boar owned by Brigit, daughter of the Dagda, was known as Orc (or Torc) Triath or Treithirne and is the equivalent of the Welsh Twrch Trwyth (*see below*).
(5) In Japan the boar was said to protect from snakes and was used as a sacrifice to the god Mi-Toshi.
(6) In Malaysia a boar may be a man in disguise.

(7) In Mesopotamian myths, the boar is regarded as a messenger of the gods and is called Papsukal or Nin-shach. It became an accursed beast after killing the god Tammuz.
(8) Norse myths include the story of Ottar who, in the form of a boar, was a lover of Freya who owned and rode a golden boar called Hildswin, and of her husband Frey who owned the golden boar, Gullinbursti, made by the dwarfs.
In Valhalla the boar Saehrimnir was slain every day to provide food for the slain warriors but was restored after each meal ready to provide the next.
Slidrugtanni was a boar which drew Frey's chariot alongside Gullinbursti.
(9) Persian mythology regards the boar as an incarnation of the god Verethragna and as the animal of the god Mithra.
(10) In Syria the boar was regarded as a sacred animal.
(11) In Welsh stories, the quest of Culhwch involved the pursuit of the huge boar Twrch Trwyth, a king who had been turned into a boar for his sins. He had a litter of young boars, among them Banw, Benwig, Gwys, Llwydawg and Twrch Llawin.
Also featuring in Culhwch's quest is the chief boar, Ysgithyrwyn, the tusk of which was required for shaving the giant Ysbadadden.

Bobbi-bobbi *Australian*
A spirit-snake of the Aborigines. He is said to have created the boomerang from one of his ribs.

bodach *Scottish*
A goblin. This malevolent spirit takes the form of an old man who frightens children at night and steals naughty ones.

bodach glas *Scottish*
A form of goblin, the 'Grey Spectre', which causes the death of any human who happens to see it.

Bodb Dearg *Irish*
'Red Bodb'
A Danaan king of Munster; son of the Dagda and Boann, the goddess of the River Boyne, some say. Some say he was the brother of Boann and the Dagda.
He became leader of the Danaans when the Dagda resigned following the defeat by the Milesians. Midir (a brother or son of the Dagda) objected to this arrangement and enlisted the Fianna to fight on his side against the new leader.
Bodb Dearg had three foster-daughters, Alva, Aobh and Aoife. Aobh married the sea god Lir, and gave him four children but died in childbirth. He then married Aoife who turned her step-children into swans. (*See also* **Children of Lir**.) When Bodb Dearg learned of this, he turned Aoife into a flying demon. (Some say that he was the father of Alva, Aobh and Aoife, rather than their foster-father.)

bogey *British*
also bogy, bogle
A goblin.

boggard *British*
also boggart, boggle, buggane
A malevolent goblin or ghost.

Bohinavlle *Baltic*
also Nail of the North;
= *Finnish* Boahje-naste
The name used in Latvia for the North Star. This star is regarded as the support round which the heavens revolve.

bokwus *North American*
In the lore of the Native American

tribes of the north-west, a spirit of the forest which pushes unsuspecting fishermen into the river.

bolla   *Balkan*

An Albanian demon in the form of a serpent. These demons open their eyes once a year and then they eat any humans they see.

Bona Dea   *Roman*

also Good Goddess;

= *Phrygian* Cybele

An obscure virgin goddess worshipped only by women and associated with snakes. In some accounts she is identified with the goddesses Fauna, Maia or Ops. Her festival was held in December.

boroka   *Pacific Islands*

In the lore of the Philippines, a four-legged, winged witch who eats children.

Borre   *British*

A Knight of the Round Table; a son of King Arthur by Lyonors, daughter of Earl Sanam.

Bors[1]   *British*

also Bors de Ganis, Bors de Gannes, Bors de Gaunes

King of Gaul. He and his brother Ban took an army to Britain to help Arthur in his fight with the rebellious barons. He died of grief when he was told of the death of his brother.

Bors[2]   *British*

also Bohort, Bors de Ganis, Bors de Gannes, Bors de Gaunes

A Knight of the Round Table; son of Bors[1] and Evaine; nephew of Lancelot.

He, with his brother Lionel and Lancelot, was raised by the Lady of the Lake. He defeated Lord Bromel who, having been rejected by Elaine who loved Lancelot, was looking for Lancelot to challenge him to a fight. At the castle of

Corbin (Castle Carbonek) he passed a night of strange adventure. A spectral spear pierced his shoulder and arrows flying out of the darkness gave him further wounds. He fought and killed a lion and watched as a leopard fought with a dragon that spat out a hundred small dragons which tore the older one to shreds. An old man sang about the journey of Joseph of Arimathea to Britain. A silver sword hanging over his head blinded him with its radiance and he was told by a disembodied voice to leave. Next day he rode to Camelot and told Lancelot what had happened. (A similar story is told of both Gawain and Lancelot.) Later, when Lancelot went mad and disappeared from Camelot, Bors rode out with Ector and Lionel to search for him. He joined the other knights in the quest for the Holy Grail and came to a tower where the owner, a lovely maiden, daughter of King Love, begged him to help her fight a giant, Priadan. He resisted all her attempts to seduce him and defeated the giant when he arrived next morning. He then encountered two men beating his brother, Lionel, and a girl being attacked by a dwarf. By the time he had saved the girl and freed himself from her embraces, Lionel was dead. The girl's relatives took him to a castle and treated him royally and, when he again resisted her attempts to seduce him, the tower and all its occupants disappeared. Next day, at Castle Tubele, he found his brother alive and so angry at being deserted by Bors that he challenged him to single combat. He was saved from death at his brother's hands by the

intervention of Colgrevaunce and then both Lionel and Colgrevaunce were struck dead by a thunderbolt. Both turned out to be wraiths conjured up by the forces of evil.

Other versions say that Lionel killed Colgrevaunce and would have killed Bors as well but was struck by a thunderbolt. Bors then came to an abbey on the shore where a voice told him to go to sea. He boarded a ship covered with white samite which immediately set off at speed. On board he met Percival and later they were joined by Galahad. They came across an abandoned ship and went aboard. Here they found a marvellous sword which Galahad retained and then returned to their own ship which carried them to the Castle of Carteloise. Here a woman lay sick who could be cured only by the blood of a virgin. Percival's sister, Dindrane, gave blood but died as a result. At her own request, Percival placed her dead body in a boat and cast it adrift. Bors rode with Galahad and Percival to the Castle of Carbonek, home of the Maimed King, where they were vouchsafed a sight of the Holy Grail. They took the Grail and the Holy Lance by ship to Sarras where they found the boat bearing the body of Percival's sister which they buried. All three were imprisoned by the king, Estorause, but he released them and asked their pardon when he was dying. Galahad became king but died about a year later and the Grail and the Lance disappeared for ever. Percival entered a hermitage and Bors stayed with him until he too died, about a year after Galahad. After burying Percival alongside his sister and Galahad, Bors returned to Camelot where the story of his adventures was relayed to Lancelot and Arthur who ordered it all to be recorded for posterity.

After the death of Arthur, Bors joined Lancelot, Bedivere and other knights in a hermitage, and when Lancelot died he went to live in the Holy Land and fought the Turks.

Bosherton   *British*
A village in Wales. The lake here is said to be the one from which Excalibur appeared and from which King Arthur was taken on his final journey to Avalon.

Botis   *European*
A demon, duke or president of hell; one of the 72 Spirits of Solomon. This being may appear as a loathsome serpent or as a human being with horns.

Botoque   *South American*
A culture-hero of the Kayapo people. He was adopted by a jaguar who taught him hunting skills but he killed the jaguar's wife and stole both fire and the bow and arrow, which he then gave to his people.

Bragi   *Norse*
God of poetry and music; son of Odin and Gunlod, the daughter of the giant Suttung; husband of Iduna (goddess of youth).

Gunlod was guarding the three containers full of the blood of Kvasir in a cave in the middle of a mountain. Odin got access to her with the help of the giant Baugi, Gunlod's uncle, who bored a hole which Odin, in the form of a snake, slipped through. Odin then resumed his godlike form and stayed with Gunlod for several days, fathering Bragi.

At his birth, the dwarfs gave Bragi a golden harp and set him afloat in a boat which carried him out of the subterranean darkness, whereupon he began to sing and play the harp. Landing, he walked through the woods and met Iduna whom he married and they went off to Valhalla where he became the god of poetry and music.

He receives fallen heroes in Valhalla and is depicted with long white hair and beard and carrying his golden harp.

Bragi's Apples   *Norse*
Fruit which have the power to cure illness. It was said that, as soon as one of these magic apples was eaten, another appeared to replace it.

Brahma   *Hindu*
A four-headed creator-god, Brahman personified. Brahma, Shiva and Vishnu form the group of gods known as the Trimurti.

In some stories he was born from Vishnu's navel, in others he was asleep in the lotus floating on the primitive waters until he awoke and created the universe while other stories say that he was self-created from the primeval waters or from the creator-god Hiranya-garbha. In the *Ramayana* he is a boar which lifted the earth on its tusks, while others say that he mated in the form of a stag with the goddess Rohita as a doe to produce all the animals.

It is said that Brahma was born with only one head but grew the others so that he could behold the beauty of his wife Sarasvati from all sides. Some say that Sarasvati was born from Brahma's body and mated

with him to produce the first man, Manu. An alternative story credits him with a daughter, Satarupa, on whom he had incestuous designs and grew the four heads so that he could admire her. Some versions say that he had five heads, one of which was cut off by Shiva when he was disrespectful. Yet another version asserts that Brahma split himself into two, the male Purusha and the female Satarupa.

In some stories his consort is Vach although some say that she was the daughter on whom he incestuously fathered the human race. Others say that his consort was Gayatri.

Some say that Brahma will live for 1000 divine years at the end of which he will die and the universe will vanish. After a period of 100 divine years, Brahma will reappear and a new universe will be created. In this system, one divine year equals 3,110,400 million human years.

He is depicted as having four hands, holding an alms bowl, a sceptre, a bow and the Rig Veda. His transport is the swan or goose (hamsa).

Brahma-yuga *see* **krita-yuga**
Brahman   *Hindu*
The primordial essence; the absolute; cosmic unity; soul of the universe; the active creative force.

Brahmavati   *Buddhist*
Mother of the future Buddha, Maitreya, who will be born from Brahmavati's right side after a pregnancy lasting ten months.

Brahmayus   *Buddhist*
Husband of Brahmavati; father of Maitreya, some say.

Bran[1]   *British*

also Bran of Gower, Brandegore

A giant god; king of Britain.

When Bran agreed that his sister Branwen should marry Matholwch, king of Ireland, his crazy half-brother Efnisien maimed the Irish king's horses. Bran gave Matholwch a magic Cauldron of Rebirth, capable of restoring the dead to life, in compensation. Later his sister was made to work as a drudge and she sent him a message with a starling, whereupon Bran invaded Ireland, wading the Irish sea while his army went by ship. The Irish king abdicated without a fight in favour of Gwern, his son. When Efnisien killed Gwern by pushing him into the fire, fighting broke out again and all the Irish except five pregnant women and all except seven of the British were killed. Bran himself was wounded and died soon after and Branwen died of grief at his loss. His head was struck off, as he had instructed, and was taken back to Britain to be buried many years later at the White Mount (the Tower of London) to protect the kingdom. In the years before it was buried, the head ate and spoke as it had always done when Bran was alive.

During Bran's absence from Britain, the country was conquered by Caswallawn (Cassivellaunus).

Years later, King Arthur, saying that the kingdom should depend for its defence on him rather than on some buried relic, dug up Bran's head.

Bran[2]   *Irish*

also Brandan

A hero voyager. He picked a branch of apple blossom and carried it to his hall where a mysterious woman told him about a marvellous island across the sea. She then took the branch and disappeared. Bran followed with three boats, each with a crew of nine men. Manannan the sea god confirmed the story of the island, Emain Ablach, so they rowed on. At the Island of Joy, one of the crewmen stayed behind while Bran and the rest went on to the Island of Women where they stayed for about a year. One of his crew, Neachtan, became homesick so they returned to Ireland but when the sailor jumped ashore he immediately crumbled to dust – they had been away for centuries and nobody recognised Bran or his men, so they put to sea again and no more was heard of them.

Bran[3]   *Irish*

A hound of the Irish hero Finn mac Cool.

Finn's sister (or, in other accounts, his sister-in-law or aunt) was Uirne and she was to be married to Iollann, king of Leinster. When she was pregnant, Iollann's jealous mistress, a druidess, put a spell on Uirne, turning her into a bitch, with the result that her children, Sceolan and Bran, were born as hounds.

In other accounts, Uirne was restored to her former self by Lugaid Lagha, whom she married, and the pups were born to them at the same time as human triplets. When the god Angus Og said the hounds could never kill any of his swine, Finn set both dogs to work and they killed all the herd of one hundred, including the famous black boar.

In some versions, Bran was originally owned by a giant who stole children. When Finn killed the giant and rescued the children, he also took the giant's bitch and her two whelps. Finn kept the brindled one, Bran, and the other, called Sceolan, was left with the father of some of the stolen children, who had sought Finn's help. On one occasion, both Bran and Sceolan were stolen by Arthur, a son of the British king, Arthur, who had come to Ireland with twenty-eight warriors to seek adventure. Nine Fianna warriors followed them to Scotland and killed all of them, taking Arthur prisoner, and recovering the hounds.

Finn accidentally struck Bran with a leash and the hound was so upset at this treatment that it ran away and drowned itself in a lake. Other stories say that Finn himself killed the hound to save a fawn that he had run down.

Brandan *see* **Bran**[2]

Brandegore *see* **Bran**[1]

Brèche de Roland   *European*

A large cleft in the Pyrenees, said to have been made by the paladin Roland when he struck the mountain with his sword, Durindana.

Brer Fox   *North American*

A trickster in many stories of the Native American tribes. The Apache say that he stole fire from the fireflies and gave it to the tribes.

Brer Rabbit   *North American*

A trickster in American folklore. This being is said to be derived from the African trickster, Hare, brought to America by slaves.

Bright Star   *North American*

A Pawnee goddess, the planet Venus as the morning star.

She was given the task by

the creator-god Atius-Tirawa of forming the earth and creating the people to live there. She mated with Great Star to produce the first woman who mated with the first man to populate the earth. She gave the first man, known as Closed Man, four varieties of corn for the use of the tribes.

Brighu   *Hindu*

A sage; one of the Seven Rishis, some say; son of Brahma or Manu.

He seized Puloma, the wife of a demon, fathering Chyavana on her, and, when Agni, the god of fire, told the demon who the abductor was, Brighu cursed the god with an insatiable appetite.

In an attempt to ascertain which of the three major deities was most worthy of veneration, Brighu visited each in turn and was less than respectful to all of them. Brahma only scolded him, Shiva would have burnt him to a cinder but he saved himself with an abject apology and Vishnu, whom he kicked to wake him up, merely enquired whether the sage had hurt his foot and massaged it. As a result, Brighu advised people to worship Vishnu.

When Shiva lost his temper at being excluded from a sacrifice, he attacked many of those present, including Brighu, who had his beard pulled off.

In some accounts he is credited with the discovery of fire.

Brigit   *Irish*

Goddess of cattle, fertility, fire, healing, poetry and smiths. In some accounts she was the wife of the god known as the Dagda, in some accounts his daughter; others say that she was the wife

of Turenn, the god of night, and mother of his three sons.

Some say she owned two oxen, Fea and Feimhean, and a boar, Treithirne.

In some accounts, there were three Brigits, sister-goddesses, whom others regard as a single person. In other accounts, she was the goddess Dana.

Briseis   *Greek*

A Trojan maiden who was captured at the siege of Troy and handed to Achilles as a prize. Agamemnon had been given the girl Chryseis but was persuaded to release her, demanding Briseis in her place. This precipitated the quarrel between these two Greek heroes and the withdrawal of Achilles.

brollachan   *Scottish*

An evil spirit. These beings were said to have only a mouth and eyes and took the form of whatever they rested on. They were thought to be the offspring of fuaths (malevolent spirits).

Brown Bull of Cooley   *Irish*

A famous bull of Ulster.

The swineherds Friuch and Rucht changed shape many times in a long-running feud and, in the form of worms, were swallowed by two cows, being reborn as the bulls Whitehorn and Donn.

Queen Maev of Connaught owned Whitehorn and wanted Donn, the Brown Bull of Cooley, as well, so she and her husband, Ailell, invaded Ulster to seize it. Macha, the war goddess, had laid a spell on the warriors of Ulster and only Cuchulainn was able to defend his county. The bull was captured by Ailell's army and taken to Connaught where it fought with Whitehorn and killed it, carrying its body back to Ulster.

In the course of the battle, Bricciu (a storm god and Lord of Ulster), who had been asked to judge the battle, was trampled to death. In one account, Donn fell dead soon after, in another it died when it charged a rock, mistaking it for another bull.

brownie   *Scottish*

A domestic fairy or goblin. These benevolent beings attach themselves to a household and help with the housework. They should not be rewarded; if they are, they may take offence and become boggards, malevolent goblins.

Brunhild   *Norse*

also Brunhilda, Brunhilde

Chief of the Valkyries, also known as Victory-wafter. She was the daughter either of Odin or of a mortal king, Budli, and raised to be a Valkyrie.

She was ordered by Odin to ensure that the hunter – some say Hialmgunnar – who had abducted Siegmund's lover won the duel with Siegmund, but she disobeyed his order and Odin had to intervene. He punished her by putting her into a long, deep sleep in a castle surrounded by fire that only the bravest hero would attempt to break through. Some say that she was so punished for rejecting Odin's amorous advances.

Sigurd rode through the flames to claim her but then left her. In some stories, she married Sigurd and they had a daughter, Aslaug, but the more usual story says that Sigurd left her after a while to seek further adventures. He became a friend of Gunnar, king of the Nibelung, who wanted Brunhild as a wife but was unable to face the wall of flame. Sigurd, this time in the guise of Gunnar, rode through the flames once more and wooed Brunhild for Gunnar.

When she married Gunnar, she realised how she had been deceived and was very bitter. She quarrelled with Sigurd's wife, Gudrun, Gunnar's sister, and tried to persuade Gunnar to kill Sigurd. He refused but his younger brother, Guttorn, speared Sigurd in the back and killed him. Brunhild, who still loved Sigurd, died with him. In some versions she stabbed herself and was burned on the same pyre as Sigurd; in others she rode her horse through the flames of his pyre and immolated herself. As she rode into the flames of the funeral pyre, she threw the Ring of Power into the Rhine. The Rhine-daughters rose to claim it and a huge wave swept Brunhild and the funeral pyre into oblivion.

The *Nibelungenlied* has Brunhild as a queen of Iceland who would marry only the man who could defeat her in a trial of strength. She was promised to Siegfried but he put on the Helmet of Invisibility and defeated her in a contest. Gunther (Gunnar) claimed that he was the invisible victor and married her. At the same time, Siegfried married Gunther's sister, Krimhild, and later the young couple visited Gunther and Brunhild at their court where the two ladies had a furious quarrel. Hagen plotted to avenge the insult to Brunhild and induced Gunther to ask for Siegfried's help to repel an alleged invasion. Hagen then took advantage of Siegfried's visit to kill him.

Brutus   *Celtic*
Leader of a band of Trojans; king of Britain; great-grandson of Aeneas.

It was prophesied that he would kill both his parents and establish a great kingdom. His mother died after three days in labour when he was born and when Brutus was fifteen, he shot and killed his father, Silvius, in a hunting accident and was exiled to Greece.

There he led the Trojan slaves of King Pandrasus in a revolt, capturing the king who gave him his daughter Imogen as a wife and ships and supplies so that the Trojans could sail west. He then led the Trojans across the sea to Gaul where they met Corineus, a son of Hercules, leader of the descendants of the Trojans who had been led there by Antenor after the fall of Troy. Some of his men stayed in Gaul but Brutus and Corineus led the others north to Britain where they conquered the native race of giants, capturing Gog and Magog, and Brutus became king of Britain.

Bubastis *see* **Bast**

bucentaur   *Greek*
A human-headed bull figure such as the minotaur.

Budda of Infinite Light *see* **Amida**

Bue   *Pacific Islands*
A hero of the Gilbert Islanders. Born when the sun impregnated a woman, he attacked his father to obtain knowledge, which he passed on to humans, of how to build boats, houses, etc.

Buer   *European*
A demon, wise in the art of medicine; one of the 72 Spirits of Solomon.

This being is depicted as having the body of a lion carried on five goat-like legs and feet. Others say

that he appears as a starfish.

buffalo[1]   *East Indies*
The Dayaks regard this animal as their ancestor.

Buffalo[2]   *North American*
In the lore of Native American tribes, a race of people with horns.

By striking a knot in a cottonwood tree, these people released the humans who lived underground beneath the tree and hunted them like animals, killing them and eating their flesh. Cut-Nose, the first to emerge, managed to escape and returned safely to the tree.

Another young man who escaped married Buffalo Girl, one of the Buffalo race. They made bows and arrows and left them by the tree so that, when the Buffalo people next knocked on the tree, the humans emerged and, seizing the weapons, killed their persecutors who then turned into real buffaloes.

The children of Buffalo Girl and her husband became the ancestors of the Arikara.

buggane   *British*
A Manx water-spirit. This being is said to appear either as a horse or a calf. (*See also* **boggard**.)

bull
Bulls typify strength, fecundity, stupidity, etc and play a role as such in many mythologies:
(1) In some Asian stories the bull was said to have dug into the primordial earth and brought up water.
(2) The Assyrians revered the bull as a beneficient winged protector.
(3) In Buddhism, Yama is said to stand on a bull.
(4) The Canaanites gave the name 'bull' to the gods El and Latipan.

(5) In China the ox is regarded as one of the animals which carry the sun through the twelve houses of the Zodiac and as a symbol of spring.

(6) In Egypt, the bulls Apis, Buchis and Mnevis were revered as gods and the north wind was depicted in the form of a bull.

(7) In Greek stories, Zeus appeared in the form of a bull to carry off Europa and he sent the white Cretan Bull to give the islanders a sign that Minos was to be their king. This animal later appeared as the Marathonian Bull captured by Hercules and subsequently killed by Theseus. The bull was also regarded as an incarnation of Dionysus.

(8) Hebrew tradition depicts the bull as a source of fruitfulness and also envisages the sun god in bovine form. It was used as a sacrificial animal.

(9) Irish mythology regards bulls as reincarnated deities and one of the finest stories concerns the Brown Bull of Cooley and the bull Whitehorn.

(10) Japanese lore says that the bull broke the primeval egg from which all else came. It is the second animal of the Zodiac and a symbol of Zen Buddhism.

(11) Muslim lore says that the bull, Kujata, supports the earth.

(12) The Norse regarded the bull as sacred to the supreme god, Odin.

(13) In Persia the bull represented the rain god. The primeval bull, Geush-Urvan, was killed by Angra Mainya or Mithra while the bull Hadhayosh was said to carry people across the primordial waters.

(14) The Romans regarded the bull as sacred to Neptune.

(15) The Siberian version of things has the bull standing on a stone (fish or crab) in the ocean and holding up the world on its horns. Should the horns ever break, the world will come to an end.

(16) In the Zodiac, the bull appears as the second sign, Taurus.

Bull-by-himself   *North American*
A Blackfoot culture-hero. He befriended some beavers, four of whom turned into humans and taught him the secrets of planting and harvesting tobacco.

Bull of Heaven   *Mesopotamian*
The manifestation of the destructive power of Nergal or Gugulanna, gods of the underworld. This fearsome animal was killed by the hero king Gilgamesh with the help of the wild man Enkidu.

Buné   *European*
A demon, a duke of hell; one of the 72 Spirits of Solomon. This being is said to have three heads, those of a dog, a griffin and a man.

bungisngis   *Pacific Islands*
A monster of the Philippines which takes the form of a giant of tremendous strength who has a very large upper lip and carries a club. He also eats human beings.

Bunyan, Paul   *North American*
A giant lumberjack. This legendary hero is said to have created the Grand Canyon with his axe. His constant companion was the blue ox, Babe.

bunyip   *Australian*
A man-eating swamp monster: the source of evil in Aboriginal lore.

Burkhan   *Siberian*
also Burkhan-Bakshi
A supreme deity. He ordered

the construction of a ship to save all the species (except the mammoth) from the impending flood. When the devil Shitkur, in the form of a mouse, tried to gnaw through the ship's timbers, Burkhan created a cat to scare the mouse away.

Butes   *Greek*
One of the Argonauts; son of Pandion, Poseidon or Teleon by Zeuxippe; brother of Philomena and Procne.
     He was the only one to jump overboard when they heard the song of the Sirens but he was rescued by Aphrodite who made him her lover.

Buttercat   *Swedish*
= *Finnish* Para; *Lappish* Smieragatto
A spirit in the form of a cat which brings its owner butter, cream and milk.

butterfly
(1) In the Baltic region, a grey butterfly is said to be soul of a dead person or of one sleeping.

(2) In China, the butterfly (hu tieh) represents married happiness and longevity.

(3) East Indian lore says that the soul of a sleeping person is held by a butterfly.

(4) The Japanese say that butterflies carry human souls, and are represented as tiny fairies.

(5) In Mexico the butterfly is regarded as the soul of a dead person.

(6) In North America, Algonquin lore regards the butterfly as creator of the south wind.

(7) Scottish lore has the butterfly in the role of a fire god (Teine-de).

(8) In Siberia it is said that witches can take the form of a butterfly.

bwbach   *Welsh*
  plural bwbachod
  A household spirit or brownie. It
  is said that these beings attack
  teetotallers.

bwci   *Welsh*
  plural bwciod
  A bugbear; a ghost.

Bwlch-y-Saethu   *Welsh*
  A pass in Snowdonia, Wales. It
  was here, according to Welsh
  stories, that King Arthur

was killed after the Battle of
Tregalen.

Bylebog   *Slav*
  A sun god, the force of good
  opposing Chernobog.

C *Central American*

A Mayan deity of uncertain identity, referred to as God C (*see **alphabetical gods***); perhaps Ed (one of the Bacabs) or Kukulcan. In some instances, this deity is depicted with a halo of rays and some planetary signs, leading some to identify him as a god of the pole-star.

Caacrinolaas *European*

A demon, one of the 72 Spirits of Solomon. He is envisaged as a winged dog and is said to teach science, make humans invisible and initiate murder.

Cadbury *British*

A site in Somerset, England, where, some say, King Arthur and his men lie sleeping. Some suggest it was the site of Camelot.

For other suggested sites, *see **Alderley Edge***.

Cadmus *Greek*

also Kadmos

A sun god and king of Thebes. He was said to have founded Thebes and introduced the alphabet.

When his sister, Europa, was abducted by Zeus in the form of a bull, Cadmus spent some time searching for her but he gave up the search on the advice of the Delphic Oracle and built a city, Thebes, on the site where the cow he was told to follow stopped for rest.

He killed the serpent guarding the Castalian spring and sowed its teeth to produce a crop of Sown Men who fought amongst themselves till only five, the Sparti, were left alive and they became servants of Cadmus, helping him to build the city of Thebes. He was condemned by Athena to serve as a slave to the war god Ares for eight years for killing the serpent.

In later years, he conquered Illyria and fathered a son whom he called Illyrius. Some say that he was given the throne by his daughter Agave who had killed her husband, the king Lycotherses.

At the end of his life he was changed by Ares into a black serpent and and sent to the Islands of the Blessed, together with his wife Harmonia who was similarly changed.

Cador *British*

King of Cornwall and a Knight of the Round Table; one of the Knights of Battle. His duty was to dress and arm King Arthur before battle.

He saved his friend Caradoc who was dying from the effects of a blood-sucking snake attached to his arm by the magician Eliaures by putting his sister in a vat of milk and Caradoc in a vat of sour wine. This induced the snake to try to cross from one vat to the other, giving Cador the chance to kill it with his sword.

caduceus *Roman*

The Latin name for the wand of the god Mercury (Hermes). This symbol is in the form of a rod with wings and entwined serpents and has the power of reconciliation. The serpents were originally white ribbons.

The wand was given to Hermes by the god Apollo in exchange for the seven-stringed lyre which the youth had made from the shell of a tortoise.

Other versions of the myth make a distinction between the caduceus used as a herald's staff and the magic wand with wings, serpents, etc.

Caim   *European*
A demon, one of the 72 Spirits of Solomon. This demon, which appears in the form of a thrush, can teach any language, including the language of the birds.

Calico Bag Monk, Calico Bag Zen Master *see* **Pu T'ai Ho-shang**

Calliope   *Greek*
also Kalliope
One of the nine Muses, the Muse of epic poetry; daughter of Zeus and Mnemosyne; mother of Orpheus.

She judged the dispute between Aphrodite and Persephone for the favours of Adonis, allocating each one third of each year (*see more at* ***Adonis***).

Callisto   *Greek*
A nymph.

The god Zeus, having seduced Callisto, changed her into a bear to deceive his wife Hera who, jealous as usual, had the bear hunted by the hounds of Artemis, the huntress goddess. Another version says that Hera herself changed Callisto into a bear.

Zeus placed her in the heavens as the Great Bear and her son Arcas as the Little Bear. Some say that she was killed by Arcas.

Calpe   *Greek*
One of the Pillars of Hercules, the present-day Rock of Gibraltar.

In some accounts, this rock and Abyla opposite were originally one mountain. Hercules tore the rock into two pieces and placed them in their present positions.

Calydonian boar   *Greek*
A wild boar. This huge animal was sent by the goddess Artemis to ravage Calydon as punishment when the king, Oeneus, overlooked a sacrifice due to her. It was was killed by Meleager who was one of a large party of hunters and its skin was presented to Atalanta who had first wounded it.

Camaralzaman   *Persian*
A prince in the *Arabian Nights' Entertainment* story of *The Adventures of Prince Camaralzaman and Badoura.* In the story, neither Prince Camaralzaman nor Princess Badoura, daughter of the King of China, wish to marry anyone until they are shown to each other by jinns.

Cancer   *Greek*
A huge crab. When Hercules fought the Hydra, Hera sent this creature to help the monster. It snapped at Hercules' heels and paid with its life. The crab was placed in the heavens as the Crab constellation.

Cannibal Mother   *North American*
A man-eating monster. This demon appears in the lore of several tribes and is known as Baxbakualanuchsiwae or Tsonqua.

Cap of Hades *see* **Helmet of Invisibility**[1]

Capricorn   *Greek*
A goat. Some say that Amalthea, the goat that suckled Zeus as a child, was placed in the sky as the

constellation Capricorn. Others say that Capricorn was the god Pan.

Caradoc Briefbras   *British*
A Knight of the Round Table.

He never knew who his father was until he went to King Arthur's court to be knighted. There, an unknown knight challenged the assembly to a beheading contest which only Caradoc would accept. He decapitated the stranger who replaced his head and left. At the return match, a year later, the stranger spared Caradoc and revealed himself as his father, Eliaures.

Later a witch persuaded Eliaures, who was a magician, to cause a snake to attach itself to Caradoc's arm, sucking his blood. His friend Cador saved his life by putting his sister Guimer in a vat of milk and Caradoc in a vat of sour wine. This induced the snake to cross from one vat to the other, giving Cador the chance to kill it with his sword. Caradoc later married Guimer.

Carrefour   *West Indian*
also Maît'(re) Carrefour
A Haitian god of the night. He operates at night to open the gate that allows spirits to take possession of humans.

Cassandra   *Greek*
A princess of Troy, a prophetess; daughter of King Priam and his wife Hecuba.

She had been given the gift of prophecy by the god Apollo but when she rejected his love he decreed that her prophecies would never be believed, even when true.

Another story says that both she and her twin brother Helenus were given prophetic powers from being licked on the ears by serpents when they were young children.

She advised the Trojans not to take the wooden horse left by the Greeks into the city but, as usual, she was ignored.

At the fall of Troy she was raped by Ajax the Less at the altar of Athena's temple. She was given to Agamemnon as a prize of war and bore him two sons, Pelops and Teledamus. She returned with Agamemnon to Greece where she foretold bloodshed and was ignored as usual. She was killed by Clytemnestra and her lover Aegisthus, together with Agamemnon and her children. After her death she was deified.

Cassiopeia   *Greek*
A goddess of night; queen of Ethiopia; wife of Cepheus; mother of Andromeda.

She boasted that her daughter Andromeda was more beautiful than any goddess and was punished by a sea-serpent that devoured her people. Andromeda was offered as a propitiary sacrifice, chained to a rock in the sea. She was rescued by the hero Perseus who was returning with the severed head of Medusa and he turned Cassiopeia and Cepheus to stone by displaying it.

She and her husband were placed in the heavens by the sea god Poseidon.

Castle Carbonek   *British*
also Grail Castle
The home of King Pelles. This castle, said to be invisible to sinners, was built by Josephus (son of Joseph of Arimathea) and Evelake (king of Sarras) when they came to Britain bringing the Holy Grail, which was then housed in the castle.

In some stories, Carbonek was

in France, in others the castle was in England but called Corbin or Corby.

It was here that Lancelot was accorded a sight of the Holy Grail but was struck down and lay unconscious for many days.

Castle Eden   *British*
A village in County Durham, England. It is said that this was once the site of one of King Arthur's residences and was later haunted by his knights in the form of hens.

Castle of Light *see* **Palace of Light**

Castle of Wonders   *Welsh*
The home of Peredur's uncle. It was here that Peredur saw the Holy Grail. It is the equivalent of the Fortress of Marvels in the story of Percival.

Castle Terribil   *British*
A grim castle in Arthurian lore, besieged by King Royns of North Wales.

In other accounts, this was the castle in which Uther besieged Gorlois when he invaded Cornwall to seduce Igraine.

Castor   *Greek*
Patron of bards and sailors; son of Leda by Zeus or Tyndareus; brother of Helen and Polydeuces (Pollux).

Zeus visited Leda in the form of a swan and there are various versions of the parentage of her children, of whom Castor was one and the twin of Polydeuces.

Castor was a member of the party hunting the Calydonian boar, sailed with the Argonauts and taught Hercules fencing and tactics.

When his sister Helen was abducted by Peirithous, king of the Lapiths, and Theseus, he and

his brother raised an army to invade Aphidnae where she was kept and recovered her.

In a dispute over some stolen cattle or as the result of the abduction of Phoebe and Hilaeria, the brides of Idas and Lynceus, by Castor and his brother, he was waiting in ambush in a hollow tree when he was killed by a spear thrown by Idas. After his death, he and Polydeuces spent alternate periods on Olympus and in Hades so that they could always be together.

He was deified by Zeus and set in the heavens with Polydeuces as the Twins (Gemini), Castor and Pollux.

cat
Cats feature in many mythologies:
(1) In China the cat is said to ward off evil spirits.
(2) In Egypt the cat was sacred to Bast (a cat-goddess) and to Isis. Anybody who killed a cat was condemned to death.
(3) In Europe, a black cat is regarded as the familiar of witches and the Devil and was revered by the 13th-century Stadinghien heretics.

One story says that a cat can suck the breath from a sleeping child, causing it to die.
(4) In France the cat is regarded as a corn-spirit.
(5) Hindu stories have the cat as the steed ridden by the goddess Shastri.
(6) The Japanese regard the cat as an animal with supernatural powers which can control the dead.
(7) The Malaysians say that an evil spirit, which can take possession of humans, lives in the cat.

(8) In Norse mythology, the cat is regarded as a form of the Midgard serpent, Iormungandr.

Cavershall   *British*
A Staffordshire castle, one of the places said to have been the site of King Arthur's court.

Celestial Archer *see* **I**
Celestial Emperor *see* **Shang Ti**
Celestial Principle *see* **T'ien-li**

Centaur   *Greek*
A being part man, part horse. These beings were, some say, fathered by Ixion, king of the Lapiths, on Nephele (a likeness of the goddess Hera made of cloud), or by his son, Centaurus, on the horses known as the Magnesian mares.

They were permanently in conflict with the Lapiths, who were known as horse-tamers.

They are sometimes depicted pulling the chariot of the god Dionysus.

Centzon Totochtin   *Central American*
'Four Hundred Rabbits'
A group of Aztec gods of intoxication. The gods of intoxication were worshipped as rabbits, the number of which indicated the degree of drunkenness. The state of complete drunkenness was represented by four hundred rabbits. They were depicted with faces painted in red and black, wearing the yaca-metztli, a crescent-shaped nose ornament and long earrings and carrying a shield.

Cerberus   *Greek*
The dog guarding the gates to Hades.

This monster, which had three heads (lion, lynx and sow) and the tail of a dragon, dripped saliva

from its jaws and, where this fell to the ground, the poisonous plant aconite grew. Earlier stories give him as many as fifty or a hundred heads.

The dead were given a honey-cake to give to Cerberus when they arrived at the gates of Hades to ensure that they were allowed to enter unmolested.

Hercules captured the monster and carried it back to Mycenae as his twelfth and final Labour. It was later returned to Hades.

Ceres   *Roman*
= *Greek* Demeter
Goddess of agriculture and corn; daughter of Saturn and Ops; a consort of Jupiter; mother of Proserpina.

Cerne Abbas Giant   *British*
A huge figure cut into a chalk hillside in Dorset, England. The giant it represents is said to have been a Danish giant who was killed by the local people when he was asleep.

It has also been interpreted as portraying the Gaulish fertility god Cernunnos. Others again say it represents the Irish leader, the Dagda, or the Greek hero Hercules.

Ceryneian Hind   *Greek*
A golden-headed stag. This animal, with golden horns and bronze hooves, was the one that escaped when Artemis captured four others to draw her chariot. It was captured by Hercules as his third Labour.

Chac   *Central American*
= *Aztec* Tlaloc
The Mayan god of fertility and rain, depicted as having large curved fangs and a tapir-like nose.

Chac is sometimes manifest as one of the Bacabs, the four gods

supporting the world, one at each corner.

In later versions, there were many Chacs, minor rain gods under Chac himself. These were later downgraded to little men with beards, living in the sixth heaven, who were said to cause shooting stars when they tossed away their cigarette butts. They are said also to cause rain when they ride on horseback through the heavens, sprinkling water as they go.

Chacopee   *North American*
also White Feather
A Sioux giant-killer. His tribe had been killed by six giants and he was destined to become White Feather, the avenger. The Man of Wood (a being with a human head but a body carved from wood) gave him a pipe, the smoke from which turned into pigeons, an invisible vine and a white feather.

He ran a race against five of the giants on consecutive days and won by tripping his opponent with his vine, killing him as the loser. The sixth giant took the form of a maiden to deceive Chacopee and turned him into a dog, taking the white feather and wearing it in his hair. When the giant married a chief's daughter, her sister took the dog. At a meeting of her tribe to decide who was the real owner of the white feather, Chacopee alone could produce flocks of pigeons when he smoked the pipe, so proving his right. He then resumed his human shape while the giant was turned into a dog and killed.

Chair of Forgetfulness   *Greek*
A seat in the underworld. Souls

newly-arrived in the underworld were seated in this chair to make them forget all about their earlier existence.

Theseus and Peirithous were trapped in the chair and, although Hercules managed to rescue Theseus, Peirithous was doomed forever.

Chalmecaciuatl   *Central American*
A paradise for dead children.
A tree growing in this place provided milk to nourish the inhabitants.

In some accounts it was the home of Tlaloc and was called Tlalocan.

Chameleon   *African*
The animal which discovered mankind.

Chameleon found a man and a woman in his fish-trap and, not recognising this new species, showed them to the god Mukungu, who decreed that they should be allowed to live and be placed on earth. The people, at that time immortal, multiplied and the gods, who at that time lived on earth, retreated to the heavens, giving Chameleon a message to take to the people – they would die but return to life. They gave the lizard a different message – men would die and not return. Lizard arrived first with his message and so people became mortal.

Chamer   *Central American*
The Mayan god of death. He is depicted as a white-robed skeleton with a scythe.

Chamiabak   *Central American*
In Mayan lore, one of the rulers of Xibalba, the underworld.

Chamiaholom   *Central American*
In Mayan lore, one of the rulers of Xibalba, the underworld.

Chang Kuo-lao   *Chinese*
A 7th- to 8th-century itinerant ascetic, one of the Eight Immortals.

He was said to have the power to make himself invisible and travelled riding backwards on a white mule which he could fold up and put in his pocket, restoring it to its normal form by sprinkling it with water.

He was called to the emperor's court but dropped dead en route, only to be restored to life.

When his identity as a white bat was disclosed by a man named Fa-shan, the latter dropped dead but was restored to life when Chang Kuo-lao sprinkled the body with water.

Ch'ang-sheng-t'u Ti   *Chinese*
also God of the Place of Long Life
A god of the household, responsible for the register of births and deaths of the family.

Chang Tao-ling   *Chinese*
A Taoist immortal, founder of a magical form of Taoism; a god of the afterlife.

He is said to have become immortal by conquering five poisonous animals (centipede, scorpion, snake, spider and toad) and drinking the elixir which he brewed from their venom when he was already over 60 years old and he ascended to heaven at the age of 123.

He made exorbitant charges for advising people to cure illness while immersed in a lake and he became known as the Rice Thief.

It was said that he could divide himself into parts so as to be present in several places at the same time. On one occasion, he stretched his arms to some 30 feet to rescue a disciple stranded

on a ledge on a cliff-face.

He was said to control all the Taoist demons and spirits and owned a sword that could kill demons thousands of miles away.

He is depicted riding a tiger.

Changing Woman   *North American*
A female deity of the Apache and Navaho; the moon; wife of the sun; mother of Child-of-the-Water and Killer-of-Enemies. She was said to be able to change from woman to baby to old woman at will.

In some accounts, she is the same as Turquoise Woman, while others say that both Estanatlehi (Turquoise Woman) and Yolkai Estsan (White Shell Woman) were created by Changing Woman from flakes of dry skin from under her breasts.

Chantico[1]   *Central American*
An Aztec goddess of the hearth and volcanoes.

Chantico[2]   *South American*
An Inca goddess of the household. She was said to be made of gold and wore a crown of poisonous cactus.

ch'ao ching   *Chinese*
Lion-like dragons.

ch'ao feng   *Chinese*
A dragon said to love danger.

Chaob   *Central American*
The four Mayan wind gods. One god controls the winds from each of the cardinal points and it is said that they will eventually cause storms that will destroy the world.

Chaonia *see* **Dodona**

Chaos Goose *see* **Nile Goose**

Chaos Mother *see* **Tiamat**

chariot
A two-wheeled vehicle for personal transport, usually horse-drawn, appearing in many

mythologies as the transport of the gods.

In Greek and Roman stories, chariots of the gods were drawn by various animals and birds:

Amphitrite – dolphins and sea-horses

Aphrodite – doves, sparrows or swans

Apollo – horses

Ares – horses or wolves

Artemis – deer

Athene – owls

Ceres – serpents

Cronus – elephants

Cybele – lions

Demeter – serpents

Dionysus – leopards, lynx or tigers

Helios – horses

Hephaestus – dogs

Hera – peacocks

Hermes – lizards, rams or storks

Medea – dragons

Oceanus – whales

Pan – goats

Pluto – horses

Poseidon – dolphins or sea-horses

Zeus – eagles

In Norse myths, Frey's chariot was drawn by boars, Freya's by cocks, and Thor's by goats.

Charon *Greek*
The ferryman of Hades. He conveys the dead over the River Acheron (and/or the Styx) to Hades but will carry only those with the fare of one obol placed on their lips. Those without the fare have to wait a hundred years but are then carried across free of charge.

Charon's toll *Greek*
The obol placed on the lips of the dead to pay for their ferry journey across the river to Hades.

Charun *Roman*
= *Greek* Charon
An Etruscan god of death. He was said to accompany Mars in battle and to finish off the dying with a blow from his hammer.

Charybdis *Greek*
A sea-nymph; daughter of Poseidon and Gaea.

She was a monster under a rock, the 'sea-swallower', a whirlpool set opposite the rock Scylla, which swallowed and regurgitated the sea three times each day.

Some say that she was originally a maiden who was thrown into the sea by Zeus for robbing Hercules.

Cheeroonar *Australian*
A monster with the body of a man and the head of a dog.

This being, which had arms so long that they trailed on the ground as he walked, hunted and killed humans for food, accompanied by his wife and a pack of six huge dogs. All of them were killed by tribesmen he had preyed on when they sought the help of the Winjarning Brothers.

Chemosh *Mesopotamian*
A Moabite war god and thunder god. He is mentioned several times in the Bible.

Chemosit *see* **Nandi Bear**

Chernobog *Slav*
The force of evil opposing Bylebog.

cherry
(1) In Greek mythology, the tree of Apollo.
(2) In Japan, the cherry tree is believed to have an individual spirit.

Chi Kung *Chinese*
A 12th-century monk; one of the Eighteen Lohan.

He was somewhat eccentric and was often known as the Mad Healer, using magic to cure sickness, etc.

ch'i-lin *Chinese*
also kylin;
= *Japanese* kirin; *Tibetan* serou
A monster, part deer, part fox, with a single horn; one of the Four Auspicious Animals; chief of the hairy animals; ruler of the west and autumn.

This animal was the symbol of Kao-yao, judge in the underworld. It was said to have appeared out of the Yellow River at the birth of Confucius but has never been seen since mankind became corrupt. It is said to display five colours (black, blue, red, white and yellow) and has a voice that sounds like chiming bells. In some accounts, it has a scaly body and two backward-curving horns and may live up to 1000 years.

In some accounts, as a dragon-horse, it is described as a water-spirit which can walk on water. Others regard it as a white tiger. The male is ch'i, the female lin.

Chicchan *Central American*
Mayan rain gods. These four deities, envisaged as giant reptiles, live in deep lakes, one at each cardinal point. They cause clouds to form from which other gods cause rain to fall.

Chicomoztoc *Central American*
also Cavern of Seven Chambers
The refuge from which the Aztec people emerged.

Chicuauhmictlan *Central American*
The last of the nine regions of the Aztec underworld, Mictlan.

Some say that the soul must spend four years in the other regions of Mictlan before reaching this final resting place.

Chicunauhapan   *Central American*
One of the nine rivers of the Aztec
underworld, Mictlan.
  When a man died, his dog
was killed and buried with him.
This animal was said to carry his
master's soul across the rivers of
the underworld.

Child of the Water *North American*
A culture-hero of the Apache and
Navaho tribes; son of Changing
Woman; brother of Killer of
Enemies. He and his brother
killed monsters and all mankind's
enemies. He was able to get
close enough to monsters to be
able to kill them by wearing a
cloak of invisibility given to him
by Lizard. One of the monsters
he killed was a giant, a huge
being covered with four layers
of rock.

Childe Rowland *see* **Roland**[1]
Children of Dana *see* **Danaans**
Children of Lir   *Irish*
The four children of the sea god
Lir by his first wife, Aobh. After
her death, he married her sister
Aoife who resolved to kill the
children and turned them into
swans, condemned to spend three
successive periods, each of 300
years, on a lake, the sea-passage
between Ireland and Scotland and
the Atlantic Ocean. They survived
the ordeal and returned at the
end of their sentence to find
their father. They were sheltered
by a Christian hermit, Mo-
Caemoc, until they were seized by
Lairgnen, king of Connaught, as a
present for his bride Deoca. Then
their feathers fell off and they
appeared as old, wrinkled humans
who, after a hurried baptism by
the hermit, died and were buried
in one grave.
  The three boys were Aedh, Conn
and Fiachra, and their sister was
Fionuala.

Children of the Sun   *South
American*
Ancestors of the Incas; sons and
daughters of the sun god Inti.
  In the beginning, human
beings were confined to the
underworld and emerged from
the cave Pacari which had three
exits. The Inca royalty emerged,
wonderfully garbed, from the
central opening, the common
people from the other two.
  Various names are given for
the royal personages, children of
Inti. Some say there were four
men (Ayar Manco, Pachocamac,
Viracocha and one other) and four
females, though some give the
four men as Ayar Ayca, Ayar Cachi,
Ayar Manco and Ayar Oco. Others
name these eight as the brothers
Cusco Huanca, Huana Cauri, Manco
Capac and Topa Ayar Cachi with
their sisters Cori Ocllo, Ipa Huaco,
Mama Coya and Topa Huaco. In
some versions there are only three
males (Ayar Cachi Asauca, Ayar
Manco and Ayar Ucho) and three
females (Mama Coya, Mama Huaco
and Mama Rahua).
  There are equally varied
accounts of what happened to
these people but at least one of
them was turned into stone and
another was sealed in a cave. The
chief character, Ayar Manco, is
said to have founded the capital
city of Cuzco and married his
sister, Mama Ocllo, founding the
Inca royal dynasty.

Chimaera   *Greek*
A fire-breathing monster, part lion,
part goat, with a serpent's tail.

Chin Lung   *Chinese*
also Golden Dragon
One of the Four Dragon Kings.

Ch'in-shih Huang Ti *see* **Huang
  Ti**
Ch'ing Lung   *Chinese*
also Azure Dragon
One of the Four Auspicious
Animals, head of the scaly
animals. Guardian of the east,
controller of spring rain.

Chinigchinich   *North American*
A supreme deity of the tribes of
California. He created the first
man, Ouiot.
  At the funeral of Ouiot, the
trickster Coyote snatched a piece
of the body and ran off. Some of
the skin fell on the ground and
here Chinigchinich appeared
to the medicine-men and gave
them supernatural powers for
the benefit of the men he then
created from clay. These beings
replaced the earlier race created
by Ouiot, all of whom were
turned by Chinigchinich into
animals, birds and plants.

Chiron   *Greek*
The king of the Centaurs.
  His parentage was different from
that of the other Centaurs, as was
his disposition. He was physically
like them because the god Cronus
had adopted the form of a horse
when fathering him on Philyra,
but he was a wise Centaur who
cared for and tutored a number of
Greek heroes, including Achilles,
Asclepius, Hercules and Jason.
  He was inadvertently shot
by Hercules whose poisoned
arrows were invariably fatal to
mortals. An alternative story says
that when the Centaur Pholus
entertained Hercules in his cave
and they were attacked by other
Centaurs, one of them, Elatus,
was wounded by one of the
poisoned arrows fired by Hercules
and Chiron was accidentally

wounded in the knee when he withdrew this arrow. Chiron, not a mortal, could not die though suffering great agony. Later on, Prometheus assumed the burden of immortality to allow Chiron to die, when he was placed in the heavens as Centaurus.

He is sometimes depicted as having human rather than equine forelegs.

chough   *British*
The bird in which King Arthur's soul is said to reside. Other accounts say it is the puffin or the raven.

Chronos   *Greek*
'Time', one of two primeval deities present at the beginning of the world.

Chryseis   *Greek*
also Cressida
Daughter of Chryses, a priest of Apollo at Troy.

When she was captured at Troy, she was given as a prize to King Agamemnon. Her father pleaded for her release but Agamemnon refused to release her until a plague descended on the Greek army. He then demanded the girl Briseis who had been awarded to Achilles, so starting a quarrel that led to Achilles refusing to fight.

In some accounts, she bore a son, also named Chryses, to Agamemnon but said the boy's father was Apollo.

Chu Pa-chieh   *Chinese*
also Pig Fairy, Pigsy
A pig-like god. He controlled movement in the Milky Way, which was regarded as a river, but was banished to earth as a pig when he upset the Jade Emperor after getting drunk.

He became a devotee of Buddha when he met the goddess Kuan Yin and went to India with

Hsüan Tsang when he made the long journey to bring the Buddhist scriptures to China.

Chuan Hsü   *Chinese*
One of the Five Emperors.

The world was in a chaotic state when he came to the throne as the second of the Five Emperors and he set about putting matters right, giving his son Chung authority over the celestial realm and his other son Li over mortals.

In some accounts, he is equated with Shun, the fifth emperor, while in others Chung and Li are his grandsons.

Chukwa   *Hindu*
The tortoise supporting the elephant, Mahapadma, which supports the earth.

Churning of the Ocean   *Hindu*
also Churning of the Sea of Milk
The making of amrita.

The gods and demons coiled the World Serpent, Ananta or Vasuki, round Mount Mandara and, by pulling on each end for 1000 years, caused the Churning of the Ocean. This operation brought up fourteen things which had been lost by the early Vedic tribes in the Flood. These were:

Airavata, the god Indra's elephant;

Amrita, the drink of the gods;
Chandra (Soma), the moon god;
Dhanvantari, the Divine Doctor;
Dhanus, the magic bow;
Kaustubha, the god Vishnu's ruby;
Lakshmi, the goddess of beauty;
Parijata, the tree of knowledge;
Rambha, a nymph;
Sankha, the horn of victory;
Surabhi, the cow of plenty;
Uccaihsravas, the magic horse;
Varuni (Sura), the goddess of wine;

Visha, poison.

In other accounts, a pair of earrings, given by Indra to his mother Adita, were recovered; Kamadhenu (a sacred cow) is referred to in place of Surabhi; the Apsarases (nymphs) emerged; the jewel, Chinta-mani (an alternative to Kaustubha, perhaps) was produced.

Cihuacoatl   *Central American*
also Serpent Woman, Snake Woman
An Aztec mother-goddess, goddess of childbirth.

She is described as a snake-woman and sometimes divided herself into separate divinities such as Coatlicue, Ilamatecuhtli, Itzpapalotl, Temazcalteci and Tonantzin.

In some aspects, she was a malevolent being, preaching doom, but in a more beneficent role she is credited with the invention of the hoe.

She is depicted with a face half red, half black, and wearing a feathered headdress.

Cihuacoatl-Quilaztli   *Central American*
An Aztec creator-goddess, who made human beings from bones ground to powder and mixed with the blood of the gods.

Cihuateteo   *Central American*
also Honoured Women
In Aztec lore, spirits of women who died in childbirth. These spirits are said to live in Tamoanchan (part of the underworld) and, in some accounts, are equated with the Tzitzimime (malevolent star-spirits).

It is said that they can appear in the form either of women or of eagles.

They were depicted with white faces with golden eyebrows and arms whitened with a powder called tisatl.

Cimeries *European*
A demon, a marquis of hell; one of the 72 Spirits of Solomon. He is depicted astride a black horse and is said to teach literature.

Cin-an-ev *North American*
A culture-hero of the Ute tribe; a wolf-trickster.

Circe *Greek*
A goddess or sorceress.

She killed her husband and was exiled to the island of Aeaea. She fell in love with the fisherman Glaucus but he preferred the nymph Scylla. Circe then changed Scylla into a monster.

She turned all men who approached her into animals and some of the crew of Odysseus' ship were turned into pigs but she fell in love with Odysseus himself and returned his men to their former selves. Some say that her three sons were fathered by Odysseus, although the parentage of one son, Latinus, is disputed.

When Picus rejected her love, she turned him into a woodpecker.

She purified Jason and Medea of the murder of Apsyrtus.

Circe's grass *Greek*
The plant (mandrake) which, it is said, Circe used to change men into animals.

Cist Arthur *British*
A burial chamber in Wales, said to be the grave of King Arthur.

Cithaeronian lion *Greek*
also Thespian lion
A lion killed by Hercules at the age of eighteen. Hercules wore the skin thereafter as a cloak (but some say that this was the pelt of the Nemean lion).

In some versions, the Cithaeronian lion was killed by Alcathous, the Nemean lion by Hercules.

Cizin *Central American*
A Mayan god of death. He is said to burn the souls of the dead in Metnal, the home of the dead, and, in some accounts, is equated with Ah Puch.

He is depicted as fleshless in parts, painted black and yellow.

Clashing Rocks *see* **Planctae, Symplegades**

Clay Mother *North American*
A tutelary spirit of the Pueblo tribes. This spirit gave her flesh (clay) to the potters so that they could make utensils for her people.

Clear Sky *North American*
She quarrelled with her husband Kulshan's second wife, Fair Maiden, and left to set up her own house far to the south. She was later turned into the mountain now known as Mount Rainier.

Clio *Greek*
One of the nine Muses, the Muse of heroic poetry and history.

When she laughed at the goddess Aphrodite for loving the mortal Adonis, the goddess caused her to fall in love with Pierus by whom, in some stories, she bore Hyacinthus.

Cloacina *Roman*
Goddess of sewers; a name for Venus as 'purifier'.

Cloak of Invisibility *German*
A magic cloak owned by Siegfried which rendered the wearer invisible.

Closed Man *North American*
The first man, in the lore of the Pawnees. He was given sacred bundles which contained all the varieties of grain.

Clotho *Greek*
One of the three Moirae (Fates), the spinner of the thread of life.

Cloud-carrier *North American*
An Algonquin youth who was taken into the heavens by the Star-maiden, Nemissa, and married her. Despite the pleasures of the land of the Star-people, he came to long for his own country and was allowed to return on the condition that he did no marry one of his own kind. He soon forgot this condition and married an earthly maiden but she died a few days later. When he married again, he disappeared from the earth, called by Nemissa, and never returned.

Cloud People *see* **Shiwanna**
Cloud Serpent *see* **Mixcoatl**

club *Greek*
(1) In Greek mythology, the weapon of Hercules.
(2) In Hindu mythology, the weapon of Yama.

Clytemnestra *Greek*
A dawn goddess; wife of King Agamemnon; mother of Chrysothemis, Electra, Iphigenia, and Orestes. In some versions, she is Leda's daughter by Zeus who, in the form of a swan, seduced Leda.

She was originally the wife of Tantalus, king of Pisa, but when Agamemnon defeated him he took over his wife Clytemnestra.

While Agamemnon was away at Troy, she was seduced by Aegisthus who was seeking revenge for Agamemnon's murder of his brother, Tantalus, and when Agamemnon returned bringing with him the Trojan princess Cassandra and the twin boys she had borne to him, the two lovers killed all four of them. Agamemnon was trapped in the bath where Aegisthus attacked him with a sword and Clytemnestra cut off his head with an axe. When Orestes later returned to avenge his father's death, he killed Aegisthus and cut off Clytemnestra's head.

Another version of the story says that Clytemnestra killed Agamemnon to avenge the death of their daughter Iphigenia who had been sacrificed by Agamemnon to ensure favourable winds on their voyage to attack Troy.

Coatlicue   *Central American*
also Robe of Serpents, Serpent Skirt
The Aztec earth goddess, moon goddess, mother-goddess, earth-serpent.

She was impregnated with a ball of down or feathers that fell on to her lap and her 400 (or 4000) children planned to kill her to prevent the birth but her son, Huitzilopochtli (Quetzalcoatl, in some accounts), was born fully armed and killed many of the rebellious children.

Another version of this story tells of a widow, La, who is similarly made pregnant and saved by her son, Huitzilopochtli.

Coatlicue is represented as a terrible deity with snakes round her waist, human hearts as a necklace and with claws on hands and feet, who eats the bodies of the dead.

cock
A bird domesticated in many countries and, in many cases, regarded as sacred:
(1) In China, the cock is regarded as a divine bird which carries the sun through part of the zodiac. Some say it could become a human being while others say that it drives away ghosts when it crows at dawn. A picture of a cock, pasted on a coffin, is said to drive away demons.
(2) In Germany the bird is regarded as a weather prophet.
(3) In Greek lore, the cock is the bird of Apollo and Athene and was sacrificed to Asclepius, the god of healing, in recognition of recovery from illness.
(4) In Japan the cock is said to prepare the heart for worship.
(5) The Norse regard the cock as a guardian. In the realm of Midgard, the cock Gullinkambi lived on the tree Yggdrasil. In Valhalla, Fialar's duty was to waken the warriors for the final battle.
(6) The Romans consulted the cock as an augury, particularly on the weather.
(7) An old Scottish custom involved the sacrifice of a cock as a cure for epilepsy.

coco macaque   *West Indies*
A stick that walks by itself. In Haiti they say that such a stick can be sent off on its own to do errands and can also be used to attack enemies. Any person struck by such a stick soon dies.

Coel   *British*
also (Old) King Cole
A duke of Colchester and a king of Britain. He was said to have overthrown the king Asclepiodotus, and died a month later. Some say that he was an ancestor of King Arthur.

Coetan Arthur   *British*
A barrow in Wales where, it is said, King Arthur lies buried.

Colchian Dragon   *Greek*
The dragon which guarded the Golden Fleece at Colchis.

Companions of the Day   *Central American*
Thirteen Aztec deities, each responsible for one hour of the day.

Companions of the Night *Central American*
Nine Aztec deities, each responsible for one hour of the night.

Con   *South American*
A boneless Inca creator-god; son of the sun god Inti.

He could raise mountains and he created a race of people who so annoyed him that he turned their fruitful land into desert. He was superseded by his brother Pachacamac who turned the people made by Con into monkeys.

Concordia   *Roman*
A goddess of civic agreement, one of the five Appiades.

Consentes Dii   *Roman*
The twelve major deities in the Roman pantheon, six male, six female.

These deities are sometimes listed as Apollo, Jupiter, Mars, Mercury, Neptune and Vulcan with Ceres, Diana, Juno, Minerva, Venus and Vesta. They acted as advisers to Jupiter.

Copper Woman   *North American*
The first human. The tribes of the northwest tell of a woman alone in the world longing for a companion. On the instruction of a spirit, she collected her tears and fluid from her nose (and, some say, her menstrual blood) in a shell. This became a strange being, part crab, part man who put an end to Copper Woman's loneliness.

coral
This substance is often regarded as having the power to protect the

wearer from harm and, if carved into the shape of a serpent, will guard against venomous bites. Among other beliefs are the following:

(1) In China, coral is said to confer longevity on the wearer.

(2) The Egyptians scattered coral over the fields to ensure good harvests.

(3) The Gauls used coral as a talisman to protect their warriors.

(4) In Greece, coral was said to have been formed from the blood of the Gorgon Medusa.

(5) In India, coral is used to protect the dead from evil spirits.

(6) The Italians say that coral is effective in countering the evil eye.

(7) Russians give coral bracelets to new babies as a form of protection.

Core   *Greek*

also Persephone, the Maiden, the Mistress;

= *Roman* Proserpina

A vegetation goddess who became queen of the underworld.

The usual story is that Core was the daughter of Zeus and his sister Demeter. In some stories, Persephone is the daughter of Zeus by Rhea, both as serpents. Then Zeus mated with Core to produce Dionysus, the god of vegetation and wine. In other stories she is the daughter of Zeus by the nymph Styx and in others again Styx is the wife of Hades. Yet another version says that she resulted from the coupling of Poseidon and Demeter, both as horses.

Core was abducted and taken to the underworld by Hades. Demeter learned where her

missing daughter was to be found from the burbling of the nymph Arethusa who, in the form of a spring, had passed through the underworld en route to Sicily and had seen Core at the side of Hades.

When Demeter blighted the earth to secure her daughter's release, Zeus ordered that she should be returned provided that she had not eaten any of the food of the dead. Core said she had eaten nothing but Ascalaphus, a gardener in Hades, said he had seen her eating the seeds of the pomegranate. She was condemned to spend a quarter (or half, in some versions) of each year with Hades as Persephone.

As Persephone she was put in charge of the infant Dionysus when Hera reassembled him after he had been torn to pieces by the Titans and she raised the infant Adonis who was put in her care by Aphrodite and made him her lover.

She is depicted, as Persephone, holding a torch and a pomegranate.

Corn *see* **Deohako**

Corn Girl   *North American*

A Navaho deity. She was placed by the creators Atse Estsan and Atse Hastin on top of Mount Taylor together with Turquoise Boy.

Corn Maidens *see* **Ten Corn Maidens**

Corn Mother   *North American*

also Corn Woman

A goddess of vegetation. She released the maize which was planted by animals to produce the human race.

Other versions say that she made corn dishes from bodily sores scraped off and boiled in

a pot or told the tribes how to plant such scrapings to produce corn. Some say that corn grew when the tribes killed her and buried her body.

cornucopia   *Greek*

also Horn of Plenty

A horn always full of food and drink. Either the horn of the goat Amalthea who fed the infant Zeus or the horn broken by Hercules from the head of the river god Achelous who had taken the form of a bull to fight Hercules for the hand of Deianeira, who became Hercules' second wife.

corrigan   *French*

also korrigan(ed)

A fairy in Brittany, said to steal children.

Some say that they were former druids, while others describe the corrigan as a dwarf, about two feet tall, who can assume the form of a horse or a goat at will.

Corrigans dress in white veils and their breath is said to be fatal to human beings.

Cottontail   *North American*

A god of the tribes of the Great Basin. He is equivalent to Rabbit or Great Hare in other tribal myths. He was said to have stolen the sun to bring light to his people.

Count of the Winds *see* **Feng Po**

cow

(1) In Egyptian mythology, the animal sacred to Hathor, Nut and Isis.

(2) In Greek mythology, the cow is sacred to Hera.

(3) The cow is a sacred animal in Hinduism.

(4) In Irish mythology, the cow was sacred to Brigit.

Coyote   *North American*
A trickster-god and messenger of
the gods.

Some tribes say that he was
created from a mist. He helped
the creator-god Kodo-yanpe
make the world fit for human
beings and then made humans
from wooden images. The two
creators later quarrelled and
fought for a long time before
Coyote finally won.

To punish a giant who had
eaten children, Coyote tricked the
giant into believing that he could
break a leg and then mend it. The
giant agreed that Coyote could
perform the same trick on his leg,
whereupon Coyote smashed his
leg with a rock and left the giant
helpless.

At the funeral of Ouiot, the
first human, he snatched a piece
of flesh from the corpse and fled.
Thereafter, he was known as Eno
(the thief).

He once gave his blanket to the
magic rock, Iya, but snatched it
back as soon as he began to feel
the cold. The rock chased him,
knocked him down and flattened
him by rolling right over him.

Another story tells how he
went to the Spirit World to rescue
his sister who had died. There
he killed the frog who held the
moon-lantern and dressed himself
in the frog's skin. He doused the
lamp and was able to capture all
the spirits and put them in a sack
but he grew tired of their weight
and released them, so death still
persists.

Yet another story tells how
Coyote married a woman with
teeth in her vagina with which
she had killed many lovers. He
broke the teeth off with a metal
chisel and was safe. Her father
tried several times to kill his
son-in-law but was unsuccessful.
Coyote carved the wooden image
of a whale and threw it into the
water when he was in a canoe
with his father-in-law. The model
turned into a killer whale which
snatched the girl's father from
the canoe and ate him.

His ability as a shape-changer
is illustrated in a story in which,
to save himself after falling into
a river, he changed into a board
which was swept down the
river to a dam where a woman
retrieved it to use as a serving-
dish. She was startled when the
salmon she placed on the board
quickly disappeared, eaten by
Coyote, and she threw the board
into the fire. Coyote then changed
into a baby which the woman
saved and reared as her own.
When he grew older, he broke
down the dam to allow salmon to
go upriver to the home of his own
people but brought a plague of
insects on them when he opened
four boxes in the woman's barn
which she had told him never to
touch.

Another story relates how,
when he was starving, Woodtick
brought him some deer meat. He
went to live with her and she kept
him well supplied with meat by
calling the deer to her tent where
she pierced the ears of two and
let the others return to the wild.
Coyote thought he could do this
himself so he killed (or, some say,
expelled) Woodtick. When he
tried to do what she had done,
he failed and all the meat he had
turned into deer and ran off so
that Coyote was soon starving
again.

His own son was killed by a
snakebite but did not return to
life as expected when immersed
in a lake. Some say that Coyote
killed himself so that he might
roam free as a spirit.

The Navaho and a few other
tribes maintain that they sprang
from the excrement of Coyote
whereas all other tribes descended
from the union of Coyote and a
louse.

Coyote and Badger met the
Navaho during their ascent from
the underworld. He seized two
of the children of the monster,
Tlieholtsodi, and the monster
caused a flood which forced the
Navaho to abandon the world
they were living in at the time
and go up, through a hole made
by Badger, into the upper world.
(*See also* **Sedit**.)

Craig-y-Dinas   *British*
A site in Wales of a cave where,
some say, King Arthur and his
knights lie sleeping
For other suggested sites, *see*
Alderley Edge.

creation
Each culture has its own version of
the creation of the universe, some
of them more than one:
African
(1) In the beginning it was always
warm and bright. The creator put
the bat in charge of darkness but
he allowed it to escape. Earth was
originally linked to heaven, in
some stories by a tree, in others
by a spider's web.
(2) The Abulayia people of Kenya
say that the creator-god Wele
first made heaven which he
propped up on posts. When he
made the sun and moon they
fought until Wele separated

them into day and night. He next created the features of the atmosphere and then the earth, followed by humans and animals. All this was done in six days.

(3) The Bakongo say that Nzambi created the first man and woman, whose children were mortal because they failed to obey his instructions not to bury those that died. In another version, he created an androgynous being, Mahungu, in the form of a tree with two heads. When Mahungu tried to embrace a tree called Muti Mpungu, Mahungu was split into male, Lumbu, and female, Muzita.

(4) The Bakuba say that there was only water, ruled by the White Giant, Mbombo. From his stomach he brought up the sun, moon and stars and, later, men and women and all the other things in the world.

(5) The Bambara say that the creation-principle, Pemba, came to earth as a seed and became a tree from which came a female being with which he mated to create all the other things on earth.

(6) The Bushmen say the world was created by a god in the form of a mantis.

(7) The Dogon say that the god Amma made the sun and moon from clay pots bound with wire, black people from sunlight and white people from moonlight. He made the earth from clay and fertilised it to produce, first, two half-human beings called Nummo, and again to make all the other things.

(8) The Fon people of west Africa say that the androgynous deity Mawu-Lisa created the world from the primeval chaos and then made plants, animals and mankind from clay and water. On day two the world was made a fit home for man who was given the power of understanding and his physical senses on the third day. On the fourth and final day of creation man was given knowledge of the skills he needed in order to advance.

Another version says that the primordial goddess, Nana Buluku, created the earth and then retired, leaving the world to her children, Mawu and Lisa.

In some accounts, the first created thing was the python, Dan Ayido Hwedo, from whose excrement Mawu made the mountains.

(9) The Kono of Sierra Leone speak of one creator-god, Alatangana, above the primeval waters and another, Sa, living in the waters. The former made solid land and ran off with Sa's daughter, producing seven black and seven white children, ancestors of the human races.

(10) The Mande say that God created seeds and planted them in the corners of the world. From them came the creator-god Pemba and Faro, his twin, who became a fish, part of which became the trees, the remainder producing a new Faro who came down from heaven in a ship with eight others. Faro made the Niger, containing seed for future generations, from his own body.

(11) The Nandi say that the god Asis created first the world order, Kiet, and then the sky and the earth, some of which he took to make man and woman.

(12) The Swahili say that a self-created god first made light and then used that light to make souls. Next he made the sky, the Canopy or Arishi; the throne Kurusi on which he sits in judgement; the Luah, the tablet on which all events are recorded by the angel Kalamu; the Trumpet of the Last Day; paradise; hell; and, beneath the throne, the Lotus Tree of the End, on each leaf of which is recorded an individual life which ends when that leaf falls. Then he made the sun, moon, and stars and the earth, together with all the things in it. A great cock in heaven announces each new day. The earth itself is saucer-shaped and is supported on the four horns of a bull or cow standing on the back of a fish swimming in an unfathomable ocean.

(13) The Yoruba say that, in the beginning, Olorun ruled the sky and his brother Olokun ruled the primitive waters. Olorun sent his son, Obatala, to place a huge sphere in the sea and when this broke into the various land masses he sent his daughter Oduduwa to sow seeds.

Another version says that the earth was created by Orishanla or Olorun who scattered soil on the marshy terrain and a hen and a pigeon scattered the soil about to form dry land.

(14) The Zulu say that the Great One appeared out of the earth with the moon and sun, which he placed in the sky, and then created not only the black people but the whites as well. He sent Unwaba, the chameleon, to tell mankind that they would never die and later sent Intulo, the lizard, to tell them the opposite.

The lizard ran faster than the chameleon and delivered its message first, so all races are now mortal.

Australian

(1) The stories of the Aborigines start with the Dreamtime, the alchera, a period of indeterminate length, when the earth already existed but was unformed and unpopulated. Various beings, some human, some spirits, slept in or under the earth in this period and later woke, performed their preordained duties and returned whence they had come. Stories vary from tribe to tribe but it is commonly held that these ancestral beings created men by singing and, when they returned to their original home, left behind songlines which form a means of communication between the Aborigines.

(2) One such being was the kangaroo-man, Minawara, who appeared with his brother Multultu when the primordial waters subsided and together they created all living things.

(3) Another pair of beings, the lizard-men known as Wati-kutjara, awoke to create rocks, plants and animals. Strangely enough, the story implies that humans already existed because they found the moon-spirit, Kidilli, chasing a group of women. They killed Kidilli, who became the moon. The women became the Pleiades and the twins, Wati-kutjara, became Gemini.

(4) Two other beings, the Bagadjimbiri, rose from the earth in the form of dingos and mated a toadstool with a fungus to produce the first humans. The brothers were killed by the cat-man, Ngariman,

but were restored by the goddess Dilga. When they finally died, they became water-snakes.

(5) A different story says that the woman Imberombera mated with Wuraka. She immediately gave birth to all living things and her consort gave them names.

(6) Some say that the earth was shaped by the rain-spirits, the Wandjina, who later caused the flood.

(7) One story has three beings known as the Djanggawuls arriving from the island of the dead and creating plant life and shaping the earth with magic rods known as rangga.

(8) In the south-east of the country they tell of Ngurunderi, a creator spirit, who caught a large cod, at that time a land animal. He cut it into pieces, gave them names and threw them into the sea where they became the first fish.

(9) In the lore of the Bathurst and Melville Islands to the north of Australia, the blind ancestral heroine, Mudungkala, emerged from the earth with three children who became the ancestors of the islanders.

Basque

A huge, seven-headed serpent under the earth moved, throwing up the Pyrenees and then opened its jaws to pour out fire which cleansed the world and from which the Basque people emerged.

Buddhist

The authors and mechanism of creation are not addressed but the structure of the universe is given as consisting of several distinct regions, each occupied by a different class of being or existence. In ascending order

they are Kama Loka (desires), Rupa Loka (material form) and Arupa Loka (spirit). The Tibetans envisage a further layer occupied by the Dhyanibuddhas, the highest part of which is the home of Adi Buddha. Nirmanarati the home of the gods of creation, Paranirmita-Vasavartin the home of Mara, Trayastrinska the home of Indra, and Tushita the home of the bodhisattvas, are four of the six parts of Kama Loka; the other parts are occupied by the guardians of the four cardinal points and by Yama's realm, the kingdom of the dead. Below these come the realms of humans, the Asuras, the animals and ghosts and, at the lowest level of all, several hells.

Cambodian

(1) In the beginning there was a holy state of nothingness from which appeared the holy jewel, Prah Keo, from which arose the earth, Prah Thorni, and all that is in it. Man was created from the earth and woman from man's shadow.

(2) An alternative version says that everything arose from the original unformed uncreated state known as Prah Prohm. There are three worlds, disc-shaped, each some ten million miles in diameter and surrounded by enormously high mountains.

Central American

(1) A monster with many mouths swam in the primeval waters. The gods split the monster into two parts, making heaven and earth. The earth was supported by four crocodiles swimming in the primeval waters. One ladder lead from the centre up to heaven, another down to hell. The

supreme god was on the top rung of the ladder to heaven. The lower ladder was the road to rebirth before which ordinary mortals stayed in the paradise of the rain god Tlaloc. For initiates, there was a higher heaven and an even higher one, the House of the Sun, for the fully enlightened who were rewarded with eternal life and happiness.

(2) Heaven was supported on four pillars. The Sun sprang first from Earth, then Air, Fire and Water and, in its fifth and present form, from all four elements combined.

(3) In Mayan lore, humans were first created by the gods Gucumatz and Tepeu (or Hurakan) from soil. These proved to be unsatisfactory so the gods destroyed them and carved the next race from wood. These beings were attacked by their own tools or a flock of huge birds and turned into monkeys. Next a race of giants, led by Vucub-Caquix, was defeated by the twin gods Hanapu and Ixbalanqué and finally the present race evolved from maize planted by animals, or, in some versions, the gods used ground-up maize and broth to create four brothers, Balam Agab, Balam Quitzé, Iqi Balam and Mahucutah, together with their wives. When, after much travelling, the brothers witnessed the birth of the sun, bringing light to the darkness of the earth, they disappeared for ever.

Another Mayan story says that the creator-god Month was created first. He then created the heavens and earth and all living things over a period of nineteen days, using the twentieth day as a day of rest to recover from his labours.

(4) The Guatemalan version of the Mayan creation story says that the gods Gucumatz and Tepeu caused the primordial waters to recede to allow dry land to appear and then made animals and men from moist soil.

(5) The Mixtec tell of two beings who appeared when the earth rose out of the primeval waters. These were the deer-god, Puma-Snake, and his female counterpart, the deer-goddess, Jaguar-Snake. They placed a copper axe on edge for the sky to rest on and built a palace where they lived for hundreds of years, finally producing Wind-Nine-Snake and Wind-Nine-Cave, two sons to whom they gave the power to change into any bird or animal or to become invisible. These four became the progenitors of the human race, many of whom died in a flood, following which the creator-god formed heaven and earth and a new race of humans.

(6) The Zapotecs say that the creator-god Cozaana created the world and all the animals while the fishes and human beings were created by another god, Huichaana.

Chinese

(1) The universe was created by eight rulers – the Five Emperors and the Three Sovereigns.

(2) Chaos produced the world when pierced by lightning.

(3) Chaos, a cosmic egg, split to form yin and yang, Earth and Sky. In between was the first human, Pan-ku, who grew for 1800 years, pushing the sky away from earth. All the physical features of the earth and sky were made from his body when he died. The earth was square with a sea on each side under the dome of the sky. The Milky Way, a heavenly river, discharged into the Eastern Sea in which floated the island paradises of P'eng-lai. Pillars supported the sky but these were broken by Chuan Hsü to prevent confusion between gods and men. His grandson Chung then ruled heaven and another grandson Li ruled the earth. The sun passed from a hollow mulberry tree in the east to a jo tree in the west ten times daily in a chariot drawn by dragons. Nine of the suns were shot out of the sky by the archer I.

(4) In the beginning there was only Wu-wu, nothingness, but this changed to Wu Chi, no limit, when Tao arrived on the scene. Hun T'un, chaos, then evolved giving rise to T'ai Chi, the Great Pole, which engendered T'ai I, the Great Change. This had two stages, T'ai Ch'u, the Great First, when Hsing (form) came into being, and T'ai Shih, the Great Beginning, when Ch'i (breath) appeared. Together, these two attributes formed T'ai Shu, the Great Primordial, which had substance (Chih).

(5) A modern version says that the universe was created by Pan-ku. One story says that he was hatched from an egg and pushed the two halves apart to form earth and sky. His left eye became the sun, his right eye the moon. Some say he made men from clay others that they developed from fleas on his body. The effort took 18,000 years and he died from his efforts, parts of his body forming

mountain ranges. In another story, Pan-ku, a dwarf, chiselled the universe into its present shape for 18,000 years, growing some six feet every day as he worked.

East Indies

(1) The Dayak say that the world lay in the mouth of Watersnake. Gold Mountain and Jewel Mountain clashed together to produce all the things that make up the world. In the first epoch came the sky and the rocks, then the land and hills and finally, in the third epoch, the Tree of Life.

Another Dayak story says that a spider came down a thread from heaven and wove a web to which adhered the things such as soil and trees which fell from heaven and made the earth. Later, two spirits descended from heaven to start the human race. They carved a loom and a sword from wood and these two objects produced two human heads which bred successively more complete beings until proper beings existed in the form of Amei Ami and Burung Une, gods of agriculture. They had children who became the ancestors of the tribes and Amei Ami made various birds and animals from bark.

(2) The Elema people of New Guinea say that, in the beginning, there was only the primordial ocean in which a huge turtle swam endlessly. Finally, needing rest, it dug up mud from the bottom and formed dry land. Here it laid eggs from which emerged the first people and all the plants and animals.

(3) The Iban say that the primordial creators were Ara and Irik. They flew in the form of birds over the primitive waters from which they drew two eggs out of which they made the world. Then they made men from the soil and gave them life.

(4) In Sumatra a primordial god mated with the cosmic blue chicken Manuk Manuk which laid three eggs from which came three gods who respectively made the earth, the heavens and the underworld.

Egyptian

(1) The universe consisted only of the primordial ocean, Nun, from which arose a fertile hill. The early sun god, Atum, brought light to the world, separating earth from sky which was supported on a pillar at each of the four corners of the earth. Nun created a son, Shu, and a daughter, Tefnut. Tefnut was lost for some time and when he found her the god's tears of pleasure became the first men. Shu and Tefnut produced Geb and Nut who produced Isis, Osiris, Nephthys and Set.

(2) Alternatively, the world was hatched from an egg laid by Geb as a goose or by Thoth in the form of an ibis or from the lotus flower.

(3) The pairs Amon and Amaunet, Huh and Hauhet, Kuk and Kakuet, Nan and Naunet, swimming in the primitive waters produced an egg from which light was born. Alternative pairs of deities were Heru and Hehut, Kekui and Kekuit, Qeh and Qerhit, created by Thoth.

(4) A lotus appeared, floating on the primitive waters, and opened to reveal the sun which created the world.

(5) Thoth, a self-created deity, spoke and his words became living things.

(6) Khnum the potter-god made the universe from mud taken from the Nile and shaped humans from the same material on his wheel. In other versions, Ptah was the creator, creating all things merely by uttering their names.

Finnish

An eagle flying over the primitive waters seeking a nesting site landed on the knee of the sleeping magician, Vainamoinen, built a nest and laid an egg. When he moved, the egg fell out of the nest and broke. The shell became the sky and earth and the contents of the egg became the heavenly bodies.

Other accounts say that the bird was a teal and the eggs were laid on the knee of Ilmatar, Vainamoinen's mother.

Greek

In general, the Greeks believed that the world pre-existed the gods who were created from a union of its parts.

(1) Chaos gave rise to the goddess Euronyme who produced the serpent Ophion in conjunction with the North Wind. The union of Ophion with Euronyme produced the universal egg from which everything else hatched.

(2) In the Homeric version, all living things arose from the union of the stream Ocean with Tethys and in the Ophic version the union of the three-headed goddess Night with the wind produced a silver world-egg from which sprang Eros who created the sky and the heavenly bodies. Night continued to rule until the coming of Uranus.

(3) In another story, Earth arose from Chaos and bore Uranus who thereupon fertilised Earth to produce the plants and animals of the world. Earth also produced

the 100-handed giants, Briareus, Cottus and Gyges, the one-eyed Cyclopes and Arges, Brontes and Sterope, the original Titans.

(4) Yet another version says that from the void of Chaos there emerged Erebus (darkness), Gaea (earth) and Nyx (night). The union of Erebus and Nyx produced Hemera (day), Aether (air) and many of the forces controlling human life such as fate, fortune, etc. Gaea produced a son, Uranus, whom she married to produce the early gods such as Cronus, the Titans and the Cyclopes. Cronus castrated his father, usurped his throne and started the second divine dynasty.

A variation of this story has Aether and Hemera producing a son, Eros, who helped in the creation of Gaea and Pontus and then created all the plants and animals, breathing life into the first humans moulded from clay by Epimetheus and Prometheus.

Hindu

(1) The early Vedic version says that Varuna was the creator of all things. Prithivi (earth) and Dyaus (heaven) begot Indra who fought the deities and took over as supreme god, rearranging the universe. There were three heavens: Indra's for major gods, Varuna's for minor gods and Yama's for the less virtuous. The universal spirit was known as Brahman.

(2) In the Rig Veda, a primordial being, Purusha, was dismembered by the other gods who then built the universe from parts of his body.

(3) The universe is egg-shaped with 21 zones. The first six, from the top, are heavenly realms; earth comes next and then seven lower worlds where the nagas live and, below these, seven hells. At the start of each kalpa, Vishnu is asleep on the coils of the cosmic snake, Ananta. Brahma emerges from the lotus that grows from Vishnu's navel and makes the universe. Vishnu awakes to rule for a kalpa then sleeps again and the universe is merged with his body.

(4) Having slept in the lotus flower floating on the primitive waters, Brahma awoke and created the universe. He made some errors which resulted in the demon rakshas and yakshas. There is a cycle of life, death and rebirth governed by Vishnu, who preserves life, Shiva, who destroys it and Brahma, the creator. The life cycle of the universe takes 100 years in the life of Brahma, each day of which (a kalpa) lasts for 4320 million years. At the end of each cycle, the universe is destroyed, by drought, then flood, then fire. Men who merit it are released from the cycle of rebirth. At each re-creation of the universe, a golden lotus with 1000 petals appears, floating on the primeval waters. From this flower, Brahma is born to create the world anew.

(5) In Malaya they say that Bahua Gura (Shiva) ruled over the primeval ocean in which lay the serpent Naga Pahoda. The god's daughter jumped into the waters and he threw her some dust from which she made land. He also sent a hero with a heavy block which he placed on the serpent's back, causing it to writhe about, twisting the land into mountains and valleys. The gods and the hero became the ancestors of the human race.

Japanese

A primordial egg, formed from the male principle In and the female principle Yo, separated to form the heavens and earth and then arose the Separate Heavenly Beings and the god Kuni-toto-tachi from whom descended Izanagi and Izanami. Others say that the first deity to emerge from the primordial chaos was Minaka-Nushi; he was followed by four other gods and, after seven generations, by Izanagi and Izanami. They dipped a spear in the primordial ocean and drops from this spear formed the islands to which Izanagi and Izanami descended from the Floating Bridge. The first island was called Onogoro. Izanami gave birth to seas and rivers, trees and herbs, and physical forces such as the wind . One of these forces, the god of fire, burnt his mother to death. His father cut off his head and 16 more gods emerged, 8 each from the blood and the body. Izanagi descended to the underworld to get his wife back but failed. To purify himself, he bathed in a river, creating gods of good and evil, and then in the sea, creating sea gods. Amaterasu was created from one eye, Tsuki-yomi from the other, and Susanowa from his nose.

When Amaterasu ate Susanowa's broken sword, she breathed out three more goddesses and he, eating her necklace, breathed out five more gods. These eight became the ancestors of the royal family.

Jain

The Jains deny the concept of creation, holding that the universe has always existed.

Korean

The world was created by Miruk who pushed heaven and earth apart, supporting the heavens on a copper pillar at each corner. Having made the sun, moon and stars and set them in the heavens, he set about improving the earth. With the help of a mouse, he made fire and then made human beings. Holding a silver tray in one hand and a golden tray in the other, he prayed and the trays filled with insects that then turned into humans, men in the golden tray, women in the silver one. These people became the ancestors of the race. When the evil Sokka appeared, they fought many battles, and Miruk finally became disenchanted by the spread of evil in the world and left it to its own devices.

Mesopotamian

(1) The Akkadian version says that Abzu and Mother Tiamat, the primordial forces, created the gods of the heavens and earth, Lahmu and Lahamu. Their son Ea defeated Abzu and fathered Marduk. In the struggle between the primal forces and the gods, Marduk slaughtered Tiamat and Kingu, leader of their forces, and seized the Tablets of Destiny. He made the earth and sky from the body of Tiamat and man from the blood of Kingu mixed with clay.

(2) One Babylonian version starts with primeval waters inhabited by hideous monsters and ruled by Thalath. Belus cut Thalath in half to make earth and sky and then had Kingu cut off his head, using the blood, mixed with earth, to make the sun, moon, planets and mankind.

(3) Another Babylonian version starts with two gods, Abzu and Tiamat, who engendered all the other gods down to Belus who created the world.

(4) In the Sumerian version, Nammu the primeval waters, created An and Ki, heaven and earth.

New Zealand

(1) In the mythology of the Maori, day, night and space evolved from the primordial void, Te Kore, incorporating formless male and female beings. These produced Rangi and Papa, sky and earth. Tane-Mahuta came down from the highest of the ten heavens after creating the space between heaven and earth by forcibly separating Rangi and Papa, and brought all knowledge in three baskets. He fathered all the natural features of the earth and made a being from sand on which he fathered the first humans.

(2) A cosmic egg was dropped into the primitive waters by a bird flying overhead and from this egg emerged mankind and animals and a canoe.

Norse

In the beginning was a vast chasm known as Ginnungagap with Niflheim, land of mists and darkness, to the north and Muspelheim, the land of fire, to the south. In the middle of Niflheim, a raging torrent, Hvergelmir, supplied the twelve rivers (Elivagar) which ran into the chasm and froze to ice which condensed the mists rising from Muspelheim to form frost-maidens and giants. The gods Odin and his brothers Ve and Vili killed the first Frost Giant, Ymir, and built the world from his parts. They used his body for the earth, his blood for the seas, his skull for the sky, bones for mountains, hair for vegetation, brains for clouds and they built a wall round Midgard, the home of mankind, from his eyebrows. Sparks from Muspelheim became the stars and planets. The sky was held up by four dwarfs, Nordri, Sudri, Austri and Westri, and the whole universe was supported on the great ash tree Yggdrasil. Odin and his brothers formed a man and a woman from driftwood, or from trees, and breathed life into them.

North American

(1) The Achomawi people of California say that the world was created by a god who appeared out of a cloud and was assisted by Coyote.

(2) The Acoma of New Mexico say that two sisters, Ia'tik and Nao-tsiti, were born under the earth. They were instructed by the spirit Tstitinako and emerged into the sunlight to begin their work of creating plants, animals and gods, using the baskets of basic materials given to them by their mentor. Nao-tsiti was impregnated by the rainbow and one of the twin boys that resulted from this union mated with Ia'tik to become the progenitors of the tribe.

(3) According to the Algonquin, the good things of the earth were made by Gluskap, the evil things by his brother Malsum. The earth-mother fell through a hole in the sky carrying a tree that had magical soil round its roots and fell into a lake. Some of this soil was saved by Toad and it grew to form first an island and then the whole earth. Turtles collected the lightning and made the sun and

moon. The stars were formed from animals that crossed the rainbow bridge into heaven.

In another story, the god Michabo followed some animals into a lake which then overflowed and inundated the earth. After both a raven and an otter had failed, the musk-rat found some earth from which the god recreated solid land. He then mated with the musk-rat and started the human race.

(4) The Arapaho say that Kici Manitou assembled all the birds and animals of the primeval waters. The turtle told him where to find earth and the birds brought some back in their beaks. The god then dried the mud with his sacred pipe, so making the world.

(5) The Arikara say that humans came up out of the ground. First came a race of giants, born to spiders, who perished in a flood; then a race sprouting from the seed of maize planted by animals.

(6) Some Californian tribes say that heaven mated with the earth to produce rocks and stones, then trees and grass, then animals and, finally, Ouiot, the first being.

Other versions say that the all-powerful Nocuma made the earth like a ball and made it steady with the black rock, Tosaut. When this was broken by fishes, it exposed a large bladder which split open, spilling out the salt that made the seas salty. Nocuma then used soil to make the first man, Ejoni, and the first woman, Ae.

Other tribes say that the trickster Coyote and Kodo-yanpe dropped from the heavens on to the primeval waters in a canoe. Coyote then scattered sand on to the sea and created dry land.

(7) In the Cherokee version, animals existed in the sky but became overcrowded and sent the water beetle to look for some other place. The whole world was covered by water at that time but the water beetle brought up mud from the bottom and spread it out to form a huge land which the spirit, Someone Powerful, suspended from the sky with rawhide ropes at each corner. A buzzard was sent down to test the muddy expanse and the flapping of his wings piled some of the mud into mountains. When the land was dry enough, the animals descended from their home in the sky. They pulled the sun down so that they had light and then found that they had to push it back a bit because it was so hot. Then Someone Powerful created plants and trees and, lastly, men and women. One day, it is said, the ropes will break and the earth will fall back into the ocean.

(8) The Cree say that the beavers flooded the earth but the trickster-god Coyote and Wolf covered the surface of the waters with moss and created a new world.

(9) In the lore of the Eskimo, it is said that the earth fell from the sky but there was no light until the sun and moon mated. The girl (sun) ran off carrying a torch which grew brighter as she reached the heavens while the man's torch grew progressively weaker, ending up as the moon.

(10) The Hopi say that the two goddesses, the Huruing Wuhti, one in the east, one in the west, survived the Flood and made mankind from drying mud left behind when the waters receded.

(11) The Iroquois say that the world was created by Hahgwehdiyu from the dead body of his mother, the sky goddess Ataensic.

(12) The Maidu maintain that the world was made by Wonomi who also created mankind.

(13) The Muskhogeans say that the hill, Nunne Chaha, rose from the primordial waters and the god, Esaugetuh Emissee, fashioned men from clay and built a huge wall on which he set them to dry.

(14) The Navaho say that the four gods, Black Body, Blue Body, White Body and Yellow Body placed two ears of corn between deerskin blankets and the Mirage People walked round them in a circle. The ears were turned into the first pair of humans.

Another version says that the first man, Atse Hastin, the first woman, Atse Estsan, and Coyote lived successively in four or five worlds, the last of which was destroyed by a flood. They found themselves on an island which grew as the waters subsided. They then created the sky and earth and all that is in it and, when it was complete, they disappeared. The daughter of the first man and woman, known as Estanatlehi, produced from maize flour a man and woman, the founders of the eight tribes.

(15) The Omaha say that all living things were created by the power of the spirit Wakonda's thought and they descended to earth after first scouring the heavens for a suitable home. At that time, the earth was covered by the primordial ocean but Wakonda caused dry land to form for the living things to land on and inhabit.

(16) The Osage say that their

ancestors lived in the sky and were sent to earth only to find it covered with water. The elk called up the winds which blew until much of the water evaporated and then rolled in the mud so that the hairs from his body stuck in the mud. From these hairs grew all the plants on earth.

(17) The Pawnee say that Atius-Tirawa created the world. At first, it resembled a bowl with the stars holding it in space and protecting it. He then caused the sun to mate with the moon and the morning star to mate with the evening star. The children of these unions were the progenitors of the human race. Coyote seized the sack of stars and tipped them out to form the Milky Way.

(18) The Pomo say that Marumda and his brother Kuksu created the world and tried unsuccessfully to destroy it first with flood and then with fire, having to be rescued from their own handiwork by Ragno.

(19) The Salish say that the sky, the earth and the underworld, created by Amotken, are supported by a huge central post. The first humans he made from five hairs from his own head.

(20) The Sia of New Mexico say that, in the beginning, a spider wove a web and the god Sus'sistinnako used it as an instrument on which he played a tune while he sang. As he sang, humans appeared and set about populating the earth.

(21) The Sioux say that the first world was destroyed by fire and the second by flood. The creator-spirit then came down and floated on the waters, bringing his pipe and pipe-bag. He took a loon from the bag and asked it to bring up mud from the bottom. The loon and then the otter and then the beaver all failed in this task but the turtle succeeded. The creator used the mud to create dry land and then let all the animals out of his bag to spread over the earth. Having made humans from coloured clay, the creator rested to prepare himself for the creation of a fourth world at some future time.

Another story says that the Sioux ancestors lived underground and reached the surface by climbing up the roots of a vine.

(22) According to the Snohomish, the god Dohkwibuhch made the sky so low that people bumped their heads on it until, with a concerted effort, they used long poles to push it into its present position. A few people who were inadvertently raised into the sky were turned into the Great Bear constellation.

(23) The Washo say that, in the beginning, there was a great upheaval which set the world on fire. The heat was so intense that the flames, which reached the heavens, melted the very stars which then fell to earth. The fire was extinguished only when the deluge came. Men who tried to escape the flood by building a tall tower were turned to stone.

(24) In the lore of the Yakima, the world was originally covered by water. Whee-me-me-ow-ah, tired of living alone in the sky, dredged up mud from the bottom of the ocean and made land and mountains. He then made all the plants and animals and finally, using more mud, made a man and a woman.

(25) In the lore of the Zuni, the green scum left behind by the receding floodwaters became earth and sky and the ancestors of the tribe emerged freom the cave where they had sought refuge. In another version, men were born in a cave which soon became overcrowded until the first man, Poshaiyangkyo, interceded with the sun and secured their release.

Pacific Islands

(1) In the Gilbert Islands they say that Nareau made, from sand, Na Atibu and Nei Teukez who had many offspring, including Nareau the Second. He killed Na Atibu and used his body to build the world, using his right eye for the sun and his left for the moon, splitting the brain into pieces for the stars and using his flesh for the islands and his bones for trees. When this was done, a tree grew from the spine of the dead Na Atibu from which human beings grew.

(2) In Hawaii they say that the earth-mother Papa bore a gourd and her husband Wakea used it to make the world. The outer cover became the sky, the pulp made the heavenly bodies and the flesh became the land and sea with the juice providing rain.

Another version says that Tangaroa created the world when, in the form of a bird, he laid an egg which, after floating on the primeval waters, broke to form the earth and sky.

(3) Polynesians say that Tangaroa lived in the eternal darkness, Po, and from there he cast down rocks which became the islands. On them he planted the Peopling Vine from which sprang the human race.

Another story says that the creator-god, Lo, separated the primordial mass into earth, sea and sky and then created the sun, moon and stars.

(4) In Samoa they say that the sky gods, Ilu and Mamoa, merged to form the sky and the sea god, Tagaloa, created rocks to support it. Then they produced the children Po and Ao and these two mated to produce Rangima and Rangiuri. Tagaloa caused the rock, Papa Taoto, to rise from the sea-bed for his son Tuli, a bird, to nest on. Two grubs emerged and grew into the first humans.

(5) The Tahitians say that Ta-aroa, a self-created being, hatched from the cosmic egg and used the shell to create the earth and sky. He then created everything that exists. Others say that he created the world inside the shell of a mussel while yet another version says that he used his own body to build the universe. Some claim that he pulled the islands up on a hook and line from the bottom of the ocean.

Persian

(1) The mountain Mount Alburz grew till it reached the sky and the Chinvat bridge led from its top into heaven. A gateway led from the base into hell. The centre of the earth was Khwanirath and there were six Keshvars (sections) round it linked by the celestial ox, Srishok. The wind god, Vayu, made the ocean round Mount Alburz from rain formed by the rain god Tishtrya who, in the form of a white horse, fought Apoasha the drought-demon. The goddess Anahita purified the waters and the fire god, Atar, fought with the destructive monster Azhi Dahak.

The Gaokerena tree, the White Hom or White Haoma, provided the fruit of immortality.

(2) The Zoroastrian version proposes an earlier phase in which Ormazd and Ahriman were separated by a huge void. Ahriman retreated to hell leaving Ormazd to rule for 3000 years after which he attacks and destroys the world. This alternation is repeated three times before the final end.

Siberian

(1) The Samoyeds say that the god Num sent out birds to investigate the primitive waters and made the earth from the mud that one of the birds brought back in its beak.

(2) In the Tartar version, the god Ulgan banished the spirit of evil, Erlik, to the land of the dead. This spirit lived on land beneath the primeval waters and when he brought a piece of it to the surface, Ulgan caused it to float on the water and grow to form a whole continent. In some versions, the disc of the earth is supported by three fishes which, in moving, cause earthquakes. Ulgan also created men and went to heaven to bring down their spirits.

(3) The Voguls say that animals and fishes were sent down from the heavens by the sky god Numitorem.

(4) According to the Yakuts, the universe has always existed with a huge tree in the middle, the branches of which shelter seven heavens. Land was created by Yryn-ai-tojon, the supreme god, rather in the way attributed to Ulgan by the Tartars.

South American

(1) The Arawak version says that Makonaima created the world

and put his son Sigu in charge of the animals. Sigu chopped down a magic tree and planted its seed throughout the land until water emerging from the trunk of the tree flooded the earth. Sigu and many animals escaped, hiding in a cave.

(2) The Barasano people say that the world was created by Romi Kumu, a female shaman. She made a griddle from clay and made three mountains on which it rested. When she lit a fire under the griddle, the edifice collapsed pushing the earth down to become the underworld while other griddles became earth and sky. She then opened the Water Door and flooded the earth and all inanimate objects turned into animals. A few survived by making a canoe that landed on a mountain top.

(3) The Chaco assert that the world and the first humans were made by a beetle.

(4) The Chamacoco say that men originally lived underground. Two climbed up a rope to the surface but then a dog gnawed through the rope so that the others had to climb a tree which reached the sky from where they fell to earth. Another Chamacoco story says that men lived inside a huge hollow tree until one of their number split the tree open to let them out.

(5) The Chibcha say that the first thing to exist was light. This was brought to earth in a casket called Chiminagaga (though some say that this was the name of the deity who sent the light) and distributed by birds. The goddess Chia was turned into the moon (or, some say, an owl) as

punishment for causing the flood which few humans survived.

(6) In the lore of the Mbaya, there are several versions of how men came to earth: emerging from a cave somewhere in the north; coming up out of the ground when released by a dog; being hatched from eggs laid on top of a mountain.

(7) The Matado version is that there were animals on the earth and women in the sky. Some women climbed down to earth on a rope and were unable to get back when a bird pecked through the rope, so they stayed on earth, mating with the animals to produce the tribes.

(8) The Tereno say that men lived in a deep crevasse until they were discovered and released by two supernatural beings who came across them when they were hunting on earth.

West Indies

The Taino people say that the supreme spirit, Yaya, created the world, which has passed through five eras. In the first era, Yaya killed his son and placed his bones in the ground. When the ground was broken, water flooded out and became the oceans. In the next stage, men were created and Guahayana led his people from a cave into the upper world. In the third stage, women were created and, as a result, the fourth era in which the islands were populated, became possible. The original culture was destroyed in the final era by the arrival of the white man.

Cressida *see* **Chryseis**
Cretan Bull   *Greek*
also Marathonian Bull

A white bull sent by Poseidon. This animal came out of the sea to Crete in response to a plea by Minos to Poseidon asking for a sign which would confirm his right to the Cretan throne. Minos should have sacrificed the bull to the sea god but it was so beautiful that he kept it for himself and sacrificed a lesser animal. In anger, Poseidon arranged for the bull to mate with Pasiphae, the wife of Minos, to produce the monster known as the Minotaur. The bull later roamed wild throughout Crete and caused much damage until it was captured by Hercules as his seventh Labour and brought to Greece. It was released on the mainland and caused further havoc until it was finally killed by Theseus.

In some accounts, this is the same animal as the bull which, as a form of Zeus, carried off Europa.

cricket
(1) In the East Indies, this insect is said to conduct the dead to the underworld.
(2) To the Japanese the cricket is a sacred insect.
(3) In the Pacific Islands, it is said that only when crickets were brought from heaven did the sun set, caused by their singing.

crocodile
(1) Some African tribes regard this animal as an evil spirit, some as the home of their ancestors, others as a sacred animal not to be killed.
(2) Arabs regard the crocodile as having oracular properties.
(3) In the East Indies, some tribes

say that these beasts house the spirits of ancestors. The Dayaks regard crocodiles as servants of the underworld gods, the Jata.
(4) In Egyptian mythology the crocodile personifies divine reason and is worshipped as such. Some say that it recovered the body of Osiris from the Nile.
(5) In Indonesia they say that men can change into crocodiles by reciting the appropriate formula.
(6) In Malaya it is said that people who fall into a river can become crocodiles, which have a compartment in their stomach to store clothes.

A young crocodile that ventures into the forest may become a tiger.
(7) In Mexico the crocodile was venerated and not killed.

Crocus   *Greek*
When the nymph Smilax rejected Crocus's love, the gods changed this youth into a flower of that name.

Crodhmara   *Scottish*
Fairy cows. These animals are said to yield three times as much milk as normal cows.

Croesus   *Greek*
A king of Lydia. This king was said to be the richest of all men. At his death, he was saved from his funeral pyre and carried off to the land of the Hyperboreans (or to Persia) by Apollo.

Cronus   *Greek*
also Kronos;
= *Roman* Saturn
An early supreme god and fertility god; the youngest Titan. Son of Uranus and Gaea; husband of his sister Rhea; father of Demeter, Hades, Hera, Hestia, Poseidon, Zeus; father of Chiron, some say.

Cronus was the youngest of the Titans who led the revolt of the Titans against the elder gods. He castrated his father Uranus and took over his throne. He was warned that one of his children would dethrone him, so he swallowed each one as it was born. Rhea managed to save Zeus by giving Cronus a large pebble wrapped in baby-clothes to swallow. He was forced to regurgitate the stone and the children, who were unharmed, when Zeus served him an emetic drink. He was killed by his son, Zeus, in the war between the Titans and the younger gods or, in another account, he became the ruler of the Isles of the Blessed.

He is sometimes depicted with three pairs of wings.

Crop-eared Dog   *Irish*
A dog with no ears or tail but capable of speech.

He was really Alexander, son of the king of India. His father had taken a second wife, Libearn, who had turned the prince and his brothers into dogs so that her own son, Knight of the Lantern, would inherit the throne. King Arthur sent Gawain with the Crop-eared Dog to capture the Knight of the Lantern, who changed the dog back to his human form. He later became king of India.

Croquemitaine   *French*
An evil sprite or ugly monster.

crow
(1) In the lore of the Aborigines, this bird demonstrated the best way to die by rolling its eyes and falling on its back.

In one story, the culture hero Wagu became a crow.

(2) British stories about Branwen, a giantess and love goddess, say that she could appear in the form of a crow.

(3) In China, a three-legged crow is said to live in the sun and sometimes comes to earth to collect herbs.

A white-winged crow is regarded as an evil omen.

(4) In Greece the crow was regarded as the bird of the god Apollo and the goddess Athena. It was originally white but was changed by Apollo for bringing bad news. In some versions, it is the raven which is so treated.

(5) Hindu lore regards the crow as a messenger of death.

(6) In Irish myths, the war goddess, Morrigan, was said to appear in the form of a crow.

(7) In Japan, the crow (called karaso) is thought of as a messenger of the gods.

(8) In Malaya, the crow is regarded as the soul of a tiger.

(9) In North America, this bird appears in many legends of the native tribes.

(*See also* **sacred birds**.)

crown
Crowns, the symbol of sovereigns, made of various things, appear in many mythologies. Crowns associated with particular persons or deities include:

cypress	Thanatos
fennel	Faunus
fig	Melpomene, Pan
flowers	Flora
grapes	Bacchus/Dionysus
ivy	Bacchus/Dionysus, Thalia
laurel	Apollo, Calliope, Clio, Melpomene
lilies	Juno
mulberry and olive	Mercury
myrtle and roses	Erato
oak leaves	Hecate, Jupiter/Zeus
olives	Athena, Zeus
palm leaves	the Muses
pearls	Polyhymnia
pine twigs	Cybele, Pan
poplar leaves	Faunus
poppies	Hercules
quince blossom	Juno
rays	Apollo
stars	Thor, Uranus
vine leaves	Bona Dea, Bacchus/Dionysus
water lilies	Faunus
wheat-ears	Demeter
wool and narcissi	the Fates

Cuchulainn   *Irish*
A warrior-hero of Ulster; the greatest of the twelve Champions of the Red Branch.

His mother was Dectera, a moon goddess. His earthly father may have been Conor mac Nessa, who some say was Dectera's brother, but his real father was the sun god Lugh who, in the form of a may-fly, flew into Dectera's mouth. Dectera gave her new-born son as a gift to Ulster and he was raised by her sister, Finchoom, alongside her own son, Conal. She called the boy, who had eyes with seven pupils, hands with seven fingers and feet with seven toes, Setanta. On a visit to Culann, a wealthy smith, the six-year-old Setanta killed Culann's huge guard-dog with his bare hands when it attacked him and then, to mollify the angry smith-god, acted as guard-dog himself until another animal could be trained. From this time on, he became Cuchulainn, the 'Hound of Culann', and swore never to eat the flesh of a dog. At the age of seven he defeated 150 princes of Conor's court and became a member of that court.

He fell in love with Emer, daughter of Forgall, lord of Lusca, but she spurned him until he had proved himself a great warrior. Conor equipped him with a chariot and weapons and sent him to Scotland to learn the arts of war from the warrior-maid, Skatha. There he learned many feats of arms from the warrior Domhnall and more from Skatha. He fought alongside her against her sister, the princess Aifa, defeated her in combat and carried her off to Skatha's camp, forcing her to make peace with Skatha. He became her lover and left her a ring to be given to any son of their union, who should be called Connla. When Connla, in later years, sought out his father, they fought, neither knowing the other's identity and Cuchulainn killed his own son. It was only when he saw the ring on the dead youth's finger that he realised what he had done.

His first exploit after his training by Skatha was to challenge the sons of Nechtan who had often raided Ulster and killed many men. He killed Foill, a supernatural being, with a sling shot and cut off his head, and then, having killed Foill's two brothers, set fire to their castle. He then went to Emain Macha, the seat of the kings of Ulster, still in the grip of blood-lust, and was returned to normal only by a group of naked women, led by Mughain, the queen, who plunged him into tubs of cold water

until his ardour left him. Other accounts say that this event took place many years earlier, when Cuchulainn was a young boy.

He then attacked Forgall's castle, killed him and his men, and carried off Emer and a great deal of treasure, including a cauldron that produced gold and silver. Forgall's sister, Scenmed, raised the alarm and pursued them but Cuchulainn defeated her forces and killed Scenmed.

In a contest with Conall Cearnach and Laoghaire, Winner of Battles, for the title of Champion of All Ulster, both Conall and Laoghaire ran from the wildcats that had been put in their room, while Cuchulainn alone faced them with his sword. They were also tested by the warrior-magician Ercol, who attacked them with witches and then fought the three of them himself, losing only to Cuchulainn. In a beheading contest with the giant, Uath, all three decapitated the giant but only Cuchulainn was prepared to offer his neck to the axe. The giant intentionally missed his stroke and declared Cuchulainn the champion before disappearing into thin air. He was really Curoi, a magician-king.

In a contest with Bricciu, a storm god and lord of Ulster, he cut off the lord's head but Bricciu picked up the severed head and disappeared into a lake. Next day, fully restored, he claimed his part of the wager and Cuchulainn laid his head on the block awaiting the axe. Bricciu went through the motions of striking but spared Cuchulainn's life in admiration of his bravery.

In some accounts, he received from Seanbheag, a man of the Otherworld, arms that ensured victory and clothes that protected him from fire and water.

Another story says that Cuchulainn once met the goddess Badb, who took the form of a red-cloaked woman, driving a one-horse chariot. The horse was connected to the chariot by a pole that ran all the way through its body and was retained by a peg in the animal's forehead. Cuchulainn jumped on to the chariot, which immediately disappeared.

He was once required to find the three sons of Daol Dearmaid who had mysteriously disappeared. He journeyed in a magic boat to an island where Achtland, their sister, led him to the place where her brothers were held captive by Eochaid Glas. Cuchulainn killed this warrior and rescued the three brothers. He also rescued the princess Gruadh who had been carried off by a giant, killing her captor in the process.

Maev, queen of Connaught, coveted Cuchulainn's spear, Cletine, and sent a bard to ask him for it, knowing that one can never refuse a poet's request. Cuchulainn threw the spear at the bard, killing him. The force of the throw broke the spear and the parts fell into a stream.

He had an affair with Blathnat, wife of King Curoi, and cut off Curoi's head and, when the sea god Manannan quarrelled with his wife Fand, she and Cuchulainn had a month-long affair but he then went back to his wife Emer. Both were given magic drinks by the druids to make them forget the incident.

When Maev and Ailill sent an army against Ulster to seize the Brown Bull of Cooley, all the men of Ulster were afflicted by the 'Debility of the Ultonians', an affliction brought on them by a curse which caused them to be as weak as a woman in childbirth for five days and four nights, and could not rouse themselves to defend their province, so Cuchulainn had to do the job himself until they recovered. He harried the enemy, killing hundreds of soldiers, some of whom fell dead at the mere sight of him in battle-fury. Several single-combat fights were arranged at a ford, all won by Cuchulainn, including one against their champion Natchrantal. Despite his efforts, the raiders seized the bull and drove it back to Connaught. He was then reluctantly engaged by his friend Ferdia who fought with him for four days with all kinds of weapons. Cuchulainn was badly wounded but killed his old friend with the spear Gae Bolg or, in some versions, ran him through with his sword. When he recovered he joined the Ulstermen who had by now joined the battle and the forces of Connaught were repelled.

When, after seven years of peace, Maev renewed her assault on Ulster, Cuchulainn ignored the pleas of his mother and his wife and went once more to battle.

He and his father Sualtam defended Ulster, but three witches deprived him of the invulnerability given by the magic belt he wore and he was mortally wounded by a spear thrown by Lugaid, son of Curoi. He tied himself to a pillar and prepared to fight on but when a crow settled on his shoulder, Lugaid came in close and cut off Cuchulainn's hand. In this way, he avenged the murder of his father Curoi. The hero's blood was drunk by an otter or, some say, by a raven. As his sword fell from his hand it cut off the hand of his killer. His enemies then cut off Cuchulainn's head and carried it off with his severed hand, burying them both at Tara.

In another version, Morrigan was opposing Cuchulainn in the battle because he had rejected her advances and it was she who attacked him in the form of a crow.

Culhwch   *Welsh*

A cousin of King Arthur.

He was born when his mother went mad and ran into a field full of pigs. She then ran off, leaving the child to be found by a swineherd.

His father's second wife charged Culhwch to marry none but Olwen, the daughter of the chief giant, Ysbaddaden. Ysbaddaden laid down thirty-nine conditions that Culhwch must fulfil before he would consent to his daughter's marriage, knowing from an old prophecy that when she married he would die. Culhwch enlisted the help of his cousin, King Arthur, by reciting the names and rank of all the two hundred or more guests at Camelot and the king provided him with an escort of many talented warriors. The tasks involved, amongst other things, clearing a thicket and ploughing the land, obtaining from many widely scattered sources a huge cauldron, a drinking-horn and a wine-cup, a never-empty hamper, a harp that could play itself, bottles that kept liquids warm and others that kept milk fresh, the blood of a witch, the tusk of a boar, the sword of Gwrnach the giant, and huntsmen, hounds and horses to hunt down the boar Twrch Trwyth and seize the comb, razor and shears carried between the huge animal's ears.

After many adventures, in which he was helped by the band of warriors provided by Arthur, all these objectives were achieved and Culhwch claimed Olwen as his bride. Her father was killed by Goreu, a page at King Arthur's court, fulfilling the old prophecy, and Culhwch took over his lands.

Cupid   *Roman*

also Amor;

= Greek Eros

God of love; son of the goddess Venus by Vulcan, the god of fire; son of the gods Mercury or Jupiter, some say.

He carried off the beautiful maiden Psyche and lived with her, coming to her only at night so that she could never see him. He left her when she violated this trust but eventually they were reconciled and Psyche was deified and accepted as Cupid's wife by the other deities.

In some accounts he was carried on the back of a fish to escape the monster Typhon, as was Venus. The pair of them, in the heavens, are represented by the constellation Pisces.

Cupid is depicted as a winged god carrying a bow who fires arrows into the hearts of those he wishes to become lovers.

Curson   *European*
A demon, one of the 72 Spirits of
Solomon. He is said to know the
past, the present and the future,
and is depicted with the face of
a lion, riding astride a bear and
holding a snake.

Cybele   *Phrygian*
also Great Mother;
= *Greek* Demeter, Rhea; *Roman* Bona
Dea, Ceres, Magna Mater, Ops;
Sumerian Inanna; *Syrian* Kubaba
A Phrygian mother-goddess and
earth goddess.

Originally, she was said to
be hermaphrodite (Agdistis), a
being born from the earth where
the sperm of Zeus fell. The gods
castrated this being which became
the goddess Cybele, while the
severed member grew into an
almond tree, the fruit of which
impregnated the mother-goddess
Nana to produce Attis. The boy was
abandoned but saved by shepherds
and grew up to become Cybele's
lover. When Attis fell in love with a
nymph, Sagaritis, Cybele drove him
mad so that he castrated himself

and died. The Greeks say she was
raped by Zeus and bore Agdistis.

In another version, Cybele was
the daughter of Meion, king of
Phrygia, and Dindyme, abandoned
and suckled by leopards. In this
version, Meion killed Attis and the
baby he had fathered on Cybele
but Cybele restored Attis to life.

Her cult was brought back to
Greece by the men returning
from the Trojan War and was
later adopted by the Romans who
instituted a festival in her honour
at which self-castration took
place. Later rites included bathing
in the blood of sacrificed animals,
the taurobolium. She is said to
have intervened when Aeneas was
attacked by Turnus and prevented
him from setting fire to the Trojan
fleet, by causing the ships to turn
into nymphs.

Cyclops   *Greek*
plural Cyclopes
A one-eyed giant, offspring of
Uranus and Gaea or of Poseidon
and Amphitrite.

The Cyclopes rebelled against

Uranus and were banished to
Tartarus but were released by
Cronus when he overthrew
Uranus. Cronus locked them up
in Tartarus once again, but Zeus
freed them to help him in his
battle with the older gods.

They provided Zeus with
his favourite weapon, the
thunderbolt, Hades with his
helmet of invisibility, and
Poseidon with his trident,
and they made a silver bow
for Artemis. Other groups of
Cyclopes built the walls of Tiryns
and Mycenae.

The first three Cyclopes, Arges,
Brontes and Steropes, were killed
by Apollo to avenge the killing of
Asclepius, and their spirits inhabit
Etna.

Cycnus   *Greek*
Son of the war god Ares, Cycnus
challenged all-comers to a chariot
duel, cutting off the heads of
the losers and using the skulls
to build a temple to Ares. When
he challenged Hercules, he was
defeated and killed.

D

D *Central American*

A Mayan deity of uncertain identity, referred to as God D (*see **alphabetical gods***); perhaps Itzamna or Kukulcan.

This deity is depicted as an old man and, in some cases, has a snail on his head. He is regarded as a moon god.

Da *Tibetan*

also Dab-hla

A guardian god who sits on one's right shoulder and protects one from enemies.

He is envisaged as clad in golden armour, riding a white horse and holding a spear. From the deity's own shoulders spring a lion and a tiger. His constant companions are said to be a man-monkey, a black bear and a dog.

Dabog *Slav*

A sun god and god of justice. He rides across the sky every day in a chariot drawn by twelve white horses or three made of precious metals.

Some say that he was the progenitor of the Russian people.

Dactyls *Greek*

Beings created by either the nymph Anchiale or Rhea, the goddess of nature, as servants for the god Cronus.

In some accounts there were three Dactyls (Acmon, Celmis and Damnameneus), in others there were five, listed as Epimedes, Heracles, Idas, Jasius and Paeonius, said to have developed the art of ironwork. Others say that there were six males and five females; or thirty-two who cast spells and twenty who removed them; or a hundred.

Some say that they were created by Anchiale by grasping a handful of soil; others say that they appeared when Rhea dug her fingers into the earth. They lived below ground, mining precious metals, and are credited with the invention of poetic measures such as the dactyl.

Daedalus *Greek*

An architect and master-craftsman, he was banished from Athens for the murder of Talos, his gifted apprentice, and the son of his sister Polycaste.

In Crete he constructed the model cow in which Pasiphae, the wife of King Minos, was concealed when she mated with a white bull to produce the monster, the Minotaur. He then built the Labyrinth, the maze in which this monstrous creation was housed and made a magic thread which he gave to Ariadne and which later made it possible for Theseus to find his way out of the maze after he had killed the Minotaur. He was himself locked up in this labyrinth by Minos for helping Pasiphae but she helped him to escape with his son Icarus. They flew off on wings made by Daedalus from feathers and wax, but Icarus, with the foolhardiness of youth, flew too near the sun, melting the wax in his wings. When he fell into the sea and drowned it was Daedalus who retrieved the body.

In another version, Pasiphae released them and they left Crete in a boat using the sail that Daedalus had invented.

He then flew on to Sicily where he was welcomed by the king, Cocalus. When Minos came in search of him, he recognised Daedalus when he solved the problem set by Minos, of passing a thread through a triton shell by tempting an ant through the coils of the shell with honey. Some say, Daedalus killed Minos with scalding water when he was in the bath.

He is regarded as the inventor of the auger, the axe, the saw and masts, sails and yards for ships.

Dagan[1]   *Mesopotamian*
also Dagon
A Babylonian fertility god.

He is said to have invented the plough. In some accounts, he is equated with Ea or envisaged as a fish.

Dagan[2]   *Phoenician*
also Baal-Dagon, Dagon
A corn god or fish god.

Dagda, the   *Irish*
God of life and death, the 'good god'; chief of the Tuatha De Danann (the 'people of the goddess Dana'); son of Dana and her husband Eladu.

The Dagda's family connections are confused; in some versions Brigit is his mother, in others his wife; others say she was one of his three daughters, all of the same name. Where his wife is not Brigit, she is a woman with three names, Breng, Meabel and Meng. Some versions have Boann as his

wife but she is more often the wife of Elcmar, seduced by Dagda to produce Angus, or of Nechtan. In some versions, Bodb Dearg is also a son by Boann. Some say the goddess Morrigan was his consort, while some say that he seduced her to enlist her help in a battle to come, the second Battle of Moytura, in which the Danaans defeated the Fomoire.

He owned a magical cauldron, known as Undry, which was always full, and used both to satisfy his enormous appetite and which was also capable of restoring the dead to life. He also owned a huge club which could kill nine men at one blow but he could restore them to life with a touch of the other end of the weapon.

When the Fomoire stole his harp, he went to their hall and demanded its return. The harp flew from the wall where it had been hung, killed those who stole it and put the others to sleep with its music.

When the Danaans were defeated by the Milesians and went to live underground as fairies, the Dagda handed over the leadership to his son, Bodb Dearg.

Dagon *see* **Dagan**[1,2]

Daikoku   *Japanese*
A Shinto god of farmers and wealth; one of the Seven Gods of Luck (Shichi Fukujin).

He became so popular that the other gods plotted to get rid of him and sent the cunning Shiro, an evil power, to deal with him. Shiro found Daikoku in a storehouse but the god's faithful rat seized a bough of holly and drove Shiro away.

He carries a hammer from which, it is said, money falls out when he shakes it. He is depicted as a dark-skinned fat man sitting on two bales of rice or standing on the bales holding the Red Sun and his mallet.

Dain   *Norse*
One of the four stags of the gods. These animals grazed on the world-tree Yggdrasil, producing water for the rivers and honeydew for the earth.

Daksha   *Hindu*
A sage and a sun god; one of the Adityas; leader of the Prajapatis; son of Brahma.

He was born from the right thumb of Brahma and is said to be reborn in each generation. In his first appearance, he had thousands of sons and 24 (26, 27, 50 or 60) daughters. One of these, Sati, married the god Shiva while the others became consorts of the sage Dharma and the sage Kashyapa.

In a later incarnation, he had 27 daughters, all of whom were consorts of the moon god, Chandra.

Daksha also acted as creator, under the supervision of Brahma, making all animals, demons, gods and minor gods.

When he forgot to include Shiva in a sacrifice, Shiva's wife Sati immolated herself and Shiva (as Virabhadra) wreaked havoc among the worshippers, cutting off Daksha's head, which was then burnt. Shiva repented and Brahma (or in some stories, Shiva) revivified Daksha, giving him the head of a goat or ram as a replacement.

Dakuwanga   *Pacific Islands*
A Fijian shark-god.

Damballah Wedo
West Indan

The serpent-god of Haiti; husband of Aida-Wedo; one of three husbands of Erzulie, the goddess of love.

This deity derives from the Fon snake-god, Dan Ayido Hwedo. He and his wife appear as a rainbow of serpents.

Damocles
Roman

A 4th-century courtier of Dionysius, king of Syracuse. He was seated at a feast with a sword hanging over his head, suspended by a single hair, to demonstrate the unpredictability of life.

Damura
Pacific Islands

An Indonesian Cinderella figure. She befriended a crocodile who provided her with wonderful clothes for the king's ball. When she left at dawn, the prince found her sandal and proposed to marry her. Her stepmother threw Damura into the river but the crocodile saved her and she married the prince.

Dan Ayido Hwedo
African

also Rainbow Snake;
= *Haitian* Damballah Wedo

A divine python of the Fon people of Benin and Nigeria.

He was made by Mawu ('God') and carried him on his journeys when Mawu created the earth. The python's excreta was used to make the mountains and, when the work was complete, he coiled himself in the sea beneath the earth to support it. If he moves there is an earthquake and, when he has eaten all the iron bars in the sea, he will start to eat himself, starting at the tail, and soon the earth will fall into the sea, from lack of support.

In some accounts, he has 3,500 coils above the earth and 3,500 below, holding it safe. One of his arched coils is seen as the rainbow.

(*See also* **Damballah Wedo.**)

Dana
Irish

also Danu

A supreme goddess and water goddess. In some accounts she was the mother of the Dagda, in others his daughter Brigit.

When her people, the Danaans, were defeated by the Milesians, she found them homes underground.

Other accounts refer to her descendants as Feini and claim that they were the first settlers in Ireland.

In some accounts she is identified with the goddess Morrigan.

Danaans
Irish

also Children of Dana, People of Dana, Tuatha De Danann

A legendary tribe of invaders. The Danaans were descendants of earlier invaders, the Nemedians, some of whom had returned to Greece, whence they later returned to Ireland. It was said that they came by sea to settle in Ireland and burnt their boats so that they could never leave.

They fought the Fir Bolg and won; in some accounts they expelled the Fir Bolg, in others they made peace and confined them to Connaught. Some say this was the first Battle of Moytura.

They were opposed by the indigenous Fomoire and defeated them in the second Battle of Moytura. Some say that both the first and second battles at Moytura were against the Fomoire. When they were later overcome by the invading Milesians at the Battle of Tailltinn, they retreated to the underground world of the fairies.

They were said to have originated in Falias, Finias, Gorias and Murias, seats of knowledge and craftsmanship, and, in some stories, came to Ireland borne on a magic cloud.

Danae
Greek

Mother of Perseus by Zeus. Her father Acrisius had been warned that a son of Danae would kill him, so he locked her in a chamber made of bronze. This did not prevent Zeus visiting her in the form of a shower of gold or golden rain, to produce a son who was called Perseus. Her father put her and her son in a chest and cast them adrift in the sea, from where they were rescued by a fisherman named Dictys on the island of Seriphos. When she later refused to marry Polydectes, brother of Dictys and the ruler of the island, he hounded her. Perseus found her hiding with Dictys and took her back to Greece.

Danaids
Greek

The fifty daughters of Danaus and the nymph Io. All these girls married the fifty sons of Aegyptus and each one killed her husband on their joint wedding-night, except Hypermnestra who spared her husband, Lynceus. They were purified of the murders by the goddess Athena and the god Hermes but in Tartarus they were condemned forever to carry water in leaking cans or to fill their jars with water using sieves.

Some accounts say that Lynceus killed not only Danaus but all the Danaids except Hypermnestra to avenge the murder of his brothers.

In some versions, two other sisters, Amymone and Berbyce, also spared their husbands.

Danaus *Greek*

King of Libya or Argos; twin brother of Aegyptus. He was the father of fifty daughters (*see* **Danaids**), and took them off to Greece to escape the murderous intentions of his brother Aegyptus. Here he became king of Argos in place of Gelanor and was attacked by the fifty sons of Aegyptus. He eventually agreed to allow them to marry his fifty daughters but armed the girls with a pin or dagger with which all except Hypermnestra killed their husbands. The spared bridegroom, Lynceus, later killed Danaus and took over his throne.

Dantalian *European*

A demon, a duke of hell; one of the 72 Spirits of Solomon.

He is depicted as having many faces, of both sexes, and holding a book. He is said to give instruction in the arts and sciences.

Danu *see* **Dana**

Daphne *Greek*

A nymph, a priestess of Mother-Earth.

Leucippus disguised himself as a nymph to woo her, but he was exposed and killed by the nymphs.

The god Apollo fell in love with her but she ran away at his approach calling on her father, the river god Peneus, for help. Just as Apollo was about to overtake her, she changed into a laurel tree which became the tree sacred to Apollo. Some say that the goddess Gaea carried her to Crete as Pasiphae, leaving the laurel in her place.

Daphnis[1] *Greek*

A shepherd of Sicily; son of the god Hermes by a nymph; half-brother of Pan. (In some accounts, Hermes was his lover rather than his father.)

Daphnis is credited with the invention of bucolic verse. Aphrodite caused him to fall in love with the water-nymph, Nais, to whom he promised always to be faithful. When he proved unfaithful by preferring Xenia, a mortal lover, Nais blinded him. He later drowned and the water-nymphs refused to go to his aid. Hermes then took him up to heaven.

In another version, he resisted all Aphrodite's attempts to make him unfaithful and died rather than give way to her tempting. Others say that he died of longing for Xenia.

In another account, he loved the nymph Pimplea who was abducted by pirates. When Daphnis found her, a slave at the court of King Lityerses in Phrygia, he was challenged to a reaping contest by the king. Hercules took the place of Daphnis, won the contest, killed Lityerses and made Daphnis, who married Pimplea, king of Phrygia.

Daphnis[2] *Roman*

A goatherd in love with Chloe, a shepherdess.

Both Daphnis and Chloe were abandoned by their parents, in adjoining fields, and grew up to become ideal lovers.

Darana *Australian*

A spirit of the Dreamtime. He could chant spells to bring rain to the desert.

He killed two young men who had opened his bags of grubs and turned their bodies into stones,

known as Duralu, which the tribes were instructed to protect since disaster would occur if the stones were damaged or broken.

He planted many trees in the wasteland and, after the Flood, he climbed a mountain and rose into the sky where he remains as a guardian sky god, meeting the souls of the dead (tulugals) and caring for them. He also superintends the initiation rites of some tribes, pretending to cut the initiates into pieces and restoring them to life. He then knocks out one of the front teeth of each initiate.

Darawigal *Australian*

The force of evil in the lore of the Aborigines.

Dardanus *Greek*

Founder of the Trojans; son of the god Zeus by Electra, one of the Pleiades. Some say that his earthly father was Corytus.

In one version of the story of the Flood, he appears in place of Deucalion.

Dausos *Baltic*

The Lithuanian kingdom of the dead. It was said to be situated in the sky behind a very tall and slippery hill.

Davy Jones *European*

A seaman's term for the devil or sea-spirit.

Davy Jones's locker *European*

The sea regarded as the grave of drowned seamen.

Day of Brahma *see* **kalpa**[1]

Dayunsi *North American*

also Water Beetle

A creator-god of the Cherokee.

He lived in the sea while all the other beings lived in the sky. He brought up from the bottom of the sea mud which, when hung on ropes by the Powerful One, dried to form the earth which was then made available for the sky beings.

De-Ai, De-Babou *Pacific Islands*
In the lore of the Gilbert Islands, twins, the first pair of humans.

Decarabia *European*
also Carabia
A demon, one of the 72 Spirits of Solomon. He may appear as a man or as a diagram (a star in a pentagram) and can impart knowledge of plants and stones.

Decuma *Roman*
A goddess of birth, one of the three Parcae or Fates.

Dedi *Egyptian*
A magician who was said to eat 500 loaves and drink 100 jugs of beer each day and had the power to cut off the head of any living thing and then restore it.

deer
(1) Some Buddhists believe that the Buddha was born in the form of a deer.
(2) In China, the deer is a symbol of longevity and is said to be the only animal that can find the fungus that confers immortality. It turns blue when it is 1000 years old, white at 1500 and black at 2000. Any person eating the flesh of such a deer will live to the same age.
(3) The Greeks regarded the deer as sacred to Aphrodite, Apollo, Artemis, Athena and Hercules.
(4) In Irish lore, Oisin, son of Finn mac Cool and king of the Land of Youth, was born to the mortal woman Saba who was then in the form of a deer, and would himself have been a deer had she licked him at birth as a female deer would.
(5) In Japan the deer is associated with Jurojin, a god of longevity.
(6) In Mexico brown deer represent

the god of the north and drought, white deer the god of the east and rain.

Deer Kachina Cloud *North American*
A horned god of the Hopi.

Deerhunter *North American*
This young Tewa man was the finest hunter in his village and fell in love with White Corn Maiden, the prettiest and most talented girl of his tribe. They married and became inseparable, neglecting everything so that they could be together. When White Corn Maiden died soon afterwards, Deerhunter was inconsolable and wandered the plains seeking her spirit. He found her, apparently unchanged, and persuaded her to return with him. Soon the smells and signs of death appeared and her husband was repelled but she would not be parted from him and followed him wherever he went. Eventually a spirit in the form of a tall hunter with a huge bow appeared and told the couple that they had offended the gods by their behaviour. To ensure that they always remained together, he shot each of them into the heavens where they now appear as two stars, the smaller one forever following the other across the sky.

Degei *Pacific Islands*
A primeval serpent, in the lore of Fiji.
This serpent incubated the eggs laid by the hawk, Turukawa, and hatched the first humans, a boy and a girl. He then created crops for them to live on. In the underworld, he interrogates the souls of the dead and allocates punishment.

Deianeira *Greek*
Second wife of Hercules. She was won by Hercules in a contest with Achelous who took the form of a bull to fight for her hand.
When Nessus the Centaur tried to rape her and was shot by Hercules, she collected his semen and blood mixed with olive oil in a jar to be used, according to Nessus, as a love potion. When she feared that she might lose Hercules to another woman, Iole, she smeared the mixture on a shirt she sent to him, so condemning him to an agonising death. When she found out what she had done, she killed herself.

Deileon *Greek*
He and his brothers Autolycus and Phlogius helped Hercules in his ninth Labour and later joined the Argonauts.

Deirdre *Irish*
A dawn goddess. When she cried out in her mother's womb, it was foretold by the druid Cathbad that she would wed a foreign king who would bring sorrow to Ireland, so the High-king Conor reared her himself, with Lavarcham for nurse, with a view to making her his wife when she was old enough. She preferred a younger man and ran away with the warrior Naisi. The king gave them safe conduct to return but then had Naisi and his brothers killed by Eoghan mac Durthacht and forcibly married Deirdre. She refused even to speak to him and, after a year, he gave her to Eoghan, whom she hated. She killed herself by throwing herself from a chariot and smashing her head against rocks. The tree that grew over her grave became entwined with the one that grew

over Naisi's grave and they could never be separated.

A different version says that Deirdre threw herself into Naisi's grave, kissed his dead lips and died with him.

Dekanawida   *North American*
A chief of the Hurons or the Mohawks.

It was prophesied that he would cause much trouble in later life so his mother dropped him through a hole in the ice when he was born. Three times she tried and each time she found him safe and sound next morning. He grew to manhood in a few years and became an ally of Hiawatha and promulgated the laws of the confederacy of tribes.

Delphic Oracle, Delphic Sibyl
see **Pythia**

Demeter   *Greek*
= *Egyptian* Isis; *Phrygian* Cybele; *Roman* Ceres
Goddess of agriculture, corn and fertility; daughter of Cronus and Rhea or of Uranus and Gaea; sister of Hades, Hera, Hestia, Poseidon and Zeus.

When Erysichthon cut down a tree on her sacred grove, she punished him with everlasting hunger, and she changed the boy Stellio into a lizard when he made a joke about the speed at which she ate her food.

At the banquet where Tantalus served up his dismembered son Pelops, she ate the shoulder part and made a new one from ivory which was built in when the boy was reassembled by the gods.

When her daughter Core was abducted by Hades she wandered the land in the guise of an old woman looking for her daughter. She was taken in by Celeus, king

of Eleusis, and employed as Deo, a wet nurse to his newly-born son. To repay his kindness, Demeter tried to make the infant immortal by plunging him into the fire but his frightened mother, Metaneira, snatched him away. In some stories the baby was Demophoon, in others he was Triptolemus: some say the baby died, others that it survived the ordeal. Abas, the eldest son of Celeus, made a foolish jest about Demeter's own son, Iacchus, and, in a fit of temper, she turned him into a lizard.

She taught Celeus the Eleusinian mysteries and he became her first priest.

She eventually discovered what had happened to Core. In one version she was told by Triptolemus whose brothers had seen the abduction, in another she heard the truth in the burbling of the nymph Arethusa who had been turned into a stream and who had seen Core seated on a throne with Hades as she passed through the underworld en route to Sicily. Others say that the goddess Hecate, who had heard Core's cries, took Demeter to see Helios who, as sun god, had seen all that had occurred and told them what had happened to Core. Demeter now caused a blight to descend on the earth and refused to lift it until Zeus intervened to order Hades to release Core, who had been made queen of the underworld, as Persephone.

She is sometimes depicted as horse-headed. Her symbol is a sheaf.

Demeter's people   *Greek*
The dead.

Demogorgon   *European*
A mysterious deity of the underworld; the spirit king of the elves.

King Arthur was said to have gone into the cave which was the home of the Demogorgon on his way to Morgan's palace.

In Spenser's *Faerie Queene*, he is said to live in a deep ravine with the three Fates, but the Italian poet Ariosto has him living in the Himalayas.

demon
An evil spirit, a devil; in some accounts, demons are said to have a life-span of 680,000 years while others calculate it as only 9720 years. They are variously classified as:
  1. armies (or hordes)
  2. demons from sexual intercourse
  3. demons attacking saints
  4. demons inducing women to attend Sabat
  5. demons of nightmare
  6. disguised demons
  7. fates
  8. familiars
  9. incubi and succubi
  10. poltergeists,
or as those of the
  1. atmosphere
  2. earth
  3. heavens
  4. night
  5. sea
  6. underground regions
or as
  1. gnomes (of the underground regions)
  2. ondines or nymphs (of the seas)
  3. salamanders (of fire)
  4. sylphs (of the air)
Other lists deal with individual

demons associated with various
forms of temptation, including:
Ashtaroth (sloth)
Asmodeus (lust)
Baalberith (blasphemy)
Beelzebub (pride)
Belial (arrogance)
Carnivean (obscenity)
Carreau (lack of pity)
Cresil (slovenliness)
Juvant (reincarnation)
Leviathan (loss of faith)
Oillet (riches)
Olivier (cruelty)
Rosier (love)
Sonneilloun (hate)
Verin (impatience)
Verrier (disobedience)
or ascribe various attributes
Abaddon (evil war)
Ashtaroth (inquisitions)
Asmodeus (vengeance)
Beelzebub (false gods)
Belial (trickery)
Mammon (temptation)
Merizim (pestilence)
Pytho (falsehood)
Satan (sorcery)
In black magic, demons are
classified in hierarchies.
1. Grand Dignitaries or Princes:
Baalberith, master of alliances
Beelzebub, supreme chief
Euronymus, prince of death
Leonard, grand master of the
Sabbath
Moloch, ruler of the land of
tears
Pluto, lord of fire
Proserpine, ruler of evil spirits
Satan, leader of the opposition
2. Ministers:
Adrameleck, chancellor
Astaroth, treasurer
Leviathon, chief admiral
Nergal, head of secret police
3. Ambassadors:
Mamma, in England

Belial, in Turkey
Belphegor, in France
Hutgin, in Italy
Martinet, in Switzerland
Thamuz, in Spain
4. Judges:
Alastor, commissioner for
public works
Lucifer, chief justice
5. Royal Household:
Behemoth, steward
Chamos, chamberlain
Dagon, steward
Melchom, paymaster
Misroch, chief steward
Mullin, valet
Siccor-Benoth, chief eunuch
Verdelet, master of the court
6. Master of Revels:
Antichrist, juggler
Asmodeus, supervisor
Kobal, stage manager
Nybras, director
Generally, demons can appear
in many different forms, in
many different locations, usually
during the hours of darkness;
are born, grow, have children
and die; intermarry with humans
and have the same appetites
and desires as humans. Most are
harmful, some are benevolent to
mankind.
Some traditions maintain that
demons are born from the union
of gods and mortals, others that
they are sexless beings.
The number of such beings
has been variously estimated as
44,435,556 and 133,306,668.
In Dante's *Inferno*, where the
demons are employed in pushing
barrators under the surface of
boiling pitch, there are twelve
demons whose names (English
versions in brackets) are given as
Alichino (Hellkin)
Barbariccia (Barbiger)

Cagnazzo (Harrow-hound)
Ciriato (Guttlehog)
Draghignazza (Dragonel)
Farfarello (Farfarel)
Grafficane (Grabbersnitch)
Malacoda (Belzecue)
Malebranche (Hellraker)
Rubicante (Rubicant)
Scarmiglione (Scaramallion)

dendan   *Arabian*
A sea monster in the *Arabian
Nights' Entertainments*. It was
said that if this monster touched
human flesh or even heard a
human voice, it died.

Deohako   *North American*
Iroquois plant spirits. This is
the name given to the three
daughters of Earth Mother. Their
individual names were Bean, Corn
and Squash.

Dercynus   *Greek*
Son of the sea god Poseidon. He
was killed by Hercules when he
tried to steal some of Geryon's
cattle that Hercules was driving
on his tenth Labour.

Desana   *South American*
also Master of Animals
A deity responsible for all animals.
Some of the Amazon tribes regard
this deity as a shape-changer who
sometimes takes the form of a
squirrel.

Desired Knight *see* **Galahad**

Deucalion   *Greek*
King of Phthia. He was forewarned
by his father of the coming Flood
and saved himself and his wife
Pyrrha. In some stories, they
stood on Mount Parnassus which
projected above flood level but
in others he built an ark and
saved himself and his wife when
Zeus caused the whole world to
flood. They repopulated the world
by throwing stones over their

shoulder, each of which turned into a human being.

In other versions of the story, Dardanus and Ogyges appear in place of Deucalion and others have Clymene as Deucalion's wife.

Devi   *Hindu*
also Durga, Kali, Mahadevi, Parvati, Sati, Shakti, Uma

Wife of the god Shiva. She is conceived as a personification of the primeval essence, Brahman. As Sati, she was Shiva's consort and as Parvati she was the reincarnation of Sati. She also appeared as Durga or Kali and is depicted as having four heads and four arms.

Devil's Dandy Dogs   *British*
A version of the Wild Hunt. This phenomenon consists of a pack of fire-breathing hounds said to appear on stormy nights in the south-west of England, where they are led over the moors by the Devil himself.

Dhakhan   *Australian*
The rainbow-god of the Aborigines. He is part fish, part man, and appears as the rainbow when he moves from one waterhole to another.

Dharmapala   *Buddhist*
Any of the eight 'protectors of the truth' or 'Eight Terrible Ones'. These beings are depicted as giants with sharp fangs and three eyes, one of which, in the middle of the forehead, beams perfect knowledge to the unbelievers. They are listed as Beg-Tse, Hayagriva, Kubera, Mahakala, Sitabrahma, Sri, Yama and Yamataka.

Diamond Jousts   *British*
A series of tournaments organised by King Arthur.

It was said that Arthur, as a

young man in Lyonesse, had found the dead bodies of two kings who had killed each other and took the jewelled crown which was lying beside them. The jewels from this crown were used as prizes for the champions of his tournaments. Lancelot won all the diamonds and gave them to Guinevere who, jealous at that time of Elaine, threw them into the river.

Diamond Sow *see* **Dorje**

Diana   *Roman*
= *Greek* Artemis

Goddess of birth, chastity, hunting, light, moon, plebians and wild things; daughter of Jupiter and Latona. (*See also* **Hecate**[2].)

Diana of Ephesus   *Roman*
A tutelary goddess and fertility goddess. A many-breasted statue of the goddess is said to have fallen from heaven.

dibbuk *see* **dybbuk**

Dido   *Greek*
A sorceress, founder and queen of Carthage. Her real name was Elissa; she was called Dido after leaving Tyre.

Her husband was Sychaeus, the wealthy king of Tyre, who was killed by Dido's brother Pygmalion. She fled to Libya with much of her husband's wealth and there she bargained with the king, Iarbas, for a piece of land on which to build a new home, buying an area which could be covered by the hide of an ox. By cutting the hide into thin strips she was able to enclose a very substantial area. Within it, she built the city of Carthage.

When the Trojan Aeneas and his crew landed in North Africa when their ship was blown off course, Dido fell in love with him

and kept him in luxury. Eventually he forced himself and his crew to leave to seek their destiny in Italy, whereupon Dido immolated herself, though some say that it was her sister Anna who died on the pyre for love of Aeneas.

Another story says that Dido killed herself to escape marriage to the neighbouring king, Iarbas.

She became identified with Tanit, guardian goddess of Carthage.

Dike   *Greek*
The goddess of human justice; daughter of Zeus. One of the Horae.

Dikpala   *Hindu*
A guardian deity. Each of these eight deities guards one of the eight points of the compass in the form of, or with the help of, an elephant. They are listed as Agni (south-east), Indra (east), Kubera or Agni (north), Surya (south-west), Vayu (north-west), Varuna (west) and Yama (south).

Another version gives Kubera (north), Virudhaka (south), Dhritarashtra (east) and Virupaksha (west).

Other lists, giving the name of the elephants or the deities as elephants, have Airavata, Anjana, Kumuda, Pundarika, Pushpadanta, Supratika, Suryabhauma and Vamana.

Dilga   *Australian*
An earth goddess of the Aborigines. When the Bagadjimbiri brothers were killed by Ngariman and his followers, she drowned the killers in the flood of milk from her breasts and revivified the victims.

Dilmun   *Mesopotamian*
The Sumerian paradise, inhabited by the creator-god Enki and the

earth goddess Ninhursaga, and home of the deified hero Tagtug and other heroes.

Dinewan   *Australian*

The emu personified. It is said that the emu lost its wings as the result of a trick played on him by Goomblegubbon, the bustard.

Diomedes[1]   *Greek*

King of Argos. He fought bravely and well at Troy, wounding Aeneas and even the war god Ares and the goddess Aphrodite. He and Odysseus entered the city by night and captured the image of Athena known as the Palladium, and he was one of those concealed in the wooden horse. He also exchanged armour with Glaucus, who was fighting on the side of the Trojans, receiving a set made of gold, and rescued Nestor whose horse had been killed.

In some accounts, he was a lover of the Trojan girl, Chryseis (Cressida).

On his return from Troy, he discovered that his wife, Aegialeia, had been unfaithful, so he went to Italy and married Euippe. With him went Abas, Acmon, Idas, Lycus, Nycteus and Rhexenor, all of whom, after the hero's death, were turned by Aphrodite into swans which sprinkled water on his grave every day.

In some accounts, he died naturally in old age, while others say that he was murdered by Euippe's father, Darnas.

Diomedes[2] *see* **Jason**

Diomedes[3]   *Greek*

King of the Bistonians in Thrace; son of the war god Ares, some say. He owned four flesh-eating horses and was eaten by them when Hercules seized them as his eighth Labour.

Dionysus   *Greek*

also Dionysos;

= *Egyptian* Osiris; *Etruscan* Fufluns; *Hindu* Rudra; *Roman* Bacchus

God of vegetation and wine. Some say that he was the son of Zeus by the goddesses Core or Demeter but it is more often said that he was fathered on Semele by Zeus, who killed her before the child was born. The infant was saved by the god Hermes who planted him in Zeus' thigh from which, at full term, he became 'twice-born'. In another version, Zeus himself planted the infant in his own side and other accounts say that Zeus, in the form of a serpent, fathered the boy on Persephone. He was reared by Athamas and Ino but, when Hera discovered the baby's whereabouts, she drove Athamas mad. The infant was torn to pieces by the Titans, on the instructions of Hera but Rhea rescued the pieces and reassembled them, restoring him to life to be reared by the nymphs of Mount Nysa and tutored by the satyr Silenus.

One variation says that the Titans ate the body with the exception of the heart which was rescued by the goddess Athena who gave it to Zeus. He swallowed the heart and immediately produced another Dionysus by Semele.

Another account says that he was born to Semele in the normal fashion but, when she claimed that Zeus was the father, her father Cadmus threw both Semele and the baby into the sea in a chest. Semele died but Dionysus was rescued and reared by Ino.

In the war between the gods and the giants, he killed Eurytus with his thyrsus (staff). Some say he was changed into a kid (or ram) by Hermes.

He is credited with the invention of wine and became its patron god. During his life on earth he was accompanied by a band of satyrs and frenzied women, the Maenads. He drove mad the three daughters of King Minyas of Thessaly (Arsippe, Alcithoe and Leucippe), when they declined his invitation to join his drunken revels.

He once led an army of Amazons in Egypt to defeat the Titans and restored King Ammon to the throne. He is also said to have conquered India.

On one occasion he was captured by pirates but he turned himself into a lion and they all jumped overboard and were turned into dolphins. In another version, the ship suddenly stopped and vines grew from the sea to envelop it, after which a group of his Maenads took over the ship and the bemused sailors jumped into the sea.

It was Dionysus who gave King Midas the golden touch as a reward for the kindness shown to his old tutor, Silenus. He rescued Ariadne after she had been abandoned by Theseus on Naxos and married her. When, soon after, she died, he threw her wedding crown into the sky to become the constellation Corona, and Zeus, taking pity on him, made Ariadne immortal and restored her to Dionysus.

He descended to Tartarus to demand the release of Semele, the mother he had never seen, and took her up to Olympus.

He was depicted originally as a mature bearded man and later as a handsome young man crowned with leaves and carrying his emblem, the thyrsus. His chariot is shown being drawn by leopards or panthers.

Some accounts suggest that Orpheus was an incarnation of Dionysus.

Dioscuri *Greek*
A name of Castor and Polydeuces as 'sons of a god'.

In the Roman pantheon, as Castor and Pollux, they are sometimes identified with the Penates.

They are said to have led the Roman cavalry at the Battle of Lake Regillus in the 5th century BC.

discus
(1) In Buddhist tradition, the weapon of Mara, king of the demons.
(2) In Hinduism, the weapon of the god Vishnu.

Disemboweller *Inuit*
A female demon. She was said to be the banished cousin of the moon goddess and attacked humans by night, sometimes killing them by causing them to laugh until their stomachs split open and their bowels fell out.

Distinguished Name *see* **Mahucutah**

Djambu Boros *East Indies*
The Sumatran tree of life. Each leaf of this tree, which grows in the highest heaven, has a word written on it. Each soul (tondi) which leaves heaven for birth on earth, takes a leaf. The nature of the inscription determines the fortunes of that individual.

Djanbun *Australian*
The man who became the duck-billed platypus. His efforts to kindle a fire by blowing a fire-stick caused his mouth to enlarge. He jumped into the river and became the platypus.

Djanggawuls *Australian*
also Djunkgao
A trinity of Aboriginal deities, parents of the Wawalag sisters.

There were two sisters and a brother who came from Bralgu, the island of the dead, and created all forms of plants and animals and shaped the earth with their sacred sticks known as rangga.

In some accounts, Djanggawul was male, the others, Bildjiwuaroju and Miralaldu, were male and female combined until Djanggawul cut off their male genitalia.

djinn, djinni *see* **jinnee**

Djuskaha *North American*
also Little Sprout, Sapling
An Iroquois culture-hero, twin brother of Othagwenda.

These boys were born to a maiden, daughter of the goddess Ataensic, impregnated by the West Wind, and Othagwenda was abandoned at birth, only to be rescued by his brother.

When they reached maturity, they went their separate ways, making plants and animals, later meeting to compare their handiwork.

Djuskaha made a number of improvements to things created by his brother, so that they were more beneficial to man, whereas Othagwenda spoiled much of his brother's work. As a result, they quarrelled and Othagwenda was killed.

dMu-rgyal *Tibetan*
Early ancestors of the race. These were the first beings to employ ritual and magic. They were followed by the 'dre

Do *African*
A fertility god and rain god of the Upper Volta. He is said to be incarnate in the butterfly.

Dobooz *European*
A Czech robber-king. He, like King Arthur and others, is said to lie sleeping, waiting for the call to help his country.

Dodona *Greek*
also Chaonia
The oracle of Zeus; the grove of the talking oak trees.

The oracle was established when a pigeon, flying from Egypt, settled on a branch and ordered that an oracle be set up. The oracle was interpreted from the rustling of the leaves, the noise of a fountain or the cooing of doves.

The grove was attended by the Selli (priests) and the Peleiai (priestesses).

dog
This animal appears in many myths, some of which are mentioned below:
(1) An Australian Aboriginal story tells how the dog Marindi fought a primeval lizard and was killed. The dog's blood is said to make the rocks red.
(2) In Central America it is said that the dog Maya Pek controls the lightning.
(3) Chinese lore says that the huge celestial dog, T'ien Kou, in the form of a shooting star, is forever trying to swallow the sun.
(4) In Egypt, the dog was sacred to Anubis and the funerary dog, Khenti Amentiu, was king of the underworld.

(5) The Inuit speak of a mythical eight-legged dog called Quiquern.

(6) In European lore, the French have story of Aubry's dog, an animal called Dragon, who harried and finally killed the man who had murdered his master.

Dogs appearing in *Reynard the Fox* are called Courtoys, Roonel and Wackerloo.

Gabriel's Hounds appear under several different names throughout Europe and are described as a pack of hounds racing through the sky led by any one of many famous figures such as King Arthur, Charlemagne and so on. It is often referred to as the Wild Hunt.

Isolde was given the fairy dog Petitcrieu by her lover, Tristram. Tristram also had dogs called Houdain and Leon.

On the Isle of Man, Peel Castle is said to be haunted by the ghostly Mauthe Dog.

The Seven Sleepers, who slept in a cave for 200 years, were guarded by the dog Kratim (or Katmir).

(7) In Greek myths, the dog was sacred to the gods Ares and Hermes. Another, Laelaps, was owned by Europa but later passed to Cephalus on his marriage to Procris. It was said to catch anything it chased but met its match in the Cadmaeian Vixen which could outrun any other animal. Zeus solved the dilemma by turning both animals to stone.

The hunter, Actaeon had a large pack of dogs which tore him to pieces when he watched the goddess Artemis bathing.

Geryon, the twin-bodied giant killed by Hercules, had two dogs, Gargittos and Orthrus, which guarded his huge herds.

In Hades, there was a dog called Laon, and the three-headed dog, Cerberus, guarded the entrance.

An Athenian farmer, Icarius, owned a dog called Maera which was originally the woman Hecuba who had turned herself into a bitch. When Icarius was killed by shepherds, Maera led his daughter Erigone, a harvest goddess, to his grave.

Odysseus owned a dog called Argos which waited twenty years for his master to return and, having recognised him, died.

The giant hunter, Orion, had several dogs including Archophonus, Ptoophagos and Sirius.

(8) In Hindu lore, the rain god, Indra, had a dog called Sharama which he had himself created to find the cloud-cattle which had been stolen. When the bitch was bribed with milk by the thieves, she reported failure and Indra was forced to undertake the search himself.

In the underworld, two four-eyed dogs, Sabala and Syama, guarded Kalichi, the god Yama's palace and rounded up the souls of the dead for judgement.

(9) In Irish stories, the warrior Celtchair owned a dog called Daolchu; Cuchulainn had Luath; Dermot O'Dyna, lover of Grania, owned a dog called Mac an Choill; Finn mac Cool had Adhnuall, Bran and Sceolan; Lugh, the sun god, had a dog called Fail Innis which could turn water into wine, catch any animal it chased and win every fight it engaged in; Mac Da Tho, king of Leinster, had a very famous dog called Ossar and two other kings fought a war to decide who should have it; Mail

Fothartaig, a Leinster hero, had Daitlenn and Doilin.

Celtchair killed a fierce dog called Brown Mouse which was ravaging the countryside by putting his hand down the beast's throat and tearing its heart out.

(10) In Japan they tell of Shippeitaro, a dog which waited in a cage for the cat-monster which demanded the annual tribute of a maiden which it ate, and held the monster while a knight killed it with his sword.

(11) In Norse mythology, the hero Frithiof had a dog called Bran and the goddess Hel had two dogs, Garm and Gurme, to guard her underworld kingdom.

(12) The trickster Coyote, who appears in so many Native American stories, had a dog called Rattlesnake.

(13) In the Pacific Islands they regard the dog Kimat as the controller of lightning and say that the monster Ku takes the form of a huge dog but can assume the shape of a man at will. It changed into a handsome prince when it fell in love with a maiden but, when his suit was rejected by her father, he reverted to his canine form and killed and ate many of her father's kin.

(14) Scottish stories refer to the fairy dog, Cu Sith, said to be green in colour and as large as an ox.

15) Welsh stories say that two dogs Aethlem and Aned were engaged in the hunt for the huge boar, Twrch Trwyth, and chased it into the sea. Another dog, Drudwyn, was the leader of the pack which was largely composed of the offspring of yet another dog, Gast Rymhi.

The king of the fairies, Gwynn ap Nudd, owned a dog called Dormath.

Llewellyn left his dog Gelert to guard his baby son and returned to find the baby missing and the dog spattered with blood. He killed the dog, thinking it had killed the child, only to discover the child alive and well beside the body of a wolf which Gelert had killed to protect the child.

dogai   *Pacific Islands*
Melanesian mischief-making female spirits.

These beings are said to be very ugly with huge ears, one of which is used as a bed, the other as a covering blanket. They can turn themselves into such things as trees and rocks and sometimes are said to kill children.

The queen of the dogai is Metakorab.

doggabi   *Korean*
A goblin.

Dogheads   *Baltic*
In Estonian lore, a race of beings, half-man, half-dog. These being were said to be manlike on one side, doglike on the other, or like a man with a dog's head with one central eye. They killed and ate human beings.

Dohkwibuhch   *North American*
The creator-god of the Snohomish people.

Dokibatl   *North American*
A trickster-god of the Chinook.

Dolorous Blow *see* **Dolorous Stroke**

Dolorous Gard   *British*
The name Lancelot used for his estate, Garde Joyeuse, after he had returned Guinevere to her husband, King Arthur.

Dolorous Mound   *Welsh*

The home of a serpent, the Black Worm of the Barrow.

Dolorous Stroke   *British*
also Dolorous Blow
When this stroke was delivered, the country (Wales or, some say, the whole of Britain) was laid waste and the barrenness could be removed only by the Grail Quest. The blow which precipitated this state was either the stabbing of Pelham, king of Listinoise, by Balin, a Knight of the Round Table, who used the Sacred Spear, or else the sword-stroke with which Varlan, king of Gales, killed Lambor, king of Terre Foraine.

dolphin
(1) In Greece, the dolphin was sacred to the god Apollo.
   This animal is also regarded as an emblem of the goddess Aphrodite and the sea god Poseidon and was ridden by the Nereids.
(2) In Mesopotamia, the dolphin was the animal of the sea god Ea or of Oannes, the god of wisdom.
(3) Some Native American tribes regard the dolphin as the incarnation of the Great Spirit.
(4) In Roman myths these animals are ridden by cupids and conduct the souls of the dead to the underworld.
(5) In South America some tribes believe that the dolphin can take on human form at night.

Dolya   *Russian*
A female deity who determines the fate of mortals at their birth.

Domovik   *Russian*
A male house spirit, a type of karlik; husband of Domovikha.

He was expelled from heaven

by the god Svarog and fell down a chimney. He is said to live near the fire or on the threshold of the house and to ensure prosperity. If not properly propitiated, he may burn the house down.

He is envisaged as a grey-bearded old man.

Domovikha   *Russian*
A female house spirit; wife of Domovik.

She is said to live in the cellar of the house and, if not properly propitiated, wakens the children in the night to annoy the parents.

Some house-spirits are even more vicious and suck the blood of sleeping children or suffocate them.

It is said that these beings have two souls, the normal one and a second which can transfer itself to another body.

Donar   *German*
= *Anglo-Saxon* Thunor; *Norse* Thor
A thunder god.

Doquebuth   *North American*
A survivor of the Flood, in the lore of the Salish tribe. He rode out the flood in his canoe which, like Noah's Ark, held two of every species plus five other humans. The creator-god told Doquebuth how to re-start life on earth after the waters had subsided.

Dorje   *Tibetan*
also Diamond Sow;
= *Buddhist* Marichi; *Chinese* Ju-I;
Japanese Nyoi
The thunderbolt, embodying the power of the law, personified.

In some accounts, she was the wife of the demon Tamjin. She took the form of a wild sow to destroy the Mongols.

Dorobo   *African*
A pygmy, the first man, in the lore of the Maasai.

dragon

A fire-breathing monster, usually with wings. Also often referred to as a 'drake' or a 'worm'. This beast appears in many forms in many mythologies. Some dragons have the power to become invisible.

(1) In alchemy, dragons were said to have different characteristics and could affect substances such as metals. Those with wings, for example, represented volatile substances.

Other dragons are described as having the body of a leopard and the feet of a bear, others as having two horns. Some were said to be able to heal their own wounds.

(2) In China, the dragon is a monster with a camel's head, fish scales, the hooves of a deer and clawed legs like a tiger. This beast, which can be very small or quite enormous, is said to carry a jewel under its chin and may disgorge pearls. Some say that it lives in the oceans during the winter months and ascends to the heavens in the spring.

In some versions, there are three main types, the lung (or long), the li and the chiao.

Other accounts have it as a fierce winged beast which breathes fire, while some claim that it can expand or contract and change into any shape.

The Dragon Kings, who guard the seas, are Kuang-te (east), Kuang-li (south), Kuang-jun (west) and Kuang-she (north). An alternative listing gives Ao Kuang (east), Ao K'in (south), Ao Jun (west) and Ao Shun (north).

(3) In Greek stories the dragon was the animal of the god Bacchus.

A dragon appears in various stories, often as a guardian of treasure such as the Apples of the Hesperides sought by Hercules and the Golden Fleece in the story of the Argonauts. In the story of Cadmus, he killed a dragon and sowed its teeth like seed, producing a crop of soldiers. Some of these teeth appear again in the story of the Argonauts, again producing soldiers from the earth.

(4) In Japan the dragon is a mythical beast thought to hatch from an egg after 3000 years. The first 1000 years are spent in the sea, the second in the mountains, and the third in a village. The egg contains a tiny snake which, as soon as it is hatched, grows into a huge dragon which flies into the sky.

Five of the many dragons in Japanese lore are regarded as guardians of the various quarters of the world; the Black Dragon rules the north, the Red Dragon the south, the Blue Dragon the east and the White Dragon the west, while the Yellow Dragon rules the centre.

Dragon-King of the Sea *see* **Ryujin**

Dragon Kings   *Japanese*

Rulers of the earth. There were said to be four such creatures, each responsble for one particular aspect and one of the oceans of the world. They were known as the Celestial Dragon, the Dragon of Hidden Treasure, the Earth Dragon and the Spiritual Dragon.

Dragon Kings are also found in Chinese mythology: *see* **Ao Ch'in, Ao Jun, Ao Kuang, Ao Shun**.

'dre   *Tibetan*

Early ancestors of the race. These people abandoned the great forests to live on bare mountain slopes. Next came the Ma-sang.

Dreamtime, Dreaming *see* **alchera**

Driant   *British*

A Knight of the Round Table. He was killed by Gawain.

Drifta   *Norse*

A Frost giantess; goddess of snowdrifts; sister of Frosti, Jokul and Snoer.

Drink-all   *African*

A frog which can empty a lake by drinking its water.

Drip-hall   *Norse*

A name for heaven.

Drudwas   *British*

One of the twenty-four Knights of King Arthur's court.

He had arranged to meet King Arthur in single combat and sent his tame griffins ahead with orders to kill the first man to arrive at the scene of the combat. His sister, a paramour of the king, delayed Arthur's arrival and Drudwas was killed by his own griffins.

dryad   *Greek*

A tree nymph, originally of oak trees. (*See also* **hamadryad**.)

Dubiaku   *African*

A man who almost cheated death.

A mother with eleven sons asked Death to take some of them because they ate so much. In the house of Death, they slept on mats, each with a child of Death, but Dubiaku kept awake, sent Death on an errand and escaped with his brothers. When Death returned, she ate her own children in mistake for the brothers. Dubiaku lured Death into a tree when they were followed and caused her to fall to the ground and be killed. She was revived inadvertently by Dubiaku and took up the chase again. Ten of the brothers escaped by swinging themselves across a river and Dubiaku turned himself into a stone to escape Death.

Dudugera   *Pacific Islands*

A Papuan leg-child. He was born from his mother's leg after a sea god in the form of a fish or a dolphin had rubbed against it, and was returned to the sea where his father seized him in his mouth. He became the sun and his heat killed nearly all the people until his mother threw lime or mud into the air to form protective clouds.

Dugnai   *Slav*

A household spirit which causes dough to rise.

Duke of Thunder *see* **Lei Kung**

Dumuzi   *Mesopotamian*

= *Babylonian* Tammuz; *Greek* Adonis

The Sumerian god of fertility, flocks, grain, herds and god of the underworld.

When Inanna was released from the underworld where she had gone to challenge the authority there of her sister Erishkegal, she was required to provide a substitiute. She nominated her consort Dumuzi along with the wine goddess Geshtinanna and these two served alternate periods in the underworld. In an effort to escape this fate, Dumuzi changed himself into a gazelle, helped by his sister, Belili.

Duneyr   *Norse*

One of the four stags of the gods. (*See* **Dain**.)

duppy   *West Indies*

also jumby

A Caribbean spirit or ghost. These spirits can be invoked to attack

one's enemy but they can be warded off by a ring of tobacco seeds.

Duranda(l) *see* **Durindana**

Durathor   *Norse*

One of the four stags of the gods. (*See* **Dain**.)

Durga   *Hindu*

An aspect of Devi, Kali or Parvati as 'the inaccessible'.

The demon Durga had taken over nearly all the world, so the gods concentrated all their powers in the goddess Devi who went out to do battle on their behalf. The demon had millions of soldiers and elephants on his side but Devi defeated them with a thunderbolt and came face-to-face with Durga himself. After many shape-changes, the goddess finally killed Durga and took his name as her own.

In another story, this four-, ten-, eighteen- or hundred-armed goddess of strength, the destroyer, was a warrior-maid who was born fully grown. She slew the monster water-buffalo, Mahisha, who had terrorised all the other gods, despite the fact that he changed successively into a lion, a giant, an elephant and a buffalo during the course of their battle.

In some accounts, she is depicted as twelve-armed, each arm holding a weapon. These are given as an arrow (Tir), an axe (Parashu), a bow (Dhanus), a bell (Ganta), a club (Khitaka), a discus (Chakra), a goad (Ankas), a javelin (Satki), a noose (Pasha), a shield (Sipar), a sword (Khagda) and a trident (Trisula).

She is depicted as yellow-skinned and riding a lion or a tiger.

Durindana   *European*

also Duranda(l)

In the Charlemagne cycle of legends, a sword of Roland. This sword, which could split a mountain, was said to have belonged originally to Hector, prince of Troy. Hector's armour had come into the possession of Roland when he killed the Saracen warrior Almontes. In another account, Roland acquired the sword and his famous horn when he defeated the giant, Jutmundus. When Roland went mad, he abandoned his armour and sword which was then seized by the Tartar Mandricardo who killed Zerbino in a fight for its possession.

Some say that King Charlemagne or the enchanter Malagigi gave Roland this sword and that it had been made by the fairies.

It was said that the hilt contained a number of relics such as a thread from the cloak of the Virgin Mary, a hair from the head of St Denis, a drop of blood from St Basil and one of St Peter's teeth.

Other stories say that, when he was dying of his wounds after the Battle of Roncesvalles, Roland threw the sword into a stream, having failed to break it on a rock.

Dvalin[1]   *Norse*

A dwarf who, at the request of the god Loki, fashioned the unerring spear Gungnir, the magic ship Skidbladnir and the golden hair to replace that stolen by Loki from the head of Sif.

Dvalin[2]   *Norse*

One of the four stags of the gods. (*See* **Dain**.)

dvapara-yuga   *Hindu*
The 3rd or bronze age of the world. In this age, people live for 200 years, wickedness increases and people are afflicted by disasters and disease. (*See also* ***yuga***.)

Dvarakala   *Hindu*
A keeper of the crossroads in Patala, the underworld.

The four roads lead to heaven or hell. To the north lies the realm of Kubera, home of the valiant dead; to the east, the realm of the god Indra where those who have achieved supernatural powers reside; to the west lies the home of the generous in the realm of Buddhapada; to the south, the road leads to the realm of Yama, god of death.

Dvorovoi   *Slav*
A spirit of the farm-yard. He is depicted as an old man with a grey beard and covered with hair.

Dwales-doll   *Norse*
A name for the sun used by the Dwarfs. Dwarfs caught in the light of the sun were turned to stone unless they were protected by the Tarnkappe, a red cap.

dwarfs   *Norse*
Beings created from the maggots which bred in the flesh of the dead giant Ymir.

These beings were banished to their own realm, Svartalfheim, below the earth, where they extracted and hoarded precious metals and stones. If they were exposed to daylight they turned to stone unless they happened to be wearing the Tarnkappe, a red cap. Their ruler was Volund.

They were said to have dark skins, green eyes and long beards. Their short legs ended in crow's feet.

In some accounts they are the same as the elves; in others they are separate beings.

Dwyvan   *Welsh*
also Dwyfan
The builder of the Ark. He and his wife Dwyvach built the ark Nefyed Nav Nevion and embarked many animals to escape the Flood caused by the Addanc.

Dxui   *African*
An ancestor of the Bushmen. He was first a flower, then a man, a tree, a man, a fly, water, a bird and a man again. When he died, he became a lizard.

dybbuk   *Hebrew*
also dibbuk
An evil spirit. The dybbuk is said to be the soul of a person who has died with some unforgiven sin and seeks to inhabit the body of some human. This spirit could be exorcised and the victim could tell when it had left his body because a red spot, together with a cracked nail, would appear on his big toe.

dzalob   *Central American*
In the mythology of the Maya, the creator-god Hunab repopulated the earth three times after floods. The second race were the dzalob, who became demons (the first were dwarfs, the third were the Maya).

Dzelarhons   *North American*
A frog-princess of the Haida people. She arrived on the north-west coast with six canoe-loads of her people and married the bear-god, Kai'ti.

Dzhe Manitou   *North American*
A benevolent god of the Chippewa; a wood-spirit; brother of Kitshi Manitou.

dziwozony   *European*
Wild-women of the Polish forests. These women are very swift runners and sometimes attack men or seduce them.

Dzokhk   *Armenian*
also Dzoxk
The underworld. In this fiery abyss, souls wear iron shoes, have their mouths filled with vermin and are burnt with hot irons. When they cross the bridge that leads to heaven, those heavy with sin cause the bridge to break and they are cast back into torment.

E

E *Central American*
A Mayan deity of uncertain
identity, known as God E (*see*
alphabetical gods).

This deity is depicted wearing
maize ears as a headdress and is
regarded as a maize god such as
Yum Caax.

E-u *Burmese*
The first woman, made by the god
Ea-pe; consort of Thanai, the first
man.

Ea *Mesopotamian*
A Babylonian sea god, the primeval
ocean personified, and a god of
wisdom; brother of Enlil; father of
Marduk and others.

He represented water and Enlil
represented earth. Mixed together
they produced humans. He is
credited with having instructed
people in the arts of agriculture,
magic, architecture, etc and
warned Atrahasis (Utnapishtim) of
the impending Flood.

He is depicted as half man, half
fish, with two heads or dressed
in fish-skins or, in the role of
creator-god, as a snake. It is said
that he was the serpent in the
story of Adam and Eve.

Ea-pe *Burmese*
The supreme deity of the Karen. He
created the first man, Thanai, and
the first woman, E-u.

eac uisge *Irish*
also each uisge;
= *Scottish* kelpie
A malicious water horse.

eagle
(1) In Babylonian lore, the eagle
was a demon. When he ate the
offspring of Mother Serpent, the
sun god Samas condemned him to
death. Mother Serpent hid inside
a slaughtered ox and killed Eagle
when he came to feed on the
carcase.

A two-headed eagle was
regarded as an attribute of
Nergal.
(2) In Greek myths, the eagle
was sacred to Zeus since it had
brought nectar to nourish the
infant god when he was hidden
from Cronus.
(3) Hindu lore identifies the eagle
with Garuda and Gayatri.
(4) The Japanese regard the eagle as
representing Uye Minu, an aspect
of the Buddha.
(5) Norse myths have the eagle as
the guardian of Asgard. The god
Odin himself often took the guise
of an eagle and the eagle sitting
in the world-tree, Yggdrasil,
represented light and wisdom. The
eagle Egder, generator of storms,
will appear at Ragnarok.
(6) Some tribes of North America
say that this bird, which they call
Master of Height, represents the
Great Spirit of the Thunderbird.
(7) Persian lore regards the eagle as
a form of the storm god and as an
emblem of the large Persian empire.

It was believed that the
feathers of this great bird carried
the prayers of the tribe up to
heaven.

(8) The Romans regarded this bird as an aspect of Jupiter.

(9) The Sumerians said that the eagle brought children into the world and took the souls of the dead out of it. It appeared as the storm bird, Zu.

Eagle Prey God   *North American*
One of the six Prey Gods guarding the home of the first man, Poshaiyangkyo. He is responsible for the space above.

Earth-bearer   *North American*
In the lore of the Seneca, the turtle which carries the world on its back.

Earth Diver   *North American*
A diving-bird, the coot.

Birds flying over the primeval ocean grew tired and needed somewhere to rest, so Earth Diver went to the ocean floor and brought back mud from which the creator-god Maheo built land on the back of a huge turtle.

This epithet is appled to various other animals and birds said to have brought up mud from the bottom.

Earth Dragon   *Japanese*
One of the four Dragon Kings. He is responsible for the rivers.

Earth Initiate   *North American*
The creator, in the lore of the Maidu people of California.

Earth Lion   *Mesopotamian*
A demon which, in the form of snake, stole the plant of life from Gilgamesh.

Earth-maker[1]   *North American*
A creator-god of the Pima tribe. He created the world which was later destroyed by the flood sent by his enemy, Great Eagle.

Earth-maker[2]   *North American*
The supreme deity of the Winnebago. He created five

(or eight) great spirits, each responsible for a particular aspect of life, who rid the earth of giants and evil spirits. He was opposed by the evil spirit Herecgunina.

Earth-maker[3] *see* **Pachacamac**

Earth-monster   *Central American*
A primeval monster of the Aztecs. This female monster swam in the primordial ocean until Quetzalcoatl and Tezcatlipoca tore it to pieces to make the sky and the earth and all that is in it.

Earth Mother[1]   *Greek*
Earth personified (*see* **Gaea**).

Earth Mother[2]   *North American*
also Mother Earth;
= *Zuni* Awitelin Tsta
The consort of Sky Father.

According to the Pueblo Indians, she produced One Alone (Poshaiyangkyo) from the fourth of her four wombs.

earthquake

(1) In classical mythology, earthquakes arise when the giants, buried under mountains by the gods, move their limbs.

(2) Indian lore asserts that earthquakes are caused when the elephant, on whose head the world rests, moves.

(3) In Tibet, earthquakes are said to be caused when the frog, on whose back the world rests, moves.

Earthshaker *see* **Poseidon**

Eastern Paradise   *Chinese*
A heaven situated on the Isle of P'eng-lai.

Eastre   *Anglo-Saxon*
also Eostre;
= *German* Ostara; *Norse* Freya, Frigga
A fertility goddess and goddess of spring. She owned a hare in the moon which loved eggs, and was

sometimes depicted as having the head of a hare.

Eater of Dreams *see* **Baku**

Ebisu   *Japanese*
A Shinto god of commerce, fishermen, good fortune and self-effacement; one of the Seven Gods of Fortune (Shichi Fukujin); son of Daikoku.

He was originally the premature son of Izanagi and Izanami, born in the form of a jellyfish or leech, and known as Hiru-ko.

He is regarded as the patron of good workers and is depicted as a cheerful fat man holding a fishing rod and a fish.

Some say he was banished for some crime and lived for many years on an island where he spent most of his time fishing, laying his catch on the shore of the mainland as food for the locals. It was said that he could spend several days under water.

Echidna   *Greek*
A monster in the form of a serpent-woman; mother of Cerberus, the Chimaera, the Colchian dragon, the Harpies, the Hydra, the Nemean Lion and others including, some say, the Sphinx. In some accounts, Echidna was the mother of the Blatant Beast.

In one version of the story in which Hercules seized Geryon's cattle, the snake-woman with whom he slept was Echidna, and she later bore three sons.

Echo   *Greek*
A nymph of Mount Helicon; mother of Iambe and Iynx by Pan.

She amused Hera with stories while Zeus entertained his concubines and was punished by the loss of her voice. She could say nothing other than repeat the words uttered by others. Rejected by Narcissus, she pined away leaving only her voice behind, still repeating what others say.

An alternative version says that Narcissus killed her accidentally, piercing her with a lance.

Another version has it that when she rejected the advances of Pan, he caused some shepherds to tear her to pieces, leaving only her voice; or he rendered her capable of repeating only what others said, which so annoyed the shepherds that they dismembered her.

eclipse

Eclipses inevitably perplexed early, unsophisticated peoples, who invented many stories to account for the phenomenon, many of them asserting that the heavenly body was being devoured by some huge animal.

Armenia

It was said that the primeval ox gave birth to two offspring which appear as dark bodies in the heavens, blotting out the sun or the moon.

Baltic

The Letts say that the body being eclipsed is being devoured by some huge animal.

Cambodia

The belief here is that some huge monster is devouring the heavenly body and young girls are allowed out during this period to do homage to the monster.

China

The Chinese say that the body being eclipsed is under attack from some huge celestial animal and kick up a great din to frighten it away.

Egypt

On the occasion of an eclipse, the king walked sunwise round the temple.

India

It is said that an eclipse of the sun is caused by the asura (demon) Svarbanhu while an eclipse of the moon occurs when it is swallowed by the demon Rahu.

Mexico

The Mexicans sacrificed humans (dwarfs and hunchbacks) to propitiate the spirits causing the eclipse.

North America

(1) The Cherokee say that eclipses are caused when the moon visits his wife, the sun.

(2) The Inuit say that the sun and moon are brother and sister who have sexual intercourse during an eclipse.

3) The Ojibway believe that the sun will be totally extinguished in an eclipse and shoot flaming arrows to keep it alight.

(4) The Tlingit believe much the same as the Cherokee except that they regard the moon as female and the sun as her husband.

(5) In the Yukon the women invert their cooking pots to avoid contamination by the unclean vapours thought to descend during an eclipse.

Pacific Islands

The Tahitians regard the two heavenly bodies as male and female and say that an eclipse occurs when they are having sexual intercourse.

Siberia

(1) The Buriats say that the sun or moon disappears when eaten by the monster Alka.

(2) The Tatars say that an eclipse is caused by a vampire which lives on a star.

South America

(1) The Bakaira of Brazil say that an eclipse is caused by a huge bird which obscures the moon with its wings.

(2) In Bolivia, Nicaragua and Peru, they say that the body being obscured in an eclipse is being eaten by a huge jaguar and shoot arrows to drive the beast away.

(3) The Cavina of Bolivia and Brazil say that the moon is being eaten by ants when it disappears during an eclipse.

(4) The Vilela people of Argentina believe much the same as the Bakaira but substitute a huge bat for the bird.

Ector[1]   *British*

also Ector of the Forest Sauvage
Foster-father of King Arthur; father of Kay. He raised the young Arthur alongside his own son, Kay, until Arthur was fifteen, at which time he took them both to London and Arthur became king.

He was killed in a battle with the Romans outside Rouen.

Ector[2]   *British*

also Ector de Maris, Hector de Marys
A Knight of the Round Table; son of King Ban; brother of Lancelot.

He rescued the maiden Perse, whom he loved, from the hands of her suitor Zelotes.

He was one of the many knights captured by Turkin and later released by Lancelot. He, with Bors and Lionel, searched for Lancelot when he went mad and disappeared from Camelot. Percival finally found him at Castle Bliant and persuaded him to return to the court.

Ector joined the other knights in the Grail quest and rode for some days with Gawain, finally reaching a deserted chapel where he fell asleep in a pew and dreamed that Lancelot was beaten and placed on a donkey and that he himself was turned away from a house where a wedding was in progress. A voice told them they were not fit for the Grail quest, so they went to Nascien the hermit who interpreted the dreams and confirmed what the voice had told them.

After the death of King Arthur and Lancelot, Ector went to live in the Holy Land where he fought the Turks.

Edjo　　　　　　　　　*Egyptian*

A cobra-goddess of the Lower Kingdom.

She is regarded as a goddess of the primordial darkness, later as a nurse of Bast and Horus. She is represented by the uraeus worn in the headdress of the pharaoh and is associated with the udjat, Ra's third eye. In some accounts, Edjo is the same as Wadjet.

Eeyeekalduk　　　　　　　*Inuit*

A god of healing. He was envisaged as an old man, so small that he lived in a pebble. He cured illness merely by looking at the patient, drawing the cause from the patient's eyes into his own. He could also transmit sickness from his eyes to another person's.

Efé　　　　　　　　　　*African*

The first man in the lore of the Pygmies. When he was born, his parents were swallowed by a monster but Efé killed it and saved them.

He spent some time in heaven acting as a hunter for the gods and returned to earth with three magic spears.

Egeria　　　　　　　　　*Roman*

A nymph, goddess of childbirth and fountains. She married Numa Pompilius, second king of Rome, and when he died she was

changed into a fountain by the goddess Diana. In some accounts she is identified with Diana and typifies the wise adviser.

Egil[1]　　　　　　　　　*Norse*

When the swan-maidens Alvit, Olruns and Svanhvil came to earth to bathe, they left their wings on the shore. Egil and his brothers Slagfinn and Volund seized the wings and kept the maidens as their wives for nine years before they recovered their wings and flew away. Egil searched for his wife in vain.

Egil[2]　　　　　　　　　*Norse*

A peasant, father of Roskva, Thialfi and Uller.

When he entertained Thor and Loki who were journeying to Jotunheim, he killed the only two goats he owned to feed them. Thor instructed him to place the bones inside the skins of the animals so that he could restore them to life but Thialfi broke one of the bones and sucked the marrow. The angry god would have killed them all but Egil placated him by giving him the children to act as the god's servants. The restored goat turned out to be lame.

Egres　　　　　　　　　*Baltic*

A Finnish fertility god, protector of turnips.

Ehecatl　　　　*Central American*

An Aztec creator-god and wind god; an aspect of Quetzalcoatl.

He brought the girl Mayahuel from the underworld and mated with her to show mankind the secret of reproduction.

When the guardians of the underworld broke the branch of a tree which sprang up on the site of the mating of Ehecatl and Mayahuel, the maiden died. From

her body grew a magical plant that produced a liquid which acted as a love potion.

Ehecatl ruled over the second of the five ages of the world which ended when it was destroyed by storms and men turned into monkeys.

Eight Ancestors　　　　　*African*

Gods of the Dogon, deified ancestors of the race. These beings were four pairs of twins born to the first man and woman created by Amma.

Eight Auspicious Signs *see* **Eight Precious Things**

Eight Diagrams　　　　　*Chinese*

also Pa Kua

A series of signs composed of straight lines. The lines employed in these diagrams, invented by the serpent-bodied Fu-hsi, are either continuous lines (Yang I) or broken lines (Yin I) representing the Yang (male) and Yin (female) principles. The signs, which are used in divination and as talismans guarding against demons, are listed, together with the elements and animals they represent, as follows:

Ch'ien – sky, heaven, horse
Chen – thunder, dragon
Li – fire, sun, heat, pheasant
K'an – lake, rain, moon, pig
Ken – mountains, dog
K'un – the earth, ox
Sun – wind, wood, fowl
Tui – sea, water, goat

Eight Fairies *see* **Eight Immortals**

Eight Gods　　　　　　　*Chinese*

The eight forces revered as controllers of the universe. These entities are Earth, Moon, Seasons, Sky, Sun, War, Yang and Yin.

Eight Immortals　　　　　*Chinese*

also Eight Fairies, Pa Hsien

A group of mortals who became Taoist divinities. These personages are listed as

Chang Kuo-lao
Han Chung-li
Han Hsiang-tzu
Ho Hsien-ku
Lan Ts'ai-ho
Li T'ieh-kuai
Lü Tung-pin
Ts'ao Kuo-chiu

Together they travelled to the undersea world in craft which they made simply by throwing anything they carried into the sea. They fought and defeated the Dragon-king of the Eastern Sea who had captured Lan Ts'ai-ho.

Eight Glorious Symbols   *Tibetan*
Religious symbols in Tibet. These symbols, often seen on some types of prayer-flag, are listed as Conch-shell trumpet, Golden fish, Lotus, Lucky Diagram, Umbrella, Vase, Victorious banner and Wheel.

Eight Imperial Deities   *Japanese*
A group of Shinto tutelary deities; guardians of the royal household. These deities are given as Ikumusubi, Kamimusubi, Koto-shiro-nushi, Miketsu, Omiya, Takamimemusubi, Tamatsumusubi and Taramusubi.

Eight Ordinary Symbols *see* **Eight Precious Things**

Eight Precious Organs of Buddha *see* **Eight Precious Things**

Eight Precious Things   *Chinese*
also Eight Treasures, Pa Pao
Groups of Taoist symbols appearing as charms. There are several such groups, some of which are:

1. book, coin, leaf, lozenge, mirror, pearl, rhinoceros horn, stone chime – these are the Eight Ordinary Symbols;

2. castanets, drum, fan, flower-basket, flute, gourd, lotus, sword – these are the symbols of the Eight Immortals;

3. gall-bladder, heart, intestines, kidney, liver, lungs, spleen, stomach – these are the Eight Precious Organs of Buddha;

4. canopy, conch-shell, fish, fan, lotus, mystic knot, umbrella, wheel of the law – these are the Eight Auspicious Signs;

5. artemisia leaf, cash, double lozenge (or two books), hollow lozenge, inverted V, pair of horns, pearl, solid lozenge.

Eight Terrible Ones *see* **Dharmapala**

Eight Thunders   *Japanese*
Guardians of the underworld. They, together with the Eight Ugly Females, chased the primeval father-god Izanagi from the underworld.

Eight Treasures *see* **Eight Precious Things**

Eight Ugly Females   *Japanese*
Female demons. They, together with the Eight Thunders, were sent to chase Izanagi from the underworld.

Eighteen Lohan   *Chinese*
Disciples of the Buddha. Each of these disciples is depicted in a distinctive pose with his own symbols. Sixteen of them, the arhats, were adopted from the Hindu tradition and two others were added by the Chinese themselves. There are a number of lists, some of them of purely Chinese and Tibetan origin. The original sixteen are listed as:

Angida (Angaja)
Asita
Chota Panthaka
Gobaka

Kalika
Kanaka-vatsa
Nagasena
Nakula
Nandimitra
Panthaka
Pindola
Pindola the Bharadvaja
Rahula
Tamra-Bhadra
Vajraputra
Vanavasa

One of the other two is sometimes given as Ajita though others equate Ajita with Asita. The other is given as Po-lo-to-she but this is said to be a form of Pindola the Bharadvaja. Other names sometimes given are Bhadra, Kanakabharadvaja and Upadhyaya.

An alternative Chinese list has only seven from the original Hindu tradition. This list is as follows:

Asvagosha
Feng-kan
Gonamati
Han-shan Tzu
Hui-tsang
Hui-yüan
Isvara
Kumarajiva
Mahakasyapa
Pu T'ai (Ho-shang)
Rahulata
Shen-tsan
Shih-te Tzu
Singhalaputra
Tao-t'ung
Tao-yüeh
Ts'ung-shen
Wu-k'o

Eighty Myriad Gods   *Japanese*
Early deities. All these deities descended to the cave where the sun goddess Amaterasu once hid herself, in an effort to persuade

her to come out and so restore the light of the sun.

einheriar *Norse*

also einherjar

The souls of slain warriors. These, the warriors of the god Odin, are resident in Valhalla awaiting the final battle, Ragnarok.

Eire *Irish*

A fertility goddess; an aspect of the Triple Goddess.

She, Banba and Fohla were the three goddesses regarded as the original rulers of Ireland.

When her husband Mac Greine and the other Danaan kings, Mac Cool and Mac Cecht, were killed by the invading Milesians, she and her sisters said they would give up their kingdoms if their names were given to the land. When they were refused, war broke out between them. Her name, however, did become the name for Ireland.

Eirene *Greek*

also Irene;

= *Roman* Pax

A goddess of peace; one of the Horae.

Eitumatupua *Pacific Islands*

A god of the Tonga Islanders. He is said to have taken the mortal Ilaheva as his wife and, having fathered the boy Ahoeitu, returned to the sky. When he grew to manhood, Ahoeitu was reunited with his father but the heavenly sons of Eitumatupua were jealous and tore him to pieces. The father ordered them to regurgitate the pieces of their brother's body that they had eaten and he reassembled them and restored Ahoeitu to life, making him king of Tonga.

Ek Chuah *Central American*

The Mayan war god and god of

merchants and travellers. He is the black-eyed (or black-skinned) god who carried off the souls of warriors killed in battle.

Ekadanta *see* **Ganesha**

Ekseri *Siberian*

One of the two aspects of the supreme being of the Evenk people. *See* **Amaka**.

Ekutsihimmiyo *North American*

The Cheyenne name for the Milky Way, regarded as a hanging road.

El Cid *Spanish*

also El Campeador

A Spanish hero, Rodrigo Diaz de Vivar.

When Don Gomez insulted his father, El Cid killed him. He then went to the court of King Ferdinand but his manner was so haughty that the king banished him. He raised a force of warriors and went off to fight the Moors and, in the first encounter, took five Moorish kings prisoner, forcing them to pay a tribute and foreswear hostilities as the price of their release. In this fight he won the sword Tizona.

Soon after, he married Ximena, daughter of Gomez, the man he had killed, and the king gave them four cities as a wedding gift.

He was said to have seen a vision of St Lazarus and gave money for the establishment of a leper-house.

Ferdinand was in dispute with Ramiro of Aragon and appointed El Cid as his champion to meet Martin Gonzalez in combat to settle the matter. He was also appointed as champion of Ferdinand to fight the Pope's champion when Ferdinand refused to submit to the Pope's authority, and was again victorious.

In a later battle with the Moors,

it was said that his army was led by St James riding a white horse.

When Ferdinand died, El Cid served his son, Sancho. One of Ferdinand's sons, Garcia, seized the city of Zamora which had been given to his sister, Urraca, and she sought help from Sancho who sent an army under El Cid to her aid. Both El Cid and Garcia were captured by their opponents but El Cid broke his bonds and escaped, charging into the opposing forces and capturing Alfonso who was helping his brother Garcia. Sancho then took over the realms of both Garcia and Alfonso, seized Toro from their sister Elvira and laid siege to Zamora. When El Cid failed to persuade Urraca to surrender, Sancho dismissed him but soon called him back to his service.

Sancho was killed during the siege and the throne passed to Alfonso who dismissed El Cid from his service. He went into exile with a small band of followers and waged war against the Moors, capturing two of their strongholds and winning another marvellous sword, Colada. His successes restored him to favour with Alfonso but they quarrelled again and El Cid took his followers to attack Castile, leaving the siege of Toledo, on which he had been engaged, to Alfonso. When Alimaymon died, the city of Toledo passed to his son, Yahia, and he broke the siege during El Cid's absence in Castile, whereupon Alfonso recalled El Cid who soon completed the capture of the city. El Cid then became ruler of Valencia where he settled with his wife and daughters.

When his daughters were

ill-treated by the Counts of Carrion whom they had married, El Cid demanded redress and appointed three knights to meet the two counts and their uncle in single combat. The girls later married princes from Navarre and Aragon. Valencia was attacked by the Moors but El Cid drove them off. They returned some years later, under the leadership of Bucar, the king of Morocco, and El Cid prepared for further battles. He saw a vision of St Peter who told him he would die within thirty days but would defeat his enemies. On the thirtieth day, El Cid died and, in accordance with his instructions, his embalmed body, flourishing the sword Tizona, was strapped into the saddle of his horse, Babieca, and his men emerged from the city with El Cid in the van, driving off the Moors in terror.

His body was seated in state for ten years before it was buried.

El Dorado   *South American*
also the Gilded Man
A city or country of fabulous wealth, or the priest-king of this city.

The report that the king of this city was covered every day with powdered gold led many to go in fruitless search for the place.

Another version says that a new king was stripped and covered with gold before being sent out on a raft to an island in the lake, Guatavita. Here he stripped off the gold and threw it into the lake, returning to the shore where he was then accepted as king.

In some accounts, the name referred to a golden statue of the king.

Elaine[1]   *British*
also Elayne

Wife of King Ban; mother of Lancelot.

Her husband's kingdom was attacked by Claudas, the giant king of the Desert Land, and he left for Britain to seek help from King Arthur, taking his wife Elaine and the infant Lancelot with him. He died of grief when his steward, whom he had left in charge, surrendered to Claudas without a fight. When Lancelot was seized by the Lady of the Lake, Elaine retired to a nunnery.

An alternative story says that Elaine was pregnant when they left their castle and died in childbirth on the shores of a lake. Ban died of grief after wrapping the baby in a blanket. The Lady of the Lake heard the infant's cries and took it to her underwater home where she reared Lancelot until he reached manhood.

Elaine[2]   *British*
also Elaine of Corbenic, Elaine sans Pere, Elayne the Fair
Daughter of King Pelles; mother of Galahad by Lancelot.

Her father invited Lancelot to his castle in Carbonek in the hope that he would marry Elaine and produce Galahad, the only knight worthy of the Holy Grail guarded by Pelles, whose arrival had been prophesied. When Lancelot rejected her advances, Pelles used a potion to deceive Lancelot into thinking that Elaine was Guinevere. Another version says she was trapped in a vat of boiling water by the sorceress Morgan le Fay and rescued by Lancelot. Dame Brisen, a maid of Elaine, cast a spell on Lancelot who was induced to go to Castle Case to keep an assignation with Guinevere but unwittingly slept

with Elaine, who later gave birth to Galahad.

At the great feast held to celebrate Arthur's return from his conquests on the Continent, Dame Brisen played the same trick on Lancelot, deceiving him into sharing Elaine's bed once again. Aghast at what he had done, he went mad, leapt from the window and roamed the countryside for two years living like an animal. Elaine found him again after his period of madness and, when he was restored to health, she lived with him for 15 years in the castle on Joyous Isle given to them by her father, Pelles.

Elaine[3]   *British*
also Elaine le Blank, Elaine the White, Elayne, (Fair) Maid of Astolat, Lady of Astolat, Lady of Shallot
When Lancelot stayed at the castle of Bernard of Astolat (Elaine's father) en route for a major tournament, she fell in love with him and, although he wore her favour in the tournament, of which he was the anonymous champion, he refused her offer to become either her husband or her lover. She pined away and died of unrequited love and, on her instructions, her body was placed in a black-covered barge and steered by a boatman down to Westminster where it was found by King Arthur who ordered Lancelot to give the maid an honourable burial.

Elaine[4]   *British*
also Elaine of Garlot, Elayne
Sister of Morgan le Fay; half-sister of King Arthur.

Elder Brother[1]   *North American*
A hero of the Natchez tribe of Native Americans.

He and Younger Brother were

fishing were a huge fish surfaced. It was too big to catch on a line, so Younger Brother jumped into the water, tied to a rope, and grabbed the fish in his arms. The fish escaped and swallowed its attacker, cutting his life-line. Only the kingfisher offered to help – he pecked so hard at the fish that it died and Elder Brother was able to cut it open and rescue what was left of his brother. All that was left was the head, which could still talk.

When Elder Brother took Younger Brother's wife as his own, the head plotted to kill them but a bird warned them of the plan and they ran away, followed by the head rolling after them and yelling loudly. A mudwasp turned the woman into a man and the head chose the wrong one, taking the new 'man' to hunt. When they came to a river they swam across but the new man sang a chant which caused the head to be trapped for ever under water. 'He' then returned to her proper female form and, when she became pregnant, put her children inside a cane and carried it with her. She later released them and they became the ancestors of the tribe.

Elder Brother[2]　　　*North American*
A culture-hero of the Pima people of Arizona and Mexico.

He and Younger Brother completed human beings by cutting an opening in the face so that they could eat and another in the back so that they could defecate and by separating their webbed fingers and toes and removing their horns and tails.

He is involved in many tales of creation and the destruction of evil in which he dies and is revivified.

Elder Edda　　　　　　　*Norse*
The older of two major collections of myths, epic poems, etc, written in verse, and compiled by Saemund about 1090.

The first part deals mainly with the gods. The second part comprises stories of the Norse heroes.

Elder Gods *see* **Aesir, Titans**

elecampane　　　　　　*Greek*
A flower said to have sprung from the tears of Helen of Troy. In some versions, this plant was said to heal wounds and confer immortality.

Electra[1]　　　　　　　　*Greek*
also Elektra
Daughter of Agamemnon and Clytemnestra; sister of Chrysothemis, Iphigenia and Orestes.

When her father was murdered by her mother and Aegisthus, her lover during Agamemnon's absence at the siege of Troy, Electra incited her brother Orestes to kill them in revenge. She was condemned to death for her part in the affair.

Electra[2]　　　　　　　　*Greek*
also Elektra
It is said of this Electra that her tears turned to drops of amber.

Electra[3]　　　　　　　　*Greek*
also Elektra
One of the Pleiades. In some accounts she is the invisible star in the constellation, having left because she could not bear to look down on the ruins of Troy. Others say that the missing star is Merope or Sterope, two other Pleiades.

elefo　　　　　　　　　*African*
A magic bell used by the god Itonde to predict the future and foretell death. The sound of the bell is capable of killing humans.

Elegant　　　　　*North American*
An Algonquin brave.

When the maiden, Handsome, rejected his love, Elegant made a snowman, dressed it in the finest clothes and feathers and gave it life, calling it Moowis. The girl fell in love with Moowis and accompanied him when he left on a long journey. As the days grew warmer, Moowis melted in the sun and the girl was left with nothing but a heap of feathers.

Eleio　　　　　　*Pacific Islands*
A Hawaiian magician. He was a kahuna, able to see spirits invisible to others and to restore the dead.

He followed a beautiful girl to a tower on a hilltop where she vanished. Inside the tower, he found the body of the girl. Eleio invoked the spirit to appear once more and then seized it, forcing it back into the body of the dead girl, whose name was Aula. When she was restored to life, she married her saviour.

Elektra *see* **Electra**

elephant
(1) In China, the elephant is a sacred animal and one of the Seven Treasures of Buddhism. It is regarded as a previous incarnation of the Buddha and it is said that a white elephant announced the Buddha's birth.
(2) In Hindu tradition, this beast is the vehicle of Indra. In the long poem, the *Mahabharata*, the elephant was the eleventh thing to be produced at the Churning of the Ocean.

Other versions of its origins say that the elephant was created from the shavings removed on a lathe from the body of Surya, by Vishvakarma, to reduce the sun god's overpowering brightness.

Yet another version says that Brahma sang over the two halves of an eggshell and Airavata, an elephant used by the god Indra as transport, emerged from the half-shell in the god's right hand, followed by seven more, all males. Next came eight female elephants from the other half-shell. These sixteen elephants, which support the world at cardinal and intermediate points, were the ancestors of all elephants.

In the early days, elephants had wings and could fly but they lost this ability when they disturbed the teaching of an ascetic, who cursed them.

In some accounts, an elephant standing on the back of a tortoise supports the earth.

Eleusinia   *Greek*
A procession and games held every two years in honour of Demeter.

Eleusinian mysteries   *Greek*
The mysterious rites used at festivals in honour of Demeter.

Eleven Mighty Helpers
                        Mesopotamian
The group of demons enlisted by the sea dragon Tiamat to help her against the god Marduk.

These beings, armed with thunderbolts and led by Kingu, earth god and husband of Tiamat, included Fish Man, Goat Fish, Great Lion, Ravening Dog, Scorpion Man, Shining Snake, Storm Winds and Viper.

elf   *European*
A diminutive supernatural being; a malignant fairy. (*See also* ***elves***.)

elf-dance   *European*
A tune to which fairies dance. Any

mortal playing the tune would be unable to stop until he died exhausted and those dancing to the music were obliged to continue until the music stopped.

elf-locks   *European*
Tangled hair in the tail or mane of a horse. It is said that these tangled knots are made by the fairies who ride the horses during the night.

elf-shot   *European*
A prehistoric stone arrow-head. This artefact is said to have been used by the elves.

The name also refers to the illness caused by such a weapon.

Elimiel   *Hebrew*
One of the Seven Intelligences, governing the moon.

Elivagar   *Norse*
The twelve rivers of Niflheim. These rivers, fed by water flowing from the antlers of the deer Eikthyrnir feeding on the branches of Laerad, a tree near Odin's hall, are given as Fimbul, Fiorm, Giall, Gunnthra, Hrith, Leiptur, Slid, Svaul, Sylgil, Thulr, Vith and Yigr.

Another account gives Vimur as one of the twelve, while others say that the rivers were fed from the spring of Hvergelmir.

Ellal   *South American*
A hero of the Patagonian Indians. He was hidden by Rat to save him from being eaten by his own father, Nosjthej. As a man, he became lord of the earth by killing all the giants with his bow and arrow, which he is said to have invented. He killed the giant-king, Goshy-e, by turning into a gadfly and poisoning him with his sting. Having instructed the tribes in the use of the bow and arrow, he flew to heaven on a swan, leaving men to fend for themselves.

Elle folk   *German*
A race of tiny people living in mounds or in elder trees. These people ae reputed to be the offspring of the first man Adam and his first wife Lilith. The males look like little old men while the females appear as beautiful but hollow dancers.

Ellerkonge   *Danish*
also Erl-king
= *German* Erlkonig
The alder-king who abducts children to the Otherworld.

Ellil   *Mesopotamian*
= *Sumerian* Enlil
A Hurrian god of floods and storms.

ellyll   *Welsh*
plural ellyllon
A small fairy or elf. In some accounts, ellyllon are fiends or ghosts, the souls of druids which are destined to roam the earth until the day of judgement.

Elma, Eloma *see* **Embla**

elves   *Norse*
Beings created from the maggots breeding in the flesh of the dead giant Ymir.

The black elves were the dwarfs living in Svartalfheim, the light elves (Liosalfar) were the fairies living in Alfheim.

In some accounts they are the same as the dwarfs; in others, they are separate beings.

Elves of Light   *North American*
In the lore of the Algonquin, fairies created by the creator-god Gluskap.

Elwe'kyen   *Siberian*
also Wild Reindeer Buck
The Koryak name for the Great Bear constellation, Ursa Major.

The Koryaks say that the creator obtained reindeer for his people from this constellation.

Elysium *Greek*

also Elysian Fields, Islands of the Blessed

A pleasant island, part of Tartarus; the home of the immortals. Originally the home of the gods, later the home of heroes, this paradise was variously said to lie in the western ocean, at the western edge of the world, somewhere suspended in the air, in the sun, in the underworld, in islands off the coast of Africa or somewhere in Italy. (*See also* **Tartarus**.)

Emain Ablach *Irish*

also Island of Apple Trees;
= *British* Avalon

An earthly paradise ruled by Manannan which was sought by Bran on his voyages. Some accounts equate it with the Isle of Arran (*See also* **Ablach**.)

Emakong *East Indies*

In the lore of New Britain, a spirit which brings birds, crickets, fire and night from the underworld.

Embla *Norse*

also Elma, Emola

The first woman, made by Odin from an elm tree; wife of Ask.

Eme'mqut *Siberian*

A Koryak spirit. When his wife was abducted, he threw an arrow into the fire to open the road to the underworld. Here he found his wife and, when they returned to the upper world, he removed the arrow, so closing up the road again.

In another story, his wife was Fox Woman. When a lodger in their house remarked on her foxy odour, she ran away.

Emma-O *Japanese*

= *Chinese* Yen Wang; *Hindu* Yama

A Buddhist god of death, lord of hell. He is the ruler of Yomi-tsu-kuni and has a magic mirror

which detects sin but he judges men only. (*See also* **Emma-ten**.)

Emma-ten *Japanese*

= *Buddhist* Yamadeva

An underworld deity associated with Emma-O. In some accounts, he is the same as Emma-O.

Emperor of the Northern Seas

see **Hu**

Emperor of the Southern Seas

see **Shu**[1]

Enceladus *Greek*

One of the Earthborn Giants; son of Uranus or, some say, of Tartarus.

He was killed by Athena during the battle between the Giants and the gods. She threw a rock which crushed him and he became the island of Sicily.

In another story, it was Zeus who defeated him and chained him under Mount Etna.

end of the world

Each culture has its own version of how the world will end:

Hindu

At the end of the present cycle, the god Vishnu's tenth and final avatar, Kalki, will appear as a winged white horse. He will destroy evil in a final battle, preparing the world for the next cycle of existence.

Norse

In the final battle, Ragnarok, the gods were destined to be defeated by the forces of evil led by Loki. After a winter of exceptional severity that lasted three years (seven in some accounts), known as the Fimbul winter, the Midgard serpent came out of the sea breathing out poisons and causing great floods; the wolves Hati, Managarm and Skoll finally swallowed the sun and the moon; Garm, Fenris and Loki broke

their bonds; the dragon Nidhogg finally ate through the roots of the world-tree Yggdrasil; the cockerels crowed and Heimdall blew his horn to warn the gods that the end was approaching, Loki's ship landed a force from Muspelheim and another ship brought the Frost Giants from the north. They were reinforced by Hel and the monster Nidhogg and by the Fire Giant Surtur and his sons who smashed the Bifrost bridge as they rode over it. In the ensuing battle on Vigrid plain the gods were defeated. Odin was eaten by the wolf Fenris; Frey was killed by Surtur, Heimdall by Loki, Tyr by Garm, and Thor drowned in the poison of the Midgard serpent after he had killed it. The god Vidar, arriving late, put his one large foot on the bottom jaw of Fenris and, taking the top jaw in his hands, pulled the wolf apart. Surtur then set the world on fire with his flaming sword and the earth sank beneath the waves. A man, Lif, and a woman, Lifthrasir, sheltering either under Yggdrasil or in the forest of Mimir, survived ready to repopulate the world. The gods Vali and Vidar, as predicted, also survived, as did Magni and Modi, sons of Thor, who recovered Thor's hammer from the ashes. Balder, son of Odin and god of light, reconciled with Hoder, the god of darkness, rose again to rule a regenerated world.

North American

(1) The Cheyenne say that the whole world is supported on a huge pole. A beaver is continuously gnawing at the bottom of the pole and, when he gnaws all the way through, the

world will fall into an abyss and that will be the end.

(2) The Sioux envisage an old woman in a cave sewing porcupine quills into a blanket. When she gets up to stir the fire, her dog chews some of the quills so that the blanket never gets finished. If she ever does manage to complete her work, the world will come to an end.

Persian

The early version says that the forces of good will overcome evil and the original cosmic god, Rapithwin or Saoshyant, will supervise the world's regeneration.

In the later, Zoroastrian, version the saviour Saoshyant will supervise the final triumph of good when all demons, except Ahriman and Az, who will be confined to hell, will be killed, men will be resurrected and reunited with their souls, the universe will revert to its original pure state and evil will be gone forever.

South American

Many tribes say that the world will be destroyed by fire caused by demons, a spark from the sky, or by part of the moon (or even the sun) falling from the heavens.

Some blame the men of fire who, having been insulted by a bird, set the world ablaze in retaliation. Others say that the blaze will occur when one of the props under the earth is removed by the creator-god.

In the cold south of the continent, they say that a bird will cause a great deal of snow to fall and, when the snow melts, the resulting flood will destroy the earth.

Endymion   *Greek*

A shepherd, and king of Elis.

The goddess Artemis, as Selene, the moon, caused the beautiful youth to sleep for ever, immortal, so that she could visit him every night and caress him, hiding him a cave on Mount Latmus.

He is said to have had fifty sons (or, some say, daughters) by Selene, and is regarded as the founder of the Olympic Games.

Enigorio, Enigohatgea   *North American*

Iroquois creator-gods. Enigorio created the useful things such as trees and fertile land while his twin brother Enigohatgea tried to make the land into deserts.

Enki   *Mesopotamian*

= *Babylonian* Ea

A Sumerian creator-god and water god; god of justice, magic and wisdom. He was said to have risen from the waters of the Persian Gulf as a fish-god.

The gods created humans from clay as servants, but when they got tired of people and Enlil sent a flood, Enki warned Ziusudra (Atrahasis).

In one creation story he exposed the heads of buried mankind with his hoe before his wife Ninhursaga gave them life.

He lived in Dilmun, the earthly paradise, with Ninhursaga until they quarrelled. The quarrel arose over his pursuit of his own daughters and an affair with Uttu, the goddess of weaving. Ninhursaga recovered some of the semen from Uttu's body and grew eight plants from it. Enki foolishly ate the plants and became ill, recovering only when Ninhursaga placed him in her own body so that he was born again. In other

versions, he gave birth to eight children to replace the plants he had eaten, or Ninhursaga gave birth to eight deities, each of which cured one of the ailments that afflicted Enki as a result of eating the plants.

Enkidu   *Mesopotamian*

A warrior. He was created by the goddess Aruru from clay and spittle as a friend for Gilgamesh, king of Uruk, and lived as wild man until Gilgamesh tamed him by using a prostitute named Shamhat to seduce him and made him his companion in many adventures. He helped Gilgamesh to kill the giant Huwawa and the Bull of Heaven but was struck with a fatal illness as a result. In an effort to save him, Gilgamesh sought immortality and got hold of a piece of the 'Never Grow Old' plant but it was stolen from him by a snake.

In another version, Enkidu was trapped in the underworld when he went down to retrieve a drum that Gilgamesh had accidentally dropped. He is envisaged as having the legs and hoofs of a goat or as half man, half bull.

Enkimdu   *Mesopotamian*

A Sumerian god of farming. He was a suitor for the hand of Inanna, the goddess of fertility, who rejected him in favour of Dumuzi, the god of fertility.

In some accounts, he is equated with Enbilulu, the god of canals and rivers, or with Enkidu (*see above*).

Enlightener of Darkness   *Chinese*

A monstrous dragon. This beast is reputed to be a thousand miles long and can change its colour at will. Opening its eyes brings light, closing them brings darkness. The wind is his breath which congeals into rain or, depending on the dragon's colour, gold, crystal or glass.

Enlil   *Mesopotamian*
also Lord of the Storm;
= *Babylonian* Adad, Ea, Elil; *Hurrian* Ellil, Kumarbi
The Sumerian god of air, earth, storms and wind.

In one story it is said that he mated with his mother Ki to produce the human race; in another he was one of the gods who fashioned humans from clay as their servants.

When the gods became angry at the noise people made, Enlil first sent a plague, then a drought, then a ban on reproduction and finally the flood that exterminated all the human race except Ziusudra who had been warned by Enki.

Enlil raped the grain goddess, Ninlil, and was sentenced to death for the crime. Ninlil followed him to the underworld, where their son Nanna was born.

When the god Marduk came to power, he blinded Enlil and killed his father, An.

He is depicted as part man, part fish or as part goat, part fish.

Ennead   *Egyptian*
A group of nine gods. The list varied from place to place: for Heliopolis it consisted of Atum, Geb, Isis, Nephthys, Nut, Osiris, Seth, Su and Tefnut. Other names sometimes included are Hu, Horus, Khenti Amentiu, Ra, Saa and Wadjet.

Eno   *North American*
A name of Coyote as 'thief'.

Enuma Elish   *Mesopotamian*
The Akkadian story of creation which begins with these words, meaning 'When on high ...'.

Enumclaw   *North American*
The thunder-spirit of the tribes of the north-west.

He learned the art of throwing fireballs like spears while his twin brother Kapoonis became adept at hurling huge boulders. To prevent them from doing much damage, the gods took them up to heaven and made Enumclaw lord of thunder and Kapoonis lord of lightning.

In some accounts, their roles are reversed.

Eos   *Greek*
also Hemera, Hespera;
= *Roman* Aurora, Mater Matuta
Goddess of the dawn. In her journeys across the sky with her brother Helius, the sun god, she is Hemera in the morning but Hespera in the evening.

She asked Zeus to make her husband Tithonus immortal but forgot to ask for eternal youth with the result that he grew old and shrivelled. In the end Eos changed him into a grasshopper.

In some accounts, she is the mother of the winds Boreas, Eurus, Notus and Zephyrus. She abducted the boy Ganymede, and handed him over to Zeus, after which he became cup-bearer to the gods.

Eostre *see* **Eastre**

Ephialtes   *Greek*
A giant. He and his twin brother Otus were known as the Aloadae, 'sons of Aloeus', but their real father was the sea god Poseidon. Unlike the other Giants, they were noble beings.

He and Otus imprisoned the war god Ares to demonstrate their power and threatened to pile Mount Pelion on Mount Ossa to attack the Olympians but either

were persuaded by Poseidon not to try or were killed by Apollo or Hercules.

They planned to carry off the goddess Artemis but she knew what they were about and set a trap for them. She flew over the sea to Naxos, where they followed. She then set a white hind in their path, which they immediately set out to hunt. Each threw his javelin from opposite sides of the hind which then disappeared and each died from the other's throw. An alternative version says that, when they tried to abduct Artemis and the goddess Hera, Artemis ran between them. Each aimed a shot at her but she avoided the arrows and each brother inadvertently killed the other.

They were said to have been bound back to back and fastened to a column by snakes when they went to Tartarus.

In some accounts, Ephialtes was one of the Earthborn Giants (*see* ***giants***), son of Uranus and Gaea, and was killed during the battle of the giants with the gods when Apollo shot him in one eye and Hercules in the other.

Epimetheus   *Greek*
One of the Titans; brother of Atlas and Prometheus; husband of Pandora; father of Pyrrha.

With his brother Prometheus he was given the task of creating humans and fitting them for life on earth.

He fought with the gods against the Titans and rejected the beautiful Pandora when offered her hand by Zeus. He changed his mind and married her when Prometheus was punished by Zeus.

Epinogrus   *British*
A Knight of the Round Table; son of
the king of Northumberland.
  He was unhorsed by Dinadan in
a joust and defeated by Lancelot
at a tournament.

Epona[1]   *Celtic*
A goddess of horses and horsemen
in Gaul. She was also worshipped
in Rome where her festival was
held on December 18th. She has a
key which gives her access to the
underworld, and is often depicted
half-naked, riding a horse.

Epona[2]   *Roman*
A name of Demeter as mare-
goddess.

Epunamun   *South American*
A supreme god or war god of the
Araucanian people.

Erato   *Greek*
One of the nine Muses, the Muse of
lyric poetry.

Eravan   *Siamese*
= *Hindu* Erewan
A sun-deity, depicted as an
elephant with three heads. (*See
also* ***Airavata***.)

eré   *African*
In Yoruba lore, childlike beings
which take over people
undergoing initiation.

Erebus   *Greek*
also Erebos
The cavern between earth and
hell: the darkest depths of
the underworld; hell. (*See also*
Tartarus.)

Ereshkigal   *Mesopotamian*
A Babylonian goddess of death and
the underworld. In some accounts
she started out as a sky goddess
but was abducted by the dragon
Kur to the underworld. When
her husband Nergal came to the
underworld at her command, she
saved herself from death at his
hands only by sharing power with

him. In other versions, her consort
is Gugulanna.
  A different version says that
she fell in love with Nergal when
he came down from heaven with
food and she threatened to raise
all the dead unless Anu sent Nergal
back as her husband. The plague
god Namtar was sent to heaven
as an envoy and Nergal hurriedly
returned to the underworld and
became the queen's consort.

Erewan   *Hindu*
A three-headed elephant ridden by
Indra. (*See also* ***Airavata***.)

Eridu   *Mesopotamian*
The Sumerian paradise, home of the
mother-goddess Zikum.

Erin-bird   *Mesopotamian*
A monstrous bird. This bird, which
has a poisonous tooth, was
regarded as a form of the lion-
headed storm bird Zu.

Erinnyes *see* **Furies**

Eris   *Greek*
= *Roman* Discordia
The goddess of discord; daughter
of Zeus and Hera or Nyx; sister of
the war god Ares.
  In some stories she is the
daughter of Erebus and Nyx.
Some say that Ate is Eris, others
that Ate is the daughter of Zeus
by Eris. Some say she was the
consort of Ares.
  She was thrown down to
earth by Zeus in one of his angry
moods. It was Eris ('strife') who
precipitated the Judgement of
Paris and all that followed from
it by throwing the golden apple,
inscribed 'for the fairest', into a
gathering of the deities at the
wedding of Peleus and Thetis.
  (*See also* ***Ate***[1].)

Erlkonig   *German*
also Erl-king;
= *Danish* Ellerkonge

The king of the elves, the alder-
king who abducts children to the
Otherworld. Some say that he is
one of the leaders of the Wild
Hunt.

Eros   *Greek*
= *Hindu* Kama; *Roman* Amor, Cupid
The god of love.
  He is depicted as a winged
youth with a bow, sometimes
blindfolded, shooting gold-tipped
arrows into the hearts of those
he wishes to become lovers. He
sometimes used lead-tipped
arrows to cause lovers to spurn
those who loved them.
  In one story, he caused Dido
to fall in love with Aeneas by
taking the form of Ascanius and
shooting Dido with one of his
arrows.

Erymanthian boar   *Greek*
A huge wild boar. This animal was
captured by Hercules as his fourth
Labour.

Erzulie   *West Indies*
A Haitian goddess of love. She is
represented as wearing three
rings, one for each of her
husbands Agwé, Damballah and
Ogoun.
  'Erzulie-Ge-Rouge' is a name of
Erzulie lamenting the brevity of
life and love.

Es   *Siberian*
A creator-god of the Ket people.
He is said to have made mankind
from clay, producing men with his
right hand, women with his left.

Esaugetuh Emissee *North American*
also Master of Breath
Creator-god and wind god of the
Creek Indians. He made the Creek
Indians from wet clay when the
Flood subsided, drying them in
the sun. Some swam away before
they were properly baked and
these became the white races.

Those who stayed in the sun long enough became the brown races.

Escanor   *British*

A knight of King Arthur's court. It was said of him, as of Gawain, that his strength increased until noon and then diminished. When he carried off a serving-maid from Arthur's court, Gawain killed him.

Eshu   *African*

= *Fon* Legba

An angel-trickster, messenger-god and god of fate among the Yoruba.

As an attendant on the creator-god, Fa, he was responsible for opening some of the god's eyes each morning.

He was a servant of the god Orisha but hated him so much that he rolled a huge rock on to his house, killing Orisha and splitting him into 401 pieces.

He was said to have persuaded the sun and the moon to swap functions on one occasion, causing great chaos.

He keeps a watchful eye on events and reports to the creator god Olorun, judging the actions of men.

Estanatlehi   *North American*

also Turquoise Woman

Earth goddess and goddess of time of the Navaho.

She was created by the Yei (gods) from turquoise and found on a mountain by the sun god Tsohanoai. The gods Hastehogan and Hasteyalti fed her on pollen so that she was fully matured in eighteen days. She produced a man and a woman from maize-flour to serve as the ancestors of each of the eight tribes and then became the goddess of Sunsetland, a land far to the west where the sun sets.

In another version she made men and women from pieces of her own skin and became queen of the underworld. She was said to rejuvenate herself when she grew old.

Some say that she is the same as Changing Woman.

Estonea-pesta   *North American*

also Lord of Cold Weather

Controller of the north wind and snow. He gave Sacred Otter, a chief of the Blackfoot tribe, the Snow-lodge and a magic pipe which protected him from the winter storms.

Etana   *Mesopotamian*

A Babylonian king of Kish, a demi-god. He was said to have flown to heaven on an eagle to establish his divine right to rule and to obtain a plant that would procure a son for him and his wife. In some stories, he fell to earth and was killed, in others the eagle was killed but he survived and had a son. Some say that he ruled for 1500 years, In some accounts he is regarded as the leader of the revolt that led to the construction of the Tower of Babel.

Eteocles   *Greek*

Co-king of Thebes with his brother Polyneices.

After the abdication of Oedipus from the throne, his two sons Eteocles and Polyneices were cursed by their father for some slight: he prayed that each should kill the other. They agreed to rule in alternate years but Eteocles refused to yield at the end of his year and banished Polyneices. He was killed by Polyneices in single combat during the Argive attack on Thebes (the Seven against Thebes) and killed his brother in the same fight.

Etzalqualiztli   *Central American*

A festival in honour of the rain god Tlaloc, held around the middle of May. On this occasion, the officiating priests dived into a lake, acting the part of frogs, animals associated with the rain god.

Etzel *see* **Atli**

Eumenides   *Greek*

also Kindly Ones

Goddesses later identified with the Furies (*see* **Furies**).

Eunomia   *Greek*

The goddess of spring and good government; daughter of Zeus and Themis. One of the Horae.

Euphemus   *Greek*

One of the Argonauts; son of the sea god Poseidon and the moon goddess Europe.

He was an excellent swimmer and it was said that he ran on water. When the *Argo* was stranded in Libya, the sea god Triton gave him a clod of earth which he later dropped into the sea. From this grew the island of Calliste, later Thera.

Euphrosyne   *Greek*

One of the three Graces, the Grace of mirth or good cheer.

Europa   *Greek*

She was carried off to Crete by Zeus in the form of a handsome bull. Changing form to an eagle he ravished her and she bore the three sons, Minos, Rhadamanthus and Sarpedon. The god gave her the dog, Laelaps, a spear which never missed its mark and Talus, the bronze guardian of Crete. She later married Asterius, king of Crete, who adopted her three sons. After her death, she was deified. Other accounts say that she was the mother of the Minotaur.

Euryale *Greek*
One of the three Gorgons; sister of Medusa and Stheno.

Eurydice *Greek*
A Thracian nymph, a dryad; wife of Orpheus.

She died when bitten by a snake as she was running to escape an attempted rape by Aristaeus. Orpheus went down to the underworld and charmed Hades into releasing her, but, when Orpheus broke the rules by looking back to make sure she was following him, Hades reclaimed her and she was lost for ever.

Eurynome *Greek*
An ancient goddess, produced from Chaos; daughter of Oceanus and Tethys; mother of the Graces by Zeus.

She created Ophion the serpent-god with the co-operation of the North Wind and coupled with Ophion to produce all the things in the world.

She later banished Ophion to the underworld and then created the Titans and the first man, Pelasgus.

She rescued the smith-god of fire Hephaestus from the sea when he fell, or was thrown by Hera, from Mount Olympus.

She is depicted in the form of a mermaid.

Eurystheus *Greek*
King of Argos.

His birth was accelerated by Hera so that he inherited the kingdom which should have fallen to Hercules.

He set the tasks for Hercules to perform as his Labours but was so scared of his bondsman that he hid in a large bronze jar when issuing his orders, which were then relayed to Hercules by his herald, Copreus.

When he later invaded Attica, he was either killed or captured and put to death.

His head was buried in a pass on the road to Athens to protect the city.

Eurytion *Greek*
A herdsman; son of the war god Ares. He tended the herds of Geryon and was killed by Hercules when the latter seized the cattle as his tenth Labour.

In some accounts, Eurytion was a seven-headed dragon.

Euterpe *Greek*
One of the nine Muses, the Muse of music. She is said by some to have invented the double flute.

Evadeam *British*
A Knight of the Round Table. He was once turned into a dwarf by sorcery and when he met Gawain he regained his full stature but Gawain became a dwarf.

Evergreen Land *Pacific Islands*
The site of the palace of the sea god.

Excalibur *British*
King Arthur's sword. This marvellous weapon was said to have been created by the sorcerer Merlin. Some say it came to King Arthur from Avalon, others that it was a gift from Vivien, Lady of the Lake.

In some accounts, the Sword in the Stone which Arthur pulled out, so demonstrating his right to the throne, was Excalibur and was engraved with that name on the blade.

In other versions, that was a different sword and when it was broken in combat with an unnamed knight who had challenged Arthur, not knowing he was the king, Merlin took Arthur to a lake where an arm 'clothed in white samite' rose out of the water holding Excalibur which Arthur claimed and used until his death, when it was returned by Bedivere to the lake where the hand rose to receive it and carry it below the surface of the water.

Yet another version says that Excalibur was made by Merlin and given to Uther Pendragon as a symbol of his office as king. When Uther objected to handing over the baby Arthur, as he had promised, Merlin blinded Uther, taking both the child and the sword.

Some say that Excalibur was given to Arthur by Morgan le Fay; certainly she once stole it from Arthur and gave it to her lover, Accolon, in revenge for the execution of another of her lovers, but Arthur soon recovered it.

While Arthur was wearing the scabbard, he could never lose blood if wounded.

Eye of Horus *Egyptian*
The left eye of the god Horus. Horus lost this eye, which was the moon, in his battles with Set, the god of darkness, but it was restored by Hathor. As the udjat (or udjat eye), it became the symbol of healing.

Also a name of Thoth as the moon.

Eye-juggler *North American*
A trickster. When he lost his eyes, he found others to take their place but they turned out to be made of pitch.

F

F *Central American*
A Mayan deity of uncertain identity known as God F (*see **alphabetical gods***); perhaps Nacon or Xipototec.

This deity is depicted with black lines painted all over his body and face, which some interpret as wounds.

Fa *African*
= *Yoruba* Ifa
The Fon god of destiny. He is said to have sixteen eyes and lives in a palm-tree in the sky. The messenger-god, Eshu, is responsible for opening some of Fa's eyes each morning.

Fa'ahotu *Pacific Islands*
An earth goddess; wife of Atea. Fa'ahotu, the earth, was created from one half of the cosmic egg. Atea, the sky, was created from the other half.

faerie
also faery
Fairyland. Humans may enter this realm if they abstain from eating and drinking and carry something, such as a knife, made of iron.

Fafnir *Norse*
Brother of Otter and Regin; brother of Fasolt, in some accounts.

Fafnir's father Hreidmar had received a hoard of gold and a magic ring from the god Loki as compensation when Loki killed Otter but he refused to share it with Fafnir and Regin. Fafnir then killed his father and seized the treasure, turning himself into a dragon to guard it. Sigurd killed not only the dragon but also Regin who had persuaded him to do it and appropriated the treasure for himself.

In the Wagnerian version, Fafnir and his brother Fasolt, both Frost Giants, built Valhalla for Odin but demanded the goddess Freya as payment. When they were given the Rhinegold as ransom, they fought over the treasure. Fafnir killed his brother and then used the Helmet of Invisibility to change himself into a dragon.

Fair Maid of Astolat *see* **Elaine**[3]
fairy
also fay, fey
A diminutive supernatural being. Some say that these immortal beings are the children of Adam and his first wife Lilith.

falcon garb *see* **Valhamr**
Falling Eagle *Mexican*
A giant, in Aztec lore. He was one of four giants who supported the sky at the beginning of the Fifth Sun. He was regarded as the symbol of divine power on earth. (*See **Thorny Flowers**.*)

Fama *Roman*
= *Greek* Pheme
The 100-tongued goddess of rumour.

familiar
A spirit, also known as a 'sending', often in the form of a cat, attending when called, usually by a witch.
(1) In Africa, Basuto witches have huge animals known as obe, while the Zulu sorcerer uses an exhumed

corpse which he revivifies in the form of an umkovu.

(2) In Arabia, the magician's familar is known as a tabi.

(3) Aborigine sorcerers use a lizard as a familiar.

(4) In the Baltic countries, flies are used in this connection.

(5) In the East Indies, a snake or crocodile is used as a sending or the sorcerer may cause slivers of bone, etc to fly through the air and embed themselves under a victim's skin.

(6) The Inuit medicine-men use an artificial seal, known as a tupilaq, as a familiar.

(7) In Malaya, a sorcerer's familiar may be a badger or an owl.

(8) In North America, some medicine-men stuff the skin of an owl and make it fly against an intended victim, causing him to starve to death.

(9) In the islands of the Pacific, sorcerers have familiars in the form of sea-snakes.

(10) The Siberian shaman's familiar is known as a yekeela.

(11) In other parts of the world, dogs, hares or toads may act as familiars.

Farasi Bahari   *Arab*
Green horses said to live in the Indian Ocean. Horses bred from these stallions and normal mares can run forever without pause since, having no lungs, they are never short of breath.

Fata Morgana   *European*
A name of Morgan le Fay (Both 'Fay' and 'Fata' mean 'fairy'.)

Morgan was reputed to have a home in Sicily, where she was known as Fata Morgana.

Also the name for a mirage seen in the Straits of Messina.

The generation of a mirage to lure ships on to the rocks would be consistent with Morgan's role as a trouble-maker. This vision, a scene of architectural wonders, was seen by Roland, the paladin of Charlemagne, in the garden of the enchantress, Falerina. Some say that it represented a palace of Morgan le Fay.

Fate Trinity   *Irish*
The trio Ana, Badb and Macha as the goddess Morrigan.

Fates *see* **Moirae, Norns, Parcae**

Father Atoja   *South American*
A rain spirit of the Aymara.

To bring rain, a magician collects several basins of water with frogs in from Lake Titicaca and places them on top of the mountain, Atoja, praying to the spirits of that mountain, Father Atoja and Mother Atoja. When the sun has evaporated the water in the basins, the frogs croak loudly and the spirits then cause rain to fall.

Father Sky *see* **Sky Father**[1]

Fatima   *Arabian*
A female hermit. In the *Arabian Nights' Entertainments* she was killed by a sorcerer who, disguised in her clothes, entered Aladdin's home.

faun   *Roman*
= *Greek* satyr
A being part man, part goat; a woodland spirit; a descendant of the god Faunus.

Fauna   *Roman*
= *Greek* Damia, Semele
Goddess of fertility, fields, herds; daughter or sister and wife of Faunus; wife of Jupiter or Vulcan, some say.

In some accounts she is identified with Bona Dea.

Faunus[1]   *Roman*
= *Greek* Pan

A vegetation god, god of prophecy and shepherds; father or consort and brother of Fauna.

In some accounts, he was the son of the war god Mars and a princess and was raised to become the god of the countryside. Others make him the son of Mercury, and say that he killed strangers and offered them in sacrifice to his father, who then gave him the hind quarters and hoofs of a goat in punishment. Some say he was the son of Picus.

Faunus[2]   *Roman*
A king of Italy; the father of Latinus, king of Latium. In some accounts, the same as Faunus, the god of vegetation (he too killed strangers and sacrificed them to his father Mercury).

He was killed by Hercules en route back to Mycenae with Geryon's cattle (his tenth Labour) and some say that it was Hercules who fathered Latinus, not Faunus.

His spirit was said to have warned Latinus not to allow his daughter, Lavinia, to marry any but a stranger who would soon arrive from over the sea. This turned out to be Aeneas, who had journeyed from Troy.

Faust   *German*
also (Dr) Faustus
A man who sold his soul to the Devil in return for unlimited knowledge and youth.

Favonius   *Roman*
= *Greek* Zephyr
The West Wind personified.

fay *see* **fairy**

Faylinn   *Irish*
also the Good Folk, the Little People, the Wee Folk
Fairies or leprechauns. This race of people, much smaller than dwarfs, was ruled by Iubdan and Bebo.

In some accounts, it is lubdan's realm, rather than his people, that is referred to as Faylinn.

Feast of Goibhniu   *Irish*

A feast in the underworld at which the smith-god Goibhniu gave his guests food and drink that made them immortal.

This was one of three gifts from the god Manannan to the Danaans. The other two were the Veil of Invisibility and the Pigs of Manannan.

Feather Cloak *see* **Valhamr**

Feathered Serpent, Feathered Staff *see* **Quetzalcoatl**

Fe'e   *Pacific Islands*

A Polynesian war god and god of the dead. He gave birth to all the rocks and islands.

He is depicted as a giant cuttlefish encompassing the world with his tentacles. His undersea palace was known as Bale-Fe'e.

Feini   *Irish*

Early settlers in Ireland. While most accounts refer to the descendants of Dana as the Danaans, the fifth in the series of invaders of Ireland, others refer to her descendants as the Feini and regard them as the first settlers of that country.

Fene   *European*

One of a race of Hungarian demons, or their realm.

Feng   *Chinese*

also feng huang, Vermilion Bird
= *Japanese* ho-o

The Chinese version of the phoenix; one of the Four Auspicious Animals; chief of the feathered animals; ruler of the south and the summer season.

This fabulous bird is described as being composed of parts of many other birds and the tail of a fish, although it is sometimes depicted as the Oriental pheasant. It is reputed to alight only on the wu t'ung tree and lives on the seeds of the bamboo.

Another version describes it as a scarlet or vermilion bird, one of four supporting the corners of the earth.

Feng Po   *Chinese*

also Count of the Winds

A sky god, in charge of the sack which contains the winds, hunger and drought. He tried to overthrow his father Huang Ti and was defeated. He was banished to a mountain-top cave where he sent winds to cause trouble until the archer I shot a hole in his wind-bag. Feng Po was wounded in the leg at the same time and was left with a permanent limp.

He is depicted as a white-bearded old man or as a dragon with the head of a deer or as having the body of a stag, a sparrow's head, the horns of a bull and a snake's tail.

Feng-p'o-p'o   *Chinese*

also Madame Wind

A wind goddess; wife of Feng Po. She is said to ride a tiger in the sky.

Fenodyree   *Manx*

also Fenoderee, Phynnodderee

A brownie.

Fenris   *Norse*

also Fenrir

A wolf, offspring of the god Loki and the giantess Angerbode.

Odin took the wolf to Asgard hoping to tame him but it grew to such size and strength that the gods tied him up for safety. They bound him first with the chain, Laeding, from which he broke free; then with a stronger chain, Droma, which he also broke; then with Gleipnir, a thin cord fashioned by the dwarfs which none could break, fixed with the fetter, Gelgia. Fenris allowed himself to be tied only if one of the gods would put a hand into his mouth as a surety. Tyr complied and when Fenris found himself unable to break free, he bit off Tyr's right hand. When he opened his huge jaws and howled, the gods thrust a sword into his mouth causing an outflow of blood that formed the river Von.

Fenris remained tied through the rock Gioll to a large boulder called Thviti on the island of Lyngvi until the final battle of Ragnarok, when he broke free and fought on Loki's side against the gods. He was killed by Vidar who, arriving late in the battle, put his one foot on the wolf's lower jaw and, grasping his upper jaw in his bare hands, tore him apart.

fey *see* **fairy**

Fianna   *Irish*

An élite military order, bodyguard of the king of Ulster. This order required that members passed stringent tests of skill and stamina and flourished under the leadership of Finn mac Cool. It was organised originally by Fiachald into 150 groups of 27 men, each with its own leader.

They fought on the side of Midir in the war with the Danaan gods.

The High-king, Cairbre Lifeachear, became fearful of their power and broke it by defeating them at the Battle of Gabhra. The dead were consigned to hell but in later years, they were released by the prayers of St Patrick.

Field of Asphodels   *Greek*

A part of the underworld where

souls wait while their fate is determined.

Field of Celestial Offerings
Egyptian
A part of the underworld where the deeds of the dead are weighed.

Field of Truth   *Greek*
The home of the three judges Aeacus, Minos and Rhadamanthus, in the underworld.

Fifth Sun   *Central American*
The fifth age of the Aztec creation cycle. This is the present age ruled by the god Nanautzin.

The gods' first choice for the ruler was Tecciztecatl but, when it came to the final ceremony in which the chosen one is required to commit himself to the fire, he could not summon the necessary courage. Nanautzin threw himself into the flames and became the sun while Tecciztecatl had to content himself with the moon. It is said that this age will end in destruction by earthquake. (*See also* **Five Suns**.)

fig tree
(1) In some accounts, the Biblical Tree of Knowledge was a fig tree.
(2) Some say that the bo-tree under which the Buddha meditated was a fig tree.
(3) In the Pacific Islands the fig tree is a sacred tree, said to be the home of spirits.

Find   *Irish*
A seer, the personification of wisdom. He was said to have emerged, already mature, from the water and became a great seer who, as with Finn mac Cool, could summon up knowledge by sucking his thumb.

Fine Weather Woman   *North American*
Daughter of an Indian chief.

Digging on the sea-shore, she found a tiny baby under a cockleshell. She reared the child, who was called Sin, and he grew very quickly, later changing into a bird and ascending into the heavens as a sky god.

She could cause storms simply by loosening her robe.

Finn mac Cool   *Irish*
= *Scottish* Fingal
A warrior, leader of the Fianna.

Some say that, when he was born, he was thrown into the sea and emerged with an eel in each hand.

When Finn's father Cumaill was killed by Goll mac Morna, Cumaill's wife, fearing for the life of his son, hid herself in the hills until the child, Demna, was born. She then handed him over to her sister (or sister-in-law) Murna and the warrior-maid Liath Luachra who reared the boy in the wild. When Goll heard of him, he set the Connaught Fianna to hunt the boy down and kill him. Demna fled and soon gathered a band of warriors and found the survivors of the Battle of Knock in which his father had been killed. He then sought out the druid Finegas who tutored him.

Finegas caught the Salmon of Knowledge and cooked it. When Demna, now named Finn, accidentally touched the fish and sucked his thumb, he acquired supernatural knowledge and the power to change his shape. Thereafter, putting his thumb in his mouth enabled Finn to foretell the future and heal the sick.

Finn killed Lia, the treasurer of the Fianna, and gave his bag of money to the survivors of

the Battle of Knock, including his uncle Crimmal, and won the captaincy of the Fianna by killing the demon Aillen who set fire to the palace at Tara every year, killing it with the magic spear given to him by the Fianna warrior Fiacha.

While Finn was hunting in Scotland, the king of Dublin landed from his ship and asked for Finn's help. Two (or seven) of his children, on the night they were born, had been seized by a huge hand which came down the chimney. His wife was now at the point of birth once again and he was afraid that they would lose another child in the same way. Finn and some of his men sailed to the king's home and, when the hand appeared, one of them seized it and tore off the arm of the giant who nevertheless seized the baby with his other hand. They tracked the giant over the sea to his tower and rescued not only the baby but several children the giant had previously stolen and two young hounds. When the giant pursued them, one of the men shot him through the only vulnerable part of his body – a mole on his left hand – and killed him. As a reward, Finn claimed one dog, a brindle whelp, which he called Bran, leaving the other, Sceolan, with the grateful parents. Finn was later captured by Lochlanners who left him bound in a glen where Sceolan, now gone wild, roamed. By showing the hound the golden leash he used for Bran, Finn tamed the ravaging hound and, when he was rescued by the Fianna, took Sceolan with him.

On another occasion, a very

ugly man called Gilla Dacar, who had a broken-down mare, took service with Finn but left when the Fianna mocked him. Some who had climbed on to the horse's back were unable to dismount and were carried off to sea. Finn searched for them and found an island where he and his men entered a cave, emerging into a land under the sea, Tir-fa-Tonn 'Land under the Waves'. Here they helped a prince, Abharthach, who had previously appeared as Gilla Dacar, to rout the forces of his brother who had deprived Abharthach of his half-share of the kingdom.

One day when hunting, Finn and his men captured a hind which they took back to their fortress and which then turned into the maiden Saba who had been changed into a hind by the Dark Druid whose love she had rejected. She married Finn and stayed with him until he was called away to fight the Northmen. While Finn was away, the druid appeared in the form of Finn and turned Saba back into a hind. Finn searched for Saba for years but never found her. He once followed a hind (who was really the girl Milucra in disguise) to an enchanted island. Here she turned Finn into an old, grey-haired man because she knew that he would never marry her and she wanted to ensure that he would never marry her sister, Aine, of whom she was jealous. He was restored to his youth by Aine who gave him a drink when the Fianna dug down into the fairy mound where she lived. Finn refused a drink which would have restored his fair hair and

remained grey-haired for the rest of his life. Years later, in another hunt, Finn found Oisin, 'little fawn', his son by Saba.

Another version of how he became grey-haired says that he was inveigled into diving into a lake to retrieve a bracelet dropped by the daughter of the magician Cuilleann and was transformed into an old man. Cuilleann gave him a drink which restored his youth but left him with grey hair.

He lived for some time with Ailbe, daughter of Cormac mac Airt, who had answered a set of riddles he put to her.

He was betrothed to Grania, also a daughter of Cormac, but, at the betrothal feast, she fell for the charms of Dermot and eloped with him. Although Finn and Dermot were later apparently reconciled, Finn never forgave Dermot and when Dermot was mortally wounded by a boar, Finn refused to give him the drink of water that would have saved his life. Finn later married Grania.

A woman named Mair fell in love with Finn and sent him some magical nuts which would have put him in her power had he eaten them. Finn merely buried them.

On one occasion, a being from the Otherworld made off with a pig that Finn and his men were roasting but Finn retrieved it when he followed this being, Culdubh, and killed him with a spear.

It is said that Finn recruited magicians and warrior-maidens from all parts of the world to save Leinster from a flood by sucking up the waters.

He is reputed to have built the

Giant's Causeway as stepping stones across to Scotland. In a Scottish story, the giant Cucullin crossed the Causeway to find and challenge Finn who bit off the giant's middle finger, the source of all his strength, whereupon he crumbled to dust.

He is said to have been 230 years old when he died. The accounts of his end vary considerably. One version says that he was killed by a man referred to as Black Arcan or by Aichleach during a rebellion among the Fianna. Another says that, in the Battle of Gabhra, the five sons of Uigreann, who had been killed by Finn, each threw a spear so that each could claim a part in his death. Some say he was drowned when he tried to jump across the River Boyne and still others say that, like King Arthur, Finn is merely sleeping, awaiting a call to serve his country again. Others say that he was reincarnated as Mongan, king of Ulster.

Fintan *Irish*

also Finntain, Fionntan

He was one of the three men who came to Ireland with Cessair and fifty women and was the only one of the party to survive the Flood, which he did by taking shelter in a cave and changing himself into a salmon. He is said to have lived for thousands of years, acquiring great wisdom and may be regarded as a manifestation of the seer, Find. Others say that this fish is the same as the Salmon of Knowledge. (*See also* **Salmon of Knowledge**.)

Fir Bolg *Irish*

An early invading tribe.
Descendants of the earlier

invaders led by Nemed, in some stories they were said to have been defeated by the Danaans at the first Battle of Moytura and exiled. Other versions say that they made peace and lived in Connaught. Some say they came from Spain, others from Greece where, it was said, they were forced to carry soil, in leather sacks, from the fertile valleys to the rocky mountain tops. They rebelled, made boats from their leather bags and sailed to Ireland where they ruled for 37 years, dividing the country into five parts.

There were in fact three groups: the Fir Bolg, the Fir Domnan and the Fir Gailean.

Fir Chlis   *Scottish*
'Nimble Men'; *also* Merry Dancers
The Aurora Borealis, regarded as being made up of the souls of fallen angels.

Fir Dhearg   *Irish*
'Red Men'
Imps, the forerunners of the leprechauns.

fire
Fire plays a part in many mythologies, sometimes for the benefit of man, sometimes to destroy the world, sometimes to carry a soul to heaven.
(1) In China fire is said to typify summer, destroy metal and produce earth. It came into being when earth and sky separated.
(2) In the East Indies, the inhabitants of Woodlark Island say that a young man stole fire from the heavens and gave it to man, whereupon the angry deity split what remained into two parts and threw it into the sky, forming the sun and moon.

(3) The ancient Greeks said that Prometheus stole fire from the heavens for the benefit of mankind and, for this crime, was chained to a rock for 30,000 years while a vulture pecked his liver.
(4) In Hindu lore, fire was used to control dragons and is regarded as sacred. There are three forms: Dakshinagni, the fire of the atmosphere, the fire of Vayu, associated with dead ancestors; Ahavaniya, the fire of the sky, the fire of Surya; Garhaptya, the fire of Agni, associated with mankind.
(5) In Japan, as in China, fire was produced when earth and sky separated and is regarded as a symbol of the phoenix.
(6) The Mexicans regard fire as a life-giving force and keep a fire burning for four days when a child is born to protect it from evil.
(7) In Muslim lore, fire is the source of genii.
(8) Norse mythology says that the final battle between the forces of good and evil, the Battle of Ragnarok, ends with the world destroyed by fire started by the flaming sword of the giant Surtur.
(9) In the Pacific, fire is said to protect the living from onslaughts by the dead.
(10) Some North American tribes keep a fire alive perpetually in the belief that, if the fire dies, the people will also perish.
(11) In Persian lore, fire is the purest element and is regarded as sacred. There are five forms of sacred fire: Bahram fire, composed of sixteen different types of fire and kept always alight with sandalwood; Spenishta, the most sacred fire, which burns in paradise; Urvazishta, fire caused by friction;

Vazishta, the fire of lightning; Vohu Fryana, the fire producing the internal body heat of animals and men.
(12) The Phoenicians regarded fire as an element, offspring of primal beings Genos and Genea.

Fire Dogs   *Korean*
Animals living in Gamag Nara, one of the heavens, a land of near-darkness. The king of this realm sends out the Fire Dogs to capture the sun or the moon so that he can have light in his country. They always fail but, when they bite the sun or the moon, they cause an eclipse.

Fire Giant *see* **giants**

Fire Mocassins   *North American*
A monster in tribal lore. This ogre wore mocassins which set alight everything they touched as he walked.

firedrake   *European*
A fire-breathing dragon. These beasts lived in caves, usually guarding treasure. One such monster was killed by Beowulf but inflicted wounds on the hero from which he died.

firefly
(1) In Japan, these insects are regarded as the souls of the dead.
(2) In the Pacific, the Balinese believe that certain people known as leyaks can turn into fireflies (or tigers).

First Ancestor   *Australian*
The creator according to the Dieri Aborigines. He first created tiny black lizards but, when he found that they could not stand properly, he cut off their tails and they became human beings, ancestors of the tribe.

First Creator   *North American*

A deity of the Mandan tribe. He created the mountains, trees, streams and some animals while Lone Man created the flat lands.

first humans

Most cultures have stories of the first human beings and how they came into existence.

African

(1) The Abaluyia people of Kenya, Uganda and Tanzania say the first couple were Mwambu and Sela who lived in a house on stilts.

(2) In Angola they say that the first man was Nambalisita, created by the god Kalunga.

(3) The Bakongo say that the first man, made by Nzambi, was Ndosimou, who married the woman Breaker of Prohibitions or, in another version, the androgynous Mahunga was split by the tree, Muti Mpurgu, into a man, Lumbu, and a woman, Musita.

Another version says that Nzambi created a being called Muntu Walunga, with male and female faces, in the form of a palm tree.

(4) The Bakuba say the first man, Kihanga, was created by the creator-god Imana and descended from heaven on a string. His skin was black and white. The first woman, Nchienge, produced a son, Woto, and a daughter, Labama, who married.

(5) The Bambara say that Pemba the wood-spirit created a woman, Musso-koroni, who produced animals and humans.

(6) The Banyarwanda say the first man was Kazikamunti.

(7) In Botswana the first man is known as Tauetona.

(8) The Baganda say that the first man was Kintu.

(9) The Bushongo people living around the Congo River say the first man was called Woto.

(10) The first man of the Dinka was Garang and the first woman was Abuk.

(11) The Dogon say the first human, made by Amma, was Amma-Serou.

(12) The Efe say that Baatsi was made from the earth by God, who also made a woman. She developed a pre-natal craving for the forbidden fruit nahu, and Baatsi picked it for her. As punishment, God took away their immortality.

(13) In Liberia they regard Gonzuole as the first woman.

(14) In Madagascar they claim the first man was Andrianbahomanana and the first woman was Andriamahilala.

(15) For the Makoni people of east Africa, the first man was Mwuetsi for whom was made a girl, Massassi, who bore the grass, trees, etc. and a woman, Morango, who bore animals, birds and human children.

(16) The Mande say that Faro and Pemba were twins generated from seeds planted by the gods at the four corners of the earth. Faro's body was cut up and the pieces scattered to become trees.

(17) The Masai say the first human was a pygmy named Dorobo.

(18) The Orandonga called the first man Amangundu.

(19) In Potomo lore the first man was Mitsotsozini or Vere.

(20) The Shilluk say that the first man was Omara.

(21) In Uganda they say that the first woman was Nambi.

(22) The Yoruba say that Oreluere was the first of sixteen men made by Olodumare.

(23) In Zaire they say the first man was Mokele.

Australian

The first men of the Aborigines were the rangga. The Dieri tribe say that the creator-god known as First Ancestor created tiny black lizards and, when he found that they could not stand properly, he cut off their tails and they became the first humans.

Balkan

In Slovenia it is said that, when God was making the world from a grain of sand, a drop of his sweat fell on to the sand and from this mixture human beings were created.

Burmese

(1) The first man, Thanoi, and the first woman, E-u, were created by the supreme god Ea-pe.

(2) The creator-spirit, Hkun Hsang Long, created the first couple, Ta-hsek-khi and Ya-hsek-khi, who were born in the form of tadpoles living in the lake Nawng Hkeo. After eating a gourd, they mated and the creator renamed them as Ta-hsang-kahsi (Yatawn).

Central American

(1) The Aztecs say that the first couple were Cipactonal and Oxomoco, created by the sun god Pilzintecuhtli. Other accounts say that the god Xolatl retrieved bones from the underworld and produced the first man and woman from ground-up bones mixed with the blood of the gods.

(2) The Mayans say the gods created four brothers, Balam Agab, Balam Quitzé, Iqi Balam and Mahucutah, from whom the human race descended.

Chinese

The first man was Pan Ku; or he modelled mankind from clay; or they developed from fleas on Pan Ku's body; or they were the children of the serpent-headed being Fu-hsi and his wife Nü-kua; or Nü-kua made people from clay.

East Indian

(1) In the Admiralty Islands, the primordial being known as Hi-asa cut her finger and collected the blood in a shell. Two eggs formed from the blood and the first man and woman emerged from the eggs.

(2) In Borneo the first man was Bujang.

(3) The Dayaks say that the first two beings were Amei Awi and Buning Une, gods of agriculture, who had twelve children, eight of whom became the ancestors of the tribes while the other four became the phases of the moon.

An alternative version says that the first man was Tunggal Garing and the first woman was Puteri Bualu.

(4) In the Moluccas the first two men were known as Maapita and Masora. In another story the first human was Patinaya Nei who took the form of a banana-tree, the fruit of which produced further humans. (*See also* (12).)

(5) In New Guinea the first woman was Namora. She swallowed a fish and produced a son, Maruka Akore. These two mated to produce the tribes.

(6) In the New Hebrides they say that the first woman was Jujumishanta and that the first man was Morfonu, who was made from her body.

(7) On Nias the first man was called Sihai.

(8) Some Papuans say that the maggots that bred in the body of a dead female wallaby became the first humans.

Another Papuan story says that a huge turtle swimming in the primordial waters laid eggs from which emerged the first man, Kerema Apo, and the first woman, Ivi Apo. Next came Avo Akore and Ohare Akore who became coconut trees.

(9) In Sulawesi, the first two beings were the brothers Sangkuruwira and Guru ri Seleng. Their children, Batara Guru and Nyilitimo, came to earth to produce ancestors of the people.

Another story says the sun god, Ilai, and the earth goddess, Indara, made humans by breathing life into stones.

Yet another version says that the first human being was the woman, Lumimu'ut, born from a stone. Her son, Toar, produced when she was made pregnant by the wind, mated with her to produce the people and their gods.

(10) It is said that the first man stole the feathers of one of a flight of cassowaries which had taken off their feathers to bathe, when they appeared as women. He kept the woman and mated with her to produce the forerunners of the human race.

(11) The creator-god, Mahatala, carved a stick into the shape of make and female human figures. When he threw it down, it broke into male and female halves. He was Tunggal Garing and she was Puteri Bualu. Her menstrual blood produced all the demons in the world but, following instructions from Mahatala, they were able to procreate properly and produced

many children, ancestors of the tribes.

(12) Some tribes believe that the first humans emerged from trees or came from the fruit of a tree which became the god Lowalangi. (*See also* (4).)

(13) Other tribes say that the first man was Turer who now acts as the guide for souls on their journey to Boigu, the land of the dead, from Beg, a resting-place on that journey.

(14) Still other tribes say that man came from larvae and worms living in the soil.

Egyptian

The first humans were formed from the tears of the god Ra-Atum. Some said that all humans (except Negroes) were born from the eyes of Horus.

Greek

(1) The Argive story says that Phoroneus was the first man and his daughter Niobe was the first woman.

(2) The first man was Pelasgus. The first woman was Pandora, created by Zeus as a gift for Prometheus, or in some stories for his brother Epimetheus, who rejected her.

(3) People were created by the gods, first the golden race like gods whose spirits lived on; then the silver race, less intelligent, whose spirits did not live on; then the brass race who were very violent and killed themselves; then the heroes, who had great adventures and departed to the Islands of the Blessed; and finally the iron race, the present race, who will get worse until the gods destroy them.

(4) The first man, created by Prometheus, was Phaenon, who became the planet Jupiter.

The other humans created by Prometheus grew so wicked that Zeus destroyed them in a flood. Only Deucalion, son of Prometheus, and his wife Pyrrha escaped, warned of the coming disaster by his father. They were told to throw the bones of their mother behind them. They interpreted this to means stones and did what they were told. From the stones came the Stone People from whom the present races are descended.

Hindu

In the early Vedic scheme of things, the first male being was Purusha from whose body the world was made; the first couple were Manu and Parsu.

In the later Hindu version, the first man was Yama and the first woman was Yami, born of Vivasvat, the rising sun.

Others say that the first man was Nara who acted as the god Vishnu's bow-carrier.

Indian

In the Andaman Islands they say that the first man, Juptu, was born inside a bamboo cane and that he made himself a wife from clay.

Maori

(1) The god Tane made Hine-ahu-one from sand and fathered Tiki, the first man, and the Dawn Maiden.

(2) Another account has it that the first woman was Papa-hanau-moku and the first man was Wakea.

(3) Another Maori story has Marikoriko as the first woman, created by the goddess Arohirohi.

Mesopotamian

(1) The Akkadians regard Adapa as the first man. He was made from clay by the god Ea and was consequently half-human, half-divine.

(2) The Babylonians said that the first humans were made from the blood of the earth god Kingu.

(3) The Sumerian version has it that the first man was made from clay by Ninmah.

Norse

The first man was Ask, made from an ash tree; the first woman was Embla, made from an elm tree.

North American

(1) The Acoma say say that the first man was Tiamuni.

(2) Some Californian tribes say that Ejoni and Ae, created from the soil by Nocuma, were the first couple. Others say that the first man was Ouiot. In some accounts, humans were made from flakes of the creator's skin.

(3) The Cherokee say that the first man was Kanati and his wife was Selu.

(4) The Chinook tell a story in which Too-lux, the god of the south wind, cut open a whale and out flew the raven, Hahness. The giantess Quoots-hooi ate the raven's eggs, from which the first humans appeared.

(5) The Fox say that the first man was Mama'sa'a.

(6) The Hopi say that Sky Father and Earth Mother produced One Alone, the progenitor of mankind.

Another story says that the god Kloskurbeh created two beings, one from his breath and the other from one of his tears. These two mated to produce the first humans.

(7) The Huchnom of California say that the first humans were made from sticks of wood.

(8) The Kato name the first man Nagaitco.

(9) The Keres call the first man Pashayani.

(10) The Maidu say that the first man was Kuksu and the first woman, Laidamlulum-Kule. They were given the power to rejuvenate themselves by immersion in water.

(11) The Mandan name for the first man is Numokh Mukana.

(12) The Navaho say that First Man and First Woman produced a daughter, Estanatlehi, who created the progenitors of the tribes from maize-flour or ears of corn. In another version, she produced humans from pieces of her own skin.

Another version says that the first man, Aste Hastin, mated with the first woman, Aste Estsan, who produced five sets of twins who became the ancestors of the Navaho.

(13) The Papago say that the first man was Montezuma who later proclaimed himself all-powerful.

(14) The Pawnee say that Bright Star mated with Great Star to produce the first woman while Sakuru and Pah produced the first male, Closed Man. The man and woman mated to populate the earth.

(15) The Pueblo Indians call the first men the Koshare, made from the skin of a goddess. The first man was Poseyemu.

(16) The Shawnee version has it that men were created from ashes, clay and beads.

(17) Sia lore says that two sisters, created by the god Sus'sistinnako, were the first humans and the ancestresses of the Indian tribes. Nowutset was the progenitor of the other human races.

(18) The Tagua of New Mexico call the first man Puspiyama.

(19) The Sioux say that the first man was We-Ota-Wichusa (Rabbit Boy), who was born from a tear shed by the sun. He mated with First Woman, created by the Great Spirit, to produce the forerunners of the tribes.

(20) The Zuni Indians envisage a dual-sex deity, Awonawilona, who formed the sun which mated with the sea which consolidated and split into earth and sky, Awitelin Tsta and Apoyan Tachi. These produced the first humans, the first man being Poshaiyangkyo. These first beings were said to have several animal features, including webbed feet.

Mongolian

In Altaic lore the first man was Torongai and his mate was Edji.

Pacific Islands

(1) On Fiji, the hawk Turukawa laid two eggs which were incubated by the primeval serpent, Degei, and hatched a human boy and girl who started the human race. The first woman was called Vitu.

(2) In the Gilbert Islands the creator-god, Nareau, made the first couple, Debabou and De-ai.

(3) In Hawaii the first man was called Kumu-honua, and was made from mud by Kane; the first woman was Lalo-honua.

Another version says Wakea was the first man and his wife was Papa-hanau-moku while yet another says that Tiki was the first man and Iowahine the first woman, both created by Tane.

(4) In the Marshall Islands they say that the first man, Wulleb, and his female consort, Limdunanji, were born from the leg of the god Loa.

Another story says that Wulleb

and Lejman, two worms, in a shell, became the first couple.

(5) In Melanesia, it is said that the god Hasibwari came down to earth and made the first woman from clay and the first man from one of her ribs.

(6) In Micronesian lore the first woman was La'i-La'i.

(7) In New Britain, the first man was To-Kabinana who was formed from the earth and the blood of the creator-god. His brother, To-Karvuvu, was formed next. To-Kabinana found a mate when a woman emerged from a tree which he had felled.

(8) In the Philippines, the Tagalog account says that humans emerged when bamboo canes cast ashore from the sea were split open by birds.

(9) The Polynesians have a story that Matuenga or, some say, Tane, created Tiki, the first man, who mated with Hina.

(10) Samoans say that the first man was Atu and the first woman was Ele'ele, the consort of the god Fetu.

Other accounts says that the first man was Tele or Tutu and the first woman was Ila, Tonga or Upolu. Some say that the first couple grew from a pair of grubs.

(11) In Tahiti they say that the god Ta-aroa made a man from red clay and later put him to sleep, took a bone from the man's body and, with it, made a woman.

(12) In Tonga, the first man was named Kohai.

Persian

(1) The primeval man, Gayomart or Gaya Martan, was poisoned by Ahriman, the embodiment of evil. From his seed came the first couple, Mashye and Mashyane,

who were in the form of plants with fifteen leaves from which came ten races. They ate their own offspring until the good god Ormazd made them unpalatable.

(2) Another version has Yima and Yimeh as the first mortals. Some say that people were made from the body of a cow which was killed by Yima.

(3) Another story says that the first mortal couple were Tazh and Tazhak.

Siberian

(1) The Buriats say that the first man was Erlik, created by Ulgan.

(2) The Chukchee people say that the first human was Ku'urkil.

(3) The Koryak call the first man Quikinna'qu.

(4) The first couple according to the Tungus were Khadau and Mamaldi.

South American

(1) The first men were killed in a flood after the animals and their tools revolted. The sun re-emerged after five days and hatched five eggs from which emerged five falcons who became humans.

(2) The Arawak say that the first woman was the stone-woman, Maiso.

(3) The Castunawa say that, when the giants who inhabited the earth were killed in the Flood, their bodies rotted in the sun and men emerged from the maggots that appeared on the corpses.

Another story says that people grew from seeds planted in the earth.

(4) The Chaco say that the first people were made of stone, the second race of wood and the final race from clay.

(5) The Chamacoco say that people

come out of trees when they are split open.

(6) The Incas were said to have issued forth from a cave, Pacari, which had three exits. Eight ancestors of the royal family, four male, four female, emerged from the central exit, the common people from the other two.

Another story says that the god Inti sent his son and daughter, Manco Capac and Mama Occlo, down to earth to teach mankind.

Another version says that Viracocha made the first people but they were unsatisfactory so he turned them all into stone and made a new race.

Another Inca story says that an early race was made by Con, the boneless man, but they were turned into monkeys by the creator-god Pachacamac who made a new race. Unfortunately Pachacamac overlooked the fact that they would need food. The man died but the woman bore a son to the sun god. Pacahacamac then produced fruit and vegetables from the body of this boy, whom he killed.

Another Peruvian story says that men emerged from eggs produced by the sun god. The status of the person was determined by the type of egg (gold, silver or copper) he came from. Other accounts say that the eggs were produced by a huge bird.

Yet another version says that the first man was Guamansuri, father of the twins Apocatequil and Piguerao.

(7) The Mbaya people along the Paraguay River say that men were dug up from the earth by a dog which had picked up their scent

or, in another version, hatched from eggs laid on top of a mountain by a huge bird.

(8) In the lore of the Paressi tribe, the first man was Uazale, son of the stone-woman, Maiso.

(9) The Quiche Indians say that the first humans, made from mud, were too weak to stand and had no mind; a second race, made of wood, were totally self-centred and were destroyed by the animals and tools; the third and final race was made from clay.

Another story says that the first man was Hurakan, created by Gucamatz and Qubanil.

(10) The Taulipang say that the first men were made from wax but they melted in the heat of the sun so the culture-hero who made them tried again and made men from clay.

(11) The Terero say that the first humans emerged from a hole in the earth.

(12) In Tierra del Fuego some say that the first man was Keros who made sexual organs from peat. These mated to produce the forerunners of the people.

(13) In the lore of the Tupari of the Amazon region, the first man was Valedjad, a giant born from a rock.

(14) The Warrau say the first humans descended from the sky.

(15) The Yaruro (and others) say that the first humans came up from an underground world.

Taiwanese

The early Formosans said that humans emerged from a rock when it split open.

West Indian

The first man was Louquo who came down from the sky.

First Made Man   *North American*

One of the early humans in the lore of the Tewa pueblo tribe.

It appears that people existed before the earth dried out from the primordial ocean, living in two caves, the bright home of Summer Mother and the gloomy abode of Winter Mother. These beings sent First Made Man to the surface from time to time to see the state of the world and he continually reported that it was not fit for humans. Finally he went up again and was attacked by various animals but his wounds healed and the animals gave him symbols to take back to his people. He led his people up from the cave of Mother Summer and settled them in the plains and then brought up those from the cave of Mother Winter and settled them along the shore-lines. He then went off to live among the animals where he was made Hunt Chief. (*See also* **Poseyemu, Poshaiyangkyo**)

First Man   *North American*

A name used by Coyote in his dispute with Lone Man.

First Sun   *Central American*

The first of the five ages of the Aztec creation cycle. In this first era, the world was populated by giants who lived on acorns and were ruled by Tezcatlipoca. His reign lasted for 676 years and at the end of that time he was killed by the god Quetzalcoatl and became a jaguar who killed the giants.

Another version, called the Sun of Water, says that animals and humans existed in total darkness. The animals ate the humans and the world was overwhelmed by a flood from which only two humans escaped. (*See also* **Five Suns**.)

fish
Fish are sacred in some cultures, in others they play an active role in myths:
(1) Some African tribes regard fish as the embodiment of departed souls.
(2) In China the fish is regarded as a symbol of regeneration.
(3) In Egypt, where several types of fish are sacred, a talisman in the shape of a fish was said to bring good fortune. As an emblem of Osiris, it signified rebirth; as an emblem of Set, it signified evil.
(4) Hindu mythology tells of ten avatars of Vishnu, the first of which was in the form of a fish known as Matsya, in which form he towed the boat of Manu to safety when the Flood came.
(5) In parts of India, as in China, the fish is regarded as a symbol of regeneration.
    In the far north, some tribes throw fish-bones back into the sea in the belief that they will become fish for the next season.
(6) According to East Indian legend, the fish Maivia Kivivia grew tired of swimming and came ashore, became a two-legged being and had two sons who became the ancestors of the tribes of New Guinea.
(7) In Persian lore, the fish Mah supports the universe.

Fisher King   *Celtic*
also Grail Keeper, Grail King, Maimed King, Sinner King, Wounded King
The keeper of the Holy Grail.
    In some accounts a distinction is made between the Fisher King who was said to be Pelles and the Maimed King, variously known as Parlan, Pelham, Pell(e)am, Pellean or Pelleham. Others say his name was Bron, and that he was a friend of Joseph of Arimathea, while others identify him with Joseph. Some Grail stories refer to him as Amfortas.
    A common feature is that he somehow became wounded, usually in the thigh(s). Some accounts say the wound was caused by the Sacred Spear or by Balin or by the fragments of the sword which killed his brother Goon Desert; some say it was punishment for drawing the Sword of Strange Girdles. It was said that, because of this wound, his only occupation was fishing – hence his title. (Note that the medieval French name 'Roi Pecheur' is capable of two translations, 'Fisher King' or 'Sinner King'.)

Five Emperors   *Chinese*
Creator-gods. These were Chuan Hsü, Huang Ti, K'u, Shun and Yao and they, with the Three Sovereigns, created the universe.

Five Holy Mountains *see* **Wu Yüeh**

Five Sisters   *North American*
Primordial beings in the lore of the tribes of British Columbia. These daughters of the creator-god, the Old One, were created from hairs taken from his beard. Three of them became earth, sea and sky, the others became the progenitors of the human race.

Five Suns   *Central American*
In Aztec myth, the intervals in the development of the world.
    The first period, which lasted for 676 years, was ruled by Tezcatlipoca who was superseded by Quetzalcoatl, who ruled the Second Sun. The Third Sun was the period of Tlaloc's rule which ended when then earth was destroyed by fire. The fourth period, ruled by Chalchihuitlicue, ended with a world-wide flood. The present Sun, the Fifth, ruled by Nanautzin, will end when the world is destroyed by earthquakes. (*See also* **First Sun, Second Sun, Third Sun, Fourth Sun, Fifth Sun**.)

Flame God   *Australian*
A deity who devoured humans. A race of winged men, the Keen Keengs, captured humans and threw them into a hole in the cave where the fire god lived.

Flaming Teeth   *Pacific Islands*
A giant of Fiji. This huge giant was killed by a band of youths who extracted the teeth which were like flaming logs. As a result, the islanders had fire for the first time.

Flauros   *European*
A demon, one of the 72 Spirits of Solomon. This being, depicted as a leopard, is said to have the power to destroy enemies by fire.

Flesh   *North American*
A supernatural being of the Winnebago; twin brother of Stump.
    The mother of Flesh and Stump was killed by an ogre before they were born and they were rescued from her body and raised by their father, who later left them.
    They killed many monsters, including the one who had killed their mother, but when they killed a beaver, one of the animals said to support the world, the supreme god, Earthmaker, intervened to stop their activities.

Flint *see* **Othagwenda**

Flint Boys   *North American*
  Tutelary deities of the Pueblo
  tribes, flint personified. These
  spirits gave freely of themselves
  so that the people could fashion
  tools and weapons.

Flint Man   *North American*
  A monster, in the lore of the
  Apache. This monster, one of
  many killed by Killer-of-Enemies,
  took the form of a huge rock.

Flood

Many cultures have myths relating
  to one or more inundations,
  referred to as the Flood or the
  Deluge, sent to eliminate the
  human race, usually with an
  advance warning to enable a few
  people to survive to repopulate the
  world.

Australia
The rain-spirits of the Aborigines,
  known as the Wandjina, were
  so disgusted with the behaviour
  of the first humans that they
  vomited, producing a Flood
  that wiped out the entire race.
  Thereafter, they set about
  creating a new race and taught
  them how to behave properly.

Baltic
It is not made clear what caused
  the Flood but there are various
  stories about what happened
  after the Flood had come.

  In one version, the culture-
  hero Pramzimas threw a nutshell
  into the waters. The shell became
  a boat and one man and one
  woman survived in this boat to
  restart the human race.

  In another version, all the
  animals and humans gathered
  on the top of a mountain and
  Pramzimas sent a boat in which
  they sailed away, leaving behind

only one elderly couple. This pair,
  instructed by Pramzimas, jumped
  nine times. On each occasion, a
  young couple appeared and these
  became the progenitors of a new
  race.

Central America
(1) In the lore of the Aztecs,
  the god Titlacahuan warned
  Nata and his wife Nena of the
  impending deluge which ended
  the Fourth Sun. They built a dug-
  out canoe and survived on one
  ear of maize.

  Another version has the Flood
  occurring at the end of the First
  Sun, when people became fish.
(2) The Mayan Floods, caused by
  Hunab, put an end to various
  phases of the creation cycle and,
  in one story, caused the sky to
  collapse. The god Kanzibyui raised
  the sky to its normal position and
  supported it on trees.
(3) Some Mexican tribes say that
  the Flood was sent by the god
  Hokomata. After it had subsided,
  Pukeheh, the daughter of
  Hokomata's brother Tochopa,
  mated with the gods Sunshaft and
  Waterfall to repopulate the earth.

Chinese
(1) The thunder god trapped by the
  father of Nü-kua and her brother
  Fu-hsi gave them a tooth when
  they set him free. From this grew
  a tree which produced a gourd in
  which the children survived the
  ensuing Flood. They mated but
  produced only an unformed lump
  of flesh. Fu-hsi cut this into pieces
  and scattered them over the earth
  to produce mankind.
(2) The Flood was caused when
  Kung Kung pulled down the
  pillars supporting the sky.
  Alternatively, he tore a hole in
  the sky when he tried to commit

suicide by banging his head
  against the heavenly bamboo.

Egyptian
When the god Ra tired of people
  muttering against him, he sent
  the goddess Hathor-Sekhet to kill
  them. He then brewed corn beer,
  flooding the country. The goddess
  got drunk and forgot what she
  was doing.

Greek
Prometheus warned his son,
  Deucalion, that Zeus was about
  to send a flood so Deucalion built
  an ark and survived with his wife
  Pyrrha.

Hindu
A god, Vishnu, appearing as a small
  fish found in his washing water,
  warned Manu of the coming Flood.
  It outgrew successively a bowl, a
  tank and a lake and had to be put
  in the sea. Manu built a boat and
  the fish towed him to safety on
  Mount Himavat when the Flood
  came. The gods granted him a wife
  and they became the progenitors
  of the present human race.

Irish
Cessair was Noah's grand-daughter
  but even she was refused a place
  in the Ark. She sailed for Ireland
  where she landed with fifty
  women and three men, the only
  survivors. Most of them later
  perished in the Flood.

Korean
When the Flood came, a huge bay
  tree, which had fathered a son
  on a heavenly being, was toppled
  but his son was saved by riding
  over the waves on the floating
  tree. He rescued a swarm of ants
  and another of mosquitoes and
  also a young boy. They all landed
  on a mountain where they found
  the only other survivors, an old
  woman with two daughters. The

four young people were able to repopulate the earth.

Mesopotamian

In the Babylonian account, the sea god Ea warned Atrahasis who survived in the ship *Preserver of Life*. In the Syrian version, the name of the person Ea warned is Utnapishtim. In the Sumerian version, Enki warned King Ziusudra of the Flood being sent by Enlil, enabling him to survive.

New Zealand

A story says that Tawhaki stamped on the floor of heaven, releasing the waters through the cracks his action caused.

North American

(1) Some Algonquian tribes say that the spirits of the underworld, the anamaqkiu, caused a flood when the trickster-god Manabush killed two of their number. Manabush managed to escape by climbing a tree which, by magic, he caused to grow much higher. Otter, Beaver and Mink died in an attempt to find dry land but Muskrat finally found a small piece of soil from which Manabush re-created the world.

(2) The Caddo say that four monstrous children, each with four arms and legs, stood back to back in a square and grew until they fused together and reached the sky. A man planted a rod which also reached the sky and was told to take his wife and a pair of each of the animals on earth into a reed when the Flood came. The monsters fell into the waters and were drowned and when the waters subsided, those inside the reed emerged to repopulate the earth.

(3) The Inuit say that only they existed before the Flood. After the

waters had receded the first white people appeared, fathered on one of their girls by a dog.

(4) In the lore of the Papago, only Montezuma, the first man, and Coyote, the trickster, survived the Flood in boats they had made. After the waters receded, Great Mystery repopulated the earth.

(5) The Pima say that the Flood was sent by Great Eagle and that only the creator-god Szeuka survived.

(6) A Sioux story says that the Flood was sent by Unktehi, a water-monster. One girl was rescued by the eagle Wanbhee Galeshka, who took her up to his nest on a high peak. They mated and produced twins, a boy and a girl, who became the progenitors of a new tribe.

(7) The Skagit of the west coast say that the Flood covered the world leaving only the tops of Mount Baker and Mount Rainier exposed. Two people in a canoe managed to escape and repopulated the world.

Pacific Islands

(1) In the Banks Islands, Qat was warned of the Flood and built a canoe in which he survived.

(2) In Fiji, the Flood was sent by the primeval serpent Degei to drown the people who had killed his friend, the hawk Turukawa.

(3) In Hawaiian lore, Nu'u survived in a boat that landed on a tall mountain. He had filled the boat with seeds and animals to restock the world after the waters had subsided.

(4) In the Society Islands, a fisherman's hook became entangled with the hair of a sleeping sea god, Ruahaku, who was so angry that he sent the Flood.

(5) Some say that the Flood was caused by the rising of a sea goddess from the depths of the ocean.

(6) It is also told that the Flood resulted from the efforts of the rain gods to douse the fire which started when the trickster sun god Maui stole fire from Mahuika.

Siberian

The Buriats say that the creator-god, Ulgan, warned Namu of the coming Flood and he built an ark in which he survived.

South American

(1) Advance warning of one of the Floods was given by the llama.

(2) The Araucanians blame the two huge serpents known as Kaikai and Trentran for causing the Flood when they demonstrated their powers by causing the waters to rise.

(3) The Arawaks blame the Flood on Sigu, the ruler of animals, who cut down the tree of knowledge, allowing water to gush out to cause the Flood.

(4) The land of the Chibcha Indians was flooded by the work god Chibchacum, aided by Chia, and the god Bochica appeared as a rainbow to create a channel to the sea and bring out the sun to dry the land.

(5) The Inca god Viracocha caused a flood to destroy the first humans, after which he created a new and better race.

(6) The Karaya tribe say that the Flood was sent by the demon Anatiwa but some of the tribe escaped when the water-hen, Saracura, brought soil which they used to raise the height of the hill Tupimare.

(7) The Quechua say that the only part of the world not

covered by the Flood was Mount Condorcoto. When the waters receded, five men were born from eggs that had survived the Flood on the higher part of the mountain.

(8) The Tupari say that the Flood was caused by the the first man, the giant Valedjad.

(9) In the Tupi story, Arikute and Tawenduare quarrelled and the latter split the earth when he stamped on the ground, allowing water to come gushing out.

(10) Other versions say that the god Monan tried to destroy the earth with fire and the Flood was caused when a magician, Irin Mage, brought about a heavy downpour that put out the flames.

Taiwan

The Taiwanese say that King Peiroun was warned of the coming Flood and was able to escape.

Thailand

The Flood was sent by the sky gods, the Thens, when the people refused to acknowledge the gods.

Flora   *Roman*

= *Greek* Chloris

An Italian goddess of flowers and fruitfulness. She is said to have touched Juno with a magic herb which enabled her to conceive the god Mars without the help of Jupiter.

Floris   *European*

A king of Hungary.

The Saracen king of Spain captured a group of French pilgrims and one of the ladies in the group gave birth to a girl, Blanchefleur, on the same day that the king's consort gave birth to a boy, Floris. They grew up together, but Floris was sent away

to school and Blanchefleur was sold to a slave-trader.

Floris set out to rescue her. He bribed his way into the tower in Babylon where Blanchefleur was imprisoned and was reunited with his beloved but they were later found in bed together and condemned to death. Their obvious love for each other softened the emir's heart and they were allowed to marry and return to Spain.

Flying Dutchman   *German*

Frustrated by winds that prevented his ship from rounding the Cape of Good Hope, the Flying Dutchman swore to manage it even if it took forever. An evil spirit condemned him to keep this oath from which he would be released only when a good woman promised to be faithful unto death. He was allowed to land only once every seven years, retaining his youth while his crew grew grey and wrinkled as the centuries passed.

He gave some of his cargo of treasure to Laland, the captain of a Norwegian ship, and fell in love with his daughter, Senta. She would have married him but, seeing her with her young friend Erik, who also loved her, Vanderdecken put back to sea rather than expose her to the curse which dogged him. She threw herself from the top of a cliff and her suicide, proving her faithful unto death, lifted the curse of the Flying Dutchman, whose ship sank beneath the waves.

Flying Head   *North American*

A monster, in the lore of the Iroquois. This monster, in the form of a head with huge wings

and sharp fangs, killed and ate all animals including those domesticated by the tribes. When it saw a squaw swallow some hot chestnuts, it thought to do the same but swallowed the red-hot stones of the fire and was killed.

Foam Woman   *North American*

An ancestress of the Haida people. She was said to have the power to project lightning from her eyes to repel the forces of evil and was envisaged as having many breasts at which she suckled the clan ancestors.

Fomoire   *Irish*

A one-legged, one-armed race of demons living under the sea; deities of the Fir Bolg.

These beings, some of whom had animals heads, had three rows of teeth and were said to be the descendants of Ham, son of Noah. They were in continual conflict with the later Danaans. They once stole the Dagda's harp, which flew from the wall where it had been hung, killed those who stole it and put the others to sleep with its music. They were finally defeated when the evil eye of the underworld god Balor was knocked out by Lugh's slingshot and all the Fomoire soldiers died at the sight of it.

Forcalor   *European*

A demon, one of the 72 Spirits of Solomon. He is said to have been a sea demon causing shipwreck and is depicted either as a winged human or as a man astride a griffin.

Forcas   *European*

A demon, one of the 72 Spirits of Solomon.

Fornax   *Roman*

A guardian goddess of ovens and baking; an aspect of Vesta.

Forneus   *European*
A demon, one of the 72 Spirits of
Solomon. He appears either as a
sea-monster or as a man, and is
said to have great knowledge of
the arts and sciences.

Forseti   *Norse*
The god of justice and truth. His
gold and silver palace, Glitnir,
held the throne on which he
sat to dispense laws and settle
disputes.

Fortuna   *Roman*
= *Greek* Tyche
A goddess of chance or fate; a
fertility goddess. She was said
to have acquired as one of her
attributes the horn of Achelous
broken off by Hercules when they
fought.
   She is depicted as standing
on a ball, a globe or a wheel,
sometimes blindfolded.

Fortunate Islands[1]   *Greek*
also Blessed Islands, Islands of the
Blessed
The home of the souls who have
attained Elysium three times.
Some identify these islands with
Elysium, others as a separate
place.

Fortunate Islands[2]   *Irish*
also Blessed Islands, Islands of the
Blessed
An earthly paradise somewhere to
the west of Ireland.

Fortunate Islands[3]   *Chinese*
also Blessed Islands, Islands of the
Blessed
The home of fairies and immortals.
   The fairies are said to eat
gemstones collected from
the coastline and retain their
immortality by drinking from the
fountain of life. The immortals
live on the sacred fungus which
grows on these three islands,
which are called Fang-chang,

P'eng-lai and Ying-chou.
   It is said that a large fleet was
sent to look for these islands in
the 2nd century BC but failed in
the attempt.
   Another story says that these
islands originally floated in
the eastern sea but were later
anchored by huge tortoises at the
behest of the Celestial Emperor.

Four Auspicious Animals *Chinese*
Animals which guard the four
cardinal points. These are the
Ch'ing Lung (azure dragon),
the Feng (phoenix), the Kuei
Shen (tortoise) and the Ch'i-lin
(unicorn).
   In some accounts, the Pai Hu
(white tiger) appears in place of
the unicorn.

Four Diamond Kings   *Chinese*
also Four Celestial Kings, Four
Heavenly Kings;
= *Japanese* Shi Tenno
The rulers of the four realms of the
Buddhist paradise and guardians
of Buddhist shrines.
   These deities are given as the
Land-bearer (Mo-li Ch'ing), who
guards the east; the Far-gazer
(Mo-li Hai) who guards the west;
the Well-Famed (Mo-li Shou) who
guards the north; and the Lord of
Growth (Mo-li Hung) who looks
after the south.

Four Dragon Kings   *Chinese*
The rulers of the four seas. These
kings were known as Jang Lung,
Lung Wang, Pai Lung and Chin
Lung.
   Alternative names sometimes
used are Ao Ch'in, Ao Jun, Ao
Kuang and Ao Shun, or Kuang-
jun, Kuang-li, Kuang-she and
Kuang-te.

Fourth Sun   *Central American*
The fourth age of the Aztec
creation cycle.

The Third Sun ended after 364
years when fire destroyed the
earth. Then Chalchiuhtlicue took
over as ruler of the Fourth Sun
which lasted for 312 years before
the world was inundated by a
flood from which only Nata and
Nena escaped. The next period was
the Fifth Sun which is the present
age.
   Another version calls the period
of the Fourth Sun the Sun of Earth
or the Sun of Water and says that
it was during this period that fishes
were made. (*See also* **Five Suns**.)

fox
This animal appears in myths
of many countries, often as a
trickster or shape-changer.
(1) In Chinese stories, the fox is a
   shape-changer that becomes a
   wizard when it reaches the age
   of 100 years. At the age of 1000,
   the animal goes to heaven as
   the Celestial Fox which has nine
   tails and serves as a means of
   transport for the celestial spirits.
(2) In the European classic, *Reynard
   the Fox*, the leading character
   gets into all sorts of scrapes
   but manages to escape his just
   desserts.
(3) In Japan the fox is the
   embodiment of Inari as Spirit
   of Rain. Others say that the fox,
   Kitsune, carries messages for the
   god Inari.
(4) In North America, Brer Fox is
   another trickster who becomes
   involved in many escapades.

Fox Woman   *Siberian*
Wife of Eme'mqut, a Koryak spirit.
She rejected the advances of a
man living as a lodger in their
house and when he remarked on
her foxy odour, she ran away.

Frashkart *Persian*

The final renewal after the destruction of the world by fire. At this time, all the dead will be restored to life by Saoshyant.

Freki *Norse*

One of the wolves of the god Odin, 'greedy'. (The other was known as Geri, 'ravenous'.)

Frey *Norse*

The god of earth, fertility, peace, rain and sunlight.

He was born in Vanaheim but moved to Asgard as a hostage when peace was made between the Vanir and the Aesir and was given the realm of Alfheim, home of the Light Elves.

He was also given the ship, Skidbladnir, a marvellous sword which could fight unaided, the golden-bristled boar, Gullinbursti which, with another boar, Slidrugtanni, drew his chariot and a horse, Blodighofi, which could carry him over water and through fire. His home was called Upsala.

He fell in love with the giantess, Gerda, but despaired of winning her, so his servant, Skirnir, wooed her on behalf of his master in return for the magic sword. He met Gerda nine days later and they were married. When her brother Beli attacked Frey, now without his sword, he defended himself with a stag's horn and killed Beli. At Ragnarok, he was killed by Surtur.

Freya *Norse*

Goddess of beauty, fertility, love, magic and youth.

She was born in Vanaheim but, like Frey, she moved to Asgard as a hostage when peace was made between the Vanir and the Aesir. She was given the realm of Folkvang, including the hall

Sessrymnir. The Valkyries collected many of the dead from the battlefields but Freya claimed half of them as her own and carried them to Folkvang while the others went to Valhalla. She was also given the beautiful necklace, Brisingamen, made by the dwarfs and wore it always. In addition, she had the magic falcon-garb, Valhamr, which enabled the wearer to fly, and her own chariot which was drawn by two cats.

She was said to take the form of a she-goat at night and sometimes rode the golden-bristled boar, Hildeswin.

Her necklace was once stolen by the mischievous god Loki who assumed the form of a flea to get into her bed as she slept but he was detected by Heimdall who, after a struggle in which they both assumed several forms, retrieved the necklace and returned it to Freya.

When Ottar, a man disputing the ownership of some land, appealed to her for help in tracing his ancestry, she turned him into a boar and rode on his back to the home of Hyndla, the sorceress, who not only traced his forebears but gave him a magic drink that ensured he remembered what he had learned.

When her husband, Odur, left her, she wandered the earth in search of him and the tears she shed sank into the earth and became gold. She eventually found him and they were happily reunited.

In some accounts she is assimilated with Frigga, others say she was married to Frey, Odin and perhaps others. Loki accused her of having affairs with all the gods.

In one story, she was kidnapped

by Belé, son of the king of Sogn, who took her to Jotunheim, hoping to marry her to one of his three sons but she rejected all of them.

She is depicted as wearing armour over a flowing gown and bearing a shield and spear. Her creatures are the cat, the cuckoo and the swallow.

Frigga *Norse*

Goddess of fertility, sky and wisdom.

She had her own palace, known as Fensalir, and a train of attendants.

When her son Balder told of the dreams that foretold danger to his life, Frigga extracted a promise from all things that they would not harm him. She overlooked the mistletoe and a branch of this, thrown by his blind brother Hoder at the instigation of the wicked god Loki, killed Balder.

She once stole some gold from a statue of Odin and had the dwarfs make it into a necklace. Odin could not make the dwarfs reveal the name of the thief so he tried to make the statue speak by using his knowledge of the mystic runes. This idea was thwarted by a dwarf who broke the statue into pieces.

Frigga is depicted as wearing heron plumes and carrying a bunch of keys at her belt.

Frog *North American*

A frog-spirit of the Navaho. He was involved with Bear, Snake and Turtle in a plan to capture two maidens from an undersea village. The plan went awry and the two girls were killed. Frog and Turtle were lucky to escape with their lives but Bear and Snake fared better. They captured two girls who were overcome by the smoke from the kidnappers' pipes which made Bear and Snake appear as handsome braves with whom the girls mated.

frog
(1) The Hindu *Rig Veda* asserts that the world rests on the back of a Great Frog.
(2) The Maoris regard the frog as a water god.

Frost Giant   *Norse*
also Hrimthurs (*plural* Hrimthursar)
Any of the beings that formed when the fiery clouds from Muspelheim condensed over the ice of Niflheim.

The principal Frost Giants were Beli, Kari, Thiassi and his daughter Skadi, and Thrym with his four children Drifta, Frosti, Jokul and Snoer.

Frost Maidens   *Norse*
The girls that formed when the fiery clouds from Muspelheim condensed over the ice of Niflheim.

Frosti   *Norse*
A Frost Giant; god of frosts; son of Thrym. He led the Frost Giants in their battle with the gods.

Fu-hsi   *Chinese*
One of the Three Sovereigns.

It was said that he was produced when his mother Hua-hsü was impregnated by the wind, after a gestation period of twelve years.

He was a serpent-bodied being having a human head with four faces, representing the yin principle, and credited with the introduction of fishing, silk-worm breeding, etc. and the invention of the trigrams of the I Ching (a book used in divination). He also invented the Eight Diagrams

from marks he saw on the back of a unicorn which rose out of a river beside which he was contemplating.

In the story of the Flood, Fu-hsi (Gourd Boy) and his sister Nü Kua (Gourd Girl) were the sole survivors, floating in a gourd from a tree grown from the tooth of the thunder god whom they had freed from a trap set by their father. He mated with his sister but they produced only an unformed lump of flesh. Fu-hsi cut this into pieces and scattered it over the earth to produce mankind.

Some say that he and his sister retired to heaven, others that he remained on earth and became the first emperor in the 20th century BC, originating the idea of marriage.

In later stories, they were said to be man and wife and were depicted as human with a fish's tail or a serpent's tail.

Fu-hsi runs the Ministry of Healing with Huang Ti and Shen Nung.

Fu-hsing   *Chinese*
also Star of Happiness
A god of happiness; one of the Fu Lu Shou.

He was the mortal Yang Ch'eng, an adviser to a 6th-century emperor, who achieved immortality and became one of the Three Gods of Happiness.

In other accounts he was an 8th-century general, Kuo Tzu-i.

Fu Lu Shou   *Chinese*
also Three Gods of Happiness
Three mortals who attained immortality by good works. These deities are Fu-hsing, the god of happiness, Lu-hsing, the god of good fortune and Shou Shen, the god of longevity.

Fujin   *Japanese*
A Shinto god of the winds. He is depicted wearing a leopard-skin and carrying a bag which contains the winds.

Fuku-kensaku   *Japanese*
A form of Kwannon. In this form, the goddess is depicted with two, four or six arms, seated on a lotus, and is sometimes shown with three faces each with three eyes.

Fukuro   *Japanese*
An owl which became a monk. He fell in love with the bullfinch, Uso-Dori, sending her love-letters in the care of the great tit, Shiju-Gara, and changed into an itinerant monk when the eagle, Uye-Minu, killed his beloved.

Fukurokuju   *Japanese*
= *Chinese* Shou Shen
A Shinto god of long life, luck and wisdom; one of the seven deities of fortune, the Shichi Fukujin.

He is said to be the deification of a Chinese hermit and is often depicted accompanied by a crane.

Furcas   *European*
A demon, one of the 72 Spirits of Solomon. He is depicted as an old man astride a pale horse and is said to teach many alchemical and scientific subjects.

Furfur   *European*
A demon, one of the 72 Spirits of Solomon. He is said to be able to cause thunderstorms and may appear in the form of a deer with wings and the tail of a snake.

Furies   *Greek*
also Erinnyes, Eumenides
The three Furies were Alecto, Magaera and Tisiphone. They were, some say, born from the blood of Uranus falling on Earth when he was castrated by Cronus. Others say they were the daughters of Nyx or of Hades and Persephone.

In some stories they had dogs' heads and bats' wings and writhing snakes for hair. They lived in Tartarus and judged complaints of insolence, etc. In other versions they are of grave demeanour, dressed as huntresses, and carry scourges, sickles and torches.

In anger at the acquittal of Orestes for the murder of Aegisthus and Clytemnestra – one of them had acted as public prosecutor at the trial – they harried him wherever he went and threatened to blight Athens with their blood. Athene pacified them by giving them a home in a grotto and guaranteeing that they would be worshipped by the people of Athens. After they took up this offer, they were known as the Solemn Ones, the Benignant or Kindly Ones or Eumenides.

fylgie *Norse*
also fylgja (*plural* fylgjur)

The guardian spirit which watches over each individual; the soul; a person's double.

As the double or soul, the fylgie is envisaged as some form of animal; as a tutelary spirit it may appear in a dream to give warning or advice. Fylgjur ride on wolves using a bridle made of snakes.

It is said that the fylgie passes from father to son through the generations.

G

G *Central American*
A Mayan deity of uncertain identity, referred to as God G (*see* **alphabetical gods**); perhaps Ah Kin or Kukulcan.

This deity is generally regarded as a sun god or god of death.

Ga-gaah *North American*
A divine crow. According to the Iroquois, the crow brought the gift of magic to mankind. He is said also to have brought the gift of corn and for this service he is welcome to take his share of the produce of the cornfield.

Ga-gorib *African*
A monster figure of the Hottentots. He was said to make a practice of throwing people into a pit. He was killed by the hero Heitsi-eibib in the same way.

Another version puts the deity Tsunigoab or the trickster, Jackal, in place of Heitsi-eibib.

Ga-oh *North American*
A wind giant of the Iroquois. He controlled four winds.

Gaap *European*
A demon, one of the Cardinal demons (west); one of the 72 Spirits of Solomon.

He is said to induce love or hate and has the power to make invisible any sorcerer who invokes him.

Gabriel's Hounds *British*
The English version of the Hounds of Hell.

In some versions they are said to be geese, plovers or swans or, alternatively, the souls of those who died young and unbaptised. They sweep noisily across the heavens looking for souls. (*See also* **Wild Hunt**.)

Gad *Semitic*
A god of good fortune in Canaan and Phoenicia.

Gae Bolg *Irish*
A weapon thrown with the foot. This 'belly spear' was said to open into thirty points after entering the body of an enemy and was used to great effect by Cuchulainn.

Some say that this weapon was made from the bones of a sea-monster which had been found dead on the shore after losing a battle with another of its kind.

Gaea *Greek*
also Gaia
Mother and wife of Uranus; mother by Uranus of the twelve Titans, the Cyclopes, the Giants, and others. In some versions Gaea was born of the primordial being Chaos. She was also the mother of the Furies after the blood of the castrated Uranus fell on her.

In her anger when the Giants were slaughtered in their revolt against the gods, she mated with Tartarus to produce the huge monster Typhon.

Gaea was the original founder of the oracle at Delphi which passed via Themis and then Phoebe to Apollo.

Gahe *North American*
also Mountain People;
Lipan Apache Hactci; *Navaho* Hactce;

Pueblo Katchina; *White Mountain Apache* Ga'n

Supernatural beings of the Chiricahua Apache, living inside mountains. These beings are said to be able to cure the sick, give sight to the blind and even restore missing limbs. The five chief Gahe are associated with both colour and direction: the Great Black Gahe (east), the Great Blue Gahe (south), the Great White Gahe (north) and the Great Yellow Gahe (west). The most powerful one of the five is known as Grey One.

Gahonga   *North American*

One of the three tribes of Jogah (the others are the Gandayah and the Ohdows). These dwarf beings are said by the Iroquois to live in rocky areas and in rivers.

Gaheris   *British*

A Knight of the Round Table. He found his mother in bed with Lamerock (another Knight of the Round Table) and killed her. With the help of his brothers, Agravain and Gawain, he killed Lamerock as well.

He was one of the knights captured and imprisoned by Turkin, who hated all Arthur's knights, until rescued by Lancelot.

He refused to be a party to the plan by Agravain and Mordred to betray Lancelot's secret affair with Guinevere to King Arthur and, when the queen was exposed and condemned to be burnt at the stake, he reluctantly obeyed the king's command to supervise the execution after his elder brother, Gawain, had refused. He went unarmed and was not recognised by Lancelot when he rode to the queen's rescue. Both Gaheris and his brother Gareth, who had also

been ordered to attend, as well as many other knights, were killed by Lancelot when he charged into the crowd and carried Guinevere off to safety.

Gaia *see* **Gaea**

gaki   *Japanese*

A malevolent spirit of the dead; a ghost. These beings creep into the bodies of mortals to take nourishment from the food ingested by their hosts since they have no digestive organs of their own. As a result, the gakis put on weight while their hosts become thinner.

Galahad   *British*

also the Desired Knight, the Perfect Knight, the True Prince

A Knight of the Round Table; son of Lancelot and Elaine.

Dame Brisen, a sorceress and maidservant of Elaine, deceived Lancelot into sleeping with Elaine in the belief that he was sleeping with his true love, Guinevere. The result of this union was Galahad. He was reared by monks and, at the age of fifteen, was knighted by his father and taken to King Arthur's court where he assumed his ordained place at the Round Table. As the the only knight pure enough to see the Holy Grail, he was able to sit in the Perilous Seat, the chair reserved for such a knight at the Round Table, without being swallowed up. A large red boulder appeared, floating in the river, and fixed immovably in it was a fine sword. After Gawain and Percival had tried unsuccessfully to pull it from the stone, Galahad withdrew it easily and put it in the empty scabbard he wore. The Grail appeared in the hall that night and, having fed the assembled

knights, disappeared. All the knights present, led by Gawain, vowed to devote their lives to the search for this sacred chalice.

Each knight took his own route and Galahad's led him to a chapel where he found the wounded knight Bagdemagus tended by Owain. A white shield hung behind the altar and the hermit of the chapel said that it was reserved for the best knight; any other trying to use it would come to harm. Bagdemagus had taken it and ridden off, only to be unhorsed and wounded by a knight in white armour who sent the shield back for Galahad. This knight told Galahad that the shield had been given by Joseph of Arimathea to a converted knight, King Evelake, before the battle with his cousin, the Saracen king, Tholomer. In that fight, a figure on a cross was seen on the shield and a man who had lost a hand in the battle was made whole when he touched the cross. The shield came to Britain with Joseph and Evelake, and Joseph (or Josephus, his son), on his deathbed, emblazoned a red cross on the shield with his own blood and told Evelake to leave it with Nascien the hermit who would guard it until it was claimed by Galahad.

Taking the shield, Galahad rode on, taking with him Meliad, whom he knighted. They parted at a fork in the road and Galahad, encountering a group of knights attacking Percival, routed them. He went on to further adventures, in one of which he routed the seven brothers who had been holding many young women captive in the Castle of Maidens, and was eventually led by a maiden, who turned out to be Percival's sister, Dindrane, to a ship where he found Percival and Bors already aboard. Sailing off, they found another ship and, seeing that it was deserted, boarded it. On a silk bed lay a marvellous sword, one that had been used by Varlan, king of Gales, to kill Lambor, king of Terre Foraine. It was said that the ship and the sword had originally been made by King Solomon. The Sword was called the Sword of Strange Girdles and its scabbard, Mover of Blood. In some accounts, this vessel was Solomon's ship and the sword was King David's. Galahad took the sword and scabbard and they returned to their own ship which carried them to Castle Carteloise. Here they found a woman dying who could be cured only by the blood of a virgin and Dindrane died as a result of giving her blood to help the sick woman.

In one version, following the adventure at the Castle of Maidens, Galahad came to a monastery where Evelake lay wounded and, cradling the sick man in his arms, cured him of his wounds so that he was able to die happy. This version says that he then met Percival and Bors and they rode to Castle Carbonek where they were welcomed and feasted by King Pelles and celebrated mass with Josephus who had come to Britain with Evelake 400 years before. Some say that Christ himself appeared at this celebration. The sins that had caused Pelles to be wounded were washed away by blood from the Holy Lance and he spent the rest of his life in a monastery.

Another version says that it was Galahad's sister who led him to the boat where Percival and Bors were waiting and that it was she who died giving blood to save the sick lady. This version has it that, at their first landfall, they were assailed by wraiths and goblins in a castle on a hill which disappeared when they routed their attackers.

In yet another version, they found the wounded Pelles at Carbonek and here the Holy Grail appeared on a silver altar with a spear that dripped blood. On the instructions of a voice from heaven, Galahad anointed Pelles with this blood and his wounds were healed and he died happy.

Then Galahad and his two companions took sail for Sarras in the Holy Land, taking with them the silver altar and the Holy Grail and Spear. There they found a ship bearing the body of Percival's sister which they buried. The king, Estorause, threw all three of them in prison but asked their pardon when on his deathbed. Galahad was crowned king in his place but he died about a year later while taking Mass with Josephus and was carried up to heaven by a host of angels. The Holy Grail and the Holy Spear disappeared for ever.

Galahaut the Haut Prince   *British*
A Knight of the Round Table. He helped King Bagdemagus organise a tournament to which they invited Lancelot in the hope of killing him. Instead, King Mark sent Tristram disguised as Lancelot, hoping that he would be killed. In the event, Tristram, although wounded, won the tournament.

In some accounts, he was defeated by Lancelot but became such a devoted friend that, when he believed that Lancelot had been killed, he fasted to death.

Galatea[1]   *Greek*
A sea nymph, one of the Nereids.

She was loved by the Cyclops Polyphemus but she just laughed at him, preferring the shepherd-prince Acis, who was killed by the jealous Cyclops, crushed by a huge stone. She turned the corpse of Acis into a stream. Some say that she wept so much at the loss of Acis that she turned into a fountain.

In another story, Acis is not mentioned and Galatea married Polyphemus, beguiled by his music-making, and bore a son, Galas.

Galatea[2]   *Greek*
Wife of Pygmalion, king of Cyprus. A statue carved by Pygmalion was brought to life by Aphrodite and became Pygmalion's wife.

Another version says that Pygmalion was already married to Cynisca, who became jealous of Galatea who then returned to a former state as a block of marble.

Galleron   *British*
A Scottish Knight of the Round Table; king of Galloway.

He fought Gawain for the ownership of land given by King Arthur to Gawain, who yielded to Galleron on the condition that he paid for a million masses to be said for the soul of Guinevere's mother.

In another version, they wounded each other so badly that they took weeks to recover. Then Gawain handed over the land to Galleron and joined the Round Table.

He was one of the twelve knights who helped Agravain and Mordred when they attempted to seize Lancelot in Guinevere's room. All except Mordred were killed by Lancelot.

Gamag Nara   *Korean*
One of the various heavens, a land of near-darkness. In an attempt to get light for his gloomy kingdom, the king sends out the Fire Dogs to capture the sun or the moon but they always fail in the attempt. When they bite the sun or the moon, it causes an eclipse.

Gamigin   *European*
A demon, one of the 72 Spirits of Solomon. He is said to be able to raise the souls of the dead and is depicted riding a donkey or a pony.

Gan-Ceann   *Irish*
'headless'; *also* Love-talker
A headless fairy or spirit who woos maidens and then disappears

Ganaskidi   *North American*
A harvest god of the Navaho. He is envisaged as a bighorn sheep. In some accounts there are many supernatural beings of this name.

Gandalfr   *Norse*
One of the dwarfs.

Gandarewa   *Persian*
A sea monster. This monster, the guardian of haoma, was said to be able to swallow twelve men at once. It was killed by Keresaspa after a fight which lasted nine days and nights.

In some accounts, this beast had golden heels and was so big that its body was in the sea while its head was in the sky.

Gandayah   *North American*
One of the three tribes of Jogah (the others are the Gahonga and the Ohdours). In the lore of the Iroquois, these dwarf beings

cultivate the earth to ensure that it remains fertile.

Gandreid   *Norse*
A name for the Wild Hunt.

It was said that any field over which the Gandreid passed would bear increased crops.

Ganesha   *Hindu*
also Ekadanta, Ganesh
The elephant-headed god of art, foresight, good fortune and scribes; ruler of the Ganas (minor deities); son of Shiva and Parvati; brother of Karttikeya; brother of Subrahmanya, some say; husband of Buddhi, Riddhi and Siddhi.

He is said by some to have been produced by Parvati from flaking skin or from bath-oil.

His mother asked him to guard her door while she bathed and when he tried to deny entry to his father Shiva, Shiva chopped off his head. To pacify Parvati, he replaced it with the first thing to hand – the head of an elephant.

In another version, the god Shani was asked to look after the baby and his fiery glance burned off Ganesa's head, which Parvati or Vishnu replaced with an elephant's head.

One of his tusks was knocked out by Rama when he tried to keep him from the sleeping Shiva (whence his being given the name Ekadanta, 'One-tooth').

Another account says that his stomach split open when he fell off the mouse (or rat) he was riding. He hastily put back all the sweet things that had fallen out and tied a snake round his waist like a belt. This episode made the watching moon laugh and this angered Ganesha so much that he pulled out one of his tusks and threw it at the moon.

Other versions say that he pulled out the tusk and used it as a pen to write down the alphabet dictated by Vyasa, the god of wisdom.

He is depicted as a red or yellow fat-bellied man holding a club, a discus, a shell and a water-lily in his four hands and is sometimes shown riding on a rat.

Ganis   *Baltic*
A Lappish forest spirit. This being takes the form of a beautiful maiden with a long tail who mates with mortals.

Ganymede   *Greek*
= *Roman* Catamitus
The god of rain. He was a Trojan prince who was carried away by Zeus in the form of an eagle (or by Eos, goddess of the dawn, who handed the boy over to Zeus) and who became cup-bearer to the gods after Hebe. Zeus gave Ganymede's father Tros two (or six) immortal horses, or, in some stories, a golden vine, in compensation for the loss of his son.

Garang   *African*
The first man in the lore of the Dinka; husband of Abuk. (*See* ***Abuk.***)

Garden of the Hesperides   *Greek*
The walled garden of the goddess Hera. The tree that bore golden apples was planted in this garden and it was tended by the Hesperides and guarded by the serpent Ladon. Hercules came here to obtain some of the golden apples as his eleventh Labour.

Gareth   *British*
A Knight of the Round Table; brother of Agravain, Gaheris and Gawain.

In some accounts, he refused to identify himself as Gawain's brother until he had earned a knighthood by his own efforts and was referred to as the Young Unknown. In this respect, the story is similar to that of Gingalin, Gareth's son, the Fair Unknown.

When he first joined Arthur's court with Agravain, Gaheris and Gawain he took the job of a scullion, earning the nickname Beaumains, 'Fair Hands'.

A maiden, Lynette, came to King Arthur's court seeking help for her sister, Lyonesse, who was being harassed by the Red Knight. Gareth took up the cause, defeated the Black Knight, the Blue Knight, the Green Knight and, finally, the Red Knight and married Lyonesse. In some accounts, he married Lynette.

He was one of the knights captured and imprisoned by Turkin, who hated all Arthur's knights, until rescued by Lancelot.

He refused to be a party to the plan by Agravain and Mordred to betray Lancelot's secret affair with Guinevere to King Arthur and, when the queen was exposed and condemned to be burnt at the stake, he reluctantly obeyed the king's command to supervise the execution after his elder brother, Gawain, had refused. He went unarmed and was not recognised by Lancelot when he rode to the queen's rescue. Both Gareth and his brother Gaheris who had also been ordered to attend, as well as many other knights, were killed by Lancelot when he charged into the crowd and carried Guinevere off to safety.

Gargamelle   *British*
A giantess; wife of Grandgousier; mother of Gargantua. It was said that the sorcerer Merlin created

this being from Guinevere's nail-clippings and whales' bones.

Gargantua   *British*
A giant, son of Grandgousier and Gargamelle.

He is said to have been created by Merlin. He served King Arthur and on one of his journeys he met and killed the monster, Leviathan.

Another story says that he was born from the ear of his mother, Gargamelle. Even as a boy he had an enormous appetite and it needed the milk from 17,913 cows to keep him fed. Fully grown, he needed a comb 300 yards long to comb his hair, and he once ate five pilgrims as a snack.

Garuda   *Hindu*
A demigod, part man, part eagle; the bird of the god Vishnu, sun-bird. One version of his origins says that he was hatched from an egg at the beginning of time.

He was said to devour evil people and carried Vishnu on his daily journey across the sky. In some accounts, he appears as an incarnation of Agni, the god of fire.

He protected the peak of Mount Sumeru from the first attempt by Vayu, the god of air and wind, to break it off but, when Garuda was away, Vayu tried again and snapped off the mountain top which fell into the sea as Sri Lanka.

His mother Vinata was imprisoned in the underworld by her sister, Kudra, mother of snakes, who demanded amrita as ransom. Garuda placed the drink in some grass that had sharp blades so that, when the snakes licked it, they split their tongues. The amrita was recovered by Indra only after a great struggle.

A different account says that, when Garuda stole the drink, which he intended to deliver to Indra, the archer Krsanu shot at him and dislodged one or two of his feathers. (A similar story is told of Gayatri.) Another version says that the ransom demanded was the moon itself to light the underworld. Garuda stole the moon but the other gods seized it and rescued Vinata.

Garuda was made an immortal and became the bird on which Vishnu travelled.

In one incarnation, as Jatayu, he helped Rama in his search for Sita when she was abducted.

He is depicted as half man, half bird, with red wings, a golden body and a white human face. The wind caused by the flapping of his wings was strong enough to stop the rotation of the earth.

Gaunab   *African*
The Hottentot god of darkness. He wounded the creator-god Tsunigoab in a fight for supremacy but lost the struggle and was banished.

Gawain   *British*
also the Red Knight
A Knight of the Round Table; nephew of King Arthur; son of King Arthur and Morgause, some say; brother of Agravain, Gaheris, Gareth and others.

Some say he was cast adrift in a boat as a baby, rescued by a fisherman and baptised by another Gawain known as the Brown. In this version he was said to have travelled on the Continent where he was knighted by the Pope.

In the more usual version he was knighted by King Arthur and, en route with his brothers to King Arthur's court to be made knights, they routed a band of robbers who had looted London during the king's absence at his wedding feast and killed the giants Chaos and Sanagran.

When he was knighted by the king, Gawain was jealous of Pellimore, who was given an honoured place at the Round Table, and planned to kill him because Pellimore had killed Gawain's father, Lot, in battle. When he met Evadeam, who had been turned into a dwarf by a sorcerer, Evadeam regained his normal stature while Gawain became a dwarf, but he also regained his normal size later.

At Arthur's wedding feast, a white stag ran into the hall and Gawain was sent to find the stag, which had been chased by a white bitch and a pack of black hounds. He rode off with Gaheris and found two knights, Brian and Sorlus, fighting to decide which of them should chase the stag, which had just run past. Gawain stopped them from fighting and made them ride to Arthur's court and submit themselves to the king. He and Gaheris caught up with the stag as it swam across a stream but Gawain was challenged by a knight, Alardine, and killed him in single combat before resuming the chase which led to a castle. Here he caught and killed the stag but was attacked by another knight, owner of the stag. Gawain defeated him and was about to strike off his head when a lady ran in and, flinging herself on the fallen loser, intercepted Gawain's sword stroke and was killed. He

spared the beaten knight, Blamire, and sent him too to Arthur's court. Four knights then set on the two brothers and Gawain was wounded in the arm by an arrow. They were saved by four ladies who begged for their lives and were allowed to return to court with the head of the white stag. Gawain was forced to carry the headless body of the lady he had killed in front of him on his horse.

To honour a pledge made by the king, he married the ugly old crone, Ragnell, who then reverted to her proper form of a beautiful young woman. They had a son, Gingalin, who came to Arthur's court unaware that the knight who taught him all the knightly arts was his father.

As a result of the sorceress Morgan's attempt on his life, the king felt unable to trust her son, Owain, and banished him from the court. Gawain opted to go with him and they rode off together to seek adventure. Their first encounter was with Morholt and they watched him unhorse two knights in quick succession. He then challenged the two newcomers and toppled and wounded Owain. Gawain put up much stronger resistance and they fought an honourable draw. All three then became friends and travelled on together. At a crossroads, they met three women who offered to lead them to adventure and Gawain chose the youngest of the three. They came to a clearing where they saw the knight Pelleas unhorse ten knights in succession but yield without a struggle when the defeated men tied him under his horse and carried him off (Pelleas saw this

as a means of getting another glimpse of his beloved, Ettard). Another knight and an ugly dwarf then appeared with a damsel who chose the dwarf and rode off. When another knight appeared and challenged Gawain, the first knight rode off with Gawain's young girl companion. The knight and Gawain fought a draw and the knight told Gawain the story of Pelleas and his hopeless love for Ettard. Gawain tried to help Pelleas by telling Ettard that he was dead, hoping she would realise how much he had meant to her but instead he seduced Ettard. He returned to the crossroads where he met Owain and Marholt and they all three rode back to Camelot where they were made welcome by the king.

He was one of the many knights captured and imprisoned by Turkin, who hated all Arthur's knights, until rescued by Lancelot.

In King Arthur's campaigns against Rome, he was sent to take a message to Lucius, the Roman commander. When Quintilian, a nephew of Lucius, made an insulting remark about Britain, Gawain decapitated him with his sword.

He joined the other knights on the Grail Quest and, after many fruitless weeks, met Ector who was equally frustrated. They rode on together and were soon challenged by a knight who Gawain ran through with his spear. To his dismay, the knight turned out to be his friend Owain, who died soon after in a nearby monastery. Another version says that Gawain was involved in another fight in which he was severely wounded by Galahad and it was a month before he was well enough to return to Camelot, having given up the quest. Yet another story says that Ector and Gawain arrived at a small chapel where they fell asleep in the pews and dreamed. Gawain dreamed about a great herd of bulls. A voice told them that they were not fit for the Grail Quest, so they went to Nascien the hermit, who interpreted their dreams and confirmed what the voice had said with the result that they gave up the quest and returned to Camelot.

In some accounts, he fell in love with Orgelleuse and fought many battles on her behalf. She promised to marry him if he would fight her enemy, Gramoflanz. Gawain provoked the knight by taking a twig from a tree near to his castle and they agreed to meet eight days later outside the magician Klingsor's castle. At this castle, he slept on a bed that moved of its own accord and was assailed by a shower of arrows and spears which left him unharmed. He fought a fierce lion and killed it; this turned out to be Klingsor in the form of a lion and his death broke the spell he had placed on Gawain. (A similar story is told of Bors at Castle Carbonek.) When Gawain fought Gramoflanz he was defeated but his conqueror, who turned out to be Percival, spared his life when Gawain's sister, Honje, pleaded for him. It was said that he married Orgelleuse shortly afterwards,

He refused to be a party to the plan by Agravain and Mordred to trap Lancelot and Guinevere together and was with King Arthur on a hunting trip when Mordred brought the king proof of Guinevere's secret affair with Lancelot. Gawain was ordered by the king to put the queen to death at the stake. He refused but his younger brothers, Gaheris and Gareth, felt bound to obey their king's command. Lancelot, riding to the queen's rescue as she was led to the stake, killed Gaheris, Gareth and many others. Bitter at this loss, Gawain became Lancelot's sworn enemy and was in the forefront of the battle when the king besieged the estate of Joyous Garde where Lancelot was installed with Guinevere and many of his friends from Brittany. This conflict ended on the orders of the Pope and the queen was returned to her husband. Although Arthur and Lancelot swore a truce, Gawain was unforgiving and, at his urging, the king took his army to the continent to further attack Lancelot who had returned to his home in Brittany. Once again Gawain was in the thick of the battle and when they reached Benwick, Lancelot's capital, challenged Lancelot to single combat. Gawain owned a magic belt which made him invulnerable and increased his strength until midday, after which his strength returned to normal. They fought each other on two successive days and Lancelot, waiting until Gawain's strength ebbed after midday, on each occasion dented his opponent's helmet with a tremendous sword blow that knocked Gawain senseless to the ground. Arthur was called back to England when Mordred usurped his throne and the wounded Gawain was brought back with the returning forces. He tried to take up the battle when he reached Dover but the effort proved too much and he died. He was buried at Dover Castle. On his death-bed he wrote a letter of forgiveness to Lancelot.

In a French story, Gawain survived Arthur and became king of Britain.

(*See also* **Green Knight**.)

Gayatri[1]   *Hindu*

A milkmaid who became consort of the god Brahma. She is regarded as a personification of a hymn to the sun from the *Rig Veda* which is taught at initiation ceremonies.

Some say that she became the second wife of Brahma who found his first wife lazy and not interested in intellectual matters.

Gayatri[2]   *Hindu*

In some accounts, this Gayatri took the form of a bird (a hawk or eagle) and brought the divine drink soma from heaven after her mother and two sisters had tried and failed.

Some equate her with Gayatri, second wife of Brahma.

Gayomart   *Persian*

A primeval man created from the sweat of Ahura Mazda.

He is said to have lived for 3000 years in spirit form as Gayomart before appearing in the flesh as Gaya Maretan. He was poisoned by the evil god Ahriman, at the behest of Jeh the whore, at the age of 30, but his seed generated the predecessors of the human race, Mashye and Mashyane. From his body came all the elements.

Gayomart was envisaged as a tall, white, radiant being who fought the forces of darkness.

Gbadé   *African*

A young thunder god in Dahomey. He is said to use lightning as a weapon with which he kills wrongdoers. The possessions of a man so killed are scattered by the roadside and anybody who touches them will be killed in the same way.

geanncanae *Irish*

A malicious type of fairy. In some accounts, these beings are equated with leprechauns.

Geb *Egyptian*

Greek Cronus

An earth god and god of healing.

Geb and his twin sister Nut were locked together at birth and their father Shu forced them apart so that Geb formed the earth and Nut formed the sky.

He ruled the kingdom after Shu, living for 1773 years. The uraeus (the snake symbol worn by gods and pharaohs on their forehead or headdress) gave him a fever of which he was cured by the god Ra. When he abdicated he split the kingdom, giving the north to Horus and the south to Set, and became one of the attendants in Ra's boat. His laugh was thought to be the cause of earthquakes.

Other versions make him the son of Ra and the brother of Shu. He is depicted as a goose or as a man with a goose on his head.

Gekka-O *Japanese*

A god of marriage. He binds the feet of lovers together with fine red silk thread.

Gelert *Welsh*

A hound of Llewellyn. When his master found his baby son missing and the dog covered in blood, he killed Gelert thinking that he had killed the child. In fact, the boy was safe and lying beside the body of a wolf that Gelert had fought and killed to save his master's son. (*See also* ***Beddgelert***.)

Gemdelovely *Scottish*

A princess, wife of Assipattle. Her father gave her in marriage to Assipattle as a reward for slaying the monstrous Stoorworm.

Gemini *Greek*

also the Twins

Castor and Pollux placed in the sky as stars by Zeus.

Gemori *European*

A female demon, one of the 72 Spirits of Solomon. This being is said to appear in the form of a lovely woman riding a camel and helps those seeking love.

Gendenwitha *North American*

An Iroquois princess. The hunter Sosondowah fell in love with her and, descending to earth, carried her up to heaven to the home of the goddess of the dawn, who was so angry that she changed Gendenwitha into the morning star.

genie *see* **jinnee**

genius *Roman*

plural genii;

= *Greek* daimon

A guardian spirit of the individual person, often in the form of a winged youth.

genius loci *Roman*

The guardian spirit of a place, often in the form of a serpent.

Genji *Japanese*

A legendary prince, hero of many tales.

Genko *Japanese*

A priest who became a dragon. When he died after a lifetime spent in meditation holding a single drop of water in his hand, Genko became a dragon living in Cherry Tree Pond where he sometimes answered the requests of those who brought offerings of rice.

Geraint *British*

A Knight of the Round Table; a prince of Devon (or Cornwall).

On a hunting trip, both he and the maid of Queen Guinevere were struck with a whip by a dwarf when Geraint enquired the name of the dwarf's master. He followed the knight and the dwarf to their castle and borrowed arms and armour from an old man, Yniol, who had lost his earldom to his nephew and was now in poor straits. The knight was Edern and Geraint fought him for the title of Knight of the Sparrowhawk, defeating him and forcing him to go to Guinevere and apologise for the injury to her maid. When Geraint threatened force, the nephew handed back all he had taken from Yniol whose daughter, Enid, went to Arthur's court with Geraint and married him. They had caught a white stag on the hunting trip and the head of that animal was given to Enid.

When his father Erebin grew old, Geraint took over his dominions and ruled peacefully with Enid, giving up knightly pursuits in favour of dalliance. He came to believe that Enid despised him for his weakness so he set out on a quest to prove his strength and valour, forcing her to ride ahead of him in silence. He killed many knights and took their horses and armour and defeated Gwiffred Petit who became his friend. He also killed three giants, one of whom wounded him badly. He was taken care of by Earl Limwris, but when this earl insulted Enid, Geraint killed him. They moved on and were helped by Gwiffred Petit until Geraint was fully recovered. Geraint's final battle was with a knight in the valley of mists in the domain of Ywein and, having overcome him and put an end to the enchanted games that took place there, he returned to his own lands and ruled happily again with Enid.

Some say, he was killed in battle, fighting for his king.

Geri *see* **Freki**

Geryon   *Greek*

A cowherd-king of Tartessus in Spain; brother of Echidna.

He was said to be one of the giants who had fought with the Olympian gods. When they were defeated, Geryon fled to the West or, in some versions, to the Belearides, where he became king. He was a three-bodied monster whose cattle were taken by Hercules as his tenth Labour. He was killed by Hercules during this adventure.

Gesar Khan   *Mongolian*

A warrior-hero. It was said that he was born from an egg which emerged from his mother's head. He was born with three eyes, resembling the the three eye-shaped marks on his birth-egg, but his mother was terrified by the implications and she plucked one of the eyes out of its socket.

He was sent from heaven to rid the world of evil. When he had accomplished his mission, he was purified on the mountain Margye Pongri and then taken up to heaven. He will return when evil becomes rampant again.

Ghede   *West Indies*

The Haitian god of life and death. Originally a god of love, he was later combined with Baron Samedi as the god of death. He acts as guardian of the cross-roads and

guide to the home of the souls of the dead and is envisaged as a dandy in evening clothes with a cane and sun-glasses.

ghost-sickness   *North American*

In the lore of the Navaho, illness caused by a ghost, which can be fatal.

ghoul   *Arabian*

A demon preying on the dead; a fiend. (*See also* **ghul**.)

ghul   *Arabian*

= *Persian* ghol

A female jinnee, offspring of Iblis, the Devil. These beings sometimes appear to men in the desert and eat them.

It is said that they have donkey-like hoofs and can change into any shape they choose. Some are small enough to ride on hares, others ride on ostriches. Another desert type is known as the udar. Female types, living in the forest, may carry men off to their caves and seduce them. Males do the same thing with women. The offspring of such matings are fierce savages.

Ghuls that live in the Sahara are said to have the legs of an ostrich and only one eye.

In some accounts, the ghul is the male, and the female version is the ghoula, ghulah or si'la. Some female types are said to play the flute so that men hearing their music will dance themselves to death. (*See also* **ghoul**.)

Giaia   *West Indies*

He killed his son, Giaiael, who had tried to kill him, and put the young man's bones in a calabash where they turned into fish. The water that ran from the calabash formed the first seas.

giant

Giants appear in most mythologies:

Greek

(1) The Earthborn Giants, the fourth race of monstrous beings, were originally 24 in number, half human, half serpent, who sprang from the blood of the god Uranus spattered on Earth (Gaea) when he was castrated by his son, Cronus. They were said to have six arms and, being made from earth, were virtually indestructible. If they were killed, their bodies merged with the earth they had sprung from and they were re-born. In some accounts, they had snakes for legs. Led by Alcyoneus, Eurymedon and Porphyrion, they rebelled against the gods after Zeus imprisoned the Titans in Tartarus but were defeated, largely by the efforts of Hercules, bred by Zeus as a defence against the expected rebellion.

(2) The Hundred-handed Giants were Briareus, Cottus and Gyges, three sons of Uranus and Gaea. Their father confined them to the underworld from which they were released by Cronus who later sent them back there. They were later released by Zeus to help in his fight with the Titans and, after the victory of the gods, the giants were given the job of guarding those Titans who were imprisoned in the underworld.

Norse

The generic name for the giants was Jotunn or Thursar. Their home was Jotunheim and they were the opponents of the gods, destined to win the final battle, Ragnarok.

The first giant was Ymir. Most of the original giants were killed in the torrent of blood that rushed from Ymir's body when he was killed by Odin, Ve and Vili. Only Bergelmir and his wife escaped this flood and they fled to the ends of the earth and started a new race of giants.

The Frost Giants (or Ice Giants), the Hrimthursar, were formed when the fiery clouds of Muspelheim condensed in the icy air over Niflheim. The Fire Giants, the Muspel, lived in Muspelheim and were ruled by Surtur.

North American

(1) The Inuit refer to a race of giants known as the Tornit.

(2) The Shawnee deity had four giant sons who could smell humans.

South American

A race of giants came into Ecuador from the sea and bored a well in the rock. Then they killed the women and practised sodomy. For this, the gods destroyed them with lightning.

Giant   *North American*

also Raven the Giant

A spirit of the Tsimshian people. He owned a raven costume in which he could fly and used it to reach the heavens from where he stole the box that contained light, bringing it back to light the earth for the first time.

Giant-Eagle   *Siberian*

= *North American* Thunderbird

A thunder god, said to cause thunder when he flaps his wings and lightning when he flashes his eyes.

Giants' Causeway   *British*

A natural formation of basalt columns running out into the sea from the north-east coast of Ireland. It was said that this causeway was built by giants to form a road across to Scotland.

Others say that it was built by Finn mac Cool.

Giants' Ring   *British*

A megalithic structure in Ireland. This structure was said to have been transported to Britain by the sorcerer Merlin and re-erected as Stonehenge. Alternatively, Merlin transformed himself into a whirlwind to suck the stones from the ground where they stood on Mount Killauras so that King Uther's workmen could transport them to Avebury.

Gilbert   *British*

A knight of King Arthur's court. In a fight with Gawain, his left hand was cut off. He was killed in a fight with Meliot.

Gilded Man *see* **El Dorado**

Gilgamesh   *Mesopotamian*

A giant, semi-divine Babylonian hero, king of Uruk. He was secretly abandoned as a baby but was saved from falling to earth by an eagle.

When the goddess Inanna's favourite tree was inhabited by a serpent, a Zu bird and the destructive demon Lilith, he killed the snake and drove off both Lilith and the bird. He overcame the giant Huwawa and rejected the love of the goddess Ishtar. When Ishtar arranged with Anu to send the Bull of Heaven to ravage the land, Gilgamesh killed it and cut it up. When his friend Enkidu who had helped him, was killed by the gods, he set out to achieve immortality. Advised to consult the one mortal, Utnapishtim, who had been given immortality, he journeyed to the edge of the world, running the gauntlet of scorpion-men, jewelled trees and women of pleasure and crossed the sea of death in a boat steered by Ursanapi.

He was told that immortality was a burden rather than a blessing but he did manage to get a piece of the plant that procured rejuvenation. He was taking it to Enkidu when it was stolen by a snake.

Another version of Enkidu's death arises from the story in which Gilgamesh and Inanna felled a tree and made a magic drum from its timber. When this drum was accidentally dropped into the underworld, Enkidu went down to retrieve it but was trapped.

Gilgamesh's story is told in the *Epic of Gilgamesh*, which includes the story of the Flood.

Gimokodan   *Pacific Islands*

The underworld, in the lore of the Philippine Islands. At the entrance to Gimokodan is the Black River in which souls bathe to eradicate all memories of human life. There is also a huge female with many breasts to succour the spirits of those who died young.

In Gimokodan itself, the spirit carries on much as it did on earth, but only during the hours of darkness. When daylight returns, each spirit makes a dish from leaves and is turned into a liquid in this dish until darkness returns.

Gin-sai   *Korean*

A fabulous bird, so evil that its mere shadow can poison food.

Gina   *Australian*

In Aborigine lore, the old man of the moon.

Giovava   *West Indies*

In the lore of the Taino, a cave from which the sun and moon emerged.

Girdle of Hippolyta   *Greek*

A love-girdle given to Hippolyta by her father the war god Ares. This girdle was seized by Hercules as his ninth Labour.

Gisdhubar *Mesopotamian*
= *Greek* Heracles; *Roman* Hercules
A Chaldean hero. He killed the tyrant Khumbala as one of the adventures related in an epic work in twelve volumes, each of which is connected with one of the signs of the Zodiac. The original work is attributed to Sin-liki-innini.

Gitchi Manitou *North American*
The creator-god of the Algonquins. He instructed the duck and the terrapin to dive into the primordial waters and bring up some mud. The god dried the mud on his pipe and from it created the world and human beings. (*See also* **Great Spirit**.)

Gizo *African*
= *Yoruba* Anansi
A trickster-hero of the Hausa in the form of a spider.

Gladsheim *Norse*
The region of happiness, site of Valhalla, the golden palace of Odin where the gods met in council.

An alternative version describes Gladsheim as a golden temple in Idavold which provided seating for Odin and twelve other deities.

glaistig *Scottish*
A female devil. This being is said to appear either as a beautiful female, half woman, half goat, or a goat-like hag or a small woman dressed in green.

glaistyn *Manx*
= *Scottish* kelpie
A water-horse which sometimes appears as a handsome youth.

Glas Gabnach *Irish*
also Grey Cow
A fairy cow. In some accounts, this animal appeared from the sea; in others, she was stolen from

Spain by a dwarf smith-god, Gavida. It was said that she had an inexhaustible supply of milk that could fill any vessel but when a witch placed a sieve under her, she died in the effort to keep it filled. Others say that she disappeared when she was struck by her owner and returned to the Otherworld.

Glastonbury *British*
A town in Somerset, England, reputed to be the place to which Joseph of Arimathea brought the Holy Grail in 63 AD. Some regard it as the site of Avalon.

Glauce *Greek*
Daughter of Creon, king of Thebes. When Jason divorced the sorceress Medea, he married Glauce, but Medea killed not only Glauce but all the wedding-guests by burning down the palace. Only Jason escaped.

Glaucus[1] *Greek*
Son of King Minos and Pasiphae. When, as a boy, Glaucus was drowned in a large jar of honey, his father ordered the seer Polyeidus, who found him, to be locked in the store-room with the dead boy. Polyeidus killed one snake when it approached the body but a second snake had a herb in its mouth with which it revived its dead mate. The seer used the same herb to restore Glaucus to life. Some say that it was Asclepius, the god of healing, who restored the boy to life.

Minos made Polyeides teach Glaucus the arts of prophecy which he did but, when leaving Crete, had the boy spit into his mouth, so taking away all that the boy had learned.

Glaucus[2] *Greek*
A sea god; perhaps a son of the sea god Poseidon.

He was a fisherman who fell in love with the nymph Scylla. She spurned him, and Circe, who also loved Glaucus, changed her into a monster who wrecked ships and destroyed sailors. Glaucus was changed into a sea god.

In another version of the story, the fish he caught ate the grass on which he tipped them from the net and then plunged back into the sea. Glaucus ate some of the grass and felt an irresistible desire to follow them. He entered the sea and became a sea god protecting fishermen.

Gleipnir *Norse*
The magic rope restraining the wolf Fenris. When he broke free of chains on two occasions, the gods had a special rope made by the dwarfs which could not be broken even though it was made from such insubstantial materials as the footfall of a cat, the beard of a woman and the voice of a fish. Others include the miaow of a cat, the sinews of a bear, the spittle of a bird and the root of a mountain.

Glenthorne *British*
A site on the coast of Cornwall, England. In the story that says that Joseph of Arimathea brought the young Jesus to Britain, they were said to have come ashore here in search of water. When they found none, Jesus caused a spring to appear, a source which has never dried up.

gLing-chos *Tibetan*
The myths of the early Tibetans concerning the world known as gLing. This world had three (or four) realms, each with its own distinctive colour. At the top was the heaven, sTang-lha, which was white; then came the red home

of humans, Bar-btsan; below that was usually the blue underworld known as Yog-klu. The fourth realm, which appears in some accounts, was the black or violet world of the demons known as bDud.

Glipsa   *North American*
A Navaho girl who was abducted by Bear and Snake. She and her sister were captured from their underwater village and she mated with one of her captors, Snake, who appeared to her as a handsome brave. She later escaped but he once again appeared in this form and she returned to him. He taught her many things including the Hozoni Chant and eventually allowed her to return to her people. When she returned, she was possessed of magic powers of healing that she passed on to her brother.

Glorianda   *European*
also Gloriana
A fairy. In the Charlemagne stories, she is said to be the mother of Oberon by Julius Caesar.
In Spenser's poetry she is the daughter of Oberon and queen of Faerie with whom Arthur, before he became king, fell in love.

Gluskap   *North American*
also Glooscap, Great Hare;
= *Algonquin* Manabozho; *Fox* Wisaka; *Iroquois* Ioskeha; *Menominee* Manabush: *Montagnais* Messou
A creator-god of the Abnaki people. He created the earth and mankind from his mother's body while his brother, Malsum, created all the inconvenient things. He then killed all the giants and the evil beings such as witches and sorcerers, ridding the earth of the evil spirit, Pamola. One giant, Win-pe, made himself taller than a pine tree but Gluskap grew until he reached the sky and then killed the giant with a blow from his bow. The only one unmoved by the god's power was the infant, Wasis, who merely gurgled at him.

In another story Gluskap overcame Jug Woman, an evil demon, and killed the huge monster that was blocking a stream that a tribe depended on for water and then squeezed it so hard that it became a bullfrog.

Malsum killed Gluskap with the feather of an owl, the only thing that could hurt him, but Gluskap returned to life and killed Malsum with a fern. Malsum then became an evil wolf, Lox.

Malsum's demon followers, the Kewawkqu', tried to avenge their leader's death and Gluskap had to wage a constant war against these forces of evil and the Medecolin, who were sorcerers, finally defeating them. When his work was done, he gave a great feast for all the animals on the shores of Lake Minas, and then sailed off in his canoe. After he had gone, the animals, which had all previously spoken the same language, suddenly found that each species now spoke a different language.

He was a benevolent deity, envisaged as a rabbit, and granted reasonable requests made to him by humans but those who asked for immortality were turned into stones or trees.

He is expected to return as a saviour of his people.

gNod-sByin   *Tibetan*
Black demons. These beings, armed with bows and arrows, were precursors of the human race. Next came the bDud.

gnome
A goblin or sprite; an elemental earth-spirit. It is said that these beings can move through the earth at will, much like a fish moving through water.

goat
(1) In Greek mythology, the animal of Dionysus.
(2) In Mesopotamian mythology, the animal of Marduk and Ningirsu.
(3) In Norse mythology, the animal of Thor.

Goat-god   *Greek*
also Goat-Pan
The god Pan.

Gobaka   *Chinese*
One of the Eighteen Lohan. He is depicted holding a fan or a book.

goblin
A frightening spirit or gnome. These malicious creatures are envisaged as being small and grotesque in appearance and are much given to causing damage in the house by night.

Goblin-spider   *Japanese*
An evil goblin. When the warrior-hero Raiko was ill, this goblin came to him each night in the form of a boy, giving him medicine which only served to make his condition worse. When Raiko struck him with his sword, the goblin enmeshed him in a large web. Raiko cut himself free and killed the goblin, which he found hiding in a cave.

Another version has the goblin appearing to Raiko and his servant, Tsunna, first in the form of an old woman and then as a beautiful maiden. Again the goblin was wounded, trapped

Raiko in a web and was killed when Raiko escaped.

When Raiko cut off the goblin's head, hundreds of skulls emerged from a wound in its stomach.

God of the Dunghill *see* **Beelzebub**

God of the Place of Long Life *see* **Ch'ang-sheng-t'u Ti**

Goddess of the Sea *see* **T'ien-Hou**

Godheim   *Norse*
Home of the gods: site of the city, Asgard; heaven.

Godlike Spirits   *North American*
also Godlike Ones
Four gods of the Sioux. These four are given as Nagi, Nagila, Niya and Sicun, all aspects of Wakan Tanka.

Gog and Magog   *British*
The last survivors of a giant race. These giants were captured by Brutus, leader of a band of Trojans, and Corineus, son of Hercules, and kept as porters in the royal palace. In an alternative story they were together the giant Gogmagog who Corineus threw to his death from a cliff.

Another story describes them as races which were imprisoned behind a range of mountains by Alexander the Great, who had built a huge metal gate to keep them from escaping. Others relate how they attacked King Arthur but he defeated them with the help of Gargantua who wielded a 60ft club.

In apocalyptic writings, Gog and Magog are the Devil's assistants.

Gogmagog   *British*
A pre-Celtic giant. He is represented by a figure cut in the chalk of the South Downs, the site of fertility rites. Some say that he

turned into a hill when a nymph, Granta, rejected his love. (*See also* ***Gog and Magog***.)

Gohone   *North American*
The Iroquois spirit of winter.

Goin   *Australian*
An evil spirit, said to have the claws of an eagle on legs like those of an alligator.

Gokuraku-Jodo   *Japanese*
= *Chinese* Hsi T'ien
The Buddhist paradise, home of Amida. (*See also* ***Pure Land***, ***Sukhavati***.)

Gold Mountain   *East Indian*
In the lore of the Dayaks, this mountain clashed with Jewel Mountain to form the world.

Golden Book of Fate   *Siberian*
The book in which the goddess Ajyst records each person's life.

golden bough   *Greek*
A branch carried by Aeneas which gave him access to Hades.

Golden Dragon *see* **Chin Lung**

Golden Fleece   *Greek*
The golden-coloured fleece of Chrysomallon, the ram that carried Phrixus to safety when his father intended to sacrifice him to Apollo. When he sacrificed the ram to the gods, Phrixus gave the fleece to the king of Colchis, who hung it on a tree guarded by a serpent. It was later the object of the quest undertaken by Jason and the Argonauts who seized it and returned it to Iolcus.

Golden Mountain *see* **Mount Meru**

Golden Tortoise   *Malay*
A wise animal. This tortoise, which owns the Golden Flute, is consulted by the king on certain matters. If plague is brought by the Green Demon, the king can cure it by blowing on the Golden Flute.

golem   *Hebrew*
An image brought to life; a servant automaton. It is said that Reb Low, a 16th-century Polish rabbi, created an automaton which worked non-stop when a plate was inserted under its tongue but rested when the plate (which bore the name of God) was removed for the sabbath. When the owner forgot to remove the plate, the automaton disintegrated.

Gonamati   *Buddhist*
One of the Eighteen Lohan. A very wise disciple of the Buddha, he is depicted seated under a tree.

Gonaqade't   *North American*
A sea god of the Chilkat people. He may appear as a canoe, a fish or a house rising from the waters. He is depicted as having both arms and fins.

'gong-po   *Tibetan*
Early ancestors of the race: miracle-workers. (*See also* ***klu***, ***rGyal-po***.)

Gonzuole   *African*
In the lore of Liberia, the first woman. Although she lived alone on earth she bore many girls. In some accounts, she was captured by a chieftain, Utompe.

Good Folk, the
also Good Neighbours, Little People Fairies. (*See also* ***Faylinn***.)

Good Goddess *see* **Bona Dea**

Goomblegubbon   *Australia*
The bustard personified. It is said that he played a trick on Dinewan the emu, as a result of which the bird lost its wings.

Goon Desert   *British*
Brother of the Fisher King. He had killed Espinogee, a knight, and was himself killed by Espinogee's son, Partinal. The sword with which Partinal killed Goon Desert shattered and its repair could be

accomplished only by the knight who finally found the Holy Grail.

Goonnear   *Australian*
A snake, the evil counterpart of Biggarroo. It is said that the dead pass through his body to the world of unhappy spirits.

goose
(1) In Egyptian mythology, the bird of Horus, Isis, Osiris and Seb.
(2) In Celtic mythology, the bird of the goddess Epona.

Goose-god   *Siberian*
An Ostyak deity of fate. This bird lives in a nest made of furs and skins built in the mountains.

Gordian knot   *Greek*
The knot with which King Gordius tied his oxen to their cart. This strange knot of cornel bark defied all attempts to undo it until the problem was dramatically solved, centuries later, by Alexander the Great who simply sliced through it with his sword.

Gordius   *Greek*
King of Phrygia. Gordius started life as a peasant but was elected king when he unwittingly fulfilled the prophecy of an oracle by entering the city Telmissus driving his ox-cart. The oxen were tied to his cart with what became known as the Gordian knot.

Gorgo *see* **Medusa**

Gorgon   *African*
A monster in Libya. This beast, which lived on poisonous plants, had a scaly body and long hair covering its face. If it raised its drooping head, its breath caused convulsions in anybody standing nearby.

Gorgons   *Greek*
Three snake-haired, winged female monsters; sisters of the Graiae. A glance from these monsters,

or at least from Medusa, could turn a man to stone. Their names were Euryale, Medusa and Stheno, and only Medusa was mortal.

They lived in Cisthene and were depicted as having snakes for hair, tusks like a boar, beards, hands of brass and the hindquarters of a mare.

Gortigern   *Irish*
A language said to have been spoken by all races before the episode of the Tower of Babel.

Goshye-e   *South American*
The king of the giants. In the lore of the Patagonian Indians, he was the giant killed by the culture-hero, Ellal, who turned himself into a gadfly and poisoned Goshye-e with his sting.

Goswhit   *British*
King Arthur's helmet, 'Goose-white'.

Gorlagon   *British*
King Arthur's pet wolf. He was originally a magician who had been turned into a wolf by his wife. When Arthur obtained the magic wand she had used, he was able to restore Gorlagon to his human form.

Götterdämmerung   *German*
also Twilight of the Gods
The German name for Ragnarok.

Graces   *Greek*
Dawn goddesses, daughters of Zeus or Dionysus by Aphrodite or Euronyme. These three, attendants on Aphrodite and Eros, are Aglaia (Splendour), Euphrosyne (Mirth) and Thalia (Good Cheer).

Originally there were two, Auxe and Hegemone, worshipped in Athens and two, Cleta and Phaenna, worshipped in Sparta. Other parts of Greece worshipped three – Aglaia, Pasithea and

Peitho. Another, Cale, is sometimes referred to as one of this trio.

Graiae   *Greek*
also Graeae, Grey Women
Sisters of the Gorgons. These sisters, named Deino, Enyo and Pemphredo, lived on the far side of Ocean and shared one eye and one tooth between them. Perseus seized this eye and returned it only when they gave him the directions, or the magic cap, shoes and bag, which he needed to locate the Gorgons. In some accounts, he was said to have thrown the eye away, leaving them blind.

Grail *see* **Holy Grail**

Grail Castle *see* **Castle Carbonek**

Grail King   *British*
also Grail Keeper
Any of a succession of kings charged with keeping the Holy Grail. The list of these kings includes such names as Amfortas, the Fisher King, Frimutel, Helaius and Pelles.

Grail Lance *see* **Holy Lance**

Grail Quest   *British*
The search for the Holy Grail by the Knights of the Round Table. The quest ended only when Galahad and his companions, Bors and Percival, returned the Holy Grail and the Holy Lance to their rightful home in the Holy Land.

Grail Question   *British*
A question to be asked by the True Knight of the Grail. When asked, this question, which took the form 'What is the Grail and whom does it serve?', healed the wounds of the Fisher King.

Grail Sword   *British*
The sword of Partinal. When Partinal used it to kill Goon Desert, it shattered. One of the objects of the Grail Quest involved its repair.

When Bors, Galahad and Percival arrived at Castle Carbonek, Eliazar, son of Pelles, brought in the broken sword, which was repaired by Galahad after the other two had tried to mend it and failed.

In other stories, it was the sword of David.

Grandfather　　　*South American*
A culture hero in Brazil. He was left in charge of some children while their parents were away hunting and took them up to heaven by climbing a tall tree which he then ordered the ants to fell. When the children tried to escape, the ropes they used were too short and they fell to the ground, leaving Grandfather in the sky.

He gave the tribe tobacco and extra women. Originally there was only one woman but Grandfather cut her into pieces when the men were away so that, when they returned from the hunt, each found a woman in his hut.

Grandgousier　　　*British*
A giant; father of Gargantua. It was said that the sorcerer Merlin created this being from whales' bones and the blood of Lancelot.

Grandmother　　　*North American*
A supernatural being. She found a clot of blood lying on a path and covered it with a jar. It developed into a baby which she raised as Orphan Boy.

Grandmother Earth　　　*North American*
also Unci
A creator-spirit of the Sioux.

Grandmother Turtle　　　*North American*
In the lore of the Cheyenne, the Turtle on whose back the creator built the world from mud.

Granta　　　*British*
A nymph. The giant Gogmagog fell in love with her and, when she rejected him, changed into a large hill.

Graphiel　　　*Hebrew*
One of the Seven Intelligences, ruler of the planet Mars.

Grasshopper　　　*North American*
A Choctaw spirit; daughter of Grasshopper Mother.

Grasshopper Girl　　　*North American*
A Navaho spirit. At creation, she and Pollen Boy were placed on Mount San Juan.

Grasshopper Mother　　　*North American*
A Choctaw spirit; mother of Grasshopper. When the Choctaws emerged from underground at Nanih Waya, she was killed by some of the tribe who failed to reach the upper world.

Grasshopper People　　　*North American*
The people of the Yellow World. During their ascent from the nether world, the Navaho passed through several worlds, including the Yellow World. They offended the Grasshopper People by seducing their wives and were forced to move up to the next world.

Great Awabi　　　*Japanese*
also Awabi
A sea god in the form of a huge earshell. When the fisherman, Kansuke, came to investigate a bright light rising from the sea, he fell into the water and sank. His son, Matakichi, failed to find him; he had been eaten by the Great Awabi. Matakichi became a disciple of a priest and together they prayed for the soul of Kansuke, whereupon the spirit of the Great Awabi appeared to the priest and confessed what had happened and then killed himself, giving instructions that the huge pearl inside him should be given to Matakichi.

Great Bear (Ursa major)
(1) In Central America, Aztec myths regard the constellation as the god Tezcatlipoca, in his aspect as Ocelotl, falling out of the sky into the sea.
(2) The Chinese call it the Bushel (= measure of grain), regarded as the throne of Shang-ti and a symbol of longevity, or else Pei-tou or Ch'i-chiang regarded as the emperor's chariot.
(3) In Greek myths it was the never-sleeping guardian of the universe or a form of the Muse Callisto.
(4) In Hindu lore the seven stars of the Plough are the Seven Rishis.
(5) The Inuit say that this was a real bear which took to the skies to escape hunters who, in following it, were turned into the Pleiades.
(6) The Mongols refer to the Great Bear as the god of thieves since the original six stars stole one of the Pleiades to make the seven.
(7) In North America, the Plains Indians refer to the Great Bear as Mishe-Mokwa and say that it was killed by Mudjekeewis, father of Hiawatha.

Other tribes say that three hunters follow the bear and, when they kill it, the world will come to an end.
(8) In Siberia, the seven stars are wolves pursuing the seven horses of the Little Bear. If they catch the horses, the world will come to an end. In some versions, the wolves are reindeer.

(9) Other stories have the Pole Star as the hunter and the Great Bear as a stag and, once again, the death of the hunted signals the end of the world. Yet another story says that the seven stars are seven skulls thrown into the sky after they had been used as cups.

Great Beginning *see* **T'ai Shih**

Great Canoe   *North American*
A stockade which the Mandan hero, Lone Man, built to save his people from the Flood.

Great Change *see* **T'ai I**

Great Eagle   *North American*
A water-spirit of the Pima tribe. He was an enemy of Earthmaker and preyed on the humans created by him. When he sent the Flood to destroy the world, only Szeuka survived. This son of Earthmaker fought and killed Great Eagle and restored human life.

Great Father   *Australian*
A name for the rainbow serpent as a creator and fertility god.

Great First *see* **T'ai Ch'u**

Great Goddess
A name given to an important (sometimes supreme) goddess in many cultures.
This name is used for such deities as Dorje, Hera, Juno, Mahadevi, Neith.
In some South American tribes, the Great Goddess is said to have mated with dogs and produced dog-spirits.

Great Hare   *North American*
also Cottontail, Hare, Rabbit
A trickster-god. This deity appears in the lore of many Algonquian tribes under such names as Gluskap, Manabush, Manabozho, Messou, Michabo, Nanabozho and Wabus.

Great Hawk   *North American*
A bird which helped the Navaho to reach the upper world. Great Hawk was said to have clawed a small opening in the sky through which the Navaho were able to escape after it had been enlarged by Locust.

Great Head   *North American*
A storm god of the Seneca people. He was envisaged as a large head carried on two legs and was said to live on blocks of maple wood.
He helped a young Seneca to kill the witch who had killed the boy's nine brothers and, when he next passed over in a storm, he restored the dead brothers to life.

Great-Holy-Fire-Above *see* **Ababinili**

Great Medicine   *North American*
A name for the creator-spirit of the Cheyenne.

Great Monad   *Chinese*
A primordial being. This entity split to form Yin and Yang. These split further to form four deities which gave rise to Pan-ku, the first man. (*See also* **T'ai I**.)

Great Mother
A name used in many cultures for a (mother-)goddess.
This name is used for such deities as Ama-arhus, Cybele, Damkina, Hathor, Isis, Magna Mater, Nekhbet, Nina and Tiamat. The Akkadians knew her as Ishtar, the Armenians as Anahit, the Babylonians as Mylitta, Nina or Tasmetu, the Canaanites as Anaitis; to the Cilicians she was Ate or Ateh, to the Greeks she was Aphrodite or Ma, to the Phoenicians she was Astarte or Bau, to the Romans she was Venus and to the Sumerians she was Baba, Mai or Mamitu.
In Australia, the Great Mother is a primeval goddess of the Aborigines who repeatedly swallowed and regurgitated young men.

Great Mystery *see* **Wakan Tanka**

Great One   *African*
The name of the creator-god in the Zulu story of creation. He came out of the earth with the sun and the moon, which he placed in the sky, and then created the tribes.

Great Primordial *see* **T'ai Su**

Great Spider   *Australian*
A sky deity of the Aborigines.

Great Spirit   *North American*
A name used for the supreme deity or creator-god by many tribes. This name is used for deities such as Gitchi Manitou, Ketchimanetowa, Kisha Manido, Kitshi Manitou, Maho Penekheka, Maiyun, Shilup Chito Osh, Sibu, Atius-Tirawa and Wakan Tanka.

Great Thunderbird *North American*
Chief of the Thunderbirds. He, together with three other elders, was responsible for guarding the nest holding the eggs from which all other Thunderbirds were hatched. He was also the guardian of the west and was said to be so large that he could eat whales whole.

Great Turtle   *North American*
In the lore of the Iroquois, the Turtle on which the earth is supported.
A tree dropped from heaven into the primordial waters, followed by the beautiful maiden Awenhai. The swans saved her from drowning and reported to Great Turtle who ordered diving birds and animals to dive on the spot where the tree fell and bring up some earth. Several animals died in the attempt but the toad finally succeeded. This soil, spread on Great Turtle's back, grew to form an island large

enough to support Awenhai and kept growing until it became the present earth.

Green Demon　　　　　　*Malay*

A plague demon. This monster, with the head of a snake on a body of green vapour, causes boils, plagues, sores, and other diseases. The Golden Tortoise, however, owns a magic flute which, when blown by the king, can cause a gentle breeze which blows away the disease.

Green-feathered Serpent *see* **Quetzalcoatl**

Green Knight　　　　　　*British*

An unknown knight. He arrived unheralded at Camelot one Christmas, dressed all in green and riding a green horse, and challenged Arthur's knights to a beheading contest. Gawain accepted the challenge and cut off the interloper's head. The Green Knight merely replaced it and rode off, renewing the challenge for a year later at the Green Chapel. En route to that meeting, Gawain was entertained by Bercilak (who was the Green Knight) whose wife twice tried in vain to seduce Gawain. He did, however, accept a green sash from the lady. At the chapel, the axe was swung three times – twice reflecting Gawain's resistance to temptation it stopped short of his neck; the third stroke inflicted only a very slight wound, reflecting his acceptance of the sash. The man wielding the axe turned out to be Bercilak and the whole episode was one of the destructive ploys of the sorceress Morgan le Fay.

Green Man　　　　　　*European*

An early vegetation god now represented by carvings of a face with foliage emerging from the mouth.

Greenan Castle　　　　*British*

A site in Scotland sometimes suggested as the site of Camelot.

Grendel　　　　　　*Anglo-Saxon*

This half-human man-eating monster, which, in some accounts, was a descendant of Cain, lived under a lake and was invulnerable to normal weapons. It frequently raided the castle of Hrodgar, the king of Denmark, who called in Beowulf who trapped it and fought it. In the struggle, Grendel broke free of Beowulf's grip and tore off its arm, causing a wound from which it later died. When the monster's mother tried to avenge Grendel's death, Beowulf killed her and decapitated both with a magic sword.

Grey Cow *see* **Glas Gabnach**

Grey Lady　　　　　　*British*

A ghost, said to haunt the site in Wales known as Moel Arthur to protect the king's treasure.

Grey Wolf　　　*North American*

A god of the tribes of the northwest. He appeared at creation and was placed on Mount Shasta as a guardian god.

Grey Women *see* **Graiae**

griffin[1]　　　　　　*African*

also griffon, gryphon

A monstrous bird. The Berbers say that the Ormaddu, a huge bird, mates with a female wolf to produce this monster which splits its mother apart when she gives birth.

griffin[2]　　　　　　*Greek*

also griffon, gryphon

A monster with the body of a lion and the beak and wings of an eagle. It guarded a stream flowing with gold against the Arimaspi.

In some accounts, its two front legs were those of an eagle, in others all four feet were those of a lion. Griffins were said to build their nests of gold and lay eggs made of agate.

It was regarded as the animal of the god Apollo or the goddess Nemesis and, later, of the Roman Empire.

Grimhild　　　　　　*Norse*

She was queen of the Nibelungs and a witch who could cast spells and brew magic potions. She gave one such drink to Sigurd, when he came to the king's court, to make him forget Brunhild and fall in love with Grimhild's daughter Gudrun. She supplied another brew to her son Gunnar which enabled him to exchange identities with Sigurd so that the latter could woo Brunhild for Gunnar.

Later, when Gudrun had left with her daughter, Swanhild, to live with Elf, Atli demanded compensation for the death of his sister Brunhild, prompting Grimhild to administer another potion to Gudrun which caused her to agree to marry Atli, whom she hated.

In the *Nibelungenlied*, she appears as Krimhild.

Grocland　　　　　　*British*

A polar island, possibly Greenland. It was said that King Arthur conquered this island where the native population were over 20 feet tall. Many of his men (4000 in some accounts) never returned from expeditions to the North Pole.

Gromersomer Joure　　*British*

A robber-baron of Cannock Chase. He asked travellers a riddle and killed them if they failed to answer correctly. When King Arthur was lost on the Chase and was given shelter by the outlaw, he was asked 'What do women want most?' An old crone, who turned out to be Joure's sister, Ragnell, gave him the answer –'Their own way'.

Ground-heat Girl   *North American*
A Navaho maiden; wife of the first man.

gruagach   *Scottish*
A monster, an ogre; a brownie; a household goddess; an otherworld wizard.

gryphon *see* **griffin**[1,2]

gShen-Lha-Odkhar   *Tibetan*
A Bon creator-god. He descended from the Tushita heaven in the form of a blue bird and was reborn on earth from his mother's right armpit. He then learned the art of magic and was able to manipulate bodies so that one became several or several united to form one.

gShen-Rabs   *Tibetan*
The supreme god in the Bon pantheon.

Guabonito   *West Indies*
A sea goddess. She was rescued from the sea by Guagugiana and taught him the arts of medicine and necklace-making.

Guagugiana   *West Indies*
A culture-hero of the Taino.

When the watchman Marocael was turned to stone by the rays of the sun, the people in the caves known as Amaiaua and Cacibagiagua escaped, and Guagugiana was one of the first after sending out his servant, Giadruvava, who was also turned to stone. Guagugiana led all the women out of the caves and took them to an island where he left them while he travelled on, taking the children with him. When he left the children, they were turned into dwarfs or, some say, into frogs. He later learned the arts of medicine and lace-making from

the goddess Guabonito whom he rescued from the sea.

In some stories, he was turned into a bird by the sun; in others, that was the fate of his servant Giadruvava.

Guallipen   *South American*
In Chile, a fabulous animal in the form of a sheep with the head of a calf: an amphibious monster. An alternative description of this monster says it was the result of a bull mating with a sheep and is very ugly with twisted hoofs. It is said that it will mate with either sheep or cows but the offspring of such unions are likely to be deformed, as will the children of any woman who hears or sees, or dreams about, the monster when she is pregnant.

Guamansuri   *Central American*
The first mortal in the lore of the Incas. He seduced the sister of the Guachimines who killed him in revenge. The twins Apocatequil and Piguerao were the result of the union and, after they were born, the Guachimines killed their mother as well.

Guarani   *South American*
An ancestral hero. He was one of four brothers who survived the Flood and became the ancestor of the Guarani tribe.

Guayacan   *South American*
In the lore of the Incas, a primordial lake. It is believed that the sky rested on pillars which rose out of this lake.

Gudanna   *Mesopotamian*
A Sumerian monster. This celestial bull, which caused seven years of drought, was killed by Gilgamesh.

Gudratrigakwitl   *North American*
also Old Man Above
The creator-god of the Wiyot people. He created the world by

opening his hands and could, if he chose, end it by clapping his hands together.

Guecubu   *South American*
An evil spirit of the Araucanian people. He was responsible for all the ills affecting mankind and is destined to destroy the earth with a flood. Some say that he has a benevolent aspect in the form of a vegetation god, Akakanet, but others say that they are separate beings, brothers representing good and evil.

In another story, he sent a flood but the god Guenu-Pillan raised the mountains so saving some animals and human beings.

In some versions, Guecubu is used as a generic term for all demons.

Guédé[1]   *West Indies*
The first man to die, in Haitian voodoo lore.

guédé[2]   *West indies*
A spirit of the dead, in Haitian voodoo lore. It is said that these spirits can take possession of humans.

Guenu-Pillan   *South American*
A name of the Araucanian god Menechen as 'spirit of heaven'. In this role, he saved some human beings and animals when Guecubu sent a flood, by raising the height of the mountains.

guffitar   *Baltic*
= *Norse* govetter
Lappish dwarf spirits of the forest or living underground.

Guinevere   *British*
Daughter of King Leodegrance; wife of King Arthur.

In some accounts she was regarded as a triune goddess while others say there were two Guineveres, one good, one bad, the latter being able to take the good Guinevere's place to do evil. Launfal, a knight at King Arthur's court, was the only man who realised that the False Guinevere had taken over from the real Guinevere at the wedding feast when she married King Arthur.

Guinevere brought the Round Table as part of her dowry when she married Arthur.

In the Welsh version of the story, she was once abducted by Melwas, king of Summer Land but Arthur soon recovered her. In the British version, she and ten of her knights were captured by Meliagaunt (son of King Bagdemagus of Gore),who loved her from afar, and imprisoned in his castle. When Lancelot rode to her aid, Meliagaunt begged for mercy and the queen forgave him. She slept that night with Lancelot, with whom she had a long affair, and he left blood on the sheets from a wound on his hand sustained when he forced the window bars. Meliagaunt accused Guinevere of being unfaithful to the king by sleeping with one of her ten knights, many of whom had been wounded when he captured them. The queen was saved from the stake by Lancelot who escaped from a trap set for him by Meliagaunt and killed him in single combat even though he had one hand tied behind his back.

The affair with Lancelot was resumed when the Grail quest ended but when Lancelot tried to distance himself from her Guinevere became angry and banished him from the court. When she gave a dinner for twenty-four of her knights, she was accused by Mador of killing his cousin Patrise who died after

eating an apple poisoned by Pinel and intended for Gawain. She would have been burnt at the stake unless her innocence could be proved by single combat and the king ordered Bors to fight on her behalf against Mador. At the last minute, Lancelot took the place of Bors and defeated Mador who then accepted that the queen was innocent.

When Arthur went off on a hunting trip, she was caught in bed with Lancelot by Mordred and Agravain who betrayed her affair with Lancelot to the king. He ordered Gawain to burn her at the stake but he refused to do so. Gawain's brothers, Gaheris and Gareth, had to obey the king's command but when the queen was led to the pyre, Lancelot charged into the crowd and rescued her, killing Gaheris and Gareth and many others in the process. Lancelot took her off to Joyous Gard and Arthur attacked this castle to recover her. The conflict was ended only when the Pope intervened and Guinevere was returned to Arthur, who pledged her safety. Lancelot took himself and many of his followers off to his estates in France where he was later followed by Arthur's army, intent on revenge. Mordred was left in charge of the country and he soon had designs on Guinevere. In some stories she became his mistress, in others she went through a form of marriage with him; still other versions say she merely pretended to yield and then left him, shutting herself away in the Tower of London.

On the death of Arthur Guinevere retired to a convent in Amesbury and refused to leave

despite the pleas of Lancelot to return with him to France. She died in the covent soon afterwards.

Some accounts say that Arthur had three wives, all called Guinevere.

Guli   *African*

A Hottentot hunter who killed the Sun-ram. He shot the ram and cut off some of the flesh. When he found that all water sources had dried up he replaced the flesh and prayed. The god revived and the water supplies were restored.

Gullinbursti   *Norse*

A boar with a golden pelt which pulled Frey's car. This marvellous animal was made by Sindi and presented to Frey by Brock. (*See also* **Slidrugtanni**.)

Gullinkambi   *Norse*

The cockerel 'Golden Comb' that will wake the gods at Ragnarok. This bird sits on the topmost branch of the great tree, Yggdrasil.

Gum Girl   *African*

also Gum Baby, Tar Baby

An effigy covered with sticky stuff. This effigy was placed by a farmer whose crops were being stolen. Anansi, the trickster-god who was the culprit, kicked her to make her speak her name and when his foot got stuck he hit her to make her release him. His hand also got stuck and he was unable to defend himself when the farmer arrived and gave him a good thrashing.

Gunarhnsengyet   *North American*

A hunter of the killer-whale, Gunarh. When his wife was abducted by the whale, Gunarhnsengyet dived to the bottom of the ocean where he met the Cormorant People who were blind. As a reward for cutting open their eyes so that they could see, they told him where to find his wife. Outside Gunarh's house, Gunarhnsengyet met a woodman and repaired the wedge he used for splitting logs. The woodman helped by taking pails of water into the house which, when tipped on to the hot hearth-stones, caused so much steam that Gunarhnsengyet's wife was able to escape. To stop the killer whales from following, Gunarhnsengyet blew a magic potion over Gunarh who swelled so much that he blocked the door, preventing the others from getting out.

Gungnir *Norse*
The spear of the god Odin. In some accounts, this marvellous weapon was made by the dwarf Dvalin and presented to Odin by Loki; in others, Odin fashioned it himself from a branch of the tree Yggdrasil and a blade was later added by the dwarfs. When thrown, it had the power to determine the outcome of the battle by the direction of its flight.

In some accounts, it is referred to as the sword of Odin.

Gusayn *European*
A demon, one of the 72 Spirits of Solomon. He is said to know the past and the future and has the power to reconcile enemies.

Gwen *British*
also Mantle of Invisibility
A cloak or veil of King Arthur. This garment, said to make the wearer invisible, could be worn only by women who were faithful to their husbands, which excluded Guinevere.

Gwlad Yr Hav *Welsh*
The otherworld, a land of summer from which humans came.

Gwrhyr Gwalstawt *British*
A warrior at the court of King Arthur. He was said to be able to talk to the birds and animals and was sent to accompany Culhwch on his quest for the hand of Olwen.

In some accounts he was a magician and could change into a bird; others say that he was a Knight of the Round Table.

gwyllion *Welsh*
Mischieveous spirits or cruel fairies. These spirits are said to appear in the form of ugly females, sometimes seen as goats.

gytrash *British*
A ghost haunting byways, the spirit of a horse, mule or dog. In some accounts, this is the same as the bargaist.

H

H *Central American*
A Mayan deity of uncertain identity, referred to as God H (*see **alphabetical gods***). This deity seems to be connected with the serpent.

ha *Egyptian*
An entity not dependent on the physical body, one of the five elements comprising the complete being.

Hades[1] *Greek*
also Pluto;
= *Egyptian* Serapis; *Norse* Ymir; *Roman* Dis (Pater), Dives, Pluto
God of the underworld, god of wealth; one of the Olympians.

He abducted Demeter's daughter Core and made her, as Persephone, his wife and Queen of the Dead.

When Hercules captured the dog Cerberus as his twelfth Labour, he wounded Hades, who had to go up to Mount Olympus to be healed by Asclepius, the god of healing.

He wears a helmet of invisibility

given to him by the Cyclopes and is depicted as a stern god with a beard and crowned head, holding a key and a sceptre

Hades[2] *Greek*
Hell. (*See also **Tartarus**.*)

hag *European*
An evil witch or sorceress in the form of an ugly woman; a she-devil. These beings are said to ride people, particularly young men, at night, to the extent that their victim wakes up exhausted. In extreme cases, the person affected may die.

hag-knots *European*
Tangled hair in a horse's mane, said to be caused by witches.

Hagenti *European*
A demon, one of the 72 Spirits of Solomon. He is said to have the power of transmutation and appears in the form of a bull with wings.

Hagiel *Hebrew*
One of the Seven Intelligences, ruler of the planet Venus.

Hah *Egyptian*
A god, eternity and infinity personified. He is depicted holding up the heavens with his raised arms and holding a palm-frond.

Hahai Wugti *North American*
also Spider Woman
A spirit of the Hopi people. In some accounts, she takes the place of the Navaho spider woman, Naste Estsan.

(*See also **Kokyangwuti**.*)

Hahness *North American*
The thunderbird of the Chinook. This bird, a raven, first appeared when Too-lux, the god of the south wind, cut open a whale. Its eggs were eaten by the giantess Quoots-hooi and humans appeared from the eggs.

Hall of Judgement *Egyptian*
also Hall of Two Truths
The place in the underworld where the souls of the dead are judged by forty-two judges.

Halphas *European*
A demon, one of the 72 Spirits of

Solomon. This being is said to provoke wars and appears in the form of a stork or a dove.

Ham   *Irish*
In Irish lore, this son of Noah is regarded as a progenitor of the Fomoire.

hamadryad   *Greek*
A tree nymph who lived and died with the tree for which she was responsible. (*See also* **dryad**.)

hamsa   *Hindu*
also hansa
The transport of the god Brahma, or a manifestation of Brahma; the swan (or goose) as a symbol of the sun; an avatar of the god Vishnu as a goose.

It was said that, given a mixture of milk and water, this bird drank only the milk.

Han Chung li   *Chinese*
Chief of the Eight Immortals.

He was a 1st-century soldier who became a hermit. He was said to have discovered the elixir of life and the secret of transmutation in a box which was revealed when the rock wall of his cave split open.

He is usually depicted as a fat man holding a peach and a fan.

Han Hsiang-tzu   *Chinese*
A 9th-century philosopher, one of the Eight Immortals.

He was carried to a magic peach-tree by his tutor Lü Tung-pin but he fell out of the tree, becoming immortal. He was said to be able to make flowers grow and come into bloom immediately or to produce plants with poems written in gold on their leaves.

He was a flute-player who could charm the animals and birds with his music and so became the patron of musicians. His emblem is a flute.

Han-shan Tzu   *Chinese*
An 8th-century hermit and poet; one of the Eighteen Lohan in some accounts.

He is described as an ugly man who, dressed in old rags, lived in a cave. His poetry was written on rocks since he had no paper. It was said that he could make himself so small that he could hide in cracks.

Hana   *East Indies*
A sun god in New Guinea. He mated with his sister Ni to produce the human race but then they retreated to the sky where he became the sun and his sister became the moon.

Handsome   *North American*
An Algonquin maiden. For the story of Handsome and Elegant. (*See also* **Elegant**.)

Hannya   *Japanese*
An ogress said to devour children.

hansa *see* **hamsa**

Hanuman   *Hindu*
A trickster monkey-god, a manifestation of the god Vishnu.

He was in charge of the forces that attacked Ravana's fortress when the demon-king abducted the god Rama's wife, Sita, building a bridge from India to Sri Lanka for this purpose. When swallowed by the female demon Surasa, he grew enormously to force her jaws apart and then shrank to the size of a finger and flew out of her ear. When he was captured by Ravana, whose son set his tail alight, Hanuman used the flame to burn down Ravana's stronghold.

In one account, Ravana persuaded his nephew to kill Hanuman but the monkey-god threw him back to his uncle's court in Sri Lanka.

For his help, Rama gave him the gifts of immortality and eternal youth. He could change his shape at will and owned a magic stick that could expand to a thousand miles.

He accompanied Tripitaka and Chu Pa-chieh on their journey to India and back and helped them to overcome the dangers they met en route. In one case, Tripitaka and Chu Pa-chieh were trapped by spider-women who attacked Hanuman with a swarm of insects. He conjured up a flock of birds which ate all the insects and his magic overcame that of the spider-women and the prisoners were released.

He was regarded as a huge, red-faced monkey with yellow fur and a tail that was several miles in length. He had a deformed jaw as the result of a blow from one of the god Indra's thunderbolts which broke his jaw when he tried to eat the sun.

Haokah   *North American*
A Sioux thunder god and god of the hunt. He has horns on his head and his face is divided down the middle, one side being miserable, the other cheerful. He uses the wind to beat a huge drum to cause thunder.

Haoma[1]   *Persian*
A sacred drink made from the haoma vine. The tree itself, Gaokerena, was brought by an eagle to Mount Alburz.

Haoma[2]   *Persian*
A Zoroastrian physician-god, son of the good god Ahura Mazda. He was the personification of the sacred drink made from the haoma vine.

In some accounts, Haoma is female – the moon.

Hapikern   *Central American*

A cosmic serpent. Some of the tribes in Yucatan say that this evil being will finally overcome the supreme god, Nohochacyum, and the world will end.

Happy Hunting-ground   *North American*

The heaven of the Native American tribes.

Hapy[1]   *Egyptian*

A fertility god and god of the Nile; an androgynous deity responsible for the Nile floods. He was born when a virgin cow was impregnated by moonbeams or by lightning. He helped to bring the god Osiris back to life after he had been killed and dismembered by Set, by suckling him after Isis had reassembled the parts.

He was sometimes depicted as a goose with two heads and a human body or as a naked fat man with pendulous breasts and erect phallus, holding a fan and a tray.

Hapy[2]   *Egyptian*

An ape-headed or dog-headed god. He was guardian of the north and of the lungs or, some say, the small intestine, of the dead.

Hapy[3]   *Egyptian*

A name for the bull-god, Apis, in some accounts.

hare

Hares appear in many myths, often associated with the moon:

(1) In West Africa, Hare (or Rabbit) is a trickster-god and is regarded as the precursor of Brer Rabbit, taken to America by slaves.

(2) In Buddhism the hare is regarded as a previous incarnation of Buddha.

(3) In China, the hare represents longevity. It is said that the female animal becomes pregnant either by looking at the moon or by licking its mate's fur and delivers her young through the mouth. Some say that the hare can live for 1000 years and lives in the moon where it sits at the foot of a tree pounding the drug of immortality. In this role, it is known as the Gemmeous Hare. Its transfer to the moon is said to have been the reward of self-sacrifice.

(4) In Greek myths the hare is the animal of Aphrodite, Eros and Hermes.

(5) In Hindu lore, Shasha, a hare, is said to live on the moon.

(6) In Japan also, Usagi, Hare in the Moon, is an animal said to live on the moon were it spends its time pounding rice which it makes into cakes.

(7) In Roman myths the hare is the animal of Mercury and Venus.

(*See also* **Great Hare**.)

Harpies   *Greek*

Female monsters, part woman, part bird.

Originally, there was just one such being, Podarge, on whom, it is said, Zeus (or Zephyrus) fathered the horses of Achilles known as Balios and Xanthos. Then Aello and Ocypete were added. Later stories had them as Aellopus, Calaeno, Ocythoe and Nicothoe. At first they were regarded as spirits of the air, later as foul monsters.

Amongst other horrible deeds they harried Phineus, the blind Thracian king who had offended Zeus by the accuracy of his prophecies, befouling his food until they were chased off by the two winged members of Jason's crew, Calais and Zetes. Some say they were never seen again.

On another occasion they harried Aeneas and his men when they landed on the Strophades Islands where they lived. On both occasions, the monsters were saved from destruction by the angry sailors by the intervention of Iris, the rainbow goddess and sister of the Harpies.

They also carried off the daughters of Pandareus, king of Miletus, and gave them to the Furies as servants.

They appear in the stories of Charlemagne where they harried Senapus, the blind king of Abyssinia, snatching or fouling his food so that he would have died of starvation if Astolpho had not arrived in time to drive them off and so save his life.

In medieval times they could be depicted in various forms such as centaur-like beasts with wings, rather than as bird-women.

Hasan   *Persian*

A hero of the *Arabian Nights*. He helped a magician to find the philosopher's stone and later was shipwrecked, coming ashore near a palace. The magician turned up again and Hasan killed him, after which he entered a forbidden room to find ten swan-maidens. He stole the feathered robe of one of the maidens who then became his wife but she later recovered the robe and flew off to the island of Wak Wak. With the help of a jinnee, he found this island and recovered his wife.

Hastehogan   *North American*

A Navaho house god and god of agriculture; the god of yellow maize.

Hasteyalti   *North American*

Supreme god of the Navaho, the god of white maize. He and

Hastehogan created the two goddesses, Estanatlehi and Yolkai Estsan, and helped them to create humans from maize-flour.

Hathor *Egyptian*

= *Canaanite* Baalat, Tanit; *Greek* Aphrodite; *Mesopotamian* Ishtar

A mother-goddess, goddess of childbirth, fertility, joy, love, marriage, music and the sky.

She was originally a war goddess of the Nubians and is sometimes identified with Sakhmet or with Isis, in which capacity she held the ladder by which the good dead could ascend to heaven.

She suckled the pharaohs and greeted the souls entering the underworld. On one occasion, in the form of Sakhmet, she was sent by Ra to kill all mankind but she got drunk on the red-coloured beer with which Ra flooded the land and forgot to carry out her mission.

She was originally depicted as a lioness but later as a cow (her son Horus is said to have cut off her head and replaced it with the cow's head), sometimes wearing a headdress of horns enclosing the disc of the sun. In some depictions, her four limbs support the universe.

hati[1] *Egyptian*

The corporeal heart, distinguished from ab, the symbolic heart that is judged at death.

Hati[2] *Norse*

A wolf, one of the Varns (wolves) along with Skoll and, some say, Managram; offspring of the wolf Fenris and the giantess and goddess of evil Gollweig. These two, or three, wolves pursued the sun and moon, trying to swallow them. When they managed to overtake the heavenly bodies, they swallowed them, causing an eclipse. At Ragnarok they finally devoured the sun and moon completely. They were fed on the marrow from the bones of dead criminals.

hatifa *Persian*

male hatif; *plural* hawatif

A type of jinnee that can be heard but not seen, a voice in the desert. The voice may sound like a maiden in distress calling for help and the traveller who follows its sound may find himself lost. In some cases, he may be led to an oasis where the caller appears in human form and the traveller, forgetting where he was going, stays with her.

hawk

A bird of prey featured in some myths.

(1) In Central America the hawk, Tlotli, was regarded as the messenger of the Aztec gods.

(2) In the East Indies the hawk is a revered bird, guardian of workers in the rice-fields.

(3) In Egypt the hawk was a sacred bird and the god Horus is frequently depicted with the head of a hawk (or falcon).

(4) In Greek myths the hawk is the messenger of Apollo or Hera.

(5) The Pacific Islanders regard the hawk as an incarnation of the trickster-hero and sun god Maui.

(6) In Siberia they say the hawk stole fire and gave the secret to the gods who passed it on to mankind.

(*See also* **Great Hawk**.)

heaven

Most cultures envisage some form of heaven:

African

The Bambara envisage a heaven created by the water god Faro divided into seven parts:

1. Kaba Noro, the home of Faro
2. Kaba dye, the home of the souls of the dead
3. Kaba fii, the home of spirits
4. Faro's accounting room
5. Red Heaven, the hall of judgement
6. Sleep Heaven, the store for secrets
7. Faro's store for rain

Australian

The paradise of the Aborigines is called wathi-wathi. The road leading there forks: the road to the right is clean and inviting but is the home of evil spirits whereas the road to the left, though dirty, is the realm of the good spirits.

Buddhist

The place where Buddhas and bodhisattvas wait is known as the Tushita heaven (Maya) and has thirteen layers, the highest of which is known as Paranirmita-Vasavarten.

In Mahayana Buddhism, a paradise for those en route to enlightenment is known as the Pure Land (Jodo) and is equated with the Nirvana of Hinayana Buddhism.

The heaven reserved for past Buddhas is known as Kshetra, Amitabha's heaven is known as Sukhavati and a future heaven is called Grdhakuta.

In Cambodia, there are said to be 26 paradises, the highest of which is known as Nirpean.

Central American

The Aztecs envisaged three heavens of which Tlalocan, home of the rain god Tlaloc, was the lowest, Tlillan-Tlallapan was in the middle and Tonatiuhican, the home of the sun god Tonatiuh, was the highest.

Other stories say there were thirteen heavens, the highest of which was called Zivena Vitzcatl. In later belief, heaven was like a ladder with steps, on the top rung of which lived the god Ometeotl. Other rungs, in descending order, were occupied by innocent children, tempests, night and day, shooting stars, birds and Venus, the sun and the 400 warring sons of the goddess Coatlicue, the Milky Way, the moon.

Egyptian
The paradise of Osiris, Aalu, lay far to the west and could be reached only by travelling in Ra's boat after being judged by Osiris in the underworld.

Hindu
Each god has his own heaven and Brahma lives in the highest heaven, Brahmaloka, said to be 84,000 leagues above the earth.

The heaven ruled by Vishnu is called Vaikuntha; that of Indra is Svarga; that of Krishna is Go-loka; that of Shiva is Kailasa; that of the goddess Shanti is called Shanti-Niketa and paradise for the uncremated dead is known as the Land of the Pitris.

Irish
The Irish envisage an earthly paradise in the form of the island, Emain Ablach, the Western Paradise.

Mesopotamian
Heaven was regarded as the playground of the gods and was referred to as Anduruna or, in Sumerian lore, Eridu.

Norse
The heaven to which slain warriors are conducted is known as Valhalla.

North American
The native Indian tribes believe in a Happy Hunting-ground where game is plentiful.

Pacific Islands
Burotu, the Fijian paradise, is envisaged as a land of perpetual joy where the good can rest.

The Hawaiian paradise is called Paliuli.

The Polynesian heaven is multi-layered, the highest realms being Putahi-nui-o-Rahua. The tenth heaven is Rangi-Tuarea.

Persian
Heaven is a four-cornered region known as Varena.

Shinto
Heaven is the Eternal Land, Taka-no-Hara, home of the gods, to which the mikado is allowed to ascend on his death and the paradisal land of the spirits is Tokoyo-no-kuni.

Slav
The paradise of the western Slavs is known as Rai, that of the eastern Slavs as Svarog.

Taoist
The island paradise where all the inhabitants are immortal is called Ying-chou. There are said to be 108 realms of paradise, one of which, called P'eng-lai, is the home of the Eight Immortals.

There are, alternatively, said to be 36 heavens of which the highest is Ta-lo.

The imperial heaven is known as Huang-t'ien.

Hebe   *Greek*
Goddess of youth; cup-bearer to the gods; daughter of Zeus and Hera; wife of Hercules.

She had to resign her post when she fell over and spilt wine at an important feast. She was superseded in the post by Ganymede.

After Hercules was deified, Hebe married him and they had two children, Alexiares and Anicetus.

Hebron   *British*
also Rich Fisher
He was given the Holy Grail by Joseph of Arimathea, who was his wife's brother.

Some say he was Percival's grandfather and became the Rich Fisher who was cured of his wounds and carried to heaven by angels.

Hecate[1]   *Greek*
The three-headed or three-bodied goddess of darkness, fertility, moon, streets, the underworld and witchcraft; a Titaness. In some accounts she is the goddess Artemis on earth, and Persephone carrying a torch in the underworld. Others say that she helped the the corn goddess Demeter in her search for her daughter Core (Persephone) in the underworld.

The triple aspect of her nature is represented by Artemis, Hecate and Selene but she is otherwise identified with other goddesses such as Cybele, Demeter and Rhea.

She is depicted as having six arms, three or four bodies and the heads of a dog, a horse and a lion.

Hecate[2]   *Roman*
A name for Diana as goddess of death and the underworld.

Hector   *Greek*
Son of Priam and Hecuba; brother of Paris and others; husband of Andromache; father of Astyanax.

He led the Trojans in their defence of the city against the attacking Greeks who had been angered by the treachery of Paris who carried off Helen, the wife of the Greek king Menelaus when a guest in their house. He killed Patroclus, bosom friend of Achilles, who, wearing the armour of Achilles, had rallied the Greeks for a further attack. The death of his friend brought Achilles back into action – he had been sulking in his tent, refusing to fight, after falling out with King Agamemnon over a girl captive. Now, in new armour made by the smith-god Hephaestus, he led the Greeks in a fresh onslaught and killed Hector. He tied Hector's body to his chariot and drove round the walls of the city. King Priam pleaded for his son's body and was allowed to take it for burial.

In some French accounts, the sorceress Morgan le Fay fell in love with him but turned against him when he spurned her advances.

In Charlemagne stories, his armour and sword, Durindana, are fought over by several of the paladins.

Hector de Marys *see* **Ector** [2]

Hecuba   *Greek*

Second wife of Priam, king of Troy; mother of Cassandra, Hector, Paris, Polydorus and others (she is said to have had nineteen children by Priam).

She sent Polydorus to Polymestor, king of Thrace, for safety when the Greeks attacked Troy but the king killed her son for the treasure he carried.

She was taken captive by the Greeks at the fall of Troy and given to Odysseus. When she learned from him what had happened to her son, she tore out Polymestor's eyes and killed his two sons. To escape the wrath of the king's subjects, she changed herself into a bitch, Maera, and jumped into the sea.

Hedley kow   *British*

A mischievous spirit. These spirits are said to appear as an immoveable bale of hay or a horse which cannot be restrained by harness.

Heduru   *East Indies*

A sky god of New Guinea. This god existed at a time when the sky was very close to the earth, to which it was connected by a rope ladder. Heduru often descended to earth to look after the children of those out at work but he started to steal children and take them back to the sky with him so the angry people cut the ladder, with the result that the heavens retreated to their present position.

Heimdall   *Norse*

A giant demi-god, god of the dawn; guardian of Bifrost, the rainbow bridge; son of the god Odin by nine wave-maidens (his mothers, all giantesses, simultaneously gave birth to the baby, which they reared on warmth from the sun, moisture from the sea and strength from the earth). Another account gives his mother as Angey.

He was said to have very keen eyesight, able to see 100 miles by night, hearing that could detect the grass growing and, armed with a bright sword Hofud and his trumpet Giallarhorn, he lived in a palace known as Himinbiorg built on top of the bridge, from where he had a good view. His job was to keep the Frost Giants from entering Asgard.

On one occasion he saw the mischievous god Loki, in the form of flea (or fly), steal the marvellous necklace, Brisingamen, from the sleeping goddess Freya and, after a struggle in which they both changed forms several times, Heimdall finally retrieved the necklace and restored it to Freya.

In the guise of Riger, he visited earth and became the progenitor of the human race, spending three days each with three couples, the impoverished Ai and Edda, the well-off Afi and Anima and the very wealthy Fadir and Modir. A son was born to each couple (Thrall, Karl and Jarl respectively) and these became the forerunners of humanity.

He blew his horn to warn the gods of the impending battle of Ragnarok but, by then, it was too late. In the fighting, he killed Loki but was himself killed with the other gods.

He had a horse called Gulltop and is depicted in shining white armour.

Heinzelmännchen   *German*

Friendly dwarfs who work by night to help people.

Heitaro   *Japanese*

A farmer who became so fond of a large willow tree that grew near his house that eventually the spirit of the tree appeared to him in the form of a maiden called Higo. He married her and they had a child, Chiyodo. When the emperor had the willow felled to provide timber for a new temple, Higo cried out in pain as the axes fell and then disappeared forever.

Hel [1]   *Norse*

A parti-coloured underworld goddess, daughter of the god Loki and the giantess Angerbode. She was thrown into Niflheim by Odin to rule the nine worlds of the dead. She occasionally roamed the earth on a three-legged horse, bringing famine and disease, and is envisaged as half black, half white.

In some accounts, she is the leader of the Wild Hunt.

Hel² *see* **Niflheim**

Hel-cake   *Norse*
Food used to pacify the dog Garm, the guard-dog of Hel.

Hel-gate   *Norse*
The entrance to Niflheim.

Hel-kappe *see* **Tarnkappe**

Hel Keplein   *Norse*
A mantle producing invisibility.

Hel-sko   *Norse*
'Hel-shoes', stout shoes fitted to the dead for their journey over the rough road, Helveg, leading to Niflheim.

Helaius   *British*
also Helyas
An ancestor of King Arthur. He is regarded as an earlier Grail King.

Helen   *Greek*
also Helen of Troy
Daughter of Zeus by Leda or Nemesis; wife of King Menelaus; sister of Castor, Clytemnestra and Polydeuces.

She was born from the coupling of Zeus, in the form of a swan, with Leda, or with Nemesis who took the form of a goose, to produce an egg from which Helen was hatched.

As a young girl, she was carried away by Peirithous and Theseus who drew lots for her. Theseus won and sent her to Aphidnus who cared for her until she was of marriageable age. She was rescued by Castor and Polydeuces when they invaded Attica while Theseus was imprisoned in Tartarus.

She later married Menelaus, king of Sparta, but was abducted by Paris, prince of Troy,

precipitating the Trojan War. After the death of Paris, whom she had married, in the fighting at Troy, she married his brother Deiphobus but when the city fell to the Greeks, she was reunited with Menelaus and returned with him to Greece. Menelaus was one of those who condemned Orestes to death for killing Aegisthus and Clytemnestra and Orestes would have killed Helen to punish her husband had not Zeus intervened and carried Helen off to Olympus as one of the immortals where she became, like Castor and Pollux, guardian of sailors, appearing as St Elmo's fire.

Another version says that, when Menelaus died, Helen went to Rhodes where she was hanged by Polyxo, who hated Helen because her husband had been killed in the Trojan War.

An alternative story says that, when Paris's ship was driven ashore in Egypt, the sea god Proteus took Helen to the safety of a cave and put a spirit facsimile in her place to be abducted by Paris.

In some accounts she is said to have married Achilles in Hades and borne a son, Euphorion.

Helith   *British*
A sun god. Some say that he is represented by the figure known as the Cerne Abbas Giant.

Helius   *Greek*
also Helios;
= *Egyptian* Ra; *Roman* Sol
A sun god and god of beauty; brother of Eos (goddess of the dawn) and Selene (the moon goddess).

He drove his sun-chariot across the sky from east to west every day, returning to his

eastern palace each night in a golden ferry-boat operating in Ocean. Foolishly he allowed his son Phaeton to drive his sun-chariot with disastrous results (*see* **Phaeton**).

During the war between the Giants and the gods, he was absent from the sky to prevent the growth of a herb that would have made the Giants immortal.

It was Helius who gave Hercules the golden bowl in which he crossed from Africa to Erythea en route to seize Geryon's cattle.

Helius owned seven herds of cattle and seven flocks of sheep, pastured on islands in the Mediterranean and tended by his daughters. These herds never grew larger or smaller until they were attacked by the crew of Odysseus's ship.

hell
Buddhist
The Buddhists envisage a hell with 8, 10 or as many as 136 realms, the lowest of which is called Avici, reserved for those who mock the Buddha.
Central American
The Mayan hell consisted of nine steps which required the soul to cross a river guarded by a yellow dog, pass between two mountain peaks, suffer the onslaught of bitterly cold winds, banners and arrows, and escape from a wild animal before reaching a land of peace.
Chinese
This home of departed souls, known as Ti Yü, Earth Prism, is said to be somewhere in Szechuan province and has ten departments, known as Shih T'ien-wen-yang, each of which is ruled by one of the Ten

Yama Kings, the judges of the dead.

Souls reaching this region are asked for money at the entrance and beaten if they fail to pay. After being weighed to ascertain whether they are weighed down by evil, they are segregated into good and evil in Bad Dog Village. They are allowed a glimpse of their future in a mirror and a nostalgic look at their past before crossing a bridge which, for sinners, is only about an inch wide. On the far side, they receive a drink which destroys all recollection of an earlier life and pass through the Wheel of the Law to emerge into a new incarnation.

Hindu

Hell has 28 realms. Of these, Asipatravana is for heretics, Avichimat is for liars, Kalasutra is for killers of Brahmins, Krimibhoja is for the selfish, Raurava is for sadists, Suchimukha is for misers, Sukramukha is for tyrants, Tamusra is for adulterers and thieves, Vaitarani for pillagers and those who have destroyed beehives, and Vajrakantaka is for those who married into another caste. Those who have caused religious controversy are thrown into the filthy river, also called Vaitarani.

Jain

Hell has a number of layers of which the lowest is known as Mahahima. In one realm, Valuka, the torture involves burial in hot sand.

Japanese

Yomitsu-kuni or Jigoku lies under the earth and comprises eight hells, each of which is divided into sixteen parts. In addition to these major hells there are others, each divided into four parts, known as

Kimpen-jigoku and others, the Koduko-jigoku, which appear randomly. Souls are judged by Emma-O and sent to one or more hells or, if deserving, reborn.

Helle   *Greek*
She and her brother Phrixus were rescued from being sacrificed and, carried away by Chrysomallon, a flying ram with a golden fleece, but she got giddy, fell into the sea and was drowned in what became known as the Hellespont. Some stories allege that she was saved from drowning by the sea god Poseidon and bore his son, Paeon or Edonus.

Helmet of Invisibility[1]   *Greek*
also Cap of Hades
A helmet owned by Hades. This helmet was worn by Perseus when he killed the gorgon, Medusa.

In some versions, this headgear was a cap made of dogskin which Perseus got from the Graiae.

Helmet of Invisibility[2]   *Norse*
also Helmet of Dread, Tarnhelm
A magic helmet made by the dwarf, Mime; part of the treasure surrendered under duress by Andvari, king of the dwarfs, to the god Loki to ransom himself, Odin and Hoenir who were held captive by Hreidmar, also a king of the dwarfs, for the killing of his son Otter by Loki. It was seized by Fafnir, another son of Hreidmar, who used it to turn himself into a dragon.

Helva   *Norse*
Daughter of the lord of Nesvek. Her father agreed that she could marry Esbern if he would build a church. Esbern agreed to give his eyes, heart and soul to the dwarf who undertook the work, unless he could discover the

dwarf's name before the church was completed. Helva's prayers to the gods enabled her to discover that the dwarf's name was Father Fine in time to save her lover.

Helveg   *Norse*
The rough road leading to Niflheim.

Helyas *see* **Helaius**

Hemera *see* **Eos**

Hen Wen   *Welsh*
A magical white sow. She distributed gifts of corn, bees, etc and was said to be the mother of the monstrous animal, Cath Palug, and other troublesome offspring. King Arthur chased her until she jumped into the sea.

Hephaestus   *Greek*
also Hephaistos;
= *Roman* Vulcan
God of fire, a smith-god; one of the Olympians; son of Zeus and Hera or of Hera alone; brother of Hebe and Ares.

He was a puny and ugly infant and may have been born lame, prompting his mother Hera to throw him off Mount Olympus. In another account, he was thrown down by Zeus when he had the audacity to criticise Zeus for his cruel treatment of Hera. Whether he was lame before or not, he was certainly lame thereafter as a result of breaking his legs in the fall. In the first version he fell into the sea and was rescued by the nymph Thetis and Eurynome (the goddess Artemis), in the second he fell on Lemnos. He walked on golden leg supports which, some say, were in the form of hand-maidens who supported him. He made a golden throne which trapped anyone who sat in it and sent it to Hera. After Hermes had failed,

Dionysus persuaded Hephaestus to return to Olympus and release her, whereupon he was restored to his parents' favour. Some say that he released Hera only when he was promised Aphrodite as his wife. He soon returned to his forge and made golden palaces for each of the gods and the thunderbolts that Zeus used as his personal weapons. His other works included Talos, the bronze guardian of Crete, a golden mastiff for Rhea to guard the infant Zeus, Harmonia's beautiful necklace, the bulls of Aetes, king of Colchis, and the golden basket used by the goddess Core when picking flowers. Some say that he also created Pandora.

In some accounts he married Aglaia, one of the Graces, or Charis; others say he married the goddess Aphrodite. In this latter story, he caught Aphrodite in bed with the war god Ares and trapped them both in a net of very fine metal mesh which he had made, allowing all the bystanders to see her shame. It was he who split open the head of Zeus with his axe to allow the birth, fully dressed in armour and already armed, of the goddess Athene.

His symbol is the hammer.

Hera *Greek*

also Great Goddess, Queen of Heaven;

= *Egyptian* Mut; *Hindu* Indrani; *Roman* Juno

The goddess of marriage and sky; one of the Olympians; daughter of Cronus and Rhea; twin sister and wife of Zeus; mother of Ares, Hebe, Hephaestus and Ilithyia.

She was one of the children swallowed by Cronus who was afraid that one of them might usurp his throne. Only Zeus escaped this fate and he later caused Cronus to regurgitate the children he had swallowed. She was raped by Zeus in the form of a cuckoo and later married him, receiving a tree that yielded golden apples as a wedding gift from Gaea.

She was so disgusted by the puny and ugly infant Hephaestus that she is said to have dropped him from Mount Olympus. She had the power to grant to others the gift of prophecy.

She found the infant Hercules abandoned by Alcmene and, not realising that this was another son of her errant husband Zeus, suckled it at her breast, so making him immortal. She later did all she could to harass Hercules.

She once led a revolt against the imperious Zeus and was severely punished for her treachery. She was suspended by her wrists with heavy weights attached to her ankles. Other accounts say that this resulted from her persecution of Hercules.

When Semele was having an affair with Zeus, Hera came in the form of Semele's old nurse, Beroe, and persuaded her mistress to demand that her lover should prove that he really was who he said he was. When Zeus complied, the divine radiance killed Semele. The son of this union was Dionysus and Hera ordered the Titans to destoy him. They tore him to pieces and boiled him but Rhea collected all the bits, reassembled them and restored Dionysus to life.

When Paris awarded the golden apple to Aphrodite at the wedding of Peleus and Thetis, Hera and Athene, the losing contestants, became his enemies and supported the Greeks against the Trojans during the Trojan War.

Once, when she left Zeus, he made a wooden image, dressed it in a bridal gown and displayed it as his new wife. She then came back, knocked over the statue and was reconciled with her husband.

Some say that she produced the monster, Typhon, in jealousy when Zeus produced the goddess Athena unaided.

Her animal was the cow, her bird the peacock and her symbol the cornucopia.

Heracles *Greek*

also Herakles;

= *Canaanite* Melkarth; *Roman* Hercules

When Zeus decided that there was a need for a great champion to safeguard both the gods and mortals, he slept with Alcmene during the absence of her husband Amphitryon, king of Tiryns, in wars, deceiving her into thinking he was her husband and causing the motions of the universe to slow so that one night lasted for three. The result of this union was Heracles, known in his early years as Alcides.

Alcmene, fearing the wrath of the jealous Hera, abandoned Heracles in a field where he was found by Hera who, not knowing who the infant was, suckled him, so making him immortal. When she later discovered that the boy – originally known as Alcaeus or Palaemon – was the son of her own husband she became obsessed with making his life difficult. As a start, she sent two fiery-eyed serpents to kill him but Heracles, though a mere lad at the time, strangled them both, one in each hand.

As a youth, he killed Linus who was teaching him to play the lyre by striking him with the instrument in a fit of anger. He was acquitted at his trial, quoting the law that gave him the right of self-defence against Linus who had been beating him. He also killed the outlaw Saurus and another called Termerus, the latter in a head-butting contest just as Termerus had killed many a traveller.

At eighteen, he slept with each of the fifty daughters of King Thespius, producing fifty-one sons, and went on to kill the Cithaeronian lion which had been causing havoc. He wore the skin as armour with the jaws forming a helmet. (Other accounts say that this was the skin of the Nemean Lion which he killed as the first of his twelve Labours and that the Cithaeronian Lion was killed by Alcathous.)

Reputedly the strongest man who ever strode the earth, he fought on the side of the gods when the Giants rebelled and killed Ephialtes, Porphyrion and their leader Alcyoneus.

When a Theban charioteer accidentally killed King Clymenus, king of the Minyans, his son Erginus avenged his death by exacting a tribute of a hundred cattle for twenty years. Heracles became involved when he cut the noses off the men sent to collect the cattle and, when Erginus attacked Thebes, he led the Theban youth and defeated the Minyan army, killing Erginus. As reward he was given Megara, the eldest daughter of King Creon of

Thebes in marriage and they had several sons – the number varies according to who is telling the story – who became known as the Alcaides.

Hera eventually drove Heracles mad and he tried to kill his own nephew Iolaus. Iolaus escaped but Heracles did kill six of his own sons and two of the sons of his brother Iphicles or, in an alternative version, Megara and two or three of his own sons. He was purified by King Thespius and, when he consulted the Delphic Oracle, he was told to serve King Eurystheus for twelve years and do whatever the king demanded of him. Hermes gave him a sword, Apollo donated a bow and arrows, Hephaestus a breast-plate, Athena a robe, Poseidon a team of horses and his father, Zeus, gave him a shield. So equipped, Heracles set out to perform the twelve Labours, taking with him young Iolaus as charioteer.

After his fourth Labour, he joined the Argonauts on their expedition to recover the Golden Fleece but was left behind at Mysia when he went off to look for his armour-bearer, Hylas, who had been carried off by water-nymphs.

Giving up his fruitless search, he resumed his Labours, successfully completing all twelve. He later killed Calais and Zetes who had advised Jason to sail on, leaving Heracles stranded in Mysia.

Afterwards, he gave his wife Megara to Iolaus and tried for the hand of Iole by beating her father Eurytus in an archery contest. When Eurytus reneged on his offer of Iole's hand to the

victor and an argument arose about some stolen cattle, Heracles killed Iphitus, son of Eurytus, by throwing him from a tower. As punishment, he was sold as a slave to Omphale, queen of Lydia, for one year but this proved pleasant punishment when Omphale fell in love with him and bore him three children.

To avenge himself on Augeas who had failed to hand over the promised reward of a tenth of all the herds when Heracles cleansed his stables and land, Heracles attacked Elis and later killed Eurytus and Cteatus, the twins who had acted as general for Augeas and were joined at the waist. He also sacked Pylus because the king, Neleus, had fought for Augeas, and killed his sons including Periclymenus who, given the power by Poseidon of assuming any shape he wished, attacked Heracles in the form of an eagle until killed with an arrow. Heracles gave the city to Nestor, son of Neleus.

Challenged to a chariot-duel by Cycnus, a son of Ares, he won the contest, killing Cycnus and wounding Ares who was supporting his son in the duel.

Heracles fought and defeated the many-formed river god Achelous for the hand of Deianeira and married her. He accidentally killed Eunomus when the boy spilled some wine and exiled himself and family to Trachis. A Centaur named Nessus offered to carry Deianeira and the children over the River Evenus, while Heracles swam across but ran off with Deianeira and tried to rape her. Heracles shot him from across the river. At the behest of Nessus, Deianeira collected his spilt semen and blood and mixed it with olive oil in a sealed jar, believing his story that it would act as a love-potion if she spread it on her husband's shirt. In another version, Nessus gave her his own robe, stained with his blood, which had the same effect. Deianeira sent, at Heracles' request, a new shirt for a ceremony and she, fearing that she would be abandoned in favour of another, anointed the shirt with what she believed to be the love-potion. In fact, the mixture contained the poison of the Hydra which had entered the blood-stream of Nessus from an arrow fired by Heracles and Heracles died in agony, finally immolating himself on a pyre on Mount Oeta. The pyre was lit by Philoctetes, to whom Heracles bequeathed his bow and arrows, or by his father, Poeas. Zeus conveyed the immortal part of his son to Olympus where he became one of the gods. Finally reconciled with Hera, he married her daughter Hebe and fathered two more children, Alexiares and Anicetus.

In the Roman version, where Heracles is Hercules, he is said to have married Lavinia and fathered Latinus and Pallas. As father of Celtus by Celtina, he originated the Celts.

(*See also* **Labours of Hercules**.)

Hercules   *Greek*
The Roman name for Heracles. Better known generally than the Greek form 'Heracles', this is the name used in most of the entries in this book in which this hero appears, regardless of whether it concerns a Roman or a Greek myth.

Hermaphroditus   *Greek*
Son of Hermes and Aphrodite.
When he spurned the advances of the nymph Salmakis she prayed that they might be united. When she embraced him as they bathed in a spring, their bodies merged into one. Subsequently, the spring changed all men who bathed in it into hermaphrodites.

Hermes   *Greek*
= *Egyptian* Anubis, Thoth; *Etruscan* Turms; *Roman* Mercury
God of art, commerce, eloquence, fertility, games, herdsmen, luck, markets, roads, thieves, travellers, wisdom; herald and messenger of the gods; one of the Olympians; son of Zeus by the nymph Maia.

Hera, as usual, was jealous of her husband's affair with Maia so Hermes disguised himself as the infant Ares and deceived Hera into suckling him, after which she felt obliged to regard him as her own son.

As an infant he stole some of Apollo's cattle and gave him the lyre, which he had invented when less than one day old, to earn his forgiveness. The peasant Bottus had told Apollo who had taken the cattle and Hermes turned him to stone.

When he was appointed official herald to the gods, Zeus gave him his winged sandals, his hat and his staff. Others say that Apollo gave him the staff when Hermes gave the god the lyre and they became friends.

He was also appointed by Hades to summon the dead and conduct their souls to Tartarus, as Psychopompus.

He saved the infant Dionysus when his mother was killed by

Zeus and planted him in his father's thigh until full term.

He is credited with the invention of fire, the lyre from the shell of a tortoise, the shepherd's pipe, astronomy, musical scales, measures, etc.

He killed the Giant Hippolytus during the battle between the Giants and the gods and restored to Zeus the sinews cut out by the monster Typhon.

He rescued Io (in the form of a cow) from imprisonment under the eyes of Argus (a giant with 100 eyes), killing Argus and cutting off his head. Hera, who had ordered the detention of Io, placed the 100 eyes of Argus in the peacock's tail.

He gave the hero Perseus the sickle with which he beheaded Medusa.

He is depicted as wearing the winged hat and sandals and carrying his staff, the caduceus, with wings and entwined serpents.

Hermes Trismegistus   *Greek*
A Greek derivation from the Egyptian god, Thoth.

Hermit King *see* **Pelles**

Hermod   *Norse*
The messenger of the gods; son of Odin and Frigga; brother of Balder, Hoder and Thor.

Swiftest of the gods, he received fallen heroes in Valhalla.

When Hoder inadvertently killed his twin brother Balder with a mistletoe branch, Hermod rode down to Niflheim on Sleipnir, Odin's eight-legged horse, to plead that his brother be restored to life. Hel, goddess of the underworld, agreed provided that the whole world wept for Balder. When just one giantess, Thok (thought to be

Loki in disguise), refused to shed a tear, Hela kept her own.

Herne   *British*

also Hern the Hunter;

= *Welsh* Arawn

A wind god and god of the underworld. He is depicted as a giant with the antlers of a stag. Some say that he still lives in Windsor Great Park where he roams through the woods, disappearing at midnight. In some versions he is leader of the Wild Hunt.

hero[1]   *Greek*

A demi-god, offspring of a god and a mortal.

Hero[2]   *Greek*

A priestess of Aphrodite. She was loved by Leander but they were forbidden to marry and were separated by the waters of the Hellespont. Every night she put a light in the window of her tower to guide Leander as he swam over to see her but one night a storm blew the light out and he was drowned. Hero killed herself in grief by jumping from the tower into the sea.

Herod's Hunt *see* **Wild Hunt**

Hershef   *Egyptian*

A fertility god; an aspect of the god Horus. He is said to have emerged from the primordial waters and is depicted as a ram or as a human with a ram's head. His feet rested on earth but his head was in the sky where his right eye was the sun and his left eye was the moon. He is sometimes depicted with four heads.

Herus   *Central American*

An Apache hero. He is said to have appeared among the Chiricahua Apache and told them to keep the book he gave them. When he died, the tribe followed their usual practice of burning all the dead man's possessions, including the book, with the result that they suffered many disasters.

Hesione   *Greek*

King Laomedon of Troy chained his daughter Hesione to a rock in the sea as a sacrifice to appease a sea-monster sent by the sea god Poseidon because Laomedon had refused to pay Apollo and Poseidon for building the walls of Troy. Hercules found her when he was returning from his ninth Labour, and undertook to rescue her in exchange for Laomedon's horses. He was swallowed by the monster but killed it by attacking its internal organs. Her father reneged on the promise of the horses so Hercules killed him and took Hesione as a captive to Athens where she married Telamon. She ransomed her brother, Podarces, for the price of her veil and Hercules made him king of Troy as Priam.

In other stories, Telamon helped Hercules in his later attack on Troy and, for his help, was awarded Hesione, as a prize and fathered Teucer on her.

Hespera *see* **Eos**

Hesperides   *Greek*

also Atlantides

Nymphs, daughters of the giant Atlas. In some accounts, there were three (Aegle, Erythia and Hespera), in others, four or seven, the other suggested names being Arethusa, Hespereia, Hesperusa and Hestia. They, with the dragon Ladon, were the guardians of the golden apples from Hera's tree, who helped Hercules in his quest for some of these apples on his eleventh Labour.

In some accounts the name is used for the Pleiades.

Hestia   *Greek*

= *Roman* Vesta

Goddess of the community, family, fire, hearth, house; one of the Olympians; daughter of Cronus and Rhea. A virgin-goddess whose symbol is a torch.

Hi-asa   *East Indies*

A primeval being in the Admralty Islands. When she cut her finger, she collected the blood in a shell. Two eggs formed from the blood and the first man and woman emerged from the eggs.

Hiawatha   *North American*

A 16th-century sage of the Iroquois; son of Mudjekeewis and Wenonah; husband of Minnehaha. He was reared by his grandmother, Nokomis.

His wife and daughter were killed by the magician Atotarho but the two men later became reconciled and founded the Confederacy of the Five Tribes.

He was regarded as a culture-hero who taught the tribes the arts of agriculture and medicine, killed the corn-spirit Mon-da-moin to give mankind maize, overcame the great sturgeon Mishe-Nahma and killed the evil magician Megissogwon. He was helped by a pair of mittens which enabled him to split rocks when he wore them and a pair of moccasins in which he could cover a mile at each step.

When his work was done, he sailed off to Ponemah in the west in his magic canoe.

In another version, the god Tarenyawagon took pity on the suffering tribes and came to earth as a man, Hiawatha. He led the tribes to a cave where they recovered their strength and then led them to their own homelands, separating them into the five tribes, the Cayuga, Mohawks, Oneida, Onondaga and Seneca, each with its own language and character. When they were attacked by wild tribes from the north the five appealed to Hiawatha for help. He sacrificed his daughter Minnehaha to the Great Spirit and she was taken up to heaven on the back of a great eagle. Hiawatha united the tribes into the Five Nations who repelled the invaders and brought peace to the land. Hiawatha himself entered his white canoe which then rose into the sky and disappeared.

Hidesato   *Japanese*
A warrior who undertook to kill the huge centipede that had taken all the children and grandchildren of the Dragon King of Lake Biwa. The first two arrows he shot when the monster next appeared had no effect but the third, moistened with saliva, killed it. As reward, the Dragon King gave Hidesato a never-empty bag of rice, an endless roll of silk, a cauldron that cooked without fire and two bells. He was thereafter known as My Lord Bag of Rice.

Hiisi   *Baltic*
A Finnish giant: a tree god.
    He owned an elk, the fastest creature on earth. He also owned a fierce cat which terrorised criminals into confessing their misdeeds.
    Some accounts equate him with the Devil. He is envisaged as a very ugly man with no eyelids.

hill folk   *Norse*
A race of people somewhere between elves and humans.

Hill of Aisneach   *Irish*
A hill said to be the centre of

Ireland. This was the site of one of the high-king Tuathal's four palaces and of the Giants' Ring from which the sorcerer Merlin transported the stones to build Stonehenge.

Hill of Bat   *Egyptian*
The hill which supports the heaven, home of the crocodile-god Sebek.

Himavan   *Tibetan*
A sacred mountain in Tibet. It is here that Zampu, the tree of life, grows. It is also the place where the ark landed after the Flood.

Hin-Han   *North American*
An owl. The Sioux say that this bird guards the entrance to the Milky Way, the road that leads to the home of the spirits.

Hina   *Pacific Islands*
= *Hawaiian* Mahina; *Hervey Islands* Ina; *Maori* Marama; *Samoan* (Ma) Sina
A moon goddess of Tahiti. The Tahitians say that the dark markings on the moon are the shadows of the branches of the original banyan tree from which Hina stripped bark to make clothes for the gods. She is therefore the tutelary deity of cloth-beaters. It was beating tapa that took her to the moon in the first place. The creator-god Ta'aroa got fed up of the noise and told her to stop. When she refused, the goddess Pani grabbed the mallet and struck her on the head, whereupon she flew off to the moon.
    In another story, she accidentally broke a branch from this tree and it fell to earth, took root and so the banyan was introduced to the islands.

Hinun   *North American*
also Thunderbird
A thunder god of the Iroquois.

When the serpent of the Great Lakes swallowed his helper, Gunnodoyak, Hinun killed the snake with one of his flaming arrows shot from the sky, restored the boy to life and took him back to heaven.
    He also saved his people from the Stone Giants of the west by shattering them with his divine power.
    Each year, he sent the three Thunderers to earth to destroy evil.
    He is accompanied by the eagles Keneu and Oshadagea.

hippalectryon   *Greek*
A monster in the form of a horse with the feet and tail of a cockerel.

hippocampus   *Greek*
plural hippocampi
A sea-monster like a horse with the tail of a fish or dolphin, the horse of the sea god Poseidon.

Hippocrene   *Greek*
A spring which appeared on Mount Helicon from a hoof-print of Pegasus, the winged horse of the god Apollo, and which became sacred to Apollo and the Muses.

hippogriff   *European*
also hippogryph
A monster in the form of a winged horse with the head of an eagle. This animal, fathered by a griffin on a mare, features in several stories of Charlemagne's paladins.

Hippolyta   *Greek*
A queen of the Amazons; daughter of the war god Ares.
    She was given a love-girdle by Ares which Hercules stole as his ninth Labour, killing her in the fight that ensued when her followers thought that he was adbducting her. Others say that she fell in love with him and gave

him the girdle, while another story says that Hercules captured Melanippe, one of her generals, and won the girdle as ransom for her release.

In some versions she was not killed in this way but was later captured by Theseus who fathered Hippolytus on her and, some say, married her. In this version she was killed in a battle when the Amazons invaded in an attempt to recapture her.

Another story says that she was killed when she interrupted the wedding of Theseus and Phaedra, and yet another that she was killed by accident by Penthesilea, who is described as her sister.

Hippomenes   *Greek*
Husband of Atalanta. Hippomenes was given three golden apples by Aphrodite which he dropped in the path of Atalanta during a foot-race between them. When she paused to pick up the apples, he won the race and, with it, her hand in marriage.

Both he and Atalanta were changed into lions by Zeus when they defiled the god's precinct, or by Aphrodite for failing to render thanks for her help.

hircocervus   *European*
A monster, part goat, part stag.

Hiru-ko   *Japanese*
also Leech Child
A Shinto god of fortune, the deformed son of the divinities Izanagi and Izanami.

He was so ugly that his parents abandoned him, putting him on a boat which was then cast upon the sea.

Others say that the child was born as a jellyfish or a leech (hence the name Leech Child) and was set adrift in a boat. The boat

came ashore at Ebisu Shore and the infant grew up bearing the name Ebisu and became the god of fishermen.

Historia Regum Britanniae *British*
The *History of the Kings of Britain*, a 12-volume work written in Latin by Geoffrey of Monmouth. This 12th-century work tells the stories of King Arthur's exploits and of the race of giants who were the early inhabitants of Britain. The last two giants, Gog and Magog, were said to have been captured by Brutus, leader of Trojan invaders.

Hkun Hsang Long   *Burmese*
A creator-spirit. He created the first couple, Ta-hsek-khi and Ya-hsek-khi who were born in the shape of tadpoles.

Hlakanyana   *African*
In Zulu lore, a trickster dwarf. Immediately he was born he stood up, cut his own umbilical cord and carved himself a choice portion of a recently-slaughtered beast, following it with the rest of the dead animal. Thereafter he seemed to eat anything and everything.

Hlebard   *Norse*
One of the dwarfs. A smith, he made a magic wand for the god Odin and shaped the mistletoe into the magic arrow with which Hoder, prompted by the evil god Loki, killed Balder.

Ho Hsien-ku   *Chinese*
= *Japanese* Kasenko
Goddess of housewives; one of the Eight Immortals.

She was the daughter of a 7th-century shopkeeper Ho T'ai, and, having eaten a magic peach, became a fairy who, living on moonbeams and powdered mother-of-pearl, was immortal. She was born with just six hairs

on her head and no more ever grew.

When she was attacked by a demon, her fellow Immortal Lü Tung-pin killed the demon with his magic sword.

Her emblem is the lotus flower and she is sometimes depicted with a fly-whisk or drinking wine.

ho-o   *Japanese*
= *Chinese* feng huang
The Japanese version of the phoenix.

hob   *British*
A brownie: a frightful apparition.

hobgoblin   *British*
A mischievous sprite such as a brownie.

hobyah   *Scottish*
A cannibal goblin.

Hochigan   *African*
A spirit in the lore of the Bushmen. The Bushmen say that, originally, all animals could speak but Hochigan went away forever taking their power of speech with him.

Hodag   *North American*
A water-monster of Quebec. This beast is said to have telescopic legs and kills its victims by shooting clay pellets from its long snout.

Hoder   *Norse*
The blind god of darkness; son of Odin and Frigga; twin brother of Balder; brother of Hermod and Thor.

Frigga had extracted a promise from all things that they would cause no harm to Balder but she overlooked the mistletoe. The gods made a game of throwing things at Balder and none of them could harm him until Loki, the troublemaker, persuaded the blind Hoder to throw a branch of mistletoe. This branch, guided by

Loki, killed Balder immediately.

In another story, Hoder and Balder vied for the hand of Nanna. When she married Hoder, he killed Balder with his sword, Mistillteinn 'mistletoe'.

In some versions, Hoder was killed by Vali, son of Odin and Rinda, who, having grown to manhood in one day, arrived with his bow and arrows and shot Hoder to avenge Balder, thus fulfilling a prophecy.

Some say that Hoder was sacrificed for killing Balder, others that both survived Ragnarok.

Hoenir *Norse*

Brother of Loki, Odin and others. He endowed newly-created mankind with intelligence and was one of the Aesir (gods) who went to live among the Vanir (other gods) as a hostage after the two groups made peace. Some say that he was one of the few to survive Ragnarok.

hoga *Pacific Islands*

Gnomes or dwarfs.

Hoh *Central American*

A crow; in Mayan lore, one of the birds which brought the maize from which the gods created human beings.

Hohhokw *North American*

A monster in the form of huge bird with a long beak, in the lore of the tribes of the north-west.

Hoita *North American*

A Mandan eagle-spirit. When Lone Man stole his white buckskin coat, Hoita collected all the animals and enclosed them in the Dog Den. Lone Man made an even more powerful medicine-drum than the one owned by Hoita, who was then forced to release the animals.

Holy Boy *North American*

A spirit of the Apache. He, with Red

Boy, placed the sun and the moon in their courses.

Holy Grail *British*

also Grail, Sangraal, Sangreal, Sangrail

A holy vessel. This prized object was the cup or plate which Christ was said to have used at the Last Supper and in which Joseph of Arimathea was said to have caught the blood of Christ at the Crucifixion. It was made from an emerald which fell from Lucifer's crown when he was cast out of heaven.

It was later brought by Joseph and Evelake to Britain where it was guarded by the 'undead' Fisher King. It was said that if the Grail ever fell into the hands of a sinner, the peace of the world would come to an end and the Grail would disappear.

It appeared at the banquet at Camelot when Galahad took his seat as a knight of the Round Table, inspiring the knights to set out in their search for it, the Grail-quest. Only Galahad was deemed worthy of finding the Grail, which was taken back to the Holy Land by Galahad, Percival and Bors. When Galahad died, the Grail and the Holy Lance disappeared forever.

In some versions, it was Percival who finally achieved the Grail, in others it was Gawain.

In the Wagnerian version, the Grail was sought by Titurel and his band of knights in another land. They built a temple on Mount Salvat and angels brought the Grail from heaven. Titurel spent the rest of his life guarding the Grail, day and night, and, when he died, the duty was carried on by his son, Amfortas.

In some accounts, the Grail was a stone on which had been engraved the names of the knights guarding it.

Holy Lance *British*

also Grail Lance

The weapon with which the Roman centurion Longinus pierced Christ's side at the crucifixion. This lance or spear was brought to Britain with the Holy Grail by Joseph of Arimathea and Evelake. It was used, in some accounts, by Balin to kill or to wound Pelham. In other accounts, Galahad found the lance and used it to cure Pelles, guardian of the Grail, who had been made lame for his sins. It was taken back to the Holy Land by Galahad, Percival and Bors at the end of the Grail Quest and, at the death of Galahad, the Lance and the Grail disappeared forever.

In the Wagnerian version of the story, this weapon was kept in the Temple of the Grail and Amfortas, the guardian of the Grail, took it with him when he tried to destroy the evil magician, Klingsor. Klingsor took the spear from Amfortas and struck him in the side, thereby causing a wound that healed only when Parsifal, at the end of the Grail Quest, regained the spear and laid it on the wound.

It some accounts, it was used by Charlemagne in his battles with the Saracens.

Homshuk *Central American*

An Olmec deity, maize personified. He was born from an egg and reared by an old couple who, alarmed when he killed all those who mocked him, tried to kill him but failed. He was later taken prisoner by Hurakan but survived after being locked in three rooms, one filled with snakes, another with tigers and a third with flying arrows. Hurakan finally realised that Homshuk was a deity and promised thereafter to tend him – in other words, to cultivate the maize.

Hong Do-Ryong *Korean*

A man who became a tiger. He prayed for help when his mother fell ill and a spirit advised him that a medicine made from 100 dogs would save her. Further prayer gave him the power to turn himself into a tiger and he was then easily able to catch 99 dogs. On the last night, his wife saw him change into a tiger and leave the house to catch the final dog. Foolishly, she burnt the paper in which the tiger spell was written and Hong was unable to resume his human form. In his anger, he killed his wife, who happened to be wearing a blue skirt at the time. Thereafter, the tiger killed every woman he met who was similarly dressed.

Honoured Women *see*
   Cihuateteo

Horae *Greek*

also Horai, Hours

The maidens, daughters of Zeus, who acted as the gatekeepers of Olympus and presided over the changes of the seasons.

In some accounts, there were just two – Carpo and Thallo – or three with Auxo; others list Dike, Eirene and Eunomia. Some say there were four, the daughters of the sun god Helius by his sister Selene, goddess of the moon, while yet others say that Hersilia, wife of Romulus, the founder of Rome, became one of their number when she was taken up to heaven. Some accounts have twelve.

Horatii *Roman*

Three champions of Rome. These three brothers fought three of the Curiatii to settle the war between Rome and the nearby city of Alba Longa. Two were killed and the other, Publius Horatius, killed their sister Horatia who was bewailing the loss of one of the Curiatii to whom she was betrothed.

Horatius *Roman*

A hero, Horatius Cocles, who, with two friends, Titus Herminius and Spurius Lartius, held the bridge leading to Rome against the might of the invading Etruscans under Lars Porsena.

Horn of Fidelity *British*

A horn sent by the sorceress Morgan le Fay to King Arthur. This vessel detected ladies who had been unfaithful to their husbands when they found that they could not drink from it.

Horn of Plenty *see* **cornucopia**

Horns Standing Up *North American*

A Cheyenne medicine-man. When his tribe was starving as a result of drought, Horns Standing Up commanded the wife of the chief to accompany him and they set off to seek help. After many days they came to the mountains and entered a cave where, for four days, the creator-god Maheo and Great Roaring Thunder gave them instructions in the art of the medicine dance. When the couple returned to their tribe, the men built a medicine lodge and danced round it as Horns Standing Up had instructed them. Soon the rains came and the buffalo returned.

horse

The horse features in many myths.

(1) In Arabian myth, it was said that a race of green horses, Farasi Bahari, lived in the Indian Ocean and horses bred from these stallions and normal mares could run forever because they had no lungs and therefore were never short of breath.

(2) The Babylonian mare, Silili, was said to be the progenitress of all the horses in the world.

(3) In some British stories, the spirit of a horse, haunting boggy areas, is called a gytrash.

(4) In Egypt, a sea-living horse, Sabgarifiya, was the equivalent of the Arabian Farasi Bahari.

(5) In Malaya, the Farasul Bahri were the equivalent of the Arabian Farasi Bahari.

(6) In Thailand, the mythical king Sison had a flying horse, Tipaka, which could transport its rider instantaneously to anywhere in the world.

(7) Buddhist lore says that the Buddha's horse was called Kantaka, that of Avalokiteshvara, the god of mercy, was Balaha.

(8) In Hindu lore, the horse was the seventh thing to emerge from the Churning of the Ocean.

The sun god Surya used the horse Rohita to pull his chariot.

(9) In Greek myths, one famous horse, Pegasus, sprang from the blood of the Gorgon, Medusa, slain by Perseus, and was later used by Bellerophon when he attacked and killed the monster called the Chimaera. Achilles' horses were named Balios and Xanthos. The horse of Alexander the Great was Bucephalus.

(10) In Norse myths, Odin's horse was the eight-legged Sleipnir.

(11) King Arthur had steeds named Dun Stallion, Lamri, Passelande, and Spumador.

(12) In Carolingian stories

Charlemagne's horse was called Blanchard, Oliver's horse was Ferrant d'Espagne, and the horses of Roland/Orlando were named Brigliadoro and Veillantif/ Vegliantino.

(13) In Serbian stories the hero Momtchilo had a flying horse called Yaboutchilo.

(14) Other European stories include the Brazen Horse of Cambuscan which had a pin in one ear which enabled it to accept instructions from the rider as to where he wished to go; Clavileno, a wooden horse, controlled by a peg protruding from its head, which similarly could take the rider wherever he wished to go; and Rosinante, the broken-down nag ridden by Don Quixote.

The goddess Epona, like her Welsh counterpart Rhiannon, is said to have ridden the White Mare.

Horus　　　　　　　　　　*Egyptian*

A falcon-headed sun god; in some accounts he is the son of Osiris and Isis, conceived when they were still in the mother-goddess Nut's womb, in others he is the son of Osiris and Nut.

He is the opponent of Set in the struggle for supremacy in the kingdom of Egypt. He lost an eye in the fight but it was restored by Thoth. In some versions, the eye was later given to Osiris but other accounts say that Set gouged out both the eyes of Horus and buried them. Lotus-blossom grew from the burial site but Horus had his sight restored by the gods. The case between Horus and Set was arbitrated by the gods and when the judgement was in favour of Horus he took over the whole of

the kingdom. The pharaoh of the United Kingdom was Horus in his lifetime.

In another version, the fight was over supremacy of the light and Thoth settled the argument by awarding the day to Horus and the night to Set.

Some say that Horus steered Ra's barque Manjet through the heavens; others equate him with Ra.

It was said that all human races, except the Negroes, were born from the eyes of Horus.

He was associated with the planets Jupiter, Mars and Saturn.

Hotei　　　　　　　　　　*Japanese*

= *Chinese* Mi-lo-fo

A god of laughter; one of the seven Shinto deities of fortune, the Shichi Fukujin.

Hotei is said to be based on a cheerful Buddhist monk, Pu Tai Ho-shang. He is depicted as a fat man with a naked belly and carrying a never-empty sack of precious things or riding in a decrepit carriage pulled by children. In this latter role, he is known as the Wagon Priest and is equated with the Laughing Buddha, Maitreya, whom he resembles and who also carries a sack.

hotot　　　　　　　　　　*Armenian*

Evil spirits living in rivers and marshes who lure children to their death.

Hototogisu　　　　　　　*Japanese*

A bird from the land of the dead. The call of this bird, heard in May, tells the peasants that the time has arrived for the planting of the rice. Some define this bird as the cuckoo which acts as a guide to the land of the dead.

hou　　　　　　　　　　　*Chinese*

A mythical animal, a form of lion, ridden by the goddess Kuan Yin.

hound marine　　　　　　*European*

A sea monster, part dog, part fish.

Hounds of Hell　　　　　　*Welsh*

A pack of white dogs with red ears, the hounds of Arawn, coming from the underworld, chasing a stag.

Hours[1]　　　　　　　　　*Egyptian*

= *Greek* Horae

Twelve daughters of Ra who control the individual's life-span.

Hours[2] *see* **Horae**

Housain　　　　　　　　　*Arabian*

The owner of the magic carpet featured in the *Arabian Nights' Entertainments*.

House of Bats　　*Central American*

Part of the Mayan underworld, Xibalba. Hunapu, god of the hunt, and his brother Ixbalanqué spent a night here and Hunapu's head was cut off by Camazotz, the bat-god. (On this and the following entries, *see* **Hunapu**.)

House of Cold　　*Central American*

Part of the Mayan underworld, Xibalba. Hunapu and Ixbalanqué spent a night here and managed to survive.

House of Gloom　　*Central American*

Part of the Mayan underworld, Xibalba. The culture-heroes Hunhunapu and Vucub Hanapu spent a night here when they visited Xibalba and were killed.

Hunapu and Ixbalanque, who came to avenge their deaths, also spent a night here. They were given torches and were told that they would be killed if the torches went out. They survived by painting red flames to replace the real ones.

House of Lances　　*Central American*

Part of the Mayan underworld, Xibalba. Hunapu and Ixbalanqué spent a night here and were required to produce four vases of flowers if they were to be allowed to survive. They did this with the help of ants after subduing the demons in the room.

House of Tigers   *Central American*
Part of the Mayan underworld, Xibalba. Hunapu and Ixbalanqué spent a night here and managed to survive by throwing bones to the fierce animals that appeared.

Hsi Wang Mu   *Chinese*
A Taoist goddess of medicine and immortaility She was the embodiment of the female yin principle and combined with her husband Tung Wang Kung to create the world and all that is in it.

Originally a terrible tiger/leopard woman or plague goddess, she was later regarded as a benevolent goddess, guarding the tree (or herb) of immortality. She was the ruler of the Western Paradise where she lived in a golden palace, hundreds of miles round, built of gold and precious stones, alongside the Lake of Jewels. In the garden of the palace stood the peach tree Shen T'ao, that flowered once every 3000 years. The fruit took a further 3000 years to ripen, an event which coincided with her birthday, but made immortal those who ate it.

Her personal transport was a crane and in one form this goddess was the wife of Yü Ti, the supreme ruler of heaven.

Hu   *Chinese*
also Emperor of the Northern Seas
He is manifest in the lightning which pierced Chaos to form the universe.

Hu Gardarn   *Welsh*
An oak god or sun god, regarded as the ancestor of the Cymry (Welsh) who brought them from Ceylon.

He raised the monster Addanc from a lake, using his team of oxen, causing a flood.

hu-hsien   *Chinese*
The fox as a shape-changer; a fox fairy or fox spirit. It is said that, in the form of young men or women, they can debilitate their lovers to such an extent that they die.

They are reported to be fond of wine but resume their shape as foxes if they drink too much or if they are frightened in some way.

Hua-hu Tiao   *Chinese*
A white rat. This animal was carried in a bag by Mo-li Shou, one of the Four Diamond Kings. When released, it became a winged elephant that ate human beings. In some accounts it is referred to as a monster, the Striped Marten.

Huang Ti   *Chinese*
also Ch'in-shih Huang Ti, Yellow Emperor
A sky god, ruler of the moving heavens; one of the Five Emperors; patron of doctors and tailors.

He was conceived miraculously and his gestation lasted for twenty-four months.

He is credited with the invention of armour, bamboo musical instruments, bricks, a form of script, ships and the potter's wheel.

He became a Taoist immortal and the patron saint of Taoism and runs the Ministry of Healing with Fu-hsi and Shen Nung.

He was said to have four faces and owned a chariot driven by a bird with a human face and drawn by an elephant and six dragons.

Hubur   *Mesopotamian*
= *Greek* Styx

A river of death in the underworld.

Hueytonantzin   *Central American*
An Aztec primeval goddess. Her children killed her as a sacrifice to the sun every day; every night she was reborn.

Hugon   *European*
A French ogre which travels about at night frightening children and causing injury.

Hui-yüan   *Chinese*
A 5th-century Taoist; one of the Eighteen Lohan, in some accounts. He was the founder of the Pure Land sect, a Buddhist order dedicated to Amitabha.

Huitzilopochtli   *Central American*
also Quetzalcoatl
An Aztec sun god and god of war, a humming-bird magician. In some accounts he is an aspect of Tezcatlipoca as god of war.

Born to Coatlicue, already mother of 400 children, he was delivered fully-formed and fully-armed, having been warned by his brother Quauitlicac while still in the womb that these children were planning to kill Coatlicue to prevent his birth. Some say that he had two mothers – Coatlicue and Teteionan.

In some versions, he decapitated his sister Coyolxauhqui; in others she was killed in battle between Huitzilopochtli and the other children. In either event, he threw her head into the heavens where it became the moon.

Some accounts say he, not Nanautzin, rules the Fifth Sun.

He is said to be the god Xochipilli who developed into the war god when he was given human blood to drink.

He was depicted with his limbs painted with bars of blue and wearing a cap of humming-bird feathers. His shield was made of reeds and down from an eagle and his spear was tipped with down rather than flint.

Huitziton   *Central American*
An Aztec hero. He knew the language of the birds and they advised him to lead his people into Mexico. He was a dragon-slayer and probably an aspect of Huitzilopochtli.

Huichaana   *Central American*
A creator deity of the Zapotecs. This deity, of indeterminate sex, was said to have created fishes and human beings after Cozaana created the world and all the animals.

Huldrafolk   *Norse*
A name for the dwarfs or elves. In some accounts, their backs are hollow, in others they have a long tail. They sometimes marry mortals. (*See also* **Uldra**.)

Humanmaker   *North American*
The creator-god of the Pima tribe. He made figures from clay to which Coyote added genitalia, so allowing them to breed and become the ancestors of the tribe.

Hun Pic Tok   *Central American*
A Mayan war god, the holder of 8000 spears.

Hun-tun   *Chinese*
A deity representing Chaos, which is conceived of as the state, following Wu Chi, from which the universe emerged. From Chaos, it is said, evolved time and space and a fixed point, T'ai Chi, which gave rise to much change and eventually to substance (Chih).

Other accounts make Hun-tun an emperor ruling the centre before creation, while Hu ruled the north and Shu the south. These two merged to form the

lightning which pierced the body of Hun-tun which then formed the universe.

In some versions, he was a wicked prince sent into exile by his father, the Yellow Emperor, while others say that he was a red, faceless bird with four wings and six legs.

Yet another story says that he was the Emperor of China who was born without the seven bodily openings of other humans. When well-meaning friends bored the necessary openings, he died as the last one was bored and the earth came into being at the same time.

Hunab   *Central American*
The creator-god of the Maya. He periodically flooded the earth by causing rain to fall from the belly of the sky-serpent. He repopulated the earth after three floods, first by dwarfs, then with a race called Dzalob, who became demons, and lastly with the Maya, who are themselves destined to perish in another flood.

Hunapu   *Central American*
The Mayan god of the hunt; one of the Hero Twins.

He and his twin brother Ixbalanqué were born when the decapitated head of his father, who had been killed by the rulers of Xibalba, spat into the hand of Xqiuq, a princess of the underworld, Xibalba. Their other brothers, Hunbatz and Hunchouen, were jealous of the twins' magical powers and would have killed them but the twins realised their intentions and turned them into monkeys.

They set out to dispose of the giant, Vacub-Caquix, and his sons Cabraca and Zipacna. Their

first attempt, when they shot a poisoned arrow that struck Vacub-Caquix on the cheek, was not successful so, in the guise of physicians, they pulled out his emerald teeth and gouged out his eyes and he then died. They tried to kill Zipacna by burying him and building a house over the site but the giant recovered and killed the 400 young men who had helped to bury him. Another attempt, when they threw mountains on top of him, was successful in killing him. His brother Cabraca was easily killed when the twins gave him poisoned chicken to eat.

They then went to Xibalba, at the invitation of the rulers, to play tlachtli (a ball-game) with them, hoping to be able to avenge the death of their father, Hunhunapu. Every time they won a game against the lords of Xibalba, they had to spend a night in a house of torture. They survived the House of Gloom, the House of Lances, the House of Cold, the House of Tigers and the House of Fire but, in the House of Bats, Hunapu was decapitated by the bat-god, Camazotz. He was later restored by a turtle.

Advised and helped by the magicians Bacam and Xulu, the twins burnt and restored all sorts of things, including, finally, themselves. The rulers Huncame and Vucubcame were persuaded to attempt this feat and were burnt to death.

Hunhau   *Central American*
An owl-headed Mayan god of death, a name of Ah Puch as chief of the demons.

Hunting Causeway   *British*
A roadway in Somerset, England. On Christmas Eve or on St John

the Baptist's Day (24 June), King Arthur and his knights are said to ride this route from Cadbury Castle to Glastonbury.

Hurakan   *Central American*
The one-legged creator-god and thunder god of the Maya. He or the creator-god Gucumatz is said to have made mankind first from clay and then from wood, both of which were unsuccessful, and finally from maize. He later sent a flood to kill them.

Some equate Hurakan with Gucumatz. Others say that he was the first man, created by Gucumatz.

Huruing Wuhti   *North American*
Two Hopi sister mother-goddesses. In some accounts they were creator-goddesses who fashioned humans and animals from clay. They made the good people – the less civilised were made by Kokyangwuti. They survived the Flood and became the ancestors of the tribe.

Hus Brothers   *North American*
Buzzard-gods of the Wintun people. The creator-god, Olelbis, sent these two beings down to earth with orders to build a ladder from there to heaven but they dismantled what they had built when the trickster-god Sedit persuaded them that it was better if humans were not given the right to go to heaven and return.

It is said that one lived in the east, the other in the west and the sun travelled from one to the other every day. They were said to have created death.

Husbishag   *Mesopotamian*
A Sumerian goddess of the underworld. She recorded the time of each person's death on tablets kept for that purpose.

Huveane   *African*
The creator-god of the Basuto people. Having created the earth and the sky, Huveane climbed into the heavens on pegs which he withdrew to prevent man from following.

Hyacinthus   *Greek*
A prince of Sparta who was loved by Apollo, Thamyris and Zephyrus the West Wind who, in a fit of jealousy, killed Hyacinthus by smashing his head with a discus thrown by Apollo as he was practising. From his blood sprang the hyacinth flower.

Hyades   *Greek*
Nymphs placed in the heavens by Zeus as reward for raising the infant Dionysus.

In some accounts, their names are given as Ambrosia, Coronis, Eudora, Phyto, Polyxo and Tyche (or Dione).

Hydra   *Greek*
A many-headed water monster which lived in the swamp at Lerna in Argolis, north-west Peloponnese, and had the ability to grow further heads to replace any that were cut off. The number of heads varies from seven to a hundred. It was eventually killed by Hercules, with the help of Iolaus, as his third Labour.

hydromel   *Norse*
The drink of the gods. This drink (mead) was produced by the goat Heidrun for the gods and the warriors in Valhalla.

Hyel   *African*
A supreme deity in Nigeria. When the first man died, a worm was sent to heaven to ask Hyel what men should do and he advised them to hang up the dead

man's body and throw mush at it. The lizard, Agadzagazda, overheard this and ran back with the message that they should bury the body. When the worm arrived with the god's real message, the people ignored it, with the result that men still die.

hyena
(1) The Arabs say that wizards can turn themselves into hyenas.
(2) In Africa, where the animal is native, some tribes say that the soul of a man can enter a hyena which then attacks the man's enemies. Others say that hyenas are tribal ancestors.
(3) In Egypt it is said that this animal has a stone in its eye and if this stone, known as a hyaenia, is placed under the tongue, it can bring the gift of prophecy.
(4) The Greek say the hyena can change its sex and imitate the human voice and so is able to lure men to their death.

hyena-men   *African*
Evil spirits appearing either as men or as hyenas. In South Africa they are said to have two faces, one handsome, the other like a hyena with powerful jaws.

Hymenaeus   *Greek*
= *Roman* Hymen
The winged god of marriage. In some accounts, he was a youth who saved a procession of maidens from the hands of a gang of pirates at Eleusis.

He is depicted as a young man carrying a torch.

Hyperion   *Greek*
A sun god; a Titan; son of Uranus and Gaea; father of Eos (goddess of

the dawn), Helios (the sun god) and Selene (goddess of the moon). His role as sun god was later assumed by Helios and then by Apollo.

Hypnus   *Greek*
also Hypnos;
= *Roman* Somnus
The god of sleep; brother of Thanatos ('death'). He lives in the underworld during the hours of daylight and, . in some accounts, is envisaged as a night-bird.

I

I[1] *Central American*

A Mayan deity of uncertain identity, referred to as God I (*see* **alphabetical gods**); perhaps Ix Chel. This deity is depicted as an old woman with feet like claws and wearing a snake formed into a knot on her head and holding a water-pot. Water flowing from the pot leads to the suggestion that she was a water goddess.

I[2] *Chinese*

also Celestial Archer

The archer who shot down nine suns. When ten suns appeared in the sky the heat was too much so I shot down nine of them with his magic bow.

In one version, he was a deity who was banished to earth by Ti Chün who was angry at the loss of his sons, killed by I. I's wife, Heng O, who was banished with him, stole the elixir of immortality and flew off to the moon. Some say that he later married Fu-fei. He was later forgiven by Ti Chün or, in some accounts, was given

immortality by Hsi Wang Mu and came to be identified with the sun

Other stories of his exploits say that he prevented the eclipse of the moon, which caused humans to become infertile, by shooting the Celestial Dog which devoured the moon and that he rode up on the winds created by the wind-lord, Feng Po, and shot him in the leg, forcing him to abate the storms he had caused.

I Kaggen *African*

The Bushman god, Kaang, as the spirit of the praying mantis.

I-mu-kuo *Chinese*

'one-eye-land'

A mythical land where the people have only one eye, in the middle of their forehead.

I-qong *Pacific Islands*

In Melanesian lore, a god of the night. He sold the creator-god Qat the darkness of night in exchange for some pigs.

Ia *Pacific Islands*

The first woman according to the lore of Samoa.

Iae *South American*

Moon god of the Mamaiuran Indians of Brazil.

People were in darkness because the wings of Urubutsin, the vulture-king, kept the light of the sky from reaching earth. Iae and his twin brother Kuat captured Urubutsin and released him only when he promised to allow light to pass. Then they took to the sky, with Iae becoming the moon, Kuat the sun.

Iapetus *Greek*

A Titan; son of Uranus and Gaea; brother or husband of Themis. In some accounts, he fathered Prometheus on Themis and is said to have created mankind.

Ia'tiku *North American*

A creator-goddess of the Pueblos; mother of the Katsinas. Her sister Nao'tsiti bore twin boys after being impregnated by the rainbow and gave one of them to Ia'tiku before leaving to settle in the east. The boy, Tia'munia, mated with Ia'tiku to produce the forerunners of the tribe.

ibis *Egyptian*

A sacred bird; an incarnation of the god Thoth.

Icarus *Greek*

Son of Daedalus by a slave girl. He was locked with his father in the labyrinth housing the Minotaur on Crete by King Minos but they were both freed by Pasiphae, the king's wife. They escaped from Crete by flying on wings of feathers and wax made by Daedalus. Ignoring his father's instructions, Icarus flew too close to the sun, whereupon the wax melted and he crashed into the sea and drowned. An alternative version says that Icarus was not killed but swam to the nearby island of Icaria and lived there for many years.

ichor *Greek*

The colourless fluid in veins of gods. This vital fluid never carried disease; if shed, it would generate new life where it fell.

Ictinike *North American*
also Spider Man

The trickster-god, war god of the Iowa Indians; son of the sun god. He was expelled from heaven for his trickery. He tricked Rabbit into taking off his fur coat and, while Rabbit was up a tree, put the coat on and ran off with it. He married one daughter of a local chief, and so offended the other daughter, who rescued the skinless Rabbit. He engaged in shooting matches with Rabbit in which they shot an eagle which grew each day from the feathers of the one shot the day before. When Rabbit gave back to Ictinike the clothes he had taken off to put on Rabbit's fur, the Indians drummed up such a frantic dance that Ictinike,

jumping ever higher, fell and broke his neck.

Another story has a different version of his death. It was said that he was jealous when Rabbit (in this story, Rabbit Boy) married the girl he wanted for himself and incited the youths of the village to kill Rabbit. Before they killed him, cut him up and boiled him, Rabbit Boy sang a death-song and then used his magic powers to reassemble the parts and return to life. When Ictinike tried to do the same, he sang the wrong words to the death-song and died, never to return.

Yet another story says that he rode on the back of a buzzard who threw him off into a hollow tree where he was trapped for some time. When he finally escaped, he pretended to be dead. The buzzard landed to feed on his flesh and Ictinike seized it and tore the feathers from the top of its head.

Some equate him with Ikto, a culture-hero said to have invented speech.

Ida *Hindu*

A goddess of food and law; daughter of the god Varuna, some say; consort of Manu, the creator-god or first human.

She was said to have been created from butter and milk left over from the Churning of the Ocean. She and Manu repopulated the earth after the flood which they survived on top of a mountain.

In some accounts, she was the daughter of Manu and wife of Buddha.

Another version says that Ida was originally male but she angered the goddess Parvati

who changed her into a woman. Later, Parvati relented and Ida was allowed to spend alternate months as a man, Ila.

Idomeneus *Greek*

A king of Crete. He was the leader of the Cretans in the Trojan War and was one of those hidden inside the Wooden Horse. He aimed his spear at Aeneas but killed Oenomaus instead. Returning from Troy, his ship was caught in a storm and Idomeneus vowed to kill the first person he met on shore in Crete if the sea god, Poseidon, would save his ship. The first person was his own son, Idamente. He killed him and was banished to Italy when a plague descended on the island.

In some accounts, he was driven from Crete by Leucus who had seduced Idomeneus's wife Meda while her husband was at Troy.

Iduna *Norse*

Goddess of youth. Some say she had no birth and could never die.

She owned a magic basket containing the apples of eternal youth, the supply of which was continuously renewed. She gave these to the gods, some of whom were otherwise not immortal.

Tricked by the trickster god Loki into leaving Asgard with a bowl of this fruit, she was abducted by the storm-giant Thiassi. When the gods, who found themselves ageing in the absence of the fruit, discovered what Loki had done, they ordered him to get her back. Wearing Freya's falcon-garb he flew to Thrymheim and, changing Iduna into a swallow, or a nut, brought her safely back to Asgard.

One day when she was sitting on a branch of the universe-tree

Yggdrasil, she fainted and fell into Niflheim where she was found by Bragi who wrapped her in a white wolf-skin given by Odin. She remained pale and tearful from the horrible sights she had seen in Hel's kingdom and Bragi stayed with her until she recovered.

Idzumo   *Japanese*

A part of the newly-created earth. This realm caused so much annoyance to the gods from the noise made by the trees and flowers which, in those days, could speak, that they sent the god Ninigi, preceded by three envoys, to quell the disturbance.

Igalilik   *Inuit*

A spirit of the hunt. He is said to carry a boiling cauldron large enough to hold a seal.

Igaluk   *Inuit*

The supreme god and moon god. He inadvertently had intercourse with his own sister who, in disgust, took a torch and ascended into the sky where she became the sun. Igaluk became the moon.

Igraine   *British*

Mother of Elaine, Morgan le Fay and others; mother of King Arthur by Uther.

When Uther fell in love with Igraine, her husband Gorlois shut her away in a castle. The sorcerer Merlin changed Uther into the form of Gorlois, giving him access to Igraine, on whom he fathered the infant Arthur, later king of Britain. Others say that they also had a daughter called Anna. She married Uther when Gorlois died.

In some accounts she came from Atlantis.

Ihoiho   *Pacific Islands*

A creator-god of the Society Islands. He created the primordial

ocean and, on it, the being Tino Taata who made man.

Ija-kyl   *Siberian*

In Yakut lore, a spirit-animal. This spirit is said to appear to a shaman when he takes up his office, in the middle of that period and just before his death. It dies when the shaman dies and conveys the shaman's spirit to the otherworld.

Ika Tere   *Pacific Islands*

A Polynesian fish-god. He is said to have created all the sea-creatures.

Iko   *East Indies*

The first man to die, in the lore of New Guinea. He left behind a sort of mirage which, ever since, has prevented the living (other than seers) from following him to the land of the dead.

Ikto   *North American*

A Sioux culture-hero said to have invented speech. In some accounts he is equated with Ictinike.

Iku-Ikasuchi   *Japanese*

A Shinto thunder god. He was one of the eight gods born from the charred body of Izanami.

Ikuzimu   *African*

The land under the earth, in the lore of the Banyarwanda.

Ilai   *Pacific Islands*

An Indonesian sun god, consort of Indara. Together they made men by making stones and breathing life into them.

Ila-Ilai Langit   *East Indian*

In the lore of the Dayaks, a primordial monster in the form of a fish. This fish was created in the first of the three epochs of creation.

Ilamatecuhtli   *Central American*

An Aztec goddess, a name of Cihuacoatl as 'old goddess'. In this role, she was the wife of Mixcoatl and bore seven sons, each of

whom founded a major city.

Ilé-Ifé   *African*

A sacred city of the seventeen deities of the Yoruba people. This was the site at the centre of the world where humans were created and where the dead meet to be given instructions.

Ilion

Another name for Troy.

Ilithyia   *Greek*

The goddess of childbirth; daughter of Zeus and Hera. In some versions, she was a primordial force, sister of Gaea, and laid the cosmic egg from which all else sprang. Others say that originally there were two goddesses with this name, one presiding over birth, one prolonging labour pains. They later merged. In some accounts there were several daughters (Ilithyiae) acting as goddesses of birth.

Illuyankas   *Mesopotamian*

= *Babylonian* Tiamat; *Hebrew* Leviathan

A Hittite dragon. This monster was involved in a struggle with the weather god, Teshub, and overcame him. The goddess Inara and her lover Hupasiyas trapped the dragon and its offspring and bound them for the weather god to kill.

In another version, the dragon took the eyes and heart of the weather god who then begot a son who married Illuyankas's daughter and received the missing parts as a wedding gift. Whole again, Teshub killed the dragon and his own son. In some accounts, this son was Telepini.

Ilma   *Finnish*

A spirit of the air. This primeval force preceded creation and produced the daughter, Ilmatar, who, in some accounts, fell from the heavens into the ocean where, mating with Ahti, the ocean, she produced countless sea creatures.

Ilmarinen   *Baltic*

A Finnish hero, said to have taught mankind the arts of metalwork.

His brother Vainamoinen had been promised the hand of the daughter of Louhi, a wicked ice-giantess, if he could make a sampo (a mysterious object that grants wishes). Ilmarinen was sent to her country, Pohjola, to make it. Using materials such as the feathers of a swan, barley and wool, he set about the task. From the flames of his furnace many wonderful objects appeared but he rejected them all as evil. Finally, the sampo emerged, a talisman with a mill on each of its three sides. When he presented it to Louhi's daughter, she married him instead of Vainamoinen.

When his wife Kildisin died, killed by her own cattle, he abducted her sister and, when she was unfaithful, he turned her into a bird.

He and Vainamoinen stole the sampo but it was smashed when Louhi caused a storm which wrecked their ship.

In one story, Vainamoinen caused a fir tree to grow until it reached the sky and Ilmarinen climbed the tree hoping to capture the moon. A magic wind sprang up and he was blown off the tree.

Ilmatar   *Baltic*

A Finnish creator-goddess and goddess of the air; mother of Vainamoinen and Ilmarinen.

She floated in the primordial waters for 700 years and finally either mated with a bird or a teal laid its egg on her exposed knee. The egg fell off and the shell broke, becoming the earth and sky. In some accounts, the bird laid six golden eggs and one made of iron and Ilmatar filled the universe from these eggs.

A similar story is told about Vainamoinen but in that case the bird was an eagle.

In another version, she fell into the ocean and mated with Ahti, the god of the waters, to produce Vainamoinen and countless sea creatures.

Ilu   *Pacific Islands*

A Samoan sky god. This entity merged with Mamao, another sky god, to form the sky and together they produced Ao, the god of the clouds, and Po, the primeval void.

Imana   *African*

The supreme god and creator-god of the Banyarwanda. He created the world in three layers, each supported on wooden props, one above the other. He lived in the topmost world, the next below was the world of living things, and the lowest was the world of the dead.

Imap-ukua   *Inuit*

A sea goddess, said to control all the animals in the sea.

Imbas forosnai   *Irish*

Acquisition of wisdom by chewing the thumb. This is featured in the story of Finn mac Cool.

Imberombera   *Australian*

An ancestress of the Kakadu tribe of Aborigines. When she met and mated with the creator-god Wuraka, she instantly produced all living things, to which Wuraka gave names. When it was all over, they walked out into the sea from whence they came and disappeared.

Imdugud   *Mesopotamian*

A name of the god Ninurta as rain god. In some versions, Imdugud and Ninurta were originally the same deity who developed into two widely different beings.

In one story, Imdugud (or perhaps Zu) once stole the Tablets of Destiny from the god Enlil but they were recovered by Ninurta.

He is depicted as a storm-bird with the head of a lion.

Imhotep   *Egyptian*

A god of learning, medicine and scribes; a pharaoh, later fully deified; son of Sakhmet or of Ptah and a mortal woman.

He was a scholar of the 26th century BC, said to have designed the first pyramid, and was deified as Ptah.

Imilozi   *African*

Ancestor-spirits of the Zulu. Their function was to pass on to men the secrets of and messages from the gods but their whistling language was incomprehensible and so no messages got through.

imp   *European*

A sprite; a wicked spirit.

Impundulu   *African*

An incubus in the form of a bird. This being will attack and kill any human lover of the woman it has intercourse with. The child of any such union will be a vampire.

Inanna   *Mesopotamian*

also Queen of Heaven;

= *Akkadian* Ishtar; *Phrygian* Cybele; *Babylonian* Nina

The Sumerian mother-goddess, goddess of fertility, love and war.

She descended to the underworld Kur, hoping to impose her authority on her sister Ereshkigal who ruled there. She was admitted to each of the seven realms but removed one symbol of her power at each gateway. She was then killed and suspended from a stake. The gods sent two sexless beings to revive her and bring her back but, to rid herself of the demons that continued to harry her, she was required to provide a substitute for herself and so she sacrificed her husband Dumuzi, who had been unfaithful in her absence, and the wine goddess Geshtinanna who, with Dumuzi, served alternate periods of six months in the underworld.

This is an earlier version of the same story about Ishtar. Some accounts distinguish between this goddess and Inanna, a Babylonian mother-goddess, and some say that Inanna is the same as Ereshkigal.

Inapertwa   *Australian*
Primitive, rudimentary beings. These beings were used by the Numbakulla (sky-beings) for making animals, birds and plants. Some were even made into humans.

Inara   *Mesopotamian*
A Hittite goddess. When the dragon Illuyankas overcame the weather god, Teshub (Inara's father), Inara and her lover Hupasiyas made the monster and its offspring drunk and tied them up so that Teshub could kill them. Others say they trapped the dragon by giving it so much food that it got wedged in the passage to its undergound lair.

She built a house for Hupasiyas and ordered him not to look out in case he should see his wife and family. When he disobeyed, she killed him.

In another version, Inara was a Hittite god (also known as Lama)

who usurped the heavenly throne but was overthrown by Ea.

Inari   *Japanese*
A Shinto god of food. After his wife Uke-mochi was killed by the moon god Tsukiyomi, Inari became identified with her, taking over her duties, though in some versions this is a female deity. In some accounts, both he and Uke-mochi are regarded as aspects of the goddess Ugonomitama.

He was sometimes seen as a fox (or riding on a fox) and is often depicted as a bearded man with two foxes.

incubus   *European*
plural incubi
A devil in male body; a spirit attacking women during the night. Early accounts regard the incubus as a fallen angel. In some accounts the incubus rides his victim, sometimes even to the point of death from exhaustion. The offspring of such a union are monsters of all descriptions. (*See also* **succubus**.)

Indaji   *African*
A famous Nigerian hunter who could attract animals by whistling and killed so many that the forest god ordered him to kill no more than one per day. When he killed three antelopes, they changed into lions and attacked him. They all changed shape several times until Indaji changed himself into a tree and was burnt in a forest fire.

Indra   *Hindu*
The supreme god, god of fertility, heavens, rain and war; consort of Indrani. Originally the god of the Aryan invaders of North India, or even a mortal later deified, he was adopted into the Hindu pantheon and later demoted to become god of the paradise, Svarga.

He is regarded as one of the Dikpalas, guardian of the east with his elephant, Airavata.

He was said to have been born fully developed from his mother's side, ready to fight the forces of evil.

Ahi, the drought-serpent, had swallowed all the primeval waters so Indra split open the monster's stomach with one of his thunderbolts to release the waters to create life. He also rescued the cloud cattle, the sacred cows, when they were stolen by Ahi.

Another version says that the cattle were swallowed by a different demon, Vritra, made by the sage Tvastri to kill Indra, who had killed Tvastri's three-headed son. In this story, Vritra also swallowed Indra who escaped when the other gods forced open the demon's jaws. Vishnu formed himself into a knife and cut off the monster's head. In some stories, this monster is called Namuci.

Indra then created a new universe in which the sky rested on pillars of gold and the mountains became fixed in position when he cut off their wings.

His weapon was the thunderbolt, Vajra, and he is depicted as red or gold, sometimes riding in a chariot drawn by two (1,100 or 10,000) horses, at other times riding an elephant. He is also depicted with a beard which, it is said, flashed like lightning and sometimes with seven arms bearing a diadem, a discus, a goad, prayer-beads, a sickle, a sword and the vajra. Seven rivers flow from him.

He owned the horse Uccaihsravas which appeared at the Churning of the Ocean.

Some say he could assume the form of an insect.

Inevitable River   *Chinese*

A river in hell which the travelling spirit must cross. The good pass over the Fairy Bridges, accompanied by the Golden Youth, while the evil are forced to cross a bridge only an inch or so wide.

Inkari   *South American*

An ancestor of the Q'ero people of Peru. He and his mate, Collari, were created by the Apus (mountain spirits) to repopulate the country after Roal had killed the existing people with the heat of the sun.

Another story says that Inkari was a god of the sun who was beheaded. His head was hidden in a secret location where it is still alive and growing a new body. As soon as the body is complete, the god will appear once again and restore his people to their former glory.

Inriri   *West Indies*

A woodpecker.

Once there were men but no women. Then one day four beings with no sexual organs fell out of the trees. The men tied these beings up and Inriri, thinking they were trees, pecked holes in their bodies, forming vaginas.

Intelligences   *Hebrew*

also Seven Intelligences

Cabbalistic spiritual beings controlling the movement of planets. These beings are listed as Agiel (Saturn), Elimiel (moon), Graphiel (Mars), Hagiel (Venus), Nagiel (sun), Sophiel (Jupiter) and Tiriel (Mercury).

Inti   *South American*

The sun god of the Incas. He sent his children to earth to start the Inca civilisation wherever the golden wedge he gave them sank into the earth.

He is depicted as a golden solar disc with a human face.

(*See also* **Children of the Sun**.)

Io   *Greek*

= *Egyptian* Isis

A river-nymph, a priestess of the goddess Hera. Zeus fell in love with Io and when Hera caught him with her he changed Io into a cow, denying that he had touched any woman. Hera begged to be given the cow which she then put in the charge of the hundred-eyed Argus. Hermes lulled the guardian to sleep with music and Zeus killed him and released Io. Hera sent a gadfly to torment Io which pursued her in her wanderings during which she came upon Prometheus chained to a rock but could not help him. After travelling through many lands, still in the form of a cow, she settled in Egypt where she was returned to human form by Zeus and bore his son Epaphus though married to Telegonus. She became assimilated into the goddess Isis and Epaphus to the bull-god, Hapy.

Iolaus   *Greek*

Hercules took this lad, his nephew, as his charioteer during the period of his Labours. At the end of this period, he gave his wife, Megara, to Iolaus. In some stories, Iolaus is sixteen when he takes Megara, which makes him rather young for a charioteer at the start of his adventures. In the adventure with the Hydra, when Hercules cut off each of the

monster's heads, Iolaus cauterised the wound to prevent the head from growing again.

Some say that, when old, he was restored to youth by Hebe in order to help the children of Hercules when attacked by Eurystheus, king of Argos, who, in some accounts, he killed.

Iolokiamo   *South American*

An evil trickster-god in Venezuela, opposed to the supreme deity Cachimana.

Iormungandr   *Norse*

also World Serpent

This monster, the Midgard serpent, was with the wolf Fenris and Hel, goddess of the underworld, the offspring of the secret marriage between the god Loki and the giantess Angerbode. Odin threw the serpent into the sea where it became so large that it encircled the earth. On one occasion, it was caught by Thor on a fishing trip but his companion on that trip, Hymir, cut the line in fear. It emerged to fight the gods at Ragnarok and was killed by Thor, who perished in the flood of venom that erupted from the dying monster.

Ioskeha   *North American*

= *Abnaki* Gluskap; *Algonquin* Manabozho; *Huron* Tsent(s)a; *Menominee* Manabush; *Montagnais* Messou

A sun god of the Iroquois; son of Wind-Ruler and Breath-of-Wind. He is regarded as the creator of the universe and mankind.

He fought with his twin brother Tawiscara, even in their mother's womb, and she died when they were born. From then on they fought for supremacy. In one story they fought, Ioskeha with a stag's horn and Tawiscara with a rose. Tawiscara was wounded and fled leaving Ioskeha as the principal god who killed monsters, including the Great Frog which had swallowed all the water from the lakes and rivers, and taught the people the arts of agriculture and hunting. It is said that he was taught the secrets of medicine by Hadui, a supernatural hunchbacked being.

In some accounts, Ioskeha married his grandmother, Ataensic, and renews his youth when he grows old.

Iphigenia   *Greek*
Daughter of King Agamemnon of Mycenae and Clytemnestra. Others say that she was the daughter by Theseus of Helen, who gave her to Clytemnestra to be brought up.

In one story she was sacrificed by Agamemnon so that the winds which were keeping the Greek fleet, ready to sail for Troy, confined to harbour would abate. In another version, Artemis substituted a deer (a bear or a calf in other stories) on the altar and spirited Iphigenia away to the land of the Taurians where she became a priestess of a cult which sacrificed all prisoners to a wooden image of the goddess, said to have fallen from the sky. She was there when Orestes and Pylades arrived to to seize this sacred image of Artemis. She recognised Orestes as her brother and deceived the king, Thoas, who had captured the newcomers, into releasing them and they escaped with the sacred image, taking Iphigenia back to Mycenae with them.

It is said that the goddess Artemis made her immortal as

Hecate and that she married the hero Achilles.

Ipos   *European*
A demon, one of the 72 Sprits of Solomon. In some accounts, he is described as a prince of hell and is depicted as a standing eagle. Others say that he appears as an angel with the body of a lion. He is said to foretell the future.

Iqi Balam   *Central American*
also Tiger of the Moon
One of the first four men, in Mayan lore; brother of Balam Agab, Balam Quitze and Mahucutah. He and his brothers were created from maize-flour and broth brewed by the creator-goddess Xmucané (*see more at* **Balam Agab**).

Irene *see* **Eirene**

Iri   *East Indies*
A creator-deity in Borneo. He helped the creator-bird Rinaggon to create people from the kumpong tree.

Irik   *East Indian*
In the lore of the Iban of Borneo, a primeval creator. Irik and Ara, in the form of birds, flew over the primordial ocean. They drew two eggs from the waters and from them made earth and sky. They then made people from soil and gave them life.

Iris   *Greek*
The rainbow goddess, sister of the Harpies, messenger of the gods.

She was said to keep the clouds supplied with rain and to release the souls of the dying from their bodies.

Irmin's Way   *Norse*
also Bil's Way
The Milky Way. (*See also* **Bifrost**.)

Isa Bere   *African*
A dragon. This beast swallowed all the water of the Niger. After a

battle lasting for some 800 years, King Samba of Gana managed to kill the dragon and the river began to flow again.

Isakawuate   *North American*
A trickster-god of the Crow tribe.

Ischin   *Hebrew*
also Bne-aleim
A group of seven angels. These beings are said to have consorted with men at the beginning of creation and taught them many subjects. Like the Muses, each had its own special field: Akibeel taught the meaning of signs; Amazariak, mathematics; Amers, magic; Asaradel, the motions of the moon; Azazel, weaponry; Barkayat, astrology; and Tamial, astronomy.

Ishits   *North American*
also Beetle
In the lore of the Sia tribe, an insect given a bag of stars by Utset, an ancestress of the human race, to carry to the underworld. Ishits bit a hole in the bag allowing the stars to escape. Utset blinded Ishits for disobeying her orders.

Ishtar   *Mesopotamian*
= *Babylonian* Ashtoreth; *Egyptian* Hathor; *Greek* Aphrodite; *Phoenician* Astarte; *Sumerian* Baba
An Akkadian mother-goddess, goddess of fertility, hunting, love and war. As a goddess of love, she was associated with the planet Venus.

In the Assyrian stories, Ishtar was the wife of Ashur, the war god, and she grew a beard that reached her breast.

As an Akkadian goddess she was the wife of Tammuz and descended to the underworld, Aralu, to bring back her husband when he died. She was kept in the underworld by the ruler,

Ereshkigal, until the gods created Ashushu-Namir and sent him to demand Ishtar's release. A similar story involves Inanna and Dumuzi, the Sumerian equivalents.

Other accounts have her as consort of Marduk, tutelary god of Babylon.

When King Gilgamesh rejected her advances, she persuaded the god Anu to send the Bull of Heaven to despoil the earth.

She is depicted as riding a lion and is sometimes envisaged as male.

Isis *Egyptian*
also Great Mother, Queen of Heaven;
= *Greek* Athena, Demeter
Mother-goddess, goddess of medicine, fertility goddess, moon goddess, queen of heaven; sister and wife of Osiris; mother of Anubis and Horus.

She is said to have introduced marriage and had the ability to change into any form she desired.

On one occasion when the gods Osiris and Set, both in the form of bulls, were fighting, she is said to have killed them both.

When her husband, Osiris, was put into a box and thrown into the Nile by his brother Set, she rescued his body, mourning in the form of a bird, and conceived their son Horus. When Set again took the body, cut it into fourteen pieces and threw them into the Nile, she recovered the pieces and brought her husband back to life. She and Nephthys are known as the Weeping Sisters from their wailing at the death of Osiris.

She found the infant Anubis hidden in the reeds by his mother, Nephthys, and raised him as her own.

Wearing the headdress of horns

enclosing the disc of the sun, she is Hathor, the cow-goddess. Her cow's-head was given to her by Thoth to replace her own head which had been cut off by Horus who was angry with her for releasing Set who had been captured in battle.

She became a goddess by devious means, making a serpent from earth and Ra's spittle. The snake bit the sun god and he was persuaded to speak his secret name, Ran, so conferring immortality on Isis. Her function as a goddess was, with Nephthys, guarding the coffins of the dead.

She is represented in the sky as Sirius and is often depicted with long wings, as a hippopotamus, a white heifer, a serpent or a queen standing on a crescent.

Island of Apple Trees *see* **Emain Ablach**
Island of Apples, Island of Blessed Souls *see* **Avalon**[1]
Island of the Blessed *see* **Tuma**
Islands of the Blessed *see* **Elysium, Fortunate Islands**
Isolde *see* **Tristram**
Itiwana *North American*
The underworld of the Zuni.

When the tribe were seeking a homeland they lost all their children in a lake which they had to cross. A brother and sister, who had been turned into supernatural beings after committing incest, made a road into the lake so that the parents could visit their children who declared themselves to be so happy at being in Itiwana under the lake that, henceforth, all the dead went there.

Itzam Cab *Central American*
A Mayan earth god, an aspect of Itzamna. In this form he has maize-leaves growing out of his head.

Itzamkabain *Central American*
In the Mayan creation story, a whale with the feet of an alligator.

Itzamna *Central American*
also Lakin Chan
= *Aztec* Quetzalcoatl
Mayan sun god, god of day and night, learning and writing. He is credited with the invention of books and is depicted as a benevolent old man with no teeth or as a huge serpent. In some versions he is described as a moon god or is equated with Ah Kin, Hunab or Kukulcan.

Itzpapalotl *Central American*
An Aztec mother-goddess, fire goddess and goddess of agriculture. She appeared as a beautiful woman but, when any man tried to take her, flint knives from her various orifices cut him to pieces and she squeezed out all his blood.

Itztapal Totec *Central American*
An Aztec fertility god and patron of workers in precious metals.

Iubdan *Irish*
King of the fairies. He owned a pair of shoes that enabled him to travel in or on the water with the greatest of ease. He was captured by Fergus mac Leda when he visited Ulster and fell into a bowl of porridge. His wife Bebo had an affair with Fergus, who released both her and her husband after a year and a day but demanded Iubdan's magic shoes in return.

Ivan *Russian*
A prince. When the firebird stole apples from the tsar's magic tree, the tsar sent Ivan and his two brothers to capture the bird. They seized it and the maiden Yelena but the two brothers killed Ivan before returning home. The prince

was restored to life by a wolf and returned to claim Yelena as his wife.

In another version, the tsar wanted Yelena for his wife and sent Ivan to seize her. Ivan fell in love with his captive and the wolf which had helped him in his quest resolved the problem by turning himself into a likeness of Yelena and the tsar took 'her' as his bride. When the wolf resumed its normal shape, the tsar died of shock and Ivan was able to marry Yelena and took the throne.

Ivi Apo   *East Indian*
In Papuan lore, the first woman. She was hatched from an egg laid by a huge turtle and mated with Kerema Apo, the first man, who came from another egg.

ivy   *Greek*
A plant sacred to Dionysus. It was said that this plant prevented drunkenness.

Iwazaru   *Japanese*
One of the Three Mystic Apes. He is depicted with his hands covering his mouth as 'he who speaks no evil'.

Ix Chel   *Central American*
A Mayan moon goddess, water goddess, goddess of childbirth and weaving; mother of the Bacabs.

She is said to hold a jug from which she can produce another world flood at any time and is envisaged as a combination of a waterfall and a serpent.

Ixbalanqué   *Central American*
One of the Mayan Hero Twins. For the story of Ixbalanqué and Hunapu, *see* **Hunapu**.

Ixion   *Greek*
King of the Lapiths, a race of horse-tamers in Thessaly. He arranged to marry Dia, daughter of Eioneus,

king of Magnesia, and pay for the honour, but he reneged on his promise and when her father demanded the money, Ixion killed him by luring him to fall into a pit of burning material. He fathered Peirithous on her, although the real father may well have been Zeus.

When Zeus invited him to dinner in Olympia, Ixion tried to seduce Hera but was forestalled by Zeus who created a likeness (Nephele) from cloud-material. She bore the Centaurs or, in some accounts, Centaurus who fathered the Centaurs on the Magnesian mares. Zeus punished Ixion by having him tied to a burning wheel forever revolving in the heavens or, in some stories, in Tartarus.

Iya   *North American*
A magic rock. In a rare display of generosity, Coyote gave the rock his blanket but snatched it back when he began to feel cold. The rock chased Coyote, flattening trees in its path, and finally ran over Coyote, flattening him also, so recovering the blanket.

In other versions, Iya was a cannibalistic monster of the Sioux, appearing in the form of a hurricane.

Izanagi   *Japanese*
also August Male
The Shinto primeval father-god; brother and husband of Izanami; father of Amaterasu, Hiru-Ko, Kazu-Tsuchi, Susanowa and Tsuki-yomo.

He and Izanami were two of the seventeen gods of creation. Standing on the bridge of heaven they stirred the primeval waters with a spear and created an island, Onogoro, with the brine that came

up on the blade. They also created an island called Awagi and the rest of the islands of Japan.

When Izanami died giving birth to the fire god Kazu-Tsuchi, Izanagi decapitated the boy with his magic sword, Ame-no-wo-ha-bari, and went into Yomi, the underworld, to get his wife back, but it was too late – she had already eaten the food of the dead. She was allowed to return if Izanagi did not look at her but, as in the story of Orpheus and Eurydice, he broke his promise. When he fled at the sight of her rotting corpse, Izanami sent demons, the Eight Ugly Females, after him. He escaped and blocked the entrance with a huge boulder. He fled to an island where he built a house and lived forever in silence. When he bathed in the sea to cleanse himself, his clothes became more gods, the dirt from his body became sea gods, the sun goddess Amaterasu came from his left eye, the moon god Tsuki-yomo from his right eye and the sea god Susanowa from his nose. Other versions allocate these deities to different parts of his face. In some accounts, he divided his kingdom between these three and retired to heaven.

While in the underworld Izanami also produced deities from her bodily discharges. (*See also* **Hiru-ko**.)

Izanami   *Japanese*
also August Female
The Shinto primeval mother-goddess; sister and wife of Izanagi.

Izdubar   *Mesopotamian*
A Babylonian hero or sun god. Like Hercules, he performed twelve

labours and, in some accounts, is equated with Gilgamesh.

Izoi-tamoi   *South American*
Creator-god of the Guarani.

He created the tribe and then departed to the underworld where he was encountered by all souls entering the underworld and grew bigger or smaller according to whether the traveller had been bad or good. Evil souls were split in half by Izoi-tamoi.

His two sons climbed an arrow-chain into the sky and became the sun and moon.

Izpuzteque   *Central American*
A fierce demon in the lore of the Aztecs. This demon is one of the many hazards faced by the souls of the dead in their journey through the underworld.

Iztac Ciuatl   *Central American*
A sacred mountain, home of the rain god, Tlaloc.

J

Jabme-aimo *Baltic*
The Lappish underworld, ruled by an old woman, Jabme-akka.

Jacunuam *South American*
A celestial fish. The Xingu of Brazil say that this great fish swallows the sun every night and vomits it up each morning.

Jade Ruler *see* **Yü Huang**

Jagannath *Hindu*
also Jagan-natha, Juggernaut, Lord of the World
An incarnation of Vishnu as a relentless god. He is depicted with no legs and only stumps in place of arms. One version accounts for this by saying that Vishnu was accidentally killed by a hunter and Vishvakarma undertook to revivify him by forming new flesh on the original bones. Krishna broke the undertaking that nobody should look until the job was finished with the result that it never was completed.

In some accounts, Jagannath is an incarnation of Krishna.

jaguar *South American*
also Master of Animals
Some say that the jaguar was the founder of the Quiche tribe and Tezcatlipoca became a jaguar when he was killed by Quetzalcoatl and fell into the sea.

The Toltecs regarded this animal as symbolising darkness and thunder.

Some tribes say that eclipses are caused when a supernatural jaguar swallows the sun or moon.

It is said that, when a black jaguar dies, it becomes a demon and a shaman may turn into a jaguar when he dies.

Jaguar-man *South American*
A form of werewolf. Some shamans are reputed to be able to turn themselves into jaguars, in which form they attack victims at night.

Jaguar-Snake *Central American*
A primordial goddess of the Mixtec. She and her consort Puma-Snake appeared when the earth rose out of the primeval waters and

built a palace in which they lived for hundreds of years before producing their two sons Wind-Nine-Cave and Wind-Nine-Snake. The four gods became the progenitors of the human race.

Jaik-khan *Siberian*
Son of Over-god; a prince of floods. He sends the souls for the new-born and, having deserted his father in heaven to go to the underworld, acts as receiver of souls. He also records people's good deeds.

Jalandhara *Hindu*
A demon; consort of the female demon Vrindha. He threatened to take over the universe so the gods forged a powerful sun-disc to kill him. Vishnu, in the form of Jalandhara, seduced Vrindha who, ashamed at what had happened, committed suicide. This angered Jalandhara so that he attacked the gods who then produced their secret weapon and cut off his head. He became whole again when his blood fell into the ocean

but eventually the goddesses lapped up the blood and he weakened and died.

An alternative version says that Jalandhara sent the demon Rahu to seize Shakti, wife of Shiva, but that god created the lion-headed monster, Kurttimukha, by discharging a tremendous burst of power from his eyes. This scared Rahu away and the hungry demon was forced to eat himself.

Jambavan   *Hindu*
A king of bears. He existed in the time before the Churning of the Ocean and it was he who had thrown into the sea the herbs that made amrita. In later years, he helped Rama in his struggle with Ravana. He also killed the lion which held the light of the sun in a ruby and refused to give the gem to Krishna who wanted it. It was only after they had fought for many days that Jambavan realised that he was fighting a god and immediately yielded the stone, adding the hand of his daughter, Jambavati, for good measure.

Jambridvipa   *Hindu*
The continent or island standing at the centre of the world; site of Mount Mandara or, some say, Mount Meru.

Jambu   *Hindu*
= *Buddhist* Jamabustrishring; *Tibetan* Jambutri Shring, Zampu
The Tree of Life growing on Mount Meru. In some accounts this tree is the source of soma. It is the axis of the earth with its roots on the underworld, and its topmost branches in the heavens.

Jambutri Shring   *Tibetan*
= *Buddhist* Jamabustrishring; *Hindu* Jambu
The tree of life. The roots of this tree are in Lamayin (the realm of

the demi-gods) but its branches in Lhayul (a celestial realm) so that the inhabitants of that realm can enjoy the fruit.

Jan   *Burmese*
A benevolent nat of the sun, one of the original nats (spirits or supernatural beings) created by Chinun Way Shun, the first of the nats and creator of all the others.

Jana-Loka   *Hindu*
One of the seven realms of the universe, home of Brahma's children.

Janet   *Scottish*
Lover of the magician Tam Lin. When Tam Lin was seized by the fairy queen, Janet held him firmly through several shape changes until he finally freed himself from the enchantment.

Jang Lung   *Chinese*
Red Dragon, one of the Four Dragon Kings.

Janus   *Roman*
The two-faced god of beginnings, dawn, doors, gateways, travel; son of Apollo.

In some accounts, he was made by Uranus and Hecate, using earth and water moulded into a ball. En route to the underworld, the ball became a kind of sentient pillar which Hecate reared as Janus. He ran off and dived into the Styx, arriving back in the land of the living where, in the warmth of the sun, he developed organs.

On one occasion, the nymph Carna lured him into a cave and then tried to slip away as she had done with many others, but his second face saw her behind him and he prevented her escape and seduced her. On another occasion, he saved Rome from the attacking Sabines by creating a spring of boiling water at the gateway.

He became a deity when he was rewarded for helping the gods in their fight with the Titans.

His temple in Rome had two doors (or four) which were closed only when the nation was not at war. His festival was celebrated on 9th January.

He was said to have one young face, one old, and is depicted with two, three or four heads and carrying a key and a rod.

As Janus Quadrifrons he was the four-headed god of the seasons.

Some regard Janus as a pre-Latin deity adopted into the Ronan pantheon.

Jarita   *Hindu*
A huge bird. Jaritas were female birds with no mates. A saint named Mandalpana died but returned as a male bird, Sarangika, mated with a Jarita, fathering four sons, and then went back to the underworld.

Jason   *Greek*
Husband of the sorceress Medea and leader of the Argonauts. His name at first was Diomedes and he was reared by the Centaur Chiron to escape his uncle Pelias who tried to kill anyone who might be a threat, and changed his name to Jason. As a result of his kindness to the goddess Hera whom he carried across a river in flood when she visited earth in the guise of an old woman, he was granted her protection in his later adventures.

He claimed the throne of Iolcus from Pelias who had usurped it from Aeson, Jason's father, and Pelias agreed to surrender it if Jason would lay a ghost which was haunting him and bring back the Golden Fleece to Iolcus. This initiated the quest for the Golden Fleece told in the story of the Argonauts.

Jatayu											*Hindu*

A huge bird, king of the vultures; an incarnation of the demigod Garuda (part man, part eagle); son of Garuda, some say. He saw the demon-king Ravana abducting Sita, wife of Rama, and tried to stop him but the demon tore out his feathers and left him dying. He lived long enough to tell Rama what had happened to his wife and was then taken up to heaven.

jay											*North American*

A chattering bird. In some southern states, this bird is regarded as a messenger of the Devil and, every Friday, takes him a bundle of sticks, with the consequence that the bird is not seen on that day.

Some say that medicine-men can take on the form of a jay; others say that the bird is a hero who brought up mud after the flood to make dry land.

Jewel Maiden											*Japanese*

A fox-woman. She appeared first as Hoji, consort of the emperor, then as concubine to the emperor Toba and finally as the Jewel Maiden. She set out to destroy the imperial dynasty and nearly caused the death of the Mikado. A sorcerer frustrated her plans and she reverted to her fox-self and fled the country to inhabit the Death Stone. She was saved from her evil ways by the prayers of the priest, Genno.

Jewel Mountain											*East Indies*

In the lore of the Dayaks, this mountain clashed with Gold Mountain to produce the world.

Jewel Peak *see* **Mount Meru**

Jinn bin Jann											*Arab*

The king of the jinn. He was regarded as the ruler of the world in the time before Adam and Eve.

jinnee											*Arabian*

also (d)jinni, genie; *female* jinniyah; *plural* (d)jinn, ginn, jann

A powerful spirit made of fire which assumes all kinds of shapes. They were created some 2000 years before Adam and Eve and lived on Mount Qaf but God dispersed them when they became disobedient. The survivors reassembled on an island in the Indian Ocean from where they now operate.

They are said to have magic powers over humans and to interbreed with them.

In some accounts they are described as half hyena, half wolf, with the power to take the form of any animal, serpent or giant invisible to humans. They are said to ride abroad at night on such mounts as foxes or ostriches.

Jogah											*North American*

Iroquois nature-spirits. There are said to be three different groups of these dwarf beings – the Gahonga, the Gandayah and the Ohdows.

Jokul											*Norse*

A Frost Giant; god of glaciers; brother of Drifta, Frosti and Snoer.

Joseph of Arimathea											*British*

In myth, he is regarded as Christ's uncle and is said to have collected the blood issuing from the wound in Christ's side pierced by the centurion's spear at the Crucifixion and to have laid Christ's body in the tomb at Gethsemane after he had been taken down from the cross.

In later years he is said to have come to Britain bringing with him the chalice, the Holy Grail, which had contained the blood of Christ, and the Holy Lance.

Some stories say that he once brought Jesus and Mary to Britain. Other stories say that he became king of Norway after driving the Saracens from that country and marrying the daughter of the former king. His greatest pleasure was fishing and he became the Fisher King.

Josephus											*British*

A priest, son of Joseph of Arimathea. He was imprisoned with some of his followers by the cruel king, Caudel, but released when Evelake brought an army to rescue him and Caudel was killed. It was said that he came to Britain with Evelake and built the Castle of Carbonek where the Holy Grail was kept.

In some accounts, he and his party crossed the seas floating on the outspread shirt of Josephus.

joshi											*Japanese*

The pre-ordained 'death of love'. Lovers who broke promises of marriages in one life may well find themselves prevented from marrying in a later life and may then commit suicide together in the hope that they may meet and marry in an even later existence.

jotun											*Norse*

also jotunn (*plural* jotnar)

A giant; in plural, a race of giants.

Jotunheim											*Norse*

The land of the giants.

Jove *see* **Jupiter**

Judgement of Paris											*Greek*

At the wedding of Peleus and Thetis, at which many gods were present, the uninvited Eris (goddess of discord) tossed a golden apple, inscribed 'To the fairest', into the assembly. There was a great dispute as to which goddess should claim the title and Paris, son of Priam, king of Troy, was asked to decide which of the three goddesses, Aphrodite, Athena and Hera, was the most beautiful. He gave the prize, a golden apple, to Aphrodite because she promised him the most beautiful girl in the world – Helen of Troy – so setting the scene for the Trojan War.

Juggernaut *see* **Jagannath**

Jugumishanta   *Pacific Islands*
The first woman in the lore of the people of Vanuatu. She made her husband Morufonu from her own body and they built the islands of the Pacific from their own excrement.

Jui Chu   *Chinese*
A pearl which makes every wish come true.

Jui-ch'ing-fu-jen   *Chinese*
also Noble Lady of Felicity
A household goddess; wife of Ch'ang-sheng-t'u-ti. She is responsible for promoting happiness in the house.

Julius Caesar   *British*
A Roman emperor. In Arthurian legend, a contemporary of King Arthur whose court the sorcerer Merlin visited in the form of a

deer. In some accounts, he is the father of Oberon, king of the fairies by the sorceress Morgan le Fay.

In the Charlemagne stories, he was said to be the father of Oberon by Glorianda, a fairy.

Jumala   *Baltic*
A supreme god of the Finns and Lapps. Originally a creative force in the early universe, Jumala came to be regarded as the later Ukko, the sky god.

In some accounts he is the same as Ilmarinen.

jumart   *French*
A monster, offspring of a bull and a mare or of a stallion and a cow.

jumby *see* **duppy**

Juok   *African*
A creator-god of the Shilluk and Nuer peoples of South Sudan. He is said to have made black people from the soil of the Sudan and brown ones from the sands of Egypt. When he got tired of making people, he gave them sexual organs so that they could reproduce themselves.

Juno   *Roman*
also Great Goddess, Queen of Heaven
= *Etruscan* Uni; *Greek* Hera

Goddess of childbirth, light, marriage; one of the Olympians; sister and wife of Jupiter; mother of Mars and Vulcan.

Jupiter seduced her in the form of a cuckoo and later married her. Jealous when Jupiter produced the goddess Minerva from his head, she complained to Flora who made her pregnant at the touch of a magic herb to produce a son, Mars.

Her festival is Matronalia, held on March 1st. Her bird is the peacock.

Jupiter   *Roman*
also Jove, Jupiter Optimus Maximus 'Jupiter the Best and Greatest'; Sky Father;
= *Etruscan* Tinia; *Egyptian* Amon; *Greek* Zeus
Supreme god and god of the moon, rain, sky, sun and thunder; son of Saturn and Ops; brother of Neptune; brother and consort of Juno.

Jurojin   *Japanese*
A god of long life, one of the seven Shinto deities of fortune, the Shichi Fukujin. He is depicted with a staff and book and riding on, or attended by, a deer.

K

K *Central American*
A Mayan deity of uncertain identity, referred to as God K (*see **alphabetical gods***); perhaps Ah Bolom Tzacab, Itzamna, Kukulcan or Lakin Chan. He is depicted with a tapir-like snout.

ka *Egyptian*
A person's double or genius, a vital force; one of the five essential parts comprising the individual. This creative force was thought to live on after the death of the individual and therefore needed sustenance which was provided in the form of offerings of food, etc.

Ka-Khu-Khat *Egyptian*
The triad of spirit, soul and body.

Kaang *African*
The supreme god of the Bushmen. He was swallowed by an ogre but was vomited up unharmed. When he died after being pricked by thorns, the agents of Gauna, the ants, ate all the flesh from his bones but he resurrected himself. He is said to have made the moon from an old shoe and can turn his shoes into dogs which attack his enemies.

All his power resides in one of his teeth and he operates through the agency of the caterpillar and the mantis.

Kabandha *Hindu*
A headless monster or serpent-god; son of the goddess Devi. He is described as having his face on his stomach, one eye in his chest and eight-mile-long arms on which, having no legs, he walked.

He was killed by the god Rama who was pursuing the demon-king Ravana who had abducted Rama's wife, Sita, and from his ashes came Gandharvaa who helped Rama against Ravana.

Ka'cak *Inuit*
A female sea-spirit who devours the bodies of the drowned.

Kachina *North American*
also Katchina
A spirit of an ancestor in the lore of the Pueblo Indians. These beings are said to live on the earth in winter and in the underworld in summer. Some say they live in lakes.

The chief priest will wear a mask of a god during ceremonial dances and, while so engaged, becomes the god himself.
(*See also **Katsinas***.)

Kadmos *see* **Cadmus**

Kalliope *see* **Calliope**

Kagu-hana *Japanese*
A double-faced male head. This object, capable of detecting misdeeds by smell, assists Emma-O in the judgement of souls in the underworld. It is placed on the left of the god's throne and smells everything.

Kaguya *Japanese*
also Kaguni
A moon-maiden. She was found as a baby on Mount Fuji by a bamboo-cutter, Sanugi, as he was cutting bamboo. She was only four inches tall but perfectly formed and grew into a beautiful maiden who set near-impossible tasks for the five nobles who were suitors for her hand, none

of whom succeeded. She became the consort of the emperor but had to reject him for she knew that she was an immortal and had to return to her home in the heavens. A company of moon-folk descended in a cloud and, wrapping her in the Feather Robe that erased the memory of her life on earth, took her back to the moon. She left behind a magic mirror in which her husband might always see her image.

Kahausibware   *Pacific Islands*

A creator-goddess and serpent-goddess of the Solomon Islands. She created all living things and, when the first baby was born to the woman she had created, the goddess took the form of a snake to rear the child. When the boy cried, the snake crushed it to death and the mother then killed the snake.

Kahiki   *Pacific Islands*

The home of spirits in the sky; the home of ancestors.

Kahit   *North American*

A wind god of the Wintun tribe of California. He is envisaged in the form of a bat.

When the first world was destroyed by the fire started by Buckeye Bush and two others, Kahit and the goddess Mem Loomis were given the task of putting out the fires and restarting the world.

Kahk   *North American*

A crow. In the lore of the Yuma people of Arizona, this bird brought seeds from all corners of the earth for them to cultivate.

Kai   *British*

also Kay

A steward to King Arthur. He grew as tall as a tree and had the ability to live for nine days

under water. It was perhaps he who originally refused to allow Culhwch to enter Arthur's court but was later a companion of Culhwch in his quest for the hand of Olwen.

In later stories he becomes Kay, one of the Knights of the Round Table.

Kaia   *Pacific Islands*

Demons in New Britain folklore. Originally the creators of all things, Kaia are now evil beings living underground and appearing on the surface in the form of snakes.

Kaiba   *Japanese*

A sea-horse. This fabulous beast was said to have the head of a goat but with a single horn, a thick curly tail and a shell on its back like the carapace of a turtle.

Kaibutsu   *Japanese*

Imaginary animals with three sharp talons on each paw, heavy beards and stumpy tails.

Kaikai   *South American*

A supernatural serpent. The Araucanians say that this huge serpent, and another called Trentren, caused the Flood.

Kaistowanea   *North American*

A monster in the form of a two-headed lake-serpent. In the lore of the Iroquois, this beast was caught, when young, by a boy fishing. It grew so large that the boy, now a brave, had to kill bear and deer to feed it.

Kaitabha   *Hindu*

A demon. He was born, with Madhu, another demon, from the ear of the god Vishnu. When they attacked the sleeping god Brahma and, some say, stole the Vedas (holy books), Vishnu killed them both. Brahma used their bodies to build the earth.

Kaka-Guia   *African*

A bull-headed god in Guinea. He is the conductor of the souls of the dead.

Kakaitch   *North American*

= *Chinook* Hahness; *Nootka* Tu-tutsh

The Thunderbird of the Macah tribe. His tongue causes lightning and he eats whales.

Kakuriyo   *Japanese*

The spirit world; the world after death.

kala   *Siberian*

plural kalau

These beings are sent by the supreme god to bring death and disease to mankind. Some of them live on earth and cause illness by breathing on people; some live underground, emerging to bite people, gouge out pieces of their flesh or knock them on the head, causing headaches.

They are generally invisible but can appear as humans with pointed heads or as animals.

They are the perpetual adversaries of the creator-god Quikinna'qu.

kalaloa   *Pacific Islands*

The soul, in the lore of the Philippines. The soul is envisaged as being in two parts, one on each side of the body. When a person dies, the right-hand kakaloa goes to heaven, the left-hand one goes to the underworld known as Kilot.

Kaleva   *Baltic*

= *Estonian* Kalevi

In Finnish lore, the ancestor of the cultural heroes whose stories appear in the *Kalevala*.

Kalevala   *Baltic*

Finnish epic stories of the heroes and creation. The 50 parts, over 20,000 lines, were compiled by Elias Lonrot in 1849 following a shorter version published in 1835.

Kali   *Hindu*
also Devi, Kumari, Mahadevi, the
Black One
A plague goddess, goddess of
  death; an aspect of Devi as 'the
  Black One'; consort of Shiva. She
  was said to have sprung from the
  forehead of Durga.
  Sent to earth, she fought the
  demon Raktavija and, when 1000
  giants grew from each drop of
  blood he spilled, she killed him,
  with the help of the seven copies
  she made of herself known as the
  Matrikas, and drank his blood. In
  her frenzy, she killed Shiva and
  danced on his body.
  She is depicted as a hideous,
  five-headed being standing on
  Shiva's body, holding a sword in
  one of her four (or ten) hands and
  a severed head in another or as
  standing in a boat which floats
  in a sea of blood, drinking blood
  from a skull.

kali-yuga   *Hindu*
The age of iron, the fourth and
  present age of the world. This
  age, in which wars are rife
  and possessions become more
  important than righteousness, is
  due to last for another 400,000
  years. (*See also* **yuga**.)

Kalika   *Buddhist*
One of the Eighteen Lohan. He is
  depicted as having eyebrows so
  long that they reach the ground.

Kalma   *Baltic*
A Finnish goddess of death. She
  normally lived in the realm of
  Tuonela but occasionally came
  into the realms of the living to
  seize the dead.
  In some accounts, Kalma is
  male.

kalpa[1]   *Hindu*
also Day of Brahma
A day in the life of the god Brahma,

equal to 4,320 million human
  years or 1000 mahayugas; a day
  and night equal to 8,640 million
  human years; an age of the world.

Kalpa[2]   *Jain*
One of the upper realms of the
  universe. This region is made up
  of sixteen separate heavens or
  Devalokas.

Kalpathitha   *Jain*
One of the upper realms of the
  universe. This region is made up
  of fourteen separate dwellings for
  the deities.

Kalpavrksha   *Jain*
also Kalpavriksha
The trees that provided all human
  needs in the early ages.

Kaltesh   *Siberian*
A fertility goddess. She appears as a
  goose or sometimes as a hare.

Kalunga   *African*
A giant creator-god and fertility
  god in Namibia; king of the
  underworld.
  In some accounts,
  Kalungangombe is the king of the
  underworld and Kalunga is his
  realm, sometimes vice versa.
  In neighbouring Angola,
  Kalunga is the creator-god who
  made the first man, Nambalisita.
  The African god was
  transported to Brazil and
  worshipped as a sea god.

Kalvaistis   *Baltic*
= *Greek* Hephaestus; *Roman* Vulcan
A Lithuanian smith-god. He is said
  to make the sun anew each day.

Kama   *Hindu*
also Kamadeva;
= *Buddhist* Madhukara; *Greek* Eros
God of love. One account of his
  origin has him born from the
  heart of Brahma at the birth of
  the universe and, like Eros, he fires
  arrows to inflame the passions of
  those they strike. His bow-string

is said to be a string of bees and
  he carries five arrows, each with
  its own designation – Carrier
  of Death, Exciter, Infatuator,
  Inflamer and Parcher.
  When he interrupted Shiva's
  meditation, he was burned to a
  cinder by the fierceness of the
  god's third eye but he was born
  again as Pradyumna, son of
  Krishna and Rukmini.
  He is depicted as having three
  heads and three-eyes and may be
  riding on a parrot or a peacock.

Kama-loka   *Buddhist*
One of the three regions of the
  universe, the world of desire; the
  after-death state of purgation.
  (*See also* **Kamadhatu, Tri-loka**.)

Kamadhatu   *Hindu*
The realm of worldly desire. (*See also*
  Kama-loka.)

Kamak   *Persian*
A huge bird whose wings prevented
  the rain from reaching earth;
  killed by the semi-divine hero
  Keresaspa.

Kamalamitra   *Hindu*
A sun hero. When he boasted of his
  wife's beauty, the gods separated
  them and he was forced to
  traverse the skies daily in search
  of her.

Kamapua'a   *Pacific Islands*
The hog-child god of Hawaii. He
  appeared first as a black fish but,
  when he came ashore, became
  a huge hog. Despite his hog-like
  figure and snout, he had human
  hands in which he could, and
  did, wield a club to defeat his
  enemies.
  He used his snout to push up
  land from the bottom of the sea
  to make a home for mankind.
  The giant Limaloa once tried
  to kill him but, when Kamapua'a
  turned into a handsome youth,

they became great friends. In this form, Kamapua'a tried to win Pele, the fire goddess. She rejected him and the ensuing battle between her forces and his ended only when she yielded to his embraces.

Kame *South American*
= *Arawak* Kamu

A culture-hero of the Bakairi Indians, the moon personified; son of the jaguar spirit Oka.

The mother of the twin brothers Kame and Keri conceived them by swallowing two bones. Her mother-in-law killed her but the two children were saved. The brothers pushed up the sky to make room for people to live and invented fire and water. They also produced all the animals of the earth from a hollow tree and set the sun and moon on their present courses through the sky.

In the lore of the Caingang, Kame's twin brother is known as Kayurukre while the Bororo of Brazil say that the twins were the offspring of Jaguar and the daughter of a chief. Jaguar's mother, a caterpillar, killed the girl by making her laugh until she died. Her husband rescued the twins from her womb and killed the caterpillar by burning her.

kami *Japanese*
also kame

A name given to all Shinto deities; a spirit; the powers of nature.

Kanaloa *Pacific Islands*
The Hawaiian squid-god and creator-god, ruler of the dead.
(*See also* **Ta'aroa, Tagaloa, Tagaro, Tangaloa, Tangaroa.**)

Kananeski Anayehi *North American*
A Cherokee water-spider. This insect is said to have brought fire from underground where lightning had set fire to the roots of a tree.

Kanasoka *Japanese*
A painter. His painting of a horse was so lifelike that the animal came to life. When people complained that the horse was destroying their crops, Kanasoka painted a rope tethering the horse to a post, after which the horse could not wander.

Kanassa *South American*
The creator-god of the Kuikuru tribe of Brazil. He got fire from the sky by capturing a vulture and forcing him to bring down a burning ember.

Kanati *North American*
The first man in the lore of the Cherokee; father of the Thunder Boys.

Kanchil *Pacific Islands*
The mouse-deer, a trickster-hero. In Indonesian lore, this small animal defeats many predators by pretending to magic powers it does not possess, persuading even tigers to live in peace with other animals.

Kane *Pacific Islands*
The creator-god and sky god of Hawaii. With the help of the agriculture and war god Ku and the god of heaven Lono, he made the world and mankind. (*See also* **Tane.**)

Kane-huna-moku *Pacific Islands*
The Hawaiian paradise, an island floating in the sky.

Kanisimbo *African*
A Swahili ancestor. The eldest of the eight people who came down from heaven in a ship.

Kanook *North American*
A god of darkness of the Tlingit people; an evil principle. Brother of Yetl (Raven). He refused to release water for the benefit of mankind, so his brother tricked him into releasing it.

He was envisaged in the form of a wolf.

Kanzibyui *Central American*
A Mayan god. He was charged with the duty of restoring the earth after the Flood and planted trees at the four corners of the earth to support the sky.

Kapoonis *North American*
The lightning-spirit of the tribes of the north-west. (*See more at* **Enumclaw.**)

kappa *Japanese*
A water demon of the Ainu. These beings lived and travelled on flying cucumbers and ate cucumbers and blood. They had a depression on the top of the head which held water. They would challenge travellers to fight and, if the traveller bowed, they would bow in return and the vital liquid ran out and, with it, their strength. The traveller would be afflicted by a wasting disease. They sometimes attacked swimmers, sucking their blood.

In one story, a kappa was captured when it seized a horse and its life was spared only when it promised on oath never again to attack domestic animals.

They are said to have taught humans the art of bone-setting and are depicted as having the body of a tortoise with the legs of a frog and the head of a monkey.

Karei *Malay*
A thunder god. This large and invisible creator uses thunder to indicate his disapproval of man's actions, causing the guilty party to atone for his sins by self-mutilation, mixing his blood with water and throwing it heavenwards.

Kari *Norse*
A Frost Giant; god of tempests. With his brothers Aegir and Loki, he formed a trinity of early gods.

karkadann   *Arabian*
A monster, part unicorn, part rhinoceros, sometimes winged.

karliki   *Russian*
singular karlik
Dwarfs. They were originally spirits that fell from heaven into the underworld when Satan was expelled. There are a number of varieties including Domoviks, Leshi, Vodyanoi and Vozdushnui.

Karshipta   *Persian*
A bird sent out by the first man, Yima, to look for survivors after the Flood. This bird, said to be able to speak, was also sent out to spread the teachings of Ahura Mazda.

Karwan   *North American*
A kachina of the Pueblo tribes, a nature-spirit of maize.

Karyobinga   *Buddhist*
A being half woman, half bird. This creature is depicted with the head and body of a woman, the legs, claws, wings and tail of a bird.

Kasogonaga   *South American*
The rain goddess of the Chaco Indians. She is said to appear as an ant-eater when she visits the earth.

Kassim Baba   *Arabian*
Brother of Ali Baba in the *Arabian Nights' Entertainments*. He entered the robbers' cave but forgot the magic password and could not escape. The robbers found him and cut him into four pieces which they hung up in the cave. The pieces were found by Ali and stitched together by the cobbler Mustapha Baba.

Katchina *see* **Kachina**

Katkochila   *North American*
A god of the Wintun Indians of California. Somebody stole his magic flute so he set the earth on fire. The Flood came in time to save the world.

Katsinas   *North American*
Pueblo rain-spirits. (*See also* ***Kachina***.)

kaukas   *Baltic*
= *Russian* domovik
A Lithuanian dwarf house spirit, similar to the aitvaras.

Kay   *British*
A Knight of the Round Table and a personal attendant on the king. Foster-brother of Arthur.

When Kay left behind his sword just before the gathering of nobles to elect a new king, Arthur rode back to fetch it but failed to find it. He then decided that Kay should have the sword which, set in an anvil and a block of stone, had appeared in the churchyard, and pulled it out with ease. When he handed it to Kay, the assembly realised that it was he, Arthur, who was destined to become king of Britain.

Once, when King Arthur was entrapped by the sorceress Annowre, Kay saved the king from death at her hands and killed her.

He was said to have killed Lachere, one of the king's sons, but he helped Arthur in his fight with the giant of Mont Saint Michel and killed Palug's Cat, a monstrous animal that had eaten 180 soldiers on Anglesey.

He was one of the many knights captured and imprisoned by Turkin, who hated all Arthur's knights, until rescued by Lancelot. When freed, he followed his rescuer and that night, as Kay slept, Lancelot donned his armour and rode off. In this guise, Lancelot defeated Gawter, Gilmere and Raywold and then Ector, Ewain, Gawain and Sagramore, so that Kay's reputation as a warrior was enhanced.

When Arthur conquered much of the Continent, Kay was left in charge of Anjou.

In the Welsh stories he is Cei or Kai, son of Cynyr, who grew as tall as a tree and had the ability to live for nine days and nights under water. He also generated so much heat that he remained dry in the heaviest downpour and could keep his comrades warm in winter and any burden he carried could never be seen. The knight Peredur vowed to avenge some ill-treatment by Kay and when, some time later, Kay met Peredur in single combat, he was defeated and broke an arm and shoulder.

He was one of the band of Arthur's men who helped Culhwch in his quest for the hand of Olwen and, in the guise of a sword-maker, entered the fort of Gwrnach the giant, killed him and took the sword which Culhwch had been instructed to get by Olwen's father Ysbaddaden. He also trapped the warrior Dillus and pulled out his facial hairs to make the leash which was another of the tasks Culhwch had been set.

(*See also* ***Kai***.)

Kay Kaus   *Persian*
A mythical king. He led an army to rid the land of demons but the leader of the demons, Diw-e-Safid, pelted the army with stones from above and took prisoner Kay Kaus, who had been blinded by the stones. He was later rescued by the great hero, Rustem, who cured the king's blindness. When the king, riding an eagle, pursued some of the demons to their stronghold in the mountains, God caused him to fall down the mountain.

His second wife, Sudabe, accused Siyawush, the king's son by his first wife, of making advances, though it was she who was guilty of trying to seduce the young prince. Siyawush fled from the palace but was killed by the demon Afrasiyab.

He was tempted by the evil demons, the Mazainyon, to take over the kingdom of heaven and tried to fly by tethering an eagle to each corner of his throne and urging them on with lumps of meat held in front of them on spears. He failed in the attempt and would have been killed by the god Ahura Mazda's messenger, Nairyosangha, but the spirit of his yet-to-be-born grandson, Kay Khusraw, pleaded for his life and saved him.

He ruled for fifty years before the usurper, Kay Khusraw, took over the throne.

Kazikamuntu   *African*
The first man, according to the lore of the Banyarwanda.

K'daai Maqsin   *Siberian*
In the lore of the Yakuts, a smith-god in the underworld. He is said to have introduced shamans and is regarded as the tutelary deity of blacksmiths. To make iron hard he tempers it in the blood of a lion, a young man and a maiden and tears of a seal.

He is envisaged as covered in a thick layer of dirt and rust, with closed eyes. It takes eight men above and eight below to pull his eyelids apart so that he can see.

Keagyihl Depguesk *North American*
A whirlpool. This whirlpool had claimed the lives of many young men so the tree-spirit, Hanging Hair, called a meeting in Festival House of all the river-spirits, who

agreed to curb its power. The storm spirit blew part of a cliff into the river, so diverting the flow of water and reducing the whirlpool to a gentle eddy.

Keen Kings   *Australian*
A race of men with wings. These evil beings, built like tall humans with bat-like wings attached to their arms and with only two fingers and a thumb on each hand, lived in a huge cage where, in a hole in the floor, the Flame God lived. They captured humans and sacrificed them to this god but all of them fell into the hole and were consumed by the the flames when the Winjarning Brothers led them in a frenzied dance.

Kekeko   *East Indies*
A fabulous bird, which can talk and also provides food for orphans.

Kekewage   *Pacific Islands*
The keeper of the Melanesian afterworld, Bevebweso. He and his wife Sinebomatu care for the spirits of dead children until their parents also die and can look after them.

Kelets   *Siberian*
A demon of death in the lore of the Chukchee. He is said to have a pack of dogs with which he hunts and kills men.

kelpie   *Scottish*
= *Irish/Scottish* each uisge; *Manx* cabyll ushtey
A spirit in the form of a water horse. He lures people to ride on his back, runs into the water to drown them and then eats them.

Kere'tkun   *Siberian*
The supreme sea spirit. He is said to devour the bodies of the drowned.

Kerema Apo   *East Indies*
The first man, in Papuan lore. He

was hatched from the egg of a huge turtle and mated with Ivi Apo, the first woman, who was born from another egg.

keres   *Greek*
singular ker
Female underworld spirits; winged creatures controlling destiny; souls of the dead. These beings are said to cause disease among the living and to carry off the bodies of the dead. Some say that they escaped from Pandora's box. They are envisaged as tiny human figures rather like gnats.

kerrighed   *French*
Devilish spirits in France. (*See also* ***corrigan***.)

Ketchimanetowa   *North American*
also Great Spirit
The creator-god of the Fox tribe. (*See also* **Great Spirit**.)

Kewanambo   *East Indies*
A man-eating ogre of Papua. This demon often appears in the guise of a kindly woman who lures children from their homes.

Khadir   *Arabian*
The original Khadir was born in Persia in 1077 and died in 1166. He was a prophet who became immortal after drinking from the Well of Life, the only mortal allowed to do so. It is said that he could speak every language.

He accompanied Alexander the Great into a cave in search of the well. He used a jewel to guide them but they became separated and Khadir stumbled in the darkness and fell into the well. As a result of drinking from the well, he turned a bluish-green colour. He managed to find his way out of the cave and is said to be still alive, wandering the face of the earth, returning once every 500 years to the same place.

Once when he was captured, his chains turned to dust, and when Hakim, brother of the king of Ethiopia, threw a spear at him, God deflected it so that it struck Hakim. On another occasion, the swords of soldiers ordered to kill the prophet turned against the soldiers and killed them.

When the king of Borneo, Jantam, gave his daughter to Alexander as a wife, Khadir used his magic to fill the king's storehouse with treasure.

In another version, Khadir was cook to Alexander the Great on his expedition into the desert. As he washed a dried fish in a pool, prior to cooking it for his master's supper, the fish came to life and swam away. Khadir drank some of the water and, as in other versions, turned green and became immortal. Alexander wanted to achieve immortality himself but the pool could no longer be found and he would have killed the cook had he not been invulnerable. He finally threw the unfortunate Khadir, weighted with stones, into the sea, whereupon Khadir turned into a sea god, still immortal.

His clear judgement was demonstrated when, having smashed a boat, killed a youth and rebuilt a wall, he explained that the boat was destined to be captured by pirates, the youth to become an evil man and the wall contained much treasure that would now go to two orphans and not to the greedy tenant.

Khadir is depicted as a young man but nevertheless with white hair and beard.

Khara   *Persian*
A huge donkey. This beast,

described as having only three legs but six eyes (two of which are on top of its head and two in its hump) stands in the sea called Vourukasha and is said to be able to overcome all forms of evil. In some accounts, Khara is described as a primeval fish.

Kharasvara   *Jain*
Gods of the underworld. These beings torture the wicked dead by forcing their bodies into thorn-bushes.

Khepra   *Egyptian*
A scarab-headed sun god, a manifestation of the god Ra as the morning sun.

He was regarded as a self-created creator-god, rising out of Nun, the god of the primeval waters, who, merely by saying his name, created a solid place on which he could stand, and created Shu and Tefnut. He was later assimilated with Ra, the sun god. In some accounts, he was the son of Nut who swallowed her son each evening only for him to be born again each morning.

In another version, one of his eyes wandered across the sky each day as the sun and was brought back to him by Shu and Tefnut.

In the form of a scarab, he fought the demons of the abyss from which he had emerged.

He was said to have made the world by rolling his own spittle into a ball.

Khnum   *Egyptian*
also Lord of the Afterworld
A ram-headed creator-god, god of the cataracts; one of the three Lords of Destiny (with Amen and Ptah).

He is said to have made gods and humans from mud from the Nile or from clay on a potter's

wheel and was guardian of the grotto where Hapi lived on the island of Bigeh.

He is sometimes depicted as ram-headed or as a serpent.

Kholumulumo   *African*
A monster of the Sotho people. He ate all humans except one woman, whose son, Moshanyana, killed the monster when it got jammed in a narrow pass, slit open its belly and released the imprisoned people.

Khonvum   *African*
The supreme god of the Pygmies. He made the first pygmies in the sky and lowered them down to earth on ropes.

Khosodam   *Siberian*
A cannibalistic female ruler of the dead. She was said to have created mosquitoes.

Khrodadevatas   *Buddhist*
A group of fearsome gods. These beings are depicted as red or black, with three eyes and with skulls and snakes adorning their bodies.

Khuran-Nojon   *Siberian*
A Buriat rain-deity. He stores rain in barrels each of which, when opened, causes rain to fall for three days.

Kibu   *Pacific Islands*
The Melanesian land of the dead. This land is envisaged as an island in the west. When the soul (mari) reaches Kibu, it is turned into a proper ghost of the dead when it is struck on the head with a stone club. It is then a markai and can learn about life in Kibu.

Kici Manitou   *North American*
The supreme god of the Algonquin people. He created the world from mud collected by birds and dried in his sacred pipe. His staff forms the central support for the world.

Kidilli   *Australian*
A moon-man of the Aborigines.
When he tried to rape the first
woman, he was killed by Kurukadi
and Mumba, the lizard-men of
the Dreamtime.

Kikazaru   *Japanese*
One of the Three Mystic Apes. He is
depicted with his hands covering
his ears as 'he who hears no evil'.

Killer-of-Enemies *North American*
A culture-hero or minor deity of
the Apache and Navaho; son of
Changing Woman and brother of
Child-of-the-Water and Wise One.
He and his brothers killed monsters
and all the enemies of mankind.

He is credited with the creation
of the horse, in which he used
the wing of a bat to form the
diaphragm.

kilot   *Pacific Islands*
The underworld, in some parts
of the Philippines. This place is
regarded as the home of the
left-hand kalaloa (soul); the
right-hand soul goes to a heaven
in the sky.

Kinderbrunnen   *German*
Wells in which, it is said, Frau Holle
guards the souls of children.
Kinderseen are lakes in which,
it is said, she similarly guards
children's souls.

Kindly Ones *see* **Eumenides**

Kindred Gods   *North American*
also Related Ones
Four gods of the Sioux. These
deities are given as Buffalo,
Four Winds, Two-legged and
Whirlwind, all aspects of the god
Wakan Tanka.

King Cole *see* **Coel**

King Lir *see* **Lir**

King of Cows   *Chinese*
An ugly ogre, protector of cattle.

King of Horses   *Chinese*
An ugly ogre. This being is depicted

with four hands and three eyes
and is revered by horse-breeders.

King of the Wood   *Roman*
The priest of Diana at Lake Nemi,
a short distance south of Rome.
The first of these was the god
Virbius, and the succession went
to a runaway slave or gladiator
who fought the incumbent
with a branch of a tree in the
surrounding grove.

Kings of Hell *see* **Ten Yama
   Kings**

kingfisher   *Greek*
The bird of Thetis. Some say that
this bird's beak always indicates
the direction of the wind and
that its dead body can be used to
divert thunderbolts.

It was said that it was originally
grey in colour and acquired its
brilliant colouring when it flew
near the sun while surveying the
waters after the Flood.

Kingu   *Mesopotamian*
An Akkadian earth god. He was the
leader of the evil primal forces and
the Eleven Mighty Helpers in the
struggle with the gods and acted
as holder of the Tablets of Destiny.

He was the son and second
husband of Tiamat and was killed
with her in the fight with Marduk.
In some accounts, his blood
was mixed with sand to make
mankind. Some equate him with
Tammuz.

Kinharingan   *East Indies*
A creator-god in Borneo. It is said
that Kinharingan and his wife
Munsumundok appeared out
of a rock in the sea, walking on
the water to the home of the
small-pox god Bisagit who gave
them some soil with which they
made the earth. They then made
the sky, the heavenly bodies and
human beings.

Kinharingan killed his first
son and cut his body into pieces
which he planted in various
places. From these pieces came all
the plants and animals.

One version says that Bisagit
gave them the soil on condition
that he could have half of the
people that Kinharingan made. He
achieved this by spreading smallpox through the population at 40
year intervals.

Kinnara   *Thai*
A monster, half man, half bird.

kinno   *South American*
In the lore of the Tupari of Brazil,
the people who failed to reach
the upper world.

Two primordial beings, Aroteh
and Tovapod, dug into the
earth to find the people who
had stolen their food and, in
so doing, created an opening
through which some humans,
at that time living under the
earth, escaped to the upper world.
The kinno were those that were
trapped when the hole was sealed.
It is said that they will emerge to
repopulate the earth when the
present races have all died.

Kintu   *African*
A king-god of the Buganda; the
first man. He went up to heaven
to ask for a wife and was given
Nambi, daughter of the supreme
god, Gulu, but only after he had
passed a number of tests. One
was to eat enough food for a
hundred people; another, to fill a
large, bottomless pot with dew.
He also had to split rocks with
an axe and identify his own cow
in three large herds. He passed
all the tests and took Nambi
back to earth. Her brother,
Walumbe, the god of death
followed them.

kiolu   *African*

A very small animal generated by a sorcerer from his own soul. A sorcerer can cause this animal to enter the body of another person and kill him.

kirin   *Japanese*

= *Chinese* ch'i-lin; *Mongolian* kere; *Tibetan* serou

A single-horned animal, counterpart of the Chinese ch'i-lin; a unicorn.

Kirttimukha   *Hindu*

A lion-headed monster. This being was created by the god Shiva to fight the demon Rahu which had been sent by Jalandhara to seize Shiva's wife, Sakti. When Rahu fled, the voracious monster ate its own body, leaving only the face.

Kisani   *North American*

also Mirage People

The inhabitants of the fourth world through which the Navaho passed on their way to the upper world.

Kisha Manido   *North American*

The Menominee name for the creator god, the Great Spirit. (*See also* **Gitchi Manitou**.)

Kitanitowit   *North American*

A creator god of the Algonquin Indians; a name for the Great Spirit.

Kitchen God   *Chinese*

also Stove God

A deity of the household. Each house has its own spirit which reports to heaven on the family each year.

Kitshi Manitou   *North American*

The Chippewa name for the Great Spirit. (*See also* **Gitchi Manitou**.)

Kivati   *North American*

A trickster-god of the Quinault people of Washington state. He changed the original giant animals into normal animals and made men from balls of dust mixed with his own sweat.

When his brother was swallowed by a monster in the lake, Kivati threw hot rocks into the lake until the scalding water killed the monster, whereupon Kivati slit open its belly and released his brother.

At the end of his world-forming labours, he turned into stone.

Klaus   *German*

also Peter Klaus

A goat-herd. He followed a goat into a valley where twelve men were playing skittles. Overcome by wine, he fell asleep and, when he awoke, found that he had slept for twenty years.

This tale is the inspiration for Washington Irving's story *Rip van Winkle*.

Kloskurbeh   *North American*

A creator-god of the Hopi. A being ('youth') was created from this god's breath and another ('lore') from one of his tears. These two mated to produce the first humans.

klu   *Tibetan*

Ancestors of the race: miracle-workers. (*See also* **'gong-po, rGyal-po**.)

Kmukamtch   *North American*

also Ancient Old Man

A demon; a creator-spirit. In the lore of the Klamath, he tried to set the world on fire, but the Medoc regard him as a creator-spirit.

knaninjar   *Australian*

Ancestors living as spirits in the sky.

Knecht Ruprecht   *German*

A domestic fairy.

Knight of the Cart, Knight of the Chariot *see* **Lancelot**

Knight of the Lion *see* **Owain**[1]

Knight of the Swan *see* **Lohengrin**

Knights of Battle   *British*

Three famous warriors of King Arthur's court, Cador, Lancelot and Owain.

Knights of the Round Table

    British

The chosen knights of King Arthur's court.

The Round Table provided places for 150 knights and 100 were sent by Leodegrance with the table as Guinevere's dowry on her marriage to Arthur. Merlin, authorised to find 50 more, found only 28 suitable knights. Each knight took a yearly oath to fight only in just causes and not for personal gain, to protect women and respect their persons, to use force only when necessary, never to commit murder or treason and to grant mercy when it was asked for.

Among these knights, the most honoured were Galahad, Gareth, Gawain, Kay, Lamerock, Lancelot, Mark, Mordred, Palamedes, Percival, Torre and Tristram. Others included were Accolon, Bleoberis, Bedivere, Bors, Dornar, Ector, Gaheris, Galahaut, Lionel, Marhaus, Owain, Pelleas, Pellimore, Sagramore and Vanoc.

knocker   *British*

= *German* kobold

A Cornish spirit of the tin-mines, said to indicate the presence of valuable ore; a form of bucca.

kobold   *German*

= *British* brownie, knocker

A dwarf mine-spirit; a domestic brownie.

Koftarim   *Egyptian*

A mythical king. It is said that he built the Pharos lighthouse and a gateway which, by staring with mechanical eyes, could put animals to sleep; and was the owner of a magical mirror in which he could see what each of his subjects was doing and a statue made of glass which could turn into clay any person who tried to gain entry to the king's treasury.

Kohin   *Australian*

A thunder god who lives in the Milky Way. A culture-hero of the Aborigines.

Koko   *African*

In Bantu lore, an old woman who knew the name of the tree bearing forbidden fruit. When she finds that animals to whom she has told the name of this tree have eaten some of its fruit, she punishes them. Tortoise, who had been buried in an anthill, escaped without punishment.

Kokumthena   *North American*

also Our Grandmother, Snaggletooth Woman

A creator-goddess of the Shawnee. This deity is said to be an old, grey-haired woman living with her grandson and her dog near the land of the dead. The shadows on the moon are said to be Kokumthena bending over her cooking-pot.

Kokyangwuti   *North American*

also Spider Woman

A creator-goddess of the Hopi. She made men and women from clay and brought them to life but they were rougher characters than those fashioned by the Huruing Wuhti sisters.

Others say that she made the first humans from spittle and dust in a kind of underworld. When her father flooded their world because they had become wicked, she led them to the upper world. Here she created two more beings,

Palongwhoya and Poquanghoya, who protected humans from evil demons.

(*See also* **Hahai Wugti**.)

kollo   *African*

also qollo

Ethiopian spirits of the mountains, trees and springs. These spirits appear in the form of four-horned cockerels or as tall, one-legged beings.

Koloowise   *Central American*

also Serpent of the Sea;

= *Aztec* Quetzalcoatl; *Hopi* Palulukon

A Zuni plumed serpent god of plenty; a god of lightning. In one story he was upset when a young maiden polluted the water he lived in by washing her clothes there and turned himself into a baby which she found and took home with her. There he resumed his former shape as a serpent and slept with her. Now committed to his power, she was forced to leave her family and go with Koloowise who, en route, changed into a handsome young man.

Komdei-mirgan   *Russian*

A Tartar hero. The monster Yebegen bit off Komdei-mirgan's head and his sister, Kubaiko, went down to the underworld to plead with the ruler, Erlik Khan, for its return. The god set her a number of tasks and gave her the head and some water of life when she completed the tasks successfully.

Komokwa   *North American*

A sea god of the Haida people. He is regarded as the guardian of seals and the receiver of the souls of the dead.

Kon-tiki *see* **Viracocha**

Kononatoo   *South American*

A creator-god of the Arawak Indians. He made man to live in the sky but the hunter-hero

Okonorote made a hole and they all came down to earth. When a fat woman got stuck in the hole, they found themselves unable to return.

Kornmutter   *German*

'corn mother'

A field spirit, the spirit of growing corn.

Kornwolf   *German*

'corn wolf'

A spirit of the cornfields invoked to frighten children.

korrigan, korriganed *see* **corrigan**

Kothluwalawa   *North American*

A celestial palace, in the lore of the Zuni, mountain home of the gods. This palace is a council chamber of the gods and a temporary abode for the spirits of the dead. It also contains the dance-house of the gods.

Kottche   *Australian*

A demon in the form of a bird or a snake. He goes about at night causing illness. His voice is the thunder, his breath the whirlwind.

Koyorowen   *Australian*

A cannibalistic monster. He lives on mountain tops and kills women while his wife Kurriwilban kills men. Her feet point to the rear.

kraken   *Norwegian*

A sea monster which pulled ships to the sea-bottom. It was said to be 1½ miles in circumference.

Kralj Matjaz   *Slovene*

'King Mathias', king of the Slovenes. He is said to have rescued his wife and sister Alencica from the Turks or, in other accounts, from the underworld.

In death, he is said to be sleeping in a cave on Mount Petra, awaiting a call in his country's hour of need. When that day arrives, he will emerge from his cave and hang his shield on a lime tree which, they say, grew on Christmas night, flowered at midnight and then died. It will flower again only when this hero emerges from his long sleep.

krasnoludi   *European*

= *Hungarian* lutki; *Serbian* ludki

Dwarfs of the Polish underworld.

Kremara   *Polish*

A god of pigs. He protected pigs from birth to death, taking over from Priparchis who ensured that they were safely born.

Krimhild   *German*

A princess of Burgundy, the *Nibelungenlied* version of Grimhild.

She fell in love with Siegfried when he came to the court of her brother, Gunther, to help him defeat the invading armies of Ludegar the Saxon and Ludegast of Denmark. When Gunther married Brunhild, Krimhild married Siegfried and later Gunther invited the young couple to his court where the two ladies had a furious quarrel. Krimhild foolishly told the Burgundian knight Hagen, who was angry at the perceived insult to Brunhild, that the only vulnerable spot on Siegfried's body was just between his shoulder-blades and, when Siegfried made a further visit to the court to help Gunther repel a purported invasion, he was killed by Hagen who speared him in the back.

When the dead body of Siegfried bled where Hagen touched it at the funeral, she knew that he was her husband's murderer and plotted revenge. She persuaded Gunther to claim the Nibelung treasure that Siegfried had won when he killed the dragon Fafnir, but the hoard

was seized by Hagen who sank it in the Rhine for safety.

Krimhild later married Etzel, king of the Huns, and bore a son, Ortlieb, but kept alive her loathing for Hagen. She persuaded Etzel to invite Gunther and his nobles to his court and then bribed Brodelin, Etzel's brother, to kill all the Burgundians. When the first attack left some of the visitors alive, she burned down the hall where they still held out. She forced Rudiger, a knight at Etzel's court, to attack them and many were slaughtered on each side, including Rudiger. In the end, only Gunther and Hagen remained alive and they were captured. She had Gunther beheaded and used his severed head to try to force Hagen to disclose where in the Rhine he had hidden the Nibelung treasure. When he refused, she killed him. Her wanton cruelty so enraged Hildebrand who was present at the murder that he drew his sword and killed her.

Krimibhoja   *Hindu*

A realm of hell. This region is reserved for the selfish, who are turned into worms which eat one another.

Krishna   *Hindu*

Earth god and preserver; the 8th incarnation of Vishnu.

He was born from a black hair of Vishnu with a mission to destroy the evil tyrant Kansa. When Kansa ordered the slaughter of all new-born males, Krishna escaped by being secretly hidden with the cowherds, Nanda and Yasoda.

He was constantly harried by demons sent by Kansa but overcame them all. He and his half-brother Balarama did battle with Kansa and killed not only

him and his eight brothers but the huge wrestler Chanura, the demons Arishta and Keshin, the wind-demon Trinavarta, Sakta-Sura who tried to crush him, the demoness Putana who tried to poison him with milk from her breasts, the cow-demon Vatsasura, the huge raven Bakasura, Ugrasura the snake-demon who swallowed him whole, the demon Dhenuka as a huge donkey and Kuvalayapida, the elephant posted to kill them. He also subdued the snake-demon Kaliya. On one occasion, a fire-demon started a forest fire that surrounded Krishna and some of his friends. The god merely swallowed the flames and put the fire out. Other demons killed by Krishna include Jarasandha, Kalayavana and Shankha-Sura.

In the battle between the Pandavas and the Kauravas he acted as charioteer to Prince Arjuna.

When Indra sent a flood, Krishna used Mount Govardhana as a canopy to save the people and their cattle and he rescued his grandson, Aniruddha, when he was seized by the demon, Bana.

He was said to have had affairs with, or married, over 16,000 women but his greatest love was the shepherdess Radha and, later, his wife Rukmini. Some of his other wives were Jambavati, Kalindi and Satyabhama.

When he was accidentally wounded in the only vulnerable part of his body, his heel, by an arrow fired by his brother Jara the Hunter, he died and returned to heaven.

He is sometimes envisaged as the personification of the universe with his navel encompassing the heavens in which his chest represents the stars.

krita-yuga *Hindu*
also Brahma-yuga, satya-yuga
The first age of the world, the golden age in which all men were virtuous. The destruction of the present age by Kali will herald in a new age. (*See also* **Vishnu, yuga**.)

Kronos *see* **Cronus**

Ku *Pacific Islands*
A monster in the form of a huge dog. He could turn himself into a man whenever he wished. In the guise of a small dog, he formed an attachment to Na-pihe-nui, the daughter of a chief, but ran off when her father tried to kill him. He then changed into a handsome prince to woo the maiden but her father refused to sanction the marriage. He next turned himself into a huge fierce dog and ate many of the chief's tribesmen. The warriors of the tribe finally killed him and cut him in half. Each half was turned into a large stone by the priests.

Kuan Yin *Chinese*
= *Buddhist* Avalokiteshvara; *Japanese* K(w)annon; *Taoist* Tou Mu
A Buddhist mother-goddess, goddess of mercy, the North Star, seamen, women and children.

In one version Kuan Yin was a male derived from Avalokiteshvara; in another she was a mortal princess, Maio Shan, who strangled herself but was revivified by Buddha, who put her on an island where she stayed for nine years before she became a deity. Some say that she died as a result of sacrificing her hands and her eyes to save the life of her father, Chong Wang.

Another story says that her

father sentenced her to death when she refused to marry but, when the executioner brought down the sword, it broke, leaving her unharmed. He later had her smothered and she went to hell which was transformed by her presence into a paradise. This did not suit Yama, the ruler of that gloomy place, so he returned her to life.

In some accounts, she was with Tripitaka when he brought the Buddhist culture to China and she released the monkey-god Sun Hou-tzu when Buddha imprisoned him in a mountain.

She is depicted sometimes with many heads and arms, sometimes riding the mythical Hou, a form of lion.

Kuang-jun, Kuang-li, Kuang-she, Kuang-te *see* **Ao Jun, Ao Ch'in, Ao Shun, Ao Kuang**

Kuat *South American*
Sun god of the Mamaiuran Indians of Brazil. *See more at* **Iae**.

Kudai *Russian*
The supreme god of the Tartars. He lives on a golden mountain in the sixteenth heaven and receives sacrifices of white horses.

In some accounts, Kudai refers to the seven sons of the supreme god.

kuei *Chinese*
A spirit of the dead; a wandering demon who has lost the chance of reincarnation.

Some say that the demons, the souls of suicides or of those drowned, have black or green faces.

Another version has the kuei as an animal with only one eye. One story says that the Yellow

Emperor killed it and made a drum from its skin.

Kuei Shen *Chinese*
The tortoise, chief of all the shell animals. One of the Four Auspicious Animals, guardian of the north and of water.

Kugo-jumo *Russian*
A supreme god of the Cheremis, envisaged as a manlike being, carrying on many of the earthly practices such as bee-keeping and agriculture.

Kukitat *North American*
A mischief-making deity of the Serrano people of California. He was born from the left shoulder of the creator, his brother Pakrokitat, and so upset him with his demands that people should have webbed feet, eyes in the back of their heads and suchlike ridiculous ideas that Pakrokitat departed to the otherworld and left his brother in charge. He turned out to be such a troublemaker that the people decided to get rid of him. This they achieved when a frog hid itself in the ocean and swallowed his excrement.

Kuksu *North American*
A creator-god of the Pomo people of California. He and his brother Marumda attempted to destroy the world by fire and flood.

Kuku-Lau *Pacific Islands*
A sea goddess who causes mirages to delude sailors.

Kukulcan *Central American*
= *Aztec* Quetzalcoatl; *Mayan* Yum Caax
A sun god and wind god of the Maya and Toltecs. In some accounts he is a deified king. It is said that he sometimes comes to earth and can be seen planting maize or fishing from his canoe. He is depicted as a

plumed serpent or with a long nose and serpent fangs. His symbols are a fish, maize, a lizard, a torch and a vulture.

Kulimina   *South American*
The creator of women in the lore of the Arawak Indians.

Kuling   *Australian*
The Milky Way, home of the thunder god, Kohin.

Kulshan   *North American*
His wives Clear Sky and Fair Maiden quarrelled and Clear Sky left, setting up her own home far to the south. Later, Fair Maiden left to visit her own mother and she and her children were changed into islands. Kulshan and his three other children, always stretching to try to see the missing women, became mountains while Clear Sky became Mt Rainier.

Kumarbi   *Mesopotamian*
= *Sumerian* Enlil
The supreme god of the Hurrians, creator-god and father of the gods. He castrated his father Anu by biting off his genitals and then spat out three gods, Teshub, Tasmisus and the river god Aranzakh. He married the daughter of a sea god and they produced the monster Hedammu which came out of the sea to devour animals and humans.

When he was overthrown by Teshub, he produced, by impregnating a stone pillar, the giant, Ullikummi to help him, but this being was rendered helpless by the sea god Ea.

Kumari   *Hindu*
A name for Devi.

Kumbhakharna   *Hindu*
A demon. This monster was said to be over 2000 miles tall and could eat 5000 women or 4000 cows at one meal. He was awake for only

one day in every six months but was awake long enough to help the demon Ravana in the battle with the god Rama during which he ate many of Rama's troops but was killed by Rama and Sugriva.

Kumbhika   *Hindu*
A realm of hell, reserved for the punishment of the cruel, who are boiled in oil.

kumi   *Maori*
A bulldog-headed monster.

Kumokums   *North American*
A creator-god of the Modoc people. He created the world with mud that he scooped out of Tule Lake. When he was tired from his labours, he went to sleep in a hole which he dug in the lake-bottom.

Kumu-honua   *Pacific Islands*
The first man in the lore of Hawaii. His wife, Lalo-honua, ate the forbidden fruit of the creator-god Kane's tree and they were both expelled from their garden paradise.

Kumush   *North American*
A creator-god of the Modoc people, father of Evening Sky.

He was given the task of creating the world, using the ashes of the Aurora Borealis and, having built it, populated it with plants and animals. After a long rest, he set about the task of creating mankind. He spent six days and nights in the underworld and returned with a basketful of bones of the dead. From these dry bones he made the various tribes and then ascended into the sky where he lives with his daughter.

K'un Lun *see* **Mount Meru**
Kunapipi   *Australian*
also Old Woman
A mother-goddess of the Aborigines.

Kung Kung   *Chinese*
A demon, half man, half serpent; a god of water. In one story he tilted the world when he impaled Mount Pu Chou on his horn; in another he tried to usurp the throne of the creator-goddess Nü-huang (Nü Kua) and, when he was defeated, knocked down the pillars supporting the sky, thereby causing the Flood. For these crimes he was executed.

An alternative version of the flood story says that Kung Kung tore a hole in the sky, allowing the waters to pour out, damage that was repaired by Nü Kua.

Another version says that he tried to depose his father, the fire god Chu-jung.

Kuni-toko-tachi   *Japanese*
A supreme Shinto god, spirit of the universe, god of Mount Fuji. An ancestor of Izanagi and Izanami who appeared out of the primordial mud as a reed and is manifest in Amaterasu. He lives on Mount Fuji.

Kuni-Tsu-Kami   *Japanese*
Earth gods, as opposed to Ama-tsu-Kami, the gods of heaven.

Kur   *Mesopotamian*
A dragon. He abducted Ereshkigal, goddess of the underworld, and became ruler of the underworld Kur-nu-gi-a with her. He was killed by the gods Enki and Ninurta but his body had held back the primeval waters and now a flood was threatened. The situation was saved when Ninurta, the war god and god of floods and winds, built a wall to hold the waters back.

In some versions, Kur is the underworld.

Kurangai   *New Zealand*
A Maori monster in the form of a bird-woman. She was said to be

as tall as a tree and had wings as well as arms. Some say that her nails were so long that she could spear birds with them.

In one story she carried off the Maori youth Hautupatu who promptly stole her clothes and escaped, only to return to her when he grew up. Another version says that, when he escaped, she followed him and, in trying to recapture him, fell into a hot spring and was scalded to death.

Kurdaitcha　　　　　　*Australian*
Invisible spirits. These beings accompany sorcerers and cause the death of the sick.

Kurkil　　　　　　*Siberian*
A Mongol creator-god, envisaged as a raven.

Kurma　　　　　　*Hindu*
The second incarnation of Vishnu, as a tortoise or turtle. In this incarnation he saved the lost divine drink, amrita. He stood on the bottom of the ocean bearing on his back the mountain, Mount Mandara, that was churned to produce amrita and the other precious objects.

Kurukadi　　　　　　*Australian*
One of the two lizard-men, known as Wati-kutjara, ancestors of the Aborigines. He and his twin Mumba awoke in the Dreamtime and created rocks, plants and animals. When they met Kidilli, the moon-spirit, who was chasing a group of women (or the first woman), they killed him. Kidilli appears in the sky as the moon, the women as the Pleiades and the twins as Gemini.

Kururumany　　　　*South American*
A creator-god in the lore of the Arawak Indians. When he found that men were corrupt, he created snakes and lizards to harass them and took away their immortality.

Kurwaichin　　　　　　*Polish*
A god of sheep.

Kusor　　　　　　*Mesopotamian*
also Kusorhasisu
An artisan-god. His job at creation was to fit windows in the roof of the earth to let rain in.

kut　　　　　　*Siberian*
In the lore of the Yakuts, the soul; the spirit investing all men and all natural objects. The soul, is said to have three parts known as anya-kut, buor-kut and iya-kut.

Kutchis　　　　　　*Australian*
Supernatural beings consulted by Aborigine medicine-men.

Kutkhu　　　　　　*Siberian*
= *Chukchee* Ku'urki; *Koryak* Quikinna'qu
Creator-god of the Kamchadal people of the Kamchatka Peninsula. In some accounts he bought the earth down from heaven, in others he created it from the body of his son.

Kutoyis　　　　　　*North American*
An Algonquin brave. His 'parents' had a son-in-law who treated them very badly, keeping all the meat and skins from the hunt for himself. One day, all he allowed his father-in-law was a drop of blood that he found on the arrow that had killed a buffalo. The old man put the drop of blood into a pot with some water and boiled it. When he opened the pot, he found a baby boy, Kutoyis, who instructed the old man to tie him to the lodge-pole, whereupon he grew to manhood at once. He killed the evil son-in-law and went on to rid the land of many evils before departing forever to the Shadow Land.

Kutso　　　　　　*Hindu*
A protégé of Indra. When Kutso

was fighting the drought demon Sushna, Indra stopped his sun-chariot and pulled off one of the wheels which Kutso then used as a weapon to defeat his enemy.

Ku'urkil　　　　　　*Siberian*
= *Kamchadal* Kutkhu; *Koryak* Quikinna'qu
Creator-god of the Chukchee people; the first human being.

Kuvalayapida　　　　　　*Hindu*
An elephant. The evil king Kansa invited Krishna and his half-brother Balarama to a feast and used this huge animal in one of his attempts to kill his guests. The elephant was killed instead, by Krishna.

Kuvalayaswa　　　　　　*Hindu*
A king. He sent his 21,000 sons to kill the demon Dhundhu who had burnt the saint, Uttanka. All but three of them died in the flames but the survivors killed the demon.

kuwai　　　　　　*Japanese*
An amulet in the form of water-weed, used to guard against fire.

Kuwatawata　　　　　　*Pacific Islands*
A guardian of Pou-Tere-Rangi, the entrance gate of the Polynesian heaven.

Kvasir　　　　　　*Norse*
A sage or god of wisdom. He was made from the saliva of the gods, which they spat into a vase as part of the peace ceremony between the two groups of gods, the Aesir and the Vanir, and in some accounts he is regarded as a god of wisdom.

The dwarfs Fialar and Galar became jealous of Kvasir and wanted to acquire his knowledge, so they killed him in his sleep and drained off his blood into three vessels. They added honey to make a drink which inspired all who partook of it to become poets or musicians.

(*See also* **Bragi**.)

Kwaku Ananse *African*

= *Yoruba* Anansi

The spider-god of the Ashanti.

Kwannon *Japanese*

= *Buddhist* Avalokiteshvara; *Chinese* Kuan Yin

A Buddhist mother-goddess; goddess of mercy, women and children. She is said to have renounced nirvana to bring happiness to others.

This deity is sometimes represented in masculine form as a prince. Other forms show a thousand eyes, the head of a horse or eleven arms, reflecting some of her names. As 'the Wise', she is Sho-Kwannon; as 'eleven-faced' she is Ju-ichi-men Kwannon; as 'a thousand-handed' she is Sen-ju Kwannon; as 'horse-headed' she is Bato Kwannon and as 'omnipotent' she is Nyo-i-rin Kwannon. In some manifestations, as Hito-koto Kwannon, she will answer only one prayer.

Some sects envisage groups of 6, 7 or even 33 Kwannons.

Kworrom *African*

A Hausa spirit who trips up those who pass his home under the roots of a tree.

kylin *see* **ch'i-lin**

L

L *Central American*
A Mayan deity of uncertain identity, referred to as God L (*see* **alphabetical gods**). This deity is depicted as an old man, hollow-cheeked from lack of teeth, with part of the face painted black, giving him the alternative name of Old Black God. Some identify this god as Ek Chuah or Tepeyollotl.

La Strega, La Vecchia *see* **Befana**
La velue *see* **Shaggy Beast**
Labe *Arabian*
A queen in the *Arabian Nights' Entertainment*. She was a sorceress who could turn men into animals.

Labours of Hercules *Greek*
The tasks given to Hercules as penance after he killed his children.

These stories are generally referred to as the Labours of Hercules, the name the Romans used for Heracles, although since they take place in a Greek setting and with a full cast of Greek characters it might have been more appropriate to retain the name Heracles. Not all writers agree on the order, or even the content, of the various tasks. Other versions include clearing the seas of pirates and the killing of Cycnus.

All the Labours were carried out on the instructions of Eurystheus, king of Mycenae (or Tiryns, in some versions), who was so frightened of Hercules that he hid himself in a large bronze jar buried in the ground and had his orders passed on by his herald Copreus.

For his first Labour, Hercules killed the Nemean lion which had a skin that resisted all weapons, choking it to death with his bare hands. After flaying it with its own claws, he used the skin as armour, as, in other accounts, he had done with the skin of the Cithaeronian lion.

He next killed the Hydra, a monster with a body like a dog and many heads, one of which was immortal. In this he was helped by his nephew Iolaus who burned the neck as Hercules cut off each head so that the head could not grow again. The immortal head he cut off and buried. Hercules dipped his arrows in the poison of the carcase so that the slightest wound from one of them was always fatal. In the end, this cost Hercules his own life.

He was then ordered to capture the golden-horned Ceryneian hind which he did by chasing it for a year until she was exhausted, whereupon he hoisted her on to his shoulders and carried her to Mycenae.

For his fourth task he captured alive the Erymanthian boar which was ravaging the area around Mount Erymanthus. En route, he killed several Centaurs and routed the others when they attacked him and Pholus, another Centaur who was entertaining Hercules. One of those who escaped was Nessus who was later to be instrumental in bringing about the death of Hercules. During this encounter, Hercules accidentally wounded Chiron, king of the Centaurs and the wise counsellor to many heroes, and Pholus died when he dropped one of Hercules' poisoned arrows on his foot. Hercules captured the boar alive and carried it back to Mycenae. He then went off to join the Argonauts, only returning to his Labours when he was left behind at Mysia.

His next task was to cleanse the stables of Augeas, king of Elis. The whole area was deep in dung from his huge herds and Hercules cleansed it all by diverting the rivers Alpheus and Peneius to flow through it. He claimed one tenth of the herds as reward for his efforts but Augeas reneged on the deal. On his way home, he saved the maiden Mnesimache from a Centaur intent upon rape, killing her attacker.

The sixth Labour involved the driving off of the huge flock of man-eating birds, largely made of brass, from the Stymphalian Marshes. This he did by making a terrible din with castanets (or a rattle) to scare the birds into the air where he shot them down with his poisoned arrows.

The white bull given by Poseidon to Minos, which had fathered the Minotaur on his wife Pasiphae, was still ravaging Crete and for his next task Hercules captured it and brought it to Mycenae. Eurystheus set it free

again and as the Marathonian Bull it was later captured by Theseus and killed.

Diomedes, king of the Bistones in Thrace, had four wild mares which he fed on human flesh. Hercules was given the task of capturing these animals as his eighth Labour. On his way there he stayed with his friend King Admetus who was in mourning for his wife, Alcestis, who had sacrificed her own life to save his. Hercules, penitent for getting noisily drunk in a house of mourning, wrestled with Death himself and forced him to hand over Alcestis alive again. Having collected the mares, he drove them to the shore ready to ship them back to Greece and diverted the sea into a channel to foil the pursuing Bistones. While he was thus engaged, the mares ate his armour-bearer Abderus who had been left in charge of them. He knocked out Diomedes and fed him to the mares which, when full, were tame enough to be led aboard his ship. He left the mares in charge of Laomedon, king of Troy.

For his ninth Labour, Hercules was required to get for Admete, the daughter of Eurystheus, the love-girdle given by the war god Ares to Hippolyta, an Amazon queen. The queen offered it to him as a gift but her people, incited by Hera to believe that Hercules intended to abduct their queen, attacked his ship. He killed Hippolyta, took her golden girdle and routed her army. Other accounts say that he took the Amazon Melanippe (who may be Hippolyta's sister) as hostage and returned her in exchange for

the girdle, while Theseus, who had joined the expedition, took Antiope who was in love with him. On the way back to Mycenae he defeated the champion boxer, Titias, and inadvertently killed him and rescued Hesione who had been chained to a rock by her father, Laomedon, king of Troy, as a sacrifice to a sea-monster sent by the sea god Poseidon. When Laomedon refused to hand over the mares of Diomedes that Hercules had left in his charge or, in some versions, reneged on a promise to give Hercules two immortal horses if he would rid Troy of the monster, Hercules killed Laomedon and all his sons except Podarces whom he set – as Priam – on the throne of Troy. He also shot and killed Sarpedon, the son of Poseidon, and killed both Polygonus and Telegonus, sons of the sea god Proteus, in a wrestling match.

His next task was to fetch the cattle of Geryon the winged, three-bodied king of Tartessus. He travelled via Libya and the sun god Helius gave him a golden bowl in which he sailed to the island of Erythea where Geryon ruled. En route to Spain, Hercules erected the Pillars of Hercules at the entrance to the Mediterranean Sea. In the Pyrenees, the giant Albion lay in ambush, hoping to kill Hercules to avenge the death of the other giants killed by Hercules when they attempted to overthrow the Olympian gods, but Hercules came upon him from behind and killed him. Reaching Geryon's kingdom, he killed both Orthrus, the two-headed guard-dog, and Eurytion, the herdsman, with his club and Geryon with an arrow through all three bodies and then drove the cattle to Mycenae. He mated with Galata, a princess of Gaul, fathering a son, Corin, to found the nation of the Gauls, and killed the brothers Ialebion and Dercynus and the three-headed Cacus, when they tried to steal the cattle. In some stories, Hercules killed the monster Scylla for taking some of the cattle and at Croton, where he was entertained by an old hero of the same name, an Italian robber Lacinius tried to steal some of the cattle and a fight ensued in which Hercules accidentally killed Croton. He also killed King Faunus who had the habit of killing and sacrificing all strangers. Others he killed on this adventure were Eryx, a king of Sicily who challenged all-comers to a wrestling match and was defeated by Hercules, and the giant Alcyoneus who died when the stone he threw at Hercules rebounded and killed him. Hercules' horses were stolen by a snake-woman who returned them only when Hercules agreed to sleep with her. He stayed with her for some time and fathered three sons, Agathyrsus, Gelonus and Scythes. Some say that this snake-woman was Echidna, who was Geryon's sister.

The tree that Gaea had given to Hera as a wedding-gift produced golden apples and the next Labour, the eleventh, was the task of collecting some of this fruit from the garden on Mount Atlas where it was guarded by the Hesperides, daughters of Atlas, and by the dragon Ladon. He had a great struggle, through many shape-changes, with Nereus

before the sea god would disclose the location of this secret garden. Hercules killed the dragon with an arrow and persuaded Atlas to get some of the apples from his daughters while he temporarily took on Atlas's task of holding up the heavens though others say that Hercules entered the garden and picked the apples himself. In some accounts, he killed Emathion who tried to prevent him from taking the apples. On the way home with the apples (which were later returned to Hera), he killed the giant King Antaeus of Libya in another wrestling match and both Busiris, king of Egypt, and his son, Amphidamas, when the former tried to kill Hercules on a sacrificial altar to avert drought. He also found Prometheus chained to a rock, killed the vulture that had been tearing at his liver and set him free. Prometheus then took on the immortality of Chiron who was still suffering from the wound inflicted by Hercules' poisoned arrow but could not die.

His final task was to bring the three-headed dog Cerberus, the guardian of Tartarus, to Mycenae. He freed Theseus from the Seat of Forgetfulness but failed to free Peirithous. Wrestling with Menotes, herdsman to Hades (or, in some accounts, with Hades himself), Hercules threatened to kill him unless Hades handed over Cerberus. He choked the dog into submission and dragged it to Mycenae. While he was in Tartarus, Hercules was told by the shade of Meleager of his sister's beauty and Hercules promised to marry her. She later became his second wife, Deianeira. When

Eurystheus insulted him by offering him a slave's portion of a sacrifice, Hercules killed the king's three sons, Eurybius, Erypilus and Perimedes. Cerberus was later returned to Hades.

Labyrinth   *Greek*
The maze built by Daedalus for Minos, king of Crete, to contain the Minotaur.

Lachesis   *Greek*
One of the Moirae (Fates). Lachesis measures the thread of life. She is depicted with a scroll.

Ladder of Heaven   *Japanese*
The means whereby the sun goddess Amaterasu and the moon god Tsuki-yumi rose to take their places in the sky.

Ladon   *Greek*
The 100-headed dragon guarding the apples of the Hesperides.
Hercules killed the dragon when he obtained some of the apples as his eleventh Labour and the goddess Hera placed him in the heavens as the constellation Draco.

Lady of Astolat, Lady of Shallot
see **Elaine**[3]
Lady of Avalon *see* **Morgan le Fay**
Lady of Death *see* **Mictlantecuhtl**
Lady of Heaven *see* **Wadjet**
Lady of the Lake   *British*
Guardian of a magical lake. The office of guardian of the lake, who lived in a castle in the centre of the lake with her own train of attendants, seems to have been occupied by several women in the Arthurian legends, including Morgan le Fay and Nimue.
She seized the infant Lancelot when he was left on the side of the lake and reared him in her underwater realm until he reached manhood. In one version

she is said to have given the sword Excalibur to King Arthur and to have received it when it was returned to the lake by Bedivere on Arthur's death.

Laertes   *Greek*
A king of Ithaca; father of Odysseus.

Some say that Sisyphus seduced Laertes' wife Anticleia on her wedding morning and he, rather than Laertes, was the real father of Odysseus.

Laertes was one of the Argonauts and a member of the party hunting the Calydonian Boar.

Although he was too old to defend Penelope from the harassment by her many suitors while Odysseus was away, he did help to rout them when his son returned.

Laidly Worm   *British*
also Lambton Worm
A monster in the form of a huge worm. This beast grew from a worm thrown into the river by a boy out fishing. If it were cut in half, it joined itself together again. It was killed when the son of Lord Lambton dressed in armour with sharp blades so that, when the worm coiled round him, it was cut into hundreds of small pieces. The witch who had advised him on the method of killing the worm demanded that he kill the first living thing he saw after emerging from the water. This turned out to be his own father and, when the boy refused to keep his undertaking, the witch placed a curse on his family.

Lake Avernus *see* **Avernus**
Lakin Chan *see* **Itzamna**
Lakshmi   *Hindu*
= *Buddhist* Maya

The lotus goddess, goddess of agriculture, beauty, pleasure and wealth; consort of the god Vishnu.

She sprang fully-formed from the body of the god Prajapati or from the foam, the third thing to emerge when the gods churned the ocean to produce amrita, and is reincarnated with every avatar of the god Vishnu. When Vishnu appeared as Rama, she was Sita; when he was Krishna, she was Radha and Rukmini; when he was Parasurama, she was Dharani.

She is sometimes depicted with four arms and standing on a lotus.

lamb   *Roman*
The animal of the goddess Juno.

Lambton Worm *see* **Laidly Worm**
Lamia   *Greek*
A monster in the form of a blood-sucking woman-serpent.

In one story, she was not at first a monster but a sea nymph or a queen of Libya, one of Zeus's many mistresses who bore him several children (including the monster Scylla), most of whom she ate. In this form she was a snake-goddess, queen of Libya. Later she became the blood-sucking monster that some have identified with Medusa.

Some say that she had the ability to remove her eyes.

In some stories, the jealous Hera stole all Lamia's children by Zeus and, to exact vengeance, Lamia killed all the children she encountered.

In some accounts she is equated with Lilith, the first wife of Adam.

Lamiae   *Greek*
Demons in the form of beautiful women. They were originally priestesses of Lamia but were

downgraded and became demons seducing travellers or sucking their blood.

Laminak   *Basque*
Fairies living underground. It is said that they sometimes exchange their children for mortal children. Each one is called Guillen.

Lan Ts'ai-ho   *Chinese*
One of the Eight Immortals. This being is variously regarded as male or female. In some accounts, Lan Ts'ai-ho was originally a street-singer and is said to have been carried off on a cloud after getting drunk, leaving one shoe behind. He/she is the patron saint of florists or gardeners and is depicted carrying a flower-basket and wearing only one shoe.

Lancelot   *British*
also Lancelot du Lac, Knight of the Cart, Knight of the Chariot
A Knight of the Round Table, one of the Knights of Battle; son of King Ban and Elaine; father of Galahad.

Besieged by rebellious chieftains, King Ban left his castle to seek help. His pregnant wife also escaped when their treacherous steward let the besiegers into the castle. She found her husband beside a lake where she died giving birth to the boy they would have called Galahad. Ban died of grief at the sight of her dead body. Other versions say they left together and that Ban died when he saw his castle going up in flames and realised that his steward had surrendered to the besiegers. The lake was the home of Nimue (the Lady of the Lake) who heard the baby's cries and rescued him, raising him with his cousins (in some versions, Lionel and

Bors) whom she stole to provide company for the boy she now called Lancelot du Lac ('Lancelot of the Lake'). Some accounts refer to a fairy foster-mother who raised him in Maidenland.

In the Nimue version, when the boys reached manhood she took them to Britain and set them on the road to Arthur's court at Camelot. The sorceress Morgan sent the sorceress Hellawes to entrap Lancelot but he used the hilt of his sword as a cross to ward off the evil phantoms she had conjured up. Hallowes, having fallen in love with Lancelot, perished.

When he delivered the Castle Dolorous Gard from an evil spell he found there a tomb which bore his own name. He took over the castle as his own home, calling it Garde Joyeux (Joyous Gard). (Later, after he returned Guinevere to Arthur he called it Dolorous Gard.) Some say the estate was given to him by King Arthur.

Seeking adventure with his nephew Lionel, he was put under a spell by Morgan and imprisoned in the Château de la Charette. Asked to choose between Morgan and three other fairy queens as a lover, he rejected them all. A maid helped him to escape when he promised to help her father, Bagdemagus. He kept his promise and, with four of Bagdemagus's knights specially trained by Lancelot, attended a tournament and defeated all the knights who came against him so that Bagdemagus was declared to have won the day. Lionel had been captured by Turkin, a knight who hated all Arthur's knights. Lancelot then rode to Turkin's

castle and killed him in single combat, freeing Lionel and all the other knights who had been imprisoned there. One of those freed was his old friend Kay who was unhappy that his duties as seneschal had sapped his knightly ardour so, while Kay was asleep, Lancelot donned his armour and, in the guise of Kay, defeated many knights, so enhancing Kay's reputation as a warrior.

The girl who led him to Turkin's castle asked a favour in return, as a result of which he challenged and killed Perys de Foreste Sauvage who had made a practice of attacking damsels. When he came upon a knight, Pedivere, intent upon killing his wife who, he claimed, had been unfaithful, Lancelot intervened but the man nevertheless cut off her head. Lancelot then forced him to carry the head in his hand and the headless body on his back all the way to Camelot.

He met a damsel who asked for his help to save her wounded brother, Meliot, who had fought and killed Gilbert the Bastard whose hand had been cut off in an earlier fight with Gawain. Taking the sword and a piece of cloth from the body of the dead Gilbert in Chapel Perilous, he touched Meliot's wounds with the sword, wiped them with the cloth and made him whole again. In another version of this incident, the damsel tried and failed to bewitch Lancelot into becoming her lover, the sword turned out to be a wooden imitation and the body a rag dummy. When he refused to hand over the sword, she tried to kill him with a dagger but Lancelot disarmed her.

At the request of another lady, he took off his armour and climbed a tree to rescue her falcon which was trapped there. Caught unarmed by Phelot, he broke off a branch of the tree and killed the treacherous knight, taking his sword and lopping off his head.

In Castle Carbonek he rescued a damsel who had been shut in a scalding hot room by the sorceress Morgan le Fay and had been there for five years and he slew the dragon living under a tomb. In some versions, this was Elaine with whom he slept to produce Galahad.

He was given hospitality by King Pelles in his castle where the Grail appeared carried by a mysterious damsel. Pelles wanted Lancelot to marry his daughter Elaine, knowing that the union would produce the perfect knight, Galahad. When Lancelot rejected the love of Elaine, Pelles or her maid Dame Brisen, using a magic potion, deceived Lancelot into thinking that he was sleeping with Queen Guinevere, his true love. When he realised how he had been duped, Lancelot would have killed Elaine but he relented when she pleaded for her life. The result of this union was indeed Galahad.

In King Arthur's battles on the Continent, he rode into the fray and, killed the Emperor, seizing his standard which he handed to the king. When they returned to Britain, Arthur gave a great feast to celebrate his victories. Here Lancelot met Elaine once more and was again tricked by Dame Brisen into sleeping with her in the belief that he was sharing

Guinevere's bed. When he realised what had happened he went mad, jumped from the window and roamed the country living like an animal for many months. In his wanderings he came to a pavilion where he fought and defeated Bliant. This knight and his brother Selivant, took Lancelot to their home in Castle Blank and looked after him for over a year. In other stories, he was cared for by Castor, a nephew of Pelles. He ran away and found himself back at Carbonek where he was kept as a fool by the knights and was found again by Elaine. He was taken to the room where the Grail was kept and was cured of his madness. Pelles gave him the Castle of Bliant for a home and he lived with Elaine on this island retreat for fifteen years, attended by a retinue of knights and ladies. He now called himself the Chevalier Mal Fet (the 'Sinner Lord'). He was finally found by Ector and Percival (or, some say, by Lionel and Bors) who persuaded him to return to Camelot where he was made welcome by Arthur and Guinevere.

When Galahad was of age, Lancelot made him a knight and took him to Arthur's court where he took his rightful place in the Perilous Seat. They both joined the other Knights of the Round Table in vowing to search for the Holy Grail. Each knight on the quest chose his own route and Lancelot found himself challenged by a knight who unhorsed him. When he realised that this was Galahad in disguise, he rode after him but could not catch him and found himself, at nightfall, by a stone cross outside an old chapel. Half asleep on his shield, he had

a vision in which a sick knight was healed by the Holy Grail, which appeared in front of the cross. The knight took Lancelot's horse, sword and helmet, leaving Lancelot to travel through the forest unarmed and on foot until he came to a hermitage where he confessed all his sins to a hermit and was forgiven. He reached the sea and a voice told him to go aboard a ship. There he found the dead sister of Percival. He stayed aboard the ship for several weeks until Galahad arrived. They sailed together for six months, having many adventures until a knight in white armour told Galahad it was time to leave his father and take up the quest for the Holy Grail. Lancelot stayed aboard until he arrived at Castle Carbonek where he entered a room and saw the Holy Grail but was struck down and lay unconscious for twenty-four days. From Pelles, he learned that Elaine was dead. Rendered unfit to find the Grail by reason of his affair with Guinevere, he gave up the quest and returned to Camelot where he found that many of the knights who had left on this quest were now dead.

He resumed the affair with Guinevere but tried to distance himself from her when the affair became the subject of gossip. This made the queen angry and she banished him from the court. He went to live with the hermit, Brastias. When Guinevere was accused by Mador of poisoning his cousin, Patrice, Lancelot took up the challenge on her behalf and defeated Mador in single combat, saving Guinevere from the stake.

On the way to a major tournament ordered by Arthur,

he stayed with Bernard at Astolat where the baron's daughter, Elaine le Blank, known as the Fair Maid of Astolat, fell in love with him. He wore her favour at the tournament at which he was the champion but refused her offer to become her husband or her lover and returned to Camelot accompanied by Elaine's brother, Lavaine, who had helped him in the tournament. Elaine died of unrequited love and her body was placed in a boat which drifted down the river to Westminster, where the king ordered Lancelot to give the dead maiden an honourable burial.

When Guinevere and ten of her knights were captured by Meliagaunt, who was in love with Guinevere, Lancelot rode to her rescue. When his horse was shot from under him in an ambush by Meliagaunt's archers, he compelled a woodman to drive him to the castle in his cart. He was thereafter called the Knight of the Cart or the Knight of the Chariot. He reached the castle by crossing a sword bridge and rescued the Guinevere. Lancelot would have killed Meliagaunt but he begged the queen for mercy and she pardoned him. That night, Lancelot slept with Guinevere but he left blood on the sheets from a wound on his hand sustained when he forced the window-bars. Meliagaunt accused Guinevere of being unfaithful to her husband by sleeping with one of the ten knights, many of whom had been wounded when he captured them. Lancelot took up the gauntlet and arranged to meet Meliagaunt at Westminster. Meliagaunt trapped Lancelot in a dungeon and left for Westminster. A maid released Lancelot for the price of one kiss and he rode to Westminster, where he met Meliagaunt in single combat and killed him with one hand tied behind his back.

Mordred, always jealous of Lancelot, betrayed Lancelot's affair with Guinevere to Arthur and, with his brother Agravain and twelve other knights, attempted to catch Lancelot with Guinevere as proof. Lancelot, unarmed, killed Colgrevance, the first man into the room, with a footstool and then, taking the dead man's sword and armour, killed all the others with the sole exception of Mordred who, though wounded, managed to escape. Given proof of the affair, Arthur ordered the queen to be burned at the stake. Lancelot rode to her rescue once again as she was being led to the stake and charged into the crowd, killing many of those who got in his way. Among these were Gaheris and Gareth, both of whom had been ordered by King Arthur to attend but who had turned up unarmed and were not recognised by Lancelot in the fury of his attack. As a result of their deaths, Gawain, their elder brother, became Lancelot's mortal enemy.

Lancelot took Guinevere to his castle, Garde Joyeuse, which was then attacked by Arthur's forces, and the fierce battle was ended only when the Pope intervened. Lancelot handed Guinevere back to her husband but his quarrel with Gawain, and hence with Arthur, was not settled. He left for France with about a hundred of his followers and set up court at Benwick but Arthur, at the urging of Gawain, took an army of 60,000 to France, laying waste Lancelot's domain and besieging the town. Each day for weeks on end, Gawain challenged and defeated one of Lancelot's knights in single combat and finally goaded Lancelot himself into fighting him. On two successive days Lancelot struck him down but refused to kill him. A third encounter was prevented when Arthur was called back to Britain to reclaim his throne that had been usurped by Mordred who had been left in charge during the king's absence.

When he learned of Arthur's troubles, Lancelot brought his forces to Britain to help the king but Arthur had already been badly wounded and carried off to Avalon. He tried to persuade Guinevere to return with him to France but she refused to leave the nunnery she had entered on the king's death, and so Lancelot joined Bedivere in a hermitage where other knights later joined them. When Lancelot learned of the death of Guinevere, he had her body carried to the hermitage where it was buried in Arthur's tomb. From then on he refused to eat or drink and died soon afterwards. Other stories say that he threw himself on the grave of the king and stayed there for six weeks, eating nothing, until he died. His body was carried to Garde Joyeuse and buried there.

Another version has it that Lancelot, believing Guinevere had been a willing accomplice of Mordred, killed her and shut Mordred in a room with her dead body which, driven by hunger, Mordred ate.

Land of Life, Land of the Living *see* **Tir nam Beo**

Land of Youth *see* **Tir nan Og**

langsuir   *Malayan*

A female vampire, the spirit of a woman who died in childbirth. They suck the blood of children through a hole in the back of the neck which is normally hidden under their ankle-length hair. Cutting the hair and their long nails renders a langsuir harmless if the hair is used to block the hole in the neck.

Glass beads were placed in the mouth, eggs under the armpits and needles in the hands of a dead woman to ensure that her spirit did not become a langsuir.

language

One legend has it that Adam and Eve spoke Persian, the serpent spoke Arabic and the angel Gabriel spoke Turkish.

Lao-tzu   *Chinese*

A Chinese philosopher, (c. 600–517 BC); the founder of Taoism.

One of the San Ch'ing, the Three Pure Ones; god of alchemists and potters.

His original name was Li Erh. He is said to have been born under a plum tree from a virgin birth after sixty (some say seventy or eighty) years in his mother's womb, already grey-haired with age. Others say that he was born from his mother's left side in 1321 BC.)

He is depicted riding a buffalo.

Laocoon   *Greek*

also Laokoon

A Trojan prince, probably son of King Priam and Hecuba. A prophet and priest of Apollo or Poseidon. When he warned the Trojans not to take the wooden horse left by the Greeks at its face value, Apollo or Poseidon sent two large serpents which coiled round Laocoon and his two sons and crushed them to death. In some accounts Laocoon, in others he and one of the sons, escaped.

Laomedon *Greek*
King of Troy; father of Antigone, Clytius, Hesione, Hicetaeon, Lampos, Podarces and Tithonus.

The gods Apollo and Poseidon had been ordered by Zeus to serve as slaves to Laomedon. The former tended his flocks while the latter built the walls of Troy. When the king refused to pay them, Poseidon sent a sea-monster to attack Troy. Laomedon chained his daughter to a rock in the sea as a sacrifice to propitiate the god. She was found and rescued by Hercules who had left the mares of Diomedes in charge of Laomedon. It is also said that Laomedon promised two immortal horses to Hercules if he would rid Troy of the monster. These horses had been given to the king of Troy by Zeus in compensation when he abducted Ganymede as his cup-bearer. Because Laomedon refused to hand over the mares or because he reneged on his promise of the two horses, Hercules later returned with an army, sacking Troy, killing Laomedon and setting his son Podarces on the throne as Priam.

Lapis exillis *British*
The name for the Holy Grail in those versions of the story in which it was said to be a stone rather than a cup or plate.

lapis manalis *Roman*
A stone placed over one of the entrances to the underworld. When a city was first founded,

entrances to the underworld were dug and sealed with such a stone. Three times each year the stone would be removed to allow the spirits of the dead to return.

Lapiths *Greek*
A mythical race in Thessaly. They were said to be horse-tamers and their long feud with the Centaurs started when the Centaur Eurytion tried to rape Hippodamia, wife of Peirithous, king of the Lapiths, on her wedding day.

Lara[1] *Irish*
He and his wife Balma and father Fintan were the survivors of the Flood.

Lara[2] *Roman*
A nymph who annoyed Jupiter by bearing tales to Juno so he had her tongue cut out and sent her to Hades. Her escort, Mercury, fell in love with her and they produced the two children who became the Lares, gods of the hearth.

Lares *Roman*
Household gods: ancestral spirits; good spirits; a form of lemur, some say.

Originally Etruscan guardian gods, the Lares were adopted into the Roman pantheon as spirits protecting institutions and various places. Lares Familiares protected the house and family; Lares Compitales guarded crossroads or parts of the city; Lares Premarini, the city or empire; Lares Rurales, the countryside; Lares Vicorum, the streets; and so on.

Another version regards the Lares as two sons of Lara by Mercury.

larva *Roman*
plural larvae
An evil spirit; a form of lemur.

laskowice *Slav*
Forest spirits, guardians of animals.

Latinus *Roman*
King of Latium. His parentage is not clear. Some say that he was the son of Hercules or Telemachus, others that his parents were the god Faunus and the nymph Marica.

He was warned by the spirit of his father not to allow his daughter Lavinia to marry one of her countrymen, but to keep her for a stranger from over the sea. This turned out to be Aeneas, seeking somewhere to settle after the fall of Troy. In some accounts he fought for Aeneas, in others against him, and was either killed in battle or taken up to heaven as Jupiter Latiaris.

Laufakanaa *Pacific Islands*
A wind god of the Tongan Islanders. He is credited with having invented the fishing net and having brought the banana from heaven.

Laughing Water *see* **Minnehaha**
laumé *Baltic*
= *Latvian* lauma
A Lithuanian hag or witch. Originally these beings were harmless fairies, later they became evil beings.

Lavinia *Greek*
Daughter of Latinus and Amata; second wife of Aeneas.

Amata tried to keep her daughter for Turnus, king of the Rutulians, by hiding her in the woods but she eventually married Aeneas, just as had been prophesied before the arrival of the Trojans in Italy.

Leander *Greek*
A youth of Abydus. He lived on one side of the Hellespont, Hero on the other and, although in love, they were forbidden to marry. Guided

by a light in her window, he swam the Hellespont every night but when a storm extinguished the light, he was drowned. She hanged herself from grief.

Lear   *British*
A legendary king of Britain; father of Cordelia, Goneril and Regan. He is said to have divided his kingdom between Goneril and Regan. They drove him to madness, and he was cared for by Cordelia who raised an army to depose her sisters but was killed in the attempt.

lechies   *Russian*
Forest-demons. These beings are envisaged as having the head and legs of a goat on a human body. In some accounts they are said to kill travellers by tickling them until they die laughing.

Leda   *Greek*
In one story she found the egg resulting from the union of Zeus (as a swan) with Nemesis (as a goose) and from which came Helen of Troy.

Another version has Zeus (as a swan) raping Leda, who produced two eggs from which came Helen and Clytemnestra, Castor and Polydeuces.

She was deified as Nemesis or her attendant.

Leech Child *see* **Hiru-ko**

Legba[1]   *African*
= *Yoruba* Eshu
An angel-trickster of the Fon; a god of destiny.

Legba[2]   *West Indies*
The sun god of Haiti. During the daytime he operates the gate that gives spirits access to take possession of humans. He is depicted as an old man in ragged clothes with a stick which supports the universe.

Lei Kung   *Chinese*
also Duke of Thunder
A Taoist thunder god. Originally depicted in human form with blue skin, fangs and talons, he was later shown as a monkey-faced bird.

leippya   *Burmese*
A soul which can appear in the form of a butterfly and leave the body and return as it pleases. While the soul is away, the person may become ill and, if the soul is seized by a demon, the person will die.

lemur   *Roman*
plural lemures
A ghost of the dead. In some accounts, a distinction is made between the larvae and the lemures, the former being ghosts of the wicked dead, the latter of the good dead.

Leodegrance   *British*
King of Cameliard; father of Guinevere. When Leodegrance's kingdom was attacked by Royns, a king of North Wales, King Arthur brought an army to his rescue. It was on this occasion that Arthur first met Guinevere, who later became his wife. He gave Arthur the Round Table as part of Guinevere's dowry.

leopard
(1) The Egyptians revered the leopard as the animal of Osiris.
(2) In Greece the leopard was regarded as the animal of Dionysus.

Leopard Spirit   *Chinese*
A demon. He captured Tripitaka and his friends on their journey to the West but the monkey-god Sun Hou-tzu turned into a firefly and rescued them.

leprechaun   *Irish*
A spirit or fairy of the Otherworld. When the Danaans were conquered by the invading Milesians, they retreated underground as these fairies. They are said to guard a crock of gold.

Lerajie   *European*
A demon, one of the 72 Spirits of Solomon. He is said to cause wars and can prevent the wounds of one's enemies from healing. He may appear dressed in green and carrying a bow and arrows.

Leto   *Greek*
= *Roman* Latona
A Titaness (or at least the daughter of the Titan Coeus and his Titaness sister Phoebe); goddess of darkness; mother of the god Apollo and the goddess Artemis by Zeus.

She was abandoned by Zeus when he made her pregnant and pursued by the winged serpent Python at the behest of the jealous Hera. She wandered the earth until finally carried by a dolphin to the floating island of Ortygia (later Delos) which welcomed her and gave her sanctuary for the birth of her children, Apollo and Artemis. The sea god Poseidon chained the island to the bottom of the sea so that its motion should not disturb Leto and her children and two men who, at the instigation of Hera, had stirred up the mud in a pool to prevent Leto from taking a drink were turned into frogs by Zeus.

Some accounts say that Ortygia and Delos were two separate places, while others say that the island of Asteria (Leto's sister turned into a rock by Zeus) was the site of the birth of the twins.

Some say that Leto arrived on Delos in the form of a wolf to deceive Hera.

Some accounts have Leto as the wife of Zeus before Hera.

Leviathan   *Hebrew*

= *Babylonian* Tiamat

The serpent of primeval chaos. This beast was said to emit a light even brighter than the sun. At the end of the world it will be killed by the monster Behemoth, but another version says that the giant Gargantua met and killed the monster on one of his journeys. In other versions it is a sea monster with seven heads which was killed by the gods Baal and Mot. Later, it came to symbolise hell.

leyak   *Pacific Islands*

In Balinese lore, one who can turn into a tiger or a firefly. The leyak roams about at night collecting the intestines of the dead and is said to use these entrails to make a brew with which he can turn himself into a tiger.

Leza   *African*

= *Fon* Lisa

A creator-god and sky god of the Kaonde. He sent three gourds to men in the care of the honeybird. The bird opened the gourds, including the one that should not have been opened until Leza himself came to earth. Two gourds contained seeds and other useful things but the third contained all the ills that afflict mankind.

In some areas they maintain that Leza reached the sky by climbing up a spider's web which broke when men tried to follow.

lha   *Tibetan*

Early inhabitants of Tibet. These beings, who knew the art of tempering steel, were the

precursors of the race. Next came the dMu-rgyal.

Li T'ieh-kuai   *Chinese*

also Iron Crutch

One of the Eight Immortals; god of apothecaries and the disabled.

He was originally a student known as Li Ning-yang and he developed the power of leaving his body to visit Lao-tzu in heaven. On one occasion, his disciple, Lang Ling, thinking his master truly dead, burned his body so that, when he finally returned, he was forced to find another body, that of a lame beggar. As a result, he is depicted as a beggar using a crutch given to him by Hsi Wang Mu or Lao-tzu.

Another story says that he was taught by Hsi Wang Mu who cured him when he had an ulcer on his leg. It left him lame so she gave him the iron crutch with which he is depicted. He is said, on one occasion, to have walked into a fiery furnace and emerged unscathed. On another occasion he crossed a river by standing on a floating leaf.

Lichas   *Greek*

A herald to Hercules. It was he who carried the poisoned robe sent by Deianeira which killed Hercules who, in his agony, grabbed the messenger by one foot and threw him to his death from the top of Mount Oeta. He was said to have been transformed into a rock.

Light Elves *see* **Liosalfar**

lightning

In many cultures, lightning is regarded as a weapon wielded by a god.

(1) The Chinese say that a young goddess uses a mirror to flash

light on to a chosen target so that the thunder god can release a bolt of lightning and be sure of hitting the right spot.

(2) In Central America, some tribes say that lightning first brought illness to man.

(3) The people of Dahomey say that the thunder gods use lightning to punish wrongdoers and one of them, the god Gbade, can kill people with a lightning shaft.

(4) Early inhabitants of Germany blamed witches for lightning while others said that a charred log from a midsummer bonfire, if kept in the house, would preserve it from lightning strikes. Some say that a magic coal, found under a mugwort plant, will protect the owner from lightning.

(5) In Greece, lightning was the weapon of Zeus, and the Greeks regarded as sacred any spot where lightning struck the earth.

(6) In New Guinea it is believed that many evil spirits can cause lightning.

(7) The Romans regarded Jupiter as manifest in lightning and thunder.

(8) In North America. some tribes believe that using a toothpick made from the timber of a tree that has been struck by lightning will cure toothache. Others say that a lightning strike near to the spot where a person is dying announces the arrival of the Devil to collect that person's soul. Some believe that lightning caused the raccoon or the mole while others cover their heads with raccoon skin as protection from lightning.

(9) The Tartars regard lightning as an arrow shot from the rainbow

which is the bow wielded by a great hero.

(10) The early Vedic religion taught that lightning was a weapon wielded by several gods, including Indra and Rudra.

Ligoupup   *Pacific Islands*

A creator-goddess in the Gilbert Islands. She is said to have created the world and now manifests her presence by causing earthquakes. In some accounts she is regarded as the first woman.

Likho   *Russian*

A female demon, depicted as a one-eyed hag.

Lilith[1]   *Mesopotamian*

= *Sumerian* Kiskil-lilla

A Babylonian goddess, envisaged as a winged demon-woman attacking sleeping men.

Lilith[2]   *Hebrew*

= *Assyrian* Lilitu; *Sumerian* Alu

A purported wife of Adam before Eve, and who later married the Devil. In some accounts, Lilith refused to obey Adam, was expelled from paradise and slept with the Devil, producing the jinn. God sent three angels to persuade Lilith to return to Adam, but to no avail. Other versions say that she flew off in the form of a vampire or took the form of a black cat, preying on new-born babies. In this context, her name is used to refer to the star Algol, previously known as Rosh ha Satan (Satan's Head.).

lindworm   *British*

A monster in the form of a wingless wivern.

Ling Tzu   *Chinese*

A deity regarded as a patron of tea.

ling-yü   *Chinese*

A monster in the form of a fish with the head and limbs of a human being.

Linus   *Greek*

He was a musician who taught Orpheus, his brother. He tried to teach Hercules literature and music and was killed by Hercules who struck him with his lyre when they argued about correct musical instruction.

li'oa   *Pacific Islands*

A ghost in the Solomon Islands. These beings, said to be the spirits of dead chiefs or warriors, are invoked to help the sick. In some cases, they become manifest as large fish such as sharks, when they are known as pa'ewa.

lion

Lions appear in many mythologies.

(1) In Babylonia, the demon Ugallu was a form of lion and the lion was also regarded as the steed of the war god Nergal.

(2) In Buddhism, the lion was the favoured steed of several deities including Avalokiteshvara and Maitreya.

(3) In China, the immortal, Chiu-shou, often took the form of a lion.

(4) Christian symbolism has the lion representing Christ and a number of saints, including Mark.

(5) In Egypt the lion was a symbol of the sun and the sun god and also the deities Sef and Tuau.

(5) The Greek hero, Hercules, killed the Cithaeronian Lion and the Nemean Lion and wore a lion's skin as a cloak.

(6) The Hebrews used the lion as the symbol of the tribe of Judah.

(7) In Hindu lore, the fourth avatar of Vishnu was Narasinha, the man/lion. The lion is also one of the signs of the Zodiac.

(8) In Persia the lion was used as the national emblem.

(9) The Romans regarded the lion as the animal of the god Vulcan.

(10) In Thailand this animal is regarded as the ancestor of the royal family.

Liosalfar   *Norse*

also Light Elves

Elves of light. Their home was Alfheim, suspended between earth and heaven. They were ruled by the god of light and peace, Frey, and were responsible for birds, butterflies and flowers. The fairy-rings seen in the grass are the sites of their dancing and are said to bring luck to – or, in some stories, kill – those who stand in them.

Liosalfheim   *Norse*

Home of the Light Elves; land of the righteous. (*See also* **Alfheim**.)

lipsipsip   *Pacific Islands*

Spirits of the New Hebrides. These beings, which take the form of dwarfs living in stones and trees, are quite capable of eating anybody who upsets them.

Lir   *Irish*

A sea god; father of Manannan. He had four children by Aobh and when she died, he married her sister, Aiofe, who turned the children into swans. Later, Lir returned them to human shape but they had grown old and wrinkled. Aiofe was changed by Bodb Dearg into a demon as punishment. (*See also* **Children of Lir**.)

Lit Merveile   *British*

A marvellous bed. In one of Gawain's adventures, he went to a castle to rescue some captives and came upon a bed which moved of its own accord. When he sat on it, the bed careered round the room, rebounding off the walls. (*See also* **Adventurous Bed**.)

Little Man   *North American*

A hero of the Metis nation. He was very small and hairy but extremely powerful and owned a magic knife given to him by a grateful tribe after he killed a bear monster. He met Smoking Mountain, a Metis hunter, and his brother, Broken War Club, and together they went looking for adventure. One day Broken War Club stayed in the lodge they had found to do the cooking and the other pair went hunting. When they returned, Broken War Club was still moaning from a beating he had received from a tiny dwarf and the same thing happened next day to Smoking Mountain. Little Man stayed home the next day and killed the ugly dwarf who came out from a deep hole. They lowered first Broken War Club and then Smoking Mountain into the hole in a kettle on a rope, but they were scared by the noises they heard, so Little Man went down. He was attacked successively by monsters with two, then three, and finally four heads and killed all three of them. He rescued three girls the monsters had kept locked up and sent them up in the kettle together with much plunder from the monsters' home. When it was his turn to go up, Broken War Club cut the rope and they left him to die but he managed to climb out. For helping them to settle an argument, a wasp, a worm and a woodpecker each gave him the power to assume their shape. He soon overtook the fleeing men and killed Broken War

Club, sending Smoking Mountain packing and keeping the girls and the treasure for himself. Later, he rescued another girl from a huge monster by killing first the monster himself and then the grizzly, the brown bear, panther, wolf, wolverine, fox, rabbit, and quail that successively emerged each from the previous body.

The quail produced an egg which, smashed against the original monster's horn, successfully killed him beyond hope of revival. As a result, Little Man acquired more treasure and a fourth wife.

Little Men *see* **Thunder Boys**
Little People *see* **Faylinn**
Little Sprout *see* **Djuskaha**
Little Turtle   *North American*

In the lore of the Iroquois, the animal who brought light to the world.

When the earth was formed on Great Turtle's back, it was dark, so he ordered Little Turtle to climb into the heavens to remedy the situation. She collected flashes of lightning from the thunder-clouds, rolling them into a large ball which became the sun and a smaller ball which became the moon.

Liu Tsung   *Chinese*
also Six Honoured Ones
Celestial spirits controlling the heavenly bodies, directions, rain and wind.

liwa   *South American*
In Honduras and Nicaragua, an evil water-spirit. These beings, envisaged as white worms, are said to pull canoes under the water, drowning the occupants. They are said to have ships of their own which travel under water.

Llewellyn   *Welsh*
A chieftain who owned the hound Gelert and killed it when he found it blood-spattered and his baby son missing. It turned out that Gelert had not eaten the child but had fought and killed the wolf that attacked the boy who was found safe and well. (*See also* **Beddgelert**.)

Lludd   *Welsh*
= *British* Lud; *Irish* Nuada
A sky god; a king of Britain. During his reign the country was afflicted by three plagues and he sought advice from his brother, Llefelys, king of France, as to how to deal with them. He then killed the mysterious Coranieids (dwarf beings) by using a spray made of insects crushed in water, trapped the dragons whose shrieks had been driving people mad and trapped the giant who had been stealing food from the palace. He trapped the dragons by making them drunk on mead and then had them carried to Wales and buried on Mount Erith. They were later released by Vortigern, a king of Britain, when he built his castle there.

Llyr   *Welsh*
= *British* Leir; *Irish* Lir
A king of Britain; a sea god. He is regarded as the prototype for King Lear. Some say that he was an ancestor of King Arthur.

Loa   *Pacific Islands*
Creator-god of the Marshall Islands. Having create the reefs, planets and birds, he then produced a god to rule each of the four cardinal points: Irjojrilik (west), Lajbuineamuen or Lalikian (north), Lokoman (east) and Lorok (south).

In one version he was the father of the first couple, Wulleb and Lejman, who were born from his leg. The hero Edao was later born from his leg or, in some accounts, was the son of Wulleb and Lejman.

When a poor couple, having no food to offer the god, killed and cooked their own daughter, Kavaonau, to provide a meal, Loa had the head and body buried separately. From the head grew the kava and from the body came sugar cane.

Later, when he saw how his descendants quarrelled, he jumped into the sea, causing a huge wave which drowned them all.

Loathly Lady   *British*
A hag who could transform herself into a beautiful maiden. (*See also* **Ragnell**.)

Lob-lie-by-the-fire   *British*
also lubber fiend
A hard-working brownie.

lohan   *Chinese*
also arhat;
= *Japanese* rakan; *Hindu* sthavira
A Buddhist immortal, a disciple of the Buddha.

Lohengrin   *German*
also Knight of the Swan, Swan Knight;
Son of Parsifal. When the princess Elsa was accused of murdering her brother Godfrey, heir to the dukedom of Brabant, Lohengrin was sent from the temple of the Grail to her rescue, riding on a swan. He defeated her accuser, Frederick of Telramund, and married Elsa without revealing his name. When he was later persuaded to tell her his name, he left her and was carried by the swan back to the temple of the Grail. Before leaving, he restored Godfrey, who had been

turned into a swan by the magic of Ortrud, Frederick's wife, to his human form.

He later married Belaye but her parents, believing that he had put her under a spell, had him killed.

Loki   *Norse*
The god of evil, fire and mischief.

In some versions, Loki was the son of Ymir and one of an early trinity with his brothers Aegir and Kari. He was said to have had three wives, fathering Einmyria and Eisa on his first wife, Glut; Fenris, Hel and Iormungandr on his second wife, the giantess Angerbode; and Narve and Vali on his third wife, Sigyn. He is also said to be the father of Sleipnir, Odin's eight-legged horse.

Loki was always a troublemaker. He stole the golden tresses of Sif, wife of Thor. The angry husband caught Loki and nearly strangled him, forcing him into a promise to restore the beautiful hair. Loki persuaded the dwarf, Dvalin, to fashion a replacement from golden thread which turned out to be even more beautiful than the original.

He made a wager with another dwarf, Brock, that Dvalin could make better things than Brock's brother, Sindri, the loser to forfeit his head. The gods judged the results and said that Brock was the winner. Instead of cutting off the loser's head, Brock sewed Loki's lips together to stop his chatter.

When Thor went to Jotunheim dressed in a bridal gown to deceive the Frost Giant Thrym into returning the hammer of Thor which he had stolen, Loki went with him dressed as the bridesmaid to help the deception.

On one occasion, he was carried into the sky by the Frost Giant Thiassi in the form of an eagle and was released only when he promised to lure Iduna, goddess of youth, into Thiassi's power with some of the apples of eternal youth which she guarded. He did what he had promised but when the gods discovered what he had done they forced him to get Iduna back. Wearing Freya's falcon-garb, he flew to Thrymheim, the forest glade where Iduna was being held captive, turned Iduna into a nut (or, some say, a swallow) and brought her safely back to Asgard.

On another occasion he turned himself into a flea to gain access to the goddess Freya's bed and made off with her beautiful necklace, Brisingamen. The giant Heimdall saw him stealing away and, after a struggle in which they both assumed several different forms, Loki was forced to surrender the necklace which Heimdall then returned to Freya.

To frustrate the giant Skrymsli, Loki hid the boy that the giant had won in a wager as an egg in the roe of a fish in the ocean but Skrymir still found the hiding-place, so Loki turned the boy back to his normal form, whereupon he ran off. The giant chased him but ran head-first into a pointed stake cunningly placed by Loki.

When the gods decided to build a wall round Asgard to keep out the giants, an unknown architect undertook to do the work if they would give him the sun, the moon and Freya. Loki advised acceptance but they stipulated that the work must be done in one winter and by the architect himself, aided only by his horse,

Svadilfare. When it looked as if these conditions would be fulfilled, Loki changed into a mare and enticed Svadilfare into the forest so that the architect did not finish the work in time. He would have killed all the gods but Thor threw his hammer and killed the architect who turned out to be a giant in disguise.

On a visit to earth with Odin and Hoenir, Loki killed Otter, the son of Hreidmar, a king of the dwarf-folk. In compensation, the king demanded sufficient gold to cover the skin of an otter, the form in which his son had been killed. This skin kept expanding as more gold was added and Loki forced the dwarf Andvari to hand over his hoard of gold to pay the ransom demanded by the king for the release of the three gods. When Loki snatched the dwarf's magic ring as well, Andvari put a curse on the treasure.

Loki's final act of treachery was to persuade the blind god Hoder to throw the branch of mistletoe that killed Balder and for this he was banished from Asgard.

He turned up uninvited at the feast given for the gods by Aegir and killed the sea god's servant Funfeng. He escaped death from Thor's hammer by fleeing to the mountains and hiding in a hut. When Odin, Kvasir and Thor came looking for him, he turned himself into a salmon and hid at the bottom of the stream, Fraananger. When the gods made a net and started to fish for him he jumped into the air to escape but was caught by Thor. He resumed his normal shape and the gods bound him hand and foot with the entrails of his son,

Narve, who had been killed by his other son, Vali, in the form of a wolf. They then turned the bonds to metal to make sure he could not escape. They left Loki in a cave with a huge serpent over his head which constantly dripped venom on to Loki's face. He was saved much agony by his faithful wife Sigyn who sat beside him catching the venom in a cup until the last day.

In the final battle, leading the subjects of Hel, he defeated the gods at Ragnarok and, in his role as Surtur, the fire god, burnt the whole world, killing Heimdall at whose hand he himself died.

Iolok   *Pacific Islands*
Gnomes, in the lore of Indonesia.

Lone Man   *North American*
A demi-god of the Mandan people.

He walked on the primordial waters with First Creator and, having been shown by a duck that earth would be brought up from the bottom, set about creating the world. He created the flat lands while First Creator made the mountains, trees and streams.

He met Coyote, who called himself First Man, and they quarrelled over who was the elder. Lone Man killed First Man with his spear but the dead man's skeleton returned to life as Coyote and they became partners in creating the land animals as food for the tribes.

He was later born to a Mandan maiden and became a culture-hero of that tribe, teaching them many things.

When he stole a white buckskin coat from the eagle-spirit Hoita, the latter exacted vengeance by collecting all the animals and enclosing them in the Dog Den.

Lone Man turned himself into a hare and hid in the Dog Den where he learned that Hoita's power came from a magic drum. He then made an even more powerful drum for himself and overcame Hoita, releasing all the trapped animals.

He also defeated the evil Maninga but he came again, four years later, in the form of a great flood which swamped the Mandan villages. Lone Man built a stockade he called Great Canoe and saved his people. He once again defeated Maninga, using the magic of his drum, and Maninga was swept away in the receding flood waters.

At the end of his time on earth, he placed a red-painted cedar in the centre of his village to which people could offer sacrifices and which was given to them as an assurance that he would one day return.

(*See also* **Lucky Man**.)

Long Arrow   *North American*
A hero of the Blackfoot tribe.

When his parents died, his sister was adopted by another family but Long Arrow, being deaf, was abandoned and lived on any scraps he could find. Later his hearing returned and he was taken in by Good Running. To repay the old man's kindness, Long Arrow undertook to find the elk-dogs (horses).

After travelling for many days, Long Arrow arrived at the edge of a lake where a young boy offered to take him to his grandfather's lodge under the lake. The boy then turned into a kingfisher and dived into the water and when Long Arrow followed he found himself in an underwater world where there were many horses. The grandfather had a secret – he had the legs of a horse – and when Long Arrow discovered this he was allowed to have a wish. He chose the old man's belt and robe and a herd of horses which he took back to his tribe. When his people made a pilgrimage to the lake to thank the old chief, they found nothing but water and some fish.

Longinus   *British*
A Roman centurion who was said to have pierced Christ's side with a spear. The spear he used appears in Arthurian legends as the Holy Lance, the Lance of Longinus or the Sacred Spear (*see Holy Lance*).

Lord of Air, Lord of All *see* **Shu²**
Lord of Cold Weather *see* **Estonea-pesta**
Lord of Creation *see* **Prajapati**
Lord of Death, Lord of Hades *see* **Mictlantecuhtli**
Lord of Heaven *see* **Ti Chün**
Lord of Sacred Wisdom *see* **Vishnu**
Lord of the Afterworld *see* **Khnum**
Lord of the Dance *see* **Shiva**
Lord of the Flies *see* **Beelzebub**
Lord of the Harvest *see* **Yum Caax**
Lord of the Ocean *see* **Varuna**
Lord of the Storm *see* **Enlil**
Lord of the Sun Face *see* **Ahau Kin**
Lord of the Universe *see* **Vishnu**
Lord of the World *see* **Jagannath**
Lord of Time *see* **Thoth**
Lorelei   *German*
A siren-maiden. She lured sailors on the Rhine to their deaths. When a troop of soldiers was sent to capture her, she put them all in a trance and escaped in her chariot to her underwater cave.

Lotophagi   *Greek*
A race of lotus-eaters. When Odysseus landed in their country, he had to force his men to leave, otherwise they would have stayed for ever in this land of pleasure.

lotus
(1) In Buddhism, the lotus is dedicated to the Buddha.
(2) In China, the lotus is the sacred flower of Taoism. This flower is the emblem of the immortal, Ho Hsien-ku, and represents the developing soul.
(3) In Egypt, the lotus is a symbol of rebirth from which the sun rose at creation.
    The blue lotus was taken as the emblem of the creator-god Nefertem.
(4) In Greek myth, the lotus was a plant causing forgetfulness, with roots which drew water from the River Lethe in the underworld and produced bean-like seeds which robbed any who ate the seeds of all memory.
(5) In Hinduism, the lotus (also kamala or padma) is a sacred flower, the symbol of knowledge, the female principle and procreation.
    It is the emblem of Lakshmi (goddess of agriculture, beauty, pleasure and wealth), the sun god Surya and the god Vishnu.

Lotus Mountain *see* **Mount Meru**
loupgarou   *West Indies*
A Haitian voodoo spirit. These spirits are envisaged as witches flying by night who can adopt the form of a mosquito to suck the life out of children. It is said that, if their discarded skin is sprinkled with pepper, it becomes too painful for

the owner to resume his proper form. If a loupgarou is wounded, the scar is still visible when the human form is resumed and from this the person can be identified as a werewolf and killed.

Love-talker *see* **Gan-Ceann**
Lu Hsing
Chinese
A god of good fortune and wealth; one of the Fu Lu Shou.
    He was originally the scholar Shih Fen, a 2nd-century BC official at the emperor's court.
    He is sometimes depicted as, or riding on, a deer.

Lü Tung-pin   *Chinese*
One of the Eight Immortals. He was an 8th-century prince and magistrate, reputed to be eight feet tall, who became one of the immortals. He was given a magic sword by the Fire Dragon for resisting temptation and used it to kill many dragons and evil beings. He met Chiung-li and, convinced by a dream of riches gained and then lost, that material possessions were worthless, became his disciple.
    He was said to have lived for over 400 years and is regarded as the guardian of the sick and patron of barbers.
    He is depicted with his sword slung over his back and a fly-whisk in one hand. This description is said to be that of Lu-tzu with whom Lü Tung-pin is sometimes confused.

lubber fiend *see* **Lob-lie-by-the-fire**
Lucky Man   *North American*
A creator-deity of the Arikara people. He and Wolf Man appeared over the primordial waters and created the world from soil brought up by ducks. He

created the hills and valleys while Wolf-Man created the prairies. (*See also* **Lone Man.**)

Lud   *British*

also Ludd

A river god; a king of Britain; the British version of Lludd. He is said to have founded London and defended it from many perils. In some accounts he had a silver hand.

ludki   *Slav*

= *Hungarian* lutki; *Polish* krasnoludi

Benevolent dwarfs of the Serbian Otherworld.

Lumawig   *Pacific Islands*

A deity in the Philippines. He is said to have created humans from reeds which he placed in pairs on the ground. Each pair became a male and female, each pair speaking a different language. His sons wiped out the whole population, except one brother and sister, by causing a flood. The surviving couple repopulated the islands and Lumawig came to be regarded as a culture-hero who taught the people their arts and customs.

Lumbu   *African*

The first man in the lore of the Bakongo. The androgynous being Mahungu, created by Nzambi, was split by the tree Muti Mpungu to form the man Lumbu and the woman Muzita.

Lung Wang *see* **Ao Kuang, Four Dragon Kings**

lutin   *French*

A goblin or house-spirit of Normandy. This goblin was said to be able to take on the form of a horse, when it was referred to as 'le Cheval Bayard'.

lutki   *Hungarian*

also lutky;

= *Polish* krasnoludi; *Serbian* ludki

Benevolent dwarfs of the Otherworld.

Lyonesse   *British*

A fabled lost land. This island is said to have been situated off the far south-west of Britain, supporting a happy agricultural society. Part of it, ruled by Galahad, was known as Surluse. The island was drowned under the Atlantic by water spirits jealous of the happiness and prosperity of the inhabitants. Only one man, Trevilian, escaped when the sea overwhelmed the island.

Some say it was the land where the Knight of the Round Table Tristram was born, the land from which King Arthur came and the site of the final battle where he met his death.

Others say that, when King Arthur was killed, Mordred survived and drove the remaining forces of the king to Lyonesse. The ghost of the sorcerer Merlin caused the land to sink beneath the waves taking Mordred's men with it, while the king's men escaped.

M

M *Central American*
A Mayan deity of uncertain identity referred to as God M (*see **alphabetical gods***); perhaps Ek Chuah. This deity is depicted as black with red lips and carrying a package on his head.

Ma *Egyptian*
Goddess of justice and truth; ruler of the underworld; a form of Tefnut the sun goddess as a lioness. Daughter of Ra and wife of Thoth.

She is depicted as wearing a single ostrich feather which she uses to weigh the souls of the dead.

Ma-sang *Tibetan*
Early ancestors of the race. During this period, armour was invented. Next came the miracle workers, the 'gong-po, the klu and the rGyal-po.

maahiset *Baltic*
A Finnish forest spirit. Ant hills are used as the site for making offerings to this spirit.

In an alternative version, they are small beings which live under the earth and which can cause skin diseases in humans.

Mab *Celtic*
also Maeve, Titania
A fairy-midwife, queen of the fairies. (*See also **Maev**.*)

Macha *Irish*
A war goddess and fertility goddess of Ulster. As a war goddess she, with Ana and Babd, made a trinity that equated with the goddess Morrigan.

When King Aedh died, the throne of Ulster should have been shared between his brothers, Dithorba and Kimbay, but Macha killed Dithorba, forcibly married Kimbay and took the throne herself. She captured and imprisoned the five sons of Dithorba and forced them to build the walls of the fortress Emain Macha.

She appeared mysteriously in the home of the wealthy farmer Crundchu and became his mistress. When he boasted that she could run faster than the king's horses, she was forced into a race although heavily pregnant at the time. She won the race but gave birth to twins on the spot. She cursed the men of Ulster, so that when they most needed their strength to fight they would, for five days and four nights, become as weak as a woman in labour.

Madame Wind *see* **Feng-p'o-p'o**

Mador *British*
A Knight of the Round Table; son of the king of the Hesperides.

At a dinner given by Guinevere for twenty-four of her knights, Pinel planted a poisoned apple for Gawain who had killed Pinel's cousin, Lamerock. By mistake, Patrise ate the apple and fell dead on the spot. Mador accused Guinevere of the murder. Lancelot took up the cause on behalf of the queen and defeated Mador in single combat.

Maen Arthur *British*
A rock in Wales said to retain the imprint of the hoof of King Arthur's horse.

Maev   *Irish*
also Maeve, Queen Maeve
A mother-goddess; queen of
Connaught. She coveted the
Brown Bull of Cooley and Ailill,
her husband, led an expedition
(the Cattle Raid of Cooley) into
Ulster to seize it. The bull was
captured but Cuchulainn inflicted
defeat on her army and she swore
revenge. She invaded seven years
later with another army, aided
by the Children of Catalin who
conjured up phantom battalions
to harass the Ulstermen.

She was killed by Furbaidhe,
a son of Clothra, Maev's sister,
who shot her with a piece of hard
cheese from his sling.

(*See also* **Mab**.)

Magaera   *Greek*
One of the three Furies.

magic carpet
A miraculous form of air transport
which would carry its rider
wherever he wished to go. One
such carpet was that used by
Solomon which carried his throne
and all his entourage. Another
was owned by Housain and
appears in the *Arabian Nights'
Entertainments*.

magical or miraculous birth
Many cultures have stories of
women bearing children after
being impregnated by some
magical occurrence. Stories
report conception as a result
of consuming various foods or
drinks; from being exposed to
sunlight or wind; from rain, tears,
mucus, etc.
(1) In China, it was said that the
god Yüan Shih was born through
the spine of a hermit.
(2) In Finnish lore, the virgin
Marjatta was impregnated after
eating a cranberry; the hero
Vainamoinen was so long in the
womb that he was an old man
when he was born.
(3) The Greeks have stories of
the impregnation of Danae by
Zeus in the form of a shower of
gold; of Hera bearing Ares after
picking a flower and Hebe from
a lettuce leaf; of Leto bearing
Castor and Polydeuces after an
encounter with Zeus in the form
of a swan; of Pasiphae bearing
the Minotaur, fathered by a bull.
Athena was born from the head
of Zeus and Dionysus from his
thigh.
(4) In Hindu lore, a man Yuvanasva
bore a son from his side after
drinking a potion; Brahma was
born from the god Vishnu's navel;
Kadru and Kaitabha were born
from Vishnu's ear; the god of
wisdom, Manjushri, was born
from the pistil of the lotus.
(5) The Irish say that Dectera
produced Setanta (later, the
hero Cuchulainn) as a result of
swallowing a mayfly (the god
Lugh in another form); Etain was
turned into a butterfly by her
husband's discarded first wife and
later fell into a cup of tea which
was drunk by the wife of Etar,
king of Ulster who, in due course,
produced a child, the reincarnated
Etain.
(6) In the Marshall Islands, the
creator-god Loa gave birth to
Lejman and Wulleb from his leg
and Wulleb similarly produced
Edao and Jemaliwut.
(7) Norse myths include the story
of the giant demi-god Heimdall,
said to have been fathered by
Odin on the nine Wave Maidens
who simultaneously gave birth to
the boy.
(8) In North American lore, the
Navaho goddess Nao'tsiti was
impregnated by the rainbow;
Kukitat was born from his
brother's shoulder; Malsum was
born from his mother's armpit.
(9) Persian lore refers to the god
Mithra having been born, fully-
formed, from a rock.
(10) In South American myth,
Coatlicue was impregnated
by a ball of down or feathers;
Chalchihuitlicue produced the
god Quetzalcoatl after contact
with a piece of jade; Xquiq
became pregnant when the
severed head of Hunhunapu spat
into her hand; a medicine-man,
Maira-pochy, impregnated a
maiden by giving her fish.

Magog   *British*
The last survivor, with Gog, of an
ancient race of British giants.
Some say he was the son of
Japhet, son of Noah.

magpie
(1) There is a story that this bird
was excluded from Noah's Ark
because it chattered so much and
it was forced to ride on the roof.
(2) In China the magpie is used
as the imperial emblem. It is
regarded as the bringer of good
news and, accordingly, is known
as the Bird of Joy.
(3) In Rome the magpie was
regarded as the bird of the war
god Mars.

Magpie Bridge   *Chinese*
In some accounts, a flock of
magpies formed a bridge over a
river (the Milky Way) to enable
the lovers Ch'ien Niu and Chih Nü
to meet once a year.

Maha-pudma *see* **Mahapadma**

Mahadevi *Hindu*
  also Great Goddess
  A name for Ambika, Canda, Devi,
  Durga, Kali, Parvati, Uma and
  other important goddesses.
    Mahadevi was created by
  the gods who gave the pre-
  existing Devi something of their
  own energy, making a visible
  and powerful deity capable of
  defeating the demons, enemies
  of the gods. They also gave her
  weapons and lion to ride on and,
  as Canda, she rode to do battle
  with the demons. After killing
  Chiksura and other leaders and
  hordes of their followers, she
  met their supreme leader, the
  huge buffalo, Mahisha. When she
  caught him in a noose, he became
  a lion; when she killed the lion,
  he became a warrior with 1000
  arms, each holding a weapon; she
  killed him, only to find that he had
  become a mad elephant and, when
  she cut off the animal's trunk, the
  demon became the huge buffalo
  again. Mahadevi (Canda) cut off
  his head, finally killing him.
    When two other demons,
  Nishumbha and Shumbha,
  challenged the gods, she returned,
  this time as Kali (or Durga). She
  killed Nishumbha and felled
  Shumbha but contact with the
  earth re-invigorated him. Locked
  in battle, he carried her into the
  sky but she escaped, threw him
  down to earth and killed him with
  her arrows and lance.

Mahaf *Egyptian*
  A ferryman in the underworld. He
  steers the boat (meseket) which
  carries Ra back to the east each
  night ready for his next trip
  across the heavens.

Mahapadma *Hindu*
  also Maha-pudma

The elephant standing on the back
  of the tortoise, Chukwa, which
  supports the earth. It is said that
  the earth rests on this animal's
  head and, when it moves its head,
  it causes an earthquake.

Mahasthama *Buddhist*
  A god of wisdom. He and
  Avalokiteshvara occupy thrones in
  Amitabha's heaven.

Maheo *North American*
  also All-spirit
  A creator-god of the Cheyenne
  Indians. He is said to have made
  the world from mud brought
  from the sea bottom by the coot,
  Earth-Diver; Maheo built land
  on the back of a huge turtle. He
  made mankind from one of his
  own ribs.

Mahisha *Hindu*
  A demon monster in the form of
  a water-buffalo armed with a
  mace. When she wounded him, he
  turned into a warrior with 1000
  arms, each holding a weapon. (*See*
  Mahadevi.)

Maho Penekheka *North American*
  A Mandan name for the Great
  Spirit.

Mahucutah *Central American*
  also the Distinguished Name
  One of the first four men, in Mayan
  lore; brother of Balam Agab,
  Balam Quitzé and Iqi Balam (*see
  more at* ***Balam Agab***).

Mahuika *Pacific Islands*
  A Polynesian goddess of the
  underworld. In some accounts,
  she was a fire goddess who
  married Auahi-Turoa and bore
  five sons.
    Some accounts say that her
  grandson Maui stole fire from
  Mahuika in the underworld and
  gave it to his people, while others
  say that she gave Maui one of her
  nails, in which fire resided, but it

was so hot that he dropped it in
  the sea. When he did this several
  times, she threw fire at him and
  he would have burnt to death if
  the rain gods had not doused the
  fire.
    Other stories say that Maui
  learned the secret of fire from
  mud-hens.
    In some versions, Mahuika is
  male.

Maia *Greek*
  A nymph, one of the Pleiades;
  mother of Hermes by Zeus.

Maid of Astolat *see* **Elaine**[3]

Maid of the Hairy Arms *Irish*
  also May Molloch
  A banshee who engages in games
  and sports.

Maiden *see* **Core**

Maimed King *see* **Fisher King**

Main *Siberian*
  A guardian of the sun.
    An elk once caught the sun in
  its antlers and took it into the
  forest so that the world became
  dark. Main shot the elk and
  restored the sun to the heavens.

Maît'(re) Carrefour *see*
  Carrefour

Maivia Kivivia *East Indies*
  A fish. Tired of swimming, the
  fish rested on a bank and here it
  grew limbs and became a two-
  legged being. Alone, it produced
  two sons, Mavu and Moro, who
  became the ancestors of the
  tribes of New Guinea.

Maka *Egyptian*
  The huge snake which attacked the
  god Ra's barge each night when
  it made its journey through the
  underworld.

Makara[1] *East Indies*
  A sea-monster in the form of a
  crocodile with a trunk-like snout.

Makara[2] *Hindu*
  A monster ridden by Ganga (the

goddess of the River Ganges)
or by the god Varuna. In some
accounts, this being was described
as part crocodile, dolphin and
shark, in others as a fish with the
head and legs of a deer or as a
fish-elephant.

Another story has the Makara
as the crab which outwitted a
crane and snapped off its head.

Malephar   *European*
One of the 72 Spirits of Solomon.
He is said to impart knowledge
of magic and anthropomorphism
and is depicted as a lion.

Mali   *African*
In Mali, a shape-changing monster
in the form of a hippopotamus.

This monster ate all the crops
and, when the hunter Karadigi
attacked it with his pack of
hounds, it ate those too. The hero
Fara Maka tried to kill it with
spears but was eaten. His wife,
Nana Miriam, paralysed the beast
with a magic spell.

Malpas   *European*
One of the 72 Spirits of Solomon.
He is said to be able to construct
impregnable buildings by magic
and is envisaged in the form of a
huge bird.

Malsum   *North American*
also Wolf
A creator-god of the Algonquin,
a wolf-god; twin brother of
Gluskap.

He made all the evil features of
this world. He killed his mother
at birth when emerging from her
armpit and he killed his brother
with the feather of an owl, the
only thing which could harm
him. Gluskap came back to life
and Malsum tried again with a
pine-root but Gluskap merely
laughed and drove him into the
woods. The beaver Quah-beet

heard Gluskap say that he could
be killed by a flowering rush and
he passed this on to Malsum.
When he asked for the wings of a
bird as reward, Malsum scoffed at
him, so Quah-beet told Gluskap
what he had done. Gluskap then
dug up a fern, the only thing that
could harm Malsum, and used it
to kill his brother who thereafter
lived as the wolf, Lox, in the
underworld.

Mama Ocllo   *South American*
She married her brother, Ayar
Manco or Manco Capac, and
founded the Inca dynasty.

In one story she went on
ahead of the others to look for
a suitable place to settle and
came to Cuzco. Here she killed a
peasant and disembowelled him.
Dangling his blood-covered liver
from her mouth, she entered the
village and all the inhabitants
fled, thinking they were about
to be attacked by a cannibalistic
monster. She and her brothers and
sisters were then able to take over
the village unopposed.

(*See also* ***Children of the Sun***.)

Mamlambo   *African*
A Zulu river goddess, goddess of
beer-makers.

Mamoo   *Australian*
A god of evil. The Aborigines say
that Mamoo made all the bugs,
insects, snails and other tiny
creatures to ravage the pleasant
world created by Yhi.

Man   *Chinese*
A Taoist deity, one of the Taoist
Four Diamond Kings.

Man-Eagle   *North American*
A Hopi monster in the form of a
huge eagle. This monster carried
off young women to his nest and
killed them. One of those taken
was the wife of Son of Light who,

with the help of Spider Woman,
a mole and several birds, reached
Man-Eagle's lair and saved his
wife by beating the monster in
several contests of magic. In the
final test, Man-Eagle was burned
to ashes but Spider Woman
restored him to life in the form
of a young man who promised to
mend his ways.

Man Maker   *North American*
A creator-spirit of the Pima tribe.
He made people in his own image
from clay and baked them in an
oven. Interference by Coyote
meant that the first result was a
dog followed by an underburnt
(white) couple and then an
overburnt (black) couple and
finally a perfect couple – the
Pueblo.

Manabozho   *North American*
also Great Hare;
= *Abnaki* Gluskap; *Iroquois* Ioskeha;
Menominee Manabush; *Montagnais*
Messou
A trickster-god of the Chippewa;
a shape-changer who often
appeared as a rabbit.

In some versions, he was
descended from Nokomis,
grandmother of Hiawatha, and,
when the Underwater Panthers
tried to kill her by causing a flood,
Manabozho called on the beavers
and others to bring up mud from
the bottom from which he made
dry land and saved Nokomis.

His enmity of the Underwater
Panthers was based on the fact
that they had seized and killed his
brother Chibiabos. He was later
given the secrets of the Mide
ceremony which enabled him to
resurrect his brother, whom he
made ruler of the underworld. As
a healing deity, he instituted the
medicine-feast known as Mide.

He is sometimes equated with Gluskap or Hiawatha.

His brother, Flint, had killed their mother when they were born and Manabozho killed Flint when they grew up.

Manabush *North American*

also Great Hare;
= *Abnaki* Gluskap; *Chippewa* Manabozho; *Iroquois* Ioskeha; *Montagnais* Messou

A trickster-god of the Menominee Indians; brother of Moqwaoi.

He was the only survivor of twins born to Wenonah, a daughter of Nokomis and mother of Hiawatha, who died in childbirth, and he turned into a white rabbit who later stole fire and gave it to the tribe.

When his brother, Moqwaoi, was killed by evil spirits, the anamaqkiu, he killed two of their number with the result that the other spirits caused a flood from which Manabush was the only one to escape, which he did by climbing a pine tree and causing it to grow rapidly to beat the rising waters. When Muskrat found a small piece of dry soil after Beaver, Mink and Otter had failed, Manabush was able to recreate the world.

In another story, Misikinebik, a monstrous serpent, ate nearly all the tribe, so Manabush offered himself and, once inside the beast, stabbed its heart and killed it.

Managarm *Norse*

One of the three wolves that chased the sun and moon.

This beast, together with Hati and Skoll, pursued the sun and moon and, on occasions caught and swallowed them, causing an eclipse. They were the offspring of Fenris and fed on the marrow

from the bones of dead criminals. As crime increased, they grew stronger and in the last days they overtook the sun and moon and finally swallowed them.

Manannan mac Lir *Irish*

= *Welsh* Manawyddan fab Llyr

A sea god; a shape-changer and magician; son of Lir and Aobh.

He was the ruler of Emain Ablach and owned a chariot in which he could ride over the waves, a magic boat known as Wave-sweeper, a horse called Splendid Mane and a cloak and helmet that rendered him invisible.

He was said to have three legs which, used like the spokes of a wheel, enabled him to travel at great speed.

As a shape-changer, he often took the form of a bird; as a magician he performed many wonderful feats including one in which he tossed a silken thread into the sky where it caught on a cloud, allowing a lady to climb up it.

It was said that when Aillen fell in love with Manannan's wife, Uchtdealb, the god gave her to Aillen and took his sister, Aine.

It was he who rescued the infant Lugh, the god of light, when he was thrown into the sea on the orders of his grandfather, Balor.

He once took Angus Og, god of love and beauty, on a trip to India and returned with two marvellous cows, keeping one and giving the other to Angus.

He allocated a sidh (fairy mound) to each of the various groups of Danaans after their defeat by the Milesians and he gave them the Veil of Invisibility

and some marvellous pigs which were restored to life each time they were killed and eaten.

Some of his children were divine, others mortal. He was said to have been drowned in Lake Corrib by Uillin.

Manasa *Hindu*

= *Jain* Nagini

A snake-goddess; an aspect of Parvati.

When Shiva sucked up the venom which Ananta, or Vasuki, used to poison the amrita created at the Churning of the Ocean, Manasa helped him by taking some of the poison in her own mouth and passing it on to the venomous creatures of the earth.

When the merchant Chand refused to worship her, she appeared in the form of a lovely maiden and married him. She then destroyed his livelihood and reverted to her snake form, biting all of his six sons, who died. He had another son, Lakshmindra, who married Behula and Chand tried to protect them by building a steel house. Manasa slipped into the house on the night of Lakshmindra's wedding and killed him but she restored him to life when Chand finally agreed to worship her.

She is said to have the power to cure illness caused by poison from snake-bites, etc and is depicted in the company of a snake with seven-heads.

Manawyddan *Welsh*

also Manawyddan fab Llyr

A sea god; ruler of the land of the dead; son of Llyr and Penardun; brother of Bran and Branwen.

He was one of the seven survivors of the force that his brother Bran led to Ireland to rescue their sister, Branwen, from the ill-treatment she received at the hands of her husband, Matholwch.

He was later introduced by Pryderi, a prince of Dyfed, to his mother Rhiannon and they married. By some mysterious agency, all living things disappeared from Wales, so Manawyddan and Rhiannon, together with Pryderi and his wife Cigfa, moved to England. Here they worked successively as saddlemakers, shield-makers and shoemakers but they aroused the enmity of local craftsmen and eventually returned to Wales where Pryderi and Rhiannon mysteriously disappeared. When Manawyddan set up as a farmer he was plagued by mice and, having caught the largest mouse, was about to hang it when a bishop appeared and offered a large ransom for the mouse, who was his wife. It turned out that he was the magician Llwyd who had put a curse on the country to avenge the treatment of Gwawl, the suitor rejected by Rhiannon when she married Pwyll, father of Pryderi. With the mouse freed and restored as the magician's wife, Pryderi and Rhiannon were returned, the spell was lifted and the land returned to normal.

mandrake
A plant said to have magical properties. Some say that this plant was grown in paradise.

In some accounts, a magician using the appropriate rituals can bring the plant to life so that it can speak. Other accounts say the plant could kill anybody who pulled up the root, so the job was done by tying a dog to the plant and then chasing the dog until it pulled the plant out of the ground, whereupon the dog died. The plant was said to scream when it was pulled up.

manedowikamekoiki   *North American*
Heaven, the 'happy hunting-ground' of the Shawnee.

maneko noko   *Japanese*
A charm in the form of a cat. The cat has one paw raised as if to beckon customers into the shop where it is displayed.

Manes   *Roman*
The spirits of the good dead. These spirits were honoured at the festivals of Feralia and Parentalia.

The word is used to refer to ancestral spirits, to the rulers of the underworld or to the underworld itself

In the theory of the three-part soul, the Manes was the part that was sent to heaven or hell.

Mang   *East Indies*
A goddess of night. On a visit to earth, in the time before night existed, she caught her long hair in a vine and could not fly back to heaven. She was found and released by Lejo, who married her. Unused to the continuous light, she had brought a bag full of darkness and she inadvertently allowed it to escape so that thereafter night alternated with day. After the birth of their daughter, Mang flew back to heaven.

Mangar-kunjer-kunja   *Australian*
'Flycatcher', a lizard-ancestor of the Aranda tribe. He discovered the two partly formed beings, Rella-manerinja, cut them apart and completed their development by making the appropriate openings so that they could become the ancestors of the human race.

Another story of the Aranda says that humans were originally lizards. The first one lay down in the sun and, after a while, others appeared from his body and later they all became human.

Maninga   *North American*
An evil spirit of the Mandan.
Maninga was in conflict with Lone Man who defeated him but Maninga came back four years later in the form of a great flood. Lone Man saved his people by building a stockade called the Great Canoe and Maninga was finally defeated by the powers of Lone Man's medicine-drum and was swept away as the flood receded.

Manitou   *North American*
also Great Spirit
A revered spirit or god.

Manjushri   *Buddhist*
A god of wisdom; a bodhisattva. He was said to have been a 10th-century Indian king who went to China.

In some accounts, he was born from the pistil of the lotus flower which was generated by a bright light beamed from the Buddha's forehead.

When Yama, god of the dead, was rampaging through Tibet, Manjushri turned himself into a demon with nine heads and thirty-four arms known as Yamantaka, who overcame Yama and converted him to Buddhism.

One story tells how Manjushri descended to the bottom of the ocean to spread Buddhism to the nagas (snake beings) and converted hundreds of them, including the daughter of Sagara, king of the nagas.

He is regarded as the bringer of civilisation, the founder of a branch of Mahayana Buddhism and a future Buddha. His shakti (female aspect) is Sarasvati.

He is depicted as holding a book and a sword, resting on a lotus.

Manohel-Tohel   *Central American*
A Mayan creator-god. He gave mankind bodies and souls and conducted them from the darkness of caves into the light of day.

Manta   *South American*
In the lore of Araucanians, a monster in the form of a cuttlefish. This monster, which lives in deep lakes, is said to drag people under the water and eat them. It may mate with various other animals, producing yet more monsters. It can be killed by the shrub quisco, which has many sharp spines.

The beast itself is said to have four eyes, with hundreds of smaller eyes round the edges of its mantle.

manticora   *European*
also manticore
A monster, part lion, part scorpion, with the head of a man. This blood-red beast was said to have three rows of teeth and a clump of poisonous spines on the end of its long tail. Some accounts say that it could shoot the spines like arrows, others use the beast to represent the devil.

Mantis   *African*
A trickster-hero of the Khoisan, who brought fire to his people by stealing it from the ostrich and is said to have given names to everything that exists.

Mantle of Invisibility *see* **Gwen**

Manu   *Hindu*
A primeval creator-god or the first human.

Every kalpa (period of 4,320

million years) has fourteen floods, each with its own version of the Manu story in which a fish warns of a coming flood.

Manu built a ship, filled it with specimens of each plant and animal and was towed to safety by the fish, allowing Manu to survive to become the progenitor of the human race. The fish is Matsya, the first avatar of the god Vishnu, in some stories.

An alternative story says that Manu was the first mortal, produced when Brahma mated with Sarasvati, the woman born of his own body.

In other accounts, Brahma produced ten Prajapatis who produced seven Manus. The first Manu was known as Svayam-bhuva and some say that Vaivasvata is the seventh and current incarnation.

He is said to have written *Manu Smirti*, a book of laws.

Manuai   *East Indies*
In the lore of the Admiralty Islands of Papua New Guinea, the first man. He cut down a tree which, at his command, became a woman with whom he mated to start the human race.

Manuk Manuk   *East Indies*
In the lore of Sumatra, a cosmic chicken. The primordial god mated with this blue chicken which produced three eggs from which came the three gods who created and ruled respectively the heavens, the earth and the underworld.

Marathonian bull *see* **Cretan Bull**

Marawa   *Pacific Islands*
A spider-spirit. When the creator-god Qat tried to cut a canoe from a log, Marawa replaced each night the pieces that Qat had chipped out during the day. When

Qat caught him in the act, he helped to complete the job.

In an alternative version, Qat was carving human beings from wood and Marawa buried them, so introducing death to the world.

Marbas   *European*
A demon, one of the 72 Spirits of Solomon. He is envisaged in the form of a lion.

Marchosias   *European*
A demon, one of the 72 Spirits of Solomon. He is said to impart knowledge of warfare and is depicted either as a fire-breathing, winged wolf or as a wolf with wings and the tail of a serpent.

Marduk   *Mesopotamian*
also Bel-Marduk;
= *Assyrian* Ashur; *Greek* Zeus; *Hebrew* Merodach; *Sumerian* Enlil
The double-headed creator-god, sun god and god of magic, wisdom and war; city god of Babylon.

He created a new world order after he had killed Tiamat, the demon of chaos. He cut her body in half, using one part for the earth, the other for the sky. He retrieved the Tablets of Destiny giving him complete control of the world and, mixing the blood of the earth god Kingu with clay, he made mankind. Another story says that Marduk cut off his own head and used the blood to make mankind.

He is described as having two heads, four ears, four eyes and a mouth emitting flames.

Eventually, all the gods were assimilated into Marduk, who was associated with the planets Jupiter and Mercury.

Marindi   *Australian*
An ancestral dog. During the Dreamtime, he fought the lizard

Adno-artina and was killed. His blood make the rocks red.

Marmyadose *British*

A sword of King Arthur. It was said that this sword had been made by the smith-god Vulcan for Hercules and came into the hands of the giant Retho from whom it was won by King Arthur.

Marrok *British*

also Maroc

A Knight of the Round Table. He was changed into a werewolf by his sorceress wife but was restored to human form after seven years.

Mars *Roman*

= *Egyptian* Anhur; *Etruscan* Maris; *Greek* Ares

The war god, god of agriculture, fertility, fields, woods; one of the Olympians; son of Jupiter and Juno; brother of Bellona, goddess of war; husband of Venus. In one account, he raped Ilia (Rhea Silvia) and fathered the twins Romulus and Remus on her.

One story says that he employed the old goddess Anna Perenna as a go-between when wooing the goddess Minerva. She told Mars that Minerva was willing to marry him but, when he raised the bride's veil, he found himself looking at Anna herself. A different version has the minor goddess Nerio in place of Minerva, while others say that Nerio, rather than Venus, was his wife.

His festivals were Armilustrium (in October) and Quinquatrus (in March).

Marsyas *Greek*

A satyr famous as a flute-player; a Phrygian demi-god. He challenged the god Apollo to a music-contest playing his double-flute or oboe, which Athena

had made but abandoned, while Apollo played his lyre. Apollo was adjudged to have won and flayed Marsyas alive. King Midas was one of the judges at this contest and, because he cast his vote in favour of Marsyas, Apollo gave him the ears of an ass.

Massim Biambe *African*

A creator-god of the Mundang people of Chad and Cameroon. This deity created the primeval beings, Mebeli and Phebele, progenitors of mankind.

Master of Animals *see* **Desana, jaguar**

Master of Breath *see* **Esaugetuh Emissee**

Mata *Irish*

A monster. This beast, said to have 4 heads and 100 legs, was captured and killed by the Irish leader, the Dagda.

Matsumura *Japanese*

A priest who went to the Shogun and asked for funds to repair his monastery. He took a house where the well was always full of water, even when a drought struck the city. Many people had thrown themselves into the well for some unknown reason. Matsumura saw a beautiful woman, Yayoi, in the water and she reappeared when the drought ended. She had been forced by the Poison Dragon to lure people to their death. She disappeared again and, when Matsumura cleaned out the well, he found her mirror, which he cleaned and kept safely. When she appeared again, she explained that she was the soul of the mirror. She warned Matsumura to leave as his home would be destroyed in a flood and told him to present the mirror to the Shogun. When

the priest gave the mirror to the Shogun, he was rewarded with money to repair his monastery.

Matsya *Hindu*

The first incarnation of Vishnu, as a fish. In this form, he saved Vaivasvata (Manu), the progenitor of mankind, from the Flood by advising him on how to build a ship and then towing it to safety. He also killed the demon Hayagriva when he tried to steal the Vedas from the sleeping Brahma.

Matvutsini *South American*

A creator-god of the Xingu. He first made a woman from a shell and they mated to produce a son who became the ancestor of the Xingu tribe.

When some of the people died, Matvutsini tried to restore them in a ceremony in which he decorated kuarup logs and tried to bring them to life. This failed because the people failed to carry out his instructions for honouring the logs and so death became a permanent feature of the human condition.

Maui *Pacific Islands*

A trickster-hero and sun god. As an infant, he was thrown into the sea wrapped in a tuft of his mother's or sister's hair and was saved from drowning by an ancestor, the sky god Tama.

Alone he pushed up the sky to give people more room to move, trapped the sun in a net made from the hair of his sister, Hina-ika, made it slow its motion across the heavens to give a longer day and fixed the stars in the sky. He killed his grandmother so that he could use her jawbone as a hook to fish up the islands from the sea-bottom and he stole fire from

Mahuika in the underworld for the benefit of mankind or, some say, learned the secret of fire from the mud-hens.

When Hina left her eel-husband Te Tuna, she took Maui as a lover. Twice they fought over her and on the second occasion Maui killed Te Tuna and buried his head from which sprang the first coconut tree.

Another story tells how he hooked a monstrous fish which, as he towed it behind his boat, split into many pieces to form the islands of the Pacific, or, in some versions, into two large pieces which became the two islands of New Zealand.

He crept through the body of the sleeping Hine-nui-te-po, goddess of death, in an abortive attempt to win immortality for the human race but he was killed when she squeezed him.

His blood gives the rainbow its colours and causes shrimps to be red.

His weapon was the jawbone of his ancestress Muri-ranga-whenua and he is credited with the invention of sails and fish-hooks.

Mawu-Lisa   *African*
Creator-god of the Fon. A dual-sex divinity, offspring of another androgynous deity Nana Buluku, combining Mawu the female aspect and Lisa the male aspect. (In some versions, Mawu is male and Lisa female.) They were said to have produced the first humans, seven pairs of twins.

May Molloch *see* **Maid of the Hairy Arms**

Mbomba   *African*
A creator-god of the Bakuba. He quarrelled with his fellow-deity,

Ngaan, and went to heaven where he disgorged the sun, moon and stars, followed by trees, animals and humans. Ngaan took the undersea world.

Mead of Inspiration   *Norse*
A magic brew made by the dwarfs Fialar and Galar from the blood of the sage, Kvasir. In some accounts, the giant Gilling made the brew and the dwarfs killed him to obtain it. They were later forced to hand it over to Suttung who passed it on to his daughter, Gunlod, from whom it was stolen by Odin for the use of the gods.

Mebege   *African*
A creator-god in the Congo and Gabon. He is said to have created humans by mixing a hair from under his arm with part of his own brain and a pebble which he then breathed on to form an egg. This he gave to the spider, Diaboba, and then fertilised it, whereupon it cracked open and human beings emerged. In similar fashion, he created termites and worms which built the world into which the humans ventured as soon as it had hardened.

Mebeli   *African*
The primeval female created by Massim Biambe. She mated with the primeval male, Phebele, to produce the human race.

Medea   *Greek*
A sorceress; a priestess of Hecate; daughter of Aetes, king of Colchis, and Idyia or Hecate.

She fell in love with Jason when he arrived in Colchis to get the Golden Fleece and lulled the guardian dragon to sleep while Jason took the fleece from the tree where it had been hung, fleeing with him in the *Argo*.

In one version, she took her half-brother Apsyrtus aboard with her and, when they were chased by the Colchian fleet, killed him and threw pieces overboard to delay the pursuers as Aetes stopped to collect the pieces for burial. Another version has Apsyrtus with the pursuers, catching up with Jason and agreeing a truce while the king of the Brygians adjudicated on the fate of both Medea and the fleece. She lured Apsyrtus ashore where Jason ambushed and killed him. She married Jason after they had been purified of the murder by the sorceress Circe.

On the voyage back to Iolcus they were attacked by Talos, the bronze guardian of Crete but Medea first drugged him and then removed the pin in his ankle which allowed the vital fluid to drain from his single vein, so killing him. In another version, she prayed to Hades who caused Talos to graze his ankle against a rock, so letting all his blood run out. At Iolcus, Pelias had brought about the death of Jason's parents and his young brother and Medea helped him to exact vengeance. She bewitched Pelias's daughters, Evadne and Amphinome, and induced them to kill and dismember their father and then signalled to the waiting Argonauts, who captured the city unopposed. In some stories, she rejuvenated Jason's father, Aeson, who had not died but had been imprisoned by Pelias.

Medea's father, Aetes, was also king of Corinth, and when she arrived there with Jason and found the throne vacant and she claimed it for herself, ruling with Jason as her king for ten years, bearing seven sons and seven daughters. She had, in fact, poisoned the previous king, Corinthus, and when Jason found this out he set out to divorce her with a view to marrying Glauce, the daughter of King Creon of Thebes. Others say that they lived happily in Corinth as ordinary citizens with two sons and that it was the daughter of the king of Corinth that Jason planned to marry. As a wedding-gift, Medea sent her a crown and a robe which burst into flames when the bride put them on, killing her, her father and many of the guests. Jason was lucky to escape with his life.

Zeus was greatly intrigued by her resourcefulness and fell in love with her, but she rejected his advances. His wife Hera, who was always jealous of her husband's lovers, was so grateful that she offered to make Medea's children immortal if she would offer them in sacrifice. Medea promptly complied and, handing the kingdom of Corinth over to Sisyphus, fled to Thebes to seek protection from Hercules. Having cured Hercules of his madness, she went on to Athens and became the third wife of King Aegeus whom she had met earlier, promising to procure a son for him. She herself produced a son called Medus. Augeus had left an illegitimate son, Theseus, with his mother, Aethra, in Troezen and when Theseus arrived at the court to claim his inheritance, Medea tried to poison him. Banished by Aegeus, she fled to Italy, later marrying an Asian king.

When Perses usurped the throne of Colchis, she returned

there with Medus, who killed Perses and reinstated Aetes as king. Some say that Medea herself killed Perses.

Medea is said finally to have become immortal and to have ruled in the Elysian Fields. In some versions, it was Medea, not Helen, who married Achilles in Hades.

Medusa   *Greek*
also Gorgo

One of the three Gorgons; sister of Euryale and Stheno.

She was originally a beautiful mortal but was changed into an ugly Gorgon by the goddess Athena for sleeping with the sea god Poseidon in Athena's temple or, in another story, for insulting Athena by claiming to be more beautiful than the goddess. (In some versions, Artemis appears instead of Athena.)

The only mortal of the three, she was killed and beheaded by Perseus who had promised her head to Polydectes, king of Seriphos, as a wedding-gift. The flying-horse, Pegasus, and the warrior, Chrysaor, sprang from the blood of Medusa when she was killed, though some say that Poseidon was the father of Pegasus. Medusa's blood was used by Asclepius – that from one vein to kill, that from another to restore the dead to life.

The head was finally given to Athene who bore it on the aegis, the shield of Zeus, which she carried. Another story has it that the head was buried under the market-place in Athens.

She is depicted as having snakes for hair, wings and, sometimes, a beard. It is said that her look could turn people to stone.

Meliot de Logris   *British*

A Knight of the Round Table.

His cousin Nimue was forcibly dragged by Ontelake from Arthur's court where she had gone to reclaim her white bitch which had chased a white stag into the hall where the king's wedding feast was in progress. Meliot challenged Ontelake and they were fighting each other on foot when Pellimore, sent by the king to bring the lady and the intruding knight back to his court, rode up and parted them. Pellimore killed Ontelake and, when Meliot surrendered without a fight, Pellimore took Nimue back to Camelot.

He was badly wounded in a fight in which he killed Gilbert the Bastard and was saved by Lancelot who retrieved a sword and a piece of cloth covering the dead knight in Chapel Perilous and used them to restore Meliot to health.

He was one of the twelve knights who helped Agravain and Mordred when they attempted to seize Lancelot in the queen's bedroom. All except Mordred were killed by Lancelot.

Melpomene   *Greek*

One of the nine Muses, the Muse of tragedy.

Menelaus   *Greek*

King of Sparta; son of Atreus and Aerope; brother of Agamemnon; husband of Helen; father of Hermione.

He welcomed Paris, son of the king of Troy, to his court in Sparta but when he left for Crete, Paris carried off his wife Helen to Troy, so precipitating the Trojan War. During the battle, he came face to face with Paris and would have killed him had not the goddess Aphrodite intervened to save him. The Trojans might well have agreed, at that point, to hand back Helen but Pandarus, or Athene in some stories, shot and wounded Menelaus and the battle was resumed.

At the fall of Troy he was reunited with Helen but when they returned to Sparta they found that his brother Agamemnon had been killed by his wife Clytemnestra and her lover Aegisthus. They in turn had been killed in revenge by tgheir son Orestes. Menelaus was instrumental in having Orestes condemned to death. Orestes then seized Helen and Hermione, forcing Menelaus to change his mind and the death sentence was commuted to exile. When Helen was taken up to Olympus by Zeus to escape Orestes' sword, Apollo intervened in the affair and ordered Menelaus to re-marry and to give his daughter Hermione to Orestes.

Some accounts say that the Helen he was reunited with was the substitute Helen and both of them sailed to Egypt to collect the real Helen. He was shipwrecked and rescued by Theone.

In some versions, both Helen and Menelaus were taken to Elysium.

Meraugis   *British*

A Knight of the Round Table. He was the son of King Mark by his niece Labiane as a result of rape. His mother abandoned him in the forest where he was found and brought up by foresters. After the death of King Arthur, he joined many of the other knights in a hermitage.

Mercury   *Roman*

= *Greek* Hermes

The god of eloquence, merchants, theft, wisdom; messenger to the gods; one of the Olympians; father of Cupid and of the Lares, gods of the hearth; father of Faunus, some say.

He is depicted as a handsome youth wearing winged sandals and hat and holding the caduceus.

Merlin   *British*

= *Welsh* Emrys, Myrddin (Emrys)

A bard and magician. In one account of his origins, he was created by the forces of evil to offset the effect of Christ's birth but he was baptised as a Christian, so the plan failed. There are many different stories about his parentage. Some say that he was fathered by an unkown youth, said to be a demon, on the daughter of a king and was born with a twin sister, Gwendydd. Other stories say that he came from Atlantis or that he was the wizard Taliesin reincarnated.

When he was only a few days old, he made an impassioned plea for the life of his mother, who was on trial for associating with the Devil, and so saved her life.

He foretold the advent of Arthur and the return of Aurelius Ambrosius, king of Britain, and his brother Uther who had been taken to France to escape the fate that befell their brother Constans who was murdered at the hand of Vortigern, who became king. When Aurelius or, in some accounts, Uther, wanted a fitting memorial to the knights slaughtered by the Danish chief Hengist, Merlin went to Ireland with Uther, dismantled the Giant's

Ring, transported the stones by magic to England and re-erected them as Stonehenge.

He changed himself into the form of Jordans, a knight at the court of Gorlois, and brought about the seduction of Igraine by Uther Pendragon by changing Uther into the form of her husband, Gorlois, on the promise that he would be given the son of their union. This was the future king, Arthur, and Merlin took the boy and fostered him with Ector. In some accounts, Uther objected to handing over the child, so Merlin snatched him and blinded Uther.

When Arthur was defeated in a joust with Pellimore, Merlin saved his life by putting his opponent into a trance.

He knew that his fate would be sealed by a young girl, and when the knight Pellimore brought Nimue to Arthur's court he knew that his time had come. He fell in love with Nimue and foolishly taught her his magic arts when she led him to believe that she might yield to his persuasive talk. She accompanied him when he went to Ban's court in Benwick and, back in Britain, he made a fabulous room in a rock in Cornwall where they could be together. When they entered, she sprang back, sealing the entrance with an unbreakable spell, and rode off leaving him to his fate. When Bagdemagaus, seeking adventure, found the rock prison he was unable to break in and had to leave Merlin where he found him.

In some versions, Nimue bound him in an enchanted wood or an oak tree, in others she trapped him in a rock until he promised to love her only, entangling him forever in thorns when he refused. An alternative story says he was never so trapped and still lives on Bardsey Island guarding the Treasures of Britain, a collection of marvellous objects including King Arthur's throne, while others say that he was killed in battle or forgetfully sat in the Perilous Seat and was swallowed up by the earth.

He is credited with the creation of the magic sword, Excalibur, and the building of the Round Table.

In the stories of Charlemagne, Merlin built a magic fountain from which Rinaldo drank, turning his love for Angelica into hate. The warrior-maid Bradamante, searching for Rogero, was taken to Merlin's tomb where his spirit gave her instructions on how to find him, helped by Merlin's priestess, Melissa.

merrow   *Irish*
A mermaid or merman. These are generally benevolent beings, the female like a traditional mermaid while the male is ugly, greenish in colour and has arms which resemble fins. Some say they intermarry with mortals.

Merry Dancers *see* **Fir Chlis**

Metal Old Man   *North American*
In the lore of the Apache, a giant clad in black metal. The only place where this monstrous being was vulnerable was under his armpit and it was here that the young Monster Slayer shot his arrows and killed him.

meteor   *Arabian*
A meteor is said to be a flaming firebrand thrown by angels to drive off evil spirits.

Metis   *Greek*
'Wise counsel', one of the Oceanids; the goddess of prudence; daughter of Oceanus and Gaea or Tethys; first wife of Zeus.

She helped Zeus to overthrow Cronus and was seduced by Zeus who swallowed her (in the form of a fly, some say) to prevent the birth of a child she had foretold would be greater even than Zeus. That child was Athena who burst from the head of Zeus. Metis was sent to live in the planet Mercury.

Metnal   *Central American*
The Mayan home of the dead, ruled by Cizin, the god of death.

metsanhaltia   *Baltic*
= *Estonian* metshaldijas
A Finnish guardian spirit of the forest. This being is envisaged as an old man with a grey beard, covered with lichen, and able to able to stretch his body so that his head is level with the tallest tree.

metsaneitsyt   *Baltic*
A Finnish female spirit of the forest. This 'forest virgin', said to entice humans to make love to her, appears as a beautiful woman at the front but like a tree-stump or a bough or just a pile of twigs, when seen from the rear.

metshaldijas   *Baltic*
= *Finnish* metsanhaltia
An Estonian guardian spirit of the forest. It is said that the cry of this spirit is a portent of death to the hearer.

Miao Shan   *Chinese*
A princess; the original name of the goddess Kuan Yin. She refused to marry and entered a convent where she was helped in her arduous manual work by a demon, a tiger and the birds. When her father set fire to the

convent, she put the fire out with a miracle and, when he ordered her execution, the sword broke as it touched her neck. After meditating for nine years on an island, she became a bodhisattva. Her father was made blind for his sins. She told him that he would regain his sight if he were to swallow the eyeballs of one of his children and, when none of his children was prepared to make the necessary sacrifice, she plucked out her own eyes and cut off her own hands and sent them to her father. Her own eyes and hands were miraculously restored.

Another version says that she made an eye which her father swallowed to restore his sight.

Michabo   *North American*
also Great Hare
A creator-god of the Algonquins; chief of the five gods of the tribe.

Michabo often descended to earth to hunt and, on one occasion, his hunting pack composed of wolves led him to a lake. When he followed them into the lake, the water overflowed and flooded the whole earth. Both the raven and the otter failed to find any dry land but the musk-rat brought up mud from the bottom and Michabo made a new world, mating with Muskrat to start the human race.

He killed his brother Chokanipok and scattered his entrails, which became vines.

He is said to have invented the fishing net and instructed his people in the art of fishing. The clouds in the sky are the fumes from his great pipe.

(*See also* **Manabozho**.)

Mictlan   *Central American*
The Aztec land of the dead; part of the underworld.

Mictlantecuhtl   *Central American*
also Lady of Death
An Aztec goddess of the dead,
consort of Mictlantecuhtli.

Mictlantecuhtli   *Central American*
also Lord of Death, Lord of Hades
An Aztec god of the underworld,
god of death. This deity created
the underworld Mictlan and, with
Mictlantecuhtl, made the monstrous
goddess Cipactli. Other accounts
place him as the god of the sixth
of the thirteen Aztec heavens or as
one of the four gods supporting the
corners of the lowest heaven. He is
sometimes equated with the Mayan
gods Ah Puch or Hunhau.

Midas   *Greek*
King of Phrygia. It is said that a
long line of ants fed him with
wheat when he was in his cradle,
a sign of wealth in the future.

Midas had shown kindness
to Silenus, the old tutor of
Dionysus, and the god repaid
him by granting his wish that all
he touched should turn to gold.
He soon discovered it was not a
good idea – his food became gold
and he nearly starved to death.
He was freed by Dionysus when
he washed himself in the River
Pactolus which thereafter had
gold-bearing sands.

He was given the ears of an
ass by Apollo when he objected
to the god being adjudged the
winner of a music contest with
Marsyas or, some say, with Pan. He
hid his ears under a cap but his
secret was betrayed by his barber
who whispered it into a hole in
the ground. He refilled the hole
but a plant grew there and its
leaves whispered the secret for
all to hear. He died from drinking
bull's blood when shamed by the
disclosure of his deformity.

Midgard   *Norse*
Middle-earth, home of the first
humans.

Midnight Hunter *see* **Wish Hunt**

Milesians   *Irish*
A tribe led by Milesius. The sixth
and last invaders of Ireland, who
came with 36 ships to avenge the
murder of the Milesian Ith by the
three Danaan kings of Ireland. The
Danaans caused a storm which
wrecked many of the invaders'
ships and drowned many of their
crews, but some got ashore. In
the Battle of Tailltinn which
ensued, the three kings of Ireland
and their wives were killed. The
defeated Danaans then retreated
underground as fairies.

Milesius   *Irish*
A Scythian warrior, king of Spain.
He was originally called Golamh.
He went to Scythia and married
Seang, the king's daughter.
When she died, he went to Egypt
where he met and married Scota,
daughter of the pharaoh. He
killed the pharaoh and returned
to Spain with an army to repel
invaders.

Ith, his uncle or, in some
accounts, his grandfather, was
killed by the three Danaan kings
when he landed in Ireland.
Milesius raised an army and
invaded. He died before reaching
the island and his wife died soon
afterwards, but his sons defeated
the Danaans.

Milky Way
(1) In Aztec lore, this galaxy
was personified in the goddess
Citlanlinicue or as Chicomexochtli
(2) In Greek mythology, Hera
was induced into suckling the
infant Hercules who had been
abandoned and a spurt of milk

from her breast was said to have
formed the Milky Way.

Another story says that it is the
trail blazed by Phaeton in his wild
ride across the heavens in the
chariot of his father, the sun god
Helius.
(3) The Cheyenne regard this band
of stars as a 'hanging road',
Ekutsihimmiyo, between heaven
and earth.
(*See also* **Bifrost, Irmin's Way**.)

Mime   *German*
= *Norse* Regin
A dwarf. He made the Helmet of
Invisibility and the Ring of Power,
used by his brother Alberich, from
some of the Rhinegold. When the
treasure fell into the hands of the
dragon Fafnir, Mime resolved to get
it for himself. He set up a forge and
started to make swords, hoping to
find a hero who would use one of
them to kill Fafnir. The distraught
Sieglinde arrived on his doorstep
with a young baby and died soon
after showing Mime the pieces of
the broken Sword of Need. Mime
raised the boy, Siegfried, who
later reforged the sword and killed
Fafnir. When Mime tried to poison
Siegfried to get the treasure for
himself, Siegfried killed him.

Mimi   *Australian*
A trickster-spirit of the Aborigines.
These extremely thin beings live in
cracks in the rocks, cracks which
they make by blowing on the
surface of the rocks, and are said
to have taught humans the skills of
the hunter. The males are depicted
with large genitals, the females
with large pendulous breasts.

Mimir   *Norse*
A god of the primordial ocean; a
wise sea giant; guardian of the
Well of Knowledge.

In some stories he was one of the hostages given to the Vanir (one group of gods) and was decapitated by them when he refused to give them the secrets of the Aesir (another group). His head was given to Odin who preserved it by magic, giving it the power of speech so that he could consult it when needed.

Mimisbrunnr   *Norse*
also Well of Knowledge
The well below the world-tree Yggdrasil in Asgard. In some accounts, this well was guarded by Mimir while others say that it came into being when Odin made a shrine there with the head of Mimir who had been decapitated by the Vanir and a spring erupted at that point. Others say that the head was placed next to Urda's Well in Midgard.

This was the well from which Odin drank to gain knowledge, giving up one of his eyes in payment. The eye was placed in the well.

Minawara   *Australia*
An ancestral hero of the Aborigines, a kangaroo-man. He and his brother Multultu appeared, when the primordial waters subsided, in the form of kangaroos and they created all the other living things on earth.

Minerva   *Roman*
= *Etruscan* Menrfa; *Greek* Athena
Goddess of craftsmen, education, war and wisdom; one of the Olympians. Originally she was seen as the daughter of the giant, Pallas, whom she killed when he tried to rape her. In other versions, like Athena, she was born fully grown, from the head of Jupiter.

Mink   *North American*
An animal which tried to find dry land so that Manabush could recreate the world after the Flood. Mink died in the attempt, as did two other animals, Beaver and Otter. The only one to succeed was Muskrat.

Minnehaha   *North American*
also Laughing Water
Wife (or some say daughter) of Hiawatha. She was offered to the Great Spirit as a sacrifice and was taken up to heaven on the back of an enormous eagle. As a result, her father was able to unify the Five Nations.

Minos   *Greek*
A king of Crete; son of Zeus by Europa; brother of Rhadamanthus and Sarpedon; husband of Pasiphae; father of Ariadne, Deucalion, Phaedra, and others.

He and his brothers were adopted by Asterius, king of Crete. They quarrelled, and Rhadamanthus and Sarpedon left the island. Minos claimed the throne on the death of Asterius and proved his right by inducing the sea god Poseidon to send a white bull that swam ashore from the sea.

His son Androgeus, on a visit to Aegeus, the king of Athens, was sent on an expedition to kill a dangerous bull and was himself killed. Minos blamed Aegeus for his son's death and invaded Athens. In settlement he demanded that seven youths and seven maidens be sent to Crete every year (or every nine years) to be handed over as victims to the Minotaur, the offpsring of his wife Pasiphae and the bull which he kept hidden in the labyrinth built by Daedalus.

When Theseus came to Crete as one of the sacrificial victims, Minos threw his ring into the sea and challenged Theseus to prove that he was the son of Poseidon by retrieving the ring. With the help of the Nereids (sea nymphs), Theseus recovered the ring quite easily.

Minos was said to be the father of a calf that changed colour three times each day from white, to red, to black. Pasiphae, enraged by his affairs with other women, gave him a potion that caused him to infect any woman he made love to. When Procris cured him, he gave her the dog Laelaps and an unerring spear.

He locked Daedalus and his son Icarus in the labyrinth and scoured the Meditarranean for them when they escaped after being freed by Pasiphae. When he found Daedalus at the court of King Cocalus, he demanded that he be handed over but Daedalus (or a priestess of Cocalus) killed him by pouring scalding water or pitch over him as he lay in his bath. In another version, he was killed in the fight that ensued when Cocalus refused to hand over Daedalus.

Zeus made Minos one of the three judges of souls in Tartarus.

In some accounts, the head of Minos, one of many in mythology said to act as an oracle, was taken to Scandinavia by the Norse god, Odin.

Minotaur   *Greek*
A monster, a bull-headed man or a man-headed bull born to Pasiphae after she mated with Poseidon's white bull. It was shut up in the labyrinth built on Crete by Daedalus and was fed on the seven

youths and seven maidens given every year (or every nine years) by the Athenians as compensation to Minos for the death of his son at their hands. Theseus offered himself as one of these youths and killed the monster.

In some accounts, the monster was the offspring of Europa.

Minyans *see* **Argonauts**

Miolnir   *Norse*

'Crusher'

The magic hammer of Thor. This wonderful weapon was made by the dwarf Sindri and presented by the god Loki. It was once stolen by the giant Thrym but recovered by Thor dressed as the goddess Freya in a bridal-gown.

After the final battle, in which Thor was killed, the hammer was recovered from the ashes of the world conflagration by his sons, Modi and Magni.

Mirage People *see* **Kisani**

Mirror of Retribution   *Buddhist*

A mirror in hell. The wandering spirit sees itself in this mirror; the good see themselves as they are while the evil see themselves as beasts.

Miruk   *Korean*

= *Chinese* Hsiao Fo, Mi-lo-fo; *Buddhist* Maitreya; *Hindu* Kalki; *Japanese* Miroku

A creator-god. He is said to have created the earth, pushing heaven and earth apart and supporting the heavens with a copper pillar at each corner. He created men and women from insects which appeared in the silver and gold trays which he held while praying to heaven. After many struggles with Sokka, the force of evil, he left the world to its own sinful ways.

Mistress *see* **Core**

Mistress of Animals *see* **Artemis**

Mithra   *Persian*

= *Hindu* Mitra; *Roman* Mithras, Saturn

God of justice, light and war; one of the Yazatas; son of Ahura Mazda. In some versions he was born fully-formed from a rock, in others he was the twin brother of Ahura Mazda.

He carried a knife with which he killed the primordial bull Geush Urvan, which had continually opposed Ahriman, and from its dead body came plants and animals. (Other accounts say that it was Ahriman who killed the bull.)

He came down to earth on December 25th to relieve the sufferings of man, returning to heaven afterwards. He is expected to return to fight the last battle, overcoming Ahriman and leading the elect to eternal life.

His weapons are arrows and the mace and his animal is the boar.

Mithras   *Roman*

= *Hindu* Mitra; *Persian* Mithra

A god of soldiers. He was worshipped as a bull-god by men only who asserted that the marrow and blood of the dead bull became, like Christ's body and blood, the bread and wine of the sacrament. Initiates to the cult took part in the sacrifice of the bull and were required to pass through at least seven stages.

Mitra   *Hindu*

= *Persian* Mithra; *Roman* Mithras

A sun god, god of the sky, ruler of the day; one of the Adityas.

Shiva lost his temper when excluded from a sacrifice by Daksha and wounded many of those present, including Mitra, who had his eyes gouged out.

He is one of three judges who weigh souls in the underworld and is said to have 1000 eyes and ears.

Mixcoatl   *Central American*

also Cloud Serpent, Sky Father

The Aztec god of hunting; father of Huitzilopochtli and Quetzalcoatl. Some say he was the father of Tezcatlipoca, others that they were the same.

He is depicted with white strips covering his body or with the features of an animal and is sometimes accompanied by a deer with two heads.

Mizaru   *Japanese*

One of the Three Mystic Apes. He is depicted with his hands covering his eyes as 'he who sees no evil'.

Mnemosyne   *Greek*

'memory'

A Titaness, goddess of memory; daughter of Uranus and Gaea; mother of the Muses by Zeus.

Mo-li Ch'ing   *Chinese*

'Land Bearer';

= *Buddhist* Ch'ih Kuo; *Japanese* Jikoku

A Taoist deity, one of the Four Diamond Kings. He is guardian of the east and owns the magic sword, Blue Cloud, which he uses to produce a host of flying spears to kill his enemies or a fire to burn them to death. He is depicted with a white face and holding a ring and a spear.

Mo-li Hai   *Chinese*

'Far-Gazer';

= *Buddhist* Kuang Mu; *Japanese* Zocho

A Taoist deity, one of the Four Diamond Kings. He is guardian of the west and is depicted with a blue face and holding a guitar, the music of which can destroy his enemies by fire.

Mo-li Hung   *Chinese*

'Lord of Growth';

= *Buddhist* Tseng Chang; *Japanese*

Komuku

A Taoist deity, one of the Four
Diamond Kings. He is guardian of
the south and is depicted with a
red face and holding an umbrella
with which he can cause storms
and darkness.

Mo-li Shou   *Chinese*

'Well-Famed';

= *Buddhist* To Wen; *Japanese*
Bishamon

A Taoist deity, one of the Four
Diamond Kings. He is guardian
of the north and is depicted with
a black face and holding two
whips, a pearl and a bag made of
panther skin which holds the rat,
Hua-hu Tiao.

mockingbird   *North American*

In Hopi lore, the bird who allocated
people, as they emerged from
the underworld, to a particular
tribe. It is said that, when the
mockingbird ran out of songs,
those who were still unallocated
returned to the underworld.

Modgud   *Norse*

A skeleton-like figure guarding
the crystal bridge leading over
the River Giall to Niflheim. In
some accounts Modgud is a pale
maiden guarding the bridge.

Moel Arthur   *British*

A hill in Wales where, it is said,
King Arthur's palace once stood.

Mohini   *Hindu*

An incarnation of Vishnu. In
this form Vishnu appears as an
enchanting woman to seduce
Shiva and to deceive evil spirits.
He performed this trick at the
Churning of the Ocean, when
the demons snatched the
precious amrita, by promising to
share it between them, but gave
the gods a drink first so that
they, not the demons, achieved
immortality.

Moirae   *Greek*

also Moirai;

= *Norse* Norns; *Roman* Parcae

The Fates; three sisters who control
the fate of humans. Clotho spins
the web of life, Lachesis measures
it and Atropos cuts it with her
shears. Some say that they
invented the alphabet.

   In the battle between the gods
and the giants, they killed Agrius
and Thoas.

Mokele-Mbembe   *African*

A West African monster. This beast
has one horn, the tail of a snake,
and lives in sea caves. Some say
that it lives in the forest and
sleeps on a bed of elephant tusks.

Mokerkialfi   *Norse*

'Mist-calf', a huge creature made
from clay.

   When Thor fought a duel with
the giant Hrungnir, each was
allowed a squire. The giants used
clay to make Mokerkialfi, nine
miles long and wide, to act for
Hrungnir. Thor's squire, Thialfi,
killed the monster with a spade.

Mole Prey-god   *North American*

One of the six Prey-gods guarding
the home of Poshaiyangkyo. He is
responsible for the earth below.

Moloch   *Mesopotamian*

also Molech

An Ammonite god to whom
children were sacrificed by fire. In
some accounts, the rite itself.

   He is depicted with ram's horns
and holding a sceptre or with the
head of an ox.

Monan   *South American*

A creator-god of the Tupi. He
tried to exterminate the human
race with fire. When a magician
caused rain to fall to put the fire
out, it caused the Flood.

Mongibel   *British*

A mountain in Sicily, Mount Etna.

In some accounts, this was the site
to which the sorceress Morgan le
Fay proposed to take King Arthur
when he was wounded in his final
battle with Mordred. Others say
that the king *was* taken there and
was seen alive.

monkey

(1) In Buddhist lore, the monkey is
an incarnation of the Buddha.

(2) In China, the monkey is one
of the members of the Twelve
Terrestrial Branches, the Chinese
Zodiac.

(3) In the East Indies the monkey is
regarded as holding the souls of
the dead.

   Some tribes in Borneo believe
that the souls of the dead are
translated into grey monkeys,
while in Java the black monkey
is said to hold the soul of the
scholar and the brown monkey
the soul of the poser.

(4) Hanuman, the trickster monkey-
god of Hindu lore, is regarded as a
manifestation of Vishnu.

Monkey King *see* **Sun Hou-tzu**

monoceros   *Greek*

A mythical beast, a form of
unicorn. This beast was described
as having the body of a horse, the
head of a stag, elephant's feet
and the tail of a boar, as well as
having one long black horn.

Monster Slayer *see* **Nayenezgani**

moomin   *Baltic*

In Finnish lore, one of a race of
imaginary forest-dwellers. These
small, fat people are said to be
very shy, and hibernate during the
winter.

moon

(1) Some Australian tribes regard
the moon as the creator of the

first couple.

(2) In Egypt the moon, deified as Ah, represents the male principle and is regarded as the left eye of the god Horus.

(3) Some Finno-Ugric peoples worship the moon as an old man with an evil eye.

(4) The Greeks regarded the moon as the peaceful home of the good dead, personified as Hecate (before rising and after setting), as Artemis (when riding in the sky) and as Selene (when kissing the shepherd-king Endymion).

(5) In India the moon, deified as Chanra, is again the home of the good dead.

(6) Norse myths say that the moon originated in fire ejected from Muspelheim.

(7) Slavic lore regards the moon as the home of the souls of dead sinners.

(8) In those mythologies that say the universe was made from the body of some god or giant, the moon is frequently regarded as having been made from one eye, the sun from the other. In some islands of the Pacific, for example, the moon is the right eye of Na Atibu while in Egypt it is the left eye of Horus.

(9) In some mythologies, the hare and rabbit live on the moon while others say that it is the home of the toad (3-legged, in Chinese stories) or the frog. Some say that all the things that are wasted on earth are stored on the moon including such things as wasted talent, broken promises and misspent time. In some accounts, the moon deposits a kind of dew on certain plants in response to incantations.

(10) The shadows on the moon are variously interpreted as the face of the moon god Amm (Arab), the goddess Pajon Yan (Cambodia), a frog formerly Heng O (China), a man, Wu Kang, chopping down trees (China), a girl making tapa (Cook Islands), ashes (Inuit), Cain (Europe), a man who sinned on the Sabbath (Europe), tar marks (Europe), boys' fingermarks (East Indies), Endymion (Greece), a hare painted by Sakka (Hindu), a hunchback sitting under a banyan tree (Malaya), a grumbling old woman (Maori), two children with buckets (Scandinavia), a tree, claw-marks of a bear, Coyote, a creatress with a cooking-pot (North American Indian), a girl with a bucket (Siberia), a jaguar with four eyes or the intestines of the moon exposed when the moon was attacked by ducks or rheas (South America), bruises caused when the moon was given a beating (Tierra del Fuego), In places as far apart as India, Japan, Mexico and Tibet, the shadows are regarded as spots on the fur of the hare that lives in the moon.

Moon Brother   *Inuit*

A boy who became the moon; brother of Sun Sister. When he became the clandestine lover of his sister, she identified him by putting paint or soot on her hands. She was so horrified at the discovery that she fled to the heavens where she became the sun. The boy chased after her but, failing to catch her, became the moon.

Moowis   *North American*

A snowman which came to life (*see more at* **Elegant**).

mopaditis   *Australian*

Spirits of the Aborigine dead.

Morax   *European*

A demon, one of the 72 Spirits of Solomon. He appears as a bull.

Mordred   *British*

A Knight of the Round Table; cousin, nephew or son of King Arthur. In some accounts he was the incestuous son of Arthur by the sorceress Morgan le Fay; others say he was fathered by Arthur on his sister Anna, or on Morgause, wife of Lot, king of Lothian and Orkney. Some say his wife was Gwenhwyach, sister of Guinevere.

The magician Merlin prophesied that this boy would grow up to kill King Arthur, so the king ordered that all babies of royal families born on May Day should be cast adrift in a boat. Only Mordred, saved by Nabur, an Orkney fisherman, survived the subsequent shipwreck. At the age of fourteen he was taken by Nabur to King Arthur's court.

He was jealous of Lancelot, and he and his brother Agravain told Arthur of the queen's affair with Lancelot. Told to provide proof, he and Agravain, supported by twelve other knights, broke into Guinevere's room when the unarmed Lancelot was with her. Only Mordred survived when Lancelot killed one man with a footstool and then took his sword with which to kill the others.

Given proof of her adultery, the king condemned Guinevere to the stake but she was saved by Lancelot who took her to his castle, Garde Joyeux. After a battle ended by the intervention of the Pope, Lancelot returned the queen to Arthur and sailed for his home in France. When Arthur followed with a huge army,

Mordred was left in charge of the country.

He looted Arthur's home in Cornwall and assaulted Guinevere who shut herself away in the Tower. He manufactured evidence to show that the king was dead and proclaimed himself king. When the Bishop of Canterbury protested, Mordred threatened to kill him and the bishop fled to Glastonbury where he became a hermit. Some say that Mordred and Guinevere went through a form of bigamous marriage. When Arthur hurried back from France to reclaim his throne, Mordred met him in several battles in which thousands of men were killed. He finally met Arthur in single combat at Camlan, when he inflicted a mortal wound on the king but was himself killed by Arthur's spear.

In some accounts, Mordred survived the final battle and drove the remnants of King Arthur's army to Lyonesse. Here, the ghost of Merlin caused the land to sink, taking Mordred's men with it, while Arthur's men escaped.

Another story says that Lancelot killed Guinevere believing that she had been a willing accomplice of Mordred and shut Mordred in a room with the queen's dead body which Mordred, driven by hunger, ate.

Morgan le Fay   *British*

also Lady of Avalon

A sorceress; daughter of Gorlois, Duke of Cornwall, and Igraine; half-sister of Arthur. She is named as the Lady of the Lake and in some accounts is equated with Nimue. (Other versions keep Morgan and Nimue as two separate characters, with Nimue

as one of the damsels of the Lady of the Lake.) Some say she was the mother of Mordred by King Arthur, others that she bore Oberon king of the fairies, to Julius Caesar. She was a shape-changer who was said to have wings that enabled her to fly.

Her real home was in Avalon, where she was head of a small community of women to whom she gave instruction in the magic arts. She was always accompanied by her three daughters, Carvilia, Morganetta and Nivetta, themselves fairy queens. She was reputed to have another home in Sicily, where she was known as Fata Morgana.

When King Arthur upset her by executing one of her lovers, she planned to kill both the king and her husband Urien, and marry another lover, Accolan, ruling as his queen. She stole the sword Excalibur and gave it to Accolan and, by her magic, caused Arthur to fight him. Her plans went astray when Arthur won the fight and recovered Excalibur. In the belief that Accolan had won, she prepared to kill Urien with his own sword while he slept but her son, Owain, alerted by a servant, seized her in time to prevent the murder. She duped him into believing that she had been possessed by evil spirits and he forgave her when she promised to give up her magic arts – which, of course, she did not. Accolan died of his wounds.

In another attempt on Arthur's life she sent a bejewelled mantle to the king, but, warned by Nimue, he made the damsel who brought it to the court put the

mantle on. She fell dead, burned to a cinder.

She stole the magic scabbard of Excalibur and, chased by Arthur's men, threw it into a lake. She escaped her pursuers by turning herself and her party into standing stones. When the pursuers gave up the chase, they resumed their normal shape and Morgan returned to her own country of Gore.

As Morgan, she rescued the infant Lancelot; as Nimue she was loved by the magician Merlin.

Some say that it was she who alerted Arthur to Lancelot's affair with Guinevere when she gave him a magic drink which opened his eyes to what was going on.

In some versions she was one of the queens accompanying the dying Arthur on the boat taking him to Avalon. After the fall of Camelot at the hands of King Mark, Morgan and her daughters left Britain for the Straits of Messina where they lured ships on to the rocks. (*See* **Fata Morgana**.)

(*See also* **Lady of the Lake, Morgen, Nimue**.)

Morgawr   *British*

A sea monster. This beast, said to be seen off the coast of Cornwall, is descibed as having a humped back and a long bristly neck bearing a head with stumpy horns.

Morgen   *Welsh*

A goddess of the druids. It was said that she could change shape at will and fly on artificial wings. It is generally accepted that she developed into the sorceress Morgan le Fay.

Morgiana   *Persian*

A slave of Ali Baba in the *Arabian Nights' Entertainments*. It was

Morgiana who discovered the thieves hidden in the jars and killed them with boiling oil and later killed their leader. As a reward, she was granted her freedom and married Ali Baba's son.

Morrigan   *Irish*
A war goddess; wife of the Dagda, some say.

This deity is usually regarded as a trio of war goddesses comprising Ana (or Nemain), Badb and Macha, or else Badb, Macha and Morrigan, who helped the Danaans at the Battles of Moytura.

She could appear as maiden or an old hag, a raven or a crow. She rides in a chariot drawn by red horses and is frequently dressed all in red.

In some stories, she helped Cuchulainn in the defence of Ulster, in others she opposed him because he had rejected her advances. On that occasion, she coiled herself round him in the form of an eel when he was engaged in single combat with the warrior Loch Mor. She further harassed him, in the form of a wolf and then a heifer, but he managed to kill Loch despite her efforts. At the end of his life, she attacked him in the form of crow, helping to kill him.

In one story, she turned Odras, wife of a man from whom she had stolen a bull, into a river.

In some accounts, she is the basis for Morgan le Fay.

Mors   *Roman*
'death';
= *Greek* Thanatos
God of death, controller of fate; son of Nyx, goddess of night; twin brother of Somnus, god of sleep.

He is depicted as holding an hour-glass and the scythe with

which he cut down those whose life-span had expired.

In some accounts, Mors is female.

Moshiriikkwechep   *Japanese*
A huge sea-monster. It is said that two deities are responsible for ensuring that this monster's movements, which cause earthquakes, do not destroy the whole world.

Moss Maidens   *Norse*
Wood nymphs hunted by the Wild Hunt.

Mother Corn   *North American*
An Arikana goddess. When the creator-god Nesaru, disappointed with the people he had created, drowned them all, he sent Mother Corn to the underworld to guide the inhabitants to the upper world to form the new population.

Mother of the Gods *see* **Neith**

Mother of the People *see* **Utset**

Mount Baker   *North American*
Kobath, a sacred mountain of the Skagit tribe. It is said that this was one of only two mountains which were not totally submerged by the Flood, the other being Mount Rainier.

Mount Caucasus   *Greek*
The place where Prometheus was chained to a rock.

Mount Etna   *British*
A site in Sicily where, some say, King Arthur and his knights lie sleeping.

For other suggested sites, *see* ***Alderley Edge***. (*See also* ***Mongibel***.)

Mount Fuji   *Japanese*
also Fuji San, Fujiyama
A volcano regarded as a sacred mountain, home of the gods. The smoke which issues from the summit is the result of the love

of the Emperor for the princess Kaguya-hime who, leaving him to become an immortal, left him a mirror in which he might always see her image and which burst into flame with the heat of his passion. Its permanent cap of snow stems from the anger of the god Mioya when the god of the mountain refused to offer him hospitality.

Mount Helicon   *Greek*
Home of the Muses.

Mount Ida   *Greek*
A mountain near Troy, home of the nymph Idaea. It was here that the infant Paris was abandoned and later judged the beauty contest of the three goddesses with the golden apple as prize.

Mount Mandara   *Hindu*
The mountain round which the gods coiled the World Serpent to cause the Churning of the Ocean.

Mount Meru   *Hindu*
also Golden Mountain, Jewel Peak, Lotus Mountain
= *Chinese* K'un Lun
The site of Brahmapura, Indra's heaven; home of the gods at the centre of the universe.

On the summit, some 350,000 miles up, lay Brahma's palace surrounded by the Ganges, while the homes of Krishna and Vishnu were built on the lower slopes. It is said that seven underworlds exist below the mountain, where the asuras (demons) live in caves.

This mountain is also the sacred mountain of the West, the Taoist paradise where all the inhabitants are immortal, is at the centre of the earth and is over 4000 miles high, providing a route from earth to heaven. It is regarded as the source of the winds, the Yellow River and the Ju Shui and as the home of the Lord of the Sky and Ho-Po, Count of the River. Mount Meru also appears as the centre of the universe in Buddhism. It is also said to be the home of the Shi Tenno, Japanese deities guarding the cardinal points.

Mount Ossa   *Greek*
A mountain in Thessaly. The giant Ephialtes and his brother Otus tried to pile Mount Pelion on Mount Ossa in order to attack the gods.

Mount Parnassus   *Greek*
Home of the god Dionysus. This mountain has two peaks, one dedicated to Apollo and the Muses, the other to Dionysus. It is generally said that Deucalion's ark landed here when the Flood subsided though others say it landed at other sites such as Mount Etna, Mount Olympus, Mount Orthrys, etc.

Mount Pelion   *Greek*
A sacred mountain in Thessaly, the original home of the Centaurs. (*See more at* **Mount Ossa**.)

Mount Qaf   *Arab*
The only spot on earth where the giant bird, the roc, will land; the home of giants and the jinn.
    This mountain is said to be made of emerald and is situated on the far side of the ocean which encircles the earth. Its reflection is what causes the sky to appear blue.
    In some versions, Qaf is a range of mountains rather than a single peak.

Mount Rainier   *North American*
'Takobah', a sacred mountain of the Skagit tribe. It is said that this was one of the only two mountains which were not submerged by the Flood, the other being Mount Baker.

Mount Salvat   *British*
The site in the Holy Land of the Temple of the Grail.

Mount T'ai *see* **T'ai Shan**
Mountain People *see* **Gahe**
Mountain Lion Prey-god   *North American*
One of the six Prey-gods guarding the home of Poshaiyangkyo. He is responsible for the North.

Mountain Woman   *Japanese*
A female ogre. This being is said to be able to fly and is covered with long white hair. Some say that she eats humans.

Mover of Blood   *Celtic*
The scabbard of the Sword of Strange Girdles.

Mr Spider *see* **Anansi**
Muchalinda   *Buddhist*
= *Hindu* Ananta
A serpent, king of the Nagas. This snake sheltered Buddha with his hood from the violent weather that arose at the end of Buddha's period of contemplation under the bo-tree. When the storm was over, he turned into a handsome youth.

Muchukunda   *Hindu*
A giant who could destroy by fire from his eyes anyone who dared to disturb his eternal sleep granted, at his request, for helping the gods against the Asuras (demons).
    He, like King Arthur and others, is said to be asleep but awaiting a call to help his country in its time of need.

Mudgegong   *Australian*
An evil spirit of the Aborigines. This being was created by Baime and turned all Baime's children into animals except one couple who became the ancestors of the human race.

Multultu   *Australian*
A kangaroo-man, an ancestral

hero of the Aborigines. (*See also* **Minawara**.)

Muluku   *African*
A creator-god of the tribes on the River Zambesi. Having created the world, he drew two beings, a man and a woman, from holes in the ground. They were so disobedient that he changed them into monkeys and the monkeys into humans.

Munsumundok   *East Indies*
She and her husband Kinharingan emerged from a rock in the sea and together they created the earth, using soil given to them by the god of smallpox, Bisagit, followed by the sky, the heavenly bodies, human beings and all the animals and plants.

Muramura   *Australian*
Ancestral heroes of the Aborigines, spirits of the Dreamtime now said to be invisible and living in trees.

Murmur   *European*
A demon of music in hell, one of the 72 Spirits of Solomon. He is said to appear as a huge soldier riding a vulture or a griffin.

Muses   *Greek*
= *Roman* Camenae
Daughters of Zeus and Mnemosyne.
    Originally there were just three Muses. Later there were four. The number was later increased to nine, one each responsible for a particular area of the arts, led by Apollo. The allocation of responsibilities varies from one version to another. The following list includes most of these alternatives;
    Calliope – epic poetry (chief Muse)
    Clio – history
    Erato – erotic poetry, hymns, lyric poetry

Euterpe – flute-playing, lyric poetry, and music

Melpomene – harmony, lyre-playing, song, tragedy

Polyhymnia – acting, dance, hymns, lyric poetry, mime, music, rhetoric, song

Terpsichore – dance, flute-playing, lyric poetry, song

Thalia – comedy, gaiety, pastoral poetry

Urania – astronomy

Other names include Menippe, mother of Orpheus.

They blinded Thamyris, a bard, for his presumption in challenging them to a contest of poetry. Winning a similar contest with the Pierides, they turned the losers into magpies, jackdaws or wrynecks. They are themselves sometimes referred to as the Pierides.

It is they who gave the Sphinx the riddle it posed to all travellers.

Muskrat　　　　　　　*North American*

One of the animals who tried to find dry soil for Manabush. In the lore of the Algonquians, four animals tried to find dry soil from which Manabush could remake the world after the Flood. Beaver, Mink and Otter all died in the attempt; only Muskrat succeeded.

Musmahhu　　　　　　*Mesopotamian*

= *Greek* Hydra

A monster in the form of a seven-headed snake.

Muspel　　　　　　　　　*Norse*

The Fire Giants; sons of Surtur.

Muspelheim　　　　　　　*Norse*

The land of fire, far to the south, ruled by Surtur. It is said that sparks flying up from this realm created the heavenly bodies.

Mustamho　　　　*Central American*

A creator-god of the Mohave. He created the tribes and saved them when the Flood came by holding them in his arms until the waters had subsided.

Mustapha　　　　　　　　*Arab*

In the *Arabian Nights' Entertainments*, a poor tailor, father of Aladdin.

Mustapha Baba　　　　*Arabian*

In the *Arabian Nights' Entertainments*, a cobbler who stitched together the severed parts of Kassim's body.

Mut　　　　　　　　　*Egyptian*

= *Greek* Hera

The goddess of Thebes. She is usually depicted with the head of a vulture but sometimes has the head of a lion. Some say that she was a consort of Hapi. Also a name for Isis, in some accounts. (*See also* **Ament**.)

Muurup　　　　　　　*Australian*

An evil deity said to eat children.

Myrmidons　　　　　　　*Greek*

'ant men'

When Zeus fell in love with the nymph Aegina, he fathered Aeacus who grew up to be king of the island of that name. Hera decimated the population in revenge, so Aeacus prayed to Zeus who created a whole new population from ants. These were the 'myrmidons' who followed Achilles and fought in the Trojan War.

myrtle

(1) In Egyptian myth, the tree sacred to Hathor.

(2) In European legends, Orlando was changed into a myrtle tree by the sorceress Alcina.

(3) In Greek mythology, the tree of Adonis, Aphrodite, Artemis and Poseidon.

The goddess Aphrodite caused Myrrha, the daughter of Cinyras, king of Cyprus, to sleep with her father, producing Adonis. The goddess (or, some say, Apollo) then turned Myrrha into a myrtle tree. The infant Adonis was delivered from the tree by a boar's tusk.

(4) In Hebrew lore, chewing the leaves of myrtle enables one to detect witches.

N

N *Central American*
A Mayan deity of uncertain identity referred to as God N (*see* ***alphabetical gods***.). This deity is thought by some to be the demon Uayayab who ruled the nemontemi, the five unlucky days at the year's end.

Na Kika *Pacific Islands*
The octopus-god of the Gilbert Islands. He helped the creator-god Nareau build the islands of the Pacific.

Naberius *European*
One of the 72 Spirits of Solomon. He is said to be able to teach logic and appears as a three-headed man on a crow or a black cockerel.

Nachiel *Hebrew*
One of the Seven Intelligences, ruler of the sun.

Nachuruchu *North American*
A Pueblo weaver and medicine-man. When Nachuruchu married the moon, the two witches known as the Yellow Corn Maidens were so jealous that they drowned her in a well. All the animals and birds searched for her and the buzzard spotted a mound covered with flowers. Nachuruchu had the buzzard bring him one of the white flowers and, placing it between two robes, sang magic songs over it until it turned into his wife, fully restored. He then made a magic hoop for her to play with and when she bowled it towards the witches they grabbed hold of it and were immediately turned into snakes.

Nacon *Central American*
A Mayan war god.

naga *Hindu*
female nagini
A sacred snake. These beings could appear in many forms, such as snake-necked warriors, and could mate with humans. They are said to have a navel in their forehead and live in jewelled underwater palaces in Bhagavati, the capital of the underworld Patala. Alternative versions call their home Nagaloka or say that they live in Niraya (hell).

Nagaitco *North American*
The first man in the lore of the Kato tribe of California.

As an infant, Nagaitco was saved from the Flood by the hero Tcenes.

In some accounts, he was the creator-god who made all things, including the first humans. The first world he created was destroyed by flood. He then made a second world from a huge horned monster.

Nagasena *Buddhist*
A Buddhist priest, one of the Eighteen Lohan. He taught the Indo-Greek king Menander the Buddhist doctrines and made the Emerald Buddha (a statue of the Buddha) by magical powers.

nagumwasuck *North American*
Ugly fairies of the lore of the Passemaquaddy tribe of Maine, USA.

Nail of the North *see* **Bohinavlle**

Nainuema *South American*
A creator-god of the Uitoto people of Colombia and Peru. He created

the world and made it flat by stamping on it, after which he used his own saliva to make all living things.

Nakaa *Pacific Islands*
A creator-god of the Gilbert Islands. Having created humans, he kept men and women apart and they lived as immortals, each sex with a tree in their part of the island. When Nakaa left on a journey, the men disobeyed his injunction and visited the women. The angry god deprived them of their immortality (which is why humans now die) and left, going to the land of the dead where he sits at the entrance and traps the souls of the dead in a net. If a soul can refrain from eating or drinking for three days, Nakaa allows them to return to the land of the living.

Nakk *Baltic*
= *Finnish* Nakki
An Estonian water-spirit. These spirits, which can appear as adult humans or children or horses, are the spirits of people who have drowned. The males lure victims by singing; the females, known as Nakineiu, lure their victims by sitting near the water combing their long golden hair while singing. Each has a huge mouth which can swallow almost anything.

Nakki *Baltic*
= *Estonian* Nakk
A Finnish water-spirit. These beings sometimes appear as large humans, sometimes as half man, half horse. The females, like their Estonian counterparts, have fine cattle living in water.

Nakula *Buddhist*
One of the Eighteen Lohan. It was said that he became young again

when he became a Buddhist at the age of 120. He is depicted with a rosary in his hand or, in some versions, with a mongoose or a three-legged toad.

Nama *Siberian*
God of the underworld. He, like the Biblical Noah, built an ark in which he, his family and some animals survived the world flood.

Nammu *Mesopotamian*
A Sumerian goddess of the primeval. Some accounts say that she generated An (the god of heaven) and Ki (the earth goddess), others that she was An's consort. She is said to have made humans from clay.

Namorodo *Australian*
Demons of the Aborigines. They are envisaged as being made of skin and bone with long talons, flying by night and killing all those they encounter.

Namu *Siberian*
The man who survived the Flood. He was given advance warning by the creator-god Ulgan and built an ark in which he survived.

Nan-lha *Tibetan*
A household god. This deity, with a head like a pig, occupies different parts of the house at different seasons of the year. If he should be guarding the entrance, no bride or groom or corpse can enter or leave until he has been propitiated.

Nana Miriam *African*
Both her husband Fara Maka and the hunter Karadigi failed to kill the monster hippopotamus Mali, but she paralysed it with a magic spell.

Nancomala *South American*
A culture-hero of the Guayami Indians. He met the water-maiden Rutbe when the Flood receded and

they mated to produce twins, who became the ancestors of the tribe.

Nandi Bear *African*
also Chemosit
A monster in the form of a man-eating bear. In some accounts, this being is described as half man, half bird, with only one leg and a mouth that glows in the dark.

Nandini *Hindu*
A cow of plenty, which could grant any wish. In some accounts, this was the marvellous animal owned by the sage Vashishtha, in others it was equated with another cow of plenty, Surabhi.

Nangananga *Pacific Islands*
A Fijian goddess of punishment. She lives in the underworld, Bulu, and receives the souls of bachelors which she smashes against rocks.

Nang-pyek-kha Yek-khi *Burmese*
An earth goddess, daughter of the first couple Ta-hsek-khi and Ya-hsek-khi.

She was born with the legs and ears of a tigress and her parents made her ruler of the earth and sea and gave her two gourds. When the gourds were split open by Khun Hsang L'rong, all the animals of the world emerged. Khun then married the goddess.

Nanook *North American*
= *Inuit* Nanue
A bear. This animal was chased into the sky by the Pleiades, a pack of hunting-dogs, and became the Great Bear. He sometimes comes to earth to assist hunters.

Nansi *see* **Annency**

nantena *North American*
Fairies or spirits of the Athapascans.

Nanters *British*
A Knight of the Round Table; a king of Garlot; husband of Elaine, the half-sister of King Arthur.

He was one of the rulers who rose against the king but lived and was made a Knight of the Round Table.

Nantes   *Celtic*
In some Continental stories, the site of King Arthur's court.

Nanue   *North American*
The Inuit name for Nanook.

Nao'tsiti   *North American*
A Pueblo creator-goddess; daughter of the creator-god Utc'tsiti. She and her sister Ia'tiku were born and, for many years lived, underground until, instructed by the spirit Tsitctinako, they emerged on to the surface and set about creating plants and animals, spirits and gods. Nao'tsiti was impregnated by the rainbow and bore twin boys. She gave one, Tiamuni, to Ia'tiku and, taking the other with her, moved away to the east. These children were the progenitors of the tribe.

Napi   *North American*
also Old Man
The creator-god of the Blackfoot tribe. His father had a dream from which he learned to trap animals by hanging a spider's web across the trail. When his mother took a rattlesnake as a lover, his father trapped her in the web and cut off her head. Their two children ran off pursued by the head while the headless body chased their father. The boys escaped when the head fell into the water while the body (or head in some stories), which is the moon, still pursues the father, who is the sun.

His clever brother created the white races and taught them all they needed to know while the simple Napi founded the Blackfoot tribe, creating the first humans from clay and leading

them out of the cave Nina Stahu. When the Buffalo-stealer drove off all the buffalo, he turned himself into a dog and drove the herds back to the Blackfoot tribe. He is expected one day to return.

Naraka   *Hindu*
One of the Asuras (demons). He took the form of an elephant and carried off some 16,000 women and held them in a magnificent palace that he built for them.

Narasinha   *Hindu*
The fourth incarnation of Vishnu, as an eight-armed man-lion. In this incarnation he killed the demon Hiranyakashipu.

narcissus[1]   *Greek*
The flower of Demeter. By some accounts, this flower was created by Zeus to hold the attention of Core so that his brother Hades could abduct her as she went to pick it. (But see also the legend in the following entry.)

Narcissus[2]   *Greek*
When Narcissus rejected his love, Ameinius committed suicide and, in punishment, Artemis caused Narcissus to fall in love with his own reflection in a stream. Unable to possess his own image he killed himself with a dagger. The flower that bears his name sprang from the soil that was stained with his blood. In other versions, he just pined away from unrequited longings or threw himself into the water and drowned. The voice of Echo, whom he had also rejected, grieved at his side.

Nareau[1]   *Pacific Islands*
also Nareau the Elder, Spider-lord
The creator-god of the Gilbert Islands. He made Na Atibu and Nei Teukez from sand and they mated to produce the gods the youngest of which, a trickster-god,

was known as Nareau the Younger.

Nareau[2]   *Pacific Islands*
also Nareau the Younger
Son of Na Atibu and Nei Teukez (*see more at* **Nareau**[1]). This Nareau killed his father, using the dead man's eyes to make the moon and the sun. He then planted the spine which became the tree Kai-n-tiku-aba from which people developed.

Nascien[1]   *British*
An ancestor of Galahad; brother-in-law of Joseph of Arimathea.

A Saracen, originally called Seraph, who changed his name to Nascien when he was baptised as a Christian. He approached too close to the Holy Grail and was blinded but was cured by the blood which dripped from the Holy Lance. He came upon Solomon's ship and went aboard. There he found the Sword of David which broke when he picked it up since he was unworthy. Its repair became one of the objects of the Grail Quest.

In some accounts, it was repaired by Evelake, in others by Galahad. He later came to Britain and, it was said, became king of Scotland.

Nascien[2]   *British*
also Nascien the Hermit
A hermit; grandson of Nascien[1]. He received the white shield with the red cross drawn in the blood of Josephus (in some accounts, Joseph) at the death of its owner, Evelake, to hold in trust for Galahad. He foretold that Arthur would achieve great fame in the quest for the Holy Grail and warned the knights not to take their ladies on the quest.

Nastrond   *Norse*
Hell; a part of Niflheim. This was the place to which the spirits of criminals were sent before being eaten by the serpent Nidhogg. It was also the place to which the evil gods who died at Ragnarok were sent.

nat   *Burmese*
A supernatural being. A nat may be a nature-spirit such as a spirit of the air, earth, forest, etc, a spirit of the dead, or some other supernatural being. All need to be appeased. Some may be harmful, causing death and disease, but others act as guardians, either of the indivdual or of his property or even of groups such as a tribe or village.

Nata   *Central American*
An Aztec culture-hero. He and his wife Nena were saved from the Flood when the god Tezcatlipoca (or Titlacahuan, some say) warned them of its coming and told them to build a boat.

    Another version says that they made a hole in a tree and survived by hiding in it. However, they had been told to eat only one ear of maize and, when they ignored this injunction and ate a fish as well, they were both turned into dogs.

Naubandhana   *Hindu*
The place on Mount Himavat where the first man Manu's boat came to rest after the Flood.

Nauplius   *Greek*
'seafarer'
A king of Nauplia in the Peloponnese; one of the Argonauts.

Nausicaa   *Greek*
She found Odysseus when he was shipwrecked and alone. Her parents provided him with another ship in which to continue his journey home.

navky   *Slav*
These spirits are regarded as the souls of children who died before being baptised. They could lure people into water where they drowned or they could attack women in labour. They developed into water nymphs.

Nayenezgani   *North American*
also Monster Slayer
The Navaho war god and god of light. He and his brother, Tobadzistsini, were given feathers by the spider-woman Naste Estsan, to protect them from all dangers when they travelled to the house of their father, the sun god, Tsohanoai. He accepted that they were his sons only after testing them with spikes, scalding water and poison. He then gave them weapons such as lightning with which to rid the land of monsters.

    They first killed the giant, Yeitso, and then the monster Teelgct. They also killed the enormous beasts, with talons like the eagle, known as the Tsenahale, and plucked their feathers. One of these birds had carried Nayenezgani to his nest on a high cliff and, after killing the bird, the young hero found himself stranded. He was rescued by Bat Woman who carried him down from the cliff in a basket on her back. He gave her the eagles' feathers as a reward but they all turned into small singing birds.

    Other adventures involved the killing of a huge bear, the rock-spirit Tsenagahi, and the people known as the Binaye Ahani, who were alleged to be able to kill with looks.

Ndauthina   *Pacific Islands*
A serpent, sea god and fire god of Fiji. He is regarded as the guardian of fishermen but is otherwise a malicious trickster.

Ndengei   *Pacific Islands*
A snake-god, the creator-god of Fiji. He lives in a cave in the mountains and causes earthquakes when he changes his position. He is said to have laid two eggs from which hatched a boy and a girl who became the progenitors of the human race.

Ndriananahary   *African*
A supreme god of Malagasy.
He sent his son Ataokoloinona to earth to see if it was fit for men to live in. The son burrowed into the earth to escape the intense heat and has never been seen since.

Nduli Mtwaa-roho   *African*
The Swahili angel of death. This being collects the leaves falling from the Cedar of the End and claims the persons whose names are written on them.

nectar   *Greek*
The drink of the gods which conferred beauty and immortality.

Neepec   *South American*
A mischievous spirit of the Chaco tribes. When the benevolent spirit Cotaa created a wonderful tree which would provide food and drink for the tribes, Neepec poured a jugful of tears over it so that its fruit thereafter tasted salty.

Nefertem   *Egyptian*
A creator-god and god of the lotus; a form of the god Ra as the setting sun. Some say that he was a manifestation of Ra-Atum whose tears became human beings. He is sometimes depicted as lion-headed.

Neith   *Egyptian*
also Great Goddess, Mother of the Gods;
= *Greek* Athena, Lamia

The cow-goddess, goddess of war and hunting; guardian of the dead. Originally a snake-goddess in Libya, she was adopted into the Egyptian pantheon.

Some say she emerged from the primitive waters, others that she was the daughter of the god Ra. Some accounts say she was the mother of the crocodile-god Sebek, some that she was the mother of Ra, others that she created Apep, the serpent-god of chaos, when she spat into the primitive waters.

She was said, by some, to have created the world by weaving it.

Nekhbet   *Egyptian*
also Great Mother;
= *Greek* Ilithyia
The vulture-headed mother-goddess of Upper Egypt; guardian of the pharaoh; daughter and wife of Ra. (*See also* **Mut**.)

Ne-kilst-lust   *North American*
A creator-god of the tribes of the north-west. He is said to have got the moon and sun from the supreme god, Settin-ki-jash, by deception in order to bring light to the human race.

Nekumonta   *North American*
An Iroquois brave. Most of his tribe had been wiped out by plague and his own wife, Shanewis, was on the point of death. He went in search of herbs to cure her and found none but heard a voice telling him to release the healing waters under the earth. He dug until his strength ran out and released the underground stream, the water from which made him strong again. He carried some of the water back to his wife and saved her life.

Nemain   *Irish*
A war goddess, an aspect of

Morrigan. In some accounts she is one of the trio – Badb, Macha and Nemain – represented by the single war goddess, Morrigan. In the Cattle Raid of Cooley (*see* **Maev**), she caused panic and killed soldiers by her shrieking.

Nemean lion   *Greek*
also Cleonaean lion
A lion killed by Hercules as his first Labour. Some say that this beast was formed from sea-foam by the moon goddess Selene. Hercules strangled the lion with his bare hands since its skin resisted all weapons, and then wore the skin as armour and the head as a kind of helmet. Others say that this was the skin of another beast, the Cithaeronian Lion.

Nemedians   *Irish*
Early invaders of Ireland, whose leader was Nemed. His invading fleet of 32 ships was wrecked and only five (or nine) people survived. They settled in Ireland and bred, defeating the Fomoire in three battles, but later almost all the Nemedians died of plague.

After this, the remaining few were tyrannised by the Fomoire who demanded two-thirds of all their children, produce and goods. Smol, the king of Greece, sent an army to their aid and together they defeated the Fomoire, killing their king, Conall mac Febar, and looting his castle. When the Greek army withdrew, the Nemedians were again attacked by Morc, another Fomoire leader. Most of the Fomoire were killed, and only thirty Nemedians survived. They split Ireland into three parts, each ruled by a grandson of Nemed, but this arrangement soon broke down; one grandson went to Britain, the other two to Greece

from where their descendants later returned to Ireland as the Fir Bolg and, later still, as the Danaans.

Nemesis   *Greek*
A goddess of destiny and retribution. She was pursued by Zeus, both of them frequently changing form until Zeus, as a swan, fertilised Nemesis as a goose. The resulting egg was found by Leda and hatched to produce Helen of Troy. An alternative version of the story involved Leda directly with Zeus.

Nemesis is depicted as carrying a bough of an apple tree and a wheel or, in other versions, scales and a whip or axe. Her chariot is drawn by griffins.

nemontemi   *Central American*
Five unlucky days at the end of the Mayan calendar year. Such was the baleful quality of this period, governed by the demon Uayayab, that no work was done.

Nemu   *East Indian*
Creator-gods of the Kai Islands of Indonesia. These demi-gods invented agriculture and caused the sun, which previously shone all day, to go down at night, so that they could get some sleep. They turned into stone or animals when they died and were finally destroyed in the Flood.

Nena   *Central American*
An Aztec culture-heroine. For the story of Nena and Nata, *see* **Nata**.

Nenabo   *North American*
A trickster-deity of the tribes of New England. He is said to have brought beans and maize to the people and to have instructed them in the art of hunting.

Nennius   *British*
A 9th-century monk. His *Historia Britonum*, a mixture of legend and historical fact, gives much

detail about King Arthur which has been used as the basis of many later writings.

Neptune *Roman*
= *Etruscan* Nethuns; *Greek* Poseidon
A sea god, one of the Olympians; son of Saturn and Ops; brother of Jupiter and Pluto.

Originally a god of irrigation and horse-racing, Neptune is generally depicted as bearded and holding a trident and may be riding a dolphin or a horse.

Nereid *Greek*
One of the fifty (or 3000) sea nymphs attendant on the sea god Poseidon; daughters of Nereus and the nymph Doris.

Nereus *Greek*
also Old Man of the Sea
A sea god; father of the Nereids. He was a shape-changing god who had a great struggle with Hercules before he would divulge the location of the garden of the Hesperides. In some accounts he is identified with Glaucus, Phorcos or Proteus. He is depicted with seaweed in place of hair.

Nergal *Mesopotamian*
also Bull of Heaven
= *Sumerian* Lugal-Irra; *Greek* Ares; *Roman* Mars
A Babylonian war god, god of death, fire and the underworld.

He was born in the underworld when Ninlil followed Enlil who had been banished there for raping her.

When Nergal was exiled to the underworld, or summoned there by Ereshkigal for having failed to speak to Namtar, her attendant, who had been invited to collect her share of a feast laid on by the gods, he threatened to kill her. She saved herself only by sharing power with him.

In some accounts, he raped her on the first occasion and forced her to share power with him when the god An ordered him back to the underworld.

In another version, Nergal consented to marry Ereshkigal only because she threatened to desolate the world if he refused.

In the form of the Bull of Heaven he was killed by Gilgamesh and Enkidu.

Nergal is depicted with the body of a lion, holding a sword and a decapitated head.

Nesaru *North American*
A creator-god of the Arikara.

Lucky Man and Wolf Man suddenly appeared when the whole world was covered by water and ordered ducks to bring up earth from the bottom. Lucky Man made the hills and valleys while Wolf Man made the prairies. They then dug up two spiders who brought forth all the various animals and a race of giants. Nesaru did not much care for the giants so he introduced maize which the animals planted in the earth. The seed of the maize became a new race of people underground. He then sent a flood which drowned all the giants and then created Corn Mother and sent her to the underworld to lead into the upper world the new people who lived there. These people repopulated the earth.

Nestor *Greek*
He was made king of Pylos by Hercules after Hercules had sacked the city and killed Nestor's eleven brothers.

In some accounts, he was one of the Argonauts and a member of the party hunting the

Calydonian Boar. In a cattle-raid, he killed Mulius and Itymoneus, capturing many horses and cattle and fifty chariots, and, on another occasion, killed Ereuthalion in single combat.

He was known for his eloquence and wisdom and tried to mediate when Achilles quarrelled with Agamemnon at Troy.

Nextepehua *Central American*
An evil spirit in the lore of the Aztecs. This fiend was one of the many hazards faced by the souls of the dead in their journey through the various layers of the underworld. It was said to take the form of ghost which scattered clouds of ashes in the path of the soul.

Ngandjala-Ngandjala *Australian*
A trickster-god of the Aborigines. These beings, who destroy crops and generally cause trouble, can sometimes be seen in the clouds.

Ngarara[1] *Australian*
An Aboriginal monster in the form of a huge lizard.

Ngarara[2] *Pacific Islands*
A minor deity or, some say, a demon. Some accounts describe this being as a beautiful woman with a tail, others as a form of mermaid. Some say she is a lizard-woman.

In the form of a woman with a tail, she tried to seduce the Fijian hero Ruru who had called at her island in search of water but, with the help of her servants Kiore Ta and Kiore Ti, Ruru got away. He then built a hut containing a model of himself and set fire to the building. Ngarara, who had coiled herself round the statue, was lucky to escape with the loss of her long tail.

Ngariman   *Australian*

The cat-man of the Aborigines.
He got into a dispute with the
Bagadjimbiri brothers and, with
his followers, speared them to
death. The earth goddess Dilga
drowned the killers with a flood
of milk from her breasts and
restored the two giants to life.

Ngewo   *African*

The creator-god and sky god of the
Mende. He moved up to a house
in the sky to be free of the never-
ending requests of mankind.

Ngurunderi   *Australian*

A name for the god Baime used
by the Aborigines of the Murray
River basin.

He speared a pondi (cod) which
swam away but it was again
speared by his brother-in-law
Nepele. They cut the fish into
small pieces and threw them,
one by one, into a lake, naming
each piece as they did so. In this
way, all the species of fish were
created.

He chased after his wives when
they deserted him and, having
drowned them by calling up a
great storm, placed his canoe in
the heavens as the Milky Way and
then ascended to heaven.

Niall   *Irish*

A high-king of Ireland. Abandoned
by his stepmother Mongfhinn, he
was saved and reared by the bard
Torna Eices. It was foretold by the
smith, Sithchenn, that he would
become the high-king.

In one incident, only he would
kiss an ugly old woman who
demanded a kiss, and she turned
into the lovely Flaitheas, the
embodiment of sovereignty.

When his poet, Laidcheann,
refused hospitality to Eochu, a
prince of Leinster, Eochu burnt

his house to the ground. Niall
invaded Leinster and took Eochu
hostage, later sending him in
exile to Scotland. When Niall
visited that country, the vengeful
Eochu shot and killed him. In
other accounts, he was killed by
Eochu's arrow in the Alps or in
the Channel Islands on one of his
many expeditions of conquest.

Nibelheim *see* **Alfheim**

Nibelung   *Norse*

also Niebelung

King of the dwarfs. He quarrelled
with his brother Schilbung over
sharing their father's estate.

Some accounts say that he
authorised Siegfried to divide his
treasure between his three sons.
Siegfried killed both Nibelung and
his brother.

Nibelungen   *Norse*

also Black Elves, Niebelungs, Niflungs

Supernatural dwarfs, followers of
Siegfried.

This name was later given to
the Burgundians as guardians
of the Nibelung treasure. In the
Wagnerian cycle of operas, they
are all the Germanic tribes.

Nibelungenlied, the   *German*

= *Norse* Thidrek Saga

A 13th-century epic poem from
the *Eddas* (Norse epic poems and
prose), the basis for Wagner's
cycle of operas.

Nichant   *North American*

An Algonquian god who destroyed
the world by fire and flood.

Nickard   *German*

A water-monster. This being was
said to steal a child from its bed,
leaving a monster in its place. The
mother could save her child only
if she whipped the monster.

Nicodemus   *British*

A Pharisee who helped to bury
Jesus. In Arthurian lore, his body

was brought to Britain and kept
there until it was transferred
to the Grail Castle. It was later
returned to the Holy Land in the
ship that carried Percival and his
companions on the voyage to
return the Holy Grail.

Nida   *Norse*

The site of the heavenly hall
reserved for dwarfs.

Nidhogg   *Norse*

A monster in the form of a dragon
or serpent which gnawed at the
roots of the world-tree Yggdrasil
and fed on corpses.

Niflheim   *Norse*

The land of mists and fog, far to
the north; hell; the underworld
ruled by the goddess Hel.

In some accounts, Hel is the
palace of the goddess, situated in
the realm of Niflheim.

Niflhel   *Norse*

In some accounts, Niflhel is the
lower part of Hel's region to
which one gains access through
the Gnipa cave, home of the
guard-dog Garm. In this version,
Niflhel is a place where the dead
undergo a second death and are
punished.

Other accounts make Niflhel
and Niflheim synonymous.

Niflungs *see* **Nibelungen**

Night Lord   *Mesopotamian*

A god of rain. It was he who,
ordered by the sun god Samas,
caused the heavy rains which
gave rise to the Flood.

Nightingale the Brigand   *Russian*

A monster, part human, part
bird. This being lived in a tree
and attacked passing travellers.
He was killed by the hero Ilya
Muromets.

night-raven   *European*

A bird variously identified as a
bittern, heron, nightjar or owl. In

Denmark, the bird is said to be the incarnation of one who was murdered or committed suicide and was buried, at the junction of roads, in a grave from which it frees itself by moving only one grain of soil per year.

Some say that this bird flies in front of the Wild Hunt.

Nike   *Greek*
= *Roman* Victoria

The goddess of victory. She was awarded the title of goddess of victory for the help she gave to the gods in their battle with the Titans. She is often depicted as a winged figure. In some accounts, she is identified with Athena.

Nilakantha   *Hindu*
'Blue Throat'

A name for the god Shiva. He was given this name when, at the Churning of the Ocean, he swallowed the poison that arose, so saving mankind. He is sometimes depicted with a blue throat caused by holding the poison in his throat.

Nile Goose   *Egyptian*
also Chaos Goose

The bird that laid the cosmic egg, the sun. (*See also* **Geb**.)

Nimble Men *see* Fir Chlis

Nimrod   *Hebrew*
= *Babylonian* Gilgamesh

A king of Shinar. He was a great hunter and warrior, and in non-Biblical stories was said to have owned the clothes worn by Adam and Eve which guaranteed victory to those who wore them. He was deified and ordered the construction of the Tower of Babel for an attack on heaven itself.

It is said that, no matter how heavy the dew, none ever falls on Nimrod's tomb in Damascus.

Nimue   *British*
also Lady of the Lake

One of the holders of the office of Lady of the Lake; daughter of King Pellinore or of Dyonas, son of the goddess Diana. In some stories she is a nun, in others the daughter of a Sicilian siren or of Dinas, a knight of the Round Table. Some equate her with the sorceress Morgan le Fay, others have her as a separate person. Some accounts place her as one of the attendants of the Lady of the Lake who later assumed that office.

At King Arthur's wedding feast, the proceedings were interrupted when a white stag galloped into the hall followed by a white bitch and a pack of hounds. A knight seized the dog and rode off with it. A lady on a pony then appeared claiming that the dog was hers. She was forcibly dragged away by an unknown knight who rode into the hall. The knight was Ontelake and the girl was Nimue. She was rescued by Pellinore who killed Ontelake and brought her back to Camelot, where the magician Merlin fell madly in love with her as he had always known he would despite knowing also that she would destroy him.

She travelled with Merlin to Ban's court in Benwick and back to England, always promising to sleep with her aging suitor if he would tell her all the secrets of his magic art which, foolishly, he did. In Cornwall, he used his powers to make a fabulous room inside a rock where they might be together but when they entered the room she sprang back and sealed the entrance with an unbreakable spell. She rode away leaving Merlin to his fate and came upon Pelleas, another knight of the Round Table, dying of unrequited love for the damsel Ettard. Nimue used her magic to cause Ettard to fall in love with Pelleas but then put a spell on Pelleas so that he rejected her love. She stayed with Pelleas for the rest of her life; some versions say they married.

In some stories she left Merlin tied up in the magic forest, Broceliande, trapped in an oak tree or entangled forever in a thorn-bush.

(*See also* **Morgan le Fay**.)

Notu   *Pacific Islands*

A white tortoise. Notu was caught by Yusup, a fisherman, and thereafter guided the young man's boat to places where he could be sure of a good catch. Notu also dived and found the magic ring which restored a sea monster to his proper form as a prince.

Nine Ladies   *British*

A megalithic structure in Derbyshire, England. The ladies were said to have been turned into stones for dancing on a Sunday.

Nine Worlds   *Norse*

The realms into which the world of the Norse races was divided. These divisions are listed as Godheim (home of the Aesir), Helheim (home of the dead), Jotunheim (land of the Frost Giants), Liosalfheim (land of the light elves), Mannheim (home of mankind), Muspelheim (land of the Fire Giants), Niflheim (the underworld), Svartalfheim (land of the dark elves), Vanaheim (home of the Vanir).

Other lists substitute Asgard for Godheim, Hel for Helheim, Alfheim for Liosalfheim, Midgard for Mannheim and introduce Nidavellir, the home of the dwarfs.

Nine Worthies   *European*

Heroes embodying the qualities of bravery and virtue. These men were listed in three groups of three. From the Bible and Apocrypha there were David, Joshua and Judas Maccabaeus; the classical period was represented by Alexander, Hector and Julius Caesar; the later Christian world produced King Arthur, Charlemagne and Godfrey of Bouillon.

Ningal   *Mesopotamian*

A Sumerian moon goddess. She refused to live with the moon god Sin until he had made the whole world fruitful.

Ninhursaga   *Mesopotamian*

A Sumerian earth goddess, goddess of animals, birth and productivity; wife of the creator-god Enki. When Enki was forming human beings from clay, she spoiled some of his handiwork by altering the shapes. As a result, dwarfs, cripples and giants were created.

She and Enki lived in Dilmun, the earthly paradise, until they quarrelled because Enki had seduced Uttu, the goddess of weaving, who was his own daughter or granddaughter. Ninhursaga recovered some of his semen from her body and used it to grow eight plants. Others say that Uttu gave birth to the plants. Enki ate them and became ill and would have died if Ninhursaga had not saved him by placing him in her own body from which he was born again. Another version says that she gave birth to eight deities each of which healed one of the ailments which afflicted Enki as a result of eating the plants. These deities were Abu, Dazimus, Enshag, Nazi, Ninkasi, Ninsutu, Ninti and Nintur.

Ninurta   *Mesopotamian*

= *Hittite* Bel

The Sumerian war god, god of farming, floods, and wind; son of Enlil and Ninlil or Ninmah; son of Inanna, some say; consort of Gula.

When the lion-headed storm bird Zu stole the Tablets of Destiny from the god Enlil, the mother-goddess Belet-Ili gave birth to Ninurta and sent him to recapture the Tablets. After a long battle, he killed Zu and returned the Tablets to Enlil.

He fought the demon Asag with huge stones which he later used to make mountains to hold back the flood-waters of Kur. He has a magic weapon and a double-edged scimitar. Some say that these weapons, Sarur and Sargaz, are cyclones which he controls.

Niobe[1]   *Greek*

The first woman. In the lore of the Argives, she was the daughter of the first man, Phoroneus, by the nymph Teledice. She was seduced by Zeus and bore a son, Argus, who became king of Phoronea, later called Argos. Another version says that she was the wife of Phoroneus.

Niobe[2]   *Greek*

Daughter of Tantalus; wife of Amphion, king of Thebes.

She had seven sons and seven daughters (or six sons and six daughters, in some accounts) and boasted that, having so many children, she was greater than the goddess Leto, mother only of Apollo and Artemis, and should be worshipped. Apollo and Artemis killed her husband and all her children for this slight (though some say that one boy, Amydas, and one girl, Chloris, escaped) and Zeus turned the weeping Niobe into stone, which continued to weep, on Mount Sipylus.

nis   *Scandinavian*

also nisse

A friendly goblin; a household spirit.

Nisse god-dreng   *Norse*

A domestic fairy.

nix   *Norse*

= *Icelandic* nykr

A water-spirit. These beings, who live in undersea palaces, are generally invisible but can take many forms such as horses or human beings. In the latter form, when they are said to have fish-like tails, they may mate with humans. In their normal habitat they are said by some to be old ugly beings with green skin who can assume the form of beautiful maidens to lure humans to their death by drowning. Anyone who rescues a person from drowning can expect to suffer at the hand of the nixes for robbing them of their victim.

Njal   *Norse*

An Icelandic hero, head of a family feuding with the Sigfussons. The feud seems to have started either when his wife Bergthora quarrelled with Hallgerda, wife of Gunnar Lambason, or when one of Njal's sons, Skarp-Hedin, killed Thrain, a Sigfusson, and it came to a head when the Sigfussons attacked the Njalssons, killing all but Kari (Njal's son-in-law), who escaped, and the women and children, who were allowed to the leave the house, Bergthorsknoll, before it was burnt to the ground. Njal and his wife, knowing that they could not escape, lay together on their bed, with their young grandson Thord between them, and quietly waited for the flames to overwhelm them.

Njal's Saga is the story of this feud between the Njalssons and the Sigfussons.

Noa   *East Indies*
An ancestor of the tribes of New Guinea. He killed his own son and threw pieces of the body far and wide, using a different language each time. The tribes grew out of these pieces of flesh, each with its own language.

Noble Lady of Felicity *see* **Jui-ch'ing-fu-jen**

Nocuma   *North American*
An omnipotent deity of the tribes of California. He formed the globe of earth in his hands and made it steady by inserting the black rock, Tosaut. The fish split open the rock, emptying its salt contents into the waters to make the seas. Nocuma then made the first man, Ejoni, and the first woman, Ae, from whom the tribes are descended.

Nokomis   *North American*
A love goddess of the tribes of the north-east; daughter of the moon; mother of Wenonah; grandmother of Hiawatha.

She fell from the heavens into the primeval waters when the other goddesses, jealous of her beauty, cut the rope on which she was swinging. She became pregnant and populated the world, turning herself into earth so that living things could have dry land to live on as well as the oceans.

In one account, her enemies, the Underwater Panthers, tried to drown her by causing a flood but the god Manabozho called on the beavers and otters to bring up mud from the bottom from which he made dry land, so saving her life.

Another story story says that she was the grandmother of Manabush (Manabozho) and reared him when his mother, Wenonah, died in childbirth. A twin boy died at the same time but Nokomis placed the surviving child under a dish where he turned into a white rabbit.

In more familiar stories, she raised the infant Hiawatha whose mother, Wenonah, died in childbirth.

Nona   *Roman*
One of the three Fates. She was originally regarded as a goddess of birth.

Nordri   *Norse*
One of the four dwarfs supporting the sky (north). (*See also* ***Austri, Sudri, Westri.***)

Nork   *Cambodian*
Hell, the home of the damned. This realm, which has eight levels, lies below the earth and the torment inflicted on sinners increases with the depth. The lowest hell is called Avichi. Each level is divided into sixteen separate hells with increasing levels of torture. Spirits who have suffered torment appropriate to their sins are reborn.

Norns   *Norse*
also Fates
= *Greek* Moirai; *Roman* Parcae
Daughters of the gods, giants or dwarfs. The Fates, Skuld (future, necessity), Urda (past, fate) and Verdandi (present, being), who were

the guardians of Urda's well. They watered the world-tree Yggdrasil with water from this well and were also responsible for renewing the soil round its roots and for tending the two swans that swam on Urda's well. (*See also* ***Wyrd.***)

Nsassi   *African*
The hero of a dog story. When Nsassi asked for two beautiful sisters as brides, their father agreed provided that Nsassi could discover their names. He left disappointed. Later, his dog heard the father address the girls as Lenga and Lunga but forgot their names when he tried to tell Nsassi. After hearing the names several more times, the dog finally remembered them and Nsassi was able to claim his brides.

Nü Kua   *Chinese*
also Gourd Girl, Nü-huang
A serpent-bodied creator-goddess; wife or sister of Fu-hsi. She represents the yang of Chinese philosophy, her husband representing yin.

In some stories she is the mother of the first humans, in others she made humans from clay and then splashed them with drops from a rope. The drops of clay became the upper classes while the peasants sprang from mud drops.

In the story of the Flood, she (as Gourd Girl) and Fu-hsi (Gourd Boy) were the sole survivors, floating in a gourd from the tree grown from the tooth of a thunder god whom they had freed from a trap set by their father. She mated with her brother, both in the form of snakes, to stock the earth with plants and animals. When they tried to produce human beings, they produced only a lump of unformed flesh. Fu-hsi cut this into pieces and scattered it over the world, so producing the human race.

When Fu-hsi died, she took over as ruler under the name of Nü-huang and defeated Kung Kung when he tried to usurp the throne. She repaired the hole in the heavens and the damage caused to earth when Kung Kung tore down the mountain that supported the heavens. Having set the world to rights, she climbed up a ladder and disappeared into the sky.

She is said to have invented the flute and is credited with the introduction of marriage.

nue   *Japanese*
A sky-monster. This beast is described as having the head of an ape and the body of either a badger or a tiger. In the former case, the beast had the feet of a tiger and the tail of a serpent.

Nuinumma-Kwiten   *Australian*
A monster in the lore of the Aborigines. The threat of this monstrous beast of prey was used to frighten children.

Nules-murt   *Russian*
A forest god of the Votyak. This one-eyed being, normally as tall as a forest tree, can vary his height at will. He has a hoard of precious things and moves about inside a whirlwind.

Numa Pompilius   *Roman*
The second king of Rome. He married his mistress and adviser, the water nymph Egeria, after the death of his first wife, Tatia. When the protective shield, the ancile, fell from the sky, he had eleven copies made and hung all twelve in the temple of Mars so

that any prospective thief would not know which was the real one. He is said to have started the cult of the Vestal virgins.

Numbakulla   *Australian*
A pair of beings from the sky. They came to earth to help the development of the primitive beings (inapertwa) into male and female humans. When they had finished their work, the pair became lizards.

Numitor   *Roman*
A demi-god; king of Alba Longa; father of Rhea Silvia, the mother of Romulus and Remus. He was deposed by his brother Amulius and sent into exile. When his grandchildren, Romulus and Remus, grew up, they killed Amulius and restored Numitor to the throne.

Nummo   *African*
Twin spirits of light and water in the lore of the Dogon people of Mali.

These beings were produced when the supreme god Amma first fertilised the earth, or were hatched from one of the two yolks in the primordial egg created by Amma. They were described as half human, half snake, with red eyes and forked tongues and were covered with green hair. In some accounts, one was good, the other evil, while some say that the evil one was Ogo who hatched from the other yolk with his sister, Yasigi. The evil one was said to have been changed into a jackal while other accounts say that this jackal was born of a union between Amma and Mother Earth before the Nummo were born. In some accounts, Amma killed the Nummo and, by sprinkling their

blood on the earth, made plants and animals. The twins were then restored to life as human beings.

Numokh Mukana   *North American*
The first man, in the lore of the Mandan tribe.

Nun   *Egyptian*
= *Babylonian* Apsu-Rushtu; *Sumerian* Abzu
A god of the the primitive waters; progenitor of Atum (Ra).

He represented, with his consort Naunet, the depth of the primitive water and is depicted as a man up to his middle in water, supporting the sun. In some accounts, Nun is identified with Ptah.

In another aspect he is regarded as the southern ocean, source of the Nile.

He is depicted with a frog's head or as a baboon or as a man holding up the solar bark.

Nundu   *African*
A man-eating monster of the Bantu. This monster is said to be invisible but is described as some form of dragon or huge lion.

Nunne Chaha   *North American*
also Nunne Hamgeh
A great mountain, home of the Creek gods, which emerged after the Flood and the mud of which was used to make the first men.

The Choctaws regard it as the site of the cave where some of their ancestors sheltered to survive the Flood.

Nut   *Egyptian*
'sky'
Mother-goddess and sky goddess. Nut and her twin brother and consort Geb were locked together when they were born and Shu forced them apart so that Geb became the earth and Nut became the sky. She was cursed by Ra for

consorting with Geb and would have been unable to have any children if Thoth had not gambled with the moon and won five intercalary days during which her five children could be born.

When Ra finally gave up the throne and went to heaven, he was raised aloft by Nut.

She is depicted as a giantess who supports the world on her arched back, swallowing the sun at night and giving birth to it again each new day. In other versions, she is a cow, supporting the sky, held up by her father Shu, god of the air, or a sow suckling young.

Nu'tentut   *Siberian*

An earth-spirit of the Chukchee people. He owns the world and lives in a house made of iron.

Nuts of Knowledge   *Irish*

The fruit of the hazel. These (nine) nuts dropped into the river (or into Segais's Well which became the River Boyne) and were eaten by the salmon, Fintan, which acquired great wisdom. This wisdom passed to Finn mac Cool when he sucked his thumb when cooking the salmon.

Nu'u   *Pacific Islands*

also Nu'u Pule

A survivor of the Flood in the lore of Hawaii. Like many other flood survivors, he was warned of the impending deluge by a god (Tane, in this case) and built a boat which he filled with seeds and animals to restock the world after the waters had subsided.

nykr   *Icelandic*

= *Norse* nix

A water-spirit. These beings sometimes appeared in the form of a horse. When anybody mounted, the horse would gallop back into the sea, drowning the rider.

nymphs   *Greek*

Female divinities living in some natural feature such as water, mountains, etc. The various groups of nymphs are given as:

Acheleids – nymphs of the River Achelous

Alseides – tree nymphs

Creneids – water nymphs

Dryads – tree nymphs

Epimelian nymphs – nymphs of flocks and herds

Hamadryads – tree nymphs

Hydriads – water nymphs

Leimoniads – nymphs of the meadows

Limniads – lake nymphs

Maelids – apple nymphs

Meliae – nymphs of ash trees

Naiads – nymphs of fresh water

Napaeae – nymphs of the trees and valleys

Nereids – nymphs of the Aegean

Nysiades – nymphs of Mount Nysa

Oceanides – sea nymphs

Oreads – mountain nymphs

Orestiads – mountain nymphs

Potameids – water nymphs

Stygian nymphs – nymphs of Hades

In some accounts, the Pleiades are referred to as nymphs, as are the Sirens.

Nyx   *Greek*

'night'

= *Roman* Nox

Goddess of night; daughter of Chaos. In one version of the story of creation, she is the sister and wife of Erebus 'darkness', in another she is the mother of Erebus and later his wife.

Nzambi   *African*

Creator-god and sun god of the Bakongo. He is said to have made the first pair of humans or a bisexual being in the form of a palm-tree called Muntu Walunga. This primeval being may be depicted in effigy with male and female faces on opposite sides and, in some tribes, Nzambi is regarded as female.

Other versions say that he spat out the heavenly bodies, followed by animals and then, having created human beings, returned to the sky.

O *Central American*

A Mayan deity of uncertain identity, referred to as Goddess O (see **alphabetical gods**). This deity is depicted as an old woman engaged in spinning and is therefore regarded as a goddess of married women, protector of the domestic scene.

Oa Iriarapo *East Indies*

A man who made fire. In the lore of Papua New Guinea, this man placed his hand on his daughter's stomach as her child was delivered and, when he removed his hand, flame emerged from his palm. From then on, his people had fire and could cook their food.

oaf *European*

A changeling; a child left by a fairy or a demon in exchange for another child.

oak

(1) In Celtic lore, this tree was venerated by the druids.
(2) In Greece it was sacred to Zeus, in Mesopotamia to Baal and in Norse mythology to Thor.
(3) It was a sacred tree in Hebrew lore.
(4) Some North American Indian tribes also regard the oak as sacred.

Oat Stallion *German*

= *German* Haferhengst

A field spirit personified in the last sheaf.

Oats Goat, Oat Goat *European*

= *German* Haferbock

A field spirit, invoked to frighten children to keep them out of the cornfields and, it is said, to make the reapers hurry in their work to keep out of his clutches.

Oberon *European*

also Auberon

King of the fairies; husband of Titania; father of Gloriana, some say. In some accounts, he is said to be the son of Julius Caesar and the sorceress Morgan le Fay. In the Charlemagne stories, his original name is said to be Tronc, and he is the son of Julius Caesar and the fairy Glorianda or Morgan le Fay, who had been stunted in his growth by a jealous aunt, never growing taller than a five-year-old boy. In other stories, Oberon is given as the brother of Morgan le Fay.

He befriended Huon, duke of Guienne, when he met him as the young man journeyed to find Sultan Grandisso, and gave him a goblet that provided unlimited quantities of wine for the true believer and a horn that would protect him in times of peril. When Oberon was finally taken up to Paradise by a host of angels, he handed his kingdom over to Huon, despite the objections of King Arthur, who had expected to receive the throne.

In some accounts, he was the father of Robin Goodfellow (the brownie also known as Puck) by a mortal and, in Shakespeare, his wife was Titania.

Ocean-sweeper   *Irish*

also Wave-sweeper

A magical ship, the boat of the sea god Manannan. This ship could read the sailor's thoughts and sailed without oars or sails wherever he wished to go. It was orginally brought from the Otherworld bythe sun god Lugh and given to Manannan.

Oceanids *see* **Oceanus**

Oceanus   *Greek*

A river encircling the earth, personified as a Titan; son of Uranus and Gaea; husband and brother of the sea goddess Tethys. He is the one Titan who did not join in the rebelion against the gods.

He is said to be the father of 3000 sons, 3000 daughters (the Oceanids) and all the river gods and sea gods except Poseidon. He is depicted with the horns of a bull.

Ocelopan   *Central American*

One of the leaders of the Aztecs when they left their homeland, Aztlan.

Ocelotl   *Central American*

An Aztec creator-god and sun god. He was the ruler of the first of the five ages of the world which was then populated by giants. This age ended when jaguars killed and ate the giants.

Ocnus   *Greek*

A deity, delay personified. He lives in the underworld and is perpetually engaged, like Sisyphus, in never-ending tasks, such as plaiting a straw rope which is eaten by a donkey as he works or piling sticks on to the back of the donkey, only for them to fall off on the other side.

Odin   *Norse*

also All-father, All-seer, Thunderer, Wild Huntsman;

= *German* Wotan, Wuotan; *Anglo-Saxon* Wodan, Woden

Creator-god, god of battle, the dead, inspiration and wind. He and his brothers Ve and Vili killed the Frost Giant Ymir and built the world from his body.

He had a number of wives, of whom the principal was Frigga. His first wife was Erda who produced Thor; the second was Frigga, mother of Balder, Hermod, and, some say, Tyr; and the third was Rinda, mother of Vali, the god of light. He was the father of the giant Heimdall, who was produced by nine giantesses (the wave-maidens) simultaneously.

He sent Hermod to consult the magician Rossthiof, who prophesied that one of his sons would be murdered and advised that Odin should woo Rinda. Worried by the omens for Balder's future, he went to Niflheim in the guise of Vegtam to consult the prophetess Volva whom he raised from the sleep of death. She told him that Balder would be killed by his own brother, Hoder.

He tried to win Rinda, first as the victorious general who had defeated her father's enemies, then as Rostrus, a craftsman who made her wonderful gifts, and finally as a handsome young warrior. She rebuffed him on every occasion, so he put her in a trance and appeared as Vak, an old crone who claimed to be able to break the spell. Instead, he tied her up, carried her off and fathered the boy Vali who grew to manhood in one day and avenged the death of Balder by shooting his killer, Hoder.

In his efforts to improve the lot of gods and humans, he gave up one eye for a drink from Mimisbrunnr, the Well of Wisdom, suffered untold tortures hanging for nine days from the tree Yggdrasil to learn mysterious runes, and took the skaldic mead from the giants and gave it to mankind so that those whose drank might become poets (skalds).

On one occasion, angered by the desecration of a statue of himself, he went off leaving Asgard to its own devices. The Frost Giants quickly took over, while his brothers Ve and Vili assumed his role. After seven months he returned, ousted his brothers, forced the giants to relax their icy grip and resumed his role.

On a visit to his foster-son, Geirrod, he went in disguise to test his hospitality. He was tortured for eight days and, when he finally revealed his true identity and freed himself, Geirrod fell on his own sword.

A later story of Odin makes him a god-king originating in Asia Minor, migrating across Europe to the northern realm, and leaving his sons as kings of countries he conquered.

As Wotan, he forced Alberich, king of the dwarfs, to hand over the Rhine-gold, together with the Ring and the Helmet of Invisibility made from it, but Alberich placed a curse on all of this treasure. When Fafnir killed his brother for possession of the gold and turned into a dragon to guard it, Odin decided that a warrior should kill Fafnir so that the gold could be returned to the Rhine-maidens to break the curse. He chose his own son Siegmund but, in a duel with a hunter who had abducted Siegmund's lover, broke Siegmund's sword, allowing Siegmund to be killed by the hunter whom Odin then killed with a fierce glance.

He was the owner of a magic spear, Gungnir, a magic bow that fired ten arrows at once (all of which hit their mark) and an eight-legged horse called Sleipnir.

When Odin felt that the end was near, he consulted the prophetess Haid, who told him how the world would end but could tell him nothing about what would happen after Ragnarok. Her knowledge, combined with his own, enabled him to see the rebirth of the world repopulated by Lif and Lifthrasir, the return of Balder and the happy future contrasting with the doom-laden past.

In the final battle, Odin was killed by the wolf Fenris.

In some accounts, he is said to have brought to Scandinavia the head of Minos, king of Crete, which continued to speak, and used it as an oracle.

He is represented with a long grey beard and carrying his spear, Gungnir, usually accompanied by his ravens Hugin and Munin. On his visits to earth he wore a blue cloak and a flat cap.

Odin's Tree   *Norse*
Yggdrasil; also a name for the gallows.

Odin's Wagon   *Norse*
The wind.

Odysseus   *Greek*
= *Roman* Ulixes, Ulysses
King of Ithaca; husband of Penelope; father of Telemachus. He won Penelope as his wife in a foot-race.

At the time of the Trojan War, he tried to avoid serving with the Greek army by pretending

madness and sowing his fields with salt, but this ruse did not work; Palamedes placed the infant Telemachus in front of the plough and Odysseus was sane enough to avoid the child. He eventually joined the force that had been raised to attack Troy.

After the fall of Troy he wandered for ten years before finally getting back to his home (*see* **Odyssey**). When he did get back he found that his wife Penelope had for some years been beseiged by suitors who thought her husband was dead. They refused to leave her house and were virtually eating her out of house and home. With the help of his old swineherd Eumaeus, his son Telemachus and the goddess Athena, he got his hands on his bow and arrows and shot the suitors in cold blood – all except Medon and the minstrel Phemus whom he spared to provide the music at the celebration of his homecoming. His son hanged all those servants who had not remained faithul to Odysseus during his long absence.

Another story says that the relatives of the dead suitors brought Odysseus to trial for murder and Pyrrhus, acting as judge, sent him into exile in Anatolia, where he married the daughter of the king, Thoas, and she bore him a son named Leontophonus.

He once stayed with the king of Epirus and raped his daughter, Euippe, on whom he fathered a son, Euryalus. When the boy grew up, Euippe sent him to kill his father but, warned of his coming, Odyssesus slew the youth, not knowing he was killing his own

son. Another version says that Odysseus sent the boy to live with Penelope, who later accused the boy of rape, so Odysseus killed him.

At the end of his life he assembled a fleet and sailed off to the west, never to be seen again.

Another story says that he was accidentally killed by Telegonus, his own son by the sorceress Circe, who had sent him to look for his father, and who was unaware that the man he fought and killed was his own father. In this story, Telegonus took the body back to Aeaea to be buried by Circe.

Odyssey   *Greek*
Homer's epic story, in 24 volumes, of the wanderings of Odysseus after the Trojan War.

At the fall of Troy, the Greeks angered the goddess Athena and the sea god Poseidon, who had helped them in the fighting, by violating Athena's temple and by failing to sacrifice to the gods, and they planned to make the Greeks suffer. They caused a storm to disperse the fleet on its homeward journey, during which Menelaus was blown all the way to North Africa and Ajax the Less was drowned. Odysseus was forced to wander for ten years before finally reaching home.

The first landfall for Odysseus and his crew was the island of Ismarus where they sacked the city and lost some men in battle. Next came the land of the Lotus-eaters where his men were so enchanted that he had to chain them aboard.

Next came the encounter with the Cyclops, Polyphemus, who trapped them in his cave and ate some of the crew. The others managed to escape, by hanging underneath the giant's sheep, only after Odysseus had blinded the giant with a fire-hardened wooden stake.

In the country of Aeolus, god of the winds, they were given all the storm winds in a sack to ensure a calm voyage, but some inquisitive sailor opened the sack and caused another storm which blew them off course to the land of the giant cannibals, the Lestrygones, who destroyed all the ships except one.

They next landed at Aeaea, the island of the sorceress Circe who turned all the advance party into pigs. The god Hermes gave Odysseus a herb which protected him from Circe's magic and he forced her to return his men to human form again on pain of death. She fell in love with him and Odysseus stayed with her for a year. In some accounts, they had a son, Telegonus, who later unwittingly killed his father; in others, they had two other sons called Agrius and Latinus. Circe found out what he needed to do in order to get home safely; this required Odysseus to go down to Tartarus and find the ghost of the prophet Teiresias who warned him not to harm the oxen of Helius, the sun god.

Passing the island where the Sirens lived, Odysseus made his crew block their ears with wax while he was roped to the mast. In this way they were able to resist the seductive songs of the Sirens and they also survived the passage between Scylla and Charybdis, losing six of his crew to the voracious monster Scylla, in some stories.

At Trinacria, the island of the Sun, his men killed some of the oxen for food and Helius avenged the insult by shattering the ship with a thunderbolt. All perished except Odysseus, who drifted for some days on a piece of wreckage until he landed on the nymph Calypso's island, Ogygia, where he was held virtually captive for several years by her, who fell in love with him.

Athena finally gave up her vendetta and Zeus made Calypso release her captive. She sent him off on a raft and he drifted for seventeen days until the sea god Poseidon, who hadn't relented, blew up another storm which wrecked the raft. Again Odysseus found himself in trouble but the sea goddess Ino came to his aid, giving him her veil to protect him from the sea, and he swam for two days before coming ashore naked and exhausted in the land of the Phaeacians. He was found by the king's daughter, Nausicaa, and her father, Alcinous, generously provided a ship which took Odysseus on the last leg of his journey home.

Oedipus   *Greek*
The infant Oedipus was abandoned on Mount Cithaeron by his father who pierced his feet with nails, and was raised by Polybus, king of Corinth. In other accounts, the child was cast adrift in a chest. In either event, he survived and in later life he met his real father without knowing who he was. Oedipus killed both his father Laius and his charioteer, Polyphontes, when they tried to run him down with their chariot. In some versions, Laius had four attendants with him and Oedipus killed all five.

He correctly answered the riddle of the Sphinx, who thereupon killed herself, and he was made king of Thebes by the citizens grateful for the removal of that monster.

He married Jocasta, not knowing that she was his mother, and they had four children, Antigone, Eteocles, Ismene and Polyneices. When the prophet Teiresias revealed what had happened, Oedipus blinded himself and wandered thereafter throughout the length and breadth of Greece accompanied by his faithful daughter Antigone.

He was finally killed by the Furies at Colonos and buried by Theseus.

oeh-da   *North American*
In the lore of the Seneca, mud brought up from the bottom of the primeval waters. This mud, brought up by Muskrat, was placed on the back of a turtle, Earth-Bearer, and grew to form the world which, it is said, is still carried on the turtle's back.

Oenone   *Greek*
A nymph of Mount Ida; a prophetess. She married Paris, prince of Troy, before he became aware of his royal parentage but he abandoned her in favour of Helen, wife of King Menelaus. When Paris was wounded in the siege of Troy, his attendants took him to Oenone in the belief that she knew a magic drug which would save him. She took her revenge by letting him die but then, overcome by grief, either hanged herself or threw herself on his funeral pyre and died with him.

Ogbu-ghu   *African*
A hornbill. In a story told by the Ibo, there was no land when

Ogbu-ghu's mother died and the bird could find nowhere to bury her body. He carried her body on his back and flew over the primordial waters seeking a burial site and finally spotted two people swimming in the ocean. They brought up land from the bottom and he was at last able to bury his mother properly.

Ogier   *Europe*
also Ogier the Dane

One of Emperor Charlemagne's paladins. At his baptism, six fairy queens endowed him with many qualities, one of the queens, Morgana, claiming him as her own. At the age of sixteen he was sent to Charlemagne's court as pledge for his father's continued allegiance. In some stories, he was sent to prison and later married the daughter of the prison governor. Other stories have him marrying an English princess who was given to him as a reward for killing a giant Saracen.

He went with the emperor's army to repel the Saracens besieging Rome and, in his first battle, took over the oriflamme from the cowardly Alory and distinguished himself by his bravery. He saved Charlemagne's life when the emperor's horse was killed and two Saracens were about to kill him and Ogier was rewarded for this with a knighthood. His sword, Cortana, was provided by Morgana (Morgan le Fay).

One of the Saracens who had unhorsed the emperor was Carahue, king of Mauritania, and he challenged Ogier to single combat. Charlot, the emperor's son, also accepted the challenge of Sadon, Carahue's cousin.

Charlot arrived with a troop of his followers and attacked the other three. Ogier and the two Saracens routed their attackers and became friends. He was held captive by Dannemont, a renegade Danish king fighting with the Saracens, until Carahue, in protest, surrendered himself to Charlemagne. Without their leader, the Saracens made peace with the emperor and Carahue and Ogier were exchanged.

Ogier then took an army to Denmark and repelled the forces attacking that country but his father, the king, died almost at the moment of victory. Warned by a heavenly voice, Ogier refused his father's crown and left it to his half-brother, Guyon.

When his young son Baldwin was killed by Charlot, Ogier was prevented from killing the emperor's son only by a servant who intervened. Ogier dashed a cup from the servant's hand and some of the wine splashed in the emperor's face. He left the court in disgrace but was later captured and handed over to Charlemagne who sentenced him to prison on a diet designed to starve him to death. An archbishop gave Ogier larger rations and kept him alive and in good health.

Ogier was released from prison only when the emperor needed him to accept the challenge thrown down by Bruhier, the Sultan of Arabia, who had invaded France. Ogier agreed to accept the challenge on the emperor's behalf on condition that Charlemagne would hand over Charlot for the punishment due to him for killing Ogier's son. Ogier allowed Charlot to live and

renewed his allegiance to the emperor. He then met Bruhier in the lists. Bruhier had a magic lotion that healed wounds and restored severed limbs as soon as it was applied. A sword-stroke from Bruhier killed Ogier's horse Beiffror and one from Ogier cut off Bruhier's arm. When the Arab dismounted to pick up the severed arm, Ogier was able to drive him away from his own horse so that he could not reach the flask of lotion. Ogier finally killed Bruhier and claimed his horse Marchevallée, using the lotion to heal his own wounds.

Armies under Carahue and Guyon sent to release Ogier from prison found that they were no longer needed since Ogier had been released by the emperor, so they combined forces to support the French under Ogier in an attack on the Saracens in their own countries. Ogier took with him the young Walter, son of his half-brother Guyon, and after many years in the east, handed over his responsibilities to Walter and sailed for France. His ship was wrecked on a strange shore where two sea monsters let him pass and the fire-breathing horse, Papillon, carried him to the palace of Morgana who had at last claimed him. He stayed in Avalon for a hundred (two hundred, some say) blissfully happy years, never aging. When he finally asked to be allowed to return to France, he and Papillon were carried over the sea on the backs of the two sea monsters.

Ogier rode Papillon to Paris where he recognised nothing and nobody. The king, Hugh Capet, told Ogier all that had happened while he had been away and Ogier helped him to rout a force of Saracens attacking Chartres. When the king died, it was intended that Ogier should marry the queen and rule France but a golden crown appeared on Ogier's head and he disappeared from sight. He had been reclaimed by Morgana, who transported him to Avalon where he still lives, together with King Arthur, both awaiting the call to return in the hour of need. Others say that he sleeps under the Kronenberg (Kronborg) where his beard has grown to an enormous length.

Another story says that he rescued a lady, who turned out to be the daughter of the king of England, from the hands of the Saracens, and married her.

He was said to have carried a burning brand and would die when it was extinguished.

Ogof Lanciau Eryri, Ogo'r Dinas   *British*
Caves in Wales in which it it said King Arthur lies sleeping, awaiting a call in Britain's hour of need.
For other suggested sites, *see* ***Alderley Edge***.

ogre
A man-eating monster, usually quite stupid. The ogre takes many different forms. In the Baltic regions it is a seven-headed serpent, in Greece a dragon and in Norway a troll.

Ogyges   *Greek*
King of Thebes. In one version of the story of the Flood, he appears in place of Deucalion. In other versions, the flood that occurred during the reign of Ogyges was two centuries before Deucalion's flood.

Ohdows   *North American*
One of the three tribes of Jogah (the others are the Gahonga and the Gandayah). In the lore of the Iroquois, these dwarf beings are responsible for preventing the monsters of the underworld from escaping into the upper world.

Ohrmazd *see* **Ahura Mazda**

Oisin   *Irish*
= *Scottish* Ossian
King of the Land of Youth; son of Finn mac Cool.
A deer run down by Finn's dogs turned out to be a beautiful maiden, Saba, who had been turned into a deer by a druid whose love she had rejected. She married Finn but when he was called away to fight the Norsemen, the druid turned up again and changed her back into a deer. Her baby by Finn would, it was said, have been a deer if she had licked him in the manner of a deer – instead he became the boy Oisin, who was later found by Finn and reared by him to be a great warrior and poet.

He was one of the party of nine, led by Goll mac Morna, which recovered Finn's hounds, Bran and Sceolan, when they were stolen by Arthur.

A beautiful girl, Niam, daughter of the sea god Manannan, arrived on a white horse. In some accounts, she had been given the head of a pig by some druidic magic. The spell was broken when Oisin married her and they lived happily on an island in the Land of Youth for some years, until Oisin wanted to return to his native land. Niam lent him her a white horse for the journey and warned him never to touch the ground of Ireland. When his foot

slipped and touched the soil, his eternal youth vanished, revealing a blind, centuries-old man. He had been away about 300 years (1000, some say).

Some say that he lived on to pass much ancient lore to St Patrick, though others say that this was done by the warrior-poet Cailte. It is said that Patrick tried to convert Oisin to the Christian faith but he turned down the chance of heaven if he could not take his dogs and his friends.

Oklatabashih   *North American*
In the lore of the Choctaws, the only man to survive the Flood.

Okonorote   *South American*
A hunter-hero of the Arawak tribe. He dug a hole through the floor of heaven and climbed down a huge tree (or a rope) to earth to retrieve an arrow he had dropped. He then showed other humans the way but, when some of them mated with serpents, the god Kononatoo caused a fat woman to become wedged in the hole in the sky, so preventing them from ever returning to their original home.

Okova   *Pacific Islands*
A Fijian hero. His wife was seized from their fishing-boat by the monstrous man-eating bird, Ngani-Vatu. Helped by his brother-in-law, Rokoua, Okova killed the bird and took some of its smaller feathers to use as sails.

Okulam   *North American*
A voracious giant in the lore of the Chinook. He killed four of five brothers and was pursuing the last when they came to a river where a Chinook fisherman Thunderer was fishing. The fisherman threw the youth across the river to safety and invited the giant to cross the water by

walking over his prostrate body. He then tipped the giant into the river where he drowned.

Okuni-Nushi   *Japanese*

A king of Idzumo; a Shinto god of thunder, magic and medicine; son of the sea god Susanowa.

He built the world, except the heavens, with the help of the god of medicine Sukuna-biko. Some say that he had eighty brothers, others that he married Ya-game-hime and many other maidens and their children populated the earth.

In some accounts, his brothers treated him as a servant and, on two occasions, killed him, once by rolling a piece of red-hot metal down a hill, burning him to death, and once by felling a tree which crushed him. In each case, he was restored to life by the god Musubi or, some say, by his mother. When he asked for the hand of Susanowa's daughter, Suseri-hime, Susanonwa tested his valour by putting him in a room full of snakes and, on another night, a room full of insects. From both he was saved by a scarf given to him by Suseri-hime. In a final test, a grass-fire, he was saved by a mouse who sheltered him below ground or by a hare that he had earlier helped. In some stories, Susanowa gave his consent to the marriage but Okuni-Nushi did not trust him and the couple eloped after tying her father to a beam with his hair.

He was forced to give up his earthly throne when the sun goddess Amaterasu sent her grandson Ninigi to take over.

In some accounts, he is regarded as the guardian of the royal family.

Old King Cole *see* **Coel**

Old Man   *North American*

also Old One

A creator-spirit of many tribes. The Aleuts say that he made humans by throwing stones over his shoulder. In the lore of the Blackfoot and Modoc, he was a culture-hero as well as a creator. The Blood Indians say that he originally made men and women separately and placed them far away from each other but soon realised that he had made a mistake and brought them together so that they could mate. Other tribes say that Old Man used balls of mud to make humans.

Old Man Above *see* **Gudratrigakwitl**

Old Man of the Sea[1]   *Arabian*

An evil jinnee in the *Arabian Nights' Entertainments*. This being took the form of an old man and refused to get down off the back of Sinbad the Sailor after he had carried him over a stream. Sinbad got him drunk and then killed him.

Old Man of the Sea[2] *see* **Nereus, Proteus**

Old Man of the South Pole *see* **Shou Shen**

Old Woman[1]   *East Indies*

In New Guinea, a deity who kept the moon in a jar. It is said that some mischievous boys opened the jar and released the moon. The dark markings now seen on the moon are those caused by the boys' fingers as they tried to grab the moon as it escaped.

Old Woman[2] *see* **Kunapipi**

Olelbis   *North American*

A creator-god of the Wintun people. The first world was destroyed by a fire started by Buckeye Bush

and his companions, a fire which was extinguished when the water goddess Mem Loomis caused the Flood. Olelbis set about re-creating the world, which was then fertilised by Old Man Acorn.

Olelbis wished to give the people he had created the gift of immortality, so he sent his brothers to construct a ladder between earth and his heaven, Olelpanti. The foolish brothers were persuaded by the trickster-god Sedit to desist and they demolished what they had already built. As a result, human beings are mortal.

Olivant   *European*

also Oliphant

In legends related to Charlemagne, the ivory horn of the paladin Roland. Some say that this horn originally belonged to Alexander the Great.

In some accounts, Roland acquired this horn, and the sword Durindana, when he defeated the giant Jutmundus. Others say he won them when he killed the Saracen warrior Almontes. The horn, which could be heard for twenty miles, was blown finally to great effect at the battle of Roncesvalles.

olive   *Greek*

The tree of the goddess Athena.

Oliver   *European*

One of the paladins of Charlemagne, Roland's comrade-in-arms.

When Charlemagne fell into dispute with Montglave, governor of Vienne and grandfather of Oliver, Oliver fought Roland in single combat to settle the matter. After five days, neither had gained the upper hand, so they declared an honourable draw, when they finally recognised each other.

He joined the Abyssinian forces under Astolpho at the siege of Biserta and was chosen with Roland and Florismart to do battle with Agramant, Sobrino and Grassado to settle the war between them. Only Oliver, Sobrino and Roland survived the encounter, and both Oliver and Sobrino were badly wounded. Oliver was healed by the hermit who had converted Rogero to the Christian faith and, after the end of the war, went with Roland to collect the tribute exacted by Charlemagne from the Spanish king, Marsilius. In the battle of Roncesvalles which resulted, he killed the Saracen knight Malprimo but was himself wounded. He was later stabbed in the back and died of his wounds.

In another story, Oliver was captured by Balan, the Saracen ruler of Spain whose son, Fierabras, he had defeated in single combat and converted to the Christian faith. He was later rescued by Charlemagne's men and Balan was killed when he refused to convert.

Olodumare   *African*
A creator-god of the Yoruba; a name of Olorun as 'almighty'. He created the fertility god and scuptor god Obatala as his deputy and created the earth by scattering dirt from a snail shell which was scratched over by a hen and a pigeon to make dry land. In some accounts, the scattering was done by Obatala on the orders of Olodumare.

Olofat   *Pacific Islands*
A trickster-god, fire god and god of death in the Caroline Islands.

He was a semi-divine being who ascended to heaven on a column of smoke and demanded recognition as a god. A long battle ensued, during which Olofat was killed but his father resurrected him and persuaded the other gods to accept him as the god of fire. He later brought fire down from heaven for the use of mankind.

He is said to have been involved in numerous escapades such as stealing food which he replaced by husks, pretending to be an old man with ringworm, seducing the wives of relatives, and so on. He so angered his relatives that they once put him in a post-hole and rammed the post in on top of him but he escaped, just as he did when they threw him into a fish-trap or tried to burn him.

Some say that he gave the shark its fearsome teeth.

Olorun   *African*
The creator-god and sky god of the Yoruba. In some accounts he is equated with Olodumare as 'he who owns the heavens', in others he is regarded as the chief god.

He filled a shell with dirt which was then scattered by a hen and a pigeon, so creating the earth. Having then provided some trees, he made the first sixteen human beings. In other accounts, all this was done by his son Obatala.

Olympia   *Greek*
A sacred valley in Elis, said to be the home of Zeus. It is the site of temples of Hera and Zeus.

Olympian
One of the greater gods, the gods living on Mount Olympus.

The Greek Olympians were Aphrodite, Apollo, Ares, Artemis, Athena, Hades (Pluto),

Hephaestus, Hera, Hermes, Hestia, Poseidon and Zeus. Other lists have Demeter in place of Hades; some substitiute Dionysus for Hestia; some regard Zeus as their ruler though not himself an Olympian. Others include Asclepius, Dionysus and Hercules.

The Roman Olympians were Apollo, Diana, Juno, Jupiter, Mars, Mercury, Minerva, Neptune, Pluto (Dis), Venus, Vesta and Vulcan (Mulciber).

Omam   *South American*
A creator god of the Yanomami. He caught a woman on his line when fishing and mated with her to produce the ancestors of the tribe.

Omphalus   *Greek*
also Omphalos
The seat of Apollo at Delphi, held to be the centre of the world. What was known as the navel stone at Delphi was in fact the stone which Rhea had wrapped and given to Cronus to swallow when he thought he was swallowing his son, Zeus, and which he was later forced to regurgitate together with the other children he had already swallowed.

It was said that the exact centre of the earth was ascertained by Zeus who set two eagles to fly from opposite ends of the earth. They met at Delphi.

Omumborombonga   *African*
A tree from which, in the lore of the Damara people, all humans and animals arose.

Onata   *North American*
A corn goddess of the Seneca; sister of Bean and Squash. Like the Greek Core, she was seized by the god of the underworld and the earth became barren while her mother searched for her. Her time

is now divided between the upper and lower worlds, giving summer and winter. (*See also* **Deohako**.)

ono pacakoti   *South American*
The flood sent by the Inca creator-god Viracocha to destroy the first race of beings.

onocentaur   *European*
A monster, part man, part ass.

opinicus   *European*
A monster, part lion, part dragon, a four-legged version of the griffin.

Opochtli   *Central American*
An Aztec god of hunting and fishing. This deity is depicted painted black, wearing a paper crown and feathers on his head and holding a red shield and a sceptre.

Ops   *Roman*
= *Greek* Rhea; *Phrygian* Cybele
The goddess of the harvest, plenty, wealth; second wife of Saturn; mother of Jupiter and Neptune. (*See also* **Bona Dea**.)

oracle
The revelations of a god, or a place where these revelations are made known.

The two most famous Greek oracles were those of Apollo at Delphi where the revelations were made by the Pythoness and that of Zeus at Dodona where the rustling of the leaves on the oak trees was interpreted to reveal the will of the gods. Zeus (as Ammon) had another oracle at Siwa in Libya. Others were at Amonium (Zeus), Aphaea (Aphrodite), Arcadia (Pan), Athens (Hercules), Branchidae (Apollo), Charos (Apollo), Crete (Zeus), Delos (Apollo), Epidaurus (Asclepius), Gades (Hercules), Lebadea (Trophonius), Mycenae (Athene), Paphos (Aphrodite) and Rome (Aesculapius).

Orthrus   *Greek*
A monster two-headed dog of Geryon. This animal, once owned by Atlas, guarded the herds of Geryon and was killed by Hercules on his tenth Labour. Geryon's other dog was Gargittos.

orc   *European*
A sea-monster. In the Charlemagne stories, the maiden Angelica was bound to a rock and would have been devoured by the monster if Rogero had not killed it and rescued her.

Oreads   *Greek*
Mountain nymphs.

Orestes   *Greek*
King of Argos, Mycenae and Sparta; son of Agamemnon and Clytemnestra; brother of Electra and Iphigenia.

At the time of his father's murder by his mother and her lover Aegisthus, Orestes was a boy of ten. He was saved from death at the hands of Aegisthus by his sister Electra, who hid him among shepherds. In another version, Electra sent him to the court of King Strophius, where he made an inseparable friend of the king's son, Pylades, his cousin.

As a man, he was told by the Delphic Oracle that he should avenge his father's death. He tricked his way into the palace with the story that Orestes was dead and killed both Aegisthus and Clytemnestra together with their daughter Helen. He was tried for matricide and condemned to death by stoning, a verdict commuted to suicide. His friend Pylades who had helped in the murder and Electra who had incited him were both included in the sentence. The trial had been arranged by his uncle Menelaus

and Orestes planned to kill his wife Helen and his daughter Hermione, to avenge what he regarded as a betrayal but Zeus intervened and carried Helen off to Olympus as an immortal where she became the guardian of sailors like her brothers Castor and Pollux. Hermione was released after being held captive for some time.

Orestes escaped the death sentence but was harried into madness by the Erinyes (Furies) for matricide. He stood trial again for the killings but was defended by Apollo and Athene and eventually acquitted.

The Delphic Oracle said that, to be rid of the Erinyes, he must seize the wooden image of Artemis which was said to have fallen from the sky and which was worshipped by the Taurians. As it turned out, the priestess in charge of the temple was Iphigenia, his sister, who had been saved from the sacrificial knife by Artemis, and she was easily able to deceive Thoas, the Taurian king, who had captured Orestes and Pylades so that they were able to escape, taking the image with them. Thoas followed the ship of Orestes as far as Sminthos where he was killed by Orestes.

When he finally got back to Mycenae with the image of Artemis, the Erinyes gave up their pursuit of him but he found that Aletes, a son of Aegisthus, had usurped the throne. Orestes killed him and would have killed his sister, Erigone, had she not been carried off by Artemis.

He died at Orestia when bitten by a snake and was buried at Tegea. His bones were later recovered and re-interred in Sparta.

Other versions of his expiation say that, in one case, he bit off one of his own fingers, in another that he was doused in pig's blood. One story says that the Erinyes still harried him after his death and Apollo gave him a bow with which to ward them off.

Orestiads　　　　　　　　　*Greek*
Mountain nymphs.

Orias　　　　　　　　　*European*
A demon, one of the 72 Spirits of Solomon. He is depicted riding a mule and holding a serpent in each hand or as a lion riding a horse.

Orion　　　　　　　　　*Greek*
A Giant, famous as a hunter. One account of his birth relates that Hyrieus, king of Boeotia, having entertained three gods, Hermes, Poseidon and Zeus, asked them to provide him with a child. They urinated on the hide of a bull which Hyrieus then buried and from which arose a son, Urion, later Orion. Other accounts say that Orion was the son of Dionysus and Demeter, or of Poseidon and Euryale, daughter of King Minos.

Orion pursued the Pleiades until they were changed first into pigeons and then into stars and set in the heavens by Zeus.

Oenopion, king of Chios, promised him the hand of his daughter Merope if he would rid his island of dangerous beasts but he went back on his promise. Orion got drunk and raped Merope and Oenopion enlisted the aid of some satyrs and blinded Orion. Guided by Cedalion, an assistant of Hephaestus, Orion sought out the sun god Helius who restored his sight. He looked for Oenopion to exact revenge

but failed to find him and spent the rest of his life in Crete where he met Artemis and went hunting with her. He was killed by an arrow shot by Artemis in the mistaken belief that he was the rapist of her priestess Opis, or out of jealousy of Eos, goddess of the dawn, who was also in love with Orion. In another version, Apollo, displeased with the attachment between Artemis and Orion, set her an archery test. She aimed at and struck a floating speck in the sea, which turned out to be the head of the swimming Orion. Other accounts say that he died when bitten by a scorpion sent by Artemis (or Gaea) when he boasted of his intention to kill all wild animals, or when he tried to rape Artemis.

Orion was set in the heavens as that constellation, with his dog, Sirius, beside him.

Orion
This constellation is referred to in the myths and legends of many cultures.
(1) The Arabic version is Al Jabbar (the Giant) – which equates with the Hebrew Gibbor – or Al Babadur (the Strong) or Al Shuja (the Snake).
(2) The Chinese call the constellation Shen and regard it as the realm of the White Tiger, one the Four Auspicious Animals.
(3) In early Egypt it was the demon, Sahu; in later times it was Horus or Osiris journeying across the sky.
(4) The Greeks had many names for the constellation, such as giant, warrior, double axe, etc.
(5) The Hebrew version is Kesil or Gibbor, equated with the hunter Nimrod.

(6) In Mesopotamia it was Ningirsu or Tammuz or Uru-Anna, the deity of light.
(7) The Mexicans recognise it as Atli the bowman.
(8) Norse mythology sees these stars as Odin or as the goddess Freya's spinning-wheel.
(9) In North America it is recognised as three fishermen (Micmac), a celestial hunter, or the Hanging Lines (Zuni).
(10) Siberian lore says that the stars are Erlik Khan and his three dogs and the wapiti they are chasing. In the Buriat version, a hunter, born of a cow, was carried to the heavens by the gods when he shot an arrow at three stags he was chasing.
(11) In South America it is recognised in Peru as condors holding two criminals, by others as three bolas, while some tribes say the stars are a leg, in some cases the leg of one of the Pleiades after it had been bitten off by an alligator.

Orlando *see* **Roland**[2]

Ormaddu　　　　　　　　　*African*
In Berber lore, a huge bird that mated with a female wolf to produce a griffin.

Orobas　　　　　　　　　*European*
A demon, one of the 72 Spirits of Solomon. He is said to impart knowledge of the past, present and future and appears in the form of a horse or a horse with a man's torso.

Orpheus　　　　　　　　　*Greek*
Son of Oeagrus, king of Thrace, or the god Apollo by the Muse Calliope or Menippe (sometimes included among the Muses); husband of Eurydice. He was given a lyre by Apollo and was taught

by the Muses, becoming the most famous musician of the age.

He sailed with the Argonauts and saved the crew from the Sirens by drowning their songs with the music of his lyre. Some say that he lulled to sleep the serpent guarding the Golden Fleece.

When his wife, Eurydice, running from an attempted rape by Aristaeus, was killed by snake-bite, he descended to Tartarus and charmed Hades into releasing her. Contrary to his instructions, he looked back to ensure that she was following behind, and Eurydice was reclaimed by Hades and condemned to remain in Tartarus for ever.

Some say that he was killed by a thunderbolt flung by Zeus for teaching mortals the secrets of the gods, while others say that he was torn to pieces by the maenads (wild female devotees of Dionysus) when he failed to acknowledge Dionysus. His head floated down the River Hebrus to Lesbos and continued to prophesy until silenced by Apollo. His lyre was installed in the heavens as the constellation Lyra.

In some accounts, it is suggested that Orpheus was an incarnation of Dionysus.

Orphic mysteries *Greek*
Rites practised by the followers of Dionysus, who regarded Orpheus as their founder.

Orunmila *African*
The god of fate and god of mercy among the Yoruba.

He defended humans from the sea god Olokur. He knows the destiny of all humans and can speak to them in every language through oracles.

In some accounts, he is equated with the demi-god Ifa while others regard him as the creator-god.

Osanobua *African*
also Osanobwe
A creator-god of the Edo people of Nigeria. He allowed his sons to choose whatever they wanted and then sent them to earth which was, at that time, entirely covered with water. While the others chose wealth, the youngest son took only a snail shell. He turned this shell upside down and the sand that fell out into the ocean became the first dry land and he became its king. The other brothers, having nowhere to live, gave him some of their wealth for a share of the land and he became very rich and powerful.

Ose *European*
A demon, one of the 72 Spirits of Solomon. He has the power to transform humans into animals and to cause madness. He is said to appear in the form of a leopard.

Oshossi *African*
A Yoruban god of woods and hunting. He is also worshipped in the West Indies.

Oshun *African*
A river goddess; consort of Shango. She is also worshipped in the West Indies.

Oshunmare *African*
= *Dahomey* Dan Ayido Hwedo;
Haitian Damballah Wedo
A serpent-deity of the Yoruba, also worshipped in the West Indies.

Osiris *Egyptian*
= *Babylonian* Nergal; *Greek* Dionysus, Hades
The supreme god, god of the dead, floods, harvest, sun, the underworld and vegetation; son

of Geb and Nut or of Ra and Nut; brother of Isis, Nepthys, Seth.

He married his sister Isis and when his father abdicated and split the kingdom between Osiris and Set, they ruled the northern half. Set wanted all the kingdom and he put Osiris in a chest and threw it into the Nile. In one version, the chest landed in Phoenicia (or Byblos) where a tree (Erica) grew round it. The tree was felled to make a column for the new palace of the king, Malcandie, who restored the chest to Isis. She retrieved the body and, mourning in the form of a bird, conceived and bore a son, Horus. Set again got hold of the body and cut it into fourteen (or up to 42) pieces which he threw into the river. Again Isis rescued the pieces, reassembled them and brought Osiris back to life but he went down to rule in the underworld, as Khenti-Amentiu, leaving the throne to Horus. In another version, she conceived Horus after Osiris had been reassembled from the pieces and, in yet another, Isis buried the pieces (except the penis which had been thrown to the crocodiles or carp) at various sanctuaries.

His symbols were the flail and the crook and he is depicted swathed like a mummy holding these implements.

The pharaoh of the united kingdom was Osiris after his death.

Ossian *see* **Oisin**

ostrich
(1) This bird is regarded by the Arabs as a cross between a bird and a camel, capable of becoming a jinnee.

(2) In Mesopotamian myth, a representation of Tiamat.
(3) The ostrich is a sacred bird of the Zoroastrians.

Othagwenda   *North American*
also Flint
An Iroquois culture-hero; twin brother of Djuskaha. (*See Djuskaha.*)

Otherworld[1]
A general term for some supernatural place, including fairyland, heaven, hell and paradise. In many cases, the otherworld can be reached only by the bravest heroes and after many difficulties.

Otherworld[2]   *Celtic*
= *British* Avalon; *Irish* Tir nan Og; *Welsh* Annfwn
Home of the fairies; land of the gods. A place where another existence, in many ways similar to this life, awaits those who have died. A death in this life meant a rebirth in the Otherworld and vice versa. It was said to become visible to mortals at the Feast of Samhain.

Otter   *North American*
One of the four animals which tried to find soil from which Manabush could re-create the world. In Algonquian lore, Beaver, Mink and Otter all died in an attempt to find soil after the flood and it was left to Muskrat to succeed.

Otter-Heart   *North American*
A young orphan. He grew up alone, except for his sister, and set off to find adventure. He met a chief who offered him his two daughters but, when he insisted that the young man should marry both Good and Wicked, Otter-Heart fled, pursued by the two maidens. When he hid in a pine

tree, they chopped it down and he escaped by riding on a cone and when he hid in a cedar, he was saved when his guardian spirit broke the maidens' axes. He came to a teepee where the woman who welcomed him exposed herself as Wicked by eating the best part of the beaver he had caught. At a second lodge, the woman gave Otter-Heart the best parts of the otter he brought with him and admitted that the otters were her relatives. She was the Good maiden and he married her.

Otus   *Greek*
A giant; son of the sea god Poseidon. He and his twin brother Ephialtes were noble beings, not monsters like the other giants. (*See more at **Ephialtes**.*)

Our Grandmother *see* **Kokumthena**

ouroboros   *Greek*
A symbolic serpent with its tail in its mouth, representing the cycle of life, totality, etc.

Ousous   *Phoenician*
A creator-god, a giant fire deity. He and his brother Hyposouranios were said to be the inventors of mankind.

Ovda   *Baltic*
A forest-spirit of the Lapps. This flesh-eating monster could appear as male or female, naked with the feet pointing to the rear. It killed people by tickling them to death before eating them but it could be rendered powerless if touched under its left arm.

Owain[1]   *British*
also Knight of the Lion
A knight of King Arthur's court, one of the Knights of Battle; son of Urien and Morgan le Fay or Modron.

The sorceress Morgan planned to kill King Arthur and her husband, Urien, marry her lover Accolan and make him king. Believing that Accolan had killed Arthur in a fight, she took her husband's sword and was about to kill him as he slept. Owain, alerted by a servant, was hidden in the room and seized his mother in time to prevent murder. His mother duped him into believing that she had been possessed by evil spirits and he forgave her when she promised to give up all her magic arts.

King Arthur felt that he could no longer trust Urien or Owain so he banished Owain from his court. His friend Gawain opted to go with him and they set out to find adventure which would allow Owain to prove his loyalty to the king.

Their first encounter was with the giant Morholt who challenged Owain and Gawain, disposing easily of the young Owain who sustained a leg wound, and fighting an honourable draw with Gawain. All three became friends and travelled on together. They met three women who offered to lead them to adventure and Owain chose the oldest of the three. She turned out to be Lyne, a woman who had always wanted to be a man and had made a lifetime study of knightly pursuits. She made Owain undergo ten months of intensive training at her home in Wales and then they set off to find adventure. He unhorsed thirty knights at a tournament and won the prize, riding on to the Castle of the Rock. Here lived the Lady of the Rock who

had had all her property, except
the Castle, taken from her by
the brothers Edward and Hugh.
Owain fought them both at once,
killing Edward and forcing Hugh
to surrender. The Lady of the Rock
offered him the chance to live
with her and run her regained
estates but he chose to leave. At
the crossroads, Lyne left him to
await another knight errant she
could train while Owain joined
Gawain and Morholt and returned
with them to Camelot where they
were all made welcome by the king.

He was one of the knights
captured and imprisoned by
Turkin, who hated all Arthur's
knights, until rescued by Lancelot.

In Welsh stories, he appears as
Owein. In one Welsh story, he has
an 'army' of 300 ravens given to
him by the warrior Cenferchyn,
which ensure him victory in any
battle.

Another Welsh story involves
the Lady of the Fountain. When
Cynon, a knight of the Round
Table,was unhorsed by the Black
Knight, Owain met the victor and
wounded him so severely that he
died. Imprisoned, he was rescued
by Luned, maid of the Lady of
the Fountain, who gave him a
ring which made him invisible,
and Owain took over all the
Black Knight's lands and his wife
Laudine, the Lady of the Fountain,
living with her for three years. At
the end of that time, Arthur went
in search of him and Kay met the
Knight of the Fountain in single

combat and was defeated. Each
of Arthur's knights was defeated
in turn and it was only when
Gwalchmei fought him that they
realised they were fighting Owain.
He was reunited with Arthur and
returned to his court for three
years. When he realised how he
had deserted his wife, he did
penance (or went mad, some say)
and lived the life of a mendicant,
killing a dragon and taming the
lion which had been fighting with
it. His path crossed that of Luned
once again and he rescued her
from death at the stake.

In some versions, he returned to
the Lady of the Fountain, in others
he was reunited with his wife and
they lived together at Arthur's court.

In another story, he arrived home
to find his castle occupied by the
knight Salados and his followers.
In the fight that ensued, Owain
escaped with his life only when the
lion, which had become his faithful
companion, intervened, killing
Salados and routing his followers.

Other stories include a fight
with Gawain when Owain set out
to defend a lady robbed of her
property by her elder sister. The
two finally recognised each other,
the fight was ended and Arthur
settled the dispute between the
sisters. En route to this adventure,
Owain had released 300 ladies
held captive in the Castle of
Pesme Aventure by two demons
who forced them to weave cloth.

Owain[2]   *British*
also Owein the Bastard

A Knight of the Round Table.
He was the illegitimate son of
Urien by the wife of his steward
and thus half-brother to the
other Owain. He was killed by
Gawain, whom he challenged to
a joust.

owl
A bird traditionally deemed to be
wise.
(1) The Buddhists regard the owl as
a messenger of Yama, the god of
the dead.
(2) In Central America the Aztec
refer to the owl as Tlacolotl and
regard it as a bird of ill-omen.
(3) In the Christian tradition the
owl is an attribute of both Christ
and Satan.
(4) In Egypt the owl was regarded
as a symbol of death.
(5) In Greece the owl was regarded
as sacred to Athene and Demeter.
(6) In Hindu lore, the owl (Shakra)
was regarded as an attribute of
Yama and sacred to Indra.
(7) The Japanese regard the owl as
typifying filial ingratitude, as a
form of the monk Fukuro and as a
god of villages.
(8) The Malay regard owls as ghosts.
(9) In North America, the Algonquin
people regard the owl as an
attendant on the Lord of the
Dead.
(10) In Persian lore the owl, Asho-
Zushta, could drive away demons
by reciting passages from the holy
book, the Avesta.

Owl-glass *see* **Tyll Eulenspiegel**

P

P *Central American*
A Mayan deity of uncertain identity, referred to as God P (*see **alphabetical gods***). This deity is depicted as a frog and may be sowing seed or ploughing, leading some to identify him as a god of agriculture.

Pa Hsien *see* **Eight Immortals**

Pa Kua *see* **Eight Diagrams**

pa-lis *Persian*
An evil gnome. These beings were said to kill those who slept in the desert by licking their feet to suck out their blood.

Pa Pao *see* **Eight Precious Things**

Pacari *South American*
A cave with three exits. This is the cave from which the ancestors of the Inca people were said to have emerged. Some say that there were three such caves. (*See also **Children of the Sun**.*)

pacarina *South American*
In Inca lore, dead ancestors. It was believed that these beings could intercede with the gods on behalf of their descendants.

Pachacamac *South American*
also Earth-maker
An Inca creator-god. He defeated his brother Con, the earlier creator of men, turned Con's people into monkeys and made new beings.

In another version of the story he created humans but forgot their need for food. The man died and the woman was fertilised by the sun. Pachacamac killed her first son and grew plants from pieces of his body. Her second son, Vichama, drove Pachacamac into the sea when Pachacamac killed the woman. He remained in the seas as a sea god.

Padstow *British*
The Cornish town said by some to be the place where King Arthur was born.

Paguk *North American*
A moving skeleton, in the lore of the Algonquian and Ojibwa tribes. This apparition, said to be the skeleton of a hunter who starved to death, is said to move through the woodlands at fantastic speed with much bone-rattling. Its presence portends the death of a friend.

Pahe-Wathahuni *North American*
A cannibal hill. This hill could open its mouth to form a cavern and any hunters who ventured in were swallowed up. Rabbit disguised himself as a man and entered the cavern with a band of hunters and slew the monster by slitting its heart open. The hill then split wide open and those who had been swallowed were restored to life.

Pai Hu *see* **Four Auspicious Animals**

Pai Lung *Chinese*
also White Dragon
One of the Four Dragon Kings. This being is said to have been born as a lump of flesh to a maiden given shelter by an old man when she was caught in a storm. In disgust, she threw the lump into the sea

where it became a white dragon, the cause of famine. The girl died from shock.

paiarehe   *New Zealand*

Fairies, in the lore of the Maori.

Paimon   *European*

A demon; one of the 72 Spirits of Solomon. He is said to be able to grant any wish a magician may make and to teach science and the arts. He is depicted as a crowned ruler riding a camel.

Pairekse   *Siberian*

Son of the god of heaven. He makes entries in the book of fate as instructed by the gods and sometimes visits the earth in the form of a goose to report what is happening.

Paiva   *Baltic*

A Finnish sun god. The rays of the sun formed roads between heaven and earth along which the gods could travel.

Pajan Yan   *Cambodian*

It is said that this healing goddess was banished to the moon to prevent her from restoring all the dead. Her face is now seen in the moon.

Palace of Light   *British*

also Castle of Light, Palace Adventurous

A palace within Castle Carbonek where the Holy Grail was kept.

paladin

also pair, peer

A knight-errant, one of the twelve personal companions of the emperor Charlemagne. The list varied from time to time but some of the most famous were

    Astolpho, the English duke

    Aymon

    Baldwin, son of Gano

    Fierabras

    Florismart

    Gano, the traitor

    Guido the Wild

    Malagigi, the sorcerer

    Namo, duke of Bavaria

    Ogier the Dane

    Oliver, friend of Roland

    Rinaldo

    Roland (Orlando)

    Saloman from Brittany

    Turpin, the archbishop

Others sometimes included in the list are Amulion, Anseis, Engelir, Gerard, Gerin, Gerier, Inon, Ivory, Otonne and Samson.

Palamedes   *Greek*

He accompanied Agamemnon and Menelaus when they tried to persuade Odysseus to join the invasion of Troy and, when Odysseus feigned madness by ploughing salt into the earth, Palamedes placed Odysseus's baby son Telemachus in front of the plough. Odysseus avoided the child, revealing that he was quite sane.

During the Trojan War, Odysseus exacted revenge by bribing a servant to plant money and a letter, said to be from the Trojan king Priam. As a result, Palamedes was accused of treachery and stoned to death. In another account, he was drowned by Odysseus and Diomedes during a fishing trip or buried by them under stones when he climbed down a well in search of gold which, they told him, was hidden there.

Palamedes is said to have invented dice, lighthouses, scales and some of the alphabet.

Palau Bah   *Malay*

The home of the dead. In this happy land, far to the west, the souls of the dead live on the produce of the perpetually-fruiting trees, hence its name 'Island of Fruit'.

Palladium   *Greek*

also Palladion, *plural* Palladia

A wooden statue of Pallas Athena. This image was said to have fallen from the sky and was enshrined at Troy as guardian of the city. It was said that the city would never be conquered while the statue remained at Troy, so during the siege of Troy the Greeks Odysseus and Diomedes made a night-raid into the city and stole it. Some say that this was one of many copies to be found in the city.

In some accounts, Diomedes gave this copy to Aeneas who took it with him to Italy although this could have been the original saved by Aeneas when Troy fell to the Greeks. Others say it was Numa Pompilius, the second king of Rome, who brought the Palladium to Italy.

Some say that the original Palladium was made from the shoulder-bone of Pelops.

Pallas[1]   *Greek*

Daughter of the sea god Triton. Triton reared Athena as a companion for Pallas. It was said that, having accidentally killed Pallas, Athena had the Palladium made in her memory.

Pallas[2]   *Greek*

One of the Earthborn Giants (*see* **giant**), son of Uranus and Gaea. He was killed in the war between the gods and the giants by Athena who flayed him and used his skin as cover for her breastplate. Thereafter, she used his name as Pallas Athena.

Another version says that Pallas was Athena's father and she killed him when he tried to rape her.

Pallas[3]   *Greek*

A name of Athena, adopted either in memory of the girl Pallas or of the giant Pallas, both of whom she had killed.

Pallian   *Australian*

A creator-god of the Aborigines. He and his brother, Pundjel, created beings from bark and clay but, when they proved to be evil, they cut them into pieces. The ancestors of the tribes sprang from these pieces.

Palulukon   *North American*

=*Aztec* Quetzalcoatl; *Zuni* Koloowise
The plumed serpent of the Hopi, a fertility god.

Pan

also Goat-god, Goat-Pan;
= *Roman* Faunus, Lupercus, Silvanus
God of flocks, shepherds and woods. He was part man, part goat, with horns, hoofs and tail.

When he pursued the nymph Syrinx, she was turned into a clump of reeds by Gaea. From seven of these, Pan fashioned the reed-pipe. He seduced a number of nymphs and goddesses including Echo, Eupheme and Selene. He gave Artemis three hunting dogs and seven hounds and helped Hermes restore the sinews of Zeus cut out by the monster Typhon. He was the only god to die.

He is depicted as holding reed-pipes and a crook.

Pan-ku   *Chinese*

The primeval being of the Confucians; father of Yüan Shih.

The primordial Great Monad separated to form the Yin and Yang. They both split to form four lesser beings which produced Pan-ku. Alternatively, he was hatched from an egg and pushed the two halves of the shell apart to form earth and sky. In some accounts he modelled the first humans from clay or, alternatively, people

developed from the fleas on his body after he died. It is said that it took him 18,000 years, during which he grew bigger every day, to achieve the final position and he died from the effort. His left eye became the sun, his right eye the moon and his beard became the stars. Some say that he had a snake-like body with the head of a dragon.

He is depicted working with a hammer and chisel to make the universe from blocks of granite floating in space, assisted by his companions, a dragon, phoenix, tortoise and unicorn.

In some versions of the creation story, Pan-ku was assisted by the woman Kua.

Panacea   *Greek*

A goddess of health, daughter of Asclepius, ther god of healing.

Pandora   *Greek*

The first woman; wife of Epimetheus. She was created from clay by Zeus or the smith-god Hephaestus as a gift for Epimetheus, who rejected her at first but married her in haste when his brother Prometheus was punished by Zeus. It was she who opened the box, given to her by the gods as a wedding gift, that contained all the ills that have since afflicted mankind. Another version says that these were items that Prometheus had left over from the creation of mankind and stored in a jar which Pandora foolishly opened.

In some accounts, she was the mother of Deucalion and Pyrrha, the first man and woman, by Prometheus or Epimetheus.

Pandora's box   *Greek*

A box containing all human troubles. This box was given

to Pandora as a gift when she married Epimetheus. Against instructions, she opened it and out flew all the ills that have since afflicted mankind. The last to come out of the box was Hope. In some versions it is a vase or jug, containing all the items left over when Prometheus created human beings, which was found by Pandora who could not resist looking inside.

panther   *Greek*

The animal of the god Dionysus.

Paoro   *New Zealand*

A goddess of echoes. At creation, it was she who gave women a voice.

Papa   *New Zealand*

Earth-mother of the Maori. She and her husband Rangi were so firmly intertwined that their children could not leave the womb until their son Tane-mahuta, god of light, forced them apart to form earth and sky.

In some stories, the gods Atea and Tangaroa argued about the paternity of Papa's first child, each claiming to be the father. Papa cut the child in half and gave half to each of them.

Papa Taoto   *Pacific Islands*

A rock raised from the sea-bed by the sea god Tagaloa. The Samoans say that the sea god created this rock in the primordial ocean so that his bird-child, Tuli, could have somewhere to build a nest. Tagaloa later split this first rock into many pieces to form the islands of the Pacific.

Papaztac   *Central American*

An Aztec god of intoxication, one of the Centzon Totochtin. A sacrifice made to this god would ensure that the drinker suffered no more than a headache after getting drunk.

Para   *Baltic*
  also Pukhis, Puk;
  = *Estonian* Puuk; *Lappish* Smieragatto;
  Latvian Pukis; *Lithuanian* Pukys;
  Scandinavian Buttercat
  A Finnish spirit. This spirit, which
    a man can make from stolen
    objects, is said to supply its maker
    with food, drink and money. It
    sometimes takes the form of a cat
    which carries milk in its mouth or
    intestines.

Parasol tree   *Chinese*
  The only tree on which the phoenix
    will land. This tree grows twelve
    leaves each year but thirteen in a
    leap-year.

Parcae   *Roman*
  = *Greek* Moirai/Moirae; *Norse* Norns
  The Fates, Nona, Decuma/Decima
    and Morta, equivalent to the
    Greek Moirae Clotho, Lachesis and
    Atropos. Nona spins the thread
    of life, Decuma measures it and
    Morta is the goddess of death
    who cuts it.

Paribanou   *Moslem*
  also Peri-Banou
  A fairy, wife of Prince Ahmed.
    In the *Arabian Nights'
    Entertainments*, she gave Ahmed
    a wonderful tent and became his
    wife.

Parioca   *South American*
  A creator-god of the Quechua.
    After the Flood receded, five men
    hatched from eggs left on top
    of a mountain. Parioca was one
    of these beings and he travelled
    the countryside changing the
    landscape and making water-
    channels. When some people
    mistook him for a vagrant, he
    destroyed the whole village.

Paris   *Greek*
  A prince of Troy; son of Priam and
    Hecuba; brother of Hector.
    His mother, pregnant with Paris,

dreamed that she would bear a
torch that would burn down the
city or a monster which would
destroy it. The prophet, Aesacus,
interpreted this to mean that the
boy would cause the death of his
family and the loss of Troy and
so his parents abandoned him
on Mount Ida. He was suckled
by a she-bear, sheltered by the
shepherd Agelaus, and survived to
manhood, when he was returned
to his parents.

When he was asked to judge a
beauty contest between the three
goddesses Aphrodite, Athene
and Hera, he awarded the prize,
a golden apple, to Aphrodite
because she promised him access
to the most beautiful girl in the
world – Helen, wife of Menelaus.
He abandoned his wife, the
nymph Oenone, who loved him,
in the hope of winning Helen
and returned to Troy where he
was reunited with his parents
who provided the ships for his
expedition to Greece. There he
was a welcome guest of Menelaus
but when the king was absent,
Paris abducted Helen and took her
off to Troy. In the Trojan War that
resulted from this abduction, he
met Menelaus in single combat
and would have been killed had
not Aphrodite carried him back
to safety in the city. His son,
Corythus, came to fight at Troy
and, when Helen fell in love
with the youth, Paris killed him.
He later shot and killed Achilles
from the city walls, the arrow
striking the Greek hero in the only
vulnerable spot, his ankle.

Another version of the death
of Achilles says that Polyxena,
who was given to Achilles as
a prize, persuaded the Greek

hero to divulge the secret of his
vulnerable heel. Polyxena then
told her brother Paris, and he
stabbed Achilles in the heel at the
wedding of Achilles and Polyxena.
After the death of Achilles,
Paris was shot and wounded by
Philotoctes using Hercules' bow
and was carried to Oenone who
was reputed to know of a drug
that would save Paris but she, still
angry at being deserted, just let
him die.

Parne   *Baltic*
  A malevolent Finnish forest spirit.

Parsifal   *German*
  also Parsival, Parzifal
  A guileless youth; father of
    Lohengrin. In the Wagnerian story
    of the Holy Grail, he innocently
    shot a swan in the grounds of the
    Temple of the Grail. The keeper
    allowed him to watch the knights
    at prayer and he resolved to
    regain the Sacred Spear which
    had been seized from Amfortas,
    the guardian of the Grail, by the
    evil magician Klingsor. He resisted
    the temptations of the maiden,
    Kundry, in Klingsor's garden of
    delights and took the spear from
    Klingsor, using it to banish him
    and all his works from the face
    of the earth. After wandering for
    many years he finally found his
    way back to the Temple where he
    cured the wound of Amfortas by
    laying on the Sacred Spear and he
    became the guardian of the Holy
    Grail in place of Amfortas.
    (*See also* **Percival**.)

Parsu   *Hindu*
  The first woman, consort of Manu.
    She was created, some say, from
    the drink that Manu offered to
    the gods when he survived the
    Flood; others say that she was
    created, like Eve, from his rib.

Parthenope   *Greek*

One of the Sirens. When Odysseus and his crew failed to succumb to her charms and escaped, she drowned herself in despair.

Partholan   *Irish*

Leader of the second wave of invaders of Ireland. He had killed his parents in Greece, expecting to take over their kingdom. When he did not become king, he sailed for Ireland with his followers and settled there after defeating the Fomoire at the Battle of Magh nlotha.

Partholanians   *Irish*

The second wave of invaders of Ireland, followers of Partholan. This group of invaders was said to have come from Spain and consisted of 24 married couples. They overcame the Fomoire and took over Ireland but they were afflicted by a disease which wiped out the whole race except Tuan, nephew of Partholan, who escaped to the hills.

Parvati   *Hindu*

also Devi, Durga, Gauri, Kali, Kumari, Mahadevi, Shakti

A mother-goddess; a name of Devi as 'the mountaineer'; a mild form of Durga; sister of the god Vishnu; wife of the god Shiva; mother of the gods Ganesha and Skanda.

Shiva's first wife, Sati, immolated herself but was later reborn as Parvati. When Shiva deplored her dark skin, Brahma transformed her into Gauri, 'the Yellow Devi'. Some say that it was Gauri who was burned to death to become Sati. Another version says that Brahma created Gauri as a wife for the god Rudra.

She, or Uma, once covered Shiva's eyes, putting the world in darkness, and he then developed a third eye in his forehead.

In one story, Shiva banished her to earth as a fisher-girl and then sent Nandu in the form of a shark to destroy the fishermen's nets. The foster-father of Parvati offered her as wife to any man who could kill the shark and Shiva was able to win back his wife by appearing in the form of a young man and catching the shark.

She is sometimes depicted with four arms or with an elephant's head.

Pasht *see* **Bast**

Pasiphae   *Greek*

Wife of King Minos of Crete; mother of Ariadne, Deucalion, Glaucus, Phaedra and others; sister of Circe.

She fell irrationally in love with the white bull that the sea god Poseidon sent at the behest of Minos to prove that he was the rightful heir to the throne of Crete. Daedalus fashioned a hollow wooden cow in which she concealed herself to mate with the bull. The outcome of the union was the monstrous bull-headed Minotaur. Pasiphae, together with Minos and the Minotaur, retreated to the Labyrinth, a tortuous maze constructed by Daedalus to contain the monster. When Minos imprisoned Daedalus and his son Icarus in the Labyrinth, it was Pasiphae who released them to make their famous escape on wings made by Daedalus. (In some accounts, Europa was the mother of the Minotaur.)

Patala   *Hindu*

The underworld, a place of many pleasures. Patala has seven distinct regions, known as Atala, Mahatala, Nitala (or Patala), Rasatala, Sutala, Talatala and

Vitala, each ruled by its own king. Beneath these realms are the various hells and the serpent, Sesha, supporting the world.

Others describe Patala as a magnificent house, home of the Asuras (demons).

Patrise   *British*

An Irish knight, a Knight of the Round Table; cousin of Mador.

At a dinner given by Guinevere for twenty-four of her knights, Pinel planted a poisoned apple intended for Gawain who had killed his cousin Lamerock. The apple was eaten by Patrise, who died on the spot. Mador accused the queen of murder and she was saved from the stake only by the intervention of Lancelot who killed Mador in single combat.

Payatami   *North American*

A harvest god of the Hopi and Zuni peoples. He sometimes appeared in the form of a tiny flute-player or a butterfly which fertilised plants.

Pazuzu   *Mesopotamian*

An Assyrian monster. This being is described as part lion, part eagle, with horns and two pairs of wings.

peacock

(1) To the Chinese, the peacock was a sacred bird.
(2) In Greek mythology, the peacock is sacred to Hera.
(3) In Hindu mythology it is the bird of Brahma, Laksmi and Sarasvati.
(4) For the Romans, the peacock is the 'Junonian bird', sacred to Juno.

pearl

Pearls appear in many myths.
(1) In Borneo, they say that if a pearl is placed in a bottle with

some grains of rice and the finger of a dead man is used as a stopper, more pearls will appear.

(2) In China, it was said that some dragons could spit out pearls and, if dragons fought in the heavens, pearls could fall like rain.

(3) Hindus say that pearls can be found in the head or stomach of elephants.

(4) Some say that pearls lose their lustre with age, others that they become dull if the owner is ill.

(5) Pearl powdered and dissolved in lemon juice, to form salt of pearl, was said to cure certain illnesses or act as an antidote to poison.

peer *see* **paladin**

Pegasus   *Greek*

The winged horse of Apollo; the horse of the Muses. This animal, fathered by the sea god Poseidon, sprang from the blood of the Gorgon Medusa when she was decapitated by Perseus. It was ridden by Bellerophon, prince of Corinth, when he killed the Chimaera and, in some accounts, Perseus rode Pegasus when he rescued Andromeda from the sea monster. It also carried the thunderbolts used by Zeus.

It is said that the fountain Hippocrene, on Mount Helicon, sprang from one of the horse's hoof-prints.

Peirithous   *Greek*

Having heard of the exploits of Theseus, Peirithous, king of the Lapiths, stole some of his cattle to test his mettle, and they became lifelong friends as a result. During the hunt for the Calydonian boar his rashness nearly cost him his life but he was saved by Theseus.

Some say that he was one of the Argonauts and took part in the expedition when Theseus raided the Amazons.

At his wedding to Hippodamia, the drunken Centaurs tried to rape the women attending the ceremony, so starting the long-running feud between the Centaurs and the Lapiths.

After the death of Hippodamia he helped Theseus in the abduction of Helen. Theseus won when they drew lots for Helen and accompanied Peirithous to Tartarus to demand Persephone as a bride for the loser. They were both trapped by Hades in the Chair of Forgetfulness and although Theseus was rescued by Hercules, Peirithous was doomed forever. In some versions, only Theseus was trapped in the chair while Peirithous was bound to a revolving wheel. Some say that he was killed by the dog Cerberus, others that the earth opened and swallowed him.

Pelasgus   *Greek*

also Pelasgos

The first man; son of Zeus by Niobe, the first woman, some say. He was said to have emerged from the soil and became the ancestor of the early Greeks, the Pelasgi.

Pele   *Pacific Islands*

The volcano goddess of Hawaii. She was so unruly that her father Kane-hoalani sent her off to find her own house. She excavated for the foundations of a new home on many islands, finally building on Hawaii. It is said that the earlier excavations are the volcano craters of the Pacific region.

Another story says that she challenged a chief, Kahawali, to a race down the slope of a volcano on wooden sledges and erupted in fury when she lost. The winner escaped by boat.

Her first husband deserted her for another woman and Pele married the chieftain Lohiau. She left him soon after the wedding to prepare a new home but the message to say that it was ready took so long to reach him that he died. He was restored to life and set off with his attendants to go to Pele but once again it took so long that Pele lost patience and killed them all with fire.

Another variation says that she sent her sister Hiiaka to rescue the soul of Lohiau from the underworld. When Lohiau was restored to life, he fell in love with Hiiaka, so the jealous Pele poured lava over him and he died again. When he was once again restored to life by Kane-hoalani, Pele repented and gave him up to Hiiaka.

Pele Kolese   *Baltic*

A Finnish water spirit, who floats on its back as if drowning. Those who attempt rescue are attacked and killed.

pelican

(1) It is said that this bird will kill its young and then restore them to life with blood from its own breast.

(2) The Greeks regarded it as the enemy of the quail.

(3) In Hebrew lore, it was said to be a bird of ill-omen.

Pelleas   *British*

A Knight of the Round Table.

At a tournament where he defeated 500 knights in three days, Pelleas fell hopelessly in love with Ettard who had organised the contest. When she rejected his advances, he made a nuisance of himself and she sent her knights against him. He unhorsed ten in quick succession but then allowed himself to be tied under the belly of his horse and taken prisoner so that he could catch just another glimpse of his beloved. As soon as he was released, he did the same again. Gawain tried to help by going to Ettard in the armour of Pelleas and telling her that he was dead but the ploy failed when Gawain seduced Ettard and stayed with her for some time. Pelleas, heart-broken, took to his bed and went into decline. Nimue found him in this state and put a spell on Ettard causing her to fall in love with Pelleas. She then bewitched Pelleas who rejected Ettard with scorn. Nimue then stayed with Pelleas for their lifetime. In some versions, they married.

Pelles   *British*

also Hermit King, Roi Pecheur, Rich Fisher

A king of Carbonek; keeper of the Holy Grail; cousin of Joseph of Arimathea.

He was guardian of the Holy Grail who had been made lame for his sins. In one story, he found a ship covered in white samite, the ship that was later found by Galahad and his two companions in the Grail quest, and went aboard. When he tried to draw the sword which he found there, a spectral spear pierced him through both thighs.

To ensure a follower worthy of learning the secrets of the Grail, he used a magic potion to deceive Lancelot into thinking that his daughter Elaine was Guinevere.

The result of their union was the boy Galahad.

When Galahad reached the Grail at the end of his quest, he heard a voice from heaven telling him to anoint Pelles with blood from the Holy Lance. This washed away his sins and healed his wounds. Pelles spent the last years of his life in a monastery.

Pellimore   *British*

also Rich Fisher

A Knight of the Round Table; king of the Isles; father of Nimue, Percival and others.

He issued a challenge to all comers, and jousted with King Arthur and defeated him. Merlin put a spell on Pellimore to save the king's life.

He was later welcomed at the king's court and given a place of honour at the Round Table. At Arthur's wedding feast, he was sent to find the knight who had ridden into the hall and forcefully made off with Nimue. He passed a damsel nursing a wounded knight but refused to stop and help her. When he found the lady, he found two knights fighting – Ontelake who had carried her off and Meliot, her cousin. He killed Ontelake and Meliot surrendered without a fight. He took Nimue back to Camelot and, on the way, saw the dead bodies of the damsel and the knight he had failed to help. It turned out that the girl was Elaine, his own daughter by the Lady of Rule, and the knight was her lover, Myles; they had both been attacked by Loraine le Sauvage as they travelled to Camelot to be married.

He killed Lot, king of Orkney and Lothian, and was himself killed by Gawain, Lot's son.

In some accounts, he is referred to as the Rich Fisher, is wounded in the thighs and is equated with Pelles.

Pelops   *Greek*

When Tantalus found himself short of food at a banquet he had laid on for the gods, he killed his son Pelops, cut him up and served him in a stew. The only one to eat any of the portions was Demeter (or Thetis, some say) who ate the shoulder. The gods restored Pelops to wholeness, with Demeter contributing a new shoulder made of ivory and Poseidon carried the restored youth off to Olympus as his lover or cup-bearer.

He fell in love with Hippodamia and won her hand after beating her father, Oenomaus, in a chariot race, driving a magic chariot given to him by Poseidon. Pelops had promised to allow Myrtilus, her father's charioteer, to sleep with Hippodamia, so persuading Myrtilus to sabotage her father's chariot. When it broke down, Pelops killed Oenomaus but afterwards reneged on his promise to Myrtilus and kicked him into the sea. Purified by the smith-god Hephaestus, he assumed the throne of Pisa.

On his death he was taken up to Olympus as an immortal.

Pemba   *African*

A creator-god and tree god of the Bambara; the primordial creation principle.

He was made from the void and then created the world. He came down to earth as the seed from which an acacia tree grew. He made the first woman, Musso-koroni, from the wood of the tree and mated with her to generate humans and animal life.

She planted Pemba in the earth only for his twin brother, Faro the water god, to dig him up.

penanggalan   *Malay*
A blood-sucking demon or witch. It is said that these demons are women who, by witchcraft, leave their bodies by night in the form of a disembodied head trailing intestines.

Penates   *Roman*
Household gods of the larder. Some say these deities were brought from Troy by Aeneas; some say they are Castor and Pollux, the Cabeiri (fertility gods).

Penbedw   *Celtic*
A site, in Wales, where some say King Arthur was buried.

Pendragon   *British*
A name assumed by Uther when he became king. Some accounts say that King Arthur also assumed this title, which means 'chief' or 'leader'.

Penelope   *Greek*
Because Icarius, king of Sparta, wanted a son, his wife hid their baby daughter in flocks of sheep, calling her Arnaea. Icarius discovered the deception and threw the child into the sea. When she was saved by ducks, he accepted her as his own and reared her. Odysseus won her as his wife in a foot-race.

When her son, Telemachus, was just a baby, Odysseus went off to fight in the siege of Troy. He was away for twenty years, the last ten of which were spent wandering at the whim of the gods.

Many men came to woo her, saying that Odysseus must surely be dead, and they refused to leave, slowly eating her out of house and home. She promised to give them an answer when she

had finished a robe (or shroud) she was making but by night she unpicked all she had done by day so that it was never finished.

In one account, Penelope, believing that her husband was dead, threw herself into the sea but was again saved by ducks.

When Odysseus finally came back, she contrived to get his bow and arrows to him and he very quickly disposed of the unwelcome guests.

One story says that Telegonus, a son of Odysseus by the enchantress Circe, killed Odysseus, not knowing that he was killing his own father, and then took Penelope and Telemachus to Aeaea where he married a miraculously youthful Penelope, fathering Italus, and Telemachus married Circe.

Yet another story says that she had been unfaithful to Odysseus and was the mother of Pan by Hermes.

P'eng-lai   *Chinese*
A Taoist island paradise, one of the Fortunate Islands. This realm, one of 108 paradises, floating in the Eastern sea, was where the plant of immortality grew and the water of immortality flowed in the rivers. It was the home of the Eight Immortals and could be reached only by air since the seas around it would not support a boat.

In later years, the Celestial Emperor had the islands anchored by huge tortoises and guarded by Yü-ch'iang, god of the winds.

P'eng Niao   *Chinese*
The Chinese version of the roc. This huge bird is said to carry the sky on its shoulders. In some accounts, it was originally Kun, a sea monster.

People of Dana *see* **Danaans**

Peopling Vine   *Pacific Islands*
The vine planted by Tangaroa at creation and from which sprang the human race.

Percival   *British*
also Parsifal, Percival de Gales
A knight of King Arthur's court; son of Pellimore (or of another Percival, in some accounts).

Reared in isolation, he yearned to be a knight and left home at an early age to seek his fortune. He was given a bracelet by the wife of Orilus, Duke of Lalander, and soon met his cousin, Sigune, weeping over the body of her husband, Schionatulander, killed by the Red Knight. Percival killed the murderer and took his horse and armour. He learned the skills of his trade at the hands of Gurnemans, a knight of the Round Table, and set off to seek adventure.

In some accounts, these are two separate events. In the first, Percival killed the Red Knight, who had stolen a golden goblet from Camelot, taking his horse and armour; in the second, the killer of Sigune's husband (or lover) turned out to be Orgelleuse (or Orilus) and Percival defeated him and sent him to Arthur's court.

Hearing that Condwiramur, the queen of Brobarz, was in trouble, he rode to her aid, killed the besieging enemies and married her, fathering a son, Lohenergrain. He left after a while to look for his mother, not knowing that she was dead.

In some stories, he came to the Grail Temple where he found the wounded Amfortas but failed to ask the one question that would have ended his suffering. He was later tricked into fighting Gawain but spared his life when Itonje, Gawain's sister, pleaded with him. He came to a hermit's cell where Trevrezent told him that he could cure Amfortas, his brother, if he asked the right question. He set off to find Amfortas again and was challenged by a knight who turned out to be his half-brother, Feirefiz, who joined him in his quest. When they found Amfortas, he was made whole again when Percival asked what ailed him. Then Titurel, father of Amfortas, appeared and crowned Percival as the guardian of the Holy Grail.

He drove off the nine Hags of Gloucester who were harassing the Lady of the Castle and spent three weeks with her before Arthur persuaded him to return to Camelot. One of the hags turned up at Camelot and said that the Lady of the Castle was now a prisoner in the Fortress of Marvels. Percival set off to the rescue but was trapped in the Tall Tower. The master's daughter released him and he drove off the attackers sent by the hags to kill him. At the Fortress of Marvels, Percival killed the guards and cut off the head of a unicorn. The head became a rider on a skeleton horse which disappeared in dust and smoke when Percival struck it with his sword. He killed the leader of the hags and the others turned to grease puddles. The Lady of the Castle had disappeared from the world of mortals and Percival returned to Camelot empty-handed. (In the parallel story of Peredur, the hags are the witches of Caer Llyw.)

He joined in the search for Lancelot when he went mad and disappeared from Camelot. In one story, he and Ector found him at Castle Bliant and persuaded him to return to Camelot.

He joined the other knights in the quest for the Holy Grail. Both he and Lancelot fought a knight who turned out to be Galahad in disguise. When Lancelot rode after Galahad, Percival went to the nearby home of an anchoress who turned out to be his aunt, the former Queen of the Waste Land, who advised him on his future course. He arrived at a monastery where he saw King Evelake who had lain wounded and almost blind for 400 years, awaiting the arrival of Galahad. Leaving, he was attacked by a group of knights (goblins in some versions) who killed his horse and would have killed Percival if Galahad had not appeared on the scene and routed the attackers.

In one version, he came to a river and fell asleep. When he awoke, he found himself on an island populated by wild animals and snakes. A black ship arrived bearing a damsel dressed in black velvet who offered to lead him to Galahad if he would become her lover. When he refused, she and the ship disappeared, to be replaced by a white ship. Another version says that he arrived at the sea just as the white ship came in carrying a lovely damsel with whom he fell in love. She induced him to go to bed with her but he rejected her at the last minute to keep himself pure for the Grail Quest.

Later he met the knight Bors and they were soon joined by Galahad, who was guided by Percival's sister, Dindrane, and they sailed together on their quest for the Grail. They found a deserted ship and went aboard. Galahad took the sword he found there and they returned to their own ship which carried them to Castle Carteloise. Here a woman lay sick who could be cured only by the blood of a virgin. Dindrane gave her blood but died as a result. At her request, Percival placed her body in a boat and cast it adrift.

All three rode to Castle Carbonek, home of the Maimed King, where they were vouchsafed a sight of the Holy Grail. The three then took the Grail and the Holy Lance to Sarras in the Holy Land where they found the ship bearing the body of Percival's sister which they buried. All three were imprisoned by the king, Esterause, but he released them and asked their forgiveness when he lay dying. Galahad was made king but died about a year later. Percival entered a hermitage and lived there until he too died about a year after Galahad.

(*See also* **Parsifal**.)

Pere   *Pacific Islands*
A Polynesian sea goddess. She is said to have created the seas by pouring water from a jar given to her by her mother Haumea.

Peredur   *Welsh*
A Knight of the Round Table; the Welsh version of Percival.

He was raised in seclusion by his mother who feared that he would be killed in fighting, just as his father and six brothers had been. Imbued with the spirit of adventure, he went to Caerleon armed only with a pointed stick. On arrival, he was greeted by a dwarf and his wife, neither of whom had ever spoken before in the court and they were ill-treated by Kay as a result. (In some stories, a maiden who had never smiled takes the place of the dwarfs who had never spoken.)

He killed a stranger knight who had assaulted Guinevere by throwing his pointed stick through his eye and took the knight's horse, weapons and armour, vowing never to return to the court until he had avenged the insult to the dwarfs.

At the Castle of Wonders his uncle showed him the severed head of his cousin and the spear with which he had been killed, so inciting Peredur to avenge his cousin's death. He fell in love with a maiden whose lands had been taken by a neighbouring earl and, by defeating the earl's forces, restored the property to its rightful owner. He spent three weeks at the witches' court learning more about the arts of horsemanship and weaponry.

In another version, the uncle was King Pêcheur and the spear was the Holy Lance which he saw, together with the Holy Grail. Later, King Pêcheur took these holy relics to 'a far country'.

King Arthur went searching for this young knight and when he found him, Peredur defeated many of Arthur's best knights in single combat, including Kay whose arm and shoulder were broken. He returned to Caerleon with Arthur and met Angharad Golden-hand and fell in love with her but went off to resume his adventures vowing not to speak until she came to love him. All

the many men he overthrew on his journeying he forced to go to Arthur's court to submit to the king's will. He fought with a lion and a serpent and took the golden ring on which the serpent slept. At this stage of his career he was known as the Dumb Knight but on his return to Caerleon, Angharad declared her love and he was able to speak again.

In another adventure he met and killed the Black Oppressor, a one-eyed black man who told him how to find the Black Worm of the Barrow and then the Addanc of the Lake. He then defeated 200 of the knights protecting the Black Worm of the Barrow and killed the serpent. He used the stone held in the serpent's tail to make gold with which he paid the remaining 100 knights and then gave the stone to his attendant, Edlym.

The Addanc of the Lake killed the three sons of the King of Suffering every day and every evening their wives restored them to life by bathing them. On the way to the lake Peredur met a maiden who gave him a stone that would protect him from the evil Addanc. He killed the Addanc and cut off its head, which he gave to the three princes.

At the court of the Countess of Achievements he defeated each of her 300 knights and won the hand of the Countess for Edlym.

The maiden who had given him the magic stone which protected him in his encounter with the Addanc turned out to be the Empress of Constantinople or, in some accounts, Cristonabyl the Great, and, at a great tournament

in her honour, Peredur, known as the Knight of the Mill as a result of lodging with a local miller, defeated all the knights and stayed with her for fourteen years. On his return to Caerleon, an ugly black maiden cursed him for not seeking the explanation of the bloody spear and the severed head which his uncle had shown him years before, so he set off to find the Castle of Wonders once again. En route, he was imprisoned by a king but released when he helped him defeat the forces of an attacking earl and he killed another black man at the castle of Ysbidinongyl. At the castle he was required to kill the one-horned stag that was killing all the animals in the area and to joust three times with a black man and then he encountered his uncle and the slain cousin who, unknown to Peredur, had appeared in many of his adventures in various guises including that of the ugly black girl. It appeared that he had been killed by the witches of Caer Llyw. Peredur sought out the witches and, with the help of Arthur's war-band, killed all of them. (In the parallel story of Percival de Gales, the witches are the Hags of Gloucester.)

In some accounts he married Condwiramur by whom he had a son, Lohenergrain. (*See also* **Lohengrin.**)

Perfect Knight *see* **Galahad**

peri   *Persian*
A fairy; a nymph of paradise, originally regarded as evil.

Perilous Bed *see* **Adventurous Bed**

Perilous Bridge   *British*
A bridge which led to the Grail Castle. In other accounts, this was

a bridge over the River Brue and it was here that Excalibur was thrown back into the water.

Perilous Seat *British*

A place at the Round Table reserved for the knight worthy of the Grail quest. The only knight to occupy this seat without disaster was Galahad. It had earlier killed Brumart and, some say, had cracked when Percival sat in it but it was later repaired by Percival.

Perseus *Greek*

King of Argos. He was born as the result of a visit by Zeus, as a shower of gold, to Danae who had been imprisoned in a bronze tower by her father, Acrisius.

As a baby he was cast into the sea in a chest with his mother because his grandfather, Acrisius, had been warned that a son of Danae would kill him. The castaways came ashore on the island of Seriphos where they were sheltered by the fisherman, Dictys, brother of the king, Polydectes. When the king tried to force Danae into marriage, Perseus undertook to bring him the head of the Gorgon Medusa as a wedding present if he married Hippodamia instead.

Armed with a sickle from Hermes and a bright shield from Athene and wearing the Helmet of Invisibility borrowed from Hades he flew in winged sandals to the land of the Hyperboreans where he stole the eye of the Graiae and handed it back only when they told him where to find the Gorgons. He decapitated Medusa with one stroke, using the shield to see only her reflection – a direct sight would have turned him to stone. At once, the flying

horse Pegasus and the warrior Chrysaor sprang from the corpse.

Perseus turned several people to stone by displaying the head, including the giant Atlas and Polydectes who had been persecuting his mother, Danae, who had refused the king's offer of marriage.

It was Perseus who decapitated the sea-monster, Cetus, which was about to devour Andromeda who had been chained to a rock by her father Cepheus to atone for an alleged slight to the Nereids. He married Andromeda and the wedding feast was interrupted by Phineus to whom Andromeda had been promised. In the ensuing fight, Perseus again used the Medusa mask to turn the intruder and 200 of his followers to stone. His own friend, Aconteus, was also petrified.

He inadvertently killed his own grand-father, Acrisius, with a discus and exchanged kingdoms with Megapenthes of Tiryns.

He gave the Medusa's head to Athena, who carried it on her aegis (breastplate or shield).

In another story, Perseus attacked Dionysus, at the instigation of Hera, flying high in his magic sandals. As Perseus flew higher, Dionysus grew in stature until he reached the sky. Only the intervention of Hermes prevented the god from destroying the presumptious mortal.

Some say that he was killed by Megapenthes to avenge his father, Proetus, who had been turned to stone by Perseus. When he died he was placed in the heavens near Andromeda and, in some accounts, was worshipped as a god.

Persephone *see* Core

Peter Klaus *see* Klaus

petit homme rouge, le *French*

A house spirit of Normandy, a lutin.

Phaenon *Greek*

The first man, made from clay by Prometheus. In some accounts he was the most beautiful youth made by Prometheus who kept the boy hidden instead of showing him to Zeus for his approval. This deception was exposed by Eros. Zeus placed Phaenon in the heavens as the planet Jupiter.

Phaeton *Greek*

also Phaethon

He is usually named as the son of Helius, the sun god. He persuaded his father to allow him to drive the chariot of the sun but lost control and came too low, scorching large areas of the earth and causing African tribes to turn black. Zeus slew him with a thunderbolt before he could do more damage. In some versions, Zeus had to send a flood to put out the fires caused by Phaeton.

His grieving sisters, Aegle, Lampetia and Phaetusa, whose tears became amber beads, were turned into poplars (or pine trees) and his lover Cycnus, king of Liguria, who collected his mortal remains and buried them, was turned into a swan by Apollo.

Philemon *Greek*

Husband of Baucis. He was a poor peasant but he and his wife were the only ones to offer hospitality to Zeus and Hermes on their travels. While all their neighbours perished in a flood, they were rewarded with a wonderful new house which they tended as a temple to the gods until, in great old age, he and Baucis were turned into trees, he an oak, she a lime, growing from the same trunk, so that they were never parted.

Philoctetes *Greek*

A famous archer, one of the Argonauts. It was he who, on the orders of his father Poeas, set the torch to Hercules' funeral pyre and Hercules bequeathed his bow and arrows to him as reward. (Others say that the pyre was set alight by Poeas himself.)

He went with the Greek army when it sailed to attack Troy but was left at Lemnos, then uninhabited, when he received a severe bite from a serpent sent by the goddess Hera. Others say that he dropped one of Hercules's poisoned arrows on his foot. Keeping the bow and arrows given to him by Hercules, he managed to survive by shooting game. When Helenus foretold that only someone armed with the bow of Hercules could bring about the fall of Troy, Odysseus and Diomedes (or Pyrrhus, the son of Achilles) returned to Lemnos and persuaded Philoctetes to go back with them to Troy where he was cured by the army physicians Machaon and Podaleirius. In his first action at Troy, he shot and wounded Paris who died soon afterwards. He left the siege before it ended and sailed to Italy where he spent the rest of his life.

Philomena *Greek*

also Philomela

For the story of Procne and Philomena, *see* **Tereus**.

Phlogius *Greek*

He and his brothers Autolycus and Delion helped Hercules in his ninth Labour and he later joined the Argonauts.

Phoebus Apollo *see* **Apollo**

phoenix[1] *Arabian*

= *Chinese* feng huang; *Egyptian* bennu-bird; *Japanese* ho-o

A huge bird which immolated itself at intervals of about 350 years (or 500, 1000, 1461 or up to 7000 years) only to rise again from its own ashes.

Another story said that, although the bird bred in Arabia, it flew to Greece to bury its parents.

It was said to feed only on dew and was described as having a purple body, a gold neck and a blue tail. Anyone who found one of its golden feathers was sure to have good fortune.

(*See also* **simurg**.)

Phoenix[2] *European*

A demon, one of the 72 Spirits of Solomon. This being is said to be able to teach poetry and the arts and appears in the form of a bird.

phooka *Irish*

also pooka, puca;

= *English* pucca, Puck; *Norse* puki; *Welsh* pwca

A mischievous hobgoblin, sometimes seen as an ass, a horse, a calf or a goat, or a combination of these, or as a ghostly black dog. It is said to be a pre-Celtic deity, later downgraded.

Its favourite trick is to rise out of the ground between a person's legs and carry him off. At daybreak next day, the phooka throws his victim back, usually into the mud.

It is said that a phooka can give humans the power to understand the language of animals.

Phynnodderee *see* **Fenodyree**

p'i-han *Chinese*

A type of dragon often used in effigy as prison guards.

pi-hsieh *Chinese*

A flying animal like a lion with horns.

pi-pi *Chinese*

A fox with wings which makes a honking sound like a wild goose.

Picus *Roman*

A fertility god and god of agriculture; first king of Latium; son of Saturn; father of Faunus by Canens.

He was betrothed to the river nymph Canens but the nymph Circe fell in love with him. When he rejected her advances, she changed him into a woodpecker. Others say that he changed himself into a woodpecker and made oracular pronouncements or that he proclaimed oracles by tapping on wood and was later turned into a woodpecker, the sacred bird of Mars. Some say that he helped the she-wolf to rear Romulus and Remus.

Pierian spring *Greek*

A spring on Mount Olympus associated with the Muses. The waters of this spring were said to confer poetic inspiration.

Pierides[1] *Greek*

singular Pieris

Daughters of Pierus, a king of Macedonia. These nine maidens challenged the Muses to a contest and, being defeated, were changed into magpies, jackdaws or wrynecks.

Pierides[2] *see* **Muses**

pig

(1) In the East Indies, the Sumatrans say that the souls of the dead are incarnate in wild pigs.

(2) The Egyptians regarded the pig as unclean and capable of causing leprosy if eaten, except

when used as a sacrifice at the mid-winter festival.

(3) In Greece, the pig was a sacred animal, said to have suckled Zeus.

(4) In Irish lore, the sea god Manannan gave the Danaans pigs which, killed and eaten one day, were restored for the following day.

(5) Some North American tribes regard the pig, who lives, they say, on the moon, as a bringer of rain.

Pig-fairy, Pigsy *see* **Chu Pa-chieh**

Pigs of Manannan   *Irish*

Food of the gods. These were pigs which, killed and eaten one day, were restored for re-use the next day. They were one of the three gifts from Manannan to the Danaans; the others were the Feast of Giobhniu and the Veil of Invisibility. In some accounts, these animals are the same as those given by Easal to the Sons of Turenn.

Pili   *Pacific Islands*

A gecko-god. He and his wife Sina produced five children who are regarded as the ancestors of the Polynesians.

Pilirin   *Australian*

A kestrel. When the Rainbow-snake Kunmanggur dived into the sea taking all the fire with him, Pilirin showed the tribes how to make fire by rubbing sticks together.

Pillars of Hercules   *Greek*

Rocks set at the entrance to the Mediterranean by Hercules en route to seize the cattle of Geryon; now Gibraltar and Ceuta.

One version says that the world was saucer-shaped with a rocky wall all round to keep out Ocean, the surrounding river. Geryon had climbed over the wall and swum to his island retreat and Hercules,

searching for him on his fifth Labour, battered a gap in the wall and sailed through. The exposed sides of the gap are the Pillars of Hercules on the Straits of Gibraltar.

Pinel le Savage   *British*

A Knight of the Round Table. To avenge the death of his cousin Lamerock at the hands of Gawain and his brothers, Pinel planted a poisoned apple to kill Gawain at a dinner given by Guinevere for twenty-four of her knights. The apple was eaten by Patrise, who died instantly, and Mador accused Guinevere of murdering his cousin. After Guinevere had been saved from the stake by Lancelot who defeated Mador in single combat, Nimue proclaimed Pinel's guilt and he fled the country.

pisgy   *British*

In Cornwall, a night-flying moth. These moths are said to be the souls of the dead. (*See also* **pisky, pixie**.)

pisky   *British*

A Cornish name for a pixie. (*See also* **pisgy**.)

Pitsanukukon   *Thai*

One of the sky lords, the Thens. He came to earth when the Flood waters receded and taught the new races the arts of metalworking and weaving.

pitua   *New Zealand*

A Maori demon.

pixie   *British*

also pisky, pixy

A small, mischievous fairy who sometimes leads travellers astray. To avoid being led astray by a pixie, one should carry a piece of bread or turn one's coat inside out. Pixies are said to take horses from their stables at night and ride them but a horse-shoe, nailed to the stable door, will keep them away.

A girl affected by pixies is likely to drop things, such as cooking implements, which will then chase after her. (*See also* **pisgy**.)

Place of Seven Caves   *South American*

In Aztec lore, the place where the tribes which emigrated from their homeland, Atzlan, split up and went their separate ways.

Planctae   *Greek*

also Clashing Rocks, Wandering Rocks

Rocks that could move of their own accord. These rocks were said to close and crush any ship passing between them. Some accounts say that there were two sets of such rocks, one at each end of the Mediterranean. (*See also* **Symplegades**.)

Plant Rhys Ddwfn   *Welsh*

The fairy inhabitants of an invisible island off the coast of Wales. These beings are said to be very tiny but they can grow to human size when they visit the world of humans.

Play-eye   *West Indies*

An evil demon. This being takes the form of a dog with eyes which seem to grow larger the longer one looks into them.

Pleiades   *Greek*

also Seven Sisters, Weepers;
= *Egyptian* Seven Hathors

These seven sisters, Alcyone, Celaeno, Electra, Maia, Merope, Sterope and Taygete, were changed into doves and set in the sky as stars to escape Orion who had pursued them relentlessly. Others say that they died of grief at the death of their half-sisters, the Hyades or when their brother Hylas was killed in a hunting accident. In this story, their number varies from seven to ten.

As descendants of Atlas they are sometimes referred to as the Atlantides.

Pleiades
(1) The Blackfoot tribe regard the stars of this constellation as lost children who, through poverty, were compelled to seek refuge in the heavens.
(2) The Cherokee regard this group of stars as the home of the star spirits, the Anitsutsa, which the Huron refer to as Huti Watsi Ya.
(3) The Inuit say that they represent a group of hunters and their dogs who chased a bear (the Great Bear) into the sky.

Pluto[1]   *Greek*
A name of Hades as 'wealth-giver'.

Pluto[2]   *Roman*
= *Greek* Hades
A god of the underworld.

Pollen Boy   *North American*
A spirit who, with Grasshopper Girl, was set on Mount San Juan by Aste Estsan and Aste Hastin.

Pollux *see* **Polydeuces**

Poloznitza   *European*
= *Russian* Poludnitsa; *Serbian* Psezpolnica
A Polish field goddess, said to punish those who damage growing crops.

poltergeist   *European*
A mischievous, noisy spirit alleged to throw things or move them about.

Polydeuces   *Greek*
= *Roman* Pollux
A horse-god, patron of bards and sailors; son of Zeus (as a swan) and Leda, or by Leda and her husband, Tyndareus; brother of Castor and Helen.

He was one of the party in the hunt for the Calydonian boar.

He was one of the Argonauts and accepted the challenge to a boxing match with King Amycus who had the habit of winning such fights and throwing the losers over a cliff. Polydeuces was a champion boxer and not only won the bout but killed his opponent.

When Helen was abducted by Peirithous and Theseus, he and his brother invaded Aphidnae where she was kept and rescued her.

After the death of his brother Castor they both spent alternate periods in Hades and on Olympus so that they could always be together.

He was deified by Zeus and set in the heavens with Castor as the Twins (Gemini). In this context, they are usually referred to as Castor and Pollux.

Polyhymnia   *Greek*
One of the nine Muses, the Muse of song.

Polyphemus[1]   *Greek*
A king of Crisius; one of the Argonauts. Polyphemus was left behind in Mysia when searching with Hercules for the missing Hylas. He became king of Crisius and was killed in battle with the Chalybians.

Polyphemus[2]   *Greek*
A Cyclops, son of the sea god Poseidon by the nymph Thoösa. He trapped Odysseus and twelve of his men in the cave where he lived when they came ashore on their way home from Troy. Four of them he ate but the others got away (by hanging beneath his sheep when he took them out of the cave to pasture) after Odysseus had made him drunk on wine and then blinded him with

a fire-hardened stake. He seems later to have regained the sight of his one eye (perhaps as a result of Poseidon's power) and fell in love with a nymph, Galatea, who just teased him. She fell in love with Acis but even when Polyphemus killed Acis, she failed to return his love.

Polyxo   *Greek*
She caused the women of Lemnos to kill their husbands, who had left their wives because they gave off a foul odour brought on by Aphrodite who felt that they had neglected her worship. Polyxo later advised the women to mate with the visiting Argonauts to ensure the continuity of the race.

pomegranate
(1) In Greek mythology, the food of the dead. It was alleged that Core (*see* **Core**) had eaten the seeds of the pomegranate and she was required to spend some of her time in the underworld as a result.
(2) To the Japanese, the pomegranate is the symbol of Kishimono-jin, the protectress of children.

ponaturi   *Pacific Islands*
Sea fairies; flying ogres.

Ponemah   *North American*
The land of the hereafter in the lore of the Iroquois. It was to this land that Hiawatha sailed in his canoe when his work on earth was done.

Pongo   *Italian*
A Sicilian sea monster who dragged people into the sea and ate them. He was killed by the three sons of St George.

pooka *see* **phooka**

Popul Vuh   *Central American*

Mayan sacred writings. The first
section deals with the destruction
of mankind by fire and flood and
the war between the gods and the
giants; the second deals with the
killing of the heroes Hunhunapu
and Vukub-Hanapu by the lords
of Xibalba (the underworld); the
last part deals with the origins of
the modern races.

Poseidon   *Greek*

also Earthshaker;

= *Hindu* Varuna; *Roman* Neptune

A sea god, god of earthquakes and
horses; one of the Olympians; son
of Cronos and Rhea; brother of
Demeter, Hades, Hera, Hestia and
Zeus; husband of Amphitrite.

He was said to have married the
Gorgon Medusa in the days before
she became a monster, and when
she was killed by Perseus, it was
Poseidon who created the winged
horse, Pegasus, and the warrior,
Chrysaor, which sprang from her
body. The Nereid Amphitrite ran
away from his advances, so he
persuaded Delphinus to plead his
case and she eventually agreed to
marry him. In gratitude, Poseidon
placed Delphinus in the heavens as
the Dolphin. Like many of the other
gods, he had numerous liaisons
with other deities and mortals and,
amongst others, was the father of
   Charybdis by Gaea
   Orion by Euryale, some say
   Pegasus by Medusa
   Persephone by Demeter, some
say
   Philomena by Zeuxippe, some
say
   Polyphemus by Thoōsa
   Procne by Zeuxippe, some say
   Procrustes (mother unnamed)
   Proteus by Tethys, some say
   Scylla by Crataeis

Theseus by Aethra
Triton by Amphitrite.

When Demeter, tired of his
attentions, changed herself
into a mare, he changed into a
stallion and fathered the winged
horse Arion. In similar fashion,
he changed Theophane into a
ewe to make her unattractive
to other suitors and mated
with her in the form of a ram
to produce the golden-fleeced
ram, Chrysomallon, that later
rescued Phrixus and carried him
to Colchis.

He killed the giant Polybutes
during the battle between the
giants and the gods.

When Pelops was reconstituted
by the gods after being cut up
and served as a meal to them,
Poseidon carried him off to
Olympus as his lover or cup-
bearer.

He owned a magic chariot with
which he could drive over the
surface of the sea and he lent
this chariot to Pelops when he
raced Oenomaus for the hand of
his daughter Hippodamia. He also
lent it to Idas (a son of Poseidon)
for his abduction of Marpessa.

He was compelled by Zeus to
serve as a slave to King Laomedon
for rebellion and with Apollo, who
was similarly punished, helped
to build the walls of Troy. When
the king reneged on his promise
of a reward for their labours,
Poseidon sent a sea monster every
year which caused havoc until a
young maiden was sacrificed to it.
The king's daughter, Hesione, was
one of those offered in sacrifice
but she was saved by Hercules,
who killed the monster. Later, he
supported the Greeks against the
Trojans during the siege of Troy.

It was he who caused Pasiphae,
wife of Minos, to fall in love with
the white bull he had sent to
Minos, resulting in the birth of
the Minotaur.

He is credited with giving
the horse to mankind and with
instituting horse-racing.

He is depicted as bearded,
wearing a crown of seaweed and
carrying his trident. The trident
was given to him by the Cyclopes.

Poseyemu   *North American*

= *Zuni* Poshaiyangkyo

The first man in the lore of the
Pueblo Indians. He was said to
have been born inside a nut.

Poshaiyangkyo   *North American*

also One Alone;

= *Pueblo* Poseyemu

The first man in the lore of the
Zuni Indians; son of the sky-
father Apoyan Tachi and the
four-wombed earth-mother
Awitelin Tsta. He is said to have
emerged from the primordial slime
and persuaded the creator-god
Awonawilona to allow people
and animals to emerge from the
underground caves in which they
had been created into the sunlight.

He lives in the City of Mists,
in a house guarded by the Prey
Gods, and is regarded as the
founder of the tribe and father of
medicine-men.

Potaka   *Hindu*

= *Chinese* P'u-t'o

The Sanskrit name for the island
home of Kuan Yin.

Potameids   *Greek*

Water nymphs.

pouke *see* **puck**

Powerful One   *North American*

A creator-god of the Cherokee.

Dayunsi, who lived alone in the
sea, brought up mud from the
bottom. The Powerful One hung it

on ropes and, when it dried in the form of the earth, many of the inhabitants of the overcrowded sky took up residence there.

Prah Keo *Cambodian*
A holy jewel. In one account, it is said that all things sprang from this jewel at the beginning of the universe. It may, perhaps, be a reference to the sun. (*See also* ***Prah Prohm***.)

Prah Prohm *Cambodian*
In one account, the unformed, uncreated source of all things. (*See also* ***Prah Keo***.)

Prajapati *Hindu*
also Lord of Creation
A primordial creator from the mind of Brahma; a name for Brahma as 'Lord of Creation'.

He formed the cosmic egg from his own sweat and this egg, after floating for one year in the primeval waters, split to form the earth and sky.

Alternatively, Prajapati was born from a golden egg which formed in the primordial waters. He uttered three words, each of which caused part of the universe to appear. These words are said to be bhur (the earth), bhuvar (the heavenly bodies) and svark (the sky).

He is regarded as the 34th god, the origin of the other 33 in the Vedic pantheon. One of these was his daughter, Ushas, goddess of the dawn, with whom he mated to produce all living things.

Seven rishis (later ten or fourteen) created from the mind of Brahma, were all referred to as Prajapati (*see* ***Seven Rishis***).

Prakriti *Hindu*
A goddess, nature personified. She and her consort Purusha created the living world.

Prakriti is also seen as the primitive matter from which the universe was formed. The life-force, Purusha, worked on the material, Prakriti, and together they formed the universe.

Pramzimas *Baltic*
A Latvian culture-hero. He threw into the waters of the Flood a nutshell in which two people escaped.

Precious Flower *Central American*
An Aztec goddess. She bore a son, Well Beloved, who died at birth and from whose body sprang many of the plants needed for mankind's survival.

Precious Raft *Chinese*
A vessel used to convey souls from one world to another.

Prester John *British*
A mysterious African or Asian priest-king. In some accounts, he is described as a son of Percival. Others say that, when the Holy Grail disappeared, it was transferred to the Far East and given into the care of Prester John.

In other accounts, he is said to have been a descendant of the Magi and owned magic stones that could cause various wonders such as turning water into wine.

In Carolingian lore, he was a descendant of Ogier. In some accounts Prester John is king of Nubia. His kingdom was said to contain a fountain, the water from which will confer eternal youth on those who drink it; a sea of sand in which fish live; a river of stones where salamanders can be found; herbs to drive out evil spirits; dragons which could be tamed and used as aerial transport; stones which could restore sight to the blind or

make the bearer invisible; other stones which could control the ambient temperature, turn water into wine or milk, or cause fire if sprinkled with dragon's blood; a glass chapel which expanded to suit the size of the congregation; a marvellous palace in which Prester John sleeps in a bed made of sapphire and which holds a mirror in which he can see any plots being hatched by evil-doers – the list of such marvels is endless.

Other stories describe him as the current guardian of the Holy Grail.

preta[1] *Buddhist*
= *Pali* peta
A wandering spirit of the damned. The mouth of such a being is so small that it can neither eat nor drink. They are said to look like trees that have been charred by a forest fire.

In some accounts, preta is a purgatory where souls undergo torture between death and rebirth.

preta[2] *Hindu*
= *Chinese* kuei
A spirit of the dead. These spirits are said to be about the size of a man's thumb. The spirits of the good are taken up to heaven, those of sinners are judged by Yama.

Preta[3] *Hindu*
The region of tortured souls.

Prey Gods *North American*
Deities with magic powers. There are six of these deities who guard the home of the first man, Poshaiyangkyo. They are given as Mountain Lion, guarding the north; Badger, the south; Wolf, the east; Bear, the west; Eagle, the skies above; and Mole, the

earth below. Their priests are known as the Prey Brothers.

Priam *Greek*

King of Troy; husband of Hecuba; father of Cassandra, Deiphobos, Hector, Laocoon, and others.

Podarces was the only son of Laomedon to be spared by Hercules when he sacked Troy, killing Laomedon and his family for failing to honour his promise to give Hercules two immortal horses in return for killing the sea-monster sent by Poseidon. Hercules put Podarces on the throne of Troy as Priam. He was king of Troy at the time of the Trojan War and pleaded with Achilles to be allowed to remove the body of his son, Hector, who had been killed by Achilles. Although Achilles had spared Priam, Pyrrhus (Achilles' son) killed him when the city finally fell to the Greeks.

He was said to have had fifty children, nineteen of them by Hecuba. Others say that he had fifty sons by Hecuba and many other children by various other women.

Prithivi *Hindu*

= *Greek* Gaea

The earth personified; consort of Dyaus, the sky.

She and Dyaus were forced apart by Varuna. As a pair, they are referred to as Dyavaprithivi. Some accounts say that she was the wife or daughter of Prithu, others that she was the consort of Indra.

She acted as the final arbiter in disputes and is sometimes depicted as a cow.

Prithu *Hindu*

A creator-god, an incarnation of Vishnu. He is said to have

instructed mankind in the arts of agriculture.

Priyavrata *Hindu*

Son of Brahma and his daughter, the goddess Shatarupa. It is said that the earth was cut into seven continents by the ruts made by the wheels of his huge chariot.

Procne *Greek*

For the story of Procne and Philomena, *see* **Tereus**.

Procrustes *Greek*

A giant outlaw, son of the sea god Poseidon. He had the habit of offering accommodation to travellers, killing them by stretching them or cutting them short to fit his bed. Theseus killed him in the same way, cutting off his head.

Prometheus *Greek*

A Titan, god of craftsmen; half-brother of Atlas and Epimetheus; father of the first man, Deucalion.

He is said to be the creator of mankind, making men from mud, and their saviour when he stole fire from heaven and gave it to humans. For this act of defiance, Zeus had him chained to a rock where, for 30,000 years, an eagle or vulture pecked his liver by day only for it to renew itself every night. He was finally freed by Hercules who shot the bird. In some stories, a herb impregnated with some of the blood that fell from Prometheus's mutilated body could make humans invulnerable to fire and weapons.

The centaur Chiron was suffering from a wound inflicted by the arrow shot by Hercules but, being immortal, could not die. Prometheus was allowed to assume the burden of immortality so that Chiron could die in peace.

He and Epimetheus fought on

the side of the gods in their war with the Titans.

Prometheus was able to warn his son Deucalion of the forthcoming Flood so that he and his wife Pyrrha survived.

Proteus *Greek*

also Old Man of the Sea

A sea god; son of Poseidon and Tethys, some say.

Proteus was a rather lazy god who spent much of his time lying on the shore with seals. He had the ability to foretell the future but would never do so willingly. Since he also had the power to change shape at will, it was hard to shake the truth out of him. A few, such as Menelaus and Aristaeus, were able to hold him long enough to make him deliver the prophecies they were seeking.

Psezpolnica *Serbian*

= *Polish* Poloznitza; *Russian* Poludnitsa

A field spirit which harasses workers.

Psyche *Roman*

A princess of Sicily; wife of Cupid.

A beautiful maiden who incurred the wrath of Venus when all men paid her more attention than to the goddess. Venus asked Cupid to make Psyche fall in love with some monster but, instead, Cupid fell in love with Psyche. When no man offered to marry her, the Delphic Oracle decreed that she should be placed on a bleak mountain-top to await the serpent who would be her husband. In another version, Psyche threw herself from a mountain-top to escape harassment by Venus.

In either case, she was wafted away from the mountain-top by the west wind, Zephyr, and found herself in a wonderful palace where she lived happily with Cupid whom she never saw since he came to her only at night, until her two sisters persuaded her that her husband was in fact a serpent. She lit a lamp when he was asleep and Cupid immediately left her for violating a trust. Psyche again tried to kill herself by drowning but was saved by the river god. She served as slave to Venus, doing many near-impossible tasks such as sorting out a pile of different grains, collecting wool from man-eating sheep, bringing water from the Styx and fetching a jar (said to contain beauty) from Persephone in Hades.

She was eventually reunited with Cupid, who took her up to Olympus where she was deified and accepted by Venus as her daughter in law.

Ptah　　　　　　　　　　　*Egyptian*

= *Greek* Hephaestus

A creator-god, god of artisans, artists, property and god of Memphis; one of the three Lords of Destiny (with Amen and Khnum); husband of Sakhmet; father of Nefertem.

Ptah was born from an egg which was laid by the Nile Goose or, some say, emerged from the mouth of Amen. Others say that he existed in the beginning as Nun, or as the son of Nun and Naunet, and created the world by moulding mud, the gods by thinking of them and speaking their names and humans from precious metals.

He is said to have caused a horde of rats to gnaw the bowstrings of the invading Assyrians, so saving the city of Pelusium.

He is regarded as being incarnated as the Apis bull,

a sacred bull worshipped at Memphis.

He is depicted in the bandages of a mummy holding a sceptre known as the 'was' or as a blacksmith.

Pu　　　　　　　　　　　　*Korean*

An ancestral hero.

Together with Ko and Yang, Pu emerged from the earth and survived by hunting. A box which they found on the shore contained three princesses and a number of domestic anaimals. The three men each married a princess and, determining a site for their new homes by shooting arrows, settled down and founded three clans.

Pu T'ai Ho-shang　　　　*Chinese*

also Calico Bag Monk, Calico Bag Zen Master;

= *Buddhist* Maitreya; *Japanese* Hotei

A 6th-century (or 10th-century) monk; a Taoist immortal; one of the Eighteen Lohan, some say.

He is regarded as the last incarnation of Maitreya or Amitabha. He is depicted with a calico bag, his symbol, either on a staff over his shoulder or at his feet. He is sometimes shown inside the sack.

P'u-t'o　　　　　　　　　　*Chinese*

= *Hindu* Potaka

The island home of Kuan Yin.

puca *see* **phooka**

pucca *see* **puck**

Pucel　　　　　　　　　　*European*

A demon, one of the 72 Spirits of Solomon. He is said to teach the sciences and appears in the form of an angel.

puck　　　　　　　　　　　*British*

also pouke, pucca;

= *Irish* phooka; *Norse* puki; *Welsh* pwca

A mischievous goblin.

puffin　　　　　　　　　　*British*

A bird in which King Arthur's soul

is said to reside. Other accounts substitute the chough or the raven.

Puk, Pukhis *see* **Para**

Pukeheh　　　　　　*Central American*

A Mexican goddess. When her uncle, Hokomata, destroyed the human race in a flood, she survived inside a log and, after the waters had subsided, mated with Sunshaft and Waterfall to restart the population.

Puki　　　　　　　　　　　　*Norse*

also Puke, Pukje;

= *English* puck; *Irish* phooka; *Welsh* pwca

A mischievous spirit.

Pukis　　　　　　　　　　　*Baltic*

A household spirit or dragon, the Latvian version of Para.

Pukys　　　　　　　　　　　*Baltic*

A household spirit, the Lithuanian version of Para.

Pulekekwerek　　　　*North American*

A monster-slaying hero of the Yurok. It is said that he was born in the far north and, finding the man who wove the sky, he placed the heavenly bodies in it. He then set about clearing the world of monsters and, having completed this task, went away to the land of everlasting dancing.

Puma-Snake　　　　*Central American*

A primordial god of the Mixtec; brother and husband of Jaguar-Snake. (*See more at* ***Jaguar-Snake***.)

Pundjel　　　　　　　　　*Australian*

A creator-god of the Aborigines of Victoria; brother of Pallian.

These brothers made beings from mud and bark but, because they turned out to be evil, cut them up and scattered the pieces. The ancestors of the tribes sprang from these pieces.

Punegusse　　　　　　　　*Mongolian*

A man-eating demon which was killed by the hero Itje.

Mosquitoes were created from the demon's corpse. (*See also* **Karaty-khan**.)

Pure Land   *Buddhist*
= *Chinese* Ching-t'u; *Japanese* Jodo
A paradise for those en route to enlightenment. This fabled realm is the Mahayana equivalent of the Hinayana Nirvana. Here no pain or sorrow exists and the cycle of death and rebirth ends.

The western Pure Land, Sukhavati, is ruled by Amitabha, the eastern version by Bhaisajyaguna. (*See also* **Sukhavati**.)

Putolu   *Pacific Islands*
In Tongan mythology, the land of the dead.

Puuk   *Baltic*
A household spirit, the Estonian version of Para.

Pygmalion   *Greek*
A sculptor-king of Cyprus, a man who hated real women but a fine sculptor who carved the statue of a perfect woman and fell in love with her. When Aphrodite brought the statue to life, Pygmalion named her Galatea and married her.

Another account says that he was married to Cynisca who was jealous of the statue and Galatea returned to her former state as a block of marble.

Pygmy   *Greek*
One of a race of dwarfs. In some accounts, they were in permanent conflict with the cranes who brought death to the pygmies when they migrated south each year. They were said to ride on rams or goats, sometimes disguising themselves as these animals.

Pyrrha   *Greek*
She and her husband Deucalion were given advance warning of the Flood and survived by building a boat. They repopulated the earth by throwing stones over their shoulders, each of which became a human being – in Pyrrha's case, a woman.

Pyrrhus   *Greek*
King of Epirus. His father, Achilles, was sent to the court of Lycomedes to escape military service at Troy. While he was there, he seduced the king's daughter, Deidamia, who bore Pyrrhus.

He was sent for after his father's death at Troy and fought well. He was one of those hidden in the wooden horse at Troy and killed the aged Priam and his son Polites and threw the infant Astyanax to his death from the city walls when the Greeks finally overran the city.

He took Andromache, Hector's widow, as a prize but abandoned her for Hesione after fathering three sons on her.

In some stories he was killed at Delphi for defiling the shrine, in others he was killed by Orestes. In the latter story, King Menelaus gave his daughter Hermione to Pyrrhus, even though she was promised to Orestes, who rescued her when he killed Pyrrhus.

A different version alleges that there were two sons of Achilles – the second Pyrrhus who killed the first and took his new name, Neoptolemus, was the one who so brutally killed Priam and the child Astyanax.

Pythia   *Greek*
also Delphic Oracle, Delphic Sibyl, Pythoness
The prophetess of the oracle at Delphi. For a fee, she would make prophecies which were noted for their ambiguity.

Python   *Greek*
A monster in the form of a winged female serpent. This monster lived at Delphi on the site of what became Apollo's oracle. Apollo killed the monster when he was still only a child, either because it had harassed his mother, Leto, when she was pregnant with Apollo and Artemis, or because he wanted to set up his own oracle.

Qagwaai *North American*

A monster in the form of a whale in the lore of the tribes of the north-west.

The culture-hero Stoneribs saw how this monster was killing people by smashing their canoes and lured it to the surface where it chased his own canoe with mouth agape. Stoneribs jumped into the gaping maw and killed the monster by shooting it from inside. He then skinned the whale and, wearing this skin, was able to take the form of a whale himself.

Qamai'ts *North American*

A creator-goddess of the Bella Coola people of Canada. She is said to have killed the giants who populated the world and built mountains from their dead bodies.

Qamatha *African*

A creator-god of the Xhosa. He sent the chameleon to tell the tribe that they would be immortal but the lizard found out what the chameleon's message was and ran ahead to tell the people just the opposite. When the chameleon arrived with the proper message, the people refused to believe it an, in consequence, humans are mortal.

(*See also* ***chameleon, Hyel.***)

Qat *Pacific Islands*

A creator-spirit of New Hebrides (Vanuatu).

Qat was said to have sprung from the stone, Qatgoro, which split open, and to have grown immediately into an adult. The world already existed but Qat created plants, animals and people, carving humans from trees and bringing them to life with music and dancing.

When people became tired of perpetual daylight, Qat gave the deity who controlled darkness some pigs and, in return, received sufficient darkness to provide alternate day and night.

He had eleven brothers, who were jealous of him. Once they abducted his wife Ro Lei and carried her off to another island but he rescued her. An alternative version says that his wife was a swan-maiden whom he had caught and kept earthbound by burying her wings. When she found the wings, she flew back to heaven where Qat followed her by shooting a chain of arrows up which he climbed. Unfortunately for Qat, the banyan to which the chain was attached was cut through by the hoe of a careless worker with the result that Qat fell to earth and was killed while his wife, whom he had managed to retrieve, flew back again to heaven.

On another occasion Qat's brothers put him in a land-crab's hole and sealed the entrance with a huge stone but he escaped with the help of the spider-spirit.

When his brothers were eaten by the monster, Qasavara, Qat slew him and, finding their bones hidden in a chest, re-assembled them and restored his brothers to life.

He is said to have sailed away from Banks Island with his wife and brothers, leaving the islanders to anticipate his future return.

Qormusta Tengri *Mongolian*
The creator-god and sky god, king of the gods. He made humans from fire, water and wind and populated the world with his own offspring who became rivers, trees, mountains and all the other things that make up the world.

quail   —
This small game bird appears in the mythology of various cultures.

(1) In China, the symbol of the scarlet bird used by astrologers is said to be based on the quail, a bird associated with the phoenix. It symbolises courage.

(2) In Greek stories, a maiden, Asteria, adopted the form of a quail to escape the amorous attentions of Zeus, Leto was turned into a quail by Hera, and Zeus adopted the form of a quail when he mated with Leto.

It was believed that this bird was immune to the effects of poison and some say that the birds sometimes landed on ships at sea to rest during their migration in such such numbers that the ships sank under their weight.

The bird is regarded as sacred to Apollo.

(3) The Hindus regard the quail as the harbinger of spring. It is eaten by the wolf at the onset of winter but is revived by the Aswins (messengers of the dawn) in the spring.

(4) In Russia, the quail is regarded as the embodiment of the sun.

Queen Maeve *see* **Maev**
Queen of Gods *see* **Wadjet**
Queen of Heaven *see* **Anat, Astarte, Hera, Isis, Juno, Tara, T'ien Hou**
Queen of Knowledge *see* **Tara**
Questing Beast *British*
A monster in the form of a leopard/lion/serpent, offspring of the Devil and a mortal maiden. It was said to have an unquenchable thirst and that the rumbling noise from the belly of this mysterious beast was like a pack of hounds baying. Both the Saracen knight Palamedes and the knight of the Round Table Pellimore hunted it.

Quetzalcoatl *Central American*
also Feathered Serpent, Feathered Staff, Green-feathered Serpent, Huitzilopochtli;
= *Mayan* Kukulcan, Itzamna
A god of the Aztecs, Maya and Toltecs in the form of a jade-coloured feathered serpent; the sun god of the Second Sun and god of the wind.

In the Aztec creation stories, he killed Tezcatlipoca, who had ruled in the period of the First Sun, and became the ruler of the Second Sun. He then created human beings. He is said to have made them from bones brought up from the underworld, sprinkled with his own blood. Some of the bones were dropped on the way and this accounts for the fact that some races are taller than others. In the form of an ant, he stole maize and gave it to the human race. After another 676 years, the wind god Tlaloc blew away all the humans (except a few who became monkeys) and took over as ruler of the Third Sun.

Some versions equate Quetzalcoatl with Ah Kin while others regard him as an aspect of Tezcatlipoca as guardian of the west.

In some accounts, he was made drunk by Tezcatlipoca and inveigled into incest with his sister, Quetzalpetlatl, immolating himself in remorse. After eight days he rose to heaven as Venus, the morning star.

In yet another version, he gave up the struggle with his enemy, Tezcatlipoca, and left Tollan to return to his original home, Tlapallan. Before leaving, he burned down all the houses and buried his treasures or, some say, threw them into the fountain of Cozcaapa. En route he rested at Temacpalco where the imprint of his hands was left in the rock he had sat on. He climbed the Sierra Nevada, where all his companions died of the cold, and slid down the far side to the shore. Here he was carried off on a raft borne by serpents, promising to return. In later years, the invading Cortez was regarded as the returned god.

He is depicted as a traveller carrying a staff or as a butterfly.

Quikinna'qu *Siberian*
also Big Raven
A creator-god of the Koryak people. This deity, who revealed the pre-existing universe, is also regarded as the first human and a culture-hero. He had a cloak of raven's feathers which enabled him to change his shape and to fly to heaven.

In one story he cut off his sexual organs and became a woman. The mother-goddess Miti, disguised as a man, wooed 'her' and they married, finding themselves in a dilemma which was resolved only when the organs (which had been saved) returned to their proper place.

He fought the evil spirits of the forest but was killed when he tried to swallow the sun.

quirin *British*

A stone said to be found in the nest of lapwings. These stones are used by witches and magicians who assert that, if they are placed under a person's pillow, that person will reveal all his or her secrets while he is asleep.

Quirinus *Roman*

A war god of the Sabines. Romulus, one of the founders of Rome, was later deified and sometimes identified with Quirinus.

qutrub *Arabian*

A male jinnee.

R

Ra[1] *Egyptian*

A creator-god, sun god and god of the underworld; husband of Nut; father and husband of Hathor, some say; father of Isis, Osiris, Nephthys and Set by Nut.

Some say he was self-created from Nun, others that he emerged from the primordial lotus flower, others that he was the son of Nut while in some accounts he was the father of Shu and Tefnut. Yet another version says that Ra emerged from an egg laid by Geb in the form of a goose. In some accounts, he was the first pharaoh.

He created mankind from his own tears of joy at the recovery of Shu and Tefnut who had been lost but when he became convinced that humans were plotting to overthrow him, he sent the goddess Hathor to kill them all. She got drunk on khakadi, the red-coloured beer that he used to flood the land, and forgot her mission.

Isis, wanting to know his secret name, fashioned a serpent from his saliva. The snake bit Ra and caused him violent pain from which Isis cured him in return for learning his secret name, which was Ran.

When he mutilated himself, the blood from his penis generated several other gods.

Every day Ra journeyed across the sky in a boat, opposed by the demon Apep. At the end of the day he became Auf, a mummy, and returned via the underworld to his starting point, ready for the next trip. As the morning sun he was Khepra or Menthu, at noon he was Ra-Harakhta and as the evening sun he was Ra-Atum.

As god of the underworld he is depicted as having a ram's head and riding in a barque; as sun god he appears as a falcon wearing the solar disc. In other cases, he is depicted as a scarab or dung-beetle.

In old age he retired to heaven – the Fields of Peace (Amenti)

in some versions – in favour of Thoth and was lifted into the sky by Nut.

Ra[2] *Pacific Islands*

= *Maori* Raa

In Polynesian lore, the sun, created by the god Io.

Ra[3] *German*

= *Swedish* Radare

An elf working in houses and workshops.

Ra-Atum *Egyptian*

also Atum-Ra

An assimilation of the early sun god Atum with Ra. In the form of the Bennu-bird or phoenix he dispersed the darkness of Nun while sitting on the benben stone (obelisk).

He had the ability to detach one eye and send it out alone to see what was going on and used it to locate his children Shu and Tefnut when they got lost. He grew another eye but kept the detachable one which he placed in his forehead.

Ra-Harakhta *Egyptian*

The god Horus as sun god, an

assimilation of 'Horus of the Horizon' (an aspect of Horus) with Ra; the sun god at dusk and dawn.

Rabbit[1]   *North American*
The animal who brought fire to the Hitchiti people of Georgia, USA.

Fire was once exclusive to the Sky People but Rabbit thought his people should have it as well. At the Green Corn Festival, when the fire was lit in the square, he soaked the top of his head with pure oil and, as he danced round the fire, bent his head low enough to set the hair alight. He then ran off, sheltering in a hollow tree when the Sky People sent rain in a vain effort to douse his fire.

Rabbit[2] *see* **Cottontail, Great Hare, Hare**

Rabbit Boy   *North American*
A Sioux hero. He was reared by a rabbit who had come across a blood-clot from which Rabbit Boy emerged. When he grew up, he left his foster-parents and married a girl in the next village. The spider-man, Iktinike, was jealous and incited the youths of the village to kill Rabbit Boy who sang his death-song before being killed, cut to pieces and boiled. Using his magic powers, Rabbit Boy reassembled the parts and reappeared alive. When Iktinike tried to do the same, he recited the wrong words to the death-song and was killed, never to return.

Radare   *Swedish*
= *German* Ra
An elf working in houses and workshops.

Radha   *Hindu*
A milkmaid. She was the favourite mistress (some say, wife) of

Krishna and when her husband Ayanagosha caught her with Krishna the god changed into female form as Durga to deceive him.

Other stories say that Krishna split himself into two parts, one of which was Radha, and their union produced the egg floating on the primordial waters from which the universe developed.

In some accounts Radha is regarded as an incarnation of Lakshmi, the lotus goddess.

Raft of Four Sticks *North American*
In some Native American tribes, a symbol of the four quarters of the world. Such a structure is regarded as the platform on which the creator rests and was the platform used by the animals and birds that dived into the primordial waters to bring up mud from which the gods made the earth.

Rafusen   *Japanese*
A fairy who scatters perfume amongst the blossom of the plum trees.

Raging Host *see* **Wild Hunt**

Ragnarok   *Norse*
= *German* Götterdämmerung 'Twilight of the Gods'; *Persian* Armageddon
The final battle; the end of the world. This was the final battle between good and evil, the battle in which the gods were destined to be defeated by the forces of evil, led by Loki, after which would come a new beginning under a new god greater even than Odin.

After a winter of exceptional severity known as the Fimbul winter, which lasted three years (seven in some accounts), the Midgard serpent came out of the sea breathing out poisons and

causing great floods; the wolves Hati, Managarm and Skoll finally swallowed the sun and the moon; Garm, Fenris and Loki broke their bonds; the dragon Nidhogg finally ate through the roots of Yggdrasil; the cockerels crew and the giant Heimdall blew his horn to warn the gods that the end was approaching.

Loki's ship landed a force from Muspelheim and another ship brought the Frost Giants from the north. They were reinforced by Hel and Nidhogg and by Surtur and his sons who smashed the Bifrost bridge as they rode over it. In the ensuing battle on Vigrid plain the gods were defeated.

Odin was eaten by the wolf Fenris; Frey was killed by Surtur, Heimdall by Loki, Tyr by Garm, and Thor drowned in the poison of the Midgard serpent after he had killed it. Vidar, arriving late, put his one large foot on the bottom jaw of Fenris and, taking the top jaw in his hands, pulled the wolf apart. Surtur then set the world on fire with his flaming sword and the earth sank beneath the waves.

The evil gods who died in that battle were sent to Nastrond, the good ones went to the highest heaven, Gimli, while the giants went to their own hall, Brimer. (*See also* **end of the world**.)

Ragnell   *British*
Cursed by her brother Gromersomer Joure, she appeared as an old crone, a version of the Loathly Lady, and told King Arthur the answers to the riddle posed by Joure but demanded Gawain as a husband. When Gawain married her, the spell was broken and she returned to her normal form as a beautiful young woman.

Rai-tubu　　　　　　*Pacific Islands*
A sky deity in Hawaii. At his father's command, he created the earth when he looked down and the sky when he looked up.

Raicho　　　　　　　　*Japanese*
A Shinto thunderbird. This bird, about the size of a crow, is said to have the ability to create a terrible sound by clashing together the spurs on its body. It is generally seen during thunderstorms.

Raim　　　　　　　　　*European*
A demon, one of the 72 Spirits of Solomon. This being is said to be able to evoke love and will steal money for the sorcerer. He appears in the form of a blackbird and, in some accounts, is equated with Alastor.

rainbow
The rainbow is woven into the myths of many cultures, with many different interpretations.
(1) One story from Africa says that, if one cuts the rainbow in half, one half goes up into the heavens while the other half goes down into the earth, making a hole that leads to an underworld paradise.
(2) Christians liken the seven colours to the seven gifts of the Holy Spirit: wisdom, understanding, counsel, fortitude, knowledge, piety, and fear of the Lord.
(3) In Inuit lore, the rainbow is a bow wielded by the thunder god.
(4) The general belief in Europe is that a pot of gold lies at the rainbow's end, treasure which was placed there by an angel which can be claimed only by a naked man.
　In Brittany, the rainbow is spoken of as a snake with a bull's head.

Others say that any person passing under a rainbow will be changed to the opposite sex.
(5) In Hebrew tradition, the rainbow symbolises God's covenant with Israel, rebirth, etc.
(6) The Irish regard the rainbow as Lugh's sling.
(7) In Japan it is a bridge, the one on which Izanagi and Izanami stood when dipping the spear into the primeval waters to create land.
(8) In Malaya, people avoid the places where the rainbow touches the earth, believing them to be unhealthy but they also believe, as do many others, that treasure is to be found there.
(9) The Mongols regard the arc of the rainbow as the bow of a great hero from which he fires shafts of lightning.
(10) In Norse mythology, the rainbow is the Bifrost bridge which leads from Niflheim to Asgard. This bridge is guarded by the giant Heimdall and will be destroyed by the pounding footsteps of the giants crossing it at Ragnarok.
(11) Some North American tribes allege that, if one uses the index finger to point to the rainbow, that finger will swell up. Other tribes regard it as the road to the land of the dead. Other tribes say that the rainbow causes drought by preventing rain from falling; that it is a means of transport for the Cloud People (Shiwanna) or a bridge to some afterworld; that it is a sign of ill-fortune or a shaman who paints himself with the colours of the arc.
(12) In Persia, the rainbow's position in the sky is significant in terms of one's future and the

intensity of the colours also plays a part, red indicating war, green wealth and yellow death.
　It is regarded as the bow of the hero Rustem or the sword of Ali, the prophet Muhammad's son-in-law.
(13) The Romans regarded the rainbow as a symbol of Juno's blessing.
(14) In Siberia, some tribes regard the rainbow as the hem of God's coat, others say it is the sun's tongue or the bow of the thunder god.
(15) In South America, the Arawak say that a rainbow over land brings evil but over the sea it is beneficial.
　Another story says that the rainbow is a serpent which, when small, was caught by a young girl and kept as a pet which escaped and grew to an enormous size, swallowing people as it travelled all over the country. It was finally killed by a huge flock of birds and went to the sky.

Rainbow Monster　　　*African*
A Kenyan water monster. This beast was said to emerge at night and eat both animals and men. The rainbow in the sky is its reflection.

Rainbow Snake *see* **Dan Ayido Hwedo**

Rairu　　　　　*South American*
A primordial being in the lore of the Tupi Indians. He and his father Karu existed in the primeval darkness but Rairu put a stone on his head which grew to form the sky and they had light.
　Karu was hostile to Rairu as he knew more than him, and tried to kill him. Rairu hid from his father in the underworld where he found human beings. When these

people emerged into the upper world, he and his father turned some of them, the lazy ones, into birds and butterflies.

rakshasa *Hindu*
female rakshasi

An evil spirit. It is said that these beings were created from Brahma's foot though others say that they were descended from the sage Pulashya.

They could assume any shape and usually appeared as monsters but sometimes as beautiful maidens. Descriptions of them in human form say that they may be blue, green or yellow, with eyes set vertically, fingers pointing backwards, matted hair, protruding stomachs, and five feet. They are said to eat human flesh, even fouled meat and corpses. Some say that they live in trees but haunt grave-yards and they are so poisonous that they kill mortals by a mere touch. They can also take possession of men, causing illness or death. Mortals who have been exceptionally cruel in life may be condemned to reappear as rakshasas.

In some versions rakshasas are the same as yakshas.

ram

The ram features in many mythologies.

(1) In Babylon the ram was sacrificed at New Year to expiate sins.

(2) In Celtic lore the ram is the personification of Belin, the Gaulish god of light and crops.

(3) In Egypt the ram symbolises the soul and the gods Amon-Ra, Geb, Min, Osiris and Shu.

(4) In the Greek story of the Golden Fleece, the ram, Chrysomallon, saved Phrixus and his sister Helle from death by carrying them off to Colchis.

In other contexts rams are sacred to Dionysus and Zeus.

In Crete the ram was deified as the god of the waning year.

(5) Hebrews regard the ram as a symbol of sacrifice.

(6) In Hindu lore, the ram is a generic name for god and an attribute of Agni.

(7) In Muslim lore the ram was one of the ten animals allowed into heaven.

(8) In Persia the ram symbolised virility and was the emblem of the empire.

(9) To the Romans, a ram with one horn facing forwards and the other facing backwards represented the two-faced god Janus.

Rama *Hindu*

The 7th incarnation of Vishnu, as a human; husband of Sita. He is the hero of the epic *Ramayana* and appears in the *Mahabharata*.

He killed the she-dragon, Taraka, and won the hand of Sita, daughter of Janaka, king of Videha, by bending the bow of Shiva. He should have succeeded to the throne when his earthly father died but he and his wife, Sita, together with his half-brother, Lakshmana, were exiled and Bharata, his other half-brother, took the throne.

Surpanakha, the sister of the demon-king Ravana, tried to seduce him but he and Lakshmana badly wounded her when she tried to swallow Rama when he rejected her advances. She then persuaded her brother Ravana to seize Rama's wife. When Sita was abducted by Ravana, Rama or the monkey-king Sugriva attacked Trikuta, the fortress of the demons, with the monkey forces of Sugriva led by Hanuman in a battle in which all the leaders of the demons were killed. Rama himself cut off Ravana's head.

In later years, he exiled Sita on the suspicioin that she had slept with Ravana. When she asked the gods to send a sign that she had been faithful to her husband, the earth opened up and she was taken away on a golden throne. In remorse, Rama drowned himself.

Ran *Norse*

A sea goddess and storm goddess. She lured sailors into her net and carried them down to her home in the deep.

Rangi *New Zealand*

Creator-god and sky-father of the Maori. The intertwined bodies of Earth (Papa) and Sky made it impossible for their children to leave the womb, so they tried to push their parents apart. After failures by Haumea and Rongo to push them apart, Tangaroa to blow them apart with his winds, and Tu to cut them apart, Tane, standing on Papa, managed to push Rangi, the sky, into its present position.

Rarohenga *Pacific Islands*

The home of the fairies; the underworld.

Rasa *Hindu*
= *Greek* Styx; *Norse* Leipter

The river which separates this world from the underworld.

Rashnu *Persian*

A god of the underworld; one of the Yazatas. He acts as one of the three judges of souls, with Mithra and Sraosha, holding the golden scales of justice.

rat

This animal appears in the mythologies of various countries.

(1) In China, the rat symbolises industry and prosperity and is one of the animals bearing the sun through the Zodiac. It is regarded as the guardian of the northern quarter.

(2) In Egypt, the rat symbolises destruction and is sometimes deified.

(3) In Hindu lore, the rat can be either the embodiment of a powerful demon or the favoured transport of Garuda.

(4) The Irish say that rats can be driven away by reciting poetry at them.

(5) In Japan, the rat is the messenger of the god Daikoku. It is said that if rats eat the New Year cakes, there will be a good harvest.

(6) Romans believed that rats could bring good luck.

(7) Some South African tribes wear rat-hair as a charm to guard against spears thrown at them by their enemies.

Ratna   *Hindu*

'jewel'

One of the precious objects generated at the Churning of the Ocean.

Ratovoantany   *African*

A creator-god of Madagascar. He formed the first humans from clay and the supreme god Zanahary gave them life. He is said to have grown out of the earth like a plant.

Ratu-mai-mbula   *Pacific Islands*

A fertility god and serpent-god of the Fijian underworld. He is said to have created coconuts.

Raudalo   *East Indies*

A culture-hero of New Guinea. He is envisaged in the form of a snake and was said to have caused the Flood to recede when he touched the waters with his tongue.

Ravana   *Hindu*

The ten-headed demon-king of the Rakshasas. He was originally an angel who was condemned to life on earth for some insult to Brahma. His first manifestation was as Hiranyakashipu, the second as Ravana, the third as Sisupala. In some accounts he had ten heads and twenty arms.

As Ravana, king of Ceylon, he could assume any shape, even a rock, smoke or a corpse; in one story he turned himself into a chameleon to gain access to the women's quarters to seduce them. He could become as big as a mountain in a moment and, using his twenty arms, could throw hills about. He could be killed only by a mortal, so the gods sent Vishnu in the form of the human Rama to deal with him.

Ravana abducted Rama's wife Sita and Rama attacked Trikuta, his fortress in Ceylon, with the monkey forces of Sugriva led by Hanuman, killing all the leaders of the demons. Rama himself cut off Ravana's heads. As fast as Rama cut off one of the heads, another grew to replace it and Ravana was killed only when Rama shot him with an arrow made for the purpose by Brahma.

Another version of Ravana's death says that he crawled under Mount Kailasa and tried to smash it. The shaking of the mountain so frightened Parvati, who lived there with Shiva, that the god stamped on the mountain, crushing the demon to death.

raven

This bird appears in the mythologies of various cultures.

(1) In Arthurian lore, ravens are the birds of Owain, and the birds that fought with warriors in the story of Rhonabwy's dream were ravens. In some versions, it is said that King Arthur's soul resides in this bird but others say it is the chough or the puffin.

A popular belief is that Britain will never be invaded while ravens continue to exist at the Tower of London.

(2) In China, a three-legged raven is said to live on the moon.

(3) To the Greeks, the raven was the messenger of the gods Aesculapius, Apollo and Cronos and the goddess Athena, and it was said that it was originally white or silver but was turned black by Apollo when it brought the news that the nymph Coronis was unfaithful to him.

(4) In Hindu stories, the raven is an incarnation of Brahma.

(5) In Irish lore, the goddess of war, Morrigan, often appears in the form of a raven.

(6) The Japanese regard the raven as the messenger of the goddess Amaterasu.

(7) Norse mythology has ravens Hugin and Munin as the birds of Odin which brought him news of the outside world.

Raven[1]   *North American*

also Big Grandfather

Creator-god and trickster-god of the Haida people; servant of the supreme god of the heavens, Sha-Lana. He caused the earth to rise from the primeval ocean, or after the Flood, by flapping his wings, he made humans from shells and stole fire from the heavens for their use. Some say that he made men from models carved from wood and women from clay.

In one story he was the grandson of a fisherman and persuaded the old man to let him play with the moon which he kept in ten boxes, nested one inside another. When Raven got it, he threw it into its present position in the sky.

Another version of this tale says that Raven turned himself into a leaf which was swallowed by the daughter of a chief when she drank. She became pregnant and Raven was re-born with black skin and fiery eyes. To stop him crying, the chief gave him a bag of stars which the child threw into the sky and finally he was given the box in which the chief kept light. Raven then resumed his former shape and flew off, placing the light in the sky in the form of the sun.

Raven is also Yetl, a creator-spirit of the Tlingit, and a god of light. He was created, with Heron, by the deity Nascakiyetl or, some say, was born to this deity's daughter when, on the advice of Heron, she swallowed a pebble. Others say that he was the son of Kitkaositiyika.

In Tlingit lore, Raven's first act was to steal the stars and planets from Nascakityetl, who kept them in a box, after which he made the winds and the tribes, stole water from Petrel to irrigate the barren land and caused the tides to rise and fall. He then gave the people fire and, releasing the sun from the

box, placed it in the sky. Having introduced the arts of fishing and hunting and propped the earth up with the leg of a beaver, he returned whence he came.

Raven[2]   *North American*
The Algonquians say that the bird was originally white. It was the only being who knew the whereabouts of Chibiabos, who had been captured by the Underwater Panthers (water monsters), and Manabozho, the brother of the missing man, held the bird over the fire to make him tell the truth, with the result that its feathers were black thereafter.

Raven the Giant *see* **Giant**

Red-cap   *Scottish*
also Red-cowl
A malevolent castle goblin. He is said to dye his cap in human blood.

Red Knight *see* **Gawain, Ironside**

Red World   *North American*
The first of the four worlds through which the Navaho passed on their ascent from the underworld. From there they passed to the Blue World.

reem   *Hebrew*
also re'em
Either of two huge oxen. These two animals are said to live at opposite ends of the earth, meeting once in 70 years to produce twins, after which they die. They swam behind Noah's ark, being too big to enter. In some versions, it is the unicorn.

Regin   *Norse*
= *German* Mime; *Greek* Hephaestus; *Roman* Vulcan
A smith; brother of Fafnir and Otter.

When the evil god Loki killed Otter, Regin's brother, their father Hreidmar demanded a ransom

which Loki paid with the hoard of gold and a magic ring which he had forced the dwarf Andvari to hand over. In doing so, the dwarf put a curse on the treasure. When Hreidmar refused to share the treasure with his sons, Fafnir killed his father and expelled Regin, keeping all the treasure for himself and turning into a monster to guard it.

Regin persuaded Sigurd to slay the monster to which Sigurd agreed if Regin would provide him with an unbreakable sword. Two made by Regin proved inadequate so they forged together the pieces of Sigmund's sword which proved capable of slicing through an anvil. Having killed the dragon, Sigurd cut out its heart and cooked it at Regin's request but, having tasted it, he found that he could hear the language of the birds who warned him that Regin was planning mischief. Sigurd then killed Regin and kept the treasure for himself.

Reinga   *New Zealand*
also Te Reinga
The Maori land of the dead; the route taken by departed souls.

Related Ones *see* **Kindred Gods**

Rella-manerinja   *Australian*
Two primeval partly-formed beings. These beings were cut apart by the lizard, Mangar-kunjer-kunja, to become the ancestors of mankind.

Remus   *Roman*
Son of Mars and Rhea Silvia; twin brother of Romulus.

Remus and his brother are traditionally regarded as the founders of Rome. For most of the story, see the entry for ***Romulus***. For jumping over the walls of the newly-founded city, Remus was killed by Romulus, who became king of Rome, or by Celer, his lieutenant. Others say that he was killed in a quarrel that broke out between the followers of the two brothers.

Resurrection *Central American*
In the lore of the Aztecs, one of the four giants who supported the sky at the beginning of the Fifth Sun. (*See* ***Thorny Flowers***.)

revenant
A ghost; the spirit of one returned from the dead. Such spirits can be human, parts of humans (such as head, hands, etc), animal of various sorts, lights moving over graves, vehicles, etc. They are said to be unable to rest until thay have returned to complete some unfinished task or to pass on some important information or because they were murdered or accidentally killed by violence. They are reputed to do nearly all the things that mortals do, such as coughing, playing instruments, moving furniture, etc.

rGyal-po *Tibetan*
Early ancestors of the race: miracle workers: fiend-kings. (*See also* ***gNod-sByin***.)

Rhadamanthus *Greek*
also Rhadamanthos
Ruler of part of Crete; son of Zeus and Europa; brother of Minos and Sarpedon.

He was a wise and renowned lawgiver who, every ninth year, received a new set of laws from the cave of Zeus.

After killing one of his relatives he fled to Boeotia. In Tartarus, he was appointed as one of the three judges of souls.

Rhea *Greek*
= *Phrygian* Cybele; *Roman* Magna Mater, Ops

Goddess of nature and queen of the universe; a Titaness and prophetess. Daughter of Uranus and Gaea; sister and wife of Cronus; mother of Demeter, Hestia, Hades, Hera, Poseidon and Zeus.

Cronus had been warned that one of his children would usurp his throne and to prevent this happening he swallowed each of his children as they were born. In some accounts, Rhea gave Cronus a foal to swallow instead of the infant Poseidon who was given to shepherds to rear. When Zeus was born, Rhea hid him on the island of Crete and gave her husband a large stone wrapped in baby-clothes which he promptly swallowed. She was later raped by Zeus, both in the form of serpents, and it was she who saved Dionysus when he was torn to pieces by the Titans.

Rhea Silvia *Roman*
A vestal virgin, daughter of Numitor (king of Alba Longa); mother of Romulus and Remus by Mars.

In one version of the story of Romulus and Remus, she was raped by Mars as she was fetching water from a spring. As a result, she was imprisoned for breaking her vows of chastity but she was later released by her sons. In some versions she suffered the traditional penalty and was buried alive though others say that she was drowned or beheaded and was then deified.

In some stories she is referred to as Ilia, daughter of Aeneas.

Rhine-daughters *German*
also Rhine-maidens
Nymphs who guarded the gold hidden in the Rhine. There

were three of these maidens – Flosshilde, Wellgunde and Woglinde.

Rich Fisher *see* **Pelles, Pellimore**
Richmond Castle *British*
A castle in Yorkshire under which, it is said, King Arthur and his men lie sleeping. A man named Thompson is said to have seen the sleeping knights, who started to wake up when he attempted to draw from its scabbard a sword lying on a table.

For other suggested sites, *see* ***Alderley Edge***.

riddle of the Sphinx *Greek*
A question posed by the Sphinx to all travellers: 'What moves on four legs when young, two when mature and three when old?' Those who failed to answer correctly paid with their lives. Oedipus got it right when he gave the answer 'man', who crawls on all fours as a baby, walks upright later and is supported by a stick in old age.

Rin-Jin *Japanese*
A Dragon-King of the Sea. When his wife fell ill, she said that only the liver of a monkey could save her, so Rin-Jin sent a jellyfish to bring a monkey to his undersea kingdom. Having persuaded a monkey to come with him, the foolish jellyfish told the monkey why his presence was required. The crafty monkey said that he had forgotten to bring his liver, so the jellyfish took him back to land to fetch it. The monkey quickly jumped ashore and ran off laughing at the jellyfish's gullibility. The angry king had the jellyfish torn from its shell and pounded into a jelly. (*See also* ***Ryujin***.)

riverhorse *Scottish*
A water sprite. (*See also* ***kelpie***.)

Robe of Serpents *see* **Coatlicue**

robin   *Norse*

The bird of the god Odin.

Robin Goodfellow   *English*

A brownie; puck; son of Oberon,
king of the fairies, in some
accounts.

In early tales of Robin
Goodfellow, he was the son of a
maiden and a male fairy and ran
away from home, waking up one
morning, after dreaming that his
father was a fairy, to find a scroll
beside him. This scroll told him
how to use his magic powers for
good rather than for evil. One of
these powers was the ability to
change into any animal.

In later years, he was regarded
as a household brownie which,
if suitably rewarded, will do
household chores.

(*See also* **Puck**.)

roc   *Arabian*

also rukh

A huge mythical bird. This bird,
which fed on baby elephants,
carried off Sinbad the Sailor
(hero of one of the *Arabian
Nights' Entertainments* tales)
and was said to be large enough
to carry off a full-grown
elephant. It is said to land only
on Mount Qaf on the far side
of the ocean that encircles the
earth.

Roggenwolf *see* **Rye-wolf**

Roi Pecheur   *Celtic*

A name for the keeper of the Holy
Grail, variously translated as the
Fisher King or the Sinner King.
(*See* **Fisher King, Pelles**.)

Rokola   *Pacific Islands*

A carpenter-god of Fiji. He was a
legendary boat-builder, by some
equated with Noah.

Roland[1]   *British*

also (Childe) Rowland

In Scottish lore, a son of King
Arthur.

When Roland's sister Ellen was
carried off by fairies, he and his
brothers went in search of her.
Two disappeared but Roland
obeyed the instructions of the
magician Merlin to kill everyone
he encountered in Elfland, and
was thereby able to rescue
not only Ellen but also his two
brothers when he defeated the
fairy king.

Roland[2]   *European*

= *Italian* Orlando

A count of Brittany, one of
Charlemagne's paladins; nephew
of Charlemagne.

Reared in poverty, he came
to the notice of Charlemagne
when he stole food from a royal
banquet. When Charlemagne
sent out his knights to seize
a magnificent jewel worn on
his shield by a knight in the
Ardennes, Roland, aged fifteen,
accompanied his father (Milon) as
armour-bearer. While his father
slept, Roland took his armour and
rode into the forest where he met
and defeated the knight, taking
the jewel from his shield. For this
deed of bravery, he was knighted
by the emperor.

He fought and killed the giant,
Ferragus, and then fought the
giant's nephew, Otuel, who tried
to avenge his uncle's death.
Roland defeated him and he
became a Christian in the service
of Charlemagne. Roland also
defeated a Saracen from whom
he took the sword Durindana.

When Charlemagne was in
dispute with Montglave, governor
of Vienne and grandfather of
Oliver, Roland fought Oliver
in single combat to settle the

matter. After five days, neither
had gained an advantage and
so they declared an honourable
draw, having recognised each
other.

At the great tournament
organised by Charlemagne,
Roland was enchanted by the
maiden Angelica and fought
another knight over her. When
she disappeared, he travelled
far and wide to find her. At a
bridge on the road to Albracca a
maiden gave him a drink which
made him forget the object of his
search and he was imprisoned.
He was freed by Angelica who
had escaped from the besieged
city of Albracca and, with other
knights who had been held in
the same prison, routed the
besieging Tartars and killed their
leader, Agrican. He found himself
fighting his own friend, Rinaldo,
and Angelica, who was in love
with Rinaldo, persuaded Roland to
avoid further conflict by leaving
to destroy the enchanted garden
of Falerina.

En route, he rescued a
maiden who had been tied to
a tree, and was given a book
The rescued maiden decamped,
taking Roland's horse and
sword. However, he then killed
the dragon at the entrance
to the garden of Falerina the
enchantress with the branch
of a tree and entered. He tied
the enchantress to a tree, took
her magic sword and killed
all the monsters guarding the
kingdom. Falerina told him that
the prisoners he was seeking to
free were held by an even greater
enchantress, Morgana. Her castle
was guarded by the strong man,
Arridano, who could breathe

under water. Roland fought with him and they both fell into the river. At the bottom, Roland killed Arridano and returned to the surface, entering the castle where he found Morgana asleep. Distracted by the mirage, Fata Morgana, he allowed her to escape but he chased her and finally caught her by the forelock, taking her keys and freeing Rinaldo, Florismart and several other prisoners.

He was imprisoned in an enchanted castle by the magician Atlantes but rescued by the duke Astolpho and soon came across a girl, Isabella, who had been seized by pirates. He routed her captors and they travelled on together, meeting another group of men guarding a prisoner. Roland killed or wounded all of them, freeing their prisoner who turned out to be Zerbino, a prince who had secretly married Isabella. He rode on, leaving Zerbino with his wife and found a cottage where Angelica and Modero had stayed. Learning of their marriage, Roland was driven to madness, tearing up trees and killing flocks. Zerbino came upon this devastation but was challenged by Mandricardo, a Tartar, for the possession of the sword Durindana which Roland had abandoned in his madness. Zerbino was killed and Mandricardo claimed the sword.

Roland seized a horse, rode to the coast and crossed to Africa riding the horse till it sank beneath him and swimming the rest of the way. He came upon the Abyssinian army, led by Astolpho, who, with the aid of a bottle given to him by St John, restored Roland to his proper senses.

When Agramant, king of Africa, withdrew from France to defend his capital, Biserta, which was besieged by the Abyssinians, Roland, Oliver and Florismart were chosen to do battle with Agramant, Sobrino and Grassado to decide the issue. Only Roland, Oliver and Sobrino survived the battle, the latter two being badly wounded. With Agramant dead, the Africans submitted and Roland was free to take his wounded comrades to Sicily for treatment. They landed on an island and the wounded men were cured by the hermit who had recently baptised Rogero with whom they were now reunited.

When the war in Europe ended, Charlemagne entered Spain, subdued the country and exacted tribute. In one version, Roland was the leader of the rearguard when the army withdrew from Spain; in another version, Roland and Oliver were sent to the Spanish border to collect the tribute from Marsilius, the Spanish king. In either event, Gano, a treacherous paladin who hated Roland, had arranged a trap and the Spanish had three armies hidden in ambush at the pass at Roncesvalles. In the battle, Roland killed King Falseron and many others but his force was greatly outnumbered and his friends were falling round him. For a long time he refused to summon help but with the death of Oliver, Roland realised that the end was near and blew three blasts on his horn, Olivant, to alert Charlemagne who was encamped at the foot of the mountains. The sound killed birds flying overhead and frightened

the Saracens. The main army routed the Saracens, but too late. The wounded Roland, told by Rinaldo that the enemy had been defeated, received absolution from Archbishop Turpin and died.

In one account of the battle, Oliver, blinded by blood from his wounds, struck Roland with his club, mistaking him for a Saracen. It was a mortal blow and Roland died shortly after Oliver and Turpin. In another version, Roland escaped from the scene of carnage but died of starvation when he tried to cross the Pyrenees alone.

Romulus   *Roman*
also Quirinus

A god of war; son of Mars and Rhea Silvia or Ilia; twin brother of Remus.

In an early version of the story, Tarchetius, a king of Alba Longa, ordered his daughter to mate with a phantom phallus of Vulcan seen in the flames of his fire. She made a servant girl take her place and the result of this union was the birth of the twins, Romulus and Remus. In this version, they were given to Teratius to be killed but he left them on the bank of the Tiber.

In some accounts, they were the sons of Latinus and Rhome, daughter of Aeneus. In the best-known version, they were the sons of Rhea Silvia who was raped by Mars and they were abandoned in a basket on the banks of the Tiber or, some say, cast adrift on its waters. They were found, under the fig-tree Ruminalis, by the herdsman Faustulus and reared by a she-wolf. They later killed Amulius who had usurped the throne from their grandfather,

Numitor, and restored him to the throne.

Romulus and Remus are traditionally regarded as the founders of Rome. Romulus killed his brother (or his follower Celer did) for jumping over the walls of the newly-founded city and became king of Rome, countering the shortage of women in his new city by abducting the Sabine women.

During a battle with the Etruscans, he was taken up to heaven as the god Quirinus. In another version of his story, the magistrates and senators, tired of his demands, had him killed during an eclipse and pretended that he had been transported up to heaven.

Rona   *New Zealand*
A Maori god. He fights perpetually with the moon, causing it to wax and wane, because the moon abducted his wife.

In some accounts, Rona is female, a girl carried off by the moon as she went to fetch water. Rona is also a name for Ina the moon goddess.

Roncesvalles   *European*
also Roncevaux
The site of the battle between the Franks and the Moors at which most of Charlemagne's paladins were killed. (*See also* **Battle of Roncesvalles, Roland**².)

Ronevé   *European*
A demon, one of the 72 Spirits of Solomon. He is said to be able to teach foreign languages.

Roth Fail   *Irish*
A rudimentary flying machine invented by a druid, Mogh Ruith.

Round Table, the   *British*
A large circular table used by King Arthur and his knights; an

institution of knighthood.

This table, originally known as the Old Table and capable of seating fifty knights, was said to have been made by the magician Merlin for Uther Pendragon, based on the table used at the Last Supper. It was given to Leodogrance, king of Cameliard and father of Guinevere, and brought by Guinevere as part of her dowry on her marriage to King Arthur. In some accounts, it could seat 13, 50, 150 or 250.

In another version it was made for King Arthur to seat 1600, including himself and the sub-kings of Britain, so that no-one sat above another, causing resentment.

Yet another story says that Arthur found a large flat stone, the lost altar of St Carannog, floating in a marsh where he was seeking a monster. The saint gave the king the altar which he had made into the Round Table.

One chair (the Perilous Seat) was left empty for the knight deemed worthy of the recovery of the Holy Grail. The only one ever to sit in it without harm was Galahad.

An early story says that, before Arthur had the table made, a quarrel broke out over precedence at his table and seven knights were killed. Arthur had the originator of the fracas drowned in a swamp and cut off the noses of that knight's womenfolk. The king then had the Round Table made to prevent further argument.

rowan   *British*
The druids alleged that this tree could ward off witches.

Ruahaku   *Pacific Islands*
A sea god of the Society Islands. When a fisherman's hook got entangled in his hair as he slept, Ruahaku got very angry and sent the Flood.

Ruarangi   *New Zealand*
A Maori fisherman. His wife was carried off by the king of the fairies but a priest sent a love-bird to the king's palace and its singing reminded her of her husband's love. She returned to her former home and the fairy king was repelled by incantations when he tried to get her back.

Ruaumoko   *New Zealand*
A Maori earthquake god; son of Rangi and Papa. He was being suckled by Papa when his brother Tane forced his parents apart to form earth and sky and he fell into the underworld where he grew up to be the chief stoker of the fires of hell.

rukh *see* **roc**

Rudra   *Hindu*
= *Greek* Dionysus; *Persian* Ahura Mazda
The robber-god, god of cattle, physicians, song, storms and winds. He was the embodiment of the terrible aspects of nature, eating the flesh of the dead and drinking their blood. In some accounts, he is equated with Agni, in others he is regarded as an aspect of Shiva. In the Buddhist version, the gods sent the god Vajrapani to kill this monster.

rudra-aksha   *Hindu*
A third eye, placed in the middle of the forehead, a feature of some deities.

rusalka   *Russian*
plural rusalki
A water nymph. These beings are said to be the souls of girls who

died before baptism or on their wedding night. In some accounts they are beautiful maidens living in trees near water, in others they are described as ugly hags. They are said to spend only half of the year in water, the rest of the time being spent in the woods. When in the water, they lure sailors to their death by singing and, during Rusalnaia (a festival devoted to the Rusalki, seven weeks after Easter), approach men from behind and tickle them to death. (*See also* **vodyanik**.)

Ruwa   *African*

A supreme god of the Chagga people of Tanzania. In a tale reminiscent of the Adam and Eve story, Ruwa made the first humans, who were immortal, and placed them in a garden on earth where they were forbidden to eat the fruit of just one plant, the yam called Utaho. The serpent of death tempted them and they ate some of the yam, losing their immortality. The plant itself was taken up to heaven and restored.

Another version says that Ruwa gave humans the power to renew themselves by sloughing their skins as a snake does. This worked for some time but eventually failed.

ruwakruwak   *Malay*

The heron. The nest of this bird is said to have the power to make one invisible.

Rye-wolf   *German*

also Roggenwolf

An evil spirit in the form of a ferocious animal.

Ryujin   *Japanese*

also Dragon-King of the Sea

A Shinto/Buddhist dragon-king, god of thunderstorms. One of the Raijin (Shinto weather gods). He lives in an undersea palace called Ryugu (Evergreen Land). With the help of the Tide Jewels he controls all the seas. (*See also* **Rin-Jin**.)

S

Sa *African*

A creator-god of the Kono people of Sierra Leone. He lived in the primordial swamp. The other creator deity, Alatangana, who created land and vegetation, ran off with Sa's daughter and they produced the first humans, four pairs of white children and three pairs of black. Each pair spoke a different language.

Sabala *Hindu*

One of the two dogs of the underworld, the other being Syama. These two dogs guarded Kalichi, the palace Yama, the god of the dead, in the underworld, and rounded up the souls of the dead, leading them to judgement.

Sabala was envisaged as a spotted dog but Syama was black.

Sabnak *European*

A demon, one of the 72 Spirits of Solomon. This demon is said to teach the arts of war and healing of wounds and appears as a lion-headed soldier astride a pale horse.

Sabra *European*

Daughter of a pharaoh. She was rescued from a dragon by St George, who then married her.

sacred animals

Many animals are sacred to a particular deity, race or country. Some of these are:

antelope	Set
ape	India
ass	Dionysus, Set
bat	Australian Aborigines
bear	Thor
bee	Egypt
beetle	Egypt
boar	Hera, Syria
bull	Dionysus, Egypt, Helius, Neptune, Shiva, Zeus
carp	Japan
cat	Egypt, Pasht
cobra	Wadjet
cow	Hera, Hinduism
crocodile	Egypt, Sebek, Set
deer	Hercules
dragon	Dionysus
elephant	Buddhism

fish	Atargatis
gazelle	Astarte
goat	Aphrodite, Dionysus, Venus
griffin	Apollo, Athena
hare	Kaltesh
heifer	Hestia, Isis
hippopotamus	Set
horse	Ares, Helius
ichneumon	Wadjet
jackal	Anubis, Set
kid	Dionysus
lamb	Helius, Juno
leopard	Dahomey, Dionysus, Osiris
lion	Dionysus, Vulcan
lynx	Dionysus
monkey	India, Dionysus, Jupiter
oxyrhynchus	Hathor
panther	Dionysus, Polynesia
pig	Angus Og, Greece
ram	Dionysus, Zeus
sheep	Nyx
shrew mouse	Wadjet
snake	Asclepius, Dayaks, Dionysius, Minerva, Sumeria

stag	Diana, Jurojin
tiger	Dionysus
tortoise	Aphrodite, Hercules, Hermes
weasel	Egypt
wolf	Apollo, Ares
zebu	Asia, Hinduism

(*See also* **animals**.)

sacred ape   *India*
The hanuman.

sacred beetle   *Egyptian*
The scarab.

sacred birds
Many birds are sacred to a particular deity, race or country. Some of these are

albatross	Ainu
cock	Ahura Mazda, Amaterasu, Apollo, Athena, Helius, Hermes, Mercury, Mithra, Nyx, Tammuz
crane	Arawn, Artemis, Athena, China, Hermes, Kwannon, Lares, Mannanan, Perseus, Shou Shen, Thoth
crow	Apollo, Asclepius, Amaterasu, Cronus, Odin, Saturn, Yama
cuckoo	Juno
dove	Aphrodite, Astarte, Ataragatis, Venus
eagle	Jupiter
falcon	Egypt
goose	Apollo, Brahma, Dionysus, Egypt, Eros, Epona, Hera, Hermes, Horus, Iris, Juno, Kaltesh, Kwannon, Mars,

	Ops, Osiris, Seb, Thoth, Vishnu
guinea-fowl	Isis
hawk	Apollo, Egypt, Hera
kingfisher	Tethys
ostrich	Zoroastrianism
owl	Asclepius, Athena, Minerva
peacock	Brahma, China, Hera, Juno, Lakshmi, Sarasvati
quail	Apollo
raven	Asclepius, Apollo, Cronus, Odin, Saturn
sparrow	Aphrodite, Venus
stork	Hera, Sweden
swallow	Aphrodite, Isis
swan	Aphrodite, Brahma, Venus
turkey	Aztecs, Maya
vulture	Apollo, Ares, Hercules, Isis
wagtail	Izanagi, Izanami
woodpecker	Ares
wren	Triptolemus
yatagarasu (sun-crow)	Amaterasu

sacred fish   *Egyptian*
(1) The oxyrhinchus was sacred to Hathor.
(2) The shark in West Africa.
(3) The eel in Greece, Phoenicia and Polynesia.

sacred plants
Many flowers, plants or trees are mentioned in myth as associated with a deity. These include

asphodel	Dionysus
box	Mercury
cherry	Apollo
corn	Ceres and Demeter
cypress	Hades
dittany	Artemis

erica	Egypt
fig	Dionysus, Pacific Islands, Romulus
fir	Cybele
first fruits	Hestia
grape	Dionysus
ivy	Dionysus
laurel	Apollo
lily	Hera
lotus	Buddha, Egypt
maiden hair	Hades
myrtle	Aphrodite, Venus
narcissus	Demeter, Hades
nelumbo	Egypt
oak	Baal, Jupiter, Thor, Zeus
olive	Athena
palm	Hermes
pine	Confucius, Dionysus
plane	Dionysus
poplar	Hercules
poppy	Demeter, Hades
sycamore	Egypt
vine	Dionysus
violet	Mithra
yew	Greece

In Sumerian myth, a sacred tree, Kiskanu, was used as a focal point for ceremonial rites.
(*See also* **tree worship**.)

sacred serpents
Snakes said to possess supernatural powers or to be connected with some deity include the following:
(1) The Buddha was said to have become a serpent as a healer.
(2) In Egypt, the cobra, in the form of the uraeus, represented power.
(3) In Greek myths, Asclepius is represented as, and sometimes took the form of, a snake and one manifestation of Zeus is as a huge serpent.
(4) In Indian myths, snakes play an important role (*see* **naga**).
(5) In many cases, the snake is associated with the rainbow. (*See also* **Rainbow Snake**.)

Sadko   *Russian*

A merchant; one of the bogatiri (legendary heroes).

To placate the sea god, to whom he had forgotten to pay tribute, Sadko offered himself as a sacrifice. He was taken to the undersea realm of the Tsar of the Sea and later restored to earth, having lost his fortune, and carried on his trade on the Volga where he paid tribute to the river gods. When he later went back to his home town of Novgorod, a water spirit instructed him to cast his nets into a lake and he was rewarded with a huge catch of fish which turned into coins.

In another version, Sadko was a minstrel whose music attracted a sea god who took Sadko to his underwater palace and compelled him to play his lute while he danced. On the advice of an old sage, Sadko broke the strings of his lute to stop the dance and, when the sea god offered him the choice of one of his hundreds of daughters as a wife, Sadko chose the last to appear, the lovely Chernava. He had been warned not to touch his bride but he inadvertently touched her with his foot as he turned in his sleep. He woke immediately to find himself on the bank of a river with his foot in the water but, by his side, he found a large sack of gold.

Sahar   *Arabian*

A giant jinnee. King Solomon, wishing to find out how to cut metal noiselessly, had the water in a well replaced with wine and so made Sahar drunk. He then persuaded the jinnee to tell him the secret and was referred to the raven. The king hid two of

the bird's eggs under a crystal bowl but the raven arrived with a stone called a samur in its beak and used it to crack the bowl. Solomon then despatched his jinn to find the source of this mystery stone and they returned with enough for all his workmen who could thereafter work without disturbing others.

Saiyamkoob   *Central American*

Mayan dwarfs. These beings, which existed in the early days of creation, were fed by a pipeline from heaven. They are regarded as the builders of the ancient cities of the Maya. Later, when the sun appeared, the dwarfs were turned to stone.

Sakhar   *Hebrew*

A demon. While King Solomon was doing penance in the desert, Sakhar took his place and stole his magic ring which he threw into the sea. On his return, Solomon recovered the ring from a fish's stomach, captured Sakhar and threw him into the sea weighted with stones. In later years, the ropes rotted and Sakhar escaped to carry on his evil work.

Sakhmet   *Egyptian*

Goddess of fire and war, goddess of Memphis; in some accounts, a name for Isis; daughter of Ra; wife of Ptah.

She is regarded as an aspect of the angry Hathor and in this role she ravaged the earth, killing mankind, on the orders of Ra who had become disenchanted by man's lack of respect for him. To halt the slaughter, Ra flooded the earth with khakadi, a red-coloured beer. Sakhmet got drunk and forgot her mission.

In some cases she merged with the cat-goddess Bast and with the

vulture-goddess Mut, while others say that she was the consort of Seker, the falcon-headed god of mercy.

She is often depicted as having the head of a lioness.

Sakti *see* **Shakti**

salamander

A monster in the form of a lizard living in fire; an elemental fire-spirit.

Salmon of Knowledge   *Irish*

also Salmon of Wisdom

A wise old fish who obtained its knowledge from feeding on the Nuts of Knowledge that fell into the river from an overhanging hazel tree. When it was caught and cooked by the druid Finegas, Finn mac Cool's tutor, its supernatural knowledge passed to Finn who sucked his thumb where it had been burnt on the side of the fish. (*See also* **Fintan**.)

Salt Woman   *North American*

also Salt Mother, Salt Old Woman

A tutelary spirit of the Pueblo tribes, the personification of salt. When she was refused hospitality in one town, she lured all the children away from their homes and turned them into jays. In another town where she was well received, she left some of herself so that the people could season their food. After that, she retired to her home in a lake.

Samanhach   *Celtic*

Scottish goblins said to appear at Samhain.

Samhain   *Celtic*

A festival on October 31st/November 1st, the Celtic New Year. This was the one occasion when the Otherworld became visible to mortals. The gates were opened so that those who had been wronged by those still living could exact vengeance.

It was adopted by Christianity as St Martin's Mass or All Hallows, and the night of October 31st became Hallowe'en, a night when demons are let loose on the earth to entrap the innocent.

Sampo   *Finnish*
A mysterious object which grants all wishes. In some versions it was a magic mill which produced endless supplies of salt, flour and money. One such mill was made by the culture-hero Ilmarinen, in his quest for the hand of the Maiden of Pohjola, by loading his furnace with many unusual things such as sheep's milk and swansdown, over which he recited spells. On successive days, the furnace produced a golden bowl, a ship made of copper, a golden-horned cow and a gold and silver plough. He melted these things down again and, on the following day, the furnace produced the magic mill that he was seeking.

San Ch'ing   *Chinese*
The Three Pure Ones, a trinity of Taoist celestial immortals. These beings, said to live in their separate heavens, are Lao-tzu, Tao Chun and Yü Huang.

San-kuan   *Chinese*
also Three Agents
Three deities who record good and evil. These deities are listed as Shui-kuan (water), Ti-kuan (earth) and T'ien-kuan (heaven). They could distribute various benefits and receive the confession of sinners.

Sangraal, Sangreal, Sangrail *see* **Holy Grail**

sankha *see* **shankha**

sanshi   *Japanese*
Three worms living in the body of each person. On monkey-day, the 57th day of the 60-day cycle, these three worms ascend to heaven while the person is asleep and report on that person's behaviour. It is said that the worms are black, green and white.

Saoshyant   *Persian*
A saviour-god. In some accounts, this saviour is born every 1000 years from the sperm of Zoroaster which is preserved in Lake Kasavya, so that it impregnates virgins who swim in its waters.

Sapling *see* **Djuskaha**

Sarasvati[1]   *Buddhist*
A female Bodhisattva, goddess of music and poetry. She is sometimes depicted playing the flute.

Sarasvati[2]   *Hindu*
An early mother-goddess and goddess of the River Sarasvati (= present-day Ghaggar-Hakra); goddess of the arts and wisdom; wife of Vishnu and later of Brahma.

In some stories, she was born from the body of Brahma with whom she mated to produce the first man, Manu, and was so beautiful that Brahma grew four more heads so that he could see her from all directions. The latter part of this tale is also told of Shatarupa who some equate with Sarasvati.

Shiva lost his temper when he was excluded from a sacrifice by Daksha and wounded many of those present including Sarasvati, who had her nose cut off. Vishnu found her too quarrelsome for his liking and gave her to Brahma.

She is depicted with either two or four arms, sometimes with three heads, and riding a peacock or a swan, and is credited with the invention of Sanskrit.

Sarkany   *European*
A Hungarian demon. He has the power to turn people to stone. His function is to control the weather and he can be seen riding his horse in the thunder clouds. In some versions he is regarded as a dragon. He is depicted with seven or nine heads.

Sarpedon   *Greek*
Son of Zeus by Europa; brother of Minos and Rhadamanthus.

When he was expelled from Crete by his brother Minos after they quarrelled, Sarpedon conquered and became king of what was later called Lycia.

He was said to have lived in the form of a serpent for three generations and was revered at some shrines.

Sarras   *British*
The city of the Holy Grail. It was to Sarras that Galahad returned the Holy Grail and where he was made king. Despite the fact that the Saracens were said, in some accounts, to have taken their name from this city, some say it was in Brittany, not the Holy Land.

sarvan   *European*
Elves or goblins who kept their masters informed of what was going on.

Sasabonsam   *African*
A hairy forest monster of the Ashanti. He had feet pointing both ways and ate any travellers he could capture with his feet when they passed under the tree in which he was sitting.

Sati   *Hindu*
An aspect of Devi or Parvati; an incarnation of Lakshmi or Uma; a name for Parvati as 'good wife'. The first wife of Shiva.

When her father invited all the gods except Shiva to a sacrifice she immolated herself though some say that is was Gauri who immolated herself to become Sati. Another story says that she fell in love with Shiva but he was not invited to the ceremony at which a maiden chooses her husband. She nevertheless became his consort but burnt to death from the intensity of her own purity. In both versions she was later reborn as Parvati. The practice of suttee (sati) stems from this incident.

Saturn   *Roman*
= *Greek* Cronus
God of agriculture, vine and workers; father of Juno, Jupiter, Neptune, Picus and Pluto.

In some accounts, he was regarded as an early Italian king, ruling jointly with Janus, who went to heaven as Saturn when he died.

satya-yuga *see* **krita-yuga**

satyr   *Greek*
female satyress;
= *Roman* faun, Silvanus
God of the woodlands, part man, part goat, with a long tail; a fertility spirit. Some say that the satyrs were sons of Hermes and brothers of the nymphs.

Saule   *Baltic*
A Latvian sun goddess. She drives across the sky each day in a chariot and, each night, she washes the horses in the sea.

When her husband, Meness, the moon god, had an affair with Ausrine, the morning star, Perkunas cut him in half. Berries of the shrubs on the hills were said to be her tears.

scarab   *Egyptian*
A sacred beetle; the personification of Khepra, the god Ra as the morning sun.

Sceolan   *Irish*
One of the hounds of Finn mac Cool. *See more at* **Bran**[3].

Schacabac   *Arabian*
In the *Arabian Nights' Entertainments*, a beggar who was the subject of the cruel jest of Barmecide's feast.

Scheherazade   *Arabian*
Wife of King Shahriyar. In the *Arabian Nights' Entertainments*, she told her husband a story each night for 1001 nights, always leaving the tale unfinished, to escape execution, the fate of all the king's previous wives.

scorpion
(1) In Babylonian lore, the scorpion appears as Scorpion Man.
(2) In Egypt, the scorpion was regarded as the personification of Serket and was sacred to Isis.
(3) In Greece, a scorpion was sent by Artemis or Gaea to kill the hunter Orion, who had boasted that he could kill any animal, and was set in the heavens as the constellation Scorpio as a reward.
It was said that oil extracted from a scorpion acted as an antidote to the poison from its sting.
(4) The Hebrews regarded the scorpion as a symbol of evil.
(5) In Persia this animal represents autumn and decay. Mithra is depicted as a bull, the strength of life, in summer and the scorpion nibbles away at the bull's testicles representing the fading of summer and the onset of autumn.
(6) In Toltec lore, the god Yappon and his wife Tlahuitzin were both turned into scorpions when they were killed by the drought demon Yaotl.

Scota   *Irish*
A Milesian queen, daughter of the pharaoh, Nectanebus; second wife of Milesius. She died soon after reaching Ireland, which was conquered by her sons who overcame the Danaans.

Scylla   *Greek*
A nymph, daughter of Zeus, who spurned the love of the sea god Glaucus. The enchantress Circe, who wanted Glaucus herself, turned her into a six-headed monster with three rows of teeth and twelve feet, destroying everything that came within range of the cliff on which she was fixed, opposite the whirlpool Charybdis.

Another story says that Amphitrite, annoyed when her husband Poseidon looked at Scylla, turned her into a monster by putting magic herbs into the water where she bathed.

Some accounts say that she was killed by Hercules when she stole some of Geryon's cattle from him, but she was revivified by the sea god Phorcos. Others say that she was turned into a rock.

Sechobochobo   *African*
In Zambia, a one-eyed, one-legged forest monster.

Second Sun   *Central American*
The second age ('sun') of the Aztec creation cycle.

At the end of the first era, ruled by Tezcatlipoca and which lasted for 676 years, the animals ate all the human beings. The god Quetzalcoatl killed Tezcatlipoca and ruled for the period of the Second Sun which also lasted for 676 years. When he took over, Quetzalcoatl created a new race of humans and, by sacrificing his own son in the fire, brought light to the dark world they lived in.

At the end of this period, Tlaloc caused a great wind to blow away all these humans (except a few who became monkeys) and took over as ruler of the Third Sun.

Another version calls this period the Sun of Air, and says that two humans escaped destruction at the end of the era. (*See also* **Five Suns**.)

Sedit   *North American*

also Coyote

A trickster-god of the Wintun people of California. The creator-god Olelbis sent his brothers to earth with orders to build a ladder from earth to heaven so that men could ascend to renew their youth. Sedit persuaded the brothers to dismantle the work that they had already done but suddenly realised that he himself was now cut off from heaven. He tried to reach heaven, flying on a pair of home-made wings, but they shrivelled in the heat of the sun and Sedit was killed when he fell back to earth.

Seere   *European*

A demon, one of the 72 Spirits of Solomon. This being is said to be able to make anything happen instantaneously and appears as a man riding a horse.

Selene   *Greek*

= *Roman* Luna

A moon goddess and goddess of magicians; a Titaness.

She fell in love with the mortal Endymion and put him to sleep for ever so that she might visit him every night. She is said to be the mother of his fifty sons.

Another story says that she slept with Pan, who gave her a white fleece or appeared in the form of a white ram.

Selket   *Egyptian*

A fertility goddess and mortuary goddess. She guards the entrails of the dead and, in her role as scorpion-goddess, guards the king's throne. She is also said to guard the serpent of chaos, Apep.

She is depicted as having the head of a scorpion or as a scorpion with a woman's head and is personified in the scorpion.

selkie   *Scottish*

also silkie

A being who is a seal in the sea but can shed their skin to be a human on land.

Semele   *Greek*

= *Roman* Fauna

A princess of Thebes. She was the mother of Dionysus by Zeus and, at the instigation of the goddess Hera in the guise of Semele's old nurse, Beroe, foolishly demanded that he show himself to her in all his full glory and died before the divine light. Her unborn baby was placed by Hermes in the thigh of Zeus or, in some stories, Zeus himself saved the child by inserting it into his own side. In either event, the child, Dionysus, was born at full term and, years later, descended to Tartarus and successfully demanded that Hades release the mother he had never seen. She was carried up to Olympus and, though a mortal, was received by the gods and deified by Zeus. Thereafter she was known as Thyone.

Another story says that Dionysus was born in the normal fashion but, when Semele claimed that Zeus was the father, her father Cadmus cast both Semele and her son adrift in a chest. Semele died but Dionysus was saved and reared by Semele's sister Ino.

Senkyo   *Japanese*

One of a race with a hole right through the chest. A senkyo who was tired or ill could be carried by two others on a pole passed through the hole.

senmerv   *Persian*

A fabulous bird. This enemy of snakes was said to be part bird, part mammal. (*See also* **simurgh**.)

Serapis   *Egyptian, Greek*

A god of the underworld, the Greek version of Osir-Apis, the combination of Osiris and Apis; consort of Isis. Serapis was the state god during the Greek occupation of Egypt.

He is depicted as having curly hair and beard, sometimes with a dog at his feet, or as a bearded, human-headed serpent.

Serim   *Semitic*

Mythical hairy, goat-like beings living in desert areas; satyrs.

Serpent of the Obsidian Knives
                                       Central American

An Aztec symbol of sacrifice. He was originally regarded as one of the four giants supporting the sky at the beginning of the Fifth Sun. (*See* **Thorny Flowers**.)

Serpent Skirt *see* **Coatlicue**
Serpent Woman *see* **Cihuacoatl**

serra   *European*

A griffin-like monster, said to breathe fire. In some accounts, this beast has the head of a lion and the tail of a fox.

Servius Tullius   *Roman*

The 6th king of Rome.

He was said to have been born when his mother mated with the god Vulcan in the form of a phantom phallus rising from the fire. He was reared by Tarquinius Priscus and his queen and married their daughter, becoming king when Tarquinius was assassinated.

His daughter Tullia plotted with Tarquinius Superbus to kill her husband Arruns. She then married Tarquinius, who had Servius assassinated so that he could take the throne himself.

Sesshiu *Japanese*

An artist. At a very early age he was tied up in a temple for some misdemeanour and, using his tears for ink, and his toe for a brush, painted rats on the floor. These animals came to life and freed the boy by gnawing through his bonds.

Set *Egyptian*

also Seth

When his father Geb abdicated, he divided the kingdom leaving the south to Set. Set wanted the whole of the kingdom so, in an attempt to get the north as well, he put his brother Osiris in a box and threw it into the Nile. When Isis recovered the body, Set cut it into fourteen pieces and threw them back into the river. Isis recovered and reassembled the pieces, restoring her husband to life, but he went off to rule in the underworld, leaving the northern kingdom to Horus. Set later fought a battle with Horus for the whole kingdom. Set was castrated but, in the form of a pig, put out one of Horus' eyes. In another version, he gouged out both the eyes and buried them. Lotus blossom sprouted from the ground where the eyes were buried and Horus had his sight restored by the gods. In the end, the case was put to the gods for a decision and Horus won. Set was then transferred either to the heavens as a storm god or the Great Bear or to the desert as a war god.

Set was one of the gods protecting Ra in his nightly journey through the underworld and once saved Ra when the serpent Apophis was about to swallow him.

He is sometimes depicted as a boar or as part ass, part pig, but, having been born prematurely and shapeless, he can assume many different animal shapes.

Setek *European*

In Slovenia, a hobgoblin. Originally a guardian spirit, this being was downgraded. It is envisaged as a boy with claws instead of nails, inhabiting sheep pens.

Seven against Thebes *Greek*

Seven champions who marched against Thebes.

Polyneices had been banished from Thebes by his twin Eteocles with whom he should have shared the throne and Tydeus had been banished from Calydon. King Adrastus of Argos married his daughter Aegia to Polyneices and his other daughter, Deiplya, to Tydeus, promising to restore both to their rightful kingdoms. He assembled a force led by the Seven to attack Thebes first. Tydeus tried to settle the matter by negotiation but failed and was ambushed on his way back by fifty Thebans, all of whom he killed.

Each of the Seven took station opposite one of the seven gates of the city, with Adrastus facing Megareus (Neistan Gate), Amphiarus facing Lasthenes (Homoloid Gate), Capaneus facing Polyphontes (Electrian Gate), Hippomedon facing Hyperbius (Oncaean Gate), Parthenopaeus facing Actor (Borrhaean Gate), Polyneices facing Eteocles (Hypsistian Gate) and Tydeus facing Melanippe (Proetid gate). The twin brothers Polyneices and Eteocles tried to settle the issue in face-to-face combat but each killed the other.

In some accounts, Eteoclus is given in place of Adrastus and Mecisteus in place of Polyneices. Of the seven, only Adrastus survived the battle, which ended in the defeat of the Argives.

Creon, who took over Thebes, refused to allow the Argives to collect the bodies of the dead for burial, causing grave offence. Adastrus reported this to Theseus who marched on Thebes, captured Creon and returned the dead to their families. The sons of the seven champions, known as the Epigoni, later avenged the death of their fathers when they attacked Thebes ten years later.

Seven Caves *see* **Tulkan-Zuiva**

Seven Gods of Luck *see* **Shichi Fukojin**

Seven Intelligences *see* **Intelligences**

Seven League Boots *British*

A pair of boots, made by the magician Merlin, which enabled the wearer to cover about twenty miles at each stride.

Seven Rishis *Hindu*

also Seven Sages, Seven Seers

Wise men created from the brain of Brahma. They are listed as Atri, Bharadwaja, Gotama, Jamadagni, Kashyapa, Vashishtha and Vishwamitra. Vishnu, in his 6th avatar as Parasurama, delivered the world into their hands and they now appear in the sky as the seven stars of the Plough constellation. Other accounts give other lists of seven, ten or 14 names.

Seven Sisters[1] *Australian*

Ancestral heroines of the Aborigines.

To escape the attentions of Nyiru, the sisters left their home and travelled south until they reached the coast. Here they entered the sea and then ascended into the sky as the Pleiades.

Seven Sisters² *see* **Pleiades**

Seven Sleepers   *Christian*
also the Seven Sleepers of Ephesus
Seven Christians who were persecuted. They were said to have slept in a cave on Mount Celion for 200 years until 497, guarded by their dog, Katmir. They fell asleep again, awaiting the Resurrection. Their names are given as Constantius, Dionysius, Joannes, Malchus, Martinianus, Maximianus and Serapion.

Seven Stars Mother   *Chinese*
A goddess of the constellation Ursa Major.

Seven Stars of the North   *Korean*
The Korean version of the constellation Ursa Major. It is said that these stars are seven brothers who were exceptionally good to their widowed mother and were set in the heavens as a reward.

Seven Wise Ones   *Egyptian*
Deities created in the form of hawks by the goddess Mehet-Weret to help to create the world.

Seventh Heaven   *Hebrew*
The highest, hence the happiest, of the seven heavens postulated in the secret lore of the rabbis.

Sewingshields   *British*
A site in Northumberland where King Arthur and his knights are said to be sleeping. In this case, a horn has to be blown and a garter severed with a sword to waken the sleeping warriors.
    For other suggested sites, *see* ***Alderley Edge.***

Sha-lana   *North American*
A sky god of the Haida tribe. He

was the ruler of a kingdom in the sky above the primordial waters. He threw his servant, Raven, out of the sky and the bird created the world and mankind.

shabti   *Egyptian*
also ushabti
A funerary figure in the form of a mummy which was said to do menial work for the deceased in the afterlife.

Shadowland   *North American*
The Algonquin land of the dead.

Shaggy Beast   *French*
also La velue
A monster with a green body and the head of a snake. This monster breathed fire which destroyed the crops and could shoot darts from the fur on its body which were fatal to humans. When it seized a young maiden, her lover cut off its tail and it died.

Shahriyar   *Persian*
A sultan in the *Arabian Nights' Entertainments*. He had killed each of his many wives on their wedding night, but Scheherazade managed to avoid this fate by telling him a story each night which she did not complete.

Shallott *see* **Astolat**

Shakti   *Hindu*
also Sakti
The female aspect of Shiva; a name for Devi or Sati as consort of Shiva. Also a name for Durga, Kali, Parvati or Uma.

Shang Ti   *Chinese*
also Celestial Emperor
A creator-god and sky god, regarded as a celestial emperor with his own court and ministers like the earthly institutions.
    In some accounts, he is equated with Yü Huang.

shang-yang   *Chinese*
A one-legged bird which was said

to cause rain.

Shango   *African*
A thunder god, war god and god of justice of the Yoruba. He was a king of Oyo who lived in a brass palace and owned a huge herd of horses. He was said to breathe flames. He hanged himself to escape his enemies and was deified. In some stories he climbed a golden chain to get to heaven and became a thunder god. He is depicted with the head of a ram.

shankha   *Hindu*
also sankha
The horn of victory. This was a conch-shell, one of the attributes of Vishnu, which was the twelfth object to be created at the Churning of the Ocean.

shape-changer
A being made from fire and air, capable of assuming any form, including that of a human, and of mating with mortals.

Sharabha   *Hindu*
A huge monster, a form of Shiva. This beast is envisaged as having tusks and claws and a body over 100 miles long supported on eight legs.

Shax   *European*
A demon, a duke of hell; one of the 72 Spirits of Solomon. He is said to be able to strike people dumb or blind and can find buried treasure. He appears in the form of a bird, perhaps a stork.

Shee folk   *British*
The English version of the Irish fairies, the aes sidhe.

shellycoat   *Scottish*
A water goblin.

shem   *Hebrew*
A charm such as that used to activate a golem.

Shen Nung   *Chinese*
An early emperor, one of the Three

Sovereigns. A god of agriculture and medicine.

Son of the princess An Teng and a dragon, he was the product of a miraculous birth and was nearly nine feet tall when born, with the head of a bull on a man's body.

He taught mankind the art of agriculture and was said to have a transparent stomach allowing observation of the effects of medicinal plants, etc. He died when testing a species of grass which cut open his intestines and was deified.

He runs the Ministry of Healing with Fu-hsi and Huang Ti and is credited with the invention of the plough and the discovery of medicinal herbs, becoming the patron of chemists. In some accounts he is regarded as a kitchen god. He died at the age of 168.

Sheng Ti   *Chinese*
God of the sacred mountain T'ai Shan; a Taoist god of destiny, lord of the underworld.

sheogue   *Irish*
A fairy.

Shi Tenno   *Japanese*
also Four Diamond Kings
The four guardians of the cardinal points, protecting the world from demons. These beings are said to very tall, 500 years old and living on the slopes of Mount Meru. They are listed as Bishamon (north), Zocho (west), Jikoku (east) and Komoku (south). (*See also* ***Four Diamond Kings***.)

Shichi Fukujin   *Japanese*
also Seven Gods of Luck
The seven Shinto deities of good fortune. They are listed as Benten (the only goddess), Bishamon, Daikoku, Ebisu, Fukurokuju,

Hotei and Jurojin. They travel together in their treasure-ship, Takara-Bune, and own a never-empty purse, a hat that confers invisibility on the wearer and many other magical devices.

Shield Maidens *see* **Valkyries**

Shiju-Gara   *Japanese*
A great tit. This bird carried love letters from the owl, Fukuro, to Uso-Dori, the bullfinch.

Shinje-chho-gyal   *Tibetan*
A god of justice, ruler of Nyalwa, the underworld. He is depicted as a monkey-headed monster holding scales into which monstrous angels drop white or black pebbles to represent good or evil deeds performed by the person being judged. He is regarded as a reincarnation of the monkey-god sPyan-ras-gzigs.

Shipap   *North American*
= *Zuni* Shipapulima
The Pueblo land of the dead, the underground kingdom of the corn goddess Iyatiku. This place is regarded not only as the place to which the dead go but also as the place from which the tribes emerged and where babies come from.

Shippeitaro   *Japanese*
A cat-monster every year demanded a maiden safely fastened in a cage and devoured her. This happened until a knight took pity on the villagers and put himself in the cage with the dog, Shippeitaro. When the cat appeared, the dog seized it while the knight killed it with his sword. The dog then killed all the cat's attendants.

shiqq   *Arabian*
A form of jinn. These beings were envisaged as half a human, split vertically, and were said to mate

with proper humans to produce nasnas.

Shirt of Nessus   *Greek*
The robe sent by Deianera to Hercules. This robe, impregnated with the poisoned blood of the centaur Nessus, killed Hercules when he put it on.

Shishupala   *Hindu*
The third and final manifestation of the demon Ravana. He was originally manifest as Hiranyakashipu and then as Ravana. In this form, the demon-king had three eyes and only four, instead of twenty, arms. Some say that he was the son of Shiva by a mortal woman. It was said that, should he ever sit on the knee of the one who would eventually kill him, his extra eye and arms would disappear and that is just what happened when he climbed up on to Shiva's knee. His mother made the god promise to give her son a hundred lives but that, in the end, was not enough because each time Shishupala tried to kill Shiva he failed and, when he tried once more, Shiva called upon the sun-disc which cut Shishupala in half from head to foot.

Shitkur   *Siberian*
The Devil. It was this being who pushed his stick into the earth, so creating all the harmful creatures such as the snake. He turned himself into a mouse and tried to gnaw through the timbers of the ark, ordered by the god Burkhan to save the people from the Flood, but he was frustrated when the god created the cat.

Shiva   *Hindu*
also Lord of the Dance;
= *Buddhist* Amitabha; *Greek* Cronos;
Japanese Amida
A creator-god, moon god, god

of destruction, fertility and medicine, strengthener of men. The Hindu version of the Vedic Rudra; consort of Devi, Ganga, Sakti, Sati and Uma; father of Ganesha.

He was said to have been born from Vishnu's forehead and to have had twenty-eight incarnations. In another version, he appeared when a cosmic lingam (phallus) rose out of the ocean and burst open to settle an argument between Brahma and Vishnu as to who had created the universe.

He killed Kama when he interrupted his meditations and to assert his authority he cut off Brahma's fifth head which he was condemned to carry for a long time before he was purified in the Ganges.

His first wife, Sati, immolated herself but was reborn as Parvati. When she (or Uma) covered his eyes, the world was put into darkness and Shiva developed a third eye in his forehead. This third eye can transmit his inner radiance with such power that it can destroy demons.

In a story in which Sati immolated herself because Shiva was not invited to the feast of the gods, he became Nataraja, Lord of the Dance, and performed a funeral dance in her honour. He then spent many days in meditation and restored Sati to life as Uma.

His wife Devi, as Kali, killed the demon Raktavija and in the excitement of her victory she killed Shiva and danced on his body

He is said to hold in his throat the poison visha that arose during the Churning of the Ocean to prevent mankind from being killed by it and, in some cases, he is depicted with a blue throat indicating this event.

When the sage Bhagiratha persuaded Vishnu to divert the waters of the Ganges from heaven to earth, which was barren from lack of water, Shiva allowed the torrent to pass through his hair, dividing it into seven separate streams, so that the force would not destroy the world.

At the end of each time cycle, he destroys the universe by opening his third eye and dancing the Tandava dance.

Shiva is depicted as having two, four or ten arms, four faces and three-eyes and sometimes wears a tiger skin and a snake round his neck and holds a flaming ball. Alternatively, he is represented in the form of Hari-Hara as a combined figure with Shiva on the right and Vishnu on the left. They combined thus to defeat the demon Guka since neither could defeat him single-handed. In another combination Shiva appears on the right, his female consort of the left, as Ardhanari, half man, half woman.

His weapons are the bow Ajagava, fire and lightning and his animal is the white bull, Nandi.

shiwan　　　　　　　*Japanese*
An insect cucumber-pest. This insect is the ghost of a physician who became entangled in a cucumber-vine and was killed by a pursuing enemy.

Shiwanna　　　　*North American*
also Cloud People
Rain-bringing spirits of the Pueblo tribes. These spirits, associated with the dead, live in many different places, such as mountains and holes under springs, and are represented as Kachina acting as rain-makers. They are said to travel on rainbows.

Shiwanni　　　　*North American*
A rain god, chief of the Shiwanna. A primeval being in the lore of the Zuni. He is said to have created the stars when he blew bubbles into the sky.

shojo　　　　　　　　*Japanese*
A monster, half man, half ape; the spirit of saké. These benevolent monsters have pink skin covered with red hair and are said to be very partial to saké which makes them immortal. (*See also* **shokuin**.)

Shoki　　　　　　　　*Japanese*
= *Chinese* Chung K'uei
A gigantic demon-killer. He has a red face, wears a black cap and carries a sword. He kills demons by crushing them underfoot.

shokuin　　　　　　　*Japanese*
A huge dragon. This beast was said to have had red scales covering a body some 200 miles long. Despite having a human face, it had horns, the tail oif a horse, hooves at the back and claws at the front. Its sleep pattern caused day and night and its breathing caused the seasons. (*See also* **shojo**.)

shoro　　　　　　　　*Japanese*
also shoryo
Souls; spirits of the dead.

shoryobuni　　　　　*Japanese*
'soul ships'
The ships which transport the souls of the dead back to the otherworld at the end of the Festival of the Dead.

Shoten　　　　　　　　*Japanese*
A god of wisdom. He is depicted either as a human with the head

of an elephant (compare the Hindu god Ganesha) or as two such figures embracing. The single-bodied version may have 2, 4 or 6 arms and is yellowish-red in colour.

Shou Shen   *Chinese*
also Old Man of the South Pole;
= *Japanese* Fukurokuju, Tobosaku
A god of longevity, one of the Fu Lu Shou. He was originally the mortal Shou Lao who became the head of the celestial department which determines a person's lifespan and is said to visit earth once a year.

He is depicted with a very tall forehead and sometimes riding a deer. His sacred bird is the crane and his home is in Shou Hsing, the star of longevity.

Shu[1]   *Chinese*
also Emperor of the Southern Seas
He is manifest in the lightning that pierced Chaos to form the universe.

Shu[2]   *Egyptian*
also Lord of Air, Lord of All
God of the air; father of Geb and Nut. He was created when Ra spat on the ground.

He separated the earth (Geb) and sky (Nut) by pushing them apart.

In some accounts he became the supreme ruler when Ra returned to the heavens and, when he himself became old, Geb seized the throne and took his mother Tefnut as consort.

Shui-kuan   *Chinese*
also Agent of Water
A water deity, one of the San-kuan. He had the power to prevent misfortunes and confessions made to him by sinners were written down and then placed under water. He was envisaged in the

form of a human riding a horse over the sea and followed by a fish.

Shun   *Chinese*
One of the Five Emperors. He married the two daughters of the emperor Yao and succeeded to his throne. When ten suns appeared in the sky all at once, Shun sent for the archer, I, who shot down nine of them.

In some accounts, he is said to have had two pupils in each eye; in others he is equated with Chuan Hsü.

sibyl   *Greek, Roman*
A priestess of Apollo given the power of prophecy by that god. There were up to ten sibyls in various stories. The ten (with their emblems) are listed as the
    Cumacan sibyl (cradle)
    Delphic sibyls (crown of thorns)
    European sibyl (sword)
    Erythraean sibyl (horn)
    Hellespont sibyl (T-cross)
    Libyan sibyl (lighted taper)
    Persian sibyl (dragon, lantern)
    Phrygian sibyl (banner, cross)
    Samian sibyl (rose)
    Tiburtine sibyl (dove).
    Other lists include the Agrippine sibyl (whip) and Cimmerian sibyl (crown).

In Roman myths, there was one sibyl (the Sibyl of Cumae), or 2, 4, 10 or 12 of these prophetesses.

Sibyl of Cumae   *Roman*
also Cumaean Sibyl
An Italian prophetess. She was given the power of prophecy by the god Apollo who also granted her wish to live for as many years as the number of grains of sand she could hold in her hands. When she rejected his advances, he withheld the gift of youth, so that she grew old and shrivelled

and finally asked to be allowed to die.

She offered Tarquinius Priscus, the fifth king of Rome, the Sibylline Books, nine books of prophecies written on palm leaves, in return for half his fortune. When he declined, she burnt three of the books, made the same offer, again declined, then burnt another three, and finally sold him the remaining three for the original price.

She advised Aeneas on his future when he arrived in Italy after the fall of Troy and guided him in the underworld to seek the advice of the ghost of his dead father.

Sickness Woman *see* **Yama Enda**
sid[1]   *Irish*
plural sid(h)e
A hill under which the Danaans lived after they were defeated by the Milesians; a mound-dwelling of the fairies. (*See also* **sidhe**.)

Sid[2]   *Irish*
= *Welsh* Annwfn
The underworld. (*See also* **sidhe**.)

sidhe   *Irish*
A later name for *side*, the enchanted mounds. The people of the mounds were the aes sidhe and, by extension, sidhe is used to mean 'fairies'. (*See also* **sid**[1,2].)

Sido   *East Indies*
A Papuan fertility god. He shaped the earth, stocked the seas with fish and taught humans to speak.

In one story, Sido was taught the art of shedding his skin like a snake, so achieving immortality, but he was once disturbed during the change and lost this power. His body died but his spirit survived to roam the earth until he married a mortal. At her death, his spirit first became a pig and then the pathfinder who leads the souls of the dead to the land of spirits.

Another version says that he married a mortal woman who died at their first love-making but all the plants of the earth sprouted at the spot where she was buried. Sido later married another mortal, Pekai, and became the god of agriculture.

Some say that Sido was the first man to die. He married Dirivo, the daughter of the ruler of the dead, and from their union came all the plants of Adiri, the underworld, where they lived. Here he built a house, miles long, to accommodate all those who died after him. It was said that he could make fire by rubbing his teeth with wood.

Siegfried   *German*

The Germanic version of the Norse Sigurd.

His mother Sieglinde died when he was a baby and he was raised by the dwarf Mime who was seeking a hero to kill the dragon Fafnir so that he could seize the treasure guarded by the dragon. He raised Siegfried to be such a hero and, armed with his father Sigmund's Sword of Need which he had re-forged, Siegfried killed the dragon and took the treasure. When Mime tried to poison him, Siegfried killed the dwarf as well. The blood of the dragon made him invulnerable and gave him the power to understand the language of the birds and they told him of the plight of the valkyrie Brunhild. He found her in a castle surrounded by a wall of fire which parted to allow him to pass. He wakened her with a kiss and they fell in love. When he left

her, Brunhild gave him her horse.

He met Gunther, king of Burgundy, who was seeking a wife and rode back through the flames in the form of Gunther to woo Brunhild for him, whom she married.

Siegfried married Gunther's sister, Gudrun, having been induced to take a drink that caused him to forget Brunhild. Hagen, half-brother of Gudrun, plotted to kill Siegfried to get from him the Ring of Power, part of the dragon's treasure, and stabbed him in the back. Brunhild, still in love with Siegfried, rode into the flames of his funeral pyre and tossed the Ring of Power into the Rhine. The Rhine-daughters rose on a huge wave which drowned Hagen as he tried to snatch the ring and swept the funeral pyre into oblivion.

In another version, after killing the dragon and acquiring the treasure, he married Krimhild, a princess of Burgundy. He also accompanied Gunther, her brother, on a visit to seek the hand of Brunhild who would marry only the man who could defeat her in a contest of spear-throwing and jumping. He used his magic Cloak of Invisibility to help Gunther win the contest and the hand of Brunhild. Siegfried later used the same cloak to help Gunther subdue his powerful bride who, thereafter, became a dutiful wife.

When Siegfried and Krimhild visited the court of Gunther, the two women quarrelled and Hagen plotted to avenge the perceived insult to Brunhild. He induced Gunther to invite Siegfried to help in repelling a purported

invasion and, on a hunting trip, killed Siegfried by driving his spear into his only vulnerable spot, the spot between his shoulder-blades which had been covered by a leaf when he bathed in the blood of the dragon, Fafnir.

Siegmund   *German*

The Germanic version of the Norse Sigmund; son of Odin; husband of Sieglinde; father of Siegfried.

His beloved Sieglinde was carried off by a hunter and Siegmund vowed vengeance but could not find her. One day, exhausted, he took shelter in a hut where a maiden, who turned out to be Sieglinde, gave him food and drink. Here he found the Sword of Need, left by his father Odin against his hour of need, stuck into the trunk of the oak-tree which grew through the roof of the hut. He took the sword and fled with Sieglinde from the hut which was, in fact, the home of the hunter who had abducted Sieglinde years before.

Odin ordered the valkyrie Brunhild to help Siegmund in his fight with the hunter who followed the fleeing lovers and met Siegmund in a duel. He then changed his mind when the goddess Frigga asserted that justice demanded the return of the the girl to the hunter, and he intervened in the fight to break the Sword of Need so that the hunter was able to kill Siegmund. Odin then killed the hunter with a single glance.

Sigmund   *Norse*

At the wedding of his twin sister Signy to the Goth Siggeir, Sigmund was the only one able to draw the sword Gram that Odin had planted in the oak, Branstock.

In envy, Siggeir plotted to kill the whole Volsung family for their wealth and possessions and when the family paid a visit to the land of the Goths they were ambushed. Sigmund's father Volsung was killed and his sons captured and tied to fallen trees in the forest to await death. All except Sigmund were devoured by wolves. Signy managed to have one of her attendants spread honey over Sigmund's face so that, when a wolf came and licked the honey, Sigmund seized its tongue in his teeth and, in the struggle to kill the wolf, broke his bonds. He built a hut in the forest and worked as a smith, plotting revenge. Signy, also seeking to avenge the death of her father and brothers, sent Sigmund two of her sons by Siggeir to help her brother but they proved useless and finally she disguised herself and slept with her brother producing a son, Sinfiotli, who was worthy of the task.

Sigmund raised the boy in the warrior tradition. When they discovered two werewolves asleep they took their skins and rampaged through the forest killing everything they came upon and finally fought each other. Sigmund killed his son but, by the intervention of the gods, restored him to life with a magic herb. He then told his son what they had to do and they both hid in Siggeir's palace but were betrayed by the sons of Siggeir who were promptly killed by Sinfiotli. Overpowered by the numbers of Goths, they were buried alive in tombs from which they escaped with the help of Sigmund's magic sword Gram,

which Signy managed to smuggle to them. Once free, they set fire to the palace, destroying all inside except the women. Signy, however, entered the burning building and died with her husband in true Norse tradition.

Father and son then returned to Hunaland where Sigmund married Borghild and fathered two more sons, Hamond and Helgi. When Borghild poisoned Sinfiotli, Sigmund deposed her and married Hiordis whose unsuccessful suitor, Lygni, then led an army against Sigmund. In the ensuing battle, Odin appeared and shattered Sigmund's magic sword. Deprived of any means of defence, Sigmund was killed but used his dying breath to instruct Hiordis to collect the broken pieces of his sword and save them for his son Sigurd, soon to be born. The victorious Lygni took over Sigmund's kingdom.

In the Germanic version, Sigmund becomes Siegmund and Sigurd, his son by Hiordis, becomes Siegfried.

Signy   *Norse*
Goddess of the dawn; daughter of Volsung; twin sister of Sigmund.

She married Siggeir, whom she despised for his puny stature and grim nature, without seeing him before the wedding. At the wedding, Odin appeared in disguise and planted a sword in the oak, Branstock. All tried to draw it from the tree but only Signy's twin brother Sigmund succeeded.

When Siggeir killed her father and all her brothers with the exception of Sigmund, she plotted to have him killed by Sigmund and another of the same blood.

She sent two of her children by Seggeir to Sigmund to help in the task but they proved useless so she disguised herself and slept with her brother, producing a son, Sinfiotli, who, when old enough, helped his father to kill all Seggeir's children and Seggeir himself by shutting him in their palace and setting it alight. Signy then entered the burning building and died with her husband.

Sigurd   *Norse*
= *German* Siegfried
He was born after the death of his father Sigmund in a battle with Lygni, king of the Hundings, in which Sigmund's magic sword, Balmung, was shattered by Odin, and after his mother, Hiordis, had remarried to Elf, king of the Vikings, who treated him as his own son. He was tutored in all the manly arts by a smith, Regin, and, at maturity, was given the horse, Grane.

It was Regin who told Sigurd the story of how the evil god Loki had killed his [Regin's] brother Otter and then forced Andvari, king of the dwarfs, to hand over his hoard of gold to pay the ransom demanded by their father, Hreidmar, and how his other brother, Fafnir, had killed their father for the treasure and turned himself into a monstrous serpent to guard it. He then persuaded Sigurd to seek out the monster and kill it. Sigurd agreed provided that Regin would make him an unbreakable sword. Two made by Regin broke when tested and they finally forged together the pieces of Sigmund's sword which Hiordis had saved and which proved capable of slicing through an anvil.

On the voyage back to Hunaland he picked up a man who was walking on the surface of the sea and who said his name was Feng. He was really Odin in disguise and he taught Sigurd how to look out for and recognise auspicious signs.

He killed Lygni to reclaim his father's throne and then set out with Regin to kill Fafnir. Again Odin appeared, this time advising Sigurd to dig a trench in the route used by the dragon on its way to drink. Hidden in the trench, Sigurd was able to strike at the dragon's heart as it slithered overhead. At Regin's behest, he cut out and cooked the dragon's heart and found when he tasted it that he could hear the language of the birds, who warned him that Regin was planning mischief. He killed Regin, ate the heart and blood of Fafnir, seized the Helmet of Dread and a magic ring and as much of the gold as he could carry. The birds then told him of the plight of the Valkyrie Brunhild who had been banished from Valhalla for disobeying the wishes of Odin and was imprisoned within a wall of flame on the Hindarfiall. His horse, Grane, took him straight through the flames to the palace where Brunhild, clad in armour, lay in a trance. When he removed the armour, she awoke and immediately fell in love with her saviour. Sigurd gave her the ring in betrothal. In one version, they married and had a daughter, Aslaug, who was reared by Brunhild's father, but more usually it is said that Sigurd left her after a few days to seek further adventures.

In the land of the Nibelungs he was entertained by Giuki and Grimhild, the king and queen, who had three sons, Gunnar, Guttorm and Hogni, and one daughter, Gudrun, with whom Sigurd fell in love and married. He also became the blood-brother of Gunnar and Hogni. Later, when Gunnar became king in succession to his father and wanted to claim Brunhild as his bride, his horse refused to carry him through the flames, so Sigurd took on the appearance of Gunnar, rode once again through the flaming barrier and spent three days with Brunhild, wooing her as Gunnar. He retrieved the ring he had given her, replacing it with a ring from Gunnar and later gave his ring to Gudrun.

Brunhild married Gunnar but was bitter at the trick played on her by Sigurd whom she still loved. When she quarrelled with Gudrun over Sigurd, she asked her husband to kill Sigurd. Both he and Hogni were bound by their blood-oaths but Guttorm was not so bound and he stabbed Sigurd in the back with a spear. Sigurd killed his murderer using his last ounce of strength to throw his sword which cut Guttorm in half. Brunhild, full of remorse, stabbed herself and was burned alongside Sigurd on his funeral pyre. In another version, she rode her horse through the flames of his pyre to perish at his side.

Silenus[1] *Greek*

A satyr; king of Nysa. A fat, jovial fellow who rode on a donkey because he was usually too drunk to walk. He was the tutor and friend of the god of wine Dionysus. He was once captured by King Midas who tried to extract from him the secret of life.

Silenus[2] *Greek*

plural Sileni

One of a race of beings, part horse, part man, who unlike the Centaurs, had horses' ears and walked on two feet.

silkie *see* **selkie**

Silvanus *Roman*

God of agriculture and woods; half man, half goat. In some accounts he was the son of Picus (a god of fertility and agriculture) or Mars (the god of war but also of agriculture and fertility). Some accounts identify him with Faunus, Mars or the Greek Pan, others with Cocidius, a god of the hunt.

Silvani *Roman*

= *Greek* satyrs

Deities of agriculture and woods. It was said that each estate had three such guardian deities, one each for the house, the boundaries and the workers.

Silvius *Roman*

First king of Alba Longa; grandson of Aeneas, some say. In some accounts, Silvius was the son of Aeneas and Lavinia.

He usurped the throne of his brother, Iulus. It had been prophesied that his son Brutus would kill both his parents. His mother, a cousin of Silvius, died after three days in labour when the boy was born and, when he was fifteen, Brutus accidentally shot and killed Silvius when they were out hunting. Brutus was banished and sailed with a group of Trojans to Britain.

simarghu *Persian*

also simorg

A winged dragon. This beast, invisible to human eyes, guarded the tree of life, one which produced seeds for all the other plants. (*See also* **simurgh**.)

Simbi   *West Indian*

A Haitian river-snake god, god of rain.

simurgh   *Persian*

also simorg, simurg

A fabulous bird. This huge bird, which lived on Mount Alburz, was said to have rescued the god Zal when he was abandoned as a baby by his parents. In some accounts, it lived for 1700 years and burned to death when its young hatched.

In one account, all the birds set out to look for the mysterious simurgh but only thirty survived the long search. These remaining birds merged into one, becoming the simurgh.

(*See also* **phoenix, roc, senmerv, simarghu**.)

Sinaa   *South American*

A creator and jaguar-ancestor of the Juruna Indians of Brazil. He was born a of a jaguar, Duca, and a woman, and his eyes were in the back of his head. He could remove his skin and rejuvenate himself by taking a bath. He is said to have created the world, propping up the sky on a stick.

He visited the Juruna shaman Uaica in dreams and told him how to make life better for the tribe.

The world will end when he removes the stick that holds up the heavens.

Sinbad   *Arabian*

also Sinbad the Sailor

A voyager, hero of a tale in the *Arabian Nights' Entertainments*. In one story he was carried by a rukh to a valley of diamonds where he collected as many as he could carry. He then tied himself

to the rukh and was carried to its nest. Sinbad was rescued by a merchant before the huge bird could eat him and the two of them shared the diamonds.

Singhalaputra   *Buddhist*

One of the Eighteen Lohan, in some accounts. He was originally an Indian Brahmin who became a Buddhist and a leader of that faith who was executed when he upset some officials of the court. He is depicted standing and holding a staff.

Sinh   *Burmese*

A cat. This animal shared daily worship with his master, the chief priest Mun-Ha, in front of the statue of the goddess Tsu-Kyan-Kse. When the priest was killed, the cat climbed on to his shoulders and looked hard into the face of the statue. The cat's yellow eyes became blue, like those of the goddess, and the white fur became the brown and gold of the present day Birman cat.

Sinner King *see* **Fisher King**

Sipa Korlo   *Buddhist*

The Tibetan Wheel of Life. This is a device with three circles setting out the cycle of existence, etc.

The outer circle has twelve scenes which illustrate the reasons for rebirth such as ignorance, covetousness and similar vices.

The second wheel has six triangles, each of which deals with one of the various realms, given as Chayula (home of the gods), Lamayin (home of demigods), Miyul (home of mankind), Yiddak (home of ghosts), Gholsong (home of animals) and Nyalwa (the underworld).

The third, innermost, circle

portrays the three worlds of passion using a cock to portray desire or lust, a pig for ignorance or sloth and a snake for anger or hatred.

Siren   *Greek*

A monster, part woman, part seabird. In some accounts the sirens were the daughters of the sea god Phorcus and the Muse Calliope or the sea monster Ceto, while others say that they were fathered by the river god Achelous or Phorcus on one or other of the Muses Melpomene and Terpsichore. The number and names of the group vary from one story to another and may be given as Himeropa and Thelxiepeia; or Leucosia, Ligea and Parthenope; or Aglaophone, Molpe, Peisinoe and Thelxiepeia.

They were originally winged beings but, when they were defeated by the Muses in a music competition, they lost their wings and took to the sea, living on the island of Anthemoessa, where their songs charmed the crews of passing ships and lured them on to the rocks.

Others say that they were originally maidens attendant on Core who were changed into the form of sirens for failing to prevent Core's abduction by Hades.

In some accounts, when they failed to seduce Odysseus and his crew, they jumped into the sea and were drowned, while others say that when they failed to seduce the Argonauts, being outsung by Orpheus, they jumped into the sea and were turned into rocks.

They are usually depicted as birds with human faces.

Sirius   *Greek*

The dog of Orion the hunter. He was placed as a star in the sky with Orion.

Sirrush   *Mesopotamian*

A Babylonian scaly monster with parts of a bird and a cheetah and having claws on its two rear feet.

Sisimatailaa   *Pacific Islands*

Son of the sun in the lore of the Tongans. On his marriage in Samoa, his father gave him two parcels, one of which had to remain unopened until they reached Tonga. His bride disobeyed this instruction as they sailed back to Tonga and the weight of all the things that emerged from the parcel was enough to sink the boat and they both drowned.

Sisyphus   *Greek*

King of Corinth. He is said to have founded Corinth, rearing a race from mushrooms to populate it, and to have instituted the Isthmian Games.

When Autolycus began stealing his cattle, Sisyphus fixed lead markers inscribed 'Stolen by Autolycus' to their hooves and was so able to prove the theft.

He seduced Anticleia, daughter of Autolycus, on the morning of her wedding to Laertes, king of Ithaca, either in revenge for the theft of his cattle or, some say, with the connivance of Autolycus with whom he became friends. In this way, he, rather than Laertes, became the father of Odysseus.

He raped Tyro, daughter of his brother Salmoneus, and she killed the children born of this union. Sisyphus persuaded the people that the infants were the result of incest between Tyro and her own father with the result that Salmoneus was banished and

Sisyphus took the throne.

He imprisoned Hades (or Thanatos) when he came to take him down to the underworld as punishment for the rape of Tyro or for betraying the fact that Zeus had abducted the nymph Aegina. He was handed over to Hades but he talked Persephone, goddess of the underworld, into releasing him. He was eventually brought back to Tartarus by Hermes and punished by being condemned to roll everlastingly a huge stone up a mountain, only for it to roll back to the bottom just before he reaches the top.

In some accounts he is regarded as a sun god.

Sita   *Hindu*

An earth goddess. She was said to have been born from a plough-furrow as an incarnation of Lakshmi and was the wife of Rama, the seventh incarnation of Vishnu, although some accounts have her as a consort of Indra and Parjanya. Rama was said to have won her hand by winning an archery contest organised by her father.

When she was carried off by Ravana, the king of the demons, her husband raised an attacking force under the monkey-god Hanuman and rased the demons' fortress, killing Ravana. To prove that she had been faithful during her captivity, she invoked her dharma and was taken into a furrow in Mother Earth.

In a variation of this story, Rama rejected her when she became pregnant, believing that she had slept with Ravana, and sent her into exile where she gave birth to twin sons, Kusha and Lava. Despairing of winning back her husband, she prayed to

mother-earth for help. A golden throne rose out of the ground to receive her and she returned to the earth she came from.

Yet another story says that Sita underwent trial by fire but walked unharmed from the pyre due to the intervention of the fire god Agni.

Sits-by-the-door   *North American*

A Blackfoot maiden. She was captured by Crows but the wife of the brave by whom she had been seized took pity on her and helped her to escape. On the long journey back to her own people, she would have died of hunger but for the help of a wolf which followed her and killed game to keep her alive.

Sitting Above *see* **Ababinili**

Six Honoured Ones *see* **Liu Tsung**

sjen   *Slav*

also sjenovik

The soul of a man or an animal acting as the spirit controlling features such as forests and mountains.

Skidbladnir   *Norse*

The ship of the god Frey. This magic ship, built by the dwarf Dvalin and presented to the gods by Loki, was capable of expanding to carry all the gods but could be folded up and carried in a pocket.

Skoll   *Norse*

A wolf; offspring of Fenris and Gollweig. This animal was one of the Varns, wolves which pursued the sun and moon, trying to swallow them. When he and his brother Hati succeeded, an eclipse ensued. They fed on the marrow from the bones of dead criminals. As crime increased they grew stronger and in the final days they overtook the sun and moon and finally swallowed them.

Skrymsli *Norse*

A giant. He won a wager with a peasant and demanded the peasant's son as a prize but agreed to forfeit the prize if the father could hide the child. Odin changed the boy into a grain of wheat hidden in an ear of corn in a wheat-field; Hoenir changed him into a small down feather and concealed him in the breast of a swan; Loki changed him into a fish-egg hidden in the roe of a fish swimming in the ocean; in every case, the giant found the boy. On the last occasion, the boy ran off and, chasing after him, Skrymsli ran head-first into a pointed stake cunningly placed by Loki and was killed.

Skuld *Norse*

One of the three Norns – the future, necessity.

Skuld sometimes rode with the Valkyries. She is depicted as veiled and holding an unopened book.

Sky Father[1] *North American*

also Father Sky;

= *Zuni* Apoyan Tachi

The supreme deity of the Pueblo tribes; husband of Earth-Mother; father of One Alone.

Sky Father[2] *see* **Jupiter**

Sky Father[3] *see* **Mixcoatl**

Sky Woman *see* **Ataensic**

Slidrugtanni *Norse*

One of the two boars that drew the god Frey's chariot. (*See also* **Gullinbursti**.)

Smoking Mountain *North American*

A Metis hunter. (*See* **Little Man**.)

Snaggletooth Woman *see* **Kokumthena**

snake

This reptile appears in many mythologies, often under the name of serpent.

(1) In African lore the snake is often depicted with its tail in its mouth as a symbol of eternity. (*See also* **ouroboros**.)

(2) In the East Indies some say that a woman's menstruation is produced from a snake inside her body and that babies are produced from the snake's body.

The Dayaks believe that their ancestors are reincarnated as snakes and so refuse to kill them.

In Sumatra, Naga Pahoda appears as a serpent in the primeval waters.

Some tribes believe that, if a snake enters a house, the person who sees it first will die.

(3) In Hindu tradition the snake (naga) is a sacred animal. It is said to take many forms and is described as having a navel in its forehead. Some say that the nagas can mate with humans.

(4) In Muslim lore, an evil spirit, in the form of a snake, lives inside a woman's body.

(5) Norse stories include the snakes Ofrir and Svafnir who were continuously gnawing at the twigs of the world-tree, Yggdrasil.

(6) In North America, the Navaho snake-spirit was involved in a plan with Bear, Frog and Turtle to capture two maidens from an underwater village but the plan went awry and the two girls were killed. Frog and Turtle were lucky to escape with their lives but Bear and Snake fared better. This pair captured two girls who were overcome by the smoke from the kidnappers' pipes which made Snake and Bear appear as handsome braves with whom the girls mated. One of the girls, Glipsa, escaped when Snake reverted to his former shape but

he later found her and, once again as a young man, wooed her. He taught her many things, including the ritual Hozoni chant, and eventually allowed her to return to her own people.

(7) In Sumeria, the snake was regarded as a sacred animal. They say that it acquired the ability to slough its skin when it swallowed the 'Never-grow-old' plant which it stole from Gilgamesh, the king-hero.

Snoqalm *North American*

A sky god of the tribes of the north-west. Snoqalm kept all the light in a box. Spider wove a rope for Snoqalm to descend to earth but, while he was there, Beaver climbed up the rope and stole the box, hanging the sun in the sky as he climbed down again. Other versions say that it was Fox who climbed the rope, changed into Beaver and returned to earth with trees as well as fire. Snoqalm, in his haste to catch the intruder, fell to earth and was killed.

snow snake *North American*

A fabulous snake. This venomous, pink-eyed snake has a white body and hence is virtually invisible to its enemies when there is snow on the ground.

solar bark *Egyptian*

The boat in which the sun god Ra, or a dead pharaoh, travelled through the underworld.

There is general agreement that there were two such boats, one used during the day, the other at night, but less agreeement as to what they were called. Some say the day-boat was Manjet, others that it was Meseket (Mesektet, Mesenktet, Me'enzet) or Semketet, while some say that the night-boat was Meseket or Semketet.

Solas   *European*

A demon, one of the 72 Spirits of Solomon. He is said to have wide knowledge of herbs and astrology and appears in the form of a raven.

Soma[1]   *Hindu*

A drink of the gods, later personified as a god. In some accounts, soma is the same as amrita, though others regard amrita as a food, soma as a drink. Some say that it was the juice of a climbing plant; others that (like amrita) it was created at the Churning of the Ocean; still others that it fell as rain when the gods pressed it through holes in a celestial sieve.

(*See also* **amrita, jambu**.)

Soma[2]   *Hindu*

The divine drink personified. In some accounts he married the many daughters of the sage Daksha, who cursed him when he neglected them. As Soma became weaker as a result of the curse, all the creatures on earth became weaker as well until Daksha was forced to lighten the curse. Now the moon, ruled by Soma, weakens and recovers every month.

Somnus   *Roman*

= *Greek* Hypnus, Hypnos

The god of sleep, son of Nyx (goddess of night), twin brother of Mors (god of death).

Son   *Norse*

A bowl, one of the three vessels into which the dwarfs Fialar and Galar drained the blood of Kvasir, whom they had killed to obtain his knowledge, and from which they brewed the magic drink which endowed all who drank

it with the power of poetry and music. Another was known as Boden.

Sons of Horus   *Egyptian*

also Amenti

The four gods guarding the organs of the deceased and the four quarters of the earth. These deities are given as Tuamutef, the jackal-headed guardian of the stomach and the east; Hapy, the baboon-headed guardian of the lungs and the north; Amset, the human-headed guardian of the liver and the south; Qebsehsenuf, the falcon-headed guardian of the intestines and the west.

Sophiel   *Hebrew*

One of the Seven Intelligences, ruler of the planet Jupiter.

Sotuknang   *North American*

A creator-god of the Hopi; father of Kokyangwuti.

When the first humans, created by Kokyangwuti, became wicked, Sotuknang sent a flood to kill them but their creator led many of them from the lower regions to the earth's surface and they survived to spread across the face of the land.

soul

The idea of a soul appears in many religions and mythologies and is thought variously to reside in blood, the brain, the intestines or in such organs as the heart, liver or kidneys.

(1) In some African societies, a man has four souls, women and children only three. One of these souls can leave the body during sleep.

(2) In the East Indies, the Papuans say that the soul (sovai) survives death.

(3) The Chinese envisage two types

of soul, the hun and the p'o. Everybody has three hun (the spirit soul) and seven po (the spirit which maintains the body).

(4) In Egypt, it was said that there were two souls; the ba which could leave the body and take any form, usually that of a bird, and the ka which lives on after death.

(5) Early Hebrew lore tells of a three-part soul, comprising the neshemah, the refesh and the ruach.

(6) The Malay soul (sumangat) is said to leave the body during illness.

(7) Some North American tribes also believe in two souls – a small one in the heart which goes west at death and which can be reborn four times, and a large soul. The latter was given by the hero, Wisaka, whereas the small soul is the gift of the supreme deity. Other tribes believe that the soul has a separate existence as a star. Still others believe that some animals have souls which leave the body finally only after it has been killed four times.

(8) In Siberia, the Buriats say that there are three souls in each person; one dies, one becomes a ghost and one is reborn.

(9) In South America, some equate the soul with a reflection in a mirror or in water, or with one's shadow; others say a person has several souls situated in various parts of the body. Some say there are only two souls, one kind, the other vicious. The soul is not always thought of as immortal.

(10) In the West Indies, the Haitian zombie is the body of one whose soul has been taken over by a sorcerer who uses it to control the zombie.

Soul of the Mirror *see* **Yayoi**

Sown-men *Greek*

A race of warriors. When Cadmus killed the dragon guarding the Castilian spring, he sowed its teeth in the ground. Immediately, warriors sprang into being, fully armed, and fought amongst themselves until only five were left. These five were Chthonius, Echion, Hyperenor, Pelorus and Udaeaus, and they served Cadmus and helped him to build the city of Thebes.

The teeth left over from this operation were later sown by Jason with similar results.

Spenta Mainya *see* **Ahura Mazda**

sphinx[1] *Greek*

An image of a hybrid animal with the body of a lion, representing, in some cases, a sun god. The most widely-known is the huge statue (the Great Sphinx) of a recumbent lion with a human head, sited at Giza in Egypt.

Other forms exist: the androsphinx has a male human head, the criosphinx has a ram's head and the hieracosphinx has the head of a hawk, in each case on the body of a lion.

A black sphinx symbolises evil, a white one symbolises goodness.

Aker, the Egyptian god of the underworld, is sometimes depicted as a double-headed sphinx.

Sphinx[2] *Greek*

also the Strangler

A winged monster, part woman, part lion, with the tail of a serpent. This beast, daughter either of the monster Chimaera or the serpent Echidna, was sent by the goddess Artemis to ravage Thebes after Laius, king of Thebes, had abducted Chrysippus. (Some accounts say it was sent by Hera, others by Apollo or Dionysus) In all versions, she killed and ate any traveller who failed to answer the riddle given to her by the Muses (*see* ***riddle of the Sphinx***) and was herself killed when Oedipus successfully replied. Some accounts say that she threw herself over a cliff, others that Oedipus drove her over the cliff at sword-point.

Spider[1] *African*

A trickster-god of the Temne people of Sierra Leone. This being is also regarded as a wise deity.

spider[2] *North American*

A female creator-spirit. Some tribes assert that the spider wove earthly phenomena (including plants, animals and mankind), the web of fate and the alphabet.

Spider-lord *see* **Nareau**[1]

Spider Man *see* **Ictinike**

Spider Woman *see* **Kokyangwuti**

Spirits of Solomon *European*

72 rebellious demons. King Solomon is said to have put these beings into a 'brass vessel' and thrown it into a lake from where it was recovered by the Babylonians who thought it contained treasures. When they opened it, the demons escaped.

sprite

A brownie, elf, gnome or goblin.

sPyan-ras-gzigs *Tibetan*

A monkey-god. He and his consort sGrol-ma are regarded as the progenitors of all living things.

In some accounts, this is the Tibetan name for Avalokiteshvara. He is manifest in the Dalai Lama.

Squash *see* **Deohako**

Sraosha *Persian*

Guardian of the earth during the hours of darkness; an aspect of the good god Ahura Mazda.

He was regarded as the ear that heard the cries of mankind and, with Mithra and Rashnu, a judge who weighed souls in the scales in the underworld.

srin *Tibetan*

Early inhabitants of Tibet. These beings, armed with catapults and slings, were the precursors of the human race. Next came the lha, then the dMu-rgyal.

stag

(1) In Greece, the deer was regarded as the the animal of Diana.

(2) The Japanese regard the deer as the animal of Jurojin.

(3) In Mesopotamian lore the deer was a symbol of fertility.

(4) In Norse mythology, four deer – Dain, Dvalin, Duneyr and Durathor – grazed on the shoots of the world-tree Yggdrasil.

(5) In Welsh stories the Red Stag of Redynvre is one of the animals consulted by Culhwch in his quest for the hand of Olwen.

Star Country *North American*

The sky, in the lore of the Hopi.

Star Creator *South American*

A creator-god of Tierra del Fuego. After the original giants inhabiting the earth had been killed, Star Creator made the ancestors of the present tribes from clay.

Star-folk *North American*

In the lore of the Algonquians, the beings who live in the heavens. These beings sometimes descend to earth on ropes spun by the spider.

Star-maiden *North American*

A fairy who came to earth in a basket. One such being married Algon, another married Cloud-carrier. (*See* ***Algon, Cloud-carrier***.)

Stentor   *Greek*

A herald at Troy. His voice was said to be as loud as the combined voices of fifty other men. He died in a shouting match with the god Hermes.

Stheno   *Greek*

One of the three Gorgons, sister of Euryale and Medusa.

Stone Boy   *North American*

A Sioux hero.

Five brothers lived with their sister and they survived by hunting. On each of five consecutive days, one of the brothers failed to return from the hunt and the girl was left to fend for herself. Desperate for food, she swallowed a pebble hoping to die. Instead, four days later she gave birth to a boy who grew very quickly to manhood. When she told him about her five missing brothers, he vowed to find them and bring them back. After travelling for four days he came to a teepee where an old hag offered him food. When she tried to poison him, he killed her and then unpacked the five bundles standing in the corner. Inside he found the dried bodies of the five missing men. Instructed by a pile of talking bones, he built a little sweat-house in which he restored his uncles to life.

Stone Giant   *South American*

A giant of the Yahgan people of Tierra del Fuego. The only vulnerable parts of his body were the soles of his feet and he was killed by a humming-bird who discovered this and attacked him.

Stone Giants   *North American*

The original inhabitants of the land of the Iroquois. These giants were defeated by the thunder god, Hinun, who persuaded his brother,

the west wind, to blow the giants over the edge of a deep ravine, where they all perished.

Stone People   *Greek*

A race created after the Flood. The sole survivors of the flood, Deucalion and Pyrrha, threw stones over their shoulders, which became people, creating a new race to repopulate the earth.

Stonehenge   *British*

A megalith on Salisbury Plain, England. Some say that these stones were originally standing in Ireland as the Giant's Ring. In some versions, they were brought over to England and re-erected by Merlin's magic or, some say, with the help of the Devil. In other stories, the structure was built by the druids.

Stoneribs   *North American*

A hero of the tribes of the north-west; son of Volcano Woman. He skinned the halibut which an eagle dropped on to the shore and, wearing the skin, took the form of a halibut and swam south towards the sound of voices calling for help. He found a tribe starving and helped them to collect mussels for food. When the monster whale, Qagwaai, wrecked some of the tribe's canoes, killing the occupants, Stoneribs lured the monster to the surface and, when it chased his canoe, mouth agape, Stoneribs jumped into the gaping maw and killed the monster by shooting it from the inside. He then skinned the whale and, by wearing the skin, was able to become a whale himself. Another monster trapped Stoneribs but he was able to escape by changing back to a halibut.

When he finally returned home,

he took off the halibut skin and hung it up to dry. An eagle swooped down and carried off the skin and, thereafter, Stoneribs remained his normal human shape but became known as Crystalribs.

stoorworm   *Scottish*

A huge water-monster. Assipattle killed this monster, which swallowed him when he went out in his little boat to fight it, by cutting open its liver and and pushing in burning peats which he had brought with him. The dead body became Iceland and the monster's teeth fell out to form the Orkney Islands.

stopan   *European*

In Bulgarian mythology, a spirit of an ancestor acting as guardian of the house.

stork

(1) A sacred bird in Sweden.

(2) In Greek mythology, a bird sacred to Hera.

Stormalong   *British*

A sailor-hero. One explanation for the white cliffs of Dover is that his great ship, Courser, scraped the sides of the Dover Straits as it passed through. It also carved out the Panama Canal when driven ashore by a storm.

Stove God *see* **Kitchen God**

Stump *see* **Flesh**

Stygian nymphs   *Greek*

Nymphs in Hades. These nymphs were in charge of the accoutrements of Hades – the helmet of invisibility, the winged sandals and the magic wallet – which were borrowed by Perseus when he set out to kill the Medusa.

Stymphalian birds   *Greek*

Man-eating brazen birds. These

birds which thronged the Stymphalian Marshes were dispersed or killed by Hercules as his sixth Labour. Those that escaped flew to the island of Aretius where they later harassed the Argonauts. They were described as being part crane, part eagle, part stork, and having feathers like arrows.

Styx　　　　　　　　　　*Greek*
= *Babylonian* Hubur; *Hindu* Rasa; *Norse* Leipter
One of the rivers in Hades. The Styx was said to encircle the underworld nine times and was regarded as the river of the unbreakable oath. A god who broke an undertaking sworn on the Styx was rendered unconscious for nine years, followed by nine years (some say one year) in exile. Mortals were poisoned by the waters of the river if they broke an oath.

Some say it was this river, rather than the Acheron, over which Charon ferried the souls of the dead.

Su　　　　　　　　*South Amrican*
A legendary monster. This cruel beast had the head of a woman, the forelegs of a tiger, the hindlegs of a wolf and a tail like a huge leaf which it used to protect its young in times of danger. It was reputed to kill its own young rather than allow them to be captured.

succubus　　　　　　*European*
plural succubi
A demon in the form of a female which attacks sleeping men and has intercourse with them. (*See also* ***incubus***.)

Sucunyum　　　*Central American*
A Mayan creator-god and god of the underworld. He carries the

sun god Ah Kin back through the underworld each night ready for his next journey across the sky.

Sudri　　　　　　　　　*Norse*
One of the four dwarfs supporting the sky (south). (*See also* ***Austri, Nordri, Westri***.)

Sueje-lodde　　　　　*Baltic*
A Lapp spirit which reveals the names of those about to die. This spirit is said to appear in the form of a bird.

Sukhavati　　　　　*Buddhist*
The Pure Land of the west, ruled by Amitabha. This land of pleasure is full of flowers and birds, trees covered with precious stones and lotuses which bathe the Buddha in pure light. All those who reach this land become male.

sukyan　　　　　　*West Indian*
A female vampire of Trinidad. These beings beg for salt or matches and cannot be kept out of the houses of those who give to them.

sun
The sun is central to many mythologies and systems of worship.
(1) In Australia, some tribes say that the sun is derived from an emu's egg which was thrown into the sky.
(2) In parts of Central America the sun is regarded as the home of the dead.
(3) The Chinese say that the sun was created by Pan-ku and regard it as an emblem of the emperor.
(4) In Egyptian lore the sun is Ra's golden boat in which he traverses the sky and came from a golden egg laid by the Nile Goose.
(5) Hebrews regard the sun as a symbol of Jahweh's power.
(6) Hindus regard the sun as the eye of Mitra or Varuna.

(7) In Norse mythology the sun was projected into the heavens from Muspelheim, the land of fire.
(8) In Persia the sun god, Mithra, was the supreme deity of a major cult of sun-worship.
(9) In South America, the Inca cult of sun-worship was centred on their sun god, Inti.

Sun Hou-tzu　　　　　*Chinese*
also Monkey King;
= *Hindu* Hanuman
A monkey-god, a companion of Hsüan Tsang (Tripitika) on his journey to India to bring back the Buddhist scriptures.

On the journey to India, he recovered Hsüan Tsang's robe which had been taken by the Black Bear spirit and helped to rescue him when he was captured by monks and again when he was held captive by the White Bone Lady. In one adventure, he met his identical self, in another he recovered the treasure stolen by a monster with nine heads and, when Hsüan Tsang was trapped by seven spider-women, he sought the help of a Hindu god who rescued the prisoner and his companions. In another country, he overcame a demon who had put a spell on the king who was about to eat the hearts of over 1,000 young boys and, when his companions were captured by the Leopard Spirit, he turned himself into a firefly to effect their rescue. In India, a woman killed her husband for his wealth and accused Hsüan Tsang of the crime but she received her just deserts when Sun Hou-tzu restored the man to life.

Some say that he was born from a fruit-stone and was made king of the monkeys by the emperor.

He once made war on the hosts of heaven but was captured by the celestial dog, T'ien Kou. He was said to be able to cover 3,000 miles in one leap and once leapt to the edge of the universe in a vain attempt to prove himself greater than the Buddha.

He is also described, in another story, as a monkey-fairy who stole the peaches of immortality from the magic tree at the home of Hsi Wang Mu and the pills of immortality from Lao Chün (the name of the deified Lao-tzu, the founder of Taoism). When he tried to assume the role of Governor of Heaven, the Buddha shut him up in a mountain from which he was released after 500 years by Kuan Yin.

Sun-bearer *see* **Tsenahale**
Sun Sister *see* **Moon Brother**
Superior Gods   *North American*
Four creator deities of the Sioux. These deities are given as Inyan, Maka, Skan and Wi and they are regarded as aspects of Wakan Tanka. When they felt lonely, they created other deities such as the Associated Gods, the Kindred Gods, etc until there were sixteen deities known as Tob Tob.

Surabhi   *Hindu*
The cow of plenty. This sacred animal was the tenth thing to be produced at the Churning of the Ocean. It had the power to grant wishes and was the mother of Shiva's white bull, Nandi.

Some say that Brahma granted Surabhi a heaven of her own, called Goloka, into which devotees who have given cows are permitted to enter.

Surma   *Baltic*
A monster guarding the Finnish underworld, Tuohela. This beast was envisaged as an enormous pair of fanged jaws without a body.

Surtur   *Norse*
A Fire Giant, the ruler of Muspelheim. He was armed with a flaming sword and set the world on fire in the last battle, Ragnarok, where he killed Frey.

Susanowa   *Japanese*
The ox-headed Shinto sea god and god of fertility and storms.

He was born from the nose of Izanagi and cracked the necklaces of his sister Amaterasu between his teeth and, by breathing on them, produced five new gods. It was Susanowa's depredations on earth that frightened Amaterasu and caused her to shut herself away in a cave; as a result, he was banned from heaven and thereafter lived on earth, begging food from the goddess O-Ge-Tsu-Hime-No-Kami. Some say he was banished to the land of Yomi, the underworld.

He is said to have conquered Korea and grown trees from his own hair planted on the mountainsides.

In one story, he found Ashi-nadzuchi and his wife, Te-nadzuchi, saying a tearful farewell to their daughter, Inada-hime, who was due to be devoured by an eight-headed dragon, Yamato-no-Orochi. Susanowa turned the girl into a comb, tempted the dragon with saké which made it so drunk that Susanowa was able to kill it, and then restored the girl to her normal form and married her. He retrieved the magic sword, Kusanagi, from the dragon's tail.

Sus'sistinnako   *North American*
A creator-god of the Sia/Zia people of New Mexico. He is envisaged as a spider and is said to have made mankind by singing and playing on a spider's web. The first mortals he made were Nowutset and Utset.

Svartalfar *see* **dwarfs**
Svartalfheim   *Norse*
The home of the Black Elves, the underground home of the dwarfs.

swallow
(1) A bird sacred to the goddess Aphrodite.

In Greek lore, it was said that dead children could revisit their homes in the form of swallows.
(2) In Muslim lore, a sacred bird which is said to make an annual pilgrimage to Mecca.
(3) In ancient Rome, a bird sacred to the Penates.

swan
(1) In Greek myths, the swan is sacred to Apollo whose soul was said to reside in it.

Zeus himself took the form of a swan to seduce Leto.
(2) In the German story of Lohengrin the Swan Knight, the hero travelled in a boat drawn by swans and when rescuing Elsa, restored her brother Godfrey, who had been turned into a swan, to his former self.

In a different story of the Swan Knight, the six children of Oriant and Beatrix were turned into swans. The seventh child, the boy Elias, escaped and appeared later as the Swan Knight to rescue his mother from the stake and, at that time, the other six children regained their human form.
(3) In Hindu lore the bird is sacred to Brahma and is regarded as the bird which laid the cosmic egg.

(4) In the Irish legend of the Children of Lir, the three sons and one daughter of Lir were turned into swans by Lir's second wife and were forced to spend three periods, each of 300 years, in that form.

(5) Norse legends have the Valkyries appearing in the form of swans and in another story three swan-maidens flew to earth to bathe and were unable to return to heaven when Slagfinn and his two brothers seized the wings the girls had left on the shore while bathing.

(6) In Serbian belief, the vilas (water spirits) sometimes appear as swans.

Swan Knight *see* **Lohengrin**

swan-maiden   *Norse*
A Valkyrie; a girl who can change into a swan.

swan-shift   *European*
A magic garment, made of swan feathers, which enables the wearer to turn into a swan.

sword
A sword, often with magical properties, features in many myths. Some of the more famous swords and their bearers are listed below.

sword of:	
Alberich	Rosen
Beowulf	Hrunting, Nagelring
Brahma	Asi
Charlemagne	Flamberge, Joyeuse
Cuchulainn	Caladin
El Cid	Colada, Tizona
Finn mac Cool	Mac an Luin
Heimdall	Hofud
Izanagi	Ame-no-wo-ha-bari
Kari	Life-taker
King Arthur	Caleburn, Chastiefol, Excalibur, Marmyadose, Sequence
King Ban	Courchouse
Lugh	Claidhimh Soluis (= Sword of Light), Fragarach/ Freagarthach (= Answerer)
Manannan	Dioltach (= Retaliator), Fragarach/ Freagarthach (= Answerer)
Oliver	Glorious, Hauteclaire
Roland	Durindana
Sigmund	Balmung, Gram, Nothung, Sword of Need
Sir Bevis	Morglay
Sir Galahad	Sword in the Stone, Sword of Strange Girdles
Sir Lancelot	Arondight
St George	Ascalon/Askalon
Vishnu	Nandaka

Sword in the Stone   *British*
In the Arthurian legends, a sword set in a block of stone

There are two such swords. The more famous of the two is the sword which could be drawn only by the man destined to be king of Britain. The other was destined for the knight Galahad.

When a successor to Uther was sought, the magician Merlin arranged for a sword embedded in a block of stone (and, in some versions, an anvil as well) to appear in the churchyard near to where the assembled peers were to make their choice. Only Arthur was able to draw the sword from the stone, so establishing his claim to the throne. In some stories, this sword was Excalibur and had that name engraved upon it; in other versions, Excalibur was the sword which Arthur received from the hand rising from a lake, an event organised by Merlin when Arthur told him he was without a sword.

The second sword, set in a block of red stone, floated down the river to Camelot where Galahad had just arrived. He was the only knight able to withdraw the sword which he claimed and put into his empty scabbard.

Sword of Strange Girdles   *British*
also Sword of Strange Hangings, Sword of the Strange Belt
The sword of King David of Israel appearing in the Grail Quest. The hilt of this sword was made of the rib-bones of a snake, the papalust, and a fish, the ortenax. It had been used by Varlan, king of Gales, to kill Lambor, king of Terre Foraine, and had once been found by Nascien, brother-in-law of Joseph of Arimathea, who drew the sword to defend himself from a giant, but the blade broke into two pieces. Evelake, a converted Saracen king, put the two pieces together and they became rejoined. Other versions say that it was mended by Galahad.

In another story, Parlan the Fisher King drew the sword and was pierced through the thighs by a flying lance.

This sword was found by Galahad and his companions on the Grail Quest when they boarded a ship covered in white samite. Originally the sword of David, it was placed in the ship by Solomon whose wife had made the original hangings. When it was found by Galahad and

Percival, Percival's sister Dindrane made new hangings, using her hair.

Syama   *Hindu*
One of the two dogs of the underworld (*see* **Sabala**).

sylph   *European*
An elemental spirit of the air. In some accounts, they now live on Mars or Venus.

sylphid   *European*
also sylphide
A little sylph, or the wife or daughter of a sylph.

Symplegades   *Greek*
also Clashing Rocks, Wandering Rocks
Rocks or islands at the entrance to the Black Sea. These rocks, regarded as living beings, the offspring of the earth goddess Gaea, moved towards one another threatening to smash passing ships. They finally became fixed in position after failing to smash the *Argo* on her voyage to Colchis. (*See also* ***Planctae***.)

Syrinx   *Greek*
A nymph who was changed into a tuft of reeds to escape the advances of the god Pan who took seven pieces of the reed and fashioned a set of pipes.

Sytry   *European*
A demon, one of the 72 Spirits of Solomon. This being is said to control love affairs and appears in the form of a man with wings and the head of an animal.

Szeuka   *North American*
A creator-god of the Pima tribe. His father Earth-maker had created the world and human beings but the water spirit, Great Eagle, who preyed on humans, apparently sent a flood to destroy the god's handiwork. Only Szeuka survived and, when the waters subsided, he killed Great Eagle and re-created humans from the bones and bodies left behind by the flood. It turned out that the eagle had not in fact caused the flood – it had merely brought a warning of its impending arrival.

T

Ta-hsek-khi
Burmese

The first man, created by Hkun Hsang Long. He and the female Ya-hsek-khi were born in tadpole form. After eating a gourd, they mated and were given new names. He became Ta-hsang-khi (Yatawn) and they produced a daughter called Nang-pyek-kha Yek-ki.

Ta'aroa
Pacific Islands

A Tahitian creator-god. Some say that he hatched from a cosmic egg and used the shell to create earth (Fa'ahotu) and sky (Atea), others that he created the world inside the shell of a mussel, others that he built the universe from his own body. Some say that he pulled up the islands from the bottom of the ocean on a hook and fishing-line.

He also made men from red clay and later put a man to sleep, took a bone from his body and, from it, made the first woman.

(*See also* **Kanaloa, Tagaloa, Tagaro, Tangaloa, Tangaroa**.)

Table of the Wandering Companions
British

A table at the court of King Arthur. Not all the knights were members of the Round Table. For the others, this table was used.

Tachi
African

A mischievous deity. He is said to be visible only to those married women with whom he consorts. The children of such unions are deformed.

Tagaloa
Pacific Islands

A Samoan sea god. His offspring, Tuli, was a bird and Tagaloa caused a rock to rise from the bed of the primordial ocean so that Tuli had somewhere to build a nest. He later split the rock into many parts to form the islands of the Pacific.

(*See also* **Kanaloa, Ta'aroa, Tagaro, Tangaloa, Tangaroa**.)

Tagaro
Pacific Islands

A creator-god of the New Hebrides (Vanuatu). One of the 11 brothers of Qat. He made models of humans from mud, using them as skittles. One of the figures mated with the fruit he used to bowl them over, so producing the first children.

When a group of maidens flew down from heaven and took off their wings to bathe, he stole one pair of wings and hid them. The girl could not leave without her wings so she stayed on earth and married Tagaro. She later recovered her wings and flew back to her home in the sky.

When Tagaro is on earth, he is visible only to the dead.

In some versions, there are two – Tagaro the Wise, the creator, and Tagaro the Foolish who destroyed much of the other's work.

(*See also* **Kanaloa, Ta'aroa, Tagaloa, Tangaloa, Tangaroa**.)

Tages
Roman

An Etruscan deity or first man, He was said to have been uncovered when a field was being ploughed and took the form of a grey-headed child of immense wisdom which he passed on to the rulers of Etruscan cities. He then returned to the earth from which he arose. His words were passed down the generations and recorded in the Twelve Books of Tages.

Tahekeroa *New Zealand*
The Maori land of the spirits in the centre of the earth.

T'ai Chi *Chinese*
also the Great Pole
The first fixed point in time and space to emerge from the primordial chaos; the origin of all creation; a circular symbol representing the opposing forces of Yin and Yang with black and white commas. (*See also* **Hun-tun.**)

T'ai Ch'u *Chinese*
also the Great First
The first stage of the Great Change, T'ai I. In this period, it is said that form (Hsing) developed.

T'ai I[1] *Chinese*
also the Great Change
The state which evolved after the creation of T'ai Chi, involving two periods of change, T'ai Ch'u and T'ai Shih

T'ai I[2] *Chinese*
God of the Pole Star; god of the eastern peak of T'ai Shan. He determines the date of the birth and death of all humans and animals.

T'ai Shan *Chinese*
also Mount T'ai
A sacred mountain, one of the Five Holy Mountains known as Wu Yüeh. This site is regarded as the starting point of the sun-chariot's journey or, some say, is the site of the underworld.

T'ai Shih *Chinese*
also the Great Beginning
The second stage of the Great

Change, T'ai I. In this period breath (Ch'i) developed.

T'ai Su *Chinese*
also the Great Primordial
The combination of form and breath, giving rise to substance (Chih).

Taikomo *North American*
A creator-god of the Yuki tribe of California. He created the earth and made men from sticks but it was all destroyed in a flood. The second world he made had no animals for the people to eat, so they ate each other until the world was destroyed by fire. He then made a third world and placed animals under the corners of the earth to hold it steady. When it still wobbled, he made the animals lie down and thereafter, apart from earthquakes caused when one of them moved, the world remained steady.

He again created men from sticks and, when the first one died, Taikomo buried him. He allowed him to return to life the next day but the others complained of the smell of decay so Taikomo gave up the idea of resurrecting the dead.

talaria *Greek*
The winged sandals presented by the gods to Hermes.

Taliesin *Welsh*
A bard and wizard.

Ceridwen, a witch, boiled a magic brew to yield just three drops of a liquid which would give all knowledge to whoever drank it, intending it for her ugly son, Avagddu. The boy Gwion whom she employed to stir the brew inadvertently swallowed the drops when they splashed on to his hand and he licked them off, so acquiring the supernatural

knowledge. Ceridwen chased after him when he ran off and, after several shape-changes, eventually caught him, she in the shape of a hen, he as a grain of wheat. She swallowed the wheat-grain and found herself pregnant with Gwion who, when born again, was thrown into the sea in a sack. He was caught in a fish-trap (or, some say, found inside a leather wallet at the weir) and rescued by Prince Elphin who reared him, calling him Taliesin.

Some writers have suggested that he was reincarnated as the magician Merlin.

talking heads
A frequent theme in mythology is that of the head which continues to speak after it has been severed from its body.
(1) In the Arthurian story of Gawain and the Green Knight, the Green Knight's head spoke and challenged Gawain to a rematch after Gawain had cut it off in a beheading contest.
(2) The German fairy tale, *The Goose Girl*, mentions the horse, Falada, which continued to speak to the girl through its decapitated head nailed over a gateway.
(3) The Greeks say that the severed head of Orpheus floated down the river still singing.
(4) In Irish lore, the head of Bran, a giant king of Britain, continued to speak for many years until it was buried, and the head of Conary Mor, a High-king of Ireland, spoke to thank Mac Cecht for the drink of water he had brought.
(5) In Norse mythology, Odin preserved the head of the giant Mimir and frequently consulted it, while another story says that

he brought the head of the king, Minos, from Crete and used that as an oracle.

(6) The North American Natchez tribe have the story of Elder Brother and Younger Brother in which the head of the latter harries the former.

(7) The Philippine god, Montinig, carried on speaking after being decapitated, mocking his attackers.

Talos[1]   *Greek*

An apprentice and nephew of Daedalus. He is credited with the invention of the saw and died when Daedalus, jealous of his nephew's skills, hurled him from the top of the temple of Athena. The goddess turned Talos into a partridge.

Talos[2]   *Greek*

Guardian of Crete. Talos was a bronze, bull-headed giant made by the smith-god Hephaestus for King Minos. Some say he was given by Zeus to Europa when he carried her off to Crete. He patrolled the coasts of Crete three times a day to repel invaders and could kill by enclosing people in his red-hot grasp. He had just one vein which carried all the vital fluid and which ended in one ankle where it was sealed with a stopper or membrane. He died when this stopper was removed and there are conflicting stories of how this came about when he was attempting to repel the Argonauts by throwing huge rocks at their ship. In one story, the enchantress Medea lulled him into sleep and removed the plug or cut the membrane; in another, Medea prayed to Hades, the god of the underworld, and he caused Talos to

graze his ankle on a rock. Another version says that Talos was shot in the foot by Poeas, one of the Argonauts, a story which assumes a vulnerable spot in the heel.

Tam Lin   *Scottish*

A magician who could turn himself into various animal forms. He was captured by the queen of faery but his lover, Janet, held him firmly while he changed into various animal shapes, finally freeing himself from the queen's enchantment.

Tambarinang   *East Indies*

A creator-god. Some of the people of Borneo claim that their ancestors were made by this being, who is envisaged in the form of a hornbill.

Tamboeja   *East Indies*

A hero who climbed up to heaven and stole fire for the benefit of his people.

Tammuz   *Mesopotamian*

= *Babylonian* Marduk; *Greek* Adonis; *Phrygian* Attis; *Sumerian* Dumuzi (-Abzu)

An Akkadian sun god and god of fertility. In some accounts, Tammuz was found floating on water, in others he was the son of Ishtar who had him torn to pieces and thrown into the sea. When, as a result, the earth became barren, she regretted what she had done and descended to the underworld to demand his release from her sister Ereshkigal. Some say that he died every year, rising again in the spring, others that he spent half the year with each of the sisters.

He was one of the doorkeepers of heaven and was associated with the constellation Orion.

Tane   *New Zealand*

A Maori god of light and forest. He forced apart his entwined parents

Rangi and Papa, raising the sky (Rangi) above the earth (Papa) and used the thunderbolts of Fatu-tiri to kill Atea who, in the Tahitian version, was his father.

In some stories, his first wife was Hine-Ahu-one whom he created from sand or carved from stone. He also mated with their daughter Hine Titama who died of shame and became Hine-nui-te-po, a goddess in the underworld, having produced a daughter, Hine Titamauri.

Other versions say that Tane had three other wives – Hine-tuanange who gave birth to reptiles and mountain streams, Mumuhango who produced grass and Rangahore who produced stone. The woman he made from sand was, in this version, Hine-i-tau-ira and it was she who killed herself when she realised that she had married her father, becoming goddess of the underworld.

Yet another story says that Tane made Tiki and Hina-ahu-one who mated to become the progenitors of the human race. Alternatively, Tane and his brothers Tu and Rongo worked together to create mankind.

(*See also* **Kane**.)

Tangaloa   *Pacific Islands*

A creator-god in the lore of Tonga. He made himself a wife by carving her from stone and, when he threw the spare fragments of stone into the primordial ocean, they became the islands of the Pacific.

(*See also* **Kanaloa, Ta'aroa, Tagaloa, Tagaro, Tangaroa.**)

Tangaroa   *Pacific Islands*

A creator-god and sea god; a squid-god of Hawaii; a fish-god and god of reptiles of Tuamotu.

One story of the origin of Tangaroa says that he emerged from Po, the primeval void.

In one version of the creation story he created the world when, in the form of a bird, he laid an egg which, after floating on the primeval waters, broke to form the sky and the earth.

He mated with the goddess Faumea after she had shown him how to remove the eels that normally lived in her vagina and killed men who slept with her. When Hina-a-rauriki, wife of Tangaroa's son Turi-a-faumea was abducted by a demon octopus, Rogo-tumu-here, he and Turi-a-faumea fished the monster up from the depths of the ocean and killed him, rescuing the wife.

When he and the sky god Atea both claimed to be the father of the goddess Papa's first child, she cut the baby in half and gave them half each. Atea threw his half into the heavens where it became the sun and later Tangaroa did the same, making the moon.

(*See also* **Kanaloa, Ta'aroa, Tagaloa, Tagaro, Tangalaa.**)

tanin   *Mesopotamian*
A Semitic monster in the form of a huge sea-serpent.

Tantalus   *Greek*
King of Argos, Corinth or Lydia. He killed his son Pelops, cut him into small, pieces and served him to the gods in a stew. As punishment, Zeus condemned him to eternal torment. Immersed in water up to his chin which recedes whenever he tries to drink and with a fruit tree over his head which moves away each time he reaches out a hand, he can never satisfy his hunger or thirst.

In other versions, his punishment was for divulging secrets of the gods, for stealing ambrosia and nectar or for lying about keeping a golden dog.

Tao Chun   *Chinese*
The mortal form of a Taoist deity, one of the San Ch'ing, the Three Pure Ones. He controls the yang and the yin and regulates time. His home is the Higher Azure Palace, Shang Ch'ing.

T'ao-t'ieh   *Chinese*
A monster with one head, two bodies and six legs. This beast may be a water-buffalo or it may have the face of a man, a lion or a tiger.

The term is also used to refer to the formalised depiction of some unidentified mythical animal.

Tao-yüeh   *Chinese*
One of the Eighteen Lohan, in some accounts. He is depicted in a sitting position, meditating, with his head supported on his hand.

Taoki-Ho-Oi   *Japanese*
A Shinto god of carpenters. When the goddess Amaterasu hid herself in a cave, he built a beautiful hall which, together with other lures, was used to entice her out again.

tapairu   *Pacific Islands*
Any of several Polynesian nymphs, daughter of Miru, goddess of the dead. Their mother used these nymphs to lure mortals to the underworld so that she could cook and eat them.

Tapio   *Baltic*
A Finnish god of the hunt and forests; a male version of Virava. He is envisaged as the forested landscape of Finland.

Tar-baby
A sticky figure featured in many cultures. (*See also* **Gum Girl.**)

Tara[1]   *Buddhist*
also Queen of Heaven, Queen of Knowledge;
= *Chinese* Kuan Yin; *Tibetan* Dolma, sGrol-ma
A Tibetan goddess of mercy, sailors and wisdom; wife of Avalokiteshvara, the god of mercy. The name may be applied to Maya, the mother of the Buddha (*see* **Tara**[2]). Some say that there were 21 versions of Tara. In some accounts, Tara was generated from a tear-drop shed by Avalokiteshvara.

She is depicted, sometimes with seven eyes, sitting on a lion, holding the sun, or as a maiden holding a lotus.

Tara[2]   *Hindu*
A three-eyed goddess; a sakti of Shiva; Maya, mother of Buddha.

She was carried off by the moon god Chandra but rescued by Brahma. She claimed that Chandra was the father of her son, Buddha.

Tara[3]   *Irish*
Originally, the fortress of the Fir Bolg taken over by the Danaans; later the seat of the high-kings of Ireland.

One story says that the site was abandoned after it was cursed by St Ruadan, others that it continued in use long after the suggested date of that incident.

Tarasque   *European*
A French monster. This beast was said to have the head of a lion, scales, six clawed legs and the tail of a serpent. In some accounts, it was killed by St Martha near Marseilles.

tarbh uisge   *Scottish*
= *Manx* tarroo-ushtey
The Scottish version of the water bull.

Tarchetius *Roman*
A king of Alba Longa in Italy. He
ordered his daughter to mate
with a phantom phallus of the
god Vulcan seen in the flames of
the fire but she made her servant-
girl take her place. The children
of this union were Romulus and
Remus. When the twins grew up
they killed Tarchetius. (*See also*
Rhea Silvia.)

Tarnhelm *Norse*
The Helmet of Invisibilty. (*See also*
Tarnkappe.)

Tarnkappe *Norse*
also Cap of Invisibility, Hel-kappe
The red cap worn by some dwarfs.
These tiny beings hid behind rocks
and repeated the last words of
anything they overheard, giving
rise to dwarf-talk or echoes. The
red cap protected them from the
daylight which would otherwise
have turned them to stone. (*See
also* ***Tarnhelm***.)

Tarquin *see* **Turkin**

Tarquinius Priscus *Roman*
An Etruscan, fifth king of Rome.
He became king of Rome after
Ancus Marcius, whose two sons
had a greater right to the throne.
He ruled for 38 years and was
killed either by the sons of the
fourth king, Ancus Marcius, or
by shepherds employed by them,
who axed Priscus to death. His
wife ensured that her favourite,
Servius Tullius, succeeded to the
throne.

Tarquinius Superbus *Roman*
also Tarquin the Proud
Seventh and last king of Rome; son
or grandson of Tarquinius Priscus.
He killed his first wife and
his brother Arruns and married
his brother's wife, Tullia. At her
instigation, he then killed her
father, the sixth king Servius

Tullius, and took the throne.
His son Sextus's rape of Lucretia
incensed the citizens, leading to
the abolition of the monarchy.
He fled to Caere and came back
with an Etruscan force to attack
Rome. He was driven off and
his second attempt, led by Lars
Porsena, was no more successful.
He was wounded in his final battle
with Rome, at Lake Regillus, and
died some time later at Cumae.

tarroo-ushtey *Manx*
= *Scottish* tarbh uisge
A monster in the form of a water
bull. This beast is said to have the
habit of pulling mortals under the
water and drowning them. (*See
also* ***glaistyn***.)

Tartarus *Greek*
also Hades
Hell; the home of the dead.
The underworld which was ruled
by Hades was divided into three
areas; the Asphodel Fields for the
souls of heroes, Erebus where the
palace of Hades and his queen
was situated, and Elysium, the
home of the souls of the virtuous.
Sometimes it is regarded as having
two divisions, Tartarus, the lower,
and Erebus, in which case Elysium
is regarded as a separate place
away to the west. Other stories
use either name to refer to the
underworld as a whole.
Entry was by two gates, one of
ivory for false dreams and one of
horn for true dreams.
Newly-arrived souls were
judged by three judges, Aeacus,
Minos and Rhadamanthus.

tasé *Burmese*
Evil spirits, vengeful souls of the
dead. These beings appear in
various forms known as hminza,
thabet and thaye. They can be
scared off by very loud noises.

Tatzelwurm *European*
A mythical dragon in the Alps.

Tauret *Egyptian*
A hippopotamus-goddess, goddess
of childbirth. Depicted as having
the head of a hippopotamus,
the legs of a lion and the tail
of a crocodile, her fearsome
appearance drove off evil spirits
at the birth of a child.
In later stories, the god Horus
won her from Seb and she was
put in charge of souls returning
from the underworld for rebirth.
She was later assimilated into
the goddess Hathor.

Tawhaki *New Zealand*
A semi-divine culture-hero; a
Maori thunder god. He led souls
across the rainbow bridge to
meet their ancestors while his
son, Rata, followed in his
canoe.
When he married Hine Piripiri,
her relatives tried to kill him but
he drove them off with lightning
flashes and drowned them in
a heavy rainstorm. His father,
Hema, had been killed by the
ponaturi (flying demons) and
these demons had taken over his
house. Tawhaki and his brother
Kiriki sealed the house so that
the demons could see no light
and, when dawn came, Tawhaki
opened the door and the demons
perished in the light of the sun.
Only two escaped.
At the end of his life on earth,
he climbed to heaven up a vine
lowered by his grandmother,
Whaitiri. In the sixth heaven,
Nga Atua, he was reunited with
Tangotango, a nymph who had
seduced him, and he lived with
her and their daughter, Arahuta,
thereafter.

Te Reinga *see* **Reinga**

Teelget   *North American*

A monster of the Navaho Indians in the form of a flesh-eating horned beast. Teelget lived in the middle of a huge plain with no cover so a ground-rat burrowed under the ground to a point beneath where the monster was standing. The god Nayenezgani then crawled along the tunnel and shot the beast from below.

Teiresias   *Greek*

A Theban prophet. He was said to combine male and female characteristics and lived for seven generations.

Once, when he saw two snakes mating, he struck them with a stick, killing the female, and became a woman. When this happened again, he struck the male and became a man again and was thus able to settle an argument between Zeus and Hera by saying that women got nine times more pleasure from sexual intercourse than did men. In this story, it was the angry goddess Hera who blinded him and Zeus who gave him the power of second sight.

In another version, he happened to see Athena when she was bathing, so she blinded him but gave him the gift of second sight in compensation and decreed that he should live seven times longer than the normal span.

Others say that he was blinded by the goddess Aphrodite when, asked to judge her beauty against that of the three Graces, he awarded the prize to Cale, a nymph.

It was said that he continued to make prophecies in Hades even after his death.

Telamon   *Greek*

King of Salamis. He was one of the party hunting the Calydonian boar and sailed with the Argonauts. He also sailed with Hercules in his attack on Troy and, for his help, was given Hesione, the Trojan king Laomedon's sister, as a prize.

He and Peleus killed their half-brother Phocus and were exiled by their father, Telamon being sent to Salamis. Here he married the king's daughter, Glauce, and himself became king. He later married Periboea and was the father by her of Ajax the Great.

Sculptured male figures used as supporting columns are called telamons.

Telchines   *Greek*

The original inhabitants of Rhodes, or, some say, Crete; children of the sea goddess Thalassa, some say.

These people, said to be skilled in magic and in the arts of metalwork, abandoned the island before Deucalion's flood. They were said to use their magic powers for evil purposes and Zeus came to hate them. Some say that Zeus, or Poseidon, drowned them all in the flood but others say that they were expelled by the sons of Helius and Rhodes.

In some accounts they are described as being like dogs with fins instead of feet and are said to have raised the infant sea god Poseidon.

Telemachus   *Greek*

Son of Odysseus and Penelope. He was a baby when the Trojan War broke out and his father feigned madness to escape military service, sowing his fields with salt. Palamedes put the infant Telemachus in front of the plough

and Odysseus quickly demonstrated that he was not mad.

Twenty years later he set out to find his father who had not returned from Troy. He travelled to Pylos to consult King Nestor, known for his wisdom but who knew nothing in this case, and then to Sparta only to find that King Menelaus could tell him only that his father was held captive on an island by the sea goddess Calypso. When Odysseus did finally get home after all his wanderings, Telemachus helped him in the killing of the many suitors who had been pestering his mother, Penelope, for years and rounded up all the servants who had been unfaithful to Odysseus and hanged them.

Telipinu   *Hittite*

A fertility god and god of agriculture. Once, when he disappeared wearing his boots on the wrong feet, the earth became desolate and all things started to die off. He was stung by a bee sent by the goddess Hannahanna to find him but that only further angered him and caused him to send major floods. When Kamrusepa, the goddess of magic, dispelled his anger or, some say, cured his illness, he returned to his palace and the earth was saved.

Temple of the Grail   *Celtic*

The temple in which the Holy Grail was kept. This temple was built on Mount Salvat by Titurel, the knight who first found the Holy Grail. He guarded it day and night during his lifetime, a duty taken over by his son, Amfortas, when Titurel died.

Ten Corn Maidens *North American* *also* Corn Maidens

Corn spirits in the lore of the Zuni.

These beings were underworld spirits who came to the upper world only to find themselves turned into mortals and locked up by witches. Their absence caused the crops to fail but fertility was restored when the maidens were rescued by the harvest god Payatami.

Another version of this story says that these ten deities followed the Ashiwi (Zuni) from the underworld and were given the seeds of maize and squash by two witches. They were found by the twin gods, Kowwituma and Watsusii, who took them to perform their dance in front of the tribes but they were frightened by Payatami and ran away, causing a great famine. The two gods managed to persuade the maidens to return and they performed their ritual dance once more, restoring the fertility of the land, before finally disappearing for ever.

Ten Suns *Chinese*

The suns lived in the giant tree, Fu Sang, in the east. They took it in turns to cross the sky each day, accompanied by their mother Hsi Ho. When they decided to appear in the sky all at the same time, the earth was in danger of being burnt to a cinder but was saved when the archer, I, shot down nine of them.

Ten Yama Kings *Chinese*
also Kings of Hell

Judges of the dead. Each of these beings had his own court in the underworld. The first judge, Ts'en-kuang, decided whether the soul should be released to a new life or passed on for judgement; the second, Chi-chiang, held court over the corrupt and incompetent; the third, Sung Ti, dealt with liars; the fourth, Wu Kuan, with misers and the fifth, Yen Wang, with murderers. Atheists were tried in the court of the sixth judge, Pien-ch'eng, while slavers appeared in the seventh ruled by T'ai Shan Kun. The eighth court, ruled by P'ing-teng, judged those who failed to honour their ancestors and the ninth, that of Tu-shih, dealt with arsonists. If they survived the punishments meted out by these courts, souls passed to the tenth and final court where the judge, Chuan Lun, made a decision on their future.

Tenenit *Egyptian*
A goddess of beer.

Tengu *Japanese*
= *Buddhist* Oni

Shinto demons in the form of bird-men, offspring of the god Susanowa. These beings looked human but were hatched from eggs and lived in trees. They were adept in the arts of dancing and the use of the sword and were said to take possession of humans who then became proficient in these arts. Some say that they carried off humans and hid them; when they were recovered, these people were found to be mad.

They are depicted as having wings, claws and beaks or as largely human with a fan. In some accounts, they are regarded as female demons with huge noses and long ears who could fly great distances carrying a man and could bite through steel.

Tepeu *Central American*
A Mayan creator-god. When the earth rose out of the primordial ocean, Tepeu and Gucumatz made people from soil but they were disappointed with the results and destroyed them in a flood. Next they carved a race of beings fron wood but these too were not satisfactory and the gods had them torn to pieces by four huge birds. The following race of giants was destroyed by the gods Hunapu and Ixbalanque and the final population was created by Tepeu and Gucumatz who made the ancestors of the tribes, Balam Agab, Balam Quitzé, Iqi Balam and Mahacutah. (Other accounts say it was the creator-goddess Xmucané who made them.) (*See also* **Hurakan**.)

Tepeyollotl *Central American*
An Aztec earth god, a jaguar-god. He was regarded as a manifestation of the god Tezcatlipoca as the cause of earthquakes.

Tequechmecauiani *Central American*
A god of intoxication; one of the Centzon Totochtin. A sacrifice made to this god would ensure that the drinker did not die from hanging when drunk.

Tereus *Greek*
A king of Thrace; son of the war god Ares.

He married Procne and fathered a son, Itys. He later went through a form of marriage with Philomena, Procne's younger sister, pretending that Procne was dead. In fact, she was incarcerated in the slave quarters. In some versions of the tale, Tereus had cut out Procne's tongue to prevent her from any communication with her sister, in others he cut out Philomena's tongue when she tried to denounce him as the monster he undoubtedly was.

The sisters did manage to communicate through words and pictures woven into a tapestry and they avenged themselves by killing Tereus's son Itys, cutting him up and serving him to Tereus in a stew.

Tereus would have slain them with an axe but the gods intervened and turned all four into birds, Tereus into a hawk (or owl or hoopoe), Philomena into a nightingale, Procne into a swallow and Itys into a pheasant or a sandpiper. Since the nightingale sings while the swallow can merely twitter, it seems perhaps more likely that it was Procne who had her tongue cut out.

In some accounts, the roles of Philomela and Procne *are* reversed.

Teriel   *Hebrew*
One of the Seven Intelligences, ruler of the planet Mercury.

Terpsichore   *Greek*
One of the nine Muses – the Muse of dance.

Teshub   *Mesopotamian*
= *Canaanite* Baal; *Sumerian* Ishkur
When the god Kumarbi overthrew Anu, he spat out three new gods, of whom Teshub was one. The others were Aranzakh and Tasmisu.

Teshub replaced Kumarbi as supreme god and married the daughter of the sea god, producing the giant Ullikummi who was made of diorite. Others say that Kumarbi married the sea god's daughter who bore Ullikummi or that this stone giant was created by Kumarbi to avenge his dethronement by Teshub. When Ullikummi grew so large that he threatened the whole world, Teshub (or Ea, in other

versions) cut off the giant's feet and it fell into the ocean.

In one story Teshub was defeated by the demon Illuyankas but the goddess Inara gave the dragon and his brood so much food that they got stuck in the opening to their lair. Inara's mortal lover, Hupasiyas, then tied them up so that Teshub could kill them.

Alternatively, when the dragon defeated Teshub, he took his eyes and heart. Telipinu, a son of Teshub, married a daughter of Illuyankas and received the eyes and heart as a wedding gift. He returned them to his father who then slew both his son and the dragon.

Tethys   *Greek*
A sea goddess; a Titaness. She was said to be the mother of some 3000 Oceanids. In some accounts she is equated with Thetis.

Teucer   *Greek*
A celebrated archer. He fought well at Troy and was one of the party concealed in the Wooden Horse but, because he had failed to avenge the death of his half-brother Ajax, his father Telamon refused to welcome him on his return from Troy so he went off to Cyprus and founded Salamis.

Teutates   *Celtic*
also Totates, Toutates
= *Roman* Mars
A British and Gaulish war god; also a god of wealth and fertility. Victims were sacrificed to him by being plunged headfirst into a vat of some liquid or another (beer has been suggested as a possibility).

Tevennec   *European*
In Breton lore, the land of the dead. This realm is an island to

which the souls of the dead are transferred every night in boats.

Tevne   *Mongolian*
A man who married a princess. Tevne trapped a servant of the princess in a deep pit and forced her to reveal the identity of her mistress. The king tried to frustrate Tevne by parading a number of identically-dressed girls in front of him but he picked out the real princess and married her. The king then used his book of divinations to locate the person who had betrayed him and, when he failed, burned the book. Later, some sheep ate the ashes of the book. That is why sheep, it is said, have divine insight.

tevoda   *Cambodian*
= *Hindu* devata
One of the blessed living in Indra's paradise or living in the forest to record the sins of humans. Some of these beings act as guardians of the world.

Teyu-Yagua   *South American*
A monster in the form of a jaguar-lizard. In the lore of the Guarani people of Paraguay, this beast is said to guard Paititi, the land of gold.

Tezcatlipoca   *Central American*
= *Mayan* Chac; *Mixtec* Tzahui
An Aztec sun god, giver of life and god of the smoking mirror. He was the father of 400 sons and the stars of the Milky Way, and was the opponent of Quetzalcoatl.

His left foot was replaced by a mirror when it was bitten off by the monster, Cipactli. He tore off the jaw of this monster crocodile and used it to make the earth. The mirror enabled him to foretell the future. (Some accounts say that he lost his foot when it became trapped in the door of the underworld.)

He fell in love with Xochiquetzal, wife of the god Tlaloc, and abducted her.

His story is one of continual conflict with Quetzalcoatl, representing the eternal struggle between good and evil.

In some versions, he died every year and was restored when a human heart, torn from a living man, was offered in sacrifice.

In the Aztec creation stories, he was the ruler of the First Sun, ruling for 676 years until he was killed by Quetzalcoatl who ruled during the period of the Second Sun. When he was killed, he became a jaguar.

He is usually depicted with a dart and spear-thrower in his right hand and a shield and a spare dart in his left hand, but sometimes appeared in the form of a turkey.

Tezcatlipoca also appeared in four aspects, referred to as Blue Tezcatlipoca when he was Tlaloc, guardian of the south; Red Tezcatlipoca when he was Xipetotec, guardian of the east; and Quetzacoatl, guardian of the west. The north (black) region he kept for himself as Titlacuhan.

As a warrior-god, he was Huitzilopochtli and, in some stories, was turned into a tiger by Quetzalcoatl who knocked him out of the heavens.

thabet   *Burmese*
Monsters, spirits of women who have died in childbirth; a form of tasé. These beings take the form of giants with very long, slimy tongues. (*See also* **thaye**.)

Thalia[1]   *Greek*
One of the three Graces – good cheer, jollity, and bringer of flowers.

Thalia[2]   *Greek*
One of the nine Muses – the Muse of comedy.

Thanai *see* **E-u**

Thanatos   *Greek*
= *Roman* Mors
God of night; death personified. The god Pluto as King of the Dead. He collected those whose time on earth had expired, cut a lock of hair from their beards, and took them to Hades.

Thardid Jimbo   *Australian*
A giant who was also a cannibal, hunting and killing tribesmen for their flesh. When he killed a young, newly-married man, the two wives of the dead man lured the giant into a cave and built a huge fire at the entrance so that he was burnt to death when he tried to escape.

thaye   *Burmese*
Monsters, spirits of men who have died violently; a form of tasé. These beings take the form of giants with very long, slimy tongues. (*See also* **thabet**.)

thein   *Burmese*
Rain nats. It is said that rain is caused by battles between these nats.

Themis   *Greek*
Goddess of divine justice; a Titaness. She was the second owner of the Delphic Oracle and told Deucalion and Pyrrha how to repopulate the world after the Flood.

She weighed the souls of the dead in the underworld and, in some accounts, she is equated with the earth goddess Gaea.

She is depicted as blind (or blind-folded), holding the sword and scales of justice.

Thens   *Thai*
Lords of the sky. These beings sent a flood when the people refused tribute to the gods. The Three Great Men (rulers of the earth) went to see the king of the Thens who sent them to his grandfather, Then Lo. When the waters receded, the three rulers went back to earth and repopulated it with people from gourds. Some of the Then lords came to earth and taught the people various skills before returning to the sky.

Theseus   *Greek*
King of Athens. Theseus was the son of the sea god Poseidon by Aethra (a princess of Troezen) but accepted by King Aegeus of Athens as his own son since he had slept with Aethra on the same night as Poseidon. Some say he was one of the Argonauts and a member of the party hunting the Calydonian boar.

At the age of sixteen, he recovered the sword and sandals hidden by Aegeus behind a rock and set off to Athens to meet his father, performing various labours in imitation of Hercules en route. He killed a number of outlaws, including the crippled Periphetes with his own club which he then kept for himself; then Sinis, by tying him to two trees which tore him apart when released from the bent position – just as Sinis had killed many a wayfarer; and Sciron by hurling him into the sea. He killed Cercyon by smashing him to earth and took over his kingdom of Eleusis and he killed the robber Procrustes in the way he had killed so many others – by adjusting his length (by cutting off his head!) to fit his bed.

Aegeus had married the sorceress Medea and she tried to poison Theseus, so that *her* son,

Medus, might inherit the throne, but Aegeus recognised his son in time to prevent the tragedy and Medea fled the country.

After being reunited with his father Theseus crushed the revolt by Pallas and his fifty sons and captured and killed Poseidon's white bull which had been brought to Greece from Crete by Hercules and was now known as the Marathonian Bull, sacrificing it to the gods.

The Athenians were still paying the tribute demanded by Minos and Theseus offered himself as one of those to be sacrificed to the Minotaur. When he arrived in Crete, Minos threw his ring into the sea and challenged Theseus to prove that he was a son of Poseidon by retrieving it from the sea-bed. With the help of the Nereids, Theseus recovered it easily. Using a ball of magic thread given to Minos's daughter Ariadne by Daedalus, he entered the Labyrinth, killed the Minotaur and was able to escape from the maze. He left Crete accompanied by Ariadne but soon abandoned her on Naxos. Or did he? In some versions, he put her ashore because she was seasick and returned to his ship to work on it. A storm blew him offshore and delayed his return. When he did get back, Ariadne was gone and he was told she had died. Another story has it that he saw the arrival of the ship of Dionysus, who rescued Ariadne, and was frightened off.

He went to the country of the Amazons either as part of Hercules' expedition or with Peirithous and came away with their queen, Antiope or Hippolyta and fathered Demophoon or

Hippolytus on her. In the first story, he was given the queen as his prize, in the second he abducted her when she came voluntarily aboard his ship. The Amazons invaded Greece in an effort to recover their queen but were defeated.

In some stories he married the Amazon queen and married Phaedra after her death but others say that he married Phaedra and, at that wedding, Antiope (or Hippolyta) broke in and would have killed those present had not Theseus killed her.

Aphrodite caused Phaedra to fall in love with Hippolytus who rejected her advances. She then falsely accused him of rape and hanged herself, whereupon Theseus invoked the help of his father Poseidon to kill his son to avenge her death.

When the survivors of the defeat of the Seven Against Thebes encounter sought his help, Theseus led a force against Creon, defeated him and recovered the bodies of the dead for the decent burial that Creon had refused.

With the help of Peirithous he abducted Helen and won when they drew lots for her. In compensation, he went with his friend to Tartarus and demanded Persephone as a bride for Peirithous.

Trapped by Hades in the Chair of Forgetfulness, he spent four years in torment before being rescued by Hercules. He found, on his return to Athens, that Menestheus had been installed in his place by Castor and Pollux who had invaded and rescued their sister Helen and that there was much disorder. He left for

Crete but landed on the island of Scyros where he was killed by Lycomedes, the king of that island, who pushed Theseus over a cliff and pretended that it had been an accident.

Later stories say that Theseus returned from the dead to help the Athenians at the Battle of Marathon.

Thespian lion *see* **Cithaeronian lion**

Thetis   *Greek*

A sea nymph, one of the Nereids. She reared the infant Apollo and (with Euronyme) rescued the smith-god Hephaestus from the sea when he was dropped from Mount Olympus by Hera.

She married the mortal, King Peleus, and bore him a son, the hero Achilles. She had been wooed by both Poseidon and Zeus and many of the gods attended her wedding, including the uninvited Eris, goddess of discord, who threw the 'apple of discord' into the midst of the gathering setting in motion the events that led to the Trojan War.

She had killed six sons by testing their immortality in the fire and, when she tried the same test on Achilles, Peleus rescued him and handed him over to the centaur Chiron to be reared. She later tried to make her son invulnerable by dipping him into the River Styx but the ankle she held him with did not enter the water and remained a weak spot which eventually brought about his death during the Trojan War.

After a disagreement with Peleus, she left him and returned to her home in the sea but they were later reconciled and he joined her in her undersea realm.

Thiassi *Norse*

A Frost Giant, god of storms.

He coveted Iduna, goddess of youth, and her apples of eternal youth. In the form of an eagle, he carried off the god Loki and kept him dangling from a staff with which he had struck the bird until he promised to get Thiassi the two things he wanted most. Loki tricked Iduna into going outside the borders of Asgard with a bowl of apples and she was immediately abducted by Thiassi. She refused to let him eat any of the apples and, when the gods found out what had happened, they ordered Loki to get Iduna back. He borrowed the goddess Freya's falcon-garb and flew to Thrymheim where Iduna was held, changed her into a nut – or, some say, a swallow – and carried her back to Asgard, hotly pursued by Thiassi. The gods saw them coming and lit a fire which burned Thiassi's feathers and he crashed to the ground and was killed by the angry gods. His eyes were placed in the heavens as a constellation, the two stars known as Gemini.

Third Sun *Central American*

The third age in the Aztec creation cycle.

The Second Sun, ruled by Quetzalcoatl, ended after 676 years when Tlaloc caused a great wind to blow away the race of humans that Quetzalcoatl had created. Tlaloc then took over as ruler of the Third Sun, which ended after a further 364 years when fire destroyed the earth. The next ruler was Chalchiuhtlicue.

Another story calls this period the Sun of Fire and says that the fire which destroyed the earth

either fell from heaven or was started by the couple who had escaped destruction at the end of the Second Sun.

(*See also* **Five Suns**.)

Thisbe *Greek*

A Babylonian maiden. She loved Pyramus but was forbidden to marry him. They planned to run away and arranged to meet by a certain mulberry bush near the tomb of Ninus. She arrived first but was scared by a lion and ran off, dropping her cloak. When Pyramus arrived, he drew the wrong conclusions from the paw-marks in the sand and the abandoned cloak and killed himself in grief. Thisbe found him dying and killed herself with the same sword.

Thomas the Rhymer *British*

Thomas of Ercildoune, a 13th-century Scottish nobleman, poet and seer. He was said to have visited Elfland with the queen of that realm and was given the gift of prophecy. As a result, he was able to see the future and foretold the Battle of Bannockburn.

He is said by some to be sleeping in a cave with his knights, awaiting a call to arms.

Thor *Norse*

also Thunderer;
= *Anglo-Saxon* Thunor; *German* Donar; *Lapp* Horagalles; *Slav* Perenu

A thunder god and fertility god; son of Odin.

As an infant he was so strong and unpredictable that his mother could not control him. At maturity he was given the realm of Thrudheim where he built a huge palace, Bilskirnir. It was said that, when he was angry, sparks came off his red

hair and beard and he generated so much body heat that he was not allowed to use the Bifrost Bridge, wading through the river instead. His chariot was drawn by two goats, Tanngrisnr and Tanngniostr. He was given a magic belt, Megingiord, that doubled his strength when he wore it and a magical hammer, Miolnir, which returned to his hand when thrown. The hammer, which was a thunderbolt when he hurled it and which produced lightning when struck against a rock, was so hot that he wore a special grip called Iarn-greiper.

His first wife, the giantess Iarnsaxa, bore two sons, Magni and Modi; his second, Sif, who had previously borne a son, Uller, gave him two daughters, Lorride and Thrud. When the mischievous god Loki stole Sif's long golden hair, Thor nearly strangled him, forcing him to return the tresses.

On another occasion he journeyed with Loki to Jotunheim with a view to forcing the giants to refrain from sending the icy winds which ruined the flowers. They slept one night in what they thought was a house but which, by daylight, turned out to be merely the glove of the giant Skrymir who then led them to the palace of Utgard-Loki, king of the giants. To test the powers of the gods, the king arranged various contests. Loki tried to out-eat Logi, the king's cook; Thor tried to drink the contents of the giant's horn; all to no avail. When Thor tried to lift the paw of the giant's cat he failed even to move it and he was beaten in a wrestling match by Elli, the old nurse of Utgard-Loki. When they left Jotunheim, Skrymir admitted that he had won all these events by the use of magic.

Thor once fought a duel with the giant Hrungnir who boasted that he would take over Asgard and, with it, Thor's wife, Sif. Thor killed the giant with his hammer but was himself wounded with a fragment from the giant's shattered flint club. As he fell to the ground, the dead giant's leg fell across his body so that he was unable to move until his young son, Magni, lifted the leg and freed his father. Thor gave Magni the giant's horse, Gullfaxi, as a reward. Groa, a sorceress, tried to remove the flint fragment from his forehead but, forgetting where she had got to in her recitation of runes, failed to extract it.

Thor's hammer was once stolen by the giant Thrym who would return it only if he were given the goddess Freya as a wife. Freya refused to leave her husband, so Thor, dressed in her bridal clothes and with Loki similarly attired as a bridesmaid, presented himself to Thrym in Jotunheim. When Thrym produced the hammer, Thor seized it and killed all the giants present.

When the gods were invited by Aegir, god of the deep seas, to a feast in his undersea kingdom, Thor and the war god Tyr asked the giant Hymir for a kettle large enough to hold drink for all the gods. He and Hymir went fishing for breakfast. Hymir caught two whales, just enough for their meal, and Thor fished for the Midgard serpent by baiting his hook with the head of Hymir's ox, Himinbrioter. He caught it and hauled it to the surface and would have killed it if Hymir, in fear, had

not cut the line. When the two gods left with the huge kettle, the giants attacked them but Thor killed all of them with his hammer.

In the final battle, Ragnarok, Thor killed the Midgard serpent but died in the flood of venom that poured from its jaws. Some say that he also killed Garm, the guard-dog of hell.

Thorn of Sleep   *Norse*
Odin's magic thorn which could induce sleep without ageing or loss of beauty.

Thorny Flowers   *Central American*
An Aztec giant. At the beginning of the Fifth Sun, he and three other giants, Falling Eagle, Serpent of the Obsidian Knives and Resurrection, were given the task of holding up the sky.

Thoth   *Egyptian*
also Eye of Horus, Lord of Time, Tongue of Ptah;
= *Greek* Hermes
God of art, law, magic, the moon, science, time, writing and wisdom; god of Khnum. He is sometimes regarded as the son of Ra but others say he was the son of Seth born from his father's head or from a lotus.

Originally a creator-god who brought into being the four pairs of deities from the primitive waters, he became the scribe and keeper of records, credited with the invention of hieroglyphics.

In the form of a baboon, he acted as a judge in the underworld, recording the weighing of souls in the balance.

He helped Isis in the resurrection of Osiris after he had been killed by Set, the god of darkness.

He took over when Ra retired and was elevated to the heavens,

though others say that Shu took over as supreme ruler. One of his duties was to stand in the prow of Ra's sun-barque, Manjet, to ward off enemies.

It was he who gambled with the moon and won five intercalary days which allowed the goddess Nut, who had been cursed by Ra so that she could not bear children in any normal month, to give birth to her five children.

He is depicted as having the head of an ibis or baboon.

Thousand Nights and a Night,
  Thousand and One Nights
  see ***Arabian Nights'***
  Entertainment
Three Agents *see* **San-Kuan**
Three Mystic Apes   *Japanese*
These apes are Mizaru, Kikazaru and Iwazaru. They are represented with hands covering respectively the eyes, the ears and the mouth – see no evil, hear no evil, speak no evil. They are often referred to as the Three Wise Monkeys.

Three Pure Ones *see* **San Ch'ing**
Three Sovereigns   *Chinese*
Creator-gods. These three were Fu-hsi, Shen Nung and Yen Ti and, together with the Five Emperors, they created the universe.

Thrym   *Norse*
A Frost Giant; god of ice; king of Jotunheim.

He stole Thor's hammer and said he would return it only if he were given the goddess Freya as a wife. When Freya refused to leave Odin, Thor dressed himself as a bride and, with Loki dressed as a bridesmaid in attendance, went to Jotunheim in the role of Freya. When Thrym produced the hammer, Thor seized it and killed all the giants present.

Thunder   *North American*
A god of many Native American
tribes.

The Coeur d'Alene people of
Idaho have a story that tells how
Thunder kidnapped the wife of
a hunter who then followed the
couple to the god's home. When
Thunder went to sleep, the hunter
stole all the god's shirts. These
garments enabled the god to fly
and without them he was quite
helpless.

The Huchnom tribe of California
say that Thunder challenged the
supreme god, Taikomol, but lost
and was banished to the northern
realms during the winter months.

Among the Kato of California,
he was regarded as a creator-god,
maker of mankind as well as of
the earth.

In Oregon, Thunder is regarded
as an old man married to an old
woman or, some say, to a tree.

In the lore of the White
Mountain Apache, the contest for
supremacy was between Thunder
and the Sun.

Thunder Boys   *North American*
also Little Men
Twin male spirits of thunder and
lightning. These twins were known
as Tame Boy, god of thunder, and
Wild Boy, god of lightning. They
are envisaged as wearing snakes
for necklaces and cause thunder
by playing ball in the sky.

Thunder Men   *North American*
Man-eating monsters in the lore of
the Sioux.

Thunderbird[1]   *North American*
also Thunderer
A name for the Sioux gods Hinun,
Wakan Tanka, Wakinyan and
Wakonda.

Thunderbird[2]   *North American*
also Thunderer

A spirit of thunder and lightning.
The description of these beings
varies from tribe to tribe.
Sometimes they are human with
the head of an eagle or wearing
cloaks made from eagle feathers;
others say that they are largely
without definite form but have
beaks with large fangs. They can
make thunder by flapping their
wings and lightning flashes come
from their eyes.

Some tribes regard them as
ancestors of the human race who
played a part in the creation of
the world.

Thunderbird[3]   *Siberian*
Rain-spirits. In this case, the birds
are ducks and it is said that it
rains when they sneeze.

Thunderbird[4]   *South American*
A spirit of thunder and lightning.
This being features in the lore of
several tribes who believe that the
Thunderbird causes thunder by
flapping his wings.

thunderbolt
In Buddhism, the embodiment of
the power of the law.

In Greek mythology, the
weapon of Zeus; likewise, in
Roman mythology, the weapon of
Jupiter.

In Hindu mythology, the
weapon of Indra, also called
Thunderstone or vajra.

Thunderer *see* **Odin, Thor,
Thunderbird**[1]**, Zeus**

Thunders   *North American*
Two fawns who were put in the sky
as Thunders.

A bear killed a deer and would
have killed her two young fawns,
but they ran off. When the bear
followed them, a lizard gave
them shelter and killed the bear

by inducing it to swallow some
red-hot stones. To save the fawns
from further trouble with bears,
he sent them into the skies where
they make the noise of thunder as
they move about wearing the dry,
crackly skin of the bear which the
lizard gave them.

Thunderstone   *Hindu*
The weapon of Indra; a
thunderbolt. (*See also* **vajra**.)

Ti Chün   *Chinese*
also Lord of Heaven
God of the eastern sky. He was the
father, by Hsi Ho, of the ten suns
which one day appeared in the sky
all together, instead of one per
day. The heat was so unbearable
that the archer I shot down nine
of the suns, each of which fell to
the earth in the form of a crow
with three legs.

He also had ten sons by Heng
Hsi, who were moons.

Ti-kuan   *Chinese*
also Agent of Earth
One of the San-kuan. He had the
power to grant absolution for
sinners whose confessions, written
in paper, were then buried in the
earth.

Ti Malice *see* **Annency**

Tiamat   *Mesopotamian*
also Chaos Mother, Great Mother
A Babylonian monster in the form
of a she-dragon; deity of the salt-
water; the female principle.

When the sea god Ea killed
Tiamat's consort Abzu, Tiamat
attacked him with a horde of
demons to which she gave birth.
Ea and the other gods chose
Marduk to lead them. Tiamat was
slain by Marduk and her body
was used to build the world. Her
second husband (or son), Kingu,
was killed at the same time and his
blood was used to make mankind.

Tide Jewels — *Japanese*

A set of jewels giving control of the seas. These jewels were owned by Ryujin, Dragon King of the Sea and were given by his daughter to the prince, Fire Fade, when they married.

Some versions say that there were only two jewels, both pearls. One, Kanji, controlled the ebb-tide, the other, Manji, controlled the flood-tide.

In some accounts, Ryujin's son, Isora, lent the jewels to the Empress Jingo for her conquest of Korea and later gave them to her son, Ojin.

T'ien Hou — *Chinese*

also Goddess of the Sea, Queen of Heaven;

A sea goddess, guardian of sailors. She was originally the maiden Lin who died when she was only twenty-eight and was deified. She was reputed to be able to control the forces of nature and saved her family by abating a storm at sea merely by pointing a finger at the sea.

Models of the goddess are carried in Chinese ships and she is often depicted flanked by her two attendants who are known as Thousand Mile Eyes and Fair Wind Ears.

T'ien-kuan — *Chinese*

also Agent of Heaven

One of the San-kuan. He had the power to grant happiness and confessions made to him were written down on paper and then burned. He is depicted in the robes of a mandarin, holding a scroll.

T'ien-li — *Chinese*

also Celestial Principle

The soul of the universe which emerged from the primordial chaos. T'ien-li combined with Ch'i to form matter, Chih.

t'ien-wu — *Chinese*

also wu

A monster in the form of a sky spirit with the body of an eight-footed tiger with eight human heads.

tiger

(1) In Chinese lore the tiger is third of the Twelve Terrestrial Branches (the zodiac).

The north and winter are represented by the Black Tiger; the south and fire by the Red Tiger; the east and vegetation by the Blue Tiger; the centre and the sun by the Yellow Tiger.

The tiger is also depicted as the favoured transport for various deities.

(2) In the East Indies it is said that there is a race of people who can appear as tigers.

In Sumatran lore, a sinner who prays for reincarnation may leave his grave in the form of a tiger.

(3) In Hindu lore the tiger is the mount of Shiva.

The Rajputs claim to be descended from tigers.

(4) In Japan the tiger is said to live for 1000 years and its image is used as the emblem of warriors.

(5) In Malaysia these animals are said to be the incarnation of the dead or of the souls of sorcerers.

It is said that a man can buy a magic means of transforming himself into a tiger both in life and after death.

Tiki — *New Zealand*

The first man or a creator-god; the procreative power of Tane.

In one version he was the first man, made from clay by Tane or fathered by Tane on Hine-ahu-one, the woman he made from sand. Alternatively he was the son of the creator-god Rangi and his consort Papa. In this version the first woman was Iowahine.

Another version says that both Tiki and Hina-ahu-one were made from sand by Tane and they mated to produce the human race.

Yet another version says that Tiki created a child in the sand which, when he returned later, had turned into a lovely woman, Hina. He married her and they produced children who populated the islands. Tiki created new islands as the population increased.

Tikoloshe — *African*

also Tokoloshe

A Xhosa monster. This ugly, hairy black dwarf lives in the river and chokes women who reject his sexual advances. He is said to be capable of becoming invisible from time to time.

tindalo — *Pacific Islands*

A ghost in the Solomon Islands; the spirit of one who has been posthumously deified; an oracle deity.

Tintagel — *Celtic*

Birthplace of King Arthur. In later stories, this is the home of Mark, king of Cornwall.

Tir nam Beo — *Irish*

also Land of Life, Land of the Living

The land of eternal life and good health; paradise; a fairyland away to the west.

Tir nan Og — *Irish*

also Land of Youth

The home of the blessed dead; Elysium; part of the Western Paradise.

Tisiphone — *Greek*

One of the three Furies.

Titania *see* **Mab**

Titans *Greek*

also Elder Gods

The six giants fathered by Uranus on the earth goddess Gaea, listed as Coeus, Crius, Cronus, Hyperion, Iapetus and Oceanus. Other versions include Atlas, Epimetheus and Prometheus. They had six sisters, the Titanesses.

Uranus had imprisoned his other offspring, the Cyclopes, in Tartarus and Gaea incited the Titans to attack their father and release the prisoners. In another version, all the Titans, Cyclopes and the Hundred-handed Ones, other offspring of Uranus, were chained up in Tartarus. The leader of the Titans, Cronus, castrated his father with a flint sickle and took over the throne, marrying his sister Rhea, and putting the Cyclopes back into Tartarus. When the sons of Cronus, led by Zeus, rebelled, a ten-year war between the Titans and the younger gods ensued at the end of which the Titans were defeated and Zeus took on the role of Cronus as ruler of the universe. The defeated Titans (except Atlas who was condemned to bear the sky on his shoulders) were themselves incarcerated in Tartarus.

Some say that Zeus destroyed and burnt the Titans, making mankind from their ashes.

Titurel *British*

He built the Grail Temple on top of Mount Salvat to house the Holy Grail which he guarded with the help of the Templars.

He married Richaude, a Spanish princess, when he was over 400 years old and, when she died, he handed responsibility for guarding the Grail to his son Frimutel or,

in some accounts, another son, Amfortas.

Tlacahuepan *Central American*

An Aztec war god.

On one occasion he went to Tollan (Toltec Tonatlan) with Tezcatlipoca who fascinated the inhabitants by displaying a tiny infant (in fact, the god Huitzilopochtli) dancing on the palm of his hand. Many died in the crush to see this marvel and the remainder, angry at the loss of their friends, killed both Tezcatlipoca and the infant. The bodies then gave off a stench that killed many thousands of the Toltecs and more died when they tried to remove the bodies.

Tlaloc *Central American*

also Tlaloctecuhtli;

= *Mayan* (Xib) Chac, *Mixtec* Tzahui

A rain god of the Aztecs and Toltecs; an aspect (south) of Tezcatlipoca; father of the Tlalocs.

In the Aztec creation stories, he became the ruler of the Third Sun. Quetzalcoatl had ruled for the 676 years of the Second Sun and had created a new race of people. Tlaloc caused a great wind which blew all these people away (except for a few who became monkeys) and took over for the period of the Third Sun which lasted for 364 years, after which Chalchiutlicue became ruler of the Fourth Sun.

He is regarded as the ruler of Ilhuicatl Xoxouhcan, the eighth of the thirteen Aztec heavens, or of Tlalocan, the lowest of the three heavens, in other accounts.

In some accounts he is the father of Tecciztecatl whom he burnt to make the moon. He owns four jugs from which he can pour rain, not all of it beneficial.

Other accounts make him an aspect of Tezcatlipoca as guardian of the south.

He is depicted as black, blue, red or white, with teeth like tusks, or as a toad wearing a serpent headdress or as a feathered serpent.

Tlalocan *Central American*

An Aztec heaven, lowest of three, the home of Tlaloc and reserved for those drowned or killed by storms. This realm provided a measure of happiness for the souls of the dead who spent their time eating, playing games and singing. After four years, they were reborn, allowing the possibility of improved status giving access to a higher heaven later on.

Tlalocs *Central American*

= *Mayan* Bacaba

Minor Aztec rain gods.

To-Kwatsu *Buddhist*

In Japanese lore, the eight hot hells. (*See also* **Abuda**.)

---

toad

(1) In China, a three-legged toad is said to live in the moon and is regarded as a symbol of the immortal Liu Hai.

(2) The Greeks regard the toad as a symbol of the Phrygian god of thunder and lightning Sabazius.

(3) The Romans believed that the toad carried in its head a stone known as the borax, an antidote to poison.

Tobadzistsini *North American*

A Navaho war god and god of darkness. *See more at* **Nayenezgani**.

Tokoloshe *see* **Tikoloshe**

Tom Thumb *British*

The magician Merlin foretold that

this boy would be no bigger than his thumb and this proved to be the case. He was fully formed as a man in a few minutes but grew no taller. His godmother, queen of the fairies, gave him some wonderful gifts; a ring that could make him invisible, a hat that could impart whatever knowledge he needed, a belt that could change his shape and a pair of shoes that could carry him wherever he wished to go.

He was said to have been a friend of King Arthur. He had crawled into the sleeve of the giant, Grumbo, who shook Tom into the sea where he was swallowed by a fish. He met the king when the fish was served at one of Arthur's feasts.

Tomam   *Siberian*
A mother-goddess and bird goddess of the Ostyaks. It is said that, in the spring, she shakes feathers out of her sleeves and these feathers become geese.

Tomartind   *Pacific Islands*
A hero of Luzon. He made friends with a witch who gave him a rod which made monsters harmless and he had a tunnel dug so that he could travel to the land of the dead whenever he wished.

Tongue of Ptah *see* **Thoth**

Torre   *British*
A Knight of the Round Table. He was taken to Arthur's court as a youth by his cowherd father, Aries, and Merlin disclosed that he was, in fact, a son of Pellimore, king of the Isles. At Arthur's wedding feast he was sent off to find the knight who had seized and ridden away with the white bitch that had chased the white stag into the hall, interrupting the proceedings.

He rode off and met a dwarf who required him to joust with two knights. He defeated them both and sent them to Arthur's court. The dwarf then attached himself as servant to Torre and led him to the knight he was seeking. Torre retrieved the bitch from the knight's lady and set off back to Camelot. The knight, Arbellus, rode after him and they fought, with Torre toppling his opponent. He might have spared him, but a damsel rode up and demanded his head, claiming that Arbellus had killed her brother. The knight ran away but Torre overtook and killed him. When he returned to Camelot with the white bitch and the dead Arbellus, he was rewarded by the king who gave him an earldom.

He was one of those killed by Lancelot when he rescued Guinevere from the stake.

tortoise
This animal is used to symbolise slowness of movement in many stories.
(1) The African Bulu tribe regard the tortoise as a quick-thinking trickster-deity rather than a plodder in the European tradition.

In one tale, he responded to a demand to bring water in a basket by asking for a strap on which to carry it – the strap to be made of smoke.
(2) The Chinese regard the tortoise as the animal on which the world is supported.

It is said that this animal can live for 3000 years without food or air. There are said to be ten types including a celestial tortoise which is described as having the head of snake on a dragon's neck and its skeleton on

the outside of the flesh. Its four feet represent the four corners of the world.

It is regarded as the ruler of the north and the winter season and is variously known as Black Tortoise, Kuei Shen or Sombre Warrior. It is sometimes envisaged as the Great Triad, its body representing the earth with the upper and lower shells as the sky and oceans respectively.
(3) In Greek myths the tortoise is the symbol of Aphrodite, Hermes and Pan.
(4) In Hindu lore, the tortoise is said to be the form in which Vishnu appeared in his second incarnation, as Kurma.

The tortoise Chukwa supports on its back the elephant Mahapadma which in turn supports the earth.
(5) In Japan this animal is said to support the Cosmic Mountain, home of the immortal beings known as sennin.
(6) In North America, some tribes believe that the world is supported by a turtle (or by four such animals) while others say that the world itself is a huge tortoise floating in the primordial waters.

The Delaware tribe say that the tree of life grows on the back of a tortoise.
(7) Some Siberian tribes say that Mandishire, the supporter of the earth, is a huge tortoise which carries the world on its back.

Totates, Toutates *see* **Teutates**

Totoima   *East Indies*
A monster in Papua New Guinea. Totoima married a mortal woman and they mated, both in

human form, producing children which were promptly eaten by their father who reverted to his original form as a boar when they were born. When twins were born, however, he ate the girl but a shaman saved the boy and inserted the infant into Totoima's body where it grew immediately to manhood and burst out into the world and killed Totoima.

toucan *Malay*
Buttons made from the bill of this bird are said to detect poison by turning black.

Transformer *North American*
A trickster or culture-hero of some Native American tribes. This being, variously known as Kivati, Mink, Blue Jay, Raven and Chief Child of the Root, is said to travel the country changing the scenery and animals into new forms.

transvection
The reputed flight of witches through the air. Such flight was said to be on a broomstick, a poker or a spade. In later times, animals such as a dog, a goat, a ram or a wolf were said to carry the witches on their nocturnal journeys.

Trebuchet *British*
A smith who is said to have made the Grail Sword and repaired it after it was broken when Partinal used it to kill Goon Desert.

Trébuerden *British*
A site in Brittany where a dolmen is said to be King Arthur's tomb.

Tree of Life

A tree appearing in many mythologies, often of unspecified species and having various functions, but always revered.
(1) In Africa, Kilembe, the magical tree of life, was brought by the hero Sudika-mbambi when he was born.
(2) In Central America, the Nahua call the agave, from which they make pulque, by this name. The Mexicans call it Tonacaquahuit.
(3) In the Christian tradition it was a tree that grew in Eden. Arthurian legends say that, in taking the fruit of this tree, Eve broke off a small branch which, after she and Adam had been evicted from Eden, she planted. It grew into a tree, all white, and cuttings from it produced white trees. It turned green when Abel was conceived and red when he was killed by Cain.

Solomon's wife had him build a ship which would last for hundreds of years to convey to Galahad his ancestry. The ship contained a bed with white, green and red posts, cut from trees propagated from the originals, and on this bed Solomon placed his own sword, inherited from his father, David, which later became known as the Sword of Strange Girdles.
(4) In the East Indies the Dayaks say it is a tree which links heaven and earth.
(5) The Hindu tree of life, known as Jambu and growing on Mount Meru, is regarded as the axis of the earth and the source of soma.
(6) The Irish version of the tree of life is called Crann Bethadh.
(7) In Mesopotamian lore it is the symbol of Ishtar and Tammuz.
(8) In Siberia, the Yakut tree of life is known as Zambu and is said to grow in paradise. A dragon lives at the base of the tree and the goddess Kybai-Khotun uses the tree as her home. Two rivers are said to emerge from the base of the tree.
(9) The Tibetan version is known as Zampu which grows on the sacred mountain Himavan.
(10) In the West Indies, the Haitian tree of life is referred to as Grand Bois.

tree-worship
In Crete trees were regarded as deities.

In Greece, some trees and groves were regarded as sacred, dedicated to a particular deity.

Trees were the domain of the Dryads and some individual trees were the home of the Hamadryads who died when their tree was cut down or died. (*See also* ***sacred plants***.)

Treta-yuga *Hindu*
An age of the world – the second – in which changes begin and people become less bound by duty. (*See also* ***yuga***.)

Tri De Dana *Irish*
The three artisan gods of the Danaans. Credne the bronze-worker, Goibhniu the smith and Luchta the carpenter made the weapons used at the second Battle of Moytura. Not only were the weapons made at great speed but they were always fatal to those struck by them.

In some accounts the title refers to the three sons of Turenn.

Tri-loka *Hindu*
The three realms of the universe.

In some accounts, the universe is divided into three realms, the underworld, earth and heaven, or Arupa-loka (the formless world), Kama-loka (the world of the five senses) and Rupa-loka (the formed but invisible world). An alternative version has seven or more realms (Sapta-Loka).

trickster

A deity, demigod or a culture hero in many countries.

(1) In Africa, the spider is the trickster in West Africa and in Dahomey it is Legba.

(2) In North America, Trickster is one of the five (or eight) great spirits created by Earth-maker.

The most widely known trickster is Coyote but there are other such as Inkotomi (Sioux), Manabozho (Chippewa), Nanabozho (Ojibwa), Nihansan (Arapaho), Old Man (Blackfoot), Rabbit (south-eastern tribes), Sen'dah (Kiowa), Sitkonski (Assiniboine) and Wisagatcak (Cree).

(3) In South America, Trickster is a deity in the Guianas where it is said that, in the early days, fish swam inside a large tree and humans were permitted to shoot all but the large fish. Trickster ignored this rule and shot a dorado. As a result, the earth was flooded. Trickster saved the day by using his spear to open up a channel which drained the waters off to the sea.

In other stories, the fox plays the part of the trickster in Chaco lore, the moon in Apinaye lore.

trident

(1) In Greek mythology, trident refers to the three-pronged spear of Poseidon.

(2) In Hindu mythology, a trident, also known as trisul, trisula or trishula, is the symbol of Shiva in his terrible aspect Bhairava.

Trimurti   *Hindu*

The trinity of gods, Brahma, Shiva and Vishnu. They are sometimes depicted as a triple-headed deity.

Tripitaka   *Chinese*

The name taken by Ch'en Kuang-jui (602-664) when he became a monk. He travelled from China to India to obtain the Buddhist scriptures.

In one version, the emperor gave him a white horse for the journey but this animal was swallowed by a dragon, so Tripitaka rode the dragon instead. His mortal companion on the journey was the priest, Sha Ho-shang, and they were guided and advised by the monkey-god, Hanuman, in the form of Sun Hou-tzu, and helped by Chu Pa-chieh, a piglike god. Buddha had arranged eighty-one tests for the pilgrim, all of which, with the help of his companions, he overcame.

An alternative story says that Ch'en married Wen-chiao. She caught the fancy of a boatman, Liu Hung, who killed Ch'en and assumed his identity. When her child by Ch'en was born, Wen-chiao cast the boy adrift on the Yangtze River from which he was rescued by a monk, Chang Lao. When the boy was of age, he took the name Hsüan Tsang, and went in search of his family. He found his grandmother and his mother who gave him a letter for her father, Yin K'ai Shan, who came to her aid and killed Liu Hung. The body of Ch'en then appeared out of the river and he came back to life, having been preserved by the Dragon King, Lung Wang, who had once, in the form of a carp, been treated kindly by Ch'en. Later, Hsüan Tsang was chosen to travel to India to receive the Buddhist scriptures.

Triple Goddess   *Irish*

also Triune Goddess

A group of three goddesses regarded as a triune goddess or as three aspects of the same deity. Ana, Badb and Mach were sometimes regarded as comprising the triune goddess Morrigan. Similarly, Banba, Eire and Fohla were regarded as aspects of Brigit.

Triptolemus   *Greek*

A prince of Eleusis. In some stories it was he who, as a baby, was placed in the fire to achieve immortality by Demeter who was temporarily employed as his wet nurse; in other versions, the baby was his brother Demophoon. In either case, the baby was snatched back by its mother and, though unharmed, did not achieve immortality. Some versions say that Demophoon was burned to death.

Others stories say that it was he who told Demeter where to find her daughter who had been abducted by Hades and, after Demeter had got her daughter safely back, she returned to teach Triptolemus the science of agriculture which he spread throughout the land. When Lyncus, king of Scythia, tried to kill her protégé, Demeter turned the king into a lynx.

Some versions describe him as a god depicted aboard the chariot drawn by winged serpents which Demeter gave him to compensate for the loss of his brother. Others say that he became a judge in the underworld with Rhadamanthus and Minos.

He was said to have promulgated the law of Triptolemus which requires a man to honour his parents, offer sacrifices to the gods and do nothing to harm any person or animal. He is also credited with establishing the Fleusinian mysteries.

Trismegistus   *Egyptian*
'thrice greatest'
A name and attribute of Thoth. (*See also* **Hermes Trismegistus**.)

Tristram   *British*
also Tristan
A prince of Lyonesse and Knight of the Round Table; husband of Isolde.

In some stories, his father was imprisoned by an enchantress, in others captured by highwaymen. His mother, pregnant at the time, searched for him in the forest and died giving birth to Tristram. Tristram's father Meliad later married a daughter of Hoel, king of Brittany, and they had several children. She tried to poison Tristram to ensure that her own son inherited his father's kingdom of Lyonesse but her son took the drink by mistake and died. When the king ordered his wife to be burned at the stake, Tristram interceded on her behalf and she was pardoned. Meliad sent his son to the court of King Hoel for safety and here his stepmother's younger sister, Belinda, fell in love with him. When he rejected her love, she too tried to poison him.

In one account, he was carried off by Norsemen who put him ashore in Britain when they were caught in a storm which, they believed, was due to their crime. He found his way to the court of King Mark of Cornwall where he was made welcome.

In other versions, his father then sent him to live with his uncle, Mark, king of Cornwall,

where he learned that his father had been killed by a knight, Morgan. He rode straight to Morgan's castle and killed him. The Irish king, Anguish, sent his huge brother-in-law, Morholt, to demand tribute from Mark but Tristram, though wounded by Morholt's spear, killed him in single combat, leaving a piece of his sword-blade buried in Morholt's head. In some versions he killed Morholt and sent his severed head back to Ireland. Other versions say that Morholt was merely wounded and returned to Ireland where he died. In either event, his sister, the queen, discovered the piece of the sword-blade and kept it.

Tristram's own wound refused to heal and, in one version, he sailed for Camelot to seek help from Merlin but a storm landed him in Ireland. He had been taught music at an early age and was a fine harpist and in another version he went to Ireland to recuperate in the guise of Tantris, a minstrel. He was tended by the king's daughter, Isolde, with whom he fell in love. When Palamedes, a Syrian prince, arrived and asked for the hand of Isolde, Tristram met him in single combat and defeated him, so that he sailed for home in disgrace.

The queen noticed his broken sword and, and, comparing the broken pieces, realised that it was he who had killed Morholt. She tried to kill Tristram with his own sword but failed. Leaving the court, Tristram returned to Cornwall where both he and King Mark were attracted by the wife of the knight Segwarides. She invited Tristram to meet her

and, when Mark and two knights waylaid him, he defeated Mark and killed the two knights. He later defeated Segwarides, who had challenged him for sleeping with his wife.

Mark and Tristram were now enemies and the king sent Tristram to Ireland to ask for the hand of Isolde, hoping that he would be killed. In one story, Tristram's ship was thrown back by strong winds and he landed at Camelot at the same time as King Anguish who had been summoned to Arthur's court to answer a charge of treason. Tristram repaid the king's earlier kindness by taking the charge upon himself and fighting Blamor de Ganis, one of the king's accusers. He defeated Blamor but refused to kill him and they became friends. He went on to Ireland with Anguish and sued for the hand of Isolde on behalf of Mark. In another version, he saved the Irish king who was being attacked by an ogre or, some say, he killed a fearsome dragon which was ravaging the countryside.

Isolde's mother prepared a love potion to ensure that her daughter would come to love her husband, Mark, whom she had never seen, and entrusted it to Branwen, Isolde's maid, who was to travel with them on the journey to Cornwall. The potion was drunk by the young couple who fell hopelessly in love. Despite that, Isolde went through with the marriage to Mark but continued to meet Tristram at every opportunity.

A knight, Andred, spied on Tristram and caught him in bed with Isolde. Tristram was imprisoned but escaped after seizing Andred's sword and killing ten knights. He rescued Isolde who had been immured by Mark and took her to a manor house in the forest. He was wounded by an arrow fired by a man whose brother Tristram had killed earlier and the wound refused to heal. He was told that he could be cured only by Isolde of the White Hands, another daughter of King Hoel. He went to France where this Isolde healed his wounds and he married her. While there, he defeated the giant, Beliagog, and forced him to build a palace decorated with scenes of Cornwall.

Other variations of the story say that when Mark was told of his wife's adultery, he condemned both the lovers to be burned at the stake. Tristram asked to be allowed to pray in a small chapel and made his escape through a window, dropping down the cliff to the shore where his squire Gouvernail waited with horses and armour. Mark handed over Isolde to Ivan, leader of a band of filthy lepers, instead of burning her and Tristram arrived in time to rescue her from a fate deemed worse even than the stake. Isolde was reconciled with Mark but further spying persuaded Mark that she really was unfaithful and a trial was arranged, in front of King Arthur and his knights, in which Isolde was declared innocent. The lovers then resumed their meetings. Mark finally found them together and killed Tristram with a poisoned spear.

Other stories say Tristram was banished by King Mark. During this banishment he wandered the land seeking adventure and saved the life of King Arthur, who had been ensnared by the enchantress, Vivien, who had given him a magic ring that held him in her power. Tristram killed the three robbers who were attacking the king and, taking the girl servant of Vivien who had led him to Arthur, returned to Camelot with the king, who made him a Knight of the Round Table. Mark came to Camelot intent upon killing Tristram and when Isolde was abducted by Bruce the Pitiless, it was Tristram who rescued her, killing her captor. In another story, Tristram carried off Isolde, who was being ill-treated by King Mark, and took her to Garde Joyeuse where she lived for some time with Guinevere. To avoid further conflict with Mark over his love for Isolde, Tristram went to Brittany where he married Isolde of the White Hands. His abandonment of the first Isolde was condemned by Lancelot and they fought each other to a standstill when Tristram next returned to Britain.

One version says that Lancelot and Tristram patched up their quarrel and Arthur installed Tristram as a Knight of the Round Table. Mark offered a false hand of friendship to Tristram who went back to Cornwall with the king. At the behest of Mark, who hoped to see Tristram killed, he took part in a tournament in the guise of Lancelot and frustrated Mark's scheme by defeating Lancelot's enemies. He allowed Mark to treat his wounds and was drugged and put in prison. He was rescued by Percival with the help of Dinas, who temporarily imprisoned Mark.

There are many versions of how Tristram came to receive the wound that caused his death. Some say it was inflicted in the struggle with Melot, a dwarf at King Mark's court, others that Mark wounded him with a poisoned spear, some that he was wounded in a duel with a Breton knight in defence of Isolde's brother, some that it resulted from a rock dropped on his head as he scaled a castle wall when fighting King Hoel's enemies. When he lay wounded, Tristram sent Kaherdin, his brother-in-law, or Gesnes, a mariner, to England to fetch his true love, the first Isolde, who came at his command in a ship with white sails, a pre-arranged signal (compare the story of Aegeus). Tristram's wife lied to him, saying that the ship was carrying black sails, and he died in despair. The beloved Isolde died at the sight of her dead lover and both were carried back to Cornwall and buried side by side. Two yew trees (in some accounts, a rose and a vine) planted on their graves entwined their branches and could not be separated.

In the Wagnerian version, Isolde had been betrothed to Morholt and wanted to avenge his death. She found a piece of a sword-blade embedded in Morholt's severed head and kept it hidden. Tristram had been wounded by a poisoned spear thrown by Morholt during their encounter and the wound refused to heal. He went to Ireland in the guise of Tantris, a minstrel, and Isolde ministered to his poisoned wound. When she saw his broken sword she realised that it was he who had killed Morholt. They fell in love but Tristram returned to Cornwall without her. Mark was so impressed by his description of Isolde that he sent Tristram back to Ireland to ask for her hand as his queen. Isolde, deeply unhappy that she was to be the wife of Mark, not Tristram, brewed a poisonous drink, intending to kill both herself and Tristram but Branwen, her maid, gave them instead a love-potion entrusted to her by Isolde's mother. They continued to meet after her marriage to Mark but were betrayed by Melot. Tristram was banished to France and when Isolde elected to go with him, Melot tried to prevent their departure and wounded Tristram who went off with Kurneval, who had killed Melot in the encounter, leaving Isolde in Cornwall. She came at his request when he was dying from the wound but arrived too late and died of a broken heart.

Triton   *Greek*

A sea god; a merman; son of Poseidon or Hermes and the sea goddess Amphitrite.

This god could cause storms or calm the seas by blowing on his conch-shell trumpet. In some accounts, he was king of Libya and, when the Argonauts were stranded inland, he appeared as Eurypylus and dragged the *Argo* overland to the sea. He also gave Euphemus a clod of earth which, when later dropped into the sea, developed into the island of Calliste.

As a sea god, he is depicted as half-man, half-fish.

Some accounts speak of Tritons in the plural, attendants on Poseidon, sons of Phorcus and Ceto.

Triune Goddess *see* **Triple Goddess**

Troilus   *Greek*

Son of Priam or Apollo by Queen Hecuba of Troy, Priam's wife.

He was in love with the Trojan girl Cressida and was heart-broken when she was handed over to the Greeks in exchange for a prisoner-of-war during the siege of Troy. She had promised to remain faithful to him and when she fell in love with the Greek hero Diomedes, Troilus rushed straight into the battle and was killed by Achilles.

In some accounts, he was ambushed by Achilles, who killed him when he refused to become the Greek's lover; in others he died when his horses bolted.

Trojan War   *Greek*

A war between the Greeks and the Trojans, a ten-year struggle precipitated by the abduction of the Greek Helen, the wife of King Menelaus, by Paris, the son of Priam, king of Troy.

The battle raged backwards and forwards outside the impregnable walls of the city, built by Apollo and Poseidon, with many great heroes on both sides being killed.

The arch-schemer on the Greek side was Odysseus and it was he who finally conceived the plan that led to the fall of Troy. He had a skilled carpenter, Epeius, construct a huge wooden horse. hollow inside, in which he, Pyrrhus and a few others could hide. The horse was left outside the gates of Troy at night and the Greek army embarked and sailed out of sight of the city. The Trojans were deceived into hauling the huge horse into Troy, in some accounts demolishing

part of the city walls to allow it to enter. During the following night the occupants descended and opened the city gates to the army who had sailed back under cover of darkness.

The city was sacked and burnt, nearly all the men were slaughtered and the women were taken as slaves and concubines. Aphrodite ensured that Aeneas escaped with his father and young son and Helen was returned to Menelaus.

troll   *Scandinavian*

= *Orkney* trow

A supernatural dwarf goblin, originally a giant. It was said that a troll would burst if the sun ever shone on its face.

trollkona   *Scandinavian*

Witches who rode by night. Sometimes they were mounted on wolves with snakes for bridles. They could adopt many shapes and bring storms, illness and even death.

trow   *Scottish*

= *Scandinavian* troll

A dwarf goblin of the hills and sea.

True Prince *see* **Galahad**

Ts'ao Kuo-chiu   *Chinese*

A 10th-century warrior, one of the Eight Immortals.

His young brother Ching-chih killed a man in order to get his wife for himself but she resisted him and he had her thrown into a well. She was saved and complained to the Imperial Censor, who had Ching-chih executed and his brother put in prison. He was later released under an amnesty and became a hermit as Ts'ao Kuo-chiu.

He became the patron saint of the theatre and is often depicted holding castanets.

Tsenagahi   *North American*
A rock spirit killed by the Navaho
god Nayenezgani. This monster's
favourite pastime was kicking
people off a rocky path near his
lair. His victims fell on to the
rocks below, where the monster's
wife and family cut them up
and ate them. He was safe from
falling because his long hair grew
into the rocks but Nayenezgani
cut through the hair and he fell,
suffering the same fate as his
victims.

Tsenahale   *North American*
Eagle-beasts of the Navaho Indians,
killed by Nayenezgani with
thunderbolts.

Tsohanoai   *North American*
also Sun-bearer
Sun god of the Navaho Indians;
father of Nayenezgani,
Tobadzistsini and Yeitso.
    He and the moon god Tlehanoai
found some soil and grew a reed
that allowed the Navaho, on their
journey up from the underworld,
to escape the flood. As a reward,
he was appointed Sun-bearer. He
was said to carry the sun on his
back by day and hang it from a
peg in his house by night. He may
walk over the rainbow and ride a
blue horse.

Tsonqua   *North American*
A cannibal mother, in the lore of
the Kwakiutl tribe. She is said
to have eaten corpses as well as
young children. When she fell in
love with Sky Youth, he failed to
return her affection and killed
her.
    Her offspring were said to be
wolves.

Tsuki-gumo   *Japanese*
A monstrous spider. This beast
was invulnerable to weapons
and caused much trouble. It was

finally killed when it was trapped
and asphyxiated by smoke.

tua   *East Indian*
A guardian spirit of the Iban of
Borneo. These spirits were often
manifest as deer, snakes or wildcats.

Tuatha De Danann *see* **Danaans**

Tule[1]   *African*
A spider-god of the Zande people.
He descended from the sky with
a bag of seeds with which he
produced all plant-life. He is said
to have stolen fire from his uncles
and given it to the tribe.

Tule[2]   *North American*
A lake from the bottom of which
the Modoc say soil was brought
by the creator-god Qumoqums
and used to create the earth.

Tulkan-Zuiva   *Central American*
also the Seven Caves;
= *Aztec* Chicomoztoc
The caves from which the ancestors
of the Quiche Indians emerged
after an earlier race had been
destroyed by fire and flood.

Tullus Hostilius   *Roman*
The third king of Rome. For
destroying Alba Longa and
its inhabitants, he and all his
family were killed by the sea god
Poseidon.

Tulsi   *Hindu*
A manifestation of the goddesses
Lakshmi or Sita. Knowing that
her husband Jalandhara was
invulnerable as long as she
remained faithful to him, she
rejected all advances, even
that of Shiva in the form of a
handsome young man. Vishnu
then appeared in the guise
of Jalandhara and, when she
allowed herself to be seduced
by him, her real husband lost
his invulerability. Her curse
on Vishnu turned him into

the stone, Salagrama. She was
turned into the plant basil by
Vishnu.

Tuma   *Pacific Islands*
also Island of the Blessed
The home of the spirits of the
dead, in the lore of the Tobriand
Islands. This realm is envisaged
as a paradise where everybody is
happy and each man has several
wives who do all the work.

Tumo-pas   *Baltic*
A Finnish thunder god revered in
the form of an oak tree.

Tung Wang Kung   *Chinese*
A Taoist god, husband of Hsi Wang
Mu.
    He was the embodiment of the
male yang principle and combined
with Hsi Wang Mu to produce the
world and all that is in it.
    He was said to have the face of
a bird and the tail of a tiger and
he lived in the Cloud Palace.

Tungk-Pok   *Siberian*
A Yakut deity. He chased a huge
six-legged stag across the
heavens and captured it but the
sky god turned it into a stone. The
Milky Way represents the hunter's
ski-trail.

Tuonela   *Baltic*
The Finnish underworld, ruled by
Tuoni. This realm is described as
an island which can be reached
only after crossing a black river
which is totally devoid of light.

Turenn   *Irish*
A god of night, husband of Brigit.
His family feuded with the
family of Cian, who was killed
by Turenn's sons. When his three
sons were killed and the sun god
Lugh refused to revive them,
Turenn dropped dead and was
buried with them.
    In some versions, Dana was the
mother of his children.

Turi-a-faumea   *Pacific Islands*
Son of Tangaro. *See more at*
Tangaro.

Turkey Girl   *North American*
A character in Pueblo myths. Like
Cinderella, she was a poor girl,
and was befriended by turkeys
who gave her fine clothes and a
carriage and sent her to a dance
where she met a lover.

Turkin   *British*
also Tarquin
A giant guarding the fairy kingdom.
In Arthurian legend, his brother
Caradoc had been killed by
Lancelot and Turkin hated all King
Arthur's knights thereafter. He
captured Lionel while Lancelot
slept under a tree and put him
in a dungeon with about thirty
others. Lancelot was placed under
a spell by the enchantress Morgan
le Fay but escaped from her fairy
castle with the help of a maid. He
then killed the giant, cut off his
head and freed the prisoners.

Turquoise Man   *North American*
also Turquoise Boy
Consort of Turquoise Woman.
    In one story of the ascent of the
Navaho from the underworld, Atse
Estsan and Atse Hastin, the first
woman and the first man, placed
Turquoise Boy and Corn Girl on
the newly-created Mount Taylor in
the south and other deities on the
three other cardinal points.
    Another version has Ahsonnutli,
the supreme god, as Turquoise
Man who placed men at these
points, while some accounts have
him as the companion of Salt
Woman.

Turquoise Woman *see*
    Estanatlehi

Turtle[1]   *North American*
A character in the lore of many
Indian tribes. This character is

usually regarded as the animal
on the back of which the world is
carried. (*See more at* **tortoise.**)

Turtle[2]   *North American*
A turtle-spirit of the Navaho. He
was involved with Bear, Frog and
Snake in a plan to capture two
maidens from an underwater
village. The plan went awry and
the two girls were killed. Frog and
Turtle were lucky to escape with
their lives but Bear and Snake
fared better. This pair captured
two girls who were overcome by
the smoke from the kidnappers'
pipes which made Bear and Snake
appear as handsome braves with
whom the girls mated.

Twenty-four Knights   *British*
An early list of the knights at King
Arthur's court. The more famous
of the names on this list included
Bors, Galahad, Gawain, Lancelot,
Mordred, Owain, Percival, and
Tristram. Others mentioned were
Aron, Blaes, Cadog, Cyon, Drudwas,
Eiddilig, Eliwlod, Glewlwyd, Hoel,
Llywarch, Menw, Morfran, Nascien,
Petroc and Sandda.

Twilight of the Gods *see*
    Götterdämmerung

Twins[1]   *North American*
Creators and culture-heroes of the
Pueblo tribes. These primordial
beings, Preceder and Follower,
were given power over all the
creatures on earth. Using their
thunderbolts, they made cracks
in the earth and descended into
the depths on spider webs, finding
partly-formed beings buried
in the first womb of the earth.
They led them up to the second
womb, those that failed to make
the ascent becoming monsters.
In the next womb, these beings
discovered the nature of sex and
continued up through the fourth

womb until they reached the
outer world as men and women.

Twins[2] *see* **Gemini**

twins
Twins are the subject of many
and varied beliefs in cultures
throughout the world.
(1) In Africa, the Ibo regard twins
with horror whereas other tribes,
including the Yoruba, revere
them.
(2) In Greek mythology, the twins
Castor and Polydeuces (Pollux),
sons of Zeus and Leda, were
placed in the heavens as the
constellation Gemini (Twins).
(3) In Mexico, the Aztec killed one
twin at birth, in the belief that it
saved the life of a parent, and the
surviving twin was said to have
evil power.
    The Tarascans of Mexico regard
twins as gifted in the matter
of medicine and say that the
plants grown by twins will yield
double fruits which, if eaten by
a pregnant woman, will result in
the birth of further twins.
    The Popaluca say that twins are
good horse-breakers and can cure
colic in domestic animals and such
ailments as toothache in humans.
(4) In North America, the Apache
have their heroes in the twins
Child-of-the-Water and Killer-of-
Enemies.
    The Cherokee say that twins are
able to see the 'little people'.
    The Iroquois twins, Flint and
Sapling, acted as transformers
and creators.
    The Lillooet say that twins are
the children of bears.
    The Shawnee are said to regard
twins as lucky in some cases
though in others it was said that
the elder was likely to be evil.

Among the Tubatulabal Indians it was believed that, if one twin should die, both would die, and if one joked about a woman having twins, she would do so.

The Winnebago have stories of the hero twins, Flesh and Stump.

(5) In Roman lore, the twins Romulus and Remus, founders of Rome, were suckled by a wolf after they were abandoned.

(6) In South America, the Bakairi twins, Kame and Keri, are the moon and sun respectively personified.

The Yaghan talk of divine twins, culture-heroes, who taught the tribe the use of fire and the art of hunting.

A widespread theme has one clever and strong twin, the other stupid and clumsy, often regarded as sun and moon respectively. Another common motif is that of the woman killed, by jaguars who rear her twins; they, when they discover the truth, kill the jaguars and climb up to heaven on an arrow-ladder and become the moon and sun.

(7) Other beliefs about twins are (i) that twins result from adultery; (ii) they may have separate fathers; (iii) a woman who eats a double fruit will bear twins; (iv) twins are lucky or have second sight.

Twrch Trwyth   *Welsh*

A king transformed into a huge boar for his sins. One of the the tasks set for Culhwch by the giant Ysbaddaden as a condition of marriage to his daughter Olwen was to bring to him the comb and scissors, which, together with a razor, this animal carried between its ears.

King Arthur and his men helped Culhwch in this task and they hunted the boar through Wales to Cornwall. He killed many of Arthur's men in the fights that ensued en route and lost most of his own sons who were in the form of young boars. The comb and scissors were seized by Arthur's men and given to Culhwch and Twrch Trwyth was finally chased into the sea off Cornwall and never seen again.

Tyll Eulenspiegel   *German*

also Owl-glass

A legendary trickster-clown who plays practical jokes and exposes people's vices.

Tyr   *Norse*

also Tyw;

= *Roman* Mars

A sky god and god of war. His hand was bitten off by the wolf Fenris when Tyr put it in the wolf's mouth as a guarantee of good faith when Fenris allowed himself to be bound to a rock and then found that he could not break free.

In the battle of Ragnarok, he killed Garm, the guard-dog of hell, but was himself killed by Garm.

Tylwith Teg   *Welsh*

Brownies or fairies ruled by Gwynn Ap Nudd, king of the fairies and lord of the underworld. These beings are said to vanish if they touch iron.

Tyndareus   *Greek*

A king of Sparta; husband of Leda.

He was banished from Sparta by King Hippocoon and fled to Aetolia, where he married Leda. Hercules killed Hippocoon and his sons and restored Tyndareus and his brother Icarius to the throne. Tyndareus sheltered

Agamemnon and Menelaus who fled to Sparta when Aegisthus killed their father Atreus and later he helped them to recover their father's throne. Tyndareus finally abdicated in favour of Menelaus.

Of the four children born to his wife Leda, there are conflicting stories. In some, they are the natural parents only of Clytemnestra, in others of both Clytemnestra and Castor, and in others of these two and Polydeuces, the beautiful Helen being the daughter of Zeus and Leda. It seems most likely that Clytemnestra and Castor were the children of Tyndareus and that Zeus was the father of Helen and Polydeuces. Tyndareus adopted Polydeuces as his own son.

So many princes wanted to marry Helen that Tyndareus had them all stand on the skin of a sacrificial animal and swear to support whichever of them was chosen as her husband. She married Menelaus and, when she was later abducted by Paris, they were reminded of their oath and rallied to the Greek cause against the Trojans.

Typhon   *Greek*

= *Egyptian* Set

An ass-headed or 100-headed monster, the hurricane personified. Typhon was a giant with hands in the form of serpents, serpent legs and huge wings who spewed flaming rocks from his mouth. He so frightened the gods that they concealed themselves, in the form of animals, in Egypt.

In a fight with Zeus, Typhon cut out the sinews of the god's limbs, leaving him helpless. He concealed the sinews in the Corycian cave where they were guarded by the dragon Delphyne until the monster Aegipan (or Cadmus or Pan) and Hermes recovered them and made Zeus whole again. The god then chased Typhon to Sicily where he buried him under Mount Etna. In another story Typhon was thrown into Tartarus.

Typhonian Beast   *Egyptian*
A monster, depicted as having a long snout, square ears and a tufted tail. It was the symbol of the god Set.

tzité   *Central American*
A plant, the berries of which were used, according to Aztec lore, by the gods Gucumatz and Tepeu as a divining tool, helping them to decide what form they should use to create human

beings. The wooden figures that they carved as a result proved to be unsatisfactory and were destroyed by huge predatory birds.

Tzitzimime   *Central American*
An Aztec star spirit. These malevolent spirits are said to attack humans in the form of an eagle or vulture, causing fits in children and lust in men. At the end of the world they will devour all mankind.

U

Uaithne *Irish*
The magical harp of the god, the Dagda. The Fomoire once stole this instrument, but the Dagda found where they had put it and, when he called it, it jumped from the wall where it was hanging, killed the men who had stolen it and put the rest to sleep with its music.

Uayayab *Central American*
The god or demon of the nemontemi, the five-day period of fasting and ill-luck at the end of the Mayan year.

Ubastet, Ubasti *see* **Bast**

Uchdryd *Welsh*
A warrior at the court of King Arthur. It was said that his beard could shelter many of his companions in bad weather. He was one of the party that accompanied Culhwch in his quest for the hand of Olwen.

udjat, udjat eye *Egyptian*
also wedjat, wedjat eye
A third eye, in the middle of a god's forehead, symbol of eternity. Such eyes are referred to as, for example, the Eye of Atum, the Eye of Horus, the Eye of Ra. (*See also* ***Edjo***.)

Ulay *Pacific Islands*
A Philippine prince. He fell in love with a beautiful girl, who was really a witch, but left her and married another girl. The witch was so angry that she turned his father's city into a forest, his people into animals and Ulay himself into a monkey, a form he was destined to keep for five hundred years.

Uldra *Baltic*
A fairy race in Lapland, living under the earth. (*See also* ***Huldrafolk***.)

Ulgan *Siberian*
A creator-god of the Buriats. Ulgan used fish swimming in the primeval waters to support the newly-created earth which he had formed in the shape of a huge, flat dish. Parts of the dish which broke off became the islands and land masses of earth and the god used one small part to make the first human, who was called Erlik.

He warned Nama, god of the underworld, of the impending Flood, giving him time to build an ark in which he survived.

Uller *Norse*
The god of archery, death, justice, oaths and winter. He took over from Odin and ruled during the winter months and ruled for ten years when Odin was banished from Asgard but was himself banished to Sweden when Odin returned. He was a rider with, and sometimes leader of, the Wild Hunt. His home was known as Ydalir.

Ulu-tojon *Siberian*
A Yakut thunder god. He was said to have brought fire from the heavens for the use of mankind.

Uma *Hindu*
In some accounts, Shiva's wife Sati immolated herself when Shiva was excluded from a feast of the gods and Shiva, having performed a frenzied funeral dance, restored his wife to life as Uma. In other accounts, Uma

was a formless goddess who, from time to time, entered the bodies of other goddesses. As a result, many of them are known as Uma. In this version, she could be Ambika, Devi, Durga, Parvati or Rudrani.

Umai-hulhlya-wit *North American*
A water monster of the lore of the tribes of California. His enormous body was burnt and from it came all things such as rituals and laws, songs and language.

Umashiashikabihikoji *Japanese*
A Shinto creator-god, one of the five primordial gods known as the Separate Heavenly Deities. He was created from reeds from the primeval waters and grew six branches, each of which produced a male and a female deity. The last pair were Izanagi and Izanami, from whom many other gods were descended.

umiarissat *Inuit*
Phantom boats. These boats, which are crewed by women, are said to cause storms.

Unci *see* **Grandmother Earth**

Underland *Welsh*
= *Irish* Tir nan Og
A land of eternal youth; a fairy kingdom beneath the earth; the underworld.

Underwater Panthers *North American*
Water monsters of the eastern tribes. These beasts were said to be like the creatures of the earth in reverse, living under the surface of rivers and lakes. They tried to destroy the earth by dragging it under the water or by inundation. When they tried to destroy the goddess Nokomis, grandmother of Hiawatha, in one such flood, the god Manabozho called on the beavers and others

to bring up mud from the bottom from which he made dry land, so saving her life.

underworld
Also known as the Afterworld or Otherworld, the place to which the dead (or the souls of the dead) are said to go. Each culture has its own version of what happens to people when they die. Many postulate a place where departed souls receive reward or punishment based on the deceased's conduct on earth.

African
(1) The Bantu say that the souls of the dead go to Kuzimu, an underground world and, if they cause a commotion, an earthquake results. For the Swahili, Kuzimu is variously described as a place where waiting souls shiver in the dark, a pleasant realm where the inhabitants look down on earth or an underwater realm where the inhabitants live like fish on the bottom.
(2) In Dahomey, some say that the land of the dead is in the sky, others that it is under the earth.
(3) In Ethiopia the underworld is known as Ekera.

Armenian
The Armenian underworld, Dzokhk, is envisaged as a fiery abyss below the earth's surface. A bridge known as Maze leads from hell to heaven. This bridge is very fragile and collapses under the weight of sin, casting the soul back into torment.

Assyrian
The Assyrian underworld is called Ekurra.

Babylonian
The underworld is called Arulu, a kingdom ruled by Ereshkigal. In

another story it is called Cuthah.

Buddhist
The Buddhists envisage a hell on seven levels, the lowest of which is Avici.

Central American
(1) The Aztecs envisaged a nine-layered underworld, Mictlan, the land of the dead, as a gloomy place at the centre of the earth. To reach the underworld, the dead had to cross eight forests, eight deserts and eight mountains, each full of great dangers, and finally cross a river into the first layer of the underworld itself. Included in the hazards of the journey were encounters with the fierce aligator, Xochitonal, the demon Izpuzteque and the fiend Nextepehua. Souls who survived the journey finally found rest in the last of these underworld realms, Chicuauhmictlan.
(2) The Maya envisaged hell not as a place of permanent torment but as one stage in the progress of each individual between birth and finally reaching heaven. This region was called Xibalba. The place reserved for the punishment of the wicked is Mitnal.

Chinese
In China, the underworld was known as Ti-yü, Earth Prison, and was ruled by Ti-ts'ang. (*See also* **Taoist** *below*.)

East Indies
The Papuan underworld, ruled by Tumudurere, is known as Hiyoyoa and lies under the sea.

Egyptian
The underworld, Amenti, is divided into twelve provinces containing a Hall of Judgement where souls were weighed in the balance by Anubis against a feather in front of Osiris and 42 judges. Those

who pass the test proceed to the paradise Aalu; those who fail are condemned to everlasting torment.

Inuit

(1) The home of the good dead is known as Qudlivum as opposed to Adlivum, the undersea world for sinners, some of whom suffer less torment in the lower section known as Adliparmiut.

(2) The souls of the dead of the Caribou Inuit go to the house of Pana, a realm in the sky which is full of holes to allow rain to fall. Here they are born again and brought back to earth by the moon and live out another life, sometimes as humans, sometimes as animals or birds.

Greek

Tartarus, ruled by Hades, had three sections, the Asphodel Fields, Erebus and Elysium.

Hindu

In Patala, the record of each soul is read out by Chitragupta and judged by Yama. As a result, the soul may be sent to heaven, to one of the many hells or back to earth for reincarnation.

Hell itself has 28 (or 21) regions, each reserved for a particular type of sinner. Some of these regions are

Asipatravana for heretics
Avichimat for liars
Kalasutra for those who have killed a Brahmin
Krimibhoja for the selfish
Kumbhika for the cruel
Raurava for sadists
Suchimikha for misers
Sukramukha for tyrants
Tamusra for adulterers and robbers
Vajrakantaka for those who married into another caste
The river Vaitarani is used to punish religious dissidents. (*See also* **Patala**.)

Irish

The underworld is variously Tech Duinn, envisaged as an island to the south-west of Ireland, the Land of Women (Tir nam Ban) when regarded as ruled by a goddess, or Sid, the Land of the Fairies, or Dun Scaith, ruled by Midir, the god of the underworld.

Jain

The Jain hell has seven layers, the lowest of which is Mahatuma. Another, filled with hot sand, is known as Valuka, home of the Valu. Fiendish tortures are applied by various underworld gods.

Japanese *see* **Shinto**

New Zealand

The Maori home of the ordinary dead is Lua-a-Milu under the earth or the sea; the souls of the exalted go to an island in the sky, the home of the gods. Other accounts refer to the nether world of Reinga or Uranga-o-te-Ra.

Norse

Niflheim, said to be beneath the earth and bounded by the river Giall. Spirits of the slain warriors went to Valhalla in Asgard, home of the gods, or were taken by the goddess Freya to her palace, but others entered Niflheim by crossing the bridge over the Giall guarded by the skelton-like figure of Modgud to whom they had to pay a tribute of blood. Next came the area of Ironwood where the trees had metal leaves and then the entrance gates guarded by the dog Garm. Inside, in the cold and darkness, was Elvidnir, the hall of Hel, ruler of Niflheim, where spirits were judged. Criminals were consigned to Nastrond and were eaten by the serpent Nidhogg.

North America

(1) The Cherokee envisage a world below which is the exact counterpart of their own world except that the seasons are reversed.

(2) The Klamath underworld is known as the Place of the Dark.

(3) Some tribes, including the Navaho, regard the underworld as the place where their ancestors came from, rather than as the home of the dead.

(4) The Omaha dead reach a seven-layered underworld by way of the Milky Way, directed by an old man who sits there.

Pacific Islands

(1) The Banks Islanders called the underworld Panoi.

(2) In the Carolines, the good dead go to Pachet, a paradise under the sea; the others go to Pueliko, a gloomy hell under the earth.

Another version says there is a heaven in the sky for those who can reach it in the form of sea birds, another reserved for warriors where they can carry on their profession and a third for women who die in childbirth. This last one is situated where earth and sky meet.

(3) The Fijian underworld is Bulu and only the married can go there – single men are smashed to death on the rocks by Nangananga, the goddess of punishment. The married man must be provided with the tooth of a whale which he must throw at a particular tree. Hitting it, he is allowed to proceed; if he misses, he is sent back to the grave. Those that pass now meet their former wives and they travel

on together. If he defeats the demon that attacks them, they can proceed; if not, he is eaten by the demon. Passing through the two caves, Cibaciba and Drakulu, couples are taken by boat to Nabangatai and then before Dengei who acts as their judge.

(4) In Hawaii, the underworld is known as Hawaiki or Poluta and is the home of the spirits of the dead, either in the sky or under the earth.

(5) In the Marquesas, they envisage one superior heaven for gods and three lower ones for the rest, graded from the top (the harshest) to the most pleasant at the bottom. Where the soul ends up depends on the number of pigs sacrificed by the dead man during his lifetime.

(6) In Melanesia, the afterworld is Bwebweso, ruled by the goddess Sinebomatu and her husband Kekewage. Most spirits reach this hill of the dead when sufficiently rotted, though some are condemned to roam the hill of lice, Koiakutu, and those who have been mutilated in life become fish with human heads living in a swamp at the foot of the hill. Others refer to Kibu which is envisaged as an island, home of the dead, far off to the west.

(7) The people of Mindanao call their underworld Gimokodan. One part contains the spirits of slain warriors, the other contains all the other dead. A giantess with many nipples suckles the spirits of dead infants.

(8) In the New Hebrides, the underworld is known as Banoi or Abokas.

(9) In some parts of the the Philippines the underworld is known as Maglawa, in others it is Kilot, the home of the left-hand kalaloa (soul). The right-hand one goes to a heaven in the sky.

(10) The Polynesian underworld is also known as Hawaika.

(11) In Samoa the underworld is known as Poluta. The Tongan underground is also called Poluta.

(12) In the Society Islands, some versions say that Po is the underworld where the soul is deified after being eaten three times by a god.

(13) In Tahiti, the underworld is known as Kahiki.

Persian
Souls were assessed by three judges, Mithra, Rashnu and Sraosha. The worthy crossed a bridge to heaven, the unworthy fell into a place of torment known as Druj.

Shinto
Yomi, a hell with two entrances, containing a huge chasm into which all the waters of the earth discharge, Yomi-tsu-kuni, 'land of gloom'.

South American
(1) In Bolivia it is said that the soul travels to the land of Grandfather. First it must cross two rivers, one by ferry, the other by a floating log. Those who fall off are eaten by fish. Next they are judged by Izoi-tamoi (Grandfather) who splits evil ones in half. Those who pass the test journey through a land of darkness using as a torch a small straw which had been placed in the grave. Gathering feathers from the humming-bird to give to Izoi-tamoi, they then must pass between the clashing rocks known as Hacaru. Having been tested by a gallinazo bird, tickled by a monkey and passed the speaking tree, they finally reach the land of Grandfather where live happily, much as they had done on earth.

(2) In Brazil, the Caingang Indians say that the dead are instructed by the tribal shaman on how to survive the dangerous journey to the underworld where it is always day, youth is restored and the forests are full of game to be hunted. But first the soul must avoid the path that leads to a giant spider's web, a trap in the form of a boiling pit and a slippery path where one false step will throw the soul into the lair of a giant crab. The happy life ends in a second death when the individual becomes some form of insect. When that insect dies it is the final end.

(3) The Incas believe that their ancestors came from the underworld which many tribes regard as the source of life on earth.

Sumerian
The underworld was known as Kur-nu-gi-a or Makan.

Taoist
Yellow Springs, sited on the sacred mountain of the east, T'ai Shan, was divided into ten hells for different types of sinner. (See also *Ten Yama Kings*.)

Thai
The underworld realm, Patal, is ruled by Maiyarab. Entering it through the hollow stalk of the lotus, souls must cross a lake guarded by Machanu before being judged.

Welsh
The underworld is known as Annwfn and is ruled by Arawn.

undine   *European*
An elemental spirit, guardian of water. It was said that these

beings were born without a soul but could acquire one if they married humans and bore children.

Undry *Irish*

A magic cauldron owned by the god, the Dagda. The cauldron, which was never empty, provided food for all according to their worthiness. It also had the power to restore life to the dead.

Ungud *Australian*

A creator-being living underground in the form of a serpent. He is said to have helped the sky god Wallanganda in the creation of the world, causing rain to fall.

unicorn

= *Chinese* ch'i-lin; *Greek* monoceros; *Japanese* kirin; *Mongolian* kere; *Tibetan* serou, tso'po

A monster in the form of a horse with a single horn. Other descriptions of the unicorn include:

a horse with the head of a dragon and the legs of a deer, which emits flame at its tail and its joints;

a horse with the head of a stag, the feet of an elephant and a horn three feet in length;

a white horse with cloven hoofs and spiral horns, a beard like a goat and a lion's tail;

a white horse with a red head and blue eyes, the legs of a deer and a red, black and white horn. This animal was variously described as being as big as a goat, a horse or an elephant and its horn as being four inches and four feet in length.

Some say that the unicorn was too large to enter the ark at the time of the Flood; others that it did enter but was thrown overboard and left to drown. It could be captured or killed if a maiden sat under a tree and waited for it to emerge from its lair. The animal would then lay his head on her lap, admiring her beauty and could easily be taken by a hunter. Some versions say that the unicorn died in the virgin's lap but not before suckling at her breast.

It was regarded as a symbol of purity and marriage and was said to have the power of purifying polluted water while others say that any person who drinks from the horn of a unicorn will never be ill. It was said that a unicorn could tell whether water was poisoned merely by dipping a hoof into it. An ointment made from the unicorn's liver would cure leprosy and a belt made from its hide would ward off illness. The stories of the health-giving properties of the horn led to its adoption as the symbol of the apothecaries.

Unktahe *North American*

A spirit of the Sioux in the form of a huge water snake.

In the first age, Wakan Tanka created human beings and the monstrous Unktahe and her brood, thinking they were ants, drowned them with water spouting from their horns. Wakan Tanka and the other Thunderbirds killed all the monsters with their thunderbolts.

In another version, Unktahe lived in the sea but, once in a while, came up the River Missouri, causing floods. The beast had only one vulnerable spot but this was known to twin boys who killed the monster with a well-aimed arrow. They cut out its heart and buried it, and found it gave them powers of prophecy until they allowed others to see it, when it exploded.

Unkulunkulu *African*

A creator-god and sky god of the Zulus. He was an androgynous deity, created from a reed, who made mankind from grass or reeds.

unseelie court *Scottish*

Malevolent spirits or fairies.

upas *East Indies*

A fabulous tree of Java, said to poison everything within miles.

Urania *Greek*

also Ourania

One of the nine Muses – the Muse of astronomy.

Uranus *Greek'*

also Ouranos;

= *Roman* Caelus, Coelus

One of the elder gods; son and husband of Gaea; father of the Cyclopes, the Hundred-handed Giants and the Titans; father of Aphrodite by Hemera, some say.

When he confined the unruly Cyclopes to Tartarus, his sons, the Titans, led by Cronus, rose against him. Cronus castrated his father and took over the throne of the gods. The blood from the wound fertilised Gaea and produced the Furies and Giants.

Urashima *Japanese*

A young fisherman. He married a sea maiden, Otohime, daughter of the Dragon King, whom he had caught in the form of a tortoise, and lived under the sea, never aging. When he returned to visit his parents, Otohime gave him a box to ensure his safe return to their undersea palace. On land, he found everything changed and it transpired that he had been away for 300 years, although it had seemed like a few days. He opened the box, from which a small cloud emerged and floated away and he immediately grew old and died.

Urda   *Norse*
One of the three Norns – the past, fate. She was regarded as the chief of the Norns and is depicted as an old woman looking backwards.

Urdarbrunn   *Norse*
also Urda's well
A sacred well in Midgard. This well or fountain, situated beside that root of the world-tree Yggdrasil which leads up to Asgard and guarded by the three Norns, was so holy that nobody was allowed to drink from it.

urisk   *Scottish*
A supernatural being; a brownie.

urna   *Buddhist*
A tuft of woolly hair, a third eye or a small jewel between the eyebrows of Shiva or the Buddha.

Ursanapi   *Mesopotamian*
A ferryman in the underworld. He was Utnapishtim's boatman during the Flood and carried Gilgamesh across the waters of death to meet Utanapishtim.

ushabti *see* **shabti**

ushi-oni   *Japanese*
A sea monster in the form of a whale-like dragon.

Usiququmadevu   *African*
A Zulu river monster. This huge monster swallowed the maiden Untombinde, the soldiers sent to rescue her, and all her tribe except one man. He managed to kill the monster which then disgorged unharmed all the people it had swallowed.

Utgard   *Norse*
The chief city of the giants in Jotunheim; an illusory city

conjured up by the Frost Giants to confuse Thor and Loki.

Uther Pendragon   *British*
King of Britain; father of King Arthur.

When his brother, King Constans, was killed by Vortigern, Uther and his brother Aurelius Ambrosius were sent to the court of King Budicius in Brittany to escape from Vortigern but returned later to kill him by burning him in his castle.

In one story, they reappeared as the dragons buried on Mount Erith (Snowdon) by the sky god Llud and released when Vortigern, building his castle there, uncovered the cavern where they were buried. They flew off to Brittany, returning later in human form at the head of an army, burning down Vortigern's castle and recapturing the kingdom. One version says that Uther met and defeated the invading forces of Vortigern's son Paschent, killing both Paschent and Gillomar who was helping him.

Uther became king on the death of his brother Aurelius and, from the dragon that appeared in the sky as a portent of his brother's death, he took the name Pendragon.

He fell in love with Igraine when she came to his court with her husband, Gorlois, who took her back to Cornwall and locked her in a tower. Uther invaded Cornwall and the magician Merlin gave him the form of Gorlois so that he was able to gain access to Igraine, fathering the future king, Arthur. After the death of Gorlois, Igraine and Uther married and, in some versions, they had a daughter, Anna.

He was poisoned by a Saxon, leaving the throne to a very young Arthur.

One version has it that Uther promised the offspring of his liason to Merlin in return for giving him access to Igraine. When Uther objected to handing over the baby Arthur, Merlin blinded the king and took the child. Another version says that Uther died childless and that Arthur was brought in by the sea and found by Merlin.

Utiu   *Central American*
A coyote. In Mayan lore, one of the four animals which brought the maize from which the gods created human beings.

Utnapishtim   *Mesopotamian*
= *Babylonian* Atrahasis; *Sumerian* Ziusudra
An Assyrian king. He and his wife were the survivors of the Flood, as told in Assyrian legend. They landed on Mount Nisu when the waters subsided and, like the Sumerian Ziusudra, they were made immortal and became the ancestors of a new race of human beings.

Utset   *North American*
also Mother of the People
One of two sisters, ancestresses of the human race. She was the ancestor of all the Indian tribes; her sister, Nowutset, engendered all other races. When the Flood came, Utset led her people through a hollow reed into the upper world where they now live. She took the stars with her in a sack but they were spilled and scattered throughout the heavens.

Some say that she gave the stars in a sack to Ishits and told him to take them to the underworld but he bit a hole in the bag and many stars escaped. Those remaining, she herself placed in the sky as the Great Bear, Orion and the Pleiades.

Utset planted her own heart from which grew maize and other crops to feed the tribes.

Uttuku   *Mesopotamian*
Akkadian monsters with the body of a man and the head and limbs of an animal. These monsters become the evil Sebettu who cause eclipses and other disasters.

Uzume   *Japanese*
A Shinto goddess of dancing and merrymaking. She came down to earth with the god Ninigi and some say that she became his wife, although the story of his coming relates that he gave her to the giant Deity of the Field Paths who had helped him restore order on earth.

Uzume danced in front of the cave in which the goddess Amaterasu had hidden after she had been affronted by the ox-headed god Susanowa, enticing her to emerge.

In some accounts, she was a goddess of the dawn, though others say that that post was held by her sister, Waka-hime.

V

Vafthruthnir *Norse*
The wisest of the giants. He made a practice of killing those who, in a contest of knowledge, failed to tell him something he did not already know. He took part in such a contest of knowledge with Odin who was disguised as Gangrad and who wished to test his own newly-acquired wisdom resulting from drinking at the Well of Knowledge – the loser to forfeit his life. At the end of the near-equal contest, the giant recognised his opponent and declared himself to be the loser. He was killed by Odin.

Vaikuntha *Hindu*
Heaven, the home of Vishnu on Mount Meru.

Vaimanika *Jain*
The gods inhabiting the vaimana, the flying palace of the gods.

Vainamoinen *Baltic*
A Finnish magician-hero, credited with the invention of music and the zither.

His mother Ilmatar floated in the primordial ocean for 700 years and was made pregnant by Ahti, the god of the waters. It was said that Vainamoinen was so long in the womb that he was an old man when he was born. In some accounts, he also floated in the primordial waters for many years. An eagle laid its egg on his knee and, when it fell off and broke open, the shell became the earth and sky. A similar story is told of his mother, Ilmatar.

When the sky god Ukko sent fire to earth in the form of a thunderbolt, it was swallowed by a fish. Vainamoinen caught the fish and recovered the fire from its stomach.

He fought the giant Joukahainen and buried him chin-deep in a bog. Joukahainen gave him his sister, Aino, as the price for being released but she jumped into the sea rather than marry an old man. He then sought a wife in Pohjola, the realm of the ice-giants, and the ice-giantess Louhi promised him her daughter if he would make her a sampo (an object which grants wishes). The daughter also imposed a number of near-impossible tasks, such as tying a knot in an egg, which he failed to complete only because three evil spirits caused him to cut himself with an axe.

When building a boat, he recited spells that bound the various parts securely together, but when he came to build a boat as one of the tasks set by Louhi's daughter, he forgot the appropriate words and could find them nowhere on earth, so he went to Tuonela, the underworld. He escaped the clutches of Tuonetar by turning himself into a steel serpent and returned home empty-handed. He next went to the giant Antero Vipunen who swallowed him but Vainamoinen hammered on his heart until the giant released him and told him the magic words he needed to complete the building of the ship. When the ship was finished, he returned to Pohjola where Ilmarinen had made the required sampo. Unhappily, Louhi's daughter had married Ilmarinen in preference to his brother Vainamoinen. He later returned to Pohjola with his brothers Ilmarinen and Lemminkainen and stole the sampo but it was broken when Louhi caused a storm that wrecked his ship. He saved some of the fragments of the sampo which alone brought prosperity to the land.

In one story Vainamoinen caused a fir-tree to grow until it reached the sky and Ilmarinen climbed the tree in a vain attempt to capture the moon.

Another story tells how Vainamoinen played such beautiful music on his kantele (an instrument like a zither) that even the sun and moon came down to listen and were captured by the mistress of Pohjola. Vainamoinen found them and released them.

He finally left the earth, sailing off in a copper boat.

vainnan tytto   *Baltic*
also vainnan tytar
Finnish water maidens.

vajra   *Hindu*
= *Tibetan* dorje
The thunderbolt of Indra.

Valac   *European*
A demon, one of the 72 Spirits of Solomon. He is said to be the ruler of reptiles and can indicate the site of hidden treasure. He appears as a small boy with wings, astride a two-headed dragon.

Valhalla   *Norse*
The hall of the chosen slain or palace of the dead in Asgard; heaven.

This palace of Odin was situated in the grove of Glasir and was said to have 540 huge doors. The walls were composed of shining spears, the roof of golden shields. The 800 occupants fought and died every day and were revived every night, training to fight on the side of the gods in the final battle, Ragnarok.

The building was destroyed after Ragnarok.

Valhamr   *Norse*
also falcon garb, Feather Cloak
A flying-suit owned by the goddess Freya. This garment enabled the wearer to fly. Freya occasionally lent it to others.

Valkyries   *Norse*
also Battle Maidens, Shield Maidens
Minor goddesses acting as handmaidens of Freya and choosers of the slain. It was the work of the Valkyries to decide who should fall in battle and to bring the bodies of some of the fallen to Valhalla; the others were taken by Freya. Those chosen for Valhalla were destined to fight on the side of the gods at Ragnarok and, having conducted the warriors to Valhalla, the Valkyries then waited on their needs.

Some depict them as bloodthirsty giants, rather than maidens, and various accounts put their numbers at three, six, nine or twenty-seven. They had the ability to put on swan-plumage and fly down to earth and, on one occasion, three of them (Alvit, Olrun and Svanhvit) left their wings on the shore while they bathed. The brothers Egil, Slagfinn and Volund seized the wings and kept the maidens as their wives for nine years.

Some say Valkyries could change into wolves or ravens.

Vamana   *Hindu*
The fifth incarnation of Vishnu, as a dwarf.

The king Bali tried to take over the powers of Indra. The dwarf asked him for just three paces of land and then became an enormous being whose three paces would have covered the whole world. He took only two steps, covering heaven and earth, leaving the third pace, the underworld Patala, to Bali.

Others say that he kept the whole universe when he covered it in three steps and forced Bali down into the underworld.

vampire
A monster leaving the grave to suck blood from the living; the spirit of one excommunicated, a heretic, etc. It is said that a vampire can be killed only by driving a stake through its heart or by shooting it with a silver bullet.

Vanaheim   *Norse*
The home of the Vanir under the earth or, some say, in the air and sea.

Vanavasa   *Buddhist*
One of the Eighteen Lohan. He is depicted in a contemplative posture, sitting inside a cave.

Vanir   *Norse*
singular Van
The later deities of the Norse pantheon, earth gods, deities of fertility, sea and wind.

Some accounts say that they preceded the Aesir, others that they were later arrivals from the east. They waged war with the Aesir for many years but finally made peace, exchanging hostages as a safeguard against future strife.

Vapula   *European*
A demon, one of the 72 Spirits of

Solomon. He is said to impart knowledge of science and philosophy and appears as a winged lion.

Var   *Persian*
A cave or enclosure built by the semi-divine Yima in which he and the selected species survived the Flood.

Varaha[1]   *Hindu*
In Vedic myth, a manifestation of Brahma. In this version, Brahma dived to the bottom of the primordial ocean, seeking the root of the lotus which floated on the surface, and discovered land. He changed into a huge boar and raised the land above the surface of the ocean on his back.

Another story says that the earth was so overpopulated that the weight of the people caused the earth to sink. The boar lifted it back into position on one tusk. When he moves the earth from one tusk to another, an earthquake results.

Varaha[2]   *Hindu*
The third incarnation of Vishnu, as a boar. In this incarnation he fought, for a thousand years, and finally killed the giant Hiranyaksha who had dragged the earth down to the sea-bottom.

Varuna   *Hindu*
also Lord of the Ocean;
= *Greek* Poseidon; *Japanese* Ryujin
A creator-god, ruler of the heavens, the night sky, seas and rivers. He resigned in favour of Indra and became a sea god with his own heaven, Pushpagiri, in the sea.

He is depicted as having four heads, 1000 arms and a fat stomach and may ride on a fish or in a seven-horse chariot or on the water-monster, Makara.

Vassago   *European*
A demon, one of the 72 Spirits of Solomon. He is said to be able to impart knowledge of the past and the future.

Vassilisa   *Russian*
A peasant girl. When her mother died, she gave Vassilisa a doll which would protect her. Her father then married again and his new wife and her two daughters became jealous of Vassilisa and sent her on an errand to the witch Baba-Yaga, hoping that she would be killed. The witch gave the girl several near-impossible tasks which, with the help of the doll, Vassilisa was able to accomplish. She waited until the witch fell asleep and then ran home, taking one of the many skulls from the witch's house. This skull had glowing eyes and it burned the stepmother and her daughters to ashes. Thereafter, Vassilisa lived happily with her old father.

Vedfolnir   *Norse*
A falcon which sat on an eagle perched on the highest branch of the world-tree Yggdrasil and watched and reported on all that happened in the realms below.

Veil of Invisibility   *Irish*
A protective cloak that made Danaans invisible to mortals and gave them immortality. This cloak was said to have been one of the three gifts to the Danaans by the god Manannan. The others were the Feast of Giobhniu and the Pigs of Manannan.

Venus   *Roman*
= *Greek* Aphrodite, Charis
Goddess of beauty, gardens, love and springs; one of the five Appiades; wife of Vulcan. Originally an Italic goddess of vegetation, Venus was

adopted into the Roman pantheon and was given the attributes of the Greek Aphrodite. The Romans claim that she was the mother of Aeneas.

In some accounts, she was carried on the back of, or turned into, a fish to escape the monster Typhon. The pair of them are represented in the heavens as Pisces.

Vepar   *European*
A demon, one of the 72 Spirits of Solomon. He is said to control the seas and can cause storms that wreck ships, appearing as a mermaid.

Veralden-olmai   *Baltic*
= *Norse* Frey
A Lapp supreme god, said to support the heavens.

Veralden-shuold   *Baltic*
Trees which help Veralden-olmai to support the world. These trees, which are erected at altars, are daubed with the blood of animals sacrificed.

Verdandi   *Norse*
One of the three Norns – the present, being. She is depicted as youthful and active.

Verethragna   *Persian*
= *Greek* Hercules; *Hindu* Indra
A god of victory, one of the Yazatas. This four-faced, irresistible god had ten incarnations – a wind, a golden-horned bull, a white horse, a camel, a boar, a fifteen-year-old youth, a bird (Varagna), a ram, a buck and a man with a golden sword. As a boar, he was used by Mithra to kill his enemies.

He was born in the primordial ocean and, in some accounts, overcame a demon, Azhi Dahak, chaining him to Mount Demavand.

Vermilion Bird *see* **Feng**

Vesta   *Roman*
= *Greek* Hestia

The goddess of fire, the hearth, the household; one of the five Appiades. She is depicted with a bowl and a torch.

A sacred fire in her temple, said to have been brought from Troy by Aeneas, was never allowed to go out and was tended by 6 Vestal Virgins. Each maiden had to serve, tending the fire in the temple and keeping her virginity, for thirty years. Those who broke their vows were buried alive. It is said that only eighteen failed in this way in a thousand years.

Vestri *see* **Westri**

vila   *European*
also veela

A Serbian water sprite. These beings are envisaged as beautiful girls with fair, flowing hair, who are the spirits of the unbaptised dead.

Other stories say that they are the spirits of betrothed maidens who died before they were married. In this form, they are said to roam at night, forcing young men to dance with them until they drop dead from exhaustion.

It was said that they sometimes appeared in the form of swans.

Ville au Camp   *West Indies*
An underwater city, home of the Haitian voodoo spirits.

Vilmund   *Norse*
A hero. He lived with his parents in a remote area and knew no other people. One day, he heard a voice from behind a rock declare that the owner of the shoe, which Vilmund had just found, would marry only the man who returned it to her.

Vilmund then set off to explore the greater world and came to a kingdom ruled by King Visivald and, after defeating the king's son Hjarandi in a wrestling match, became his friend. He joined forces with Hjarandi to destroy the army of a suitor for the hand of Hjarandi's half-sister, Gullbra, and then they killed Kolr who had married Soley, Gullbra's sister. In fact, the girl Kolr had married was a servant-girl substituted for Soley who had disappeared. Her father believed that Vilmund had killed her and banished him. To prove his innocence, Vilmund returned to the rock, handed over the shoe to Soley who was living there and took her back to her father's palace.

Vimana   *Hindu*
The chariot of the gods.

Vindhya   *Hindu*
A mountain. This mountain, in its efforts to grow higher than Mount Meru, threatened to block out the light of the sun. The sage Agastya, at the request of the gods, put a stop to its growth. He merely asked the mountain to pause for a while until he returned – which he never did.

Viné   *European*
A demon, one of the 72 Spirits of Solomon. He is said to be able to build impregnable towers and can impart knowledge of the past and the future. He appears as a lion on a black horse.

Viracocha   *South American*
also Kon-tiki

An ancient Peruvian creator-god, storm god and sun god, recognised by the Incas. He is said to have emerged from Lake Titicaca or from the Pacari cave. He destroyed in a flood the humans created by an earlier god, or by his own unsuccessful efforts, and made new races appropriate to their environment, travelling amongst them, teaching them the basic skills. He finally disappeared over the Pacific, walking on the water.

He is depicted as crowned with the sun and holding thunderbolts.

Virava   *Baltic*
A Finnish goddess of the woods. She can appear either as an animal, a flame or a whirlwind. (*See also* **Tapio**.)

Vishnu   *Hindu*
also Lord of Sacred Wisdom, Lord of the Universe

As a preserver of life, the god Vishnu intervenes as an avatar whenever evil becomes dominant, making it hard for men to progress upwards. In this capacity, he has ten incarnations:

1. Matsya, a fish
2. Kurma, a tortoise
3. Varaha or Keseva, a boar
4. Narasinha, a man/lion
5. Vamana, a dwarf
6. Parashurama, son of a hermit
7. Rama (Ramachandra), a mortal
8. Krishna (or Balarama)
9. Buddha

with the 10th, as Kalki, a white horse, yet to come.

Some versions say that Krishna is a god in his own right and that the eighth incarnation was as Balarama. Lakshmi appeared in each of his incarnations and married him. In addition, there are said to be between 16 and 39 minor avatars.

He gave his wife Ganga to Shiva and Sarasvati to Brahma when he found that three wives were more than he could cope with.

His weapons are the sword Handaka, the bow Sarnga and the

discus, and he is transported by the sun-bird, Garuda.

He is generally depicted as a handsome, dark blue youth with four hands in which he holds a club, a discus, a lotus blossom and a shell but is sometimes shown in a combined form with Shiva on the right and Vishnu on the left. They combined thus to defeat the demon Guha since neither could defeat him single-handed.

(*See also* **Jagannath**.)

Vishvakarma   *Hindu*

A creator-god and god of artisans; an aspect of Brahma, Indra or Prajapani.

The brilliance of Surya the sun god was too overpowering for his wife, Sanjna, so her father Vishvakarma shaved away some of his power on a lathe. He used the shavings to make Vishnu's discus, Shiva's trident, and, some say, the elephant Airavata. He is said to have established the art and science of architecture, built chariots for the gods, a hall for Yudhishthira (a brother of Arjuna) and the city of Chandrapura, and created the monkey-king, Nala. He is also credited with the creation of Jagannath when he attempted to put new flesh on the bones of the dead Vishnu and was interrupted by Krishna so that the job was never completed, leaving the deformed version.

Vision Serpent   *Central American*

A Mayan creation spirit. This being is sometimes depicted as spitting out gods or kings.

vodyanik   *Russian*

A male water spirit, one type of the karliki. These beings can take many different forms, overturning fishermen's boats and drowning swimmers. They often live in

millponds. They use the souls of the drowned as servants on the bottom and allow the dead bodies to float to the surface. They can be propitiated by the sacrifice of a black pig.

In some accounts, their youth is restored with the phases of the moon; in others they may be depicted as fat old men wearing a cap of reeds.

(*See also* **rusalka**.)

Volsung   *Norse*

Grandson of Odin; father of a daughter, Signy, and of Sigmund and nine other sons.

When his father, Rerir, bemoaned the lack of offsprnig, the goddess Frigga sent her messenger, Gna, to drop an apple from the sky. When Rerir's wife ate the apple, she gave birth to Volsung after a seven-year pregnancy. The boy's parents died soon after he was born and he became ruler of Hunaland as a child. His palace had a huge oak, Branstock, into which Odin thrust the sword Gram, growing up through the roof.

His daughter, Signy, married Siggeir, king of the Goths, and, shortly after the wedding, he and his sons paid a visit to Siggeir's country. They were ambushed by the Goths and Volsung was killed.

Volund   *Norse*

= *British* Wayland

King of the Elves; a blacksmith.

When the three swan-maidens, Alvit, Olrun and Svanhvit, flew to earth to bathe, they left their wings on the shore and Volund and his brothers seized the wings and kept the maidens as their wives for nine years until they recovered their wings and flew away. Alvit had given Volund a

ring and, instead of going on a fruitless search for her, he occupied himself with making 700 copies of this ring.

He was captured by Nidud, king of Sweden, who accused him of theft and cut the sinews of Volund's legs, forcing him to work ceaselessly making ornaments and weapons. Volund killed the two sons of Nidud and sent their heads, decorated with precious metals and stones, to their father. He also put Nidud's daughter, Bodwild, into a trance and raped her then, using wings that he had made himself, flew to Alfheim where he was reunited with Alvit. There, he carried on his trade as smith, forging many wonderful weapons including the swords Miming for his son Heime, Balmung for Sigmund, Joyeuse for Charlemagne and, some say, Excalibur for King Arthur.

Vorys-mort   *Russian*

A forest spirit. This being takes the form of a whirlwind to carry off animals and humans. Those who fear to use his real name call him Dyadya, 'Uncle'.

Votan   *Central American*

also Master of the Sacred Drum

A mysterious Mayan god. This deity, who said he was a serpent, claimed that he had been sent to earth by the sky-gods to start a new culture based on his teachings. One of his roles was as guardian of the sacred instrument, the Tepanaguaste.

In some accounts he is identified with Quetzalcoatl or Tepeyollotl.

Vu-murt   *Russian*

A Votyak river god. He is generally regarded as an evil being but is sometimes helpful to fishermen.

He is said to appear on the bank of a river, either as man or a woman, completely naked, combing his or her long black hair, disappearing if a human approaches.

Vual   *European*

A demon, one of the 72 Spirits of Solomon. He can impart knowledge of the past and the future and can cause a woman to fall in love. He appears as a camel or sometimes as a man.

Vulcan   *Roman*

= *Greek* Hephaestus

God of fire and metalwork; son of Jupiter and Juno; husband of Venus.

He was lame as the result of being thrown out of heaven and set up his forge in Mount Etna where he made a golden throne for Juno, the thunderbolts hurled by Jupiter and the arrows for Cupid's bow.

He was the owner of a mirror which could tell the past, the present and the future.

In one story, angered by the infidelities of Venus, he made a special robe. All who wore it became wicked.

vulture

(1) A scavenging bird. Some say that this bird bears live young rather than laying eggs while others say that it can, by dipping its beak into food or drink, tell if has been poisoned. Sweet smells, pomegranates or myrrh were said to kill the vulture.

(2) In Egyptian mythology, the emblem of Isis and Mat; also called Pharaoh's Hen.

(3) In Greek myth, the vulture is the bird of the gods Apollo and Ares.

This bird was also sacred to Hercules, who had killed the vulture that attacked the liver of Prometheus.

(4) To the Romans, it was the bird of Mars.

Vyasa   *Hindu*

A god of wisdom; an incarnation of Vishnu, some say.

He is said to have written the *Vedas* and the *Puranas* together with the *Mahabharata*, which, it is said, he dictated to the god Ganesha. He is said to have been extremely ugly.

W

Wabun *North American*

A sun god and Algonquin hero. He was one of the quadruplets born of the primordial being, who died in childbirth. He represented east; the other three were Kabibonokka (north), Kabun (west) and Shawano (south). He chased away darkness, heralding the day.

Wabun's wife was Wabund Annung, the morning star.

Wacabe *see* **Black Bear**[2]

Wadjet *Egyptian*

also Edjo, Lady of Heaven, Queen of Gods, Udjat

A snake-goddess of Lower Egypt. She is depicted as a cobra which breathes fire and represents the pharaoh's sovereignty. She is said to have created the papyrus swamps and to have suckled the infant Horus.

Wagu *Australian*

A culture-hero of the Aborigines. He and Biljata laid down rules of marriage to avoid incest. Both became birds as a result of tricks played on each other, Wagu becoming a crow.

Wai-ora-a-Tane *New Zealand*

A river in which the Maori say the moon bathes to restore her health.

Wainadula *Pacific Islands*

A well of forgetfulness. In Fiji it is said that the dead drink the water of this well in order to forget the sorrows of this world.

Wakan Tanka *North American*

also Great Mystery, Thunderbird, Wakonda

A creator-god of the Sioux. He created the four groups of deities known as Superior Gods, Associated Gods, Kindred Gods and Godlike Spirits, all of them regarded as aspects of himself. He then created human beings but the water monster, Unktahe, caused a flood to drown them. Wakan Tanka and his thunderbird followers did battle with the monster and its offspring, killing them with thunderbolts. He split himself into four to make Inyan, Maka, Skan and Wi.

Wakea *Pacific Islands*

An ancestral chief of Hawaii. Although a mortal, he was the husband of the earth goddess, Papa, by whom he had a daughter, Ho'ohoku-ka-lani. His wife left him when he fathered children on his own daughter; the first was a root which grew into a plant, the second was a human, Ha-loa. In one story he made the world from a gourd borne by Papa.

Wakiash *North American*

A Kwakiutl chief. Seeking a dance of his own, he was carried off on the back of a raven. He landed in a house full of animals which had adopted human form and was allowed to take some of their dances and songs. Back home, he found that he had been away not four days but four years. He taught his people the songs and his new dance and made a totem pole, Kalakuyuwish, and took this name for himself.

Wakinyan   *North American*
also Thunderbird
A Thunderbird god, a manifestation of Wakan Tanka. In the lore of the Dakota Indians, they are the Flyers, the deities which bring storm winds.

Wakonda *see* **Wakan Tanka**

Wakonyingo   *African*
Dwarfs living on Mount Kilimanjaro. It is said that these people have very large heads and sleep sitting up because, if they lie down, they cannot get up again unaided. They own ladders with which they can reach the heavens.

wallaby   *East Indies*
A progenitor of the human race. In Papua they say that the maggots that bred in the body of a dead female wallaby turned into the first human beings.

Walleyneup   *Australian*
A supreme god. His son Bindinoor was wounded and Walleyneup, though a god, could not heal his wounds and this son died. As a result, Walleyneup decided that mankind should no longer be immortal.

Wandering Jew   *Christian*
The Jew who insulted Christ as he carried his cross to Calvary. He was condemned to wander for ever the face of the earth and, in some stories, is said to be the leader of the Wild Hunt.

Wandering Rocks *see* **Planctae, Symplegades**

Wandjina   *Australian*
Rain spirits of the Aborigines. Disgusted with the behaviour of the first humans, these beings caused the flood which destoyed them all and then created another, more civilised race. Satisfied with their handiwork,

they became invisible and retreated to live in water-holes.
These beings are depicted as semi-human with a bony face which has no mouth. Sometimes limbs are missing. The Aborigines say that, if the spirit had a mouth, it would rain all the time.
They are said to control the weather and can appear in various forms such as birds and human beings.

Waq-Waq   *Arabian*
A fabulous tree, said to bear fruit in the shape of the heads of animals or humans, the latter being capable of speech.
When Alexander the Great finally reached the islands on which these trees grew (the Waq-Waq Islands, situated at the end of the earth), he was advised by these talking heads to give up further attempts at conquest.

War Brothers, War Twins *see* **Ahayuta achi**

water babies   *North American*
Spirits living in water sources such as streams, lakes, etc. These beings, met with in the lore of several Indian tribes, are small but not necessarily young. They may appear in the guise of an old man who tugs at a fisherman's line or as an old woman who appears on the bank of the stream at dusk.

Water Beetle *see* **Dayunsi**

water-bull
= *Manx* tarroo ushtey; *Scottish* tarbh uisge
An amphibious monster in the form of a bull.

Wati-kutjara   *Australian*
Two lizard-men, Kurukadi and Mumba, creator-ancestors of the Aborignes. They killed Kidilli when he tried to rape one of the first

women. Kidilli became the moon, the women became the Pleiades, and the two lizard-men became the constellation Gemini.

Wave-sweeper *see* **Ocean-sweeper**

Wawalag sisters   *Australian*
Ancestral heroines of the Aborigines. These beings were regarded as the daughters of the elder of the two Djanggawul sisters and in some accounts their names are given as Boaliri and Waimariwi. They angered the snake-spirit Yurlunggur who swallowed them and vomited them up repeatedly. Each time, the green ants revived them.
They are said to have travelled throughout northern Australia, prodding the ground with their sticks. Waterholes formed at each such site.

Wayland   *British*
also Wayland Smith;
= *German* Wieland; *Norse* Volund
The smith-god, god of craftsmen.

Wayland's Smithy   *British*
A megalithic circle in Berkshire, England. A horse left here with some money (6d in former British currency) will be shod by an invisible smith.

weasel
(1) The Chinese say that this animal has the power to bewitch humans.
(2) In Egypt the weasel was regarded as a sacred animal.
(3) In ancient Greece the Thebans worshipped the weasel.
(4) Some tribes of North American Indians say the weasel can detect hidden meanings and, using its fabled insight, it forecast the arrival of the white man.

wedjat *see* **udjat**
Wee Folk *see* **Faylinn**
Weepers *see* **Pleiades**
Well of Knowledge *see*
   Mimisbrunnr

werewolf
A human said to be able to
change into a wolf. In those
cases where people were turned
into wolves by others, it was
said that, if they refrained from
eating human flesh for eight
years, they would be restored to
their human form.
(1) Other animals take the place
of wolves in those places where
the wolf is not feared. Examples
include the bear (North America),
boar (Greece, Turkey), crocodile
(Africa), fox (China, Japan),
hyena (Africa), jaguar (South
America), leopard (Africa), lion
(Africa) and tiger (Borneo, China,
Japan.).
(2) In European belief, a werewolf
removes his skin and resumes his
shape as a human at daybreak
and will die if the skin is found
and destroyed.
(3) A German story says that a
person wearing a belt made from
the skin of a wolf or of a man
who has been hanged will become
a werewolf.
(4) In the lore of some North
American Indians, werewolves
can be either men or women.
It is said that those who can
become werewolves also practise
witchcraft when in their normal
human shape.

Westri   *Norse*
also Vestri
One of the four dwarfs supporting
the sky (west). (*See also* **Austri,
Nordri, Sudri**.)

whale
(1) Arab mythology says that a
whale supports the world on its
back.
(2) In the Judaeo-Christian
tradition, Jonah was saved
from a shipwreck when he
was swallowed by a whale and
vomited safely on shore after
three days.
(3) In Japan the whale was a
protected species, one of which is
said to have saved a shipwrecked
emperor.
(4) In Norse mythology, these
animals were often used as
transport by witches and were
credited with magical powers
(5) Slavic lore says that four of
these animals support the world.
(6) In Taiwan, the whale is said to
have introduced millet to the
island.

Whiskey Jack *see* **Wisagatcak**
White Corn Maiden   *North
                                 American*
This young Tewa maiden was the
prettiest and most talented girl
of her tribe and she fell in love
with their finest hunter, a youth
named Deerhunter. (*See more at*
***Deerhunter*.**)
White Dragon *see* **Pai Lung**
White Feather *see* **Chacopee**
**White Painted Woman, White
   Shell Woman** *see* **Yolkai
   Estsan**
White Snake of Hangchow
                                 Chinese
A monster in the form of a huge
snake. This beast lived for
thousands of years and brought
many disasters on the city. Then
she changed into a woman who
married a young man but, when
she drank some wine, she turned
back into a snake, causing her

husband to flee in terror. A priest
captured her spirit in a box, which
he buried on the shore.
White Tiger *see* **Four Auspicious
   Animals**
White World   *North American*
The fourth of the four worlds
that the Navaho passed through
before emerging into the upper
world. The Navaho arrived here
after being expelled from the
Yellow World.
Wigan   *Pacific Islands*
Brother and husband of Bugan. This
couple were the sole survivors
of the Flood in the lore of the
Philippines.
Wild Hunt   *European*
also Herod's Hunt, Raging Host,
Woden's Hunt
A noisy phantom host rushing
through the sky on horseback
accompanied by a pack of
hounds.
   One explanation of the origins
of the Wild Hunt involves the
Cornish priest, Dando, who was a
keen huntsman. Finding that all
the flasks of his hunting-party
were empty, he declared that
he 'would go to hell for a drink',
whereupon the Devil, in the form
of a huntsman, gave him a full cup
but then put Dando in front of
him on his horse which galloped
off with both of them. When they
crossed a stream, fire blazed from
the water and horse, riders and
dogs disappeared for ever.
   Anyone who sees the Wild Hunt
is likely to suffer some injury or
even death but such results can
be avoided by asking the riders
for parsley.
   Those who mocked the spirits
could be whisked away; those
who joined in the hullabaloo
might be rewarded with the leg

of a horse thrown down from the sky which would miraculously turn into gold the following day. The Hunt presaged an on-coming storm, a plague, the outbreak of war or some similar misfortune. On occasions, a black dog would be left behind by the Hunt and this could be exorcised only by brewing beer in egg-shells. Some say the hunt was led by King Arthur, others that it was chasing a criminal, Tregeagle.

(*See also* **Devil's Dandy Dogs, Gabriel's Hounds, Hounds of Hell**.)

Wild Huntsman   *European*
The leader of the Wild Hunt.
    Among suggested leaders have been Cain, Charlemagne, the Erlkonig, Gabriel, Hel, Hermes, Herne, Herod, King Arthur, Odin or the Wandering Jew.

Wild Reindeer Buck *see* **Elwe'kyen**

Winjarning Brothers   *Australian*
Two great sorcerers or medicine-men. These brothers spent the whole of their lives helping those who appealed to them for help and were responsible for the extermination of the Keen Keengs and many other monsters.

wirricow   *Scottish*
also worricow, worrycow
A hobgoblin.

Wisagatcak   *North American*
also Whiskey Jack, Wolverine;
= *Fox* Wisaka
A trickster-god of the Cree Indians. He annoyed the great god Gitchi Manitou by stirring up trouble between humans and animals, so the supreme god sent a flood which only a few (including Wisagatcak) survived to repopulate the world.
    Another version says that

when he failed to spear a beaver, he brought down their dam. The beavers used their magic to keep the waters flowing until they covered the whole world. Wisagatcak made a raft and saved as many animals as he could. Several died trying to find land under the waters and finally the wolf spread moss over the raft. Earth grew in the moss and kept on growing until it covered the raft and finally the whole world.

Wise Lord *see* **Ahura Mazda**

Wish Hunt   *British*
A version of the Wild Hunt. This version is said to have been seen over Dartmoor in the south of England, and is led by the Midnight Hunter accompanied by his pack of Wish Hounds. (*See also* **Yeth Hounds**.)

Wishpoosh   *North American*
A monster in the form of a beaver. The Nez Percé Indians, in whose lore this monster appears, are his descendants. The trickster-god, Coyote, fought a titanic battle with the monster, winning when he turned himself first into a branch that the monster swallowed and then back into his normal shape, stabbing the monster in the heart. Coyote then created new tribes from the immense carcase of Wishpoosh.

wivern   *British*
also wyvern
A winged monster in the form of a dragon with two legs. The wingless form of this beast is known as the lindworm.

Wo   *African*
Zamba, the supreme god of the Yaunde people, allowed his four sons to make human beings and Wo the chimpanzee made the inquisitive ones.

Wodan   *German*
= *Anglo-Saxon* Woden; *Norse* Odin
A war god; the German form of Odin.

Woden   *Anglo-Saxon*
= *German* Wodan; *Norse* Odin
A war god; the Anglo-Saxon form of Odin.

Woden's Hunt *see* **Wild Hunt**

Wolf[1]   *North American*
A creator-deity of the Shoshone.
    Coyote asked Wolf to restore his son who had been killed by a snake-bite but Wolf reminded him of an earlier discussion in which Coyote had said that the dead should not be brought back to life, otherwise the world would soon become overcrowded.

Wolf[2] *see* **Malsum**

wolf
(1) In Greece, the wolf was regarded as the animal of the gods Apollo and Ares.
(2) In Egypt, the wolf was sacred to Wepwawet, god of the underworld.
(3) In Irish lore, a she-wolf suckled Cormac mac Airt, a high-king of Ireland.
(4) In Norse mythology, Fenris is a monster in the form of a wolf; the wolves Hati, Managarm and Skoll forever chased the sun and moon; the god Odin had two pet wolves known as Freki and Geri; and the Valkyries were said to ride on wolves.
(5) Some North American tribes say that a man's soul can pass into a wolf while others claim wolves as their ancestors.
(6) Roman lore claims that Romulus and Remus, the founders of Rome, were suckled by a she-wolf.
    It was also said that, if a man saw a wolf with its mouth shut,

the beast would never be able to open it again. On the other hand, if a wolf saw a man with his mouth shut, that man would lose the power of speech.

Wolf-Man   *North American*
A creator-deity of the Arikara. He and Lucky Man appeared over the primordial waters and created the world from soil brought up by ducks. Wolf Man created the prairies while Lucky Man created the hills and valleys.

Wolf Prey God   *North American*
One of the six Prey Gods guarding the home of Poshaiyangkyo. He is responsible for the east.

Wolverine *see* **Wisagatcak**

Wonomi   *North American*
The creator-god of the Maidu people. He and Coyote created the first man and woman from wooden images and showed them how to revivify the dead by immersing them in a lake. He was eventually deposed by Coyote and retreated to the heavens.

woodhouse   *British*
also woodwose
A satyr or faun; a minor woodland god; a god of shepherds.

woodpecker   *Greek*
A bird sacred to the war god Ares; also, a form sometimes assumed by the god Zeus.

Woodtick   *North American*
A character in one of the stories about Coyote. She gave Coyote meat when he was starving and he went to live with her. She kept them well supplied with meat by calling the deer to her tent where she pierced the ears of two and let the rest go free. Coyote thought that he could do the same so he killed

Woodtick. When he tried to do what she had done, all the meat in the tent turned into deer and ran away and Coyote was soon starving again.

World Serpent *see* **Ananta, Iormungandr**
World Tree *see* **Yggdrasil**
worm   *British*
An old name for a dragon or serpent.

worricow, worrycow *see* **wirricow**
Wounded King *see* **Fisher King**
wren   *Norse*
In Norse stories, the wren was regarded as the king of the birds. This title was awarded to the bird which could fly nearest to the sun. The eagle flew higher than any of the other birds in the contest but lost to the wren who, cunningly, had ridden on the eagle's back.
    In another story, a siren who lured men to their death at sea escaped death herself only by turning into a wren. The bird returned every year, was killed, but always came again the following year.

wu *see* **t'ien-wu**
Wu Chi   *Chinese*
The unlimited state that arose when the Tao, the all-pervading basis of being, came into existence. It is said that from this state came Hun-tun, the state of chaos, from which evolved time and space.

Wu Kang   *Chinese*
A man in the moon. He was banished to the moon when he upset the spirits. His punishment condemned him everlastingly to chop down a cassia tree but every cut of the axe immediately closed up so that he never completed the job.

In other versions he was set to chop down cinnamon trees but, as fast he cut them down, they grew again.

Wu-k'o   *Chinese*
One of the Eighteen Lohan, in some accounts. He is said to have lived in a tree and is depicted in this situation.

Wu Yüeh   *Chinese*
also Five Holy Mountains
Five mountains regarded as the home of the gods. These are named as Heng Shan (in Hunan), Heng Shan (in Shansi), Hua Shan, Sung Shan and T'ai Shan. The celestial Ministry of the Five Sacred Mountains (also known as Wu Yüeh) is run by Tung Yüeh Ta Ti.

Wyrd   *Norse*
A goddess of fate. In some accounts, she is the same as Urda; in others she is all three of the Fates (Norns) in one; in others, she is their mother.

Wurruri   *Australian*
An old woman in the lore of the Aborigines. It was said that she was responsible for the fact that the tribes spoke different languages. In life, she had a habit of scattering fires with the stick she carried and, when she died, people celebrated and ate her body. Those eating different parts of the body thereafter spoke different languages.

Wyungare   *Australian*
A legendary hunter. He was created from excrement and grew to be a great hunter. He tied a rope to his spear and threw it into the heavens and then he and his two wives climbed the rope into the sky where they are now seen as stars.

wyvern *see* **wivern**

Xelhua *Central American*
An Aztec culture-hero. He was a giant who survived the Flood by climbing to the top of a mountain.

Another version says that he built a brick tower to escape the flood but the building was struck by lightning and destroyed.

Xhindi *Balkan*
Albanian spirits. These beings are usually beneficent and betray their presence in the house by causing stairs to creak and lights to flicker.

Xibalba *Central American*
The Mayan underworld or, in some versions, its inhabitants or its ruler Vucub-Caquix.

Xipetotec *Central American*
An Aztec flayed god of agriculture, fortune, metallurgists and spring. He is regarded as an aspect of Tezcatlipoca, Nanahuatl or Quetzalcoatl.

In one aspect he brought food to man by allowing himself to be skinned alive; in another he is responsible for many of the diseases that afflict mankind.

He could be envisaged in any one of three different forms: a spoonbill, a blue cotinga (a species of bird) or a tiger, representing heaven, earth and hell or fire, earth and water, but was most often depicted as a red god carrying a round shield.

Xithuthros *Mesopotamian*
A survivor of the Flood. He is variously described as Armenian, Babylonian and Chaldaean. In the Babylonian version he was a king of Babylon. He built an ark in which he and his family and a few others survived the Flood. When the ark landed on the sacred mountain of Ravandiz, Xithuthros became an immortal.

In some accounts, this is the Greek name for Ziusudra.

Xiuhtecuhtli *Central American*
An Aztec god of fire and volcanoes. He acted as guide to the souls of the dead and is the ruler of the Tlalticpac, lowest of the thirteen heavens.

He is said to support the

universe on a pillar of fire and acts as the guardian of the centre, and is depicted as an old man carrying a brazier or mirror and a yellow serpent.

Xochitonal *Central American*
A fierce alligator in the lore of the Aztecs. This beast was one of the many hazards faced by the souls of the dead in their journey through the various layers of the underworld.

Xolotl *Central American*
An Aztec sun god or god of misfortune, a dog-headed god of the underworld; twin brother of Quetzalcoatl.

He took the form of a dog in some aspects and his feet were said to point towards the rear. In his role as lord of the evening star he caused the sun to sink each night.

He descended into the underworld and brought out bones from which mankind was created. In the story that tells how the gods sacrificed themselves to create man, he acted as their executioner and then killed himself. Another version says that the gods died to persuade the sun to resume its journey across the sky and, in this version, Xolotl executed the other gods but refused to kill himself. To escape, he changed himself first into the maize-plant xolotl, then into the agave mexolotl and finally into the larval salamander axolotl. He was eventually sacrificed and the sun started to move again. Some say that he was killed by being boiled in a kettle.

He is depicted as a dwarf jester and has empty eye-sockets because, it is said, his eyes fell out when he cried over the death of the other gods.

Y

Ya-hsek-khi *Burmese*
The first woman, created by Hkun Hsang Long.

She and the male Ta-hsek-khi were born in tadpole form. After eating a gourd they mated and were given new names. She became Ya-hsang-kahsi (Yatai). They produced a daughter called Nang-pyek-kha Yek-ki.

Ya-o-ga *North American*
also Bear
The north wind in the lore of the Seneca. He took the form of a bear tethered at the entrance to Ga-oh's cave. (*See also* **Ga-oh**.)

Yabuling *East Indies*
A Papuan god. He is said to have created pigs.

Yaégiri *Japanese*
A mountain spirit; one of the Yama-uba. She fell in love with Sakata Kurando, a soldier. When he was dismissed from the emperor's bodyguard, he killed himself, and she went off into the mountains where her son Kintaro was born.

She was an evil spirit who became a beautiful woman to lure men into the mountains, where she became a terrible demon and killed her victims.

Yaguarogin *South American*
A green tiger. Some tribes in Bolivia say that this animal lives in the sky and causes eclipses of the sun when he first swallows and then regurgitates it.

Yajna *Hindu*
A god, personifying ritual; an avatar of Vishnu. He resides in the heavens as a minor constellation and is depicted as having the head of a deer.

yaksha *Hindu*
female yakshi(ni)
A forest or mountain demon. These beings are shape-changers and can appear in the form of handsome youths or fat black dwarfs, or even as objects such as trees. In a friendly role they are punyajana.

Yakshini often appear in the guise of attractive females who

bewitch travellers. Some, known as ashramukhi, are in the form of women with the face of a horse.

(*See also* **rakshasa**.)

Yaksha-Loka *Hindu*
The home of the yakshas.

yakshagraha *Hindu*
A version of a yaksha which can take possession of mortals and drive them mad.

yale *British*
A monster in the form of an antelope; or a horse-bodied animal, with swivelling horns, tusks and the tail of an elephant; or a combination of boar, elephant, horse, stag and unicorn.

Yalungur *Australian*
A creator-spirit of some of the northern tribes. Yalungur was orginally male but Gidja, the other creator of the Dreamtime, cut off his penis and inserted a doll into the wound (which became the vagina) where it was brought to life and born as the first human being.

Yama[1]   *Buddhist*
A god of the dead, ruler of one of
the courts of the underworld. He
was originally one of the first pair
of humans and later came to be
regarded as an evil deity who will
one day be reborn as a Buddha
known as the Universal King.

In one story of his origins,
he was a Tibetan saint who was
killed and decapitated by robbers
who had stolen and killed a bull.
The saint immediately came to
life again, took the bull's head
in place of his own and became
a rampaging demon who was
finally subdued and converted
to Buddhism by Manjushri who
had assumed the form of an
even more terrifying demon,
Yamantaka, and subdued Yama,
converting him to Buddhism, in
which faith he became god of the
dead, lord of the underworld. (*See
also* **Ten Yama Kings**.)

Yama[2]   *Hindu*
= *Chinese* Yen Wang; *Greek* Hades;
Japanese Emma-O
The first man; also god of the dead;
one of the Dikpalas.

Yama was the appointed god of
the dead, lord of underworld, who
owned two four-eyed hounds,
Sabala and Syama, which guarded
his palace, Kalichi, in Yamapura,
the capital city of his kingdom,
and rounded up the souls of dead.
Some say that his messengers,
the owl and the pigeon, tied the
spirits of the dead in a noose
and transported them across
the river Vaitarani to Yamapura.
When souls reached Yamapura, he
greeted them as Pitripati, Lord of
Ancestors, acted as their judge,
Samavurti, and, as Dandadhara,
put the judge's verdict into effect.
His verdict on a soul determined

whether it was returned for
rebirth, sent to heaven or
despatched to one of 21 hells.

As a Dikpala, he was
responsible, with his elephant
Vamana, for the southern region.

He is depicted as green, dressed
in red, carrying a club and a
noose, riding a buffalo.

Yama[3]   *Persian*
A god of the underworld, controller
of Chinvat Bridge, a bridge that
the souls of the dead have to
cross.

Yama[4]   *Tibetan*
A Buddhist guardian-god; one of
the Dharmapalas. He is one of the
guardians of the Dalai Lama.

Yama Enda   *East Indies*
also Sickness Woman
A female demon in Papua. She
takes the form of a beautiful
maiden to attract men and then
eats them.

Yama-uba   *Japanese*
A female mountain spirit. These
spirits are said to have snakes for
hair and a mouth on top of the
head.

Yamadi   *Burmese*
A lord who rescued a drowning
youth. The young man's mother
gave the rescuer a dead bird
which, though very old, had not
decayed. Yamadi found a seed
lodged in the bird's throat and
removed it, whereupon the body
immediately started to rot. The
seed, planted in holy ground,
became the first tea tree.

Yamantaka *see* **Yama**
Yamato-no-Orochi   *Japanese*
An eight-headed dragon. This beast,
which was large enough to cover
eight mountains and valleys and
even had trees growing on its
back, was attacking the maiden
Inada-hime when the ox-headed

sea god Susanowa arrived on the
scene. He killed the dragon and
married the girl.

In one of the dragon's tails,
Susanowa found the magic sword,
Kusangi.

Yami   *Hindu*
The first woman, daughter of
Vivasvat or Surya by Sanjna; twin
sister and wife of Yama[2]. She
became the goddess Yamuna,
goddess of the river Jumna.

Yanauluha   *North American*
A medicine man of the Zuni
Indians, who taught mankind
the arts of agriculture, etc.
When he tapped the earth with
his staff, four eggs appeared,
two white and two blue. Some
people chose white; these
hatched into colourful macaws
which flew south. Those who
chose blue fed the whitish birds
that emerged, only to find that
these changed into ravens. These
two groups evolved into the
active and strong on the one
hand and the gentle and wise on
the other.

Yao   *Chinese*
A sage who became one of the Five
Emperors. He ruled for seventy
years and then gave the throne to
Shun, who married his daughter.

He is credited with the
invention of the calendar and
the construction of the first
observatory.

Yao Wang   *Chinese*
A hermit-physician, later deified.
He was said to live on air and
wine and once saved the life of a
snake and removed a bone lodged
in a tiger's throat. The grateful
feline guarded the physician's
house thereafter. When he was
taken to the home of the dragon-
king Ching Yang, the king's

daughter thanked him for saving her child's life – the snake had been that child.

As a deity, he became head of the Ministry of Medicine.

Yasigi　　　　　　　　　　*African*
In the lore of the Dogon, the sister of the evil god Ogo. She and Ogo were hatched from one of the two yolks of the primordial egg created by the surpreme god Amma. She mated with Amma to populate the world.

Yaun-Goicoa　　　　　　*Basque*
A supreme god. He is said to have created three principles: Begia, the light of the body which is the eye; Egia, the light of the spirit; and Ekhia, the light of the world which is the sun.

Yaxche　　　　　*Central American*
A tree in the paradise of the Maya. The souls of warriors killed in battle were transported to Yaxche by the goddess Ixtab.

Yaya　　　　　　　　　*West Indies*
A supreme spirit. His son was rebellious, so Yaya killed him, putting his bones in a gourd hung from the roof. These bones turned to fish which Yaya and his wife lived on.

Another version says that four brothers seized the gourd and ate some of the fish but the gourd broke and the water which flooded out became the seas, full of fish.

Ya'yai　　　　　　　　　　*Siberian*
A guardian of the household. This being takes the form of a drum and speaks through a drumstick made of whalebone.

Yayoi　　　　　　　　　*Japanese*
also Soul of the Mirror
A maiden who fell into the clutches of the Poison Dragon. (*See more at* **Matsumura**.)

Yazata　　　　　　　　　*Persian*
One of the ancient gods of the Zoroastrian pantheon, attendant on Ahura Mazda; guardian spirits; the embodiment of abstract ideas.

Yder　　　　　　　　　　*British*
A Knight of the Round Table. His father Nuc abandoned his mother when Yder was born and he grew up not knowing who his father was. As a young man, he set out to find him. He fell in love with a queen, Gwenloie, but had to prove himself worthy. Having killed two knights who were attacking King Arthur, he expected the king to knight him but was disappointed. He was later made a knight by another king, Ivenant, as reward for resisting the efforts of the king's wife to seduce the young stranger.

When he came to Castle Rougemont, home of Talac, a vassal of King Arthur's, he found it besieged by Arthur's forces and decided to help Talac and defeated all Arthur's best knights in combat. When Kay treacherously plunged a sword into Yder's back, the others were so appalled that a truce was declared and Talac and the king were reconciled. Luguain, Yder's squire, took his master to a monastery where his wounds were healed and he was later welcomed at the court, where Yder he saved the queen, Guinevere, from a bear.

When Talac's castle again came under siege, Yder rode to help his friend but the siege had already been lifted when he arrived. There he found a maiden who asked him to discover the identity of a knight who visited her in her tent every day. Yder found the man and a great fight ensued which

ended only when the knight recognised Yder as his own son.

Arthur, who was jealous of Yder, decided to get rid of him, and when Gwenloie asked his help in finding a husband, told her to marry the man who could kill two giants and bring her their knife. Yder did just that and claimed her hand. Kay gave Yder some poisoned water and he was left for dead but he recovered and returned to court. Arthur then made Yder a king and he married Gwenloie.

One story tells how he went with King Arthur in a foray against three giants and went on ahead of the others. When the rest of the party arrived at the hill where the giants lived, they found all three of them dead. Yder was also killed in the fight.

Yeak　　　　　　　　　*Cambodian*
= *Hindu* Yaksha
A flying ogre. These beings are shape-changers who can fire arrows that become serpents.

Also, one of a race of underground beings, guardians of buried treasure.

yek　　　　　　　　*North American*
The spirits inherent in all things, in the lore of the Tlingit.

yekeela　　　　　　　　*Siberian*
The familiar of the Siberian shaman. If the yekeela should be killed, the shaman also dies.

Yell Hounds *see* **Yeth Hounds**

Yellow Corn-ear Maiden　　*North American*
A Hopi maiden. She quarrelled with Blue Corn-ear Maiden, who used magic to turn her into a coyote. This animal was captured and taken to Spider Woman who returned the girl to her proper form and gave her a magic cup.

When Blue Corn-ear Maiden drank from this cup, she was turned into a snake.

Yellow-corn Girl *North American*

A Navaho deity. She, together with White-corn Boy, was placed on Mount San Francisco by Atse Estsan and Atse Hastin, the first woman and first man, when they formed the land of the Navaho on their ascent from the underworld.

Yellow-corn Maiden *North American*

A corn-spirit of the Zuni, leader of the Ten Corn Maidens. She and her sisters were changed into mortals and locked up by witches. Payatami, the harvest god, who was in love with Yellow Corn Maiden, rescued them all from their prison.

Yellow-corn Maidens *North American*

Two sisters, Pueblo witches. These maidens were jealous when the chief of their village Nahchuruchu married the moon so they drowned her in a well. All the birds and animals seached in vain until the buzzard spotted a mound with flowers on it. Nahchuruchu placed one of the white flowers between two robes and sang over it until at last his wife emerged restored to life and beauty. With the help of a magic hoop made by her husband, the moon turned the Yellow-corn Maidens into snakes.

Yellow Dragon *Chinese*

Ruler of the centre. This beast is said to have emerged from the River Lo to impart the secret of writing to the emperor. Others say it brought the secret from heaven.

Yellow Emperor *see* **Huang Ti, Yü**[2]

Yellow Thunderbird *North American*

One of the elders of the Thunderbirds. He, together with the other three elders, guarded the nest containing the eggs from which all the other Thunderbirds hatched. He was also the guardian of the east.

Yellow World *North American*

The third of the four worlds that the Navaho passed through before emerging into the upper world. The Navaho arrived here after being expelled from the Blue World and found it occupied by the Grasshopper People. They were soon expelled from this world also when some of their number seduced the women of the Yellow World, advancing to the White World.

Yeman'gnyem *Siberian*

An Ostyak fish-god. The aurora borealis, it is said, is a fire that this god lights to guide travellers.

Yen Ti *Chinese*

One of the Three Sovereigns. In some accounts, he is regarded as the same as Shen Nung, in others they are separate characters.

Yen Wang *Chinese*

= *Hindu* Yama; *Japanese* Emma-O

The double-bodied Buddhist god of death, the fifth and chief of the Ten Yama Kings. He was the overseer of the ten courts of the underworld in which souls were judged and he himself presided over the first court.

Yerunthully *Australian*

A rope, which, when a person dies, is lowered from the heavens so that the spirit can climb up. When the spirit reaches the top, the rope falls as a meteor.

Yeth Hounds *English*

also Hounds of Hell, Yell Hounds

The spirits of unbaptised children in the form of headless dogs. (*See also* **Wish Hounds**.)

Yetl *see* **Raven**[1]

Yggdrasil *Norse*

also World Tree

A huge evergreen ash-tree, said to support the universe. It had three main roots, one each sheltering the underworld, the Frost Giants and mankind. In some accounts, a further root reached Asgard, the home of the gods. The shoots were eaten by the deer Dain, Dvalin, Duneyr and Durathor while the root in Niflheim was constantly gnawed away by the serpent Nidhogg and his brood, threatening one day to bring the whole universe crashing down.

Odin is said to have hung for nine days on this tree in one of his efforts to acquire wisdom.

Yhi *Australian*

A sun goddess. She awoke from her age-long sleep when the sky god Baime whispered to her and she came down to earth in the form of a radiant goddess who, with her warmth and light, woke all the plants, birds and animals into life. She then retired to the heavens in the form of a glowing ball and became the sun.

Yima *Persian*

= *Buddhist* Yen Wang; *Hindu* Yama; *Norse* Ymir

Son of one of the first four men to produce the divine drink, Haoma, from the fruit of the Gaokerena tree. Some accounts describe Yima himself as the first man, son of Vivahvant, the sun god.

He was a semi-divine being, said to have ruled for 700 years, who, in attempting to make people immortal, sacrificed a bull, so upsetting the gods whose prerogative this was. For his presumption he was killed, according to one account. In another version, he was not killed but lost his own immortality and when the great god Ahura Mazda set out to destroy mankind he was warned in advance and constructed a vast cave, Var, in which he sheltered the best of all species with which to repopulate the world.

Yimantuwinyai   *North American*
A creator-god of the south-west coastal region. A culture-hero of the Hupa. He was said to have established order in the world and was the leader of a group of Kihunai, the people who inhabited the area before the Hupa, when he left for a new home across the sea to the north.

Ymir   *Norse*
The first giant. He was formed from the frost that came from the condensing of the warm mists of Muspelheim when they met the cold from the icy rivers of Niflheim. The cow, Audhumbla, was formed at the same time and Ymir survived by drinking her milk. From the sweat of his armpit he produced a son and a daughter and from his feet came the six-headed giant Thrudgelmir.

The god Odin and his brothers Ve and Vili killed Ymir and made the earth from his body. The rush of blood from the giant's body killed all the other giants with the exception of Bergelmir and his wife, who survived to produce more giants. Dwarfs grew from Ymir's dead body, his skull became the heavens and his brains the clouds.

Yo-shin-shi   *Japanese*
Grass growing in paradise, which can confer eternal youth on those who eat it.

Yokomatis   *North American*
also Blind Old Man
A creator-spirit of the Diegueño or Kumayaay people of California and Mexico.

He and his brother Tuchaipai were born under the sea and Yokomatis was blinded by the effect of the salt water on his eyes. They pushed up the sky so that they had room to move about and then created all the things in the world, including men and women. He is regarded as the one who caused death, while his brother is the giver of life.

Yolkai Estsan   *North American*
also White Painted Woman, White Shell Woman
A sea goddess and fertility goddess of the Navaho Indians. She was created by the gods Hasteyalti and Hastchogan from white shell, though others say that both she and her sister Estanatlehi were created by Changing Woman from flakes of skin from beneath her breasts.

In some versions, she, rather than Estanatlehi, created humans from maize-flour.

Yomi-tsu-kuni   *Japanese*
The Shinto underworld ruled by Emma-O. This realm is said to have sixteen regions, eight hot and eight freezing, with sixteen sub-divisions.

Yryn-ai-tojon   *Siberian*
The supreme god of the Yakuts. He challenged Satan to bring up land from the bottom of the primordial waters and when Satan, in the form of a swallow, did what he was asked, Yryn floated down to earth and sat on it. It grew and grew until it formed the world.

Yü[1]   *Chinese*
Jade, or a drink made from it. It is said that a drink of this liquid not only imparts desirable qualities to the drinker but allows him or her to overcome gravity.

Yü[2]   *Chinese*
also Yellow Emperor
A winged dragon with horns. This monster emerged from the body of Kun, a descendant of Huang Ti, three years after he was killed for stealing the magical substance Swelling Earth from Huang Ti. Yü was given permission by Huang Ti to use the Swelling Earth and became a famous builder of dams and irrigation engineer, controlling flood-waters. He later became a master smith, making nine cauldrons on which he inscribed all the details of his works. (Others say that the inscriptions were made on a stone tablet which he erected on a mountain peak.)

He became emperor in 2205 BC, and is regarded as the founder of the first dynasty.

Yü sometimes took the form of bear and when his wife saw him in this guise she turned to stone.

Yü Ch'iang   *Chinese*
also Yü Hu
God of the winds of the Northern Sea. He guarded the islands of P'eng-lai in the form of a being with a human head, the body of a bird and with serpents hanging from his ears.

Yü Huang   *Chinese*
also Jade Ruler;
= *Buddhist* Yü Ti
A Taoist supreme god, one of the San Ch'ing, the Three Pure Ones; consort of Hsi Wang Mu.

It was said that, at his birth, a glowing light was emitted by his body. He was reared by mortal foster-parents, the emperor Ching Te and his wife Pao Yüeh. He could have succeeded to his foster-father's throne but gave it up for a life of meditation, finally being translated to heaven. He came to earth 800 times to help the sick and the poor, followed by a further 800 visits when he spread goodness throughout the world, and yet another such series when he took upon himself much suffering.

His jade palace is situated in the constellation of Ta Wei (the Great Bear).

In some accounts, he is equated with Shang Ti or Yüan Shih.

Yüan Shih   *Chinese*
also Yü Shih

A Taoist supreme god and rain god.

When the primeval being Pan-ku had finished creating the universe he entered through the mouth of an ascetic hermaphrodite in the form of a ray of light. Twelve years later the hermit gave birth to Yüan Shih, allegedly through his spine. (In another account the ascetic hermit is replaced by the holy virgin T'ai Yüan.)

Yüan Shih lives in a palace on Jade Mountain and learns about the people on earth from the kitchen god, Tsao Chün.

In some accounts, he is equated with Yü Huang.

Yüan Tan   *Chinese*

A god of wealth. He owned a magic bowl, Chu-pao P'en, which produced all the gold he could ever want. He is depicted riding a tiger and holding a club.

yuga   *Hindu*
also yug

One of four ages of the world.

These are given as:

1. krita-yuga, lasting 4000 years

2. treta-yuga, lasting 3000 years

3. dvapara-yuga, lasting 2000 years

4. kali-yuga, the present age, lasting 1000 years.

In some accounts the four ages total 12,000 years, made up as follows:

1. krita-yuga, 4800

2. treta-yuga, 3600

3. dvapara-yuga, 2400

4. kali-yuga, 1200

Including dawn and twilight periods.

The 'years' referred to are divine years, and, since each divine year equals 360 human years, the complete cycle of four ages, a mahayuga, equals 4,320,000 human years.

Yum Caax   *Central American*
also Lord of the Harvest

The Mayan maize god, an aspect of Kukulcan.

Yurlungur   *Australian*
also Copper Python, Rainbow Serpent, Rainbow Snake

A snake-spirit of the Aborigines. A bisexual fertility symbol, he was regarded as the ancestor of some of the tribes and lived in the waterhole, Mirrimina. He swallowed and regurgitated the Wawalag sisters and subsequently regurgitated all the plants and animals he had previously swallowed, before disappearing into the sky where he appears as the rainbow.

Yusup   *Pacific Islands*

A Polynesian fisherman. He caught the magic white tortoise, Notu, which he then carried in the front of his boat. The tortoise could lead him to sites where he was sure of a good catch of fish and, when they met a sea monster, Notu found the ring lost in the ocean which restored the monster to its proper form as a prince, a feat for which Yusup was well rewarded.

Z

Zagan *European*
A demon of forgers, one of the 72 Spirits of Solomon. He is said to be able to perform miracles such as turning water into wine and appears in the form of a winged bull.

Zaleos *European*
A demon, one of the 72 Spirits of Solomon. He is depicted as a soldier riding a crocodile.

Zarathustra *see* **Zoroaster**

Zepar *European*
A demon, one of the 72 Spirits of Solomon. He is said to be able to cause women to fall in love and appears as a soldier. Others say that he is a duke in hell who incites men to indulge in unnatural sexual practices.

Zephyrus *Greek*
also Zephyr;
= *Roman* Favonius
God of the west wind.

When Psyche threw herself from the top of cliff to escape the harassment of the goddess Aphrodite who was jealous of her beauty, Zephyrus caught her in mid-air and wafted her off to a splendid palace where she lived with Eros, the god of love, who visited her every night.

In one account, he killed Hyacinthus when the youth rejected him as a lover and, in remorse, changed his boisterous ways and became a gentle breeze.

Zeus *Greek*
also Thunderer;
= *Egyptian* Amon; *Etruscan* Tinia; *Hindu* Dyaus; *Persian* Ahura Mazda; *Roman* Jupiter
A supreme god, rain god and sky god; son of Cronus and Rhea; brother of Demeter, Hera, Hestia, Pluto and Poseidon; husband of Metis, Themis and finally Hera; father of Ares, Hebe, Hephaestus and Ilithyia by Hera.

His father, Cronus, had made a habit of swallowing his offspring to prevent their becoming a threat to his position, so Cronus's wife Rhea hid the infant in a cave in Crete where he was reared by the nymphs Io and Adrasteia and the goat-nymph Amaltheia whose skin he wore.

He became cup-bearer to Cronus and gave him an emetic which forced him to regurgitate all the children he had swallowed.

He led the gods in the war against the Titans and killed Campe, the female guardian of Tartarus, releasing the Cyclopes and the hundred-handed Giants who helped in the fight against the Titans. After a ten-year struggle the gods were the victors and the three brothers shared the world between them, Pluto taking the underworld, Poseidon the sea and Zeus the earth and heavens.

He was defeated in a single-handed fight with the monster Typhon who cut out all his sinews. Pan and Hermes restored them and Zeus carried on the fight with Typhon, finally burying him for all time when he threw Mount Etna at him.

Angered by the impiety of

the sons of Lycaon, he caused a universal flood from which only Deucalion with his wife Pyrrha and a few others managed to escape.

He is said to have created Pandora, the most beautiful of all women, as a gift to Epimetheus who rejected her, and to have placed the Pleiades in the sky as stars to escape the attentions of Orion who had pursued them relentlessly.

In the form of an eagle, he abducted the beautiful youth Ganymede and made him cup-bearer to the gods after Hebe.

He married his sister Hera and they had three children, Ares, Hebe and Hephaestus (and, some say, Ilithyia) but he is said to have raped his mother, Rhea, both of them in the form of serpents, and to have fathered many other children on various goddesses, nymphs and mortals.

One of these children was Athena. Zeus had seduced Metis, one of the Oceanids, and she was expecting his child. When he heard that the child would be a girl but any second child would be a boy who would dethrone him, Zeus swallowed Metis and her unborn baby. When he later developed a headache, Hephaestus split open his skull and out sprang Athena fully armed.

Another child was Hercules. When he decided there was a need for a protector of both gods and humans, he set out to produce such a champion, selecting Alcmene, the wife of Amphitryon, king of Tiryns, as his partner. He caused the motions of the earth to slow so that one night lasted for three as he lay with Alcmene in the guise of her husband. The son of this union was the hero Hercules.

In the form of a white bull he carried off Europa and then, changing to an eagle, fathered Minos, Rhadamanthus and Sarpedon on her and he also abducted Aegina, fathering Aeacus on her and turning himself into a huge rock to escape the vengeance of her father Asopus.

In the case of Castor, Pollux, Helen and Clytemnestra, there is some dispute but there is no doubt that Zeus was involved in some way with their mother Leda. In some tales he seduced Leda taking the form of a swan on a night when she had also lain with her husband Tyndareus. Four children resulted and these are attributed variously to the two potential fathers. In another version, Helen was fathered on Nemesis (as a goose) by Zeus (as a swan).

Amongst others, he was the father of

Aphrodite by Dione, some say
Apollo and Artemis by Leto (as quails)
Ares by Hera
Argus by Niobe
Athena by Metis (from his head)
Castor by Leda (as swan)
the Charities by Eurynome
Clytemnestra by Pyrrha
Core (Persephone) by Demeter
Dionysus by Semele or by Demeter
Eros by Aphrodite, some say
the Graces by Eurynome
Helen by Pyrrha
Hephaestus by Hera
Hermes by Maia
the Horae by Themis
Minos by Europa (as bull or eagle)
the Moirae by Themis
the Muses by Mnemosyne
Pan by Aphrodite, some say
Perseus by Danae
Pollux (Polydeuces) by Leda (as swan)
Rhadamanthus by Europa (as bull or eagle)
Scylla by Lamia, some say
Tantalus by Pluto, some say
He killed Tantalus when he put pieces of his son Pelops in a stew served to the gods and he killed Asclepius when the physician tried to restore Hippolytus to life.

His bird was the eagle, his tree the oak, his weapon the thunderbolt and his oracle was at Dodona

Zeus-Ammon   *Greek*

= *Roman* Jupiter-Ammon

A combined deity respresented by a bull and a ram. This version of Zeus was said to be the father of Alexander the Great.

Zimbabwe   *African*

A sun god of the Shona people.

Zipacna   *Central American*

A Mayan dawn god and god of earthquakes. He and his brother Cabraca were giants whose power threatened that of the gods. The twins Hunapu and Ixbalanqué trapped him in a pit and piled trees on top, then built a house over it. The giant broke out, killing the 400 young men who had helped the twins, but they later trapped him in a ravine and killed him by dropping huge boulders on him, finally using their magical powers to turn him into stone.

Ziusudra   *Sumerian*

= *Mesopotamian* Utnapishtim;
Babylonian Atrahasis

The Sumerian king of Sippar. A name for Atrahasis in some versions of the Flood story. (*See* also **Xithuthros**.)

Zoroaster *Persian*

also Zarathustra

The Greek form of Zarathustra (*c.* 628–551 BC), a prophet or priest.

He was the son of one of the first four men to press the divine drink, haoma, from the fruit of the Gaokerena tree and was the founder or reformer of the old Persian religion based on the writings of the Zend-Avesta.

In some accounts, as an infant he was thrown on a fire to die but the burning logs turned into a bed of roses. As a young man of twenty he left his home and took up a life of solitude, protected by Ahura Mazda when he confronted Ahriman, the evil principle, and resisted the temptations that he offered. He prophesied that, in the final battle between good and evil, Ahriman would be defeated by Saoshyant.

His sperm was preserved in Lake Kasavya (now Hamoun) and impregnates any virgin who swims in its waters. As a result, every 1000 years, a Saoshyant is born.

Zosim *Slav*

A bee-god and god of mead.

Zu *Mesopotamian*

A Babylonian lion-headed storm bird. Zu (or the god Imdugud) once stole the Tablets of Destiny, originally belonging to Tiamat, from Enlil, the god of air and earth, threatening to become supreme ruler of the world, but Lugalbanda (the father of Gilgamesh) found Zu's nest and recovered the tablets. (In some accounts, the tablets were recovered by the god Marduk, in others by Ninurta.)

Basilisk *page 41*

Phoenix *page 274*

Roc *page 292*

Unicorn *page 349*